MATTHEW

VOLUME 2

THE PREACHER'S OUTLINE & SERMON BIBLE®

MATTHEW

VOLUME 2

THE PREACHER'S OUTLINE & SERMON BIBLE®

NEW TESTAMENT

NEW INTERNATIONAL VERSION

Leadership Ministries Worldwide
PO Box 21310
Chattanooga, TN 37424-0310

The Preacher's Outline & Sermon Bible® is written for God's people to use in their preparation for preaching and teaching. The purpose of the copyright is to prevent the reproduction, misuse, and abuse of the material.

May our Lord bless us all as we preach, teach, and write for Him, fulfilling His great commission to make disciples of all nations.

Previous Editions of **The Preacher's Outline & Sermon Bible®**,
King James Version,
Copyright © 1991, 1996
by Alpha-Omega Ministries, Inc.

Please address all requests for information or permission to:
LEADERSHIP MINISTRIES WORLDWIDE
PO Box 21310
Chattanooga TN 37424-0310
Ph.# (423) 855-2181 FAX (423) 855-8616
E-Mail outlinebible@compuserve.com
http://www.outlinebible.org

Library of Congress Catalog Card Number: 98-067967
International Standard Book Number: 1-57407-077-0

Printed in the United States of America

Publisher &
Distributer

DEDICATED:

To all the men and women of the world
who preach and teach the Gospel of our
Lord Jesus Christ
and
To the Mercy and Grace of God.

- Demonstrated to us in Christ Jesus our Lord.

"In him we have redemption through his blood, the forgiveness of sins, in accordance with the riches of God's grace." (Eph. 1:7 NIV)

- Out of the mercy and grace of God His Word has flowed. Let every person know that God will have mercy upon him, forgiving and using him to fulfill His glorious plan of salvation.

"For God so loved the world, that he gave his one and only Son, that whosoever believes in him shall not perish, but have eternal life. For God did not send his Son into the world to condemn the world, but to save the world through him." (Jn 3:16-17 NIV)

"This is good and pleases God our Saviour; who wants all men to be saved and to come to the knowledge of the truth." (I Tim. 2:3-4 NIV)

The Preacher's Outline and Study Bible®
is written for God's people to use
in their study and teaching of God's Holy Word.

9/98

OUTLINE BIBLE RESOURCES

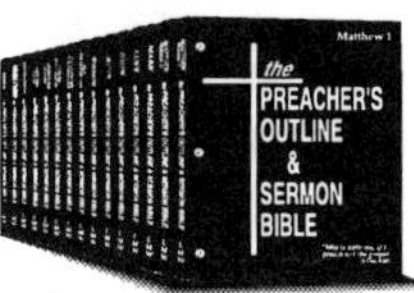

This material, like similar works, has come from imperfect man and is thus susceptible to human error. We are nevertheless grateful to God for both calling us and empowering us through His Holy Spirit to undertake this task. Because of His goodness and grace The Preacher's Outline & Sermon Bible® - New Testament is complete in 14 volumes, and the Old Testament volumes release periodically. **The Minister's Handbook** is available and *OUTLINE* Bible materials are releasing electonically on **POSB-CD** and our **Web site**.

God has given the strength and stamina to bring us this far. Our confidence is that, as we keep our eyes on Him and grounded in the undeniable truths of the Word, we will continue working through the Old Testament volumes and the second series known as **The Teacher's Outline & Study Bible.** The future includes helpful ***Outline Bible*** books and **Handbook** materials for God's dear servants.

To everyone everywhere who preaches and teaches the Word, we offer this material firstly to Him in whose name we labor and serve, and for whose glory it has been produced.

Our daily prayer is that each volume will lead thousands, millions, yes even billions, into a better understanding of the Holy Scriptures and a fuller knowledge of Jesus Christ the incarnate Word, of whom the Scriptures so faithfully testify.

As you have purchased this volume, you will be pleased to know that a small portion of the price you have paid has gone to underwrite and provide similar volumes in other languages (Russian, Korean, Spanish and others yet to come) — To a preacher, pastor, lay leader, or Bible student somewhere around the world, who will present God's message with clarity, authority, and understanding beyond their own. *Amen.*

For information and prices, kindly contact your *OUTLINE* Bible bookseller or:

LEADERSHIP MINISTRIES WORLDWIDE

P.O. Box 21310, 515 Airport Road, Suite 107
Chattanooga, TN 37424-0310
(423) 855-2181 FAX (423) 855-8616
E-Mail - outlinebible@compuserve.com
www.outlinebible.org — *FREE* download materials

9/98

PUBLISHER & DISTRIBUTOR OF OUTLINE BIBLE MATERIALS

Currently Available Materials, with New Volumes Releasing Regularly

- **THE PREACHER'S OUTLINE & SERMON BIBLE® — DELUXE EDITION** 3-Ring, looseleaf binder

Volume 1 . . . . **St. Matthew I** (chapters 1-15)
Volume 2 . . . . **St. Matthew II** (chapters 16-28)
Volume 3 . . . . **St. Mark**
Volume 4 . . . . **St. Luke**
Volume 5 . . . . **St. John**
Volume 6 . . . . **Acts**
Volume 7 . . . . **Romans**
Volume 8 . . . . **1, 2 Corinthians** (1 volume)
Volume 9 . . . . **Galatians, Ephesians, Philippians, Colossians** (1 volume)
Volume 10 . . . . **1,2 Thessalonians, 1,2 Timothy, Titus, Philemon** (1 volume)
Volume 11 . . . . **Hebrews -James** (1 volume)
Volume 12 . . . . **1,2 Peter, 1,2,3 John, Jude** (1 volume)
Volume 13 . . . . **Revelation**
Volume 14 . . . . **Master Outline & Subject Index**
FULL SET — 14 Volumes

- **THE PREACHER'S OUTLINE & SERMON BIBLE® — OLD TESTAMENT**

Volume 1 . . . . **Genesis I** (chapters 1-11)
Volume 2 . . . . **Genesis II** (chapters 12-50)
Volume 3 . . . . **Exodus I** (chapters 1-18)
Volume 4 . . . . **Exodus II** (chapters 19-40)
Volume 5 . . . . **Leviticus**

New volumes release periodically

- **THE PREACHER'S OUTLINE & SERMON BIBLE® — SOFTBOUND EDITION**
  Identical content as Deluxe above. Lightweight, compact, and affordable for overseas & traveling
- **THE PREACHER'S OUTLINE & SERMON BIBLE® — 3 VOL HARDCOVER w/CD**
- **THE PREACHER'S OUTLINE & SERMON BIBLE® — NIV SOFTBOUND EDITION**
- **The Minister's Personal Handbook - What the Bible Says...to the Minister**
  12 Chapters - 127 Subjects - 400 Verses *OUTLINED* - Paperback, Leatherette, 3-ring
- **THE TEACHER'S OUTLINE & STUDY BIBLE™ • New Testament Books •**
  Complete 45 minute lessons - 4 months of studies/book; 200± pages - Student Journal Guides
- **OUTLINE Bible Studies series: 10 Commandments - The Tabernacle**
- **Practical Word Studies: New Testament - 2,000 Key Words Made Easy**
- **CD-ROM: Preacher, Teacher, and Handbook- (Windows/STEP) - WORD*Search***
- **Translations of Preacher, Teacher, and Minister's Handbook: Limited Quantities**

Russian — Spanish — Korean *Future: French, Portuguese, Hindi, Chinese*

— Contact us for Specific Language Availability and Prices —

For quantity orders and information, please contact either:

LEADERSHIP MINISTRIES WORLDWIDE
PO Box 21310
Chattanooga, TN 37424-0310
(423) 855-2181 (9am - 5pm Eastern) • FAX (423) 855-8616 (24 hours)
E•Mail - outlinebible@compuserve.com.

Your OUTLINE Bible Bookseller

→ FREE Download Sample Pages — www.outlinebible.org

• ***Equipping God's Servants Worldwide with OUTLINE Bible Materials*** •

LMW is a nonprofit, international, nondenominational mission agency 9/98

ACKNOWLEDGMENTS

Every child of God is precious to the Lord and deeply loved. And every child as a servant of the Lord touches the lives of those who come in contact with him or his ministry. The writing ministry of the following servants have touched this work, and we are grateful that God brought their writings our way. We hereby acknowledge their ministry to us, being fully aware that there are so many others down through the years whose writings have touched our lives and who deserve mention, but the weaknesses of our minds have caused them to fade from memory. May our wonderful Lord continue to bless the ministry of these dear servants, and the ministry of us all as we diligently labor to reach the world for Christ and to meet the desperate needs of those who suffer so much.

THE GREEK SOURCES

1. Expositor's Greek Testament, Edited by W. Robertson Nicoll. Grand Rapids, MI: Eerdmans Publishing Co., 1970

2. Robertson, A.T. Word Pictures in the New Testament. Nashville, TN: Broadman Press, 1930.

3. Thayer, Joseph Henry. Greek-English Lexicon of the New Testament. New York: American Book Co, No date listed.

4. Vincent, Marvin R. Word Studies in the New Testament. Grand Rapids, MI: Eerdmans Publishing Co., 1969.

5. Vine, W.E. Expository Dictionary of New Testament Words. Old Tappan, NJ: Fleming H. Revell Co. No date listed.

6. Wuest, Kenneth S. Word Studies in the Greek New Testament. Grand Rapids, MI: Eerdmans Publishing Co., 1966.

THE REFERENCE WORKS

7. Cruden's Complete Concordance of the Old & New Testament. Philadelphia, PA: The John C. Winston Co., 1930.

8. Josephus' Complete Works. Grand Rapids, MI: Kregel Publications, 1981.

9. Lockyer, Herbert. Series of Books, including his Books on All the Men, Women, Miracles, and Parables of the Bible. Grand Rapids, MI: Zondervan Publishing House, 1958-1967.

10. -Nave's Topical Bible. Nashville, TN: The Southwestern Co., No date listed.

11. The Amplified New Testament. (Scripture Quotations are from the Amplified New Testament, Copyright 1954, 1958, 1987 by the Lockman Foundation. Used by permission.)

12. The Four Translation New Testament (Including King James, New American Standard, Williams - New Testament In the Language of the People, Beck - New Testament In the Language of Today.) Minneapolis, MN: World Wide Publications.

13. The New Compact Bible Dictionary, Edited by T. Alton Bryant. Grand Rapids, MI: Zondervan Publishing House, 1967.

14. The New Thompson Chain Reference Bible. Indianapolis, IN: B.B. Kirkbride Bible Co., 1964,

THE COMMENTARIES

15. Barclay, William. Daily Study Bible Series. Philadelphia, PA: Westminster Press, Began in 1953.

16. Bruce, F.F. The Epistle to the Ephesians. Westwood, NJ: Fleming H. Revell Co., 1968.

17. Bruce, F.F. Epistle to the Hebrews. Grand Rapids, MI: Eerdmans Publishing Co., 1964.

18. Bruce, F.F. The Epistles of John. Old Tappan, NJ: Fleming H. Revell Co., 1970.

19. Criswell, W.A. Expository Sermons on Revelation. Grand Rapids, MI: Zondervan Publishing House, 1962-66.

20. Greene, Oliver. The Epistles of John. Greenville, SC: The Gospel Hour, Inc., 1966.

21. Greene, Oliver. The Epistles of Paul the Apostle to the Hebrews. Greenville, SC: The Gospel Hour, Inc., 1965.

22. Greene, Oliver. The Epistles of Paul the Apostle to Timothy & Titus. Greenville, SC: The Gospel Hour, Inc., 1964.

23. Greene, Oliver. The Revelation Verse by Verse Study. Greenville, SC: The Gospel Hour, Inc., 1963.

24. Henry, Matthew. Commentary on the Whole Bible. Old Tappan, NJ: Fleming H. Revell Co.

25. Hodge, Charles. Exposition on Romans & on Corinthians. Grand Rapids, MI: Eerdmans Publishing Co., 1972-1973.

26. Ladd, George Eldon. A Commentary On the Revelation of John. Grand Rapids, MI: Eerdmans Publishing Co., 1972-1973.

27. Leupold, H.C. Exposition of Daniel. Grand Rapids, MI: Baker Book House, 1969.

28. Morris, Leon. The Gospel According to John. Grand Rapids, MI: Eerdmans Publishing Co., 1971.

29. Newell, William R. Hebrews, Verse by Verse. Chicago, IL: Moody Press, 1947.

30. Strauss, Lehman. Devotional Studies in Galatians & Ephesians. Neptune, NJ: Loizeaux Brothers, 1957.

31. Strauss, Lehman. Devotional Studies in Philippians. Neptune, NJ: Loizeaux Brothers, 1959.

32. Strauss, Lehman. James, Your Brother. Neptune, NJ: Loizeaux Brothers, 1956.

33. Strauss, Lehman. The Book of the Revelation. Neptune, NJ: Loizeaux Brothers, 1964.

34. The New Testament & Wycliffe Bible Commentary, Edited by Charles F. Pfeiffer & Everett F. Harrison. New York: The Iverson Associates, 1971. Produced for Moody Monthly. Chicago Moody Press, 1962.

35. The Pulpit Commentary, Edited by H.D.M. Spence & Joseph S. Exell. Grand Rapids, MI: Eerdmans Publishing Co., 1950.

36. Thomas, W.H. Griffith. Hebrews, A Devotional Commentary. Grand Rapids, MI: Eerdmans Publishing Co., 1970.

37. Thomas, W.H. Griffith. Outline Studies in the Acts of the Apostles. Grand Rapids, MI: Eerdmans Publishing Co., 1956.

38. Thomas, W.H. Griffith. St. Paul's Epistle to the Romans. Grand Rapids, MI: Eerdmans Publishing Co., 1946.

39. Thomas, W.H. Griffith. Studies in Colossians & Philemon. Grand Rapids, MI: Baker Book House, 1973.

40. Tyndale New Testament Commentaries. Grand Rapids, MI: Eerdmans Publishing Co., Began in 1958.

41. Walker, Thomas. Acts of the Apostles. Chicago, IL: Moody Press, 1965.

42. Walvoord, John. The Thessalonian Epistles. Grand Rapids, MI: Zondervan Publishing House, 1973.

MISCELLANEOUS ABBREVIATIONS

&	=	And
Arg.	=	Argument
Bckgrd.	=	Background
Bc.	=	Because
Circ.	=	Circumstance
Concl.	=	Conclusion
Cp.	=	Compare
Ct.	=	Contrast
Dif.	=	Different
e.g.	=	For example
Et.	=	Eternal
Govt.	=	Government
Id.	=	Identity or Identification
Illust.	=	Illustration
K.	=	Kingdom, K. of God, K. of Heaven, etc.
No.	=	Number
N.T.	=	New Testament
O.T.	=	Old Testament
Pt.	=	Point
Quest.	=	Question
Rel.	=	Religion
Resp.	=	Responsibility
Rev.	=	Revelation
Rgt.	=	Righteousness
Thru	=	Through
V.	=	Verse
Vs.	=	Verses
Vs.	=	Versus

"Woe to me if I do not preach the gospel!"

(I Cor. 9:16 NIV)

MATTHEW

INTRODUCTION

I. AUTHOR

Matthew. The Bible in no place says that Matthew is the author; however, the evidence for Matthew's authorship is strong.

1. Early writers have always credited the Gospel to Matthew. William Barclay quotes one of the earliest church historians, a man named Papias (A.D. 100), as saying, "Matthew collected the sayings of Jesus in the Hebrew tongue" (William Barclay. *The Gospel of Matthew*, Vol.1. "The Daily Study Bible." Philadelphia, PA: The Westminster Press, 1956, p.21.) Irenaeus (about A.D. 175), the saintly bishop of Lyons, wrote: "Matthew also issued a written Gospel among the Hebrews in their own dialect, while Peter and Paul were preaching at Rome and laying the foundations of the church" (Irenaeus, Against Heresies, 3.1.1).

2. Matthew was qualified to write the Gospel. He had been a tax collector which means that he was involved in large business transactions. A study of the Gospel shows that the author had an interest in figures, large numbers (Mt.18:24; 28:12), and statistics (Mt.1:17). The detailed messages of Jesus point to a man experienced with shorthand which he had apparently used in his business. Very little is given in the Scripture about Matthew.

a. He was one of the twelve apostles (Mk.2:14).
b. He left all to follow Christ (Lk.5:27-28).
c. He introduced his friends to Christ by inviting them to a banquet which he gave in honor of Christ (Lk.5:29).

II. DATE

Uncertain. A.D. 50-70. It was written some years after Jesus' ascension, but before A.D. 70.

1. The fall of Jerusalem, A.D. 70, is prophetic (Mt.24:1f).

2. The statements such as "to this day" (Mt.27:8) and "to this very day" (Mt.28:15) suggest a date sometime after Jesus' ascension, but not too far in the distant future.

3. The scattering of the Jerusalem Church due to persecution (Acts 8:4) suggests a date sometime after the ascension. A Gospel would not have been necessary so long as the church and apostles were together.

4. The quote by Irenaeus points to Matthew's writing during Nero's reign, "while Paul and Peter were in Rome."

III. TO WHOM WRITTEN

The Gospel was written originally to the Jews. However, it breathes a message for all, a message proclaiming the Messianic hope of the world for the Great Deliverer.

IV. PURPOSE

To show that Jesus is the Messiah, the Savior and King prophesied by the Hebrew prophets.

Matthew is a strong book, a book written to force belief in Jesus. Matthew sets out to prove that all the prophecies of the O.T. are fulfilled in Jesus, the carpenter from Nazareth. It has one recurring theme: "All this took place to fulfill what the Lord had said through the prophet:..." This is repeated approximately sixteen times, and there are ninety-three O.T. quotations.

V. SPECIAL FEATURES

1. Matthew is *The Ecclesiastical Gospel.* Remember, gospel means *the good news* or, simply stated, the *good news is the gospel.* Down through the centuries, Matthew has been widely used by the church. Its material is arranged primarily by subjects, not by a strict chronological sequence. It is somewhat a topical arrangement of the ministry and teachings of Jesus. As such, it has been extremely useful to the church: as an apology to defend the faith, as a handbook of instructions for new believers, and as a book of worship to read in church services.

2. Matthew is *The Teaching Gospel.* Much of Jesus' teaching is arranged so that it can be easily taught and easily lived. This material is clearly seen in five sections.

a. The Sermon on the Mount (Mt.5-7).
b. The Messiah's messengers and their mission (Mt.9-10:42).
c. The Messiah's parables (Mt.13).
d. The Messiah's disciples and their behavior toward one another (Mt.18).
e. The Messiah's prophecy of His return and the end of time: the great Olivet discourse (Mt.24-25).

3. Matthew is *The Royal Gospel* or *The Kingdom Gospel.* The heart of Matthew's Gospel is that Jesus is King. Jesus is the Son of David, the greatest of Israel's kings. He is the fulfillment of the Messianic prophecies that foretold the coming of a King like unto David.

a. His genealogy shows Him to be David's son by birth (Mt.1:1-17).
b. He was born King of the Jews (Mt.2:2).
c. He was called the King of David repeatedly (Mt.9:27; 15:22; 20:30; 21:9, 15; 22:42).
d. He personally claimed the power of a king by overriding the law: "But I tell you...." (Mt.5:21-22, 27-28, 31-32, 33-34, 38-39, 43-44).
e. He dramatically showed Himself to be King by His triumphal entry into Jerusalem (Mt.21:1-11).
f. He deliberately accepted the title of King before Pilate (Mt.27:11).
g. His cross bore the title, "King of the Jews" (Mt.27:11).
h. He claimed the supreme power of the King of Kings, "All authority...has been given to me" (Mt.28:18).
i. The word "Kingdom" is used fifty-four times and "Kingdom of Heaven" thirty-two times.

4. Matthew is *The Apocalyptic Gospel.* Among the Gospels, it has the most comprehensive account of the Lord's return and of the end time (Mt.24-25).

5. Matthew is *The Gospel of the Church.* It is the only Synoptic Gospel that mentions the church (Mt.16:13-23; 18:17; cp. Mk.8:27-33; Lk.9:18-22).

6. Matthew is *The Gospel of the Jew.* Matthew never failed to show that Jesus fulfills O.T. prophecy. He makes more than one hundred allusions or quotations from the O.T. He is determined to compel the Jew to believe that Jesus is the Messiah.

OUTLINE OF MATTHEW

THE PREACHER'S OUTLINE & SERMON BIBLE® is *unique*. It differs from all other Study Bibles & Sermon Resource Materials in that every Passage and Subject is outlined right beside the Scripture. When you choose any *Subject* below and turn to the reference, you have not only the Scripture, but you discover the Scripture and Subject *already outlined for you—verse by verse.*

For a quick example, choose one of the subjects below and turn over to the Scripture, and you will find this marvelous help for faster, easier, and more accurate use.

In addition, every point of the Scripture and Subject is *fully developed in a Commentary with supporting Scripture* at the bottom of the page. Again, this arrangement makes sermon preparation much easier and faster.

Note something else: The Subjects of Matthew have titles that are both Biblical and *practical.* The practical titles sometimes have more appeal to people. This *benefit* is clearly seen for use on billboards, bulletins, church newsletters, etc.

A suggestion: For the quickest overview of Matthew, first read *all the major titles* (I, II, III, etc.), then come back and read the subtitles.

OUTLINE OF MATTHEW

C. Jesus Heals Peter's Mother-in-Law: Jesus' Power and Its Purpose, 8:14-17
(Mark 1:29-34; Luke 4:38-41)

D. Jesus Attracts People: The Cost of True Discipleship, 8:18-22
(Luke 9:57-62)

E. Jesus Calms a Storm: Conquering Fear and Nature, 8:23-27
(Mark 4:35-41; Luke 8:22-25)

F. Jesus Casts Out Demons: Saving Men, 8:28-34
(Mark 5:1-20; Luke 8:26-40)

G. Jesus Heals a Paralyzed Man: Forgiving Sin, 9:1-8
(Mark 2:1-12; Luke 5:17-26)

H. Jesus Calls Matthew: Receiving Sinners, 9:9-13
(Mark 2:14-17; Luke 5:27-32)

I. Jesus Answers the Question about Fasting: Ushering in a New Age and Covenant, 9:14-17
(Mark 2:18-22; Luke 5:33-39)

J. Jesus Heals Several People: Meeting Man's Desperate and Hopeless Needs, 9:18-34
(Mark 5:21-43; Luke 8:41-56; 11:14-15)

VI. THE MESSIAH'S MESSENGERS AND THEIR MISSION, 9:35-10:42
(Mark 6:7-13; Luke 9:1-6)

A. The Mission of the Messiah, 9:35-38

B. The Messiah's Call to His Disciples, 10:1-4
(Mark 3:13-19; Lk.6:13-19; Acts 1:13)

C. The Messiah's Commission to His Disciples, 10:5-15

D. The Messiah's Warning of Persecution, 10:16-23

E. The Messiah's Encouragement Not to Fear Persecution, 10:24-33

F. The Cost of Being the Lord's Disciple, 10:34-42

VII. THE MESSIAH'S VINDICATION OF HIS MESSIAHSHIP, 11:1-30

A. The Assurance: Given to a Questioning Disciple, John the Baptist, 11:1-6
(Luke 7:18-23)

B. The Reminder: Given to a Forgetful and Fickle People, 11:7-15
(Luke 7:24-28)

C. The Message: Given to a Childish Generation, 11:16-27
(Luke 7:31-35; 10:12-15; 10:21-22)

D. The Great Invitation: Given to this Generation, 11:28-30

VIII. THE MESSIAH'S DEFENSE OF HIMSELF AGAINST OPPONENTS, 12:1-50

A. Defense 1: Messiah Is Greater than Religion, 12:1-8
(Mark 2:23-28; Luke 6:1-5)

B. Defense 2: Man Is Greater than Religion, 12:9-13
(Mark 3:1-6; Luke 6:6-11)

C. Defense 3: Messiah Is the Chosen Servant of God, 12:14-21
(Mark 3:7-12)

D. Defense 4: Messiah Is of God's Kingdom and House, 12:22-30
(Mark 3:22-30; Luke 11:14-23)

E. Defense 5: A Man's Words Determine His Destiny, 12:31-37
(Mark 3:28-30; Luke 11:14-16)

F. Defense 6: Messiah's Answer to an Evil Generation or Apostates, 12:38-45
(Luke 11:29-32)

G. Defense 7: Messiah's Answer to Doubting Relatives, 12:46-50
(Mark 3:31-35; Luke 8:19-21)

IX. THE MESSIAH'S PARABLES DESCRIBING THE KINGDOM OF HEAVEN, 13:1-52

A. The Parable of the Sower: How a Man Receives the Gospel, 13:1-9
(cp. Matthew 13:18-23; Mark 4:1-9; Luke 8:4-15)

B. The Messiah's Reasons for Speaking in Parables: Who Receives and Who Loses, 13:10-17
(Mark 4:10-12; Luke 8:9-10; 10:23-24)

C. The Parable of the Sower Explained, 13:18-23
(Mark 4:13-20)

D. The Parable of the Wheat and the Tares: The Question of Evil—Why It Exists, 13:24-30
(cp. Matthew 13:36-43)

E. The Parable of the Mustard Seed: The Growth and Greatness of Christianity, 13:31-32
(Mark 4:30-32; Luke 13:18-19)

F. The Parable of the Leaven: The Transforming Power of the Gospel, 13:33
(Luke 13:20-21)

G. The Messiah's Purpose for Speaking in Parables, 13:34-35
(Mark 4:33-34)

H. The Parable of the Wheat and the Tares Explained, 13:36-43

I. The Parable of the Hidden Treasure: Giving Up All for Christ, 13:44

J. The Parable of the Merchant Man and the Pearl of Great Price: Giving up All for Christ, 13:45-46

K. The Parable of the Dragnet: Separating the Bad from the Good, 13:47-50

L. The Parable of the Householder: Devotion and Study and Sharing, 13:51-52

X. THE MESSIAH'S MINISTRY WHILE IN EXILE FROM HEROD, 13:53-16:12

A. The Messiah is Rejected in His Home Town: Why Jesus is Rejected, 13:53-58
(Mark 6:1-6; cp. Luke 4:16-30)

B. The Messiah's Forerunner is Murdered: A Godly vs. an Ungodly Man, 14:1-14
(Mark 6:14-29; Luke 9:7-9)

C. The Messiah's Power to Feed Five Thousand: The Essentials for Ministry, 14:15-21
(Mark 6:30-44; Luke 9:10-17; John 6:1-14)

D. The Messiah's Power to Calm a Storm: The Power of His Presence, 14:22-33
(Mark 6:45-52; John 6:16-21)

E. The Messiah's Power Sought and Trusted: The Steps to Seeking and Being Made Whole, 14:34-36

F. The Messiah Teaches What Defiles a Man, 15:1-20
(Mark 7:1-23; cp. Luke 11:37-41)

G. The Messiah Teaches What It Takes to Receive Things of God, 15:21-28
(Mark 7:24-30)

H. The Messiah's Compassion for Man's Physical Need: How to Minister, 15:29-39
(Mark 8:1-9)

XI. THE MESSIAH'S DRAMATIC REVELATION: HIS MESSIAHSHIP, HIS CHURCH AND HIS CROSS, 16:13-17:27

A. The Messiah's Dramatic Revelation of Himself and His Church: Peter's Great Confession, 16:13-20
(Mk.8:27-30; Lk.9:18-21; cp. Jn.6:68-69)

13 When Jesus came to the
region of Caesarea Philippi,
he asked his disciples, "Who
do people say the Son of Man
is?"
14 They replied, "Some say
John the Baptist; others say
Elijah; and still others, Jeremiah or one of the prophets."
15 "But what about you?" he
asked. "Who do you say I
am?"
16 Simon Peter answered,
"You are the Christ, the Son
of the living God."
17 Jesus replied, "Blessed
are you, Simon son of Jonah,
for this was not revealed to
you by man, but by my Fa-
ther in heaven.
18 And I tell you that you are
Peter, and on this rock I will
build my church, and the
gates of Hades will not overcome it.
19 I will give you the keys of
the kingdom of heaven;
whatever you bind on earth
will be bound in heaven,
and whatever you loose on
earth will be loosed in
heaven."
20 Then he warned his disciples not to tell anyone that
he was the Christ.

1 Christ was in the area of Caesarea Philippi
2 This confession is not the confession of the world
- a. The first critical question
- b. The false confessions

3 This confession declares one's trust in Christ
- a. The second critical question, v.15
- b. The true confession: A personal trust in Christ

4 This confession is revealed by God alone

5 This confession is the foundation of the church[DSI]
- a. Fact 1: His church
- b. Fact 2: He builds
- c. Fact 3: He protects

6 This confession assigns great responsibility to believers for the church
- a. A resp. to use the keys to the Kingdom of heaven
- b. A responsibility to bind & loose on earth

7 This confession must be understood before being shared with others

DIVISION XI

THE MESSIAH'S DRAMATIC REVELATION: HIS MESSIAHSHIP HIS CHURCH, AND HIS CROSS, 16:13-17:27

A. The Messiah's Dramatic Revelation of Himself and His Church: Peter's Great Confession, 16:13-20

(16:13-20) **Introduction**: Jesus withdrew to be alone with His disciples. He was facing the end very, very soon. There was much to reveal and teach them. It was time for them to learn that He was *building a church*—an assembly of people who would be confessing Him to be the Messiah. The present passage is one of the most dramatic revelations ever made. It is also one of the most demanding questions ever asked. It is demanding because the answer given determines a person's eternal destiny. How a person answers the questions determines where he will spend eternity, with God in heaven or apart from God in hell. And note: there is only one answer to the question that can qualify a person for heaven: "You are the Christ, the Son of the living God." The importance of the question and its confession is clearly seen by glancing quickly at the points of the passage.

1. Christ was in the area of Caesarea Philippi (v.13).
2. This confession is not the confession of the world (v.13-14).
3. This confession declares one's personal trust in Christ (v.15-16).
4. This confession is revealed by God alone (v.17).
5. This confession is the foundation of the church (v.18).
6. This confession assigns great responsibility to believers for the church (v.19).
7. This confession must be understood before being shared with others (v.20).

1 (16:13) **Caesarea Philippi**: Christ was in the area of Caesarea Philippi. (See DEEPER STUDY # 1—Mk.8:27. This note will give the dramatic background for the Lord's pointed question. Jesus had withdrawn to be alone and to pray before this event and its profound revelation [cp. Lk.9:18].)

2 (16:13-14) **Profession, False**: Peter's confession is not the confession of the world. Note two significant points.

1. Jesus had asked a critical question: "Who do people say the Son of Man is?" We must know what others say about Jesus, just who He is. What people think of Jesus...
   - determines their destiny
   - determines how we are to reach out to them
   - determines their reaction to us as we witness to them
   - determines to a large degree the morality and justice of a society

2. There were false confessions regarding Christ. The popular opinions show that Christ was highly esteemed and greatly respected. He was considered one of the greatest of men. It should be noted that these opinions were not only untrue, but they were dangerous in that they contained only half truths. The result was tragic: people were deceived and misled by them.
   a. Some people said Jesus was John the Baptist. These people were professing Jesus to be a great spirit of righteousness, a spirit that was willing to be martyred for its faith. Herod and others thought this (Mt.14:1-2). Upon hearing of Jesus' marvelous works, Herod fancied that either John had been revived or else his spirit indwelt the man about whom he was hearing.
   The common people saw some similarity between John and Jesus: both were doing a unique and great work for God; both were divinely chosen and gifted by God; and both proclaimed the Kingdom of God and prepared men for it. Therefore, when some people looked at Jesus and His ministry, they did not consider Him to be the

Messiah, but rather the promised forerunner of the Messiah (Mal.4:5).

b. Some people said Jesus was Elijah. Elijah was considered to be the greatest prophet and teacher of all time and was also predicted to be the forerunner of the coming Messiah (Mal.4:5). William Barclay points out that even today the Jews expect Elijah to return before the Messiah. In the celebration of the Passover, they always leave a chair vacant for him to occupy (*The Gospel of Matthew*, Vol.2, p.150). Elijah had also been used by God to miraculously feed a widow woman and her son (1 Ki.17:14).The people connected Elijah's miracle and Jesus' feeding of the multitude.

c. Some people said Jesus was Jeremiah. They were professing Jesus to be a prophet who was revealing some very important things about God and religion to men. It had always been thought that Jeremiah was going to return to earth right before the Messiah and bring with him the tabernacle, ark, and altar of incense. He was said to have taken these and hid them in Mount Nebo right before he died (2 Maccabees 2:1-12; 2 Esdras 2:18).

d. Some people said Jesus was one of the prophets. They were professing Jesus to be a great prophet who had been sent for their day and time. He was thought to be one of the great prophets brought back to life or one in whom the spirit of a great prophet dwelt (cp. Dt.18:15, 18).

It should be noted that the same false confessions about Christ exist in every generation.

⇒ There are some people who think that Jesus was only a great man of righteousness who was martyred for His faith. Therefore, He leaves us a great example of how to live and stand up for what we believe.

⇒ There are other people who think that Jesus was only one of the great teachers and prophets of history.

⇒ There are still others who think that Jesus was only a great man who revealed some very important things to us about God and religion. Therefore, He can make a significant contribution to every man in his search for God.

⇒ There are some others who think that Jesus was just a great man and prophet sent to the people (Jews) of His day. We can learn about Him by studying His life.

Isn't this the carpenter? Isn't this Mary's son and the brother of James, Joseph, Judas and Simon? Aren't his sisters here with us?" And they took offense at him. (Mark 6:3)

He was in the world, and though the world was made through him, the world did not recognize him. He came to that which was his own, but his own did not receive him. (John 1:10-11)

Then they asked him, "Where is your father?" "You do not know me or my Father," Jesus replied. "If you knew me, you would know my Father also." (John 8:19)

Who is the liar? It is the man who denies that Jesus is the Christ. Such a man is the antichrist—he denies the Father and the Son. No one who denies the Son has the Father; whoever acknowledges the Son has the Father also. (1 John 2:22-23)

But every spirit that does not acknowledge Jesus is not from God. This is the spirit of the antichrist, which you have heard is coming and even now is already in the world. (1 John 4:3)

Thought 1. Note three things about the world's opinions of Jesus Christ.

1) The world is not unanimous in its opinion of Christ. There are many different opinions, yet there is only one *truth*. He either is or is not who He claimed to be: the Son of God. As long as the world does not hold to the truth, it shall wander around in a maze of opinions, following guess after guess and hypothesis after hypothesis.
2) Most of the world's opinions of Christ see Him as a good and great man. The opinions are not accurate, but they at least elevate Christ above the average man.
3) The world's opinions are false and inaccurate. There are two bases for this statement.
   a) If Christ should not be the Son of God, then He is not a good and great man. He is the worst deceiver and biggest hoax to ever arrive on the world scene. Why? Because He claimed to be the Son of God and the God of righteousness, and He built His following on the claim. If Jesus Christ is not the Son of God, then every true follower of His is living in a *dream world* of *false hope* and denying himself many of the world's goods. He is also teaching a deceptive lie to others. If Christ should not be the Son of God, then He is not worth following.
   b) Scripture emphatically declares: Jesus Christ is the Son of God. He is who He claimed to be.

3 (16:15-16) **Confession—Jesus Christ, Names and Titles**: Peter's confession was a personal trust in Christ.

1. Jesus asked a second critical question, and He asked this question much more emphatically in the Greek: "But you, who do you say that I am?" The answer to this question is critical; it is all-important. It determines a person's eternal destiny.

2. The true confession declares one's personal trust in Christ. Note Peter's words, "You are the Christ, the Son of the living God"—a simple and yet momentous confession arising from a personal conviction. It is the confession that saves the soul and the confession that lays the foundation for the church. The very life and survival of a man's soul and of the church as a whole rests upon this simple, yet profound conviction.

⇒ The *Christ*: the Messiah, the annointed One of God (see DEEPER STUDY # 2—Mt.1:18).

⇒ The *Son of God*: of the same being, the same substance; One with the Father (see note—Ph.2:6).

⇒ The *Son of the Living God*: the source and being of life; possessing the source, energy, and power of life within Himself (Jn.5:26; 17:2-3; 1 Th.1:9).

Peter probably did not understand all that was involved in Christ's being the Son of God (the cross and resurrection had not yet taken place). But his confession was made in simple trust arising from a heart that was truly convicted that Jesus was the Christ, the Son of the living God. It is simple trust which God desires and longs for—nothing more and nothing less. Peter was simply confessing step by step, "I believe you are..."

- the true Messiah,
- not a mere man,
- but the Son of God,
- sent by God,
- to fulfill all that the prophets foretold.

Thought 1. The question is personal. It is directed to every man: "Who do you say that I am?" Every man has to answer, and his eternal destiny depends upon his answer. But his answer is critical, for it is not a confession *about* Christ that Christ is after. He is after a belief, a confession in His deity, a trusting of His saving grace.

"Whoever acknowledges me before men, I will also acknowledge him before my Father in heaven. But whoever disowns me before men, I will disown him before my Father in heaven. (Mat 10:32-33)

If anyone is ashamed of me and my words in this adulterous and sinful generation, the Son of Man will be ashamed of him when he comes in his Father's glory with the holy angels." (Mark 8:38)

"I tell you, whoever acknowledges me before men, the Son of Man will also acknowledge him before the angels of God. (Luke 12:8)

That if you confess with your mouth, "Jesus is Lord," and believe in your heart that God raised him from the dead, you will be saved.For it is with your heart that you believe and are justified, and it is with your mouth that you confess and are saved. (Rom 10:9-10)

The first thing Andrew did was to find his brother Simon and tell him, "We have found the Messiah" (that is, the Christ). (John 1:41)

Philip found Nathanael and told him, "We have found the one Moses wrote about in the Law, and about whom the prophets also wrote—Jesus of Nazareth, the son of Joseph." (John 1:45)

Then Nathanael declared, "Rabbi, you are the Son of God; you are the King of Israel." (John 1:49)

"Come, see a man who told me everything I ever did. Could this be the Christ?" (John 4:29)

We believe and know that you are the Holy One of God." (John 6:69)

"Yes, Lord," she told him, "I believe that you are the Christ, the Son of God, who was to come into the world." (John 11:27)

Thomas said to him, "My Lord and my God!" (John 20:28)

As they traveled along the road, they came to some water and the eunuch said, "Look, here is water. Why shouldn't I be baptized?" (Acts 8:36-37)

4 (16:17) **Conviction—Holy Spirit, Work of**: Peter's confession was revealed by God alone. Only God can convict the soul of a man and lead a man to personally trust Christ as the Son of God. There are two reasons for this.

1 Man is only flesh and blood. A person cannot convict another person to trust Christ, not convict him in regenerating power. Conviction that leads a man to trust Christ—that leads to regeneration—is the work of God's Spirit (Jn.16:8-11).

2. The man without the Spirit does not accept the things that come from the Spirit of God (1 Cor.2:14). Man is of the earth; he is earthly. Christ is of heaven and of God; He is heavenly. God is Spirit, and they who worship Him must worship Him *in spirit* and in truth (Jn.4:23-24). Man cannot come to know Christ in a personal way through natural wisdom or study. Humanly, the fact is as clear as can be, man cannot *recreate* himself. If he is to be reborn, he has to be *recreated* by Someone other than himself. He has to be recreated by God (Jn.3:3, 5-6).

⇒ Man cannot *quicken* himself; he cannot give spiritual life to himself—only God can.
⇒ Man cannot *regenerate* himself—only God can.
⇒ Man cannot *transform* himself—only God can.
⇒ Man cannot *redeem* himself—only God can.
⇒ Man cannot *infuse* himself with eternal life—only God can.

Children born not of natural descent, nor of human decision or a husband's will, but born of God. (John 1:13)

Flesh gives birth to flesh, but the Spirit gives birth to spirit. (John 3:6)

For it is by grace you have been saved, through faith—and this not from yourselves, it is the gift of God— not by works, so that no one can boast. (Eph 2:8-9)

He saved us, not because of righteous things we had done, but because of his mercy. He saved us through the washing of rebirth and renewal by the Holy Spirit, (Titus 3:5)

For you have been born again, not of perishable seed, but of imperishable, through the living and enduring word of God. (1 Pet 1:23)

Everyone who believes that Jesus is the Christ is born of God, and everyone who loves the father loves his child as well. (1 John 5:1)

Thought 1. Natural man has been led away from the spiritual...

- by pride, power, fame, wealth, and glory.
- by the prejudices of education, the philosophy of humanism, the limitations of scientific methodology, and the materialistic results of technology.
- by the pull to disbelieve, the lack of courage to buck the crowd, and the hesitation to surrender all of self and possessions to Christ.
- by the love of the flesh, the enjoyment of looking, the stimulation of touching, the sensation of experiencing, and the consumption of tasting.
- by the deceptions of the evil one, the lusts of the human heart, and the sins of personal behavior.

5 (16:18) **Church, Foundation**: Peter's confession is the foundation of the church (see DEEPER STUDY # 1, Church—Mt.16:18. Also see notes—Eph.2:20; 4:4-6 for more discussion.) Christ replied to Peter, "You are Peter [petros] and on this rock [petra] I will build my church." No matter how a person interprets this passage, one thing is sure: this was a tremendous compliment to Peter. But what did Jesus mean? Probably this: the rock was *Peter himself and his* *confession*, not simply Peter and not just his confession. The rock was *both*, but in a very special sense.

1. Peter himself was the rock in two senses.
   a. Peter was the first person to *fully* grasp who Jesus really was. He was the first to confess with *full* understanding that Jesus is the Christ, the Son of the living God. Others had made similar confessions before (Jn.1:41, 45, 49; 6:69), but they had not yet been with Jesus long enough to *fully* grasp what being "the Son of God" really meant. Their confessions had been the earthly confessions of a simple child-like faith. But now Peter understood more fully; he *fully* grasped who Jesus was. Therefore, he became the first man, the first rock, the foundation *upon* which the church and all other "living stones" were to be built.

      Great weight is given to this meaning in Eph.2:20. The apostles and prophets are said to be the foundation of the church upon which all future believers or "living stones" are built (1 Pt.2:5). Jesus Christ is said to be the chief cornerstone. The picture is unquestionably clear. From the human perspective, the apostles and prophets work and build the church, and upon their work and effort the church depends. From God's perspective, Christ's power and work establishes the church (cp. 1 Cor.3:11; 1 Pt.2:4-8; see note—Mt.16:19).
   b. Peter was the one who launched and laid the foundation of the church. He was the early leader of the church who stood forth at Pentecost when three thousand souls were saved (Acts 2:41) and at Caesarea when the door of salvation was opened to the Gentiles (10:1f). Therefore, he was the rock and the foundation in that he was the first man who ever opened the doors of the church to both Jew and Gentile.

2. Peter's confession (or one might say, Christ Himself) was the rock. Christ said, "You are Peter and on this rock [I, Myself, the great truth of your confession] I will build my church." There is no question that the church is built upon Christ. He is unquestionably the builder of the church and the power behind its structure (1 Cor.3:11). It is He who takes every believer, every "living stone," and places him into the structure of His church (1 Pt.2:4-8). The church *depends* upon Christ, not upon Peter nor any other man or combination of men. It was first *built* by Peter after Pentecost; but it is *held up and held together* by Christ, the only foundation.

Note the exact words spoken by Christ.

⇒ Fact 1: "My church." The church is Christ's not man's.
⇒ Fact 2: "I will build." Christ builds the church.
⇒ Fact 3: "The gates of Hades will not overcome it." Christ Himself protects the church.

"Therefore everyone who hears these words of mine and puts them into practice is like a wise man who built his house on the rock. (Mat 7:24)

Jesus said to them, "Have you never read in the Scriptures: "'The stone the builders rejected has become the capstone ; the Lord has done this, and it is marvelous in our eyes'? (Mat 21:42)

For no one can lay any foundation other than the one already laid, which is Jesus Christ. (1 Cor 3:11)

Built on the foundation of the apostles and prophets, with Christ Jesus himself as the chief cornerstone. (Eph 2:20)

As you come to him, the living Stone— rejected by men but chosen by God and precious to him— you also, like living stones, are being built into a spiritual house to be a holy priesthood, offering spiritual sacrifices acceptable to God through Jesus Christ. For in Scripture it says: "See, I lay a stone in Zion, a chosen and precious cornerstone, and the one who trusts in him will never be put to shame." (1 Pet 2:4-6)

Thought 1. The *true* church is universal. It is made up of *all* who genuinely confess Jesus to be the Christ, the Son of the living God. But note: He is the Son of the *living* God. If God is living, then Christ is living. He is, therefore, "My Lord, my God." A genuine believer, that is, a true church member, becomes a person who has surrendered himself to be a servant of God's Son, of God's Lord.

Thought 2. We should go to Christ often and confess our trust and faith in Him. We should do so alone, demonstrating strength, devotion, tenderness, and warmth. He desires such strong and warm devotion, for we are the "living stones" of His church.

Thought 3. Note a fact often overlooked. Christ not only loved and died for us individually—He also loved and died for the church as a whole (universally). "Christ loved the church, and gave Himself up for her" (Eph.5:25).

DEEPER STUDY # 1

(16:18) **Church** (ekklesia): the word means to call out a gathering, an assembly. In the Greek, there is no spiritual significance ascribed to the word itself. An example is the town meeting in Ephesus which was "called out" (ekklesia). It was only an official city-wide meeting (Acts 19:32, 39, 41).

What is the difference then between such secular gatherings and the church of God?

1. It is God who calls together and gathers His church. His church is the body of people "called out" from the world by Him. They are His body of people, a people sanctified or *set apart* by Him to form the church of the living God.
2. God dwells within the very presence of believers when they gather together (see note—1 Cor.3:16-17).
3. The gathering of God meets together for two purposes—worship and mission. God is the object of worship, and His mission becomes the objective of the church. Therefore, God's church, the local assembly, gathers together to worship and to pool its resources in order to carry out the mission of God Himself. It should be noted that this is the first mention of the church in the New Testament. (See notes—Mt.16:18; Eph.2:20; 4:4-6 for more discussion.)

6 (16:19) **Christian Responsibility**: Peter's confession assigned great responsibility to believers for the church. The steward of the house is given the keys or the responsibility for the house. The steward has the responsibility to close (bind) and to open (loose) the house. The key is the gospel, the message of the Lord Jesus Christ Himself. It is the business of the steward to proclaim and teach the Gospel. By proclaiming and teaching, he opens the door; by not proclaiming and not teaching, he shuts the door.

Note: the keys are not the keys to the church but to the Kingdom of Heaven. It is entrance into the Kingdom of Heaven that is the point. Peter was the first man to preach the gospel and open the door to Israel at Pentecost (Acts 2:38-42) and to the Gentiles in the house of Cornelius (Acts 10:3-48).

Note another point of critical importance: Peter claimed no power or authority beyond preaching the gospel and opening the door to unbelievers (Acts 15:7-11). His epistles say nothing whatsoever about man's acting in God's behalf and determining who will and who will not enter the Kingdom of Heaven. Only God will determine who lives and who does not live in His presence. There is also this additional evidence: Peter claimed nothing more for himself than what other men claimed—to be gifted by God as an apostle (1 Pt.1:1) and an elder (1 Pt.5:1). This fact is clearly seen in his subservience to James. James presided over the Jerusalem church, not Peter (Acts 15:13-19; Gal.2:11-14).

> **Thought 1.** The servants of God, ministers and laymen alike, have been given the gospel, the keys to the Kingdom of Heaven. It is every believer's responsibility to use the keys. The unbeliever who rejects the gospel in hostility and begins to persecute the believer is to be turned away from (Mt.10:11-14, 23). The one who receives the gospel and the believer is to have the door of the kingdom opened to him.
>
> **Therefore go and make disciples of all nations, baptizing them in the name of the Father and of the Son and of the Holy Spirit, and teaching them to obey everything I have commanded you. And surely I am with you always, to the very end of the age." (Mat 28:19-20)**
>
> **He said to them, "Go into all the world and preach the good news to all creation. (Mark 16:15)**
>
> **Again Jesus said, "Peace be with you! As the Father has sent me, I am sending you." (John 20:21; cp.Mt.20:28; Lk.19:10)**
>
> **But you will receive power when the Holy Spirit comes on you; and you will be my witnesses in Jerusalem, and in all Judea and Samaria, and to the ends of the earth." (Acts 1:8)**
>
> **And the things you have heard me say in the presence of many witnesses entrust to reliable men who will also be qualified to teach others. (2 Tim 2:2)**
>
> **But in your hearts set apart Christ as Lord. Always be prepared to give an answer to everyone who asks you to give the reason for the hope that you have. But do this with gentleness and respect, (1 Pet 3:15)**

7 (16:20) **Witnessing**: Peter's confession must be understood before being shared with others. There were several reasons the disciples were forbidden to share that Jesus was the Son of God.

1. They still needed more preparation. They did not yet know the *full* gospel. The death and resurrection of Jesus, the very core of the gospel, had not yet taken place.

2. The disciples needed the indwelling power of the Holy Spirit if the message was to be effective, and the Spirit had not yet come. Pentecost had not yet taken place.

3. The people misunderstood the prophecies of the Messiah. If the disciples began preaching with force, the people might revolt against the Roman conquerors (see notes—Mt.1:1; DEEPER STUDY # 2—1:18; DEEPER STUDY # 3—3:11; notes—11:1-6; 11:2-3; DEEPER STUDY # 1—11:5; DEEPER STUDY # 2—11:6; DEEPER STUDY # 1—12:16; note—Lk.7:21-23).

> **Thought 1.** Two things are essential before a believer can effectively proclaim the gospel.
>
> 1) He must understand the death and resurrection of Jesus Christ (1 Cor.15:1-4).
> 2) He must be indwelt and infilled with the Spirit of God (Acts 1:8).

	B. The Messiah Foretells His Death and Future Glory (1st Time): Total Commitment, 16:21-28 (Mk.8:31-9:1; Lk.9:22-27)	24 Then Jesus said to his disciples, "If anyone would come after me, he must deny himself and take up his cross and follow me.	**2 His death demands total commitment from a man** a. Must will to follow b. Must deny self c. Must take up the cross d. Must follow Jesus
1 His death required total commitment on His part a. His death was necessary: He "must go" to suffer 1) In Jerusalem[DS1] 2) To suffer[DS2] 3) To be killed 4) To be raised	21 From that time on Jesus began to explain to his disciples that he must go to Jerusalem and suffer many things at the hands of the elders, chief priests and teachers of the law, and that he must be killed and on the third day be raised to life.	25 For whoever wants to save his life will lose it, but whoever loses his life for me will find it. 26 What good will it be for a man if he gains the whole world, yet forfeits his soul? Or what can a man give in exchange for his soul?	**3 His death offers four arguments for total commitment** a. An abandonment of this life saves a man b. A man's soul is worth more than the whole world
b. His death arouses natural man	22 Peter took him aside and began to rebuke him. "Never, Lord!" he said. "This shall never happen to you!"	27 For the Son of Man is going to come in his Father's glory with his angels, and then he will reward each person according to what he has done.	c. A day of judgment is coming
c. His death shows man to be an adversary of God d. His death reveals man's true nature	23 Jesus turned and said to Peter, "Get behind me, Satan! You are a stumbling block to me; you do not have in mind the things of God, but the things of men."	28 I tell you the truth, some who are standing here will not taste death before they see the Son of Man coming in his kingdom."	d. A promise is given—the promise of never having to taste death

DIVISION XI

THE MESSIAH'S DRAMATIC REVELATION: HIS MESSIAHSHIP HIS CHURCH, AND HIS CROSS, 16:13-17:27

B. The Messiah Foretells His Death and Future Glory (1st Time): Total Commitment, 16:21-28

(16:21-28) **Introduction**: a new stage was now launched by Jesus. Note the words, "From that time on." More plainly than ever before and without reserve, Christ revealed that *the Son of the living God* was going to be killed and raised again from the dead. Never before had so phenomenal an event happened, and never again would it happen. History would be made. "Jerusalem...that killed the prophets" was going to commit the ultimate crime—they were going to kill God's own Son (cp. Mt.23:29-31).

Note two facts.

1. Christ had already been telling His disciples about His death and resurrection for some time, but they had not understood. There were two primary reasons for their blindness. First, the idea of a suffering Messiah differed radically from their own idea of the Messiah (see notes—Mt.1:1; Deeper Study # 2—1:18; Deeper Study # 3—3:11; notes—11:1-6; 11:2-3; Deeper Study # 1—11:5; Deeper Study # 2—11:6; Deeper Study # 1—12:16; Deeper Study # 1—Mk.8:27; notes—8:30; Lk.7:21); and second, the revelation had been hidden in pictures and symbols.

> **Jesus answered them, "Destroy this temple, and I will raise it again in three days." (John 2:19)**
> **Just as Moses lifted up the snake in the desert, so the Son of Man must be lifted up, (John 3:14)**
> **I am the living bread that came down from heaven. If anyone eats of this bread, he will live forever. This bread is my flesh, which I will give for the life of the world." (John 6:51)**

Now, however, there was a significant switch in how Jesus went about preparing His disciples for His death. The difference was that Christ no longer spoke in pictures and symbols. He now taught them in simple and direct words (Mt.20:18-20; Lk.18:31-33). A new stage in the revelation of God's plan for the world was now taking place: God's Son was to die and be raised again for the sins of the world. God's plan for saving the world was to take place through a suffering Messiah, not a conquering Messiah. God's Messiah was not going to deliver a *materialistic* world into the hands of His followers. God's Messiah was going to die; and through death, He was going to usher in the Kingdom of God, making it possible for His followers to live eternally in the very presence of God Himself (see Deeper Study # 3—Mt.19:23-24; cp. Jn.3:16; 5:24f).

2. The disciples now understood *more fully* that Jesus was "the Christ, the Son of the living God" (Mt.16:16). They had taken a great leap forward in their understanding of His nature, just who He really was. Now they needed to learn two things: that the real way into God's kingdom and glory was through death, sacrifice, and self-denial. The path of suffering had to be taken not only by God's Messiah but also by the followers of God's Messiah (v.24-28).

Just imagine the radical difference between the two concepts...

- a suffering Messiah vs. a conquering Messiah
- a suffering believer vs. a conquering believer

Seeing the radical difference helps a person understand Peter's behavior and the reason why the disciples were so slow to grasp what Christ was saying. In fact, they never completely understood until after the resurrection (see outlines and notes—Mt.17:22-23; 20:17-19; Mk.8:31-33; 9:30-32; 10:32-34).

The lesson of Christ is clear: God's plan to save the world is through the death of His Son, His sacrifice and self-denial, and the way of salvation for man is the same. Man must undergo personal sacrifice, self-denial, and death (Mt.16:24-26).

1. His death required total commitment on His part (v.21-23).
2. His death demands total commitment from a man (v.24).
3. His death offers four arguments for total commitment (v.25-28).

1 (16:21-23) **Jesus Christ, Death**: Jesus' death required total commitment on His part.

1. His death was necessary: He "must go to Jerusalem and suffer." The words "must [dei] go" are strong: a constraint, an imperative, a necessity was laid upon Christ. He had no choice. His death and resurrection had been planned and willed by God through all eternity. The prophets had predicted it; He must fulfill the will of God, for God had ordained His death (cp. Mt.26:54; Lk.24:26, 46).

The resurrection of Jesus Christ was also necessary. Jesus' prediction of His resurrection is clear to us because we can look back upon it, but it was never clear to His disciples. Why? Very simply, it was to be a new experience. No one had ever risen from the dead never to die again. It was unprecedented. The apostles believed perhaps somewhat like Martha—that there was to be a future resurrection of all men (Jn.11:24-26). Such a belief is an expression of the hope that is within every man, the hope to continue on in some form of existence. Such a belief is easy to hold, but to think of a resurrection now, to think of a person's arising from the dead today is difficult. The actual resurrection of a dead person would be inconceivable to those who had not been grounded in its teaching.

Just what they thought Christ meant by *being raised again* is not known. The fact that they did not fully understand is clear from the fact that their spirits were crushed when He was killed. However, some of His followers seemed to grasp more of *a real bodily* resurrection than others. This is clear by an immediate remembrance of His words after His resurrection. There was John who believed immediately (Jn.20:8-9). Mary Magdalene was shown that He had risen just "as He said" (Mt.28:6), and she understood after seeing Him. But others were slower to understand and believe (Mk.16:11; Jn.20:24-25).

> **Jesus answered them, "Destroy this temple, and I will raise it again in three days." (John 2:19)**
>
> **Just as Moses lifted up the snake in the desert, so the Son of Man must be lifted up, (John 3:14)**
>
> **I am the living bread that came down from heaven. If anyone eats of this bread, he will live forever. This bread is my flesh, which I will give for the life of the world." (John 6:51)**
>
> **But I have had God's help to this very day, and so I stand here and testify to small and great alike. I am saying nothing beyond what the prophets and Moses said would happen— that the Christ would suffer and, as the first to rise from the dead, would proclaim light to his own people and to the Gentiles." (Acts 26:22-23)**
>
> **For what I received I passed on to you as of first importance : that Christ died for our sins according to the Scriptures, that he was buried, that he was raised on the third day according to the Scriptures, (1 Cor 15:3-4)**
>
> **And he died for all, that those who live should no longer live for themselves but for him who died for them and was raised again. (2 Cor 5:15)**
>
> **For Christ died for sins once for all, the righteous for the unrighteous, to bring you to God. He was put to death in the body but made alive by the Spirit, (1 Pet 3:18)**

Thought 1. Christ revealed His death and resurrection in stages—revealed it only as the disciples were able to receive and bear the fact. Christ always teaches us gradually and moves us along as we are able to learn. There is great truth in the saying that He does not put more upon us than we can bear.

Thought 2. Note that Jesus spoke of His resurrection when He spoke of His death. It was for the joy that was set before Him that He endured the cross (Heb.12:2). The joy and hope of spending eternity with Christ and His followers is what encourages us to bear *our cross* while here on earth (cp. Lk.9:23).

2. His death arouses natural man. Natural man rebels at the idea of the cross. Natural man wants another way other than the cross. This is what Peter was doing: rebelling against the idea that *God's Son* was to die, that His blood had to be shed for the sins of the world (1 Pt.2:24). Peter could accept Jesus as "the Son of the living God" but not as the suffering Savior. Such an idea was repulsive and unacceptable to him. Therefore, he tried to stop the idea. Note the words, "Peter took him aside" (proslabomenos). The Greek is strong; it means *caught hold of.* Peter took hold of Christ; he grabbed Christ and took Him aside for a conference.

Note also that Peter "began to rebuke [epitiman] Him." This again is strong. It is not just a wish but a forcible attempt to stop the idea of the suffering Savior. "This shall never happen to you." *This must not and cannot happen to you. God forbid it* is the equivalent idea. The point is this: Peter was out to stop the cross. He was urging Christ to be the Messiah of power, fame, and sensation whom the Jews were expecting (see notes—Mk.8:27-9:50; 8:30; Mt.1:1; DEEPER STUDY # 2—1:18; DEEPER STUDY # 3—3:11; notes—11:1-6; 11:2-3; DEEPER STUDY # 1—11:5; DEEPER STUDY # 2—11:6; DEEPER STUDY # 1—12:16; note—Lk.7:21-23). Peter was urging Christ to follow his own human schemes instead of God's way; and by such urging, he was tempting Christ with the very same compromises that Satan used to tempt Christ—the compromises of power, fame, and sensation (Mt.4:1-11). Peter was zealous for God, but he was mistaken and ignorant in his zeal. He did not understand that God was planning to save the world through the death of His Son (see note, pt.3—Mk.8:31).

Such behavior is the way of the world. It is the natural, carnal mind. Man rebels and recoils against the idea of a suffering Savior who had to die for the sins of the world—a Savior who demands the same sacrifice and denial of His followers. Such an idea is unacceptable and repulsive.

Thought 1. The natural man's idea of God and of God's plan for man is seen in three concepts.

1) Some think the path of life is love, so they live showing interest and care for others. God is seen as a giving, loving, and indulgent *grandfather type* of person—the indulgent grandfather who tolerates even the worst behavior, no matter how much human suffering and devastation is wrought by the hands of a person. To think of the cross and *the blood* of Christ as an emblem of suffering is repulsive and repelling. The cross is viewed only as an emblem of love, not of sin and shame. The way of love is thought to be the path of life which man is to follow.
2) Some think that comfort and pleasure is the path of life. God again is viewed only as an indulgent *grandfather type* who gives man the good things of life and helps man when he gets in trouble. God's will for man is thought to be comfort and pleasure, ease and plenty, health and leisure. Again the cross is only an emblem of love and care for the world, not of suffering and sacrifice and self-denial. The shame, pain, and agony of the cross and its purpose of reconciling a world lost in sin and reeling in desperate need is over-looked.

The seed that fell among thorns stands for those who hear, but as they go on their way they are choked by life's worries, riches and pleasures, and they do not mature. (Luke 8:14)

And I'll say to myself, "You have plenty of good things laid up for many years. Take life easy; eat, drink and be merry."' (Luke 12:19)

But the widow who lives for pleasure is dead even while she lives. (1 Tim 5:6)

They will be paid back with harm for the harm they have done. Their idea of pleasure is to carouse in broad daylight. They are blots and blemishes, reveling in their pleasures while they feast with you. (2 Pet 2:13)

"Now then, listen, you wanton creature, lounging in your security and saying to yourself, 'I am, and there is none besides me. I will never be a widow or suffer the loss of children.' Both of these will overtake you in a moment, on a single day: loss of children and widowhood. They will come upon you in full measure, in spite of your many sorceries and all your potent spells. (Isa 47:8-9)

3) Some feel that triumph, victory, position, authority, power, and reigning supreme is God's way. This was the idea of most Jews in Christ's day. It was Peter's concept of the Messiah (see notes—Mt.1:1; DEEPER STUDY # 2—1:18; DEEPER STUDY # 3—3:11; 11:1-6; 11:2-3; DEEPER STUDY # 1—11:5; DEEPER STUDY # 2—11:6; DEEPER STUDY # 1—12:16; note—Lk.7:21-23). The concepts of power, position, and authority are clearly seen in movements that stress *self-image*, *self-improvement*, and *personality development*. Developing one's self-image as much as possible and achieving all that one can are said to be God's plan and path for man. However, the idea of suffering and sacrifice and self-denial is rejected.

Jesus called them together and said, "You know that the rulers of the Gentiles lord it over them, and their high officials exercise authority over them. Not so with you. Instead, whoever wants to become great among you must be your servant, and whoever wants to be first must be your slave— (Mat 20:25-27)

How can you believe if you accept praise from one another, yet make no effort to obtain the praise that comes from the only God? (John 5:44)

The man who thinks he knows something does not yet know as he ought to know. (1 Cor 8:2)

For everything in the world—the cravings of sinful man, the lust of his eyes and the boasting of what he has and does—comes not from the Father but from the world. (1 John 2:16)

You say, 'I am rich; I have acquired wealth and do not need a thing.' But you do not realize that you are wretched, pitiful, poor, blind and naked. (Rev 3:17)

But man, despite his riches, does not endure; he is like the beasts that perish. (Psa 49:12)

Pride goes before destruction, a haughty spirit before a fall. (Prov 16:18)

Do you see a man wise in his own eyes? There is more hope for a fool than for him. (Prov 26:12)

3. His death shows man to be an adversary of God. The literal meaning of Satan in the words "get behind me, Satan" is "adversary" (see note—Rev.12:7-9). Calling Peter "Satan" is stern, yet such sternness was necessary. Peter was tempting Christ with the very same temptation that Christ had faced in the wilderness (see notes—Mt.4:8-10). All the worldly glory that could be His flashed across His mind. The loyalty and allegiance of men without the cross was again being suggested to Him. How this must have cut Christ! This time the temptation was coming from one of His own disciples! When a man refuses to accept God's plan for life, he becomes an adversary to God. He opposes God's will. In essence, man says that he knows what is best; that he is *wiser* than God. Think! When a man does not accept God's plan for life, the crux of what he says to God is, "The cross is not necessary. Jesus' dying to save the world was a useless plan. It was not needed."

This is what Peter was doing and saying. He was opposing God's plan for life, that is, saving the world through the death of His Son. He was saying that he was wiser than God. Note: Christ abruptly turned to Peter before Peter could say anything else and stopped him in his tracks. He charged Peter with being Satan, with being under the authority of Satan, with speaking as Satan. He had become *as* Satan, an adversary to God and God's plan for His Son and for the salvation of the world.

"You are a child of the devil and an enemy of everything that is right! You are full of all kinds of deceit and trickery. Will you never stop perverting the right ways of the Lord? (Acts 13:10)

You belong to your father, the devil, and you want to carry out your father's desire. He was a murderer from the beginning, not holding to the truth, for there is

no truth in him. When he lies, he speaks his native language, for he is a liar and the father of lies. (John 8:44)

In which you used to live when you followed the ways of this world and of the ruler of the kingdom of the air, the spirit who is now at work in those who are disobedient. (Eph 2:2)

This is how we know who the children of God are and who the children of the devil are: Anyone who does not do what is right is not a child of God; nor is anyone who does not love his brother. (1 John 3:10)

Thought 1. No man should instruct or counsel God. Our task is not to force our ideas upon God but to surrender to His will.

Who is he that condemns? Christ Jesus, who died—more than that, who was raised to life—is at the right hand of God and is also interceding for us. (Rom 8:34)

4. His death reveals man's true nature. Note the words "You do not have in mind [ou phroneis]." This means to think; to mind. Peter did not have his mind or his thoughts in line with God's mind and thoughts. His tastes were different from God's tastes. Peter's thoughts and tastes were worldly and self-pleasing, not spiritual and pleasing to God. He was using human reasoning not God's reasoning. The thought that God's Son had to die and shed His blood for the sins of the world was disgraceful to Peter. In his mind, such a concept was unfit for God.

Note how true Christ's words to Peter are! "You do not have in mind the things of God, but the things of men." The death of Christ reveals man's true nature, a nature that uses natural and carnal reasoning instead of spiritual reasoning.

Those who live according to the sinful nature have their minds set on what that nature desires; but those who live in accordance with the Spirit have their minds set on what the Spirit desires. The mind of sinful man is death, but the mind controlled by the Spirit is life and peace; the sinful mind is hostile to God. It does not submit to God's law, nor can it do so. (Rom 8:5-7)

So I tell you this, and insist on it in the Lord, that you must no longer live as the Gentiles do, in the futility of their thinking. (Eph 4:17)

For, as I have often told you before and now say again even with tears, many live as enemies of the cross of Christ. Their destiny is destruction, their god is their stomach, and their glory is in their shame. Their mind is on earthly things. (Phil 3:18-19)

Once you were alienated from God and were enemies in your minds because of your evil behavior. But now he has reconciled you by Christ's physical body through death to present you holy in his sight, without blemish and free from accusation—(Col 1:21-22)

To the pure, all things are pure, but to those who are corrupted and do not believe, nothing is pure. In fact, both their minds and consciences are corrupted. (Titus 1:15)

The LORD knows the thoughts of man; he knows that they are futile. (Psa 94:11)

O Jerusalem, wash the evil from your heart and be saved. How long will you harbor wicked thoughts? (Jer 4:14)

Thought 1. Man feels a little more humane, a little more civil by denying "the blood of Christ" for the sins of the world. To reject what is sometimes called a "blood religion" makes a person feel more acceptable in a so-called *civilized society*. Two things need to be noted.

1) The cross should be viewed as repulsive. The cross is a symbol of sin and shame. Hanging upon the cross, God's *very own Son* bore our sins and the sins of the whole world (1 Jn.2:1-2). Sin and shame are always repulsive, and the fact that God's Son hung there *becoming sin for us* is abhorrent. Nothing could be any more distasteful than what actually happened.
2) The cross should be viewed as glorious. The cross is a symbol of life and of forgiven sins (1 Pt.2:20). Through the cross, God gloriously reconciles man to Himself and to one another (see outline and notes—Eph.2:13-18). So much comes through the glorious work of the cross that Paul just exclaimed, "May I never boast except in the cross of our Lord Jesus Christ" (Gal.6:14).

DEEPER STUDY # 1

(16:21) **Jesus Christ, Opposition**: note the three Jewish groups who were to take the lead in killing Jesus. These were the three groups who made up the Sanhedrin, the supreme court of Jewish justice. It was comprised of seventy members (cp. the historical basis for this structure, 2 Chron.19:5-11).

1. The elders: these were the older and most respected men of a community. The elders were judges of the civil courts and of temporal affairs (Ex.3:29; 12:21; 24:9; Num.11:25; 1 Sam.16:4; Ezra 10:14; Mt.27:12).

2. The chief priests: these were primarily the leaders among the Sadducees. They held most of the high offices of Jewish government under Roman rule (see DEEPER STUDY # 1—Acts 23:8). The chief priests were judges of religious affairs.

3. The Scribes: these were primarily Pharisees who held the teaching positions of the nation (see DEEPER STUDY # 1—Lk.6:2).

Thought 1. Note the three groups who opposed Jesus. They were the very people who should have been following Jesus, the very leaders who should have known God. They should have known God well enough to have recognized His Son the Messiah. But, as with so many in every generation, they were blinded by their own religion, power, wealth, fame, and position.

DEEPER STUDY # 2

(16:21) **"Many things"**: the sufferings of Jesus are spelled out in some detail in two passages (Mt.20:18-19; Lk.18:31-33). (Also see DEEPER STUDY # 1—Mt.27:26-44 for a detailed description of Jesus' death.)

2 (16:24) **Jesus Christ, Death—Cross—Commitment**: Jesus' death demands the total commitment of a man. Christ gives four steps that are involved in total commitment (see note—Mt.16:25-28. The note is adequate for stirring thoughts for application.)

1. A person must *will* to follow Christ. The word "would" (thelei) means to desire, wish, design, purpose, resolve, determine. It is a deliberate willing, a deliberate choice, a determined resolve to follow Christ. If a person really wills and deliberately chooses to follow Christ, then he has to do the three things mentioned. Note: the choice is voluntary; it is made by the person. It is the individual who wills and chooses; therefore, it is the individual who must act and do the three things mentioned.

2. A person must deny self. The word "deny" (aparnesastho) means to disown, disregard, forsake, renounce, reject, refuse, restrain, disclaim, do without. It means to subdue, to disregard one's self and one's interest. Very simply, it means to say "no." But note: the call is not to say "no" to some behavior or thing but to *self*. A person is to *deny self*; and this means much more than just being negative, that is, giving up something and doing without something. It means that we are to act positively, to say "yes" to Christ and "no" to self. It means to let Christ rule and reign in our hearts and lives, to let Christ have His way completely. Of course, if a person allows Christ to rule in his life, all negative as well as positive behavior is taken care of (see note and DEEPER STUDY # 1,2,3—Mk.8:34). In the Greek the word "deny" is an ingressive aorist which means that the person enters a new state or condition. It means, "Let him at once begin to deny self."

3. A person must take up the cross. (See note and DEEPER STUDY # 1, Self-denial—Lk.9:23 for discussion.)

4. A person must follow Jesus. The word "follow" (akoloothei) means to be a follower or companion, to be a disciple. It has the idea of seeking to be in union with and in the likeness of. It is following Christ, seeking to be just like Him. Again, this is not a passive behavior but an active commitment and walk. It is energy and effort, action and work. It is going after Christ with zeal and energy, struggling and seeking to follow in His footsteps, no matter the cost. Note that the steps of Christ led to death before they led to glory (Mt.16:21).

3 (16:25-28) **Commitment**: Jesus' death offers four arguments for total commitment.

1. An abandonment of this life saves a person. What does it mean when Scripture says that a person saves his life by losing it and loses his life by finding it? The key is in the words "for me." Christ says that "whoever loses his life for me will find it." The person who abandons this life—who sacrifices and gives all that he is and has for Christ—shall save his life. But the person who *keeps* his life and what he has and *seeks* more and more of this life, shall lose his life completely and eternally.

The person who "saves his life"...

- by seeking to avoid the aging of the body and death and yet denies Christ—that person shall lose his life eternally.
- by seeking to make his life more and more comfortable, easy, and secure (beyond what is necessary) and neglects Christ shall lose his life eternally.
- by seeking to gain wealth and power and fame by compromising Christ shall lose his life eternally.
- by seeking the thrills, excitement, and stimulation of this world by ignoring Christ shall lose his life eternally.

As said above, the person who loses his life for Christ—who sacrifices and gives all he is and has for Christ—saves his life, and he saves it eternally. The person who keeps his life and what he has for himself shall lose his life, and he loses it eternally. The call of Christ is just what He says: a life of denial that takes up the cross and follows in His steps.

> **Just as the Son of Man did not come to be served, but to serve, and to give his life as a ransom for many." (Mat 20:28)**
> **For the Son of Man came to seek and to save what was lost." (Luke 19:10)**
> **Again Jesus said, "Peace be with you! As the Father has sent me, I am sending you." (John 20:21)**
> **We who are strong ought to bear with the failings of the weak and not to please ourselves. (Rom 15:1)**

2. A man's soul is worth more than the whole world. The word *soul* is the same word translated "life" (v.25). Christ uses the word *life* in two senses. There are *two stages*, two beings, two existences to the same life: the life that exists on this earth and the life that shall exist beyond this life. Once a person (life) is born into this world, he shall exist forever. It is just a matter of where he goes after this world: to be with God or to be apart from God.

No man can gain the whole world, but what if he could? All the pleasure and wealth and power and fame are nothing compared with his soul. There are four primary reasons why the soul is far superior to the things of this earth.

a. Everything fades and passes away. A person possesses something only for a short time.

b. Everything cannot be used all at once. Everything sits and remains unused most of the time.
   ⇒ Clothes sit.
   ⇒ A car sits.
   ⇒ Power goes unused.
   ⇒ Popularity and fame quickly pass and are forgotten.

c. The human soul is eternal. The soul never dies and never ceases to exist. It shall live forever either with God or apart from God.

d. The human soul is of more value than the whole world.

Once a man has lost his soul, it is lost. It cannot be bought back. The man forfeits and suffers the loss of it forever. Imagine! Even if a man possessed all the wealth of the world, he would not be able to buy back his soul. Why? Because it is gone; it has passed on forever. The man will never return to earth, not even for one day. He is gone forever.

> **What good is it for a man to gain the whole world, and yet lose or forfeit his very self? (Luke 9:25)**
> **I say to you that many will come from the east and the west, and will take their places at the feast with Abraham, Isaac and Jacob in the kingdom of heaven. But the subjects of the kingdom will be thrown outside, into the darkness, where there will**

be weeping and gnashing of teeth." (Mat 8:11-12)

'Friend,' he asked, 'how did you get in here without wedding clothes?' The man was speechless. "Then the king told the attendants, 'Tie him hand and foot, and throw him outside, into the darkness, where there will be weeping and gnashing of teeth.' (Mat 22:12-13)

You did not choose me, but I chose you and appointed you to go and bear fruit—fruit that will last. Then the Father will give you whatever you ask in my name. (John 15:16)

No, I beat my body and make it my slave so that after I have preached to others, I myself will not be disqualified for the prize. (1 Cor 9:27)

"Be careful, or your hearts will be weighed down with dissipation, drunkenness and the anxieties of life, and that day will close on you unexpectedly like a trap. (Luke 21:34)

3. A day of judgment is coming. When Christ returns, the true value of sacrifice vs. self-satisfaction will be clearly seen. Sacrifice for Christ will be abundantly rewarded; self-satisfaction will be condemned. Man is to be judged according to what he has done. The word "done" means doing, working, acting. It is not isolated acts, but continuous behavior. A person is to be rewarded on the basis of his continuous behavior, not isolated acts.

Then I will tell them plainly, 'I never knew you. Away from me, you evildoers!' (Mat 7:23)

"But he replied, 'I tell you the truth, I don't know you.' (Mat 25:12)

But he who disowns me before men will be disowned before the angels of God. (Luke 12:9)

"But he will reply, 'I don't know you or where you come from. Away from me, all you evildoers!' (Luke 13:27)

4. A promise is given—a promise of never having to taste death. This verse is much clearer when it is compared to Mark's account: "I tell you the truth, some who are standing here will not taste death before they see the Kingdom of God come with power" (Mk.9:1). It is the power of the kingdom to which Jesus refers; that is, His death and resurrection and Pentecost and to the many, many converts to His kingdom that resulted. After Pentecost the power of His Kingdom came—power beyond anything the disciples could have ever dreamed.

Outline	Scripture
	CHAPTER 17 **C. The Transfiguration: Strengthened to Bear the Cross, 17:1-13** (Mk.9:2-13;Lk.9:28-36)
1 Jesus was on a high mountain a. Time: 6 days later b. Three witnesses[DS1]	After six days Jesus took with him Peter, James and John the brother of James, and led them up a high mountain by themselves.
2 The strength of God's glory a. His face shone as the sun b. His clothes gleamed	2 There he was transfigured before them. His face shone like the sun, and his clothes became as white as the light.
3 The strength of great saints a. Moses: The lawgiver b. Elijah: The first great prophet	3 Just then there appeared before them Moses and Elijah, talking with Jesus.
4 The strength of a heavenly experience a. A taste of glory b. A staggering request	4 Peter said to Jesus, "Lord, it is good for us to be here. If you wish, I will put up three shelters—one for you, one for Moses and one for Elijah."
5 The strength of God's presence a. The cloud: The Shekinah glory was given b. The voice of God: Proclaimed Jesus to be His Son—listen to Him	5 While he was still speaking, a bright cloud enveloped them, and a voice from the cloud said, "This is my Son, whom I love; with him I am well pleased. Listen to him!"
c. The disciples' reaction: They prostrated themselves—terrified	6 When the disciples heard this, they fell facedown to the ground, terrified.
d. The Lord's intercession: His closeness & presence	7 But Jesus came and touched them. "Get up," he said. "Don't be afraid."
e. The Lord's preeminence: They saw no one but Jesus	8 When they looked up, they saw no one except Jesus.
6 The strength of the resurrection	9 As they were coming down the mountain, Jesus instructed them, "Don't tell anyone what you have seen, until the Son of Man has been raised from the dead."
a. The misconception of the Messiah	10 The disciples asked him, "Why then do the teachers of the law say that Elijah must come first?"
b. The misconception corrected	11 Jesus replied, "To be sure, Elijah comes and will restore all things.
c. The Messiah must also suffer	12 But I tell you, Elijah has already come, and they did not recognize him, but have done to him everything they wished. In the same way the Son of Man is going to suffer at their hands." 13 Then the disciples understood that he was talking to them about John the Baptist.

DIVISION XI

THE MESSIAH'S DRAMATIC REVELATION: HIS MESSIAHSHIP HIS CHURCH, AND HIS CROSS,16:13-17:27

C. The Transfiguration: Strengthened to Bear the Cross, 17:1-13

(17:1-13) **Introduction**: the transfiguration of Christ is a most unusual experience, but Christ and the disciples needed *unusual strength* to face the future. The future held the cross for both.

Christ had just entered the last stage of training for the disciples (see outline and notes—Mt.16:21-28). It was most important that they grasp God's plan for the world: He was the Messiah and He was to save the world through death and not through earthly power and conquest (see notes—Mt.1:1; DEEPER STUDY # 2—1:18; DEEPER STUDY # 3—3:11; notes—11:1-6; 11:2-3; DEEPER STUDY # 1—11:5; DEEPER STUDY # 2—11:6; DEEPER STUDY # 1—12:16; note—Lk.7:21-23). He was to bear the cross for the sins of the world (1 Pt.2:24), but they too were to bear the cross if they were to follow Him. For some days now He had been drilling this message into them. Soon He was to face the reality of the cross and they were going to fully understand the thrust of what He meant by their "taking up the cross" (see outline and notes—Mt.16:24-28). They both needed a very special portion of strength to face what lay in front of them.

The transfiguration was God's answer to their need. God used five things to strengthen Christ and the disciples. The same five things are applicable to the great needs we face. God will use the same kinds of things to strengthen us.

1. Jesus was on a high mountain (v.1).
2 The strength of God' glory (v.2).
3. The strength of great saints (v.3).
4. The strength of a heavenly experience (v.4).
5. The strength of God's presence (v.5-8).
6. The strength of the resurrection (v.9-13).

1 (17:1) **Devotion**: Jesus was on a high mountain. Note that this event took place six days after drilling His disciples with the fact of His coming death and resurrection. Christ needed to get all alone with God. He took three disciples, Peter, James and John, with Him and climbed a high mountain. The place chosen is important. It was "a high mountain," an isolated place where they would not be interrupted. It was conducive, fitted for being alone with God. Four major things drove Christ to get alone with God. The same things should always cause us to get alone with God for an extended time:

⇒ pressure (from facing the cross)
⇒ a momentous decision (to bear the cross)
⇒ intensive training
⇒ the need for renewed strength

DEEPER STUDY # 1
(17:1) **Peter, James, and John**: see DEEPER STUDY # 1—Mk.9:2 for the reasons these three were chosen.

2 (17:2) **God's Glory**: there was the strength of God's glory. The word "transfigured" (metamorphothe) means a change into another form; a transformation; a change of countenance; a complete change. Luke said, "the appearance of His face changed" (Lk.9:29). Note how the gospel writers described what happened.

There he was transfigured before them. His face shone like the sun, and his clothes became as white as the light. (Mat 17:2)

His clothes became dazzling white, whiter than anyone in the world could bleach them. (Mark 9:3)

As he was praying, the appearance of his face changed, and his clothes became as bright as a flash of lightning. (Luke 9:29)

Apparently *the glory* of His Godly nature was allowed to shine through His body. "The glory [which He] had with [God] before the world began" shone through His body right on through His clothes (Jn.17:5). Peter said, "We were eyewitnesses of His majesty." In John's vision of Christ in The Revelation, he described the glory of Christ as the sun shining in all its brilliance (Rev.1:16).

The scripture says:

This is the message we have heard from him and declare to you: God is light; in him there is no darkness at all. (1 John 1:5)

Who alone is immortal and who lives in unapproachable light, whom no one has seen or can see. To him be honor and might forever. Amen. (1 Tim 6:16)

He wraps himself in light as with a garment; he stretches out the heavens like a tent (Psa 104:2)

Thought 1. Believers experience some portion of the glory of the Lord.

And we, who with unveiled faces all reflect the Lord's glory, are being transformed into his likeness with ever-increasing glory, which comes from the Lord, who is the Spirit. (2 Cor 3:18)

Of course, our sense of God's glory is very much dependent upon our doing what Christ did: getting alone with God in an intensive session of prayer and devotion. We are to be transformed into the image of Christ, transformed in all His moral excellence. But we must learn that the change is brought about only by the Spirit of God and only as we seek His face in prayer and genuine trust.

Do not conform any longer to the pattern of this world, but be transformed by the renewing of your mind. Then you will be able to test and approve what God's will is—his good, pleasing and perfect will. (Rom 12:2)

3 (17:3) **Moses—Elijah**: there was the strength of great saints. Why did Moses and Elijah appear with Jesus? There seem to be two reasons.

1. To discuss Jesus' death (Lk.17:31). Jesus needed to be strengthened to bear the weight and pressure of the cross (see note—Mk.9:2-13. Cp. the Garden of Gethesemane experience and His cry on the cross, Lk.22:39-46; see note—Mt.27:46-49.)

2. To show that Jesus was the true Messiah, the Son of God, the One who was superior to the Law and the prophets. Moses represented the law; and Elijah, who was considered the greatest of the prophets, represented the prophets. These two men were honoring and ministering to Christ. By such they were symbolizing that the law and the prophets found their fulfillment in Christ.

⇒ Christ was the One of whom the law and the prophets spoke.

⇒ Christ was the One to whom the law and the prophets pointed. The old covenant was now to be fulfilled inand superseded by Christ who was to usher in the new covenant (see note—Mk.9:2-4. Cp. outline and notes—2 Cor.3:6-18; Mt.9:16-17.)

Thought 1. Christ was soon to fulfill His prophetic and priestly offices. Moses and Elijah were symbolically transferring the old prophetic and priestly offices to Him.

Jesus took the Twelve aside and told them, "We are going up to Jerusalem, and everything that is written by the prophets about the Son of Man will be fulfilled. (Luke 18:31)

Concerning this salvation, the prophets, who spoke of the grace that was to come to you, searched intently and with the greatest care, trying to find out the time and circumstances to which the Spirit of Christ in them was pointing when he predicted the sufferings of Christ and the glories that would follow. (1 Pet 1:10-11)

Thought 2. Something very significant is seen here. Believers who have gone on before are as *alive*, if not more alive, than we are. They are living in a dimension other than our physical world, an eternal world that is perfect and free from all sin, suffering, and death. What a glorious hope!

We are confident, I say, and would prefer to be away from the body and at home with the Lord. (2 Cor 5:8)

I am torn between the two: I desire to depart and be with Christ, which is better by far; (Phil 1:23)

4 (17:4) **Spiritual Experiences—Glory**: there was the strength of a heavenly experience. The three disciples were tasting *glory*. They were in the very presence of God Himself and were tasting some of heaven's joy, peace, security, fulfillment, and perfection. They did not want to leave this hallowed ground.

Note what Peter did.

1. He offered to build three shelters (skenas) for Jesus and the two prophets. By this act he hoped to extend the stay of the heavenly guests and the glorious experience. The shelters offered were the booths made of branches and grass which could be quickly built, the kind often built by travellers on their stops along the road night by night.

2. He said, "If you wish." Peter, even in a moment as glorious as this, would not act against his Lord's will. Imagine the devotion and loyalty!

Thought 1. There is a great need to learn something: God knows exactly how to meet every believer's need. He knows just what kind of experience is needed, and God will do whatever it takes to meet our need—if we truly seek Him.

However, we must remember something: our experiences must conform to God's Word. God will not go against His Word in order to give growth and experiences. The experiences that come from God are the experiences that conform to His Word. In fact, spiritual experiences and growth usually come about as a result of reading and studying God's Word.

Thought 2. A deep spiritual experience with God is always a glorious time. Nothing can compare to a session of deep communion with Christ, and there is always the wish that we could remain in His presence.

But such is not our calling, not now. Our present call is to bear the cross and its message, not to wallow around in deep spiritual experiences. Our spirits do occasionally need to be spiritually renewed, but they are always renewed for a purpose: to strengthen us for going out and bearing a much stronger witness for our Lord.

> **Is it not to share your food with the hungry and to provide the poor wanderer with shelter— when you see the naked, to clothe him, and not to turn away from your own flesh and blood? (Isa 58:7)**
>
> **In everything I did, I showed you that by this kind of hard work we must help the weak, remembering the words the Lord Jesus himself said: 'It is more blessed to give than to receive.'" (Acts 20:35)**
>
> **We who are strong ought to bear with the failings of the weak and not to please ourselves. (Rom 15:1)**
>
> **Carry each other's burdens, and in this way you will fulfill the law of Christ. (Gal 6:2)**
>
> **Remember those in prison as if you were their fellow prisoners, and those who are mistreated as if you yourselves were suffering. (Heb 13:3)**
>
> **Religion that God our Father accepts as pure and faultless is this: to look after orphans and widows in their distress and to keep oneself from being polluted by the world. (James 1:27)**
>
> **Finally, all of you, live in harmony with one another; be sympathetic, love as brothers, be compassionate and humble. (1 Pet 3:8)**

5 (17:5-8) **Spiritual Experience—Heaven**: there was the strength of God's presence. The cloud also covered the disciples. It and the voice of God terrified the disciples and caused them to fall immediately upon their faces, prostrated and unable to look up. As mortal men, they were crouched in fear and paralyzed in terror. Note four facts.

1. The cloud was "a bright cloud." This was the Shekinah glory, the cloud that symbolized God's presence. It was the cloud that guided Israel out of Egypt and that rested upon the tabernacle (Ex.40:34-38) and above the Mercy Seat or Atonement Cover in the Most Holy Place. God dwells in unapproachable light upon which no man can look. The Shekinah glory is a light so glorious and brilliant that there is no need for a sun. It is a light that radiates splendor (cp. Rev.21:11, 23). Peter later called it "the Majestic Glory" (2 Pt.1:17).

> **Who alone is immortal and who lives in unapproachable light, whom no one has seen or can see. To him be honor and might forever. Amen. (1 Tim 6:16)**

The "bright cloud" overshadowing Christ was in contrast to the dark and threatening cloud that overshadowed the giving of the old covenant to Moses, that is, the law (Ex.19:18; 20:21). There is a point to be made here.

⇒ The law (old covenant) was dark and threatening (see DEEPER STUDY # 2—Gal.3:10).

⇒ The new covenant (the love of Christ) is bright and is given to save and bless, not to threaten and condemn (Heb.12:18-24. Cp. Heb.8:6-13.)

2. The voice speaking actually says in the Greek, "This is My Son, the Beloved One." Note the two facts stressed: Christ is God's Son and He is the One whom God loves. The idea is that Christ is the "one and only Son" who was to be given for the world (Jn.3:16).

3. Note the disciples experienced a clear, intense sense of God's presence. They fell prostrate on their faces before the Lord.

4. The Lord stood there alone. The representatives of the Old Testament and covenant (law) had faded away. The bondage and darkness and terror of the law were now gone. Christ now stood in the law's place (see note—Mt.5:17-18). The new covenant was soon to take effect; the new covenant of light, love, and liberty was now replacing the old covenant of darkness, fear, and bondage.

The disciples' experience can be applied to the believer's future, to his appearance before God in *the great Day of Redemption*. In fact, that is just what is happening to Peter, James, and John. They find themselves in God's presence. The believer's experience when he meets Christ face to face will undoubtedly be very much like what they experienced.

1. The believer will experience the Shekinah glory and see its full manifestation upon Christ.

2. The believer will hear the voice of God proclaiming Christ to be His Son; expressing perfect approval of His redemptive work; and rejoicing that He has been heard and is to be heard throughout all eternity.

3. The believer will fall upon his face, prostrating himself before Christ in awe and adoration and worship.

4. The believer will experience the Lord's intercessory work. He will feel the Lord's hand reaching out to touch him and to lift him up, and the believer will stand in the Lord's righteousness and perfection, living in a state of glory forever.

> **Thought 1.** How often God would grant a clear, intense sense of His presence—if we would only get alone with Him for long sessions of meditation and prayer! How much power would be present in our lives and ministries if we often got alone with God for long periods!

5. The believer will witness and experience the Lord's preeminence throughout all eternity.

> **Thought 1.** The message of God was, is, and ever will be…
>
> - this is my Son, whom I love
> - in whom I am well pleased,
> - listen to Him.

6 (17:9-13) **Jesus Christ, Resurrection**: there was the strength of the resurrection. The resurrection proves two things.

- ⇒ First, the resurrection proves that Jesus Christ is definitely the Son of God.
- ⇒ Second, the resurrection proves that the transfiguration actually happened—that it actually foreshadowed the supremacy of the new covenant and to some degree the believer's experience of heaven.

Jesus did not allow the three disciples to share their experience because it could not be understood. It was just too incredible to grasp until after the resurrection. This charge to keep silent baffled the disciples because the Scribes had always taught that Elijah was to come and proclaim the Messiah (cp. Mal.4:5). They had just seen Elijah with Christ. When would Elijah begin announcing Jesus to be the Messiah? And if he were going to proclaim the message, why should they keep silent about Jesus' Messiahship? Should they not also proclaim Him as Messiah? Jesus told them that John the Baptist was the prophesied prophet like Elijah who was to come. The people killed him, and the Messiah too was to suffer at the hands of the people.

Thought 1. Jesus Christ is the Messiah, the Son of God. Belief in Him is absolutely essential.

I told you that you would die in your sins; if you do not believe that I am the one I claim to be, you will indeed die in your sins." (John 8:24)

The woman said, "I know that Messiah" (called Christ) "is coming. When he comes, he will explain everything to us." Then Jesus declared, "I who speak to you am he." (John 4:25-26)

We believe and know that you are the Holy One of God." (John 6:69; cp. Jn.11:25-27)

Yet Saul grew more and more powerful and baffled the Jews living in Damascus by proving that Jesus is the Christ. (Acts 9:22; cp. Acts 17:2-3)

Everyone who believes that Jesus is the Christ is born of God, and everyone who loves the father loves his child as well. (1 John 5:1)

Outline	Scripture	Scripture	Outline
	D. The Powerless Disciples: A Great Lesson on Faith & Power, 17:14-20 (Mk.9:14-29; Lk.9:37-42)	plied," "how long shall I stay with you? How long shall I put up with you? Bring the boy here to me."	always be available b. His patience was limited
		18 Jesus rebuked the demon, and it came out of the boy, and he was healed from that moment.	c. His power broke the power of Satan
1 Jesus after the transfiguration a. Joined the crowd b. Was approached by a desperate man	14 When they came to the crowd, a man approached Jesus and knelt before him.	19 Then the disciples came to Jesus in private and asked, "Why couldn't we drive it out?"	**4 The clear reason for no power: Unbelief**
2 The tragedy of no power a. A desperate need unmet	15 "Lord, have mercy on my son," he said. "He has seizures and is suffering greatly. He often falls into the fire or into the water.	20 He replied, "Because you have so little faith. I tell you the truth, if you have faith as	**5 The great power of faith promised**[DS3]
b. A frantic disappointment[DS1] c. An embarassing situation	16 I brought him to your disciples, but they could not heal him."	small as a mustard seed, you can say to this mountain, 'Move from here to there'	
3 The rebuke of no power[DS2] a. His presence will not	17 "O unbelieving and perverse generation," Jesus re-	and it will move. Nothing will be impossible for you."	

DIVISION XI

THE MESSIAH'S DRAMATIC REVELATION: HIS MESSIAHSHIP HIS CHURCH, AND HIS CROSS, 16:13-17:27

D. The Powerless Disciples: A Great Lesson on Faith and Power, 17:14-21

(17:14-21) **Introduction**: this is an excellent study on *power and faith.* The points speak for themselves.

1. Jesus after the transfiguration (v.14).
2. The tragedy of no power (v.15-16).
3. The rebuke of no power (v.17-18).
4. The clear reason for no power: little faith or unbelief (v.19-20).
5. The great power of faith promised (v.20).

1 (17:14) **Devotion—Prayer**: Jesus after the transfiguration. What a contrast—the heavenly glory and the mountain top experience of the transfiguration vs. the earthly problems and the valley experiences of the next day (Lk.9:37)! What a lesson for all of us! The glory of devotions is for the purpose of going out and meeting the crowds in all their need. We do not stay on the mountain top; we come down to the valley, down to earth where people are.

No experience of Christ teaches the necessity for both devotions and ministry any more forcibly than this experience.

⇒ The transfiguration is an *end* in itself, but it is also a *means* to service.

⇒ The transfiguration calls us to a monastic life, but it also prepares us for going out and meeting the needs of a corrupt world.

⇒ The mount of prayer calls us to be renewed, but it also strengthens us to go forth and labor in a mixed up world.

⇒ God wants to meet us *daily* for our own soul's nourishment, but He also wants to send us out to meet the daily needs of a crying world.

⇒ God wants our private attention and fellowship, but He also wants to send us out to give attention and godly fellowship to a lost world.

2 (17:15-16) **Powerlessness—Unbelief—Little Faith**: the tragedy of no power (see DEEPER STUDY # 1—Mt.17:16).

The son's illness seems to have been both physical and spiritual. The description of the illness in the gospel of Mark points toward what is known today as epilepsy and demon-possession (Mt.17:15; Mk.9:17-18; Lk.9:39). The demon-possession in particular seems to have heightened and aggravated the condition, perhaps causing some suicidal tendencies (Mt.17:15; Mk.9:22). Throughout the gospels, this seems to be one of the major works of evil spirits: to *heighten and aggravate* existing conditions. The great tragedy of the event was unbelief (little faith) and having no power. These tragedies plague so many servants of God. But note: they plague us only because "we do not ask" (Jas.4:2). We fail to go up to the high mountain of transfiguration and receive the renewing of God's presence. Our lack of power too often results in three things.

1. So many *desperate needs* going unmet.
2. So many frantic disappointments being experienced.
3. So many *embarassing situations* happening.

> **He will call upon me, and I will answer him; I will be with him in trouble, I will deliver him and honor him. (Psa 91:15)**
>
> **Then you will call, and the LORD will answer; you will cry for help, and he will say: Here am I. "If you do away with the yoke of oppression, with the pointing finger and malicious talk, (Isa 58:9)**
>
> **'Call to me and I will answer you and tell you great and unsearchable things you do not know.' (Jer 33:3)**

Thought 1. Note two things.

1) The father was seeking and interceding for his child.

---

[21] *But this kind does not go out except by prayer and fasting.*

2) Christ's heart was tender and compassionate toward the child. There had been only one thing lacking—someone with faith and power to stand in the gap. There simply was no one.

How many children are gripped by desperate needs both physical and spiritual? How many are trapped by sin? Where are the parents who are concerned enough to seek Jesus, not half-heartedly and haphazardly, but genuinely? Where are the parents who seek Him, persevering until He answers? As in the above case, Jesus is willing to meet the needs of our children, but where are the parents who seek Jesus with the fervency of the father? And where are the servants of God who can lead parents to trust Christ?

DEEPER STUDY # 1
(17:16) **Power, Lack of**: Why do men lack power? (See DEEPER STUDY # 3—Mk.9:18 for discussion.)

3 (17:17-18) **Powerlessness—Unbelief—Little Faith**: the rebuke of no power. Christ rebuked the lack of power. A person with no power saddens and brings sorrow to His heart. What can He do to stir faith and power? He does all He can: He warns, yet He offers hope.

1. He warns that His presence will not always be available (Gen.6:3. See note—Mt.12:14-16.)
2. He warns that His patience is limited (cp.Pr.29:1. See note—Mt.12:31-32.)
3. He assures that His power breaks the power of Satan. Note that it is the Word of Christ that breaks the devil's power. Satan cannot stand before God's Word. Christ has disarmed the authorities and principalities and powers under Satan's control (Col.2:15).

Thought 1. A *faithless* person…
- cannot receive the blessing which he *might have had.*
- cannot do the works which he *might have done.*

Note the tone and ache of Christ's heart and words. He aches for us to receive what we should have and to do the works which we should do. He longs for us to live an abundant life of power and fulfillment (Jn.10:10).

Thought 2. There is a critical point to remember: the longer Christ has to put up with our *faithless* and *powerless* behavior, the more He is displeased with us. We must learn and learn quickly. His presence will not always be with us, and His patience is limited.

Thought 3. Note the glorious message of the gospel proclaimed and illustrated in this event. When the faith and power of men fail, when all other hope and help fails, we can go to Christ and know that He will hear and help us. He will have compassion and use His power to meet our need—no matter how desperate.

DEEPER STUDY # 2
(17:17) **Perverse** (diastrepho): to distort, to twist; to turn aside or away; to be torn in two; to be corrupted (cp. Acts 20:30; Ph.2:15).

pure, children of God without fault in a crooked and depraved generation, in which you shine like stars in the universe (Phil 2:15)
Even from your own number men will arise and distort the truth in order to draw away disciples after them. (Acts 20:30)
and constant friction between men of corrupt mind, who have been robbed of the truth and who think that godliness is a means to financial gain. (1 Tim 6:5)
The integrity of the upright guides them, but the unfaithful are destroyed by their duplicity. (Prov 11:3)
A man is praised according to his wisdom, but men with warped minds are despised. (Prov 12:8)
The tongue that brings healing is a tree of life, but a deceitful tongue crushes the spirit. (Prov 15:4)
Better a poor man whose walk is blameless than a rich man whose ways are perverse. (Prov 28:6)

4 (17:19-20) **Unbelief—Little Faith—Powerlessness**: the clear reason for no power was little faith or unbelief. What is little faith? Why does faith weaken and turn into unbelief? The disciples had been given and promised unusual power earlier, and they had ministered effectively (Mt.10:1; Lk.10:17). But now the power seemed to be gone, and they were unable to minister. "Why?" they asked.

Pointedly, Jesus answered, "Because you have so little faith." Little faith or unbelief is four things, or to put it in the form of a question, "What is unbelief?"

1. Little faith or unbelief is doubting Christ Himself, the object of one's faith. It is questioning the power of Christ. Is He really strong enough to do what is needed: to save, deliver, heal, and help; and to remove evil empires, entrenched wickedness, destructive greed, and the threat of wars?
2. Little faith or unbelief is doubting the power of the Lord *within* oneself. It is questioning if one is close enough to Christ for Him to hear and answer or to grant enough power to meet the need.
3. Little faith or unbelief is doubting one's own faith. It is questioning the strength of one's own dependence and confidence in Christ.
4. Little faith or unbelief is doubting if the thing needed is God's will. It is questioning if one should be seeking such a thing or if God is willing to do what is needed.

He said to his disciples, "Why are you so afraid? Do you still have no faith?" (Mark 4:40)
Later Jesus appeared to the Eleven as they were eating; he rebuked them for their lack of faith and their stubborn refusal to believe those who had seen him after he had risen. (Mark 16:14)
He said to them, "How foolish you are, and how slow of heart to believe all that the prophets have spoken! (Luke 24:25)
Whoever believes in him is not condemned, but whoever does not believe stands condemned already because he has not believed in the name of God's one and only Son. (John 3:18)
Whoever believes in the Son has eternal life, but whoever rejects the Son will not

see life, for God's wrath remains on him." (John 3:36)

I told you that you would die in your sins; if you do not believe that I am the one I claim to be, you will indeed die in your sins." (John 8:24)

When he comes, he will convict the world of guilt in regard to sin and righteousness and judgment: in regard to sin, because men do not believe in me; (John 16:8-9)

See to it, brothers, that none of you has a sinful, unbelieving heart that turns away from the living God. (Heb 3:12)

Let us, therefore, make every effort to enter that rest, so that no one will fall by following their example of disobedience. (Heb 4:11)

The answer to little faith or unbelief is hungering and thirsting after God so much that we spend a great deal of time in God's presence—so much time that even food is forgotten. We do without in order to meet God (see note—Mt.6:16-18).

Consequently, faith comes from hearing the message, and the message is heard through the word of Christ. (Rom 10:17)

He said to his disciples, "Why are you so afraid? Do you still have no faith?" (Mark 4:40)

And without faith it is impossible to please God, because anyone who comes to him must believe that he exists and that he rewards those who earnestly seek him. (Heb 11:6)

"If you are the Christ, " they said, "tell us." Jesus answered, "If I tell you, you will not believe me, (Luke 22:67)

I tell you the truth, we speak of what we know, and we testify to what we have seen, but still you people do not accept our testimony. (John 3:11)

The Jews gathered around him, saying, "How long will you keep us in suspense? If you are the Christ, tell us plainly." Jesus answered, "I did tell you, but you do not believe. The miracles I do in my Father's name speak for me, (John 10:24-25)

Even after Jesus had done all these miraculous signs in their presence, they still would not believe in him. (John 12:37)

Who has believed our message and to whom has the arm of the LORD been revealed? (Isa 53:1)

Thought 1. When things are not going well and we are not successful in life or marriage or ministry, note two things.

1) It tends to lead everyone to blame others:
   ⇒ spouse blames spouse
   ⇒ workman blames fellow workman
   ⇒ congregation blames minister
   ⇒ minister blames congregation

2) The fault usually lies at our own feet (not always, of course, but usually), and the cause is our little faith or unbelief. We are not trusting and seeking God like we should, not diligently.

Thought 2. Something displeases God enormously: distrusting any power or gift given by Him. So many confuse personal strength and gifts with God's strength and gifts. To deny His power and gifts is not humility; it is distrust. His power and gifts are to be used to the utmost.

5 (17:20) **Faith—Power**: the great power of faith is promised. The Jews clearly understood what Jesus meant by "removing mountains." The phrase was a Jewish idiom or proverb meaning "to remove difficulties" (cp. Zech.4:7; 1 Cor.13:2). The greatest difficulties in human life can be removed by faith. Prayer and faith can do anything for God. They can remove all kinds of mountains: fear, disappointment, depression, despair, sickness, temptation, guilt, weariness, loneliness, persecution, heartache. Such mountains loom ever so large as a barrier before man's path. Such mountains can really defeat life. How can they be overcome? By prayer and faith—praying and believing God even to the point of fasting (see DEEPER STUDY # 3—Mt.17:20).

Thought 1. Every believer has two strengths and two gifts to offer the world. He has both his own strength and gifts (talents) and God's strength and gifts. (Cp. Ro.12:6f; 1 Cor.12:4-11; Eph.4:11.)
1) God's strength and gifts are as high as the heavens above our strength and gifts.
2) Our call is to learn to use God's strength and gifts.

Thought 2. An *active* faith can remove mountains (see note and DEEPER STUDY # 1—Heb.11:6).

DEEPER STUDY # 3
(17:20) **Faith—Power—Mustard Seed**: what does Christ mean by "faith as small as a mustard seed"? The mustard seed was known for its small size, the smallest of all plants; yet it grew to be one of the largest bushes (see note—Mt.13:32). Picture a mustard seed lying in a person's hand. It is *real* and it is *small*. Just imagine the potential for *growth and use*. So it is with faith: faith is "as small as a mustard seed." It is real and small, yet it has enormous power for growth and for use and for ministry.

If you believe, you will receive whatever you ask for in prayer." (Mat 21:22)

"'If you can'?" said Jesus. "Everything is possible for him who believes." (Mark 9:23)

	E. The Messiah Foretells His Death and Resurrection (2nd Time): Delivered Up By God, 17:22-23 (Mk.9:30-32; Lk.9:43-45)
1 He foretold His betrayal 2 He foretold the guilty party	22 When they came together in Galilee, he said to them, "The Son of Man is going to be betrayed into the hands of men.
3 He foretold His death 4 He foretold His resurrection	23 They will kill him, and on the third day he will be raised to life." And the disciples were filled with grief.

DIVISION XI

THE MESSIAH'S DRAMATIC REVELATION: HIS MESSIAHSHIP HIS CHURCH, AND HIS CROSS, 16:13-17:27

E. The Messiah Foretells His Death and Resurrection (2nd Time): Delivered Up by God, 17:22-23

(17:22-23) **Introduction**: the death and resurrection of Jesus Christ cannot be overstressed. They are of paramount importance: a person's destiny is determined by his response to the death and resurrection of Jesus Christ. His death and resurrection are the pivotal points of human history, the hub of God's plan for eternity. History itself revolves around the death and resurrection of God's dear Son. God works all things out for good to the praise of His dear Son. Even the evil and devastation of men are turned around and worked out for the good of Christ and for those for whom He died and arose again. All that the Scripture says about the death and resurrection of Jesus Christ speaks to every generation of men. (See outline and notes—Mt.16:21-23; 20:17-19; Mk.8:31-33; 9:30-32; 10:32-34.)

1. He foretold His betrayal (v.22).
2. He foretold the guilty party (v.22).
3. He foretold His death (v.23).
4. He foretold His resurrection (v.23).

1 (17:22) **Jesus Christ, Death**: Christ foretold His betrayal. Note two facts.

1. The phrase "when they came together" (anastrephomenon) means went to and fro, back and forth. The point is this: while Jesus and the disciples went all about Galilee, He was drilling into them the fact that He was to be killed and raised from the dead.

Jesus had been in the extreme northern country for several weeks (see notes—Mt.15:21-22; 15:29; 16:13). At some point He returned to the country of Galilee, but quietly (Mk.9:30). Apparently He just kept moving about rather secretly so that He could indoctrinate His disciples to the fact of His impending death and resurrection (see notes—Mt.15:21-22; 15:29; 16:21-28). Interestingly, this fact is referred to by the angels in announcing His resurrection: "Remember how he told you, while he was still with you in Galilee: 'The Son of Man must be delivered into the hands of sinful men, be crucified and on the third day be raised again'" (Lk.24:6-7).

Jesus had to continue talking about His death and resurrection because it was so hard to understand. There were three primary reasons why the disciples had difficulty in grasping the fact.

a. The Messiah's death and resurrection were new experiences, new happenings. History was to be made. The talk of a literal death and resurrection was bound to be understood in symbolic and spiritual language (see note—Mt.18:1-2). (How like so many to spiritualize the two events—even though the events really took place and are so strongly proclaimed by the disciples.) (Cp. 1 Cor.15:3-8. See notes—Mk.9:32; 9:34.)

b. The Messiah's death and resurrection were thought to be impossible. How could God die? Most men proclaim that God cannot die. Of course, the disciples had not yet seen what death really is—basically separation from God (see DEEPER STUDY # 1—Heb.9:27). They had to learn that God was dealing with spiritual and eternal life (and death), not just with physical and temporal life (and death) on this earth.

c. The Messiah's death and resurrection were contrary to all their hopes and expectations. It was just different from all the disciples had ever heard or been taught. The Messiah was thought to be a Messiah of power and sovereign rule not a Messiah who had to suffer and die in order to save man. (See notes—Mt.1:1; DEEPER STUDY # 2—1:18; DEEPER STUDY # 3—3:11; notes—11:1-6; 11:2-3; DEEPER STUDY # 1—11:5; DEEPER STUDY # 2—11:6; DEEPER STUDY # 1—12:16; notes—22:42; Lk.7:21-23.)

2. The word "betrayed" is actually *delivered up* (paradidosthai) which means that His death was ordained. Christ was saying that He was about to be *delivered up* to death—it was ordained, that is, determined in the counsel and plan of God. Christ was delivered up to death by three persons.

a. God delivered Christ up to be betrayed.

> **"For God so loved the world that he gave his one and only Son, that whoever believes in him shall not perish but have eternal life. (John 3:16)**
>
> **This man was handed over to you by God's set purpose and foreknowledge; and you, with the help of wicked men, put him to death by nailing him to the cross. (Acts 2:23)**

He who did not spare his own Son, but gave him up for us all—how will he not also, along with him, graciously give us all things? (Rom 8:32)

God made him who had no sin to be sin for us, so that in him we might become the righteousness of God. (2 Cor 5:21)

Thanks be to God for his indescribable gift! (2 Cor 9:15)

b. Christ delivered Himself up to be crucified.

Who gave himself for our sins to rescue us from the present evil age, according to the will of our God and Father, (Gal 1:4)

And live a life of love, just as Christ loved us and gave himself up for us as a fragrant offering and sacrifice to God. (Eph 5:2)

Husbands, love your wives, just as Christ loved the church and gave himself up for her (Eph 5:25)

Who gave himself for us to redeem us from all wickedness and to purify for himself a people that are his very own, eager to do what is good. (Titus 2:14)

This is how we know what love is: Jesus Christ laid down his life for us. And we ought to lay down our lives for our brothers. (1 John 3:16)

c. Judas betrayed and delivered Christ up to be crucified (see notes—Mt.26:21-25; 27:3-5; Mk. 14:10-11; Lk.22:4-6; Jn.13:18; 13:21-26).

And while they were eating, he said, "I tell you the truth, one of you will betray me." (Mat 26:21)

Then Judas Iscariot, one of the Twelve, went to the chief priests to betray Jesus to them. (Mark 14:10)

"I am not referring to all of you; I know those I have chosen. But this is to fulfill the scripture: 'He who shares my bread has lifted up his heel against me.' (John 13:18)

2 (17:22) **Jesus Christ, Death**: Christ foretold the guilty party. Jesus had already named the men who would kill Him (see DEEPER STUDY # 1—Mt.16:21). The order of the betrayal would be *Judas*, who identified Him for the *elders*, *chief priests*, and *teachers* or *Scribes*, who in turn would deliver Him to the *Gentiles* or Romans for execution (Mt.20:19).

Peter, in preaching to the Jews right after Pentecost, accused the Jews: "This man was handed over to you by God's set purpose and foreknowledge and you, with the help of wicked men, put him to death by nailing him to the cross" (Acts 2:23).

Thought 1. Men killed Jesus—men who so desperately needed Him.

1) The men who plotted and caused His death were the Jews. They were His own people by race and by God's choice. They were even expecting the Messiah, yet they did not know Him (Jn.1:11). They did not want the kind of Messiah He was claiming to be. They wanted a Messiah of power and fame and wealth that would give Israel the glory of an international government or theocracy (see notes—Mt.1:1; DEEPER STUDY # 2—1:18; DEEPER STUDY # 3—3:11; notes—11:1-6; 11:2-3; DEEPER STUDY # 1—11:5; DEEPER STUDY # 2—11:6; DEEPER STUDY # 1—12:16; note—Lk.7:21-23).
2) The men who carried out His death were the Romans. They were the very ones for whom He had come to open the door of salvation. Salvation had been closed to them. Now in Him, they could be saved and live eternally. They should have been grateful and received Him with open arms, yet they too rejected His claims. They tried and executed Him—all for political purposes.

"For God so loved the world that he gave his one and only Son, that whoever believes in him shall not perish but have eternal life. For God did not send his Son into the world to condemn the world, but to save the world through him. Whoever believes in him is not condemned, but whoever does not believe stands condemned already because he has not believed in the name of God's one and only Son. This is the verdict: Light has come into the world, but men loved darkness instead of light because their deeds were evil. (John 3:16-19)

3 (17:23) **Jesus Christ, Death**: Christ foretold His death. As simply as possible, Jesus Christ was killed for two reasons.

1. The religionists delivered Him up to the Gentiles because He was a threat to them (see notes and DEEPER STUDY # 1—Mt.12:10; cp. 12:1-8. These are important notes for understanding just why the religionists killed Jesus.) Three passages will show this clearly.

Again the Jews picked up stones to stone him, but Jesus said to them, "I have shown you many great miracles from the Father. For which of these do you stone me?" "We are not stoning you for any of these," replied the Jews, "but for blasphemy, because you, a mere man, claim to be God." (John 10:31-33)

"Men of Israel, listen to this: Jesus of Nazareth was a man accredited by God to you by miracles, wonders and signs, which God did among you through him, as you yourselves know. This man was handed over to you by God's set purpose and foreknowledge; and you, with the help of wicked men, put him to death by nailing him to the cross. (Acts 2:22-23)

For you, brothers, became imitators of God's churches in Judea, which are in Christ Jesus: You suffered from your own countrymen the same things those churches suffered from the Jews, who killed the Lord Jesus and the prophets and also drove us out. They displease God and are hostile to all men (1 Th 2:14-15)

2. God delivered Him up to die for the sins and the life of the world. Most of the passages in the New Testament dealing with the death of Christ follow (see JESUS

CHRIST, Death—Master Subject Index, for additional information on the death of Christ).

For as Jonah was three days and three nights in the belly of a huge fish, so the Son of Man will be three days and three nights in the heart of the earth. (Mat 12:40)

A wicked and adulterous generation looks for a miraculous sign, but none will be given it except the sign of Jonah." Jesus then left them and went away. From that time on Jesus began to explain to his disciples that he must go to Jerusalem and suffer many things at the hands of the elders, chief priests and teachers of the law, and that he must be killed and on the third day be raised to life. (Mat 16:4,21; cp. Lk.11:30; Lk.9:22)

But I tell you, Elijah has already come, and they did not recognize him, but have done to him everything they wished. In the same way the Son of Man is going to suffer at their hands." Then the disciples understood that he was talking to them about John the Baptist. (Mat 17:12-13)

When they came together in Galilee, he said to them, "The Son of Man is going to be betrayed into the hands of men. (Mat 17:22)

Now as Jesus was going up to Jerusalem, he took the twelve disciples aside and said to them, "We are going up to Jerusalem, and the Son of Man will be betrayed to the chief priests and the teachers of the law. They will condemn him to death and will turn him over to the Gentiles to be mocked and flogged and crucified. On the third day he will be raised to life!" (Mat 20:17-19)

Just as the Son of Man did not come to be served, but to serve, and to give his life as a ransom for many." (Mat 20:28; cp. Mk.10:32, 34)

Last of all, he sent his son to them. 'They will respect my son,' he said. "But when the tenants saw the son, they said to each other, 'This is the heir. Come, let's kill him and take his inheritance.' So they took him and threw him out of the vineyard and killed him. (Mat 21:37-39)

"As you know, the Passover is two days away—and the Son of Man will be handed over to be crucified." (Mat 26:2)
The Son of Man will go just as it is written about him. But woe to that man who betrays the Son of Man! It would be better for him if he had not been born." (Mat 26:24)

This is my blood of the covenant, which is poured out for many for the forgiveness of sins. (Mat 26:28)

Going a little farther, he fell with his face to the ground and prayed, "My Father, if it is possible, may this cup be taken from me. Yet not as I will, but as you will." (Mat 26:39)

He went away a second time and prayed, "My Father, if it is not possible for this cup to be taken away unless I drink it, may your will be done." (Mat 26:42)

Do you think I cannot call on my Father, and he will at once put at my disposal more than twelve legions of angels? But how then would the Scriptures be fulfilled that say it must happen in this way?" (Mat 26:53-54; cp. Mk.14:24, 36, 39)

Because he was teaching his disciples. He said to them, "The Son of Man is going to be betrayed into the hands of men. They will kill him, and after three days he will rise." (Mark 9:31)

"We are going up to Jerusalem," he said, "and the Son of Man will be betrayed to the chief priests and teachers of the law. They will condemn him to death and will hand him over to the Gentiles, who will mock him and spit on him, flog him and kill him. Three days later he will rise." (Mark 10:33-34; cp. Mt.20:18, 19; Lk.18:31-33)

And he said, "The Son of Man must suffer many things and be rejected by the elders, chief priests and teachers of the law, and he must be killed and on the third day be raised to life." (Luke 9:22)

As the time approached for him to be taken up to heaven, Jesus resolutely set out for Jerusalem. (Luke 9:51)
But I have a baptism to undergo, and how distressed I am until it is completed! (Luke 12:50; cp. Lk.22:15)

But first he must suffer many things and be rejected by this generation. (Luke 17:25)

And he said to them, "I have eagerly desired to eat this Passover with you before I suffer. And he took bread, gave thanks and broke it, and gave it to them, saying, "This is my body given for you; do this in remembrance of me." In the same way, after the supper he took the cup, saying, "This cup is the new covenant in my blood, which is poured out for you. (Luke 22:15, 19-20)

It is written: 'And he was numbered with the transgressors' ; and I tell you that this must be fulfilled in me. Yes, what is written about me is reaching its fulfillment." (Luke 22:37)

"Father, if you are willing, take this cup from me; yet not my will, but yours be done." (Luke 22:42)

The next day John saw Jesus coming toward him and said, "Look, the Lamb of God, who takes away the sin of the world! (John 1:29)

Just as Moses lifted up the snake in the desert, so the Son of Man must be lifted up, that everyone who believes in him may have eternal life. "For God so loved the world that he gave his one and only Son, that whoever believes in him shall not perish but have eternal life. For God did not send his Son into the world to condemn the world, but to save the world through him. (John 3:14-17)

I am the living bread that came down from heaven. If anyone eats of this bread,

he will live forever. This bread is my flesh, which I will give for the life of the world." (John 6:51)

"I am the good shepherd. The good shepherd lays down his life for the sheep. just as the Father knows me and I know the Father—and I lay down my life for the sheep. The reason my Father loves me is that I lay down my life—only to take it up again. No one takes it from me, but I lay it down of my own accord. I have authority to lay it down and authority to take it up again. This command I received from my Father." I give them eternal life, and they shall never perish; no one can snatch them out of my hand. My Father, who has given them to me, is greater than all ; no one can snatch them out of my Father's hand. I and the Father are one." Again the Jews picked up stones to stone him, (John 10:11, 15, 17-18, 28-31)

You do not realize that it is better for you that one man die for the people than that the whole nation perish." He did not say this on his own, but as high priest that year he prophesied that Jesus would die for the Jewish nation, and not only for that nation but also for the scattered children of God, to bring them together and make them one. (John 11:50-52)

I tell you the truth, unless a kernel of wheat falls to the ground and dies, it remains only a single seed. But if it dies, it produces many seeds. Now is the time for judgment on this world; now the prince of this world will be driven out. But I, when I am lifted up from the earth, will draw all men to myself." He said this to show the kind of death he was going to die. (John 12:24, 31-33)

"I am not referring to all of you; I know those I have chosen. But this is to fulfill the scripture: 'He who shares my bread has lifted up his heel against me.' "I am telling you now before it happens, so that when it does happen you will believe that I am He. After he had said this, Jesus was troubled in spirit and testified, "I tell you the truth, one of you is going to betray me." (John 13:18-19, 21; cp. Mt.26:21; Mk.14:18; Lk.22:21)

"Do not let your hearts be troubled. Trust in God ; trust also in me. In my Father's house are many rooms; if it were not so, I would have told you. I am going there to prepare a place for you. And if I go and prepare a place for you, I will come back and take you to be with me that you also may be where I am. (John 14:1-3)

Before long, the world will not see me anymore, but you will see me. Because I live, you also will live. (John 14:19)

"You heard me say, 'I am going away and I am coming back to you.' If you loved me, you would be glad that I am going to the Father, for the Father is greater than I. I have told you now before it happens, so that when it does happen you will believe. I will not speak with you much longer, for the prince of this world is coming. He has no hold on me, but the world must learn that I love the Father and that I do exactly what my Father has commanded me. "Come now; let us leave. (John 14:28-31)

Greater love has no one than this, that he lay down his life for his friends. (John 15:13)

I tell you the truth, you will weep and mourn while the world rejoices. You will grieve, but your grief will turn to joy. (John 16:20)

Jesus commanded Peter, "Put your sword away! Shall I not drink the cup the Father has given me?" (John 18:11)

Jesus answered, "You would have no power over me if it were not given to you from above. Therefore the one who handed me over to you is guilty of a greater sin." (John 19:11)

"Now, brothers, I know that you acted in ignorance, as did your leaders. But this is how God fulfilled what he had foretold through all the prophets, saying that his Christ would suffer. Repent, then, and turn to God, so that your sins may be wiped out, that times of refreshing may come from the Lord, and that he may send the Christ, who has been appointed for you—even Jesus. He must remain in heaven until the time comes for God to restore everything, as he promised long ago through his holy prophets. (Acts 3:17-21)

The God of our fathers raised Jesus from the dead—whom you had killed by hanging him on a tree. (Acts 5:30)

Keep watch over yourselves and all the flock of which the Holy Spirit has made you overseers. Be shepherds of the church of God, which he bought with his own blood. (Acts 20:28)

But I have had God's help to this very day, and so I stand here and testify to small and great alike. I am saying nothing beyond what the prophets and Moses said would happen— that the Christ would suffer and, as the first to rise from the dead, would proclaim light to his own people and to the Gentiles." (Acts 26:22-23)

You see, at just the right time, when we were still powerless, Christ died for the ungodly. Very rarely will anyone die for a righteous man, though for a good man someone might possibly dare to die. But God demonstrates his own love for us in this: While we were still sinners, Christ died for us. Since we have now been justified by his blood, how much more shall we be saved from God's wrath through him! For if, when we were God's enemies, we were reconciled to him through the death of his Son, how much more, having been reconciled, shall we be saved through his life! Not only is this so, but we also rejoice in God through our Lord Jesus Christ, through whom we have now received reconciliation. (Rom 5:6-11)

Or don't you know that all of us who were baptized into Christ Jesus were baptized into his death? We were therefore buried with him through baptism into death in order that, just as Christ was raised from the dead through the glory of the Father, we too may live a new life. If we have been united with him like this in his death, we will certainly also be united with him in his resurrection. (Rom 6:3-5)

For we know that since Christ was raised from the dead, he cannot die again; death no longer has mastery over him. The death he died, he died to sin once for all; but the life he lives, he lives to God. (Rom 6:9-10)

For what the law was powerless to do in that it was weakened by the sinful nature, God did by sending his own Son in the likeness of sinful man to be a sin offering. And so he condemned sin in sinful man, (Rom 8:3)

He who did not spare his own Son, but gave him up for us all—how will he not also, along with him, graciously give us all things? (Rom 8:32)

Who is he that condemns? Christ Jesus, who died—more than that, who was raised to life—is at the right hand of God and is also interceding for us. Who shall separate us from the love of Christ? Shall trouble or hardship or persecution or famine or nakedness or danger or sword? (Rom 8:34-35)

No, in all these things we are more than conquerors through him who loved us. For I am convinced that neither death nor life, neither angels nor demons, neither the present nor the future, nor any powers, neither height nor depth, nor anything else in all creation, will be able to separate us from the love of God that is in Christ Jesus our Lord. (Rom 8:37-39)

For this very reason, Christ died and returned to life so that he might be the Lord of both the dead and the living. (Rom 14:9)

For Christ did not send me to baptize, but to preach the gospel—not with words of human wisdom, lest the cross of Christ be emptied of its power. (1 Cor 1:17)

For I resolved to know nothing while I was with you except Jesus Christ and him crucified. (1 Cor 2:2)

Get rid of the old yeast that you may be a new batch without yeast—as you really are. For Christ, our Passover lamb, has been sacrificed. (1 Cor 5:7)

You were bought at a price. Therefore honor God with your body. (1 Cor 6:20)

So this weak brother, for whom Christ died, is destroyed by your knowledge. (1 Cor 8:11)

For what I received I passed on to you as of first importance : that Christ died for our sins according to the Scriptures, that he was buried, that he was raised on the third day according to the Scriptures, (1 Cor 15:3-4)

We always carry around in our body the death of Jesus, so that the life of Jesus may also be revealed in our body. For we who are alive are always being given over to death for Jesus' sake, so that his life may be revealed in our mortal body. (2 Cor 4:10-11)

For Christ's love compels us, because we are convinced that one died for all, and therefore all died. And he died for all, that those who live should no longer live for themselves but for him who died for them and was raised again. (2 Cor 5:14-15)

That God was reconciling the world to himself in Christ, not counting men's sins against them. And he has committed to us the message of reconciliation. We are therefore Christ's ambassadors, as though God were making his appeal through us. We implore you on Christ's behalf: Be reconciled to God. God made him who had no sin to be sin for us, so that in him we might become the righteousness of God. (2 Cor 5:19-21)

For you know the grace of our Lord Jesus Christ, that though he was rich, yet for your sakes he became poor, so that you through his poverty might become rich. (2 Cor 8:9)

Who gave himself for our sins to rescue us from the present evil age, according to the will of our God and Father, (Gal 1:4)

I have been crucified with Christ and I no longer live, but Christ lives in me. The life I live in the body, I live by faith in the Son of God, who loved me and gave himself for me. (Gal 2:20)

Christ redeemed us from the curse of the law by becoming a curse for us, for it is written: "Cursed is everyone who is hung on a tree." (Gal 3:13)

But when the time had fully come, God sent his Son, born of a woman, born under law, to redeem those under law, that we might receive the full rights of sons. (Gal 4:4-5)

To the praise of his glorious grace, which he has freely given us in the One he loves. In him we have redemption through his blood, the forgiveness of sins, in accordance with the riches of God's grace (Eph 1:6-7)

But now in Christ Jesus you who once were far away have been brought near through the blood of Christ. For he himself is our peace, who has made the two one and has destroyed the barrier, the dividing wall of hostility, (Eph 2:13-14)

And in this one body to reconcile both of them to God through the cross, by which he put to death their hostility. (Eph 2:16)

For through him we both have access to the Father by one Spirit. (Eph 2:18)

And live a life of love, just as Christ loved us and gave himself up for us as a fragrant offering and sacrifice to God. (Eph 5:2)

Husbands, love your wives, just as Christ loved the church and gave himself up for her (Eph 5:25)

Who, being in very nature God, did

not consider equality with God something to be grasped, but made himself nothing, taking the very nature of a servant, being made in human likeness. And being found in appearance as a man, he humbled himself and became obedient to death— even death on a cross! (Phil 2:6-8)

In whom we have redemption, the forgiveness of sins. (Col 1:14)
and through him to reconcile to himself all things, whether things on earth or things in heaven, by making peace through his blood, shed on the cross. Once you were alienated from God and were enemies in your minds because of your evil behavior. But now he has reconciled you by Christ's physical body through death to present you holy in his sight, without blemish and free from accusation— (Col 1:20-22)

Having canceled the written code, with its regulations, that was against us and that stood opposed to us; he took it away, nailing it to the cross. And having disarmed the powers and authorities, he made a public spectacle of them, triumphing over them by the cross. (Col 2:14-15)

And to wait for his Son from heaven, whom he raised from the dead—Jesus, who rescues us from the coming wrath. (1 Th 1:10)

We believe that Jesus died and rose again and so we believe that God will bring with Jesus those who have fallen asleep in him. (1 Th 4:14)

For God did not appoint us to suffer wrath but to receive salvation through our Lord Jesus Christ. He died for us so that, whether we are awake or asleep, we may live together with him. (1 Th 5:9-10)

Here is a trustworthy saying that deserves full acceptance: Christ Jesus came into the world to save sinners—of whom I am the worst. But for that very reason I was shown mercy so that in me, the worst of sinners, Christ Jesus might display his unlimited patience as an example for those who would believe on him and receive eternal life. (1 Tim 1:15-16)

This is good, and pleases God our Savior, who wants all men to be saved and to come to a knowledge of the truth. For there is one God and one mediator between God and men, the man Christ Jesus, who gave himself as a ransom for all men—the testimony given in its proper time. (1 Tim 2:3-6)

Who has saved us and called us to a holy life—not because of anything we have done but because of his own purpose and grace. This grace was given us in Christ Jesus before the beginning of time, but it has now been revealed through the appearing of our Savior, Christ Jesus, who has destroyed death and has brought life and immortality to light through the gospel. (2 Tim 1:9-10)

For the grace of God that brings salvation has appeared to all men. It teaches us to say "No" to ungodliness and worldly passions, and to live self-controlled, upright and godly lives in this present age, while we wait for the blessed hope—the glorious appearing of our great God and Savior, Jesus Christ, who gave himself for us to redeem us from all wickedness and to purify for himself a people that are his very own, eager to do what is good. (Titus 2:11-14)

But when the kindness and love of God our Savior appeared, he saved us, not because of righteous things we had done, but because of his mercy. He saved us through the washing of rebirth and renewal by the Holy Spirit, whom he poured out on us generously through Jesus Christ our Savior, so that, having been justified by his grace, we might become heirs having the hope of eternal life. (Titus 3:4-7)
but in these last days he has spoken to us by his Son, whom he appointed heir of all things, and through whom he made the universe. The Son is the radiance of God's glory and the exact representation of his being, sustaining all things by his powerful word. After he had provided purification for sins, he sat down at the right hand of the Majesty in heaven. (Heb 1:2-3)

But we see Jesus, who was made a little lower than the angels, now crowned with glory and honor because he suffered death, so that by the grace of God he might taste death for everyone. In bringing many sons to glory, it was fitting that God, for whom and through whom everything exists, should make the author of their salvation perfect through suffering. (Heb 2:9-10)

Since the children have flesh and blood, he too shared in their humanity so that by his death he might destroy him who holds the power of death—that is, the devil— and free those who all their lives were held in slavery by their fear of death. For surely it is not angels he helps, but Abraham's descendants. For this reason he had to be made like his brothers in every way, in order that he might become a merciful and faithful high priest in service to God, and that he might make atonement for the sins of the people. Because he himself suffered when he was tempted, he is able to help those who are being tempted. (Heb 2:14-18)

During the days of Jesus' life on earth, he offered up prayers and petitions with loud cries and tears to the one who could save him from death, and he was heard because of his reverent submission. Although he was a son, he learned obedience from what he suffered and, once made perfect, he became the source of eternal salvation for all who obey him (Heb 5:7-9)

Therefore he is able to save completely those who come to God through him, because he always lives to intercede for them. Such a high priest meets our need—one who is holy, blameless, pure, set apart from sinners, exalted above the heavens. Unlike the other high priests, he does not need to offer sacrifices day after day, first for his own sins, and then for the sins of the peo-

ple. He sacrificed for their sins once for all when he offered himself. (Heb 7:25-27)

He did not enter by means of the blood of goats and calves; but he entered the Most Holy Place once for all by his own blood, having obtained eternal redemption. The blood of goats and bulls and the ashes of a heifer sprinkled on those who are ceremonially unclean sanctify them so that they are outwardly clean. How much more, then, will the blood of Christ, who through the eternal Spirit offered himself unblemished to God, cleanse our consciences from acts that lead to death, so that we may serve the living God! For this reason Christ is the mediator of a new covenant, that those who are called may receive the promised eternal inheritance—now that he has died as a ransom to set them free from the sins committed under the first covenant. In the case of a will, it is necessary to prove the death of the one who made it, because a will is in force only when somebody has died; it never takes effect while the one who made it is living. (Heb 9:12-17)

Nor did he enter heaven to offer himself again and again, the way the high priest enters the Most Holy Place every year with blood that is not his own. Then Christ would have had to suffer many times since the creation of the world. But now he has appeared once for all at the end of the ages to do away with sin by the sacrifice of himself. Just as man is destined to die once, and after that to face judgment, so Christ was sacrificed once to take away the sins of many people; and he will appear a second time, not to bear sin, but to bring salvation to those who are waiting for him. (Heb 9:25-28)

And by that will, we have been made holy through the sacrifice of the body of Jesus Christ once for all. (Heb 10:10)

But when this priest had offered for all time one sacrifice for sins, he sat down at the right hand of God. (Heb 10:12)
because by one sacrifice he has made perfect forever those who are being made holy. The Holy Spirit also testifies to us about this. First he says: "This is the covenant I will make with them after that time, says the Lord. I will put my laws in their hearts, and I will write them on their minds." Then he adds: "Their sins and lawless acts I will remember no more." And where these have been forgiven, there is no longer any sacrifice for sin. Therefore, brothers, since we have confidence to enter the Most Holy Place by the blood of Jesus, by a new and living way opened for us through the curtain, that is, his body, (Heb 10:14-20)

Let us fix our eyes on Jesus, the author and perfecter of our faith, who for the joy set before him endured the cross, scorning its shame, and sat down at the right hand of the throne of God. (Heb 12:2)

To Jesus the mediator of a new covenant, and to the sprinkled blood that speaks a better word than the blood of Abel. (Heb 12:24)

The high priest carries the blood of animals into the Most Holy Place as a sin offering, but the bodies are burned outside the camp. And so Jesus also suffered outside the city gate to make the people holy through his own blood. (Heb 13:11-12)

Who have been chosen according to the foreknowledge of God the Father, through the sanctifying work of the Spirit, for obedience to Jesus Christ and sprinkling by his blood: Grace and peace be yours in abundance. (1 Pet 1:2)

For you know that it was not with perishable things such as silver or gold that you were redeemed from the empty way of life handed down to you from your forefathers, but with the precious blood of Christ, a lamb without blemish or defect. He was chosen before the creation of the world, but was revealed in these last times for your sake. Through him you believe in God, who raised him from the dead and glorified him, and so your faith and hope are in God. (1 Pet 1:18-21)

To this you were called, because Christ suffered for you, leaving you an example, that you should follow in his steps. (1 Pet 2:21)

He himself bore our sins in his body on the tree, so that we might die to sins and live for righteousness; by his wounds you have been healed. (1 Pet 2:24)

For Christ died for sins once for all, the righteous for the unrighteous, to bring you to God. He was put to death in the body but made alive by the Spirit, (1 Pet 3:18)

Therefore, since Christ suffered in his body, arm yourselves also with the same attitude, because he who has suffered in his body is done with sin. (1 Pet 4:1)
But if we walk in the light, as he is in the light, we have fellowship with one another, and the blood of Jesus, his Son, purifies us from all sin. (1 John 1:7)

He is the atoning sacrifice for our sins, and not only for ours but also for the sins of the whole world. (1 John 2:2)

This is how we know what love is: Jesus Christ laid down his life for us. And we ought to lay down our lives for our brothers. (1 John 3:16)

This is love: not that we loved God, but that he loved us and sent his Son as an atoning sacrifice for our sins. (1 John 4:10)

And from Jesus Christ, who is the faithful witness, the firstborn from the dead, and the ruler of the kings of the earth. To him who loves us and has freed us from our sins by his blood, and has made us to be a kingdom and priests to serve his God and Father—to him be glory and power for ever and ever! Amen. (Rev 1:5-6)

And they sang a new song: "You are worthy to take the scroll and to open its seals, because you were slain, and with your blood you purchased men for God

from every tribe and language and people and nation. You have made them to be a kingdom and priests to serve our God, and they will reign on the earth." In a loud voice they sang: "Worthy is the Lamb, who was slain, to receive power and wealth and wisdom and strength and honor and glory and praise!" (Rev 5:9-10, 12)

This calls for wisdom. If anyone has insight, let him calculate the number of the beast, for it is man's number. His number is 666. (Rev 13:18)

4 (17:23) **Jesus Christ, Resurrection**: Christ foretold His resurrection. God raised Christ for several reasons (see outline and notes—Acts 2:29-31; Col.3:1-4).

1. He was raised to reign with God.
2. He was raised to deliver His soul from hell.
3. He was raised to deliver His body from corruption.
4. He was raised to do seven wonderful things for us (see note—Col.3:1-4 for discussion).

(See JESUS CHRIST, Resurrection—Master Subject Index, for additional information on the resurrection of Christ.)

Most of the passages in the New Testament dealing with the resurrection follow. One of the most precious and profitable studies a person can make is to place each passage under some subjects such as: Purpose, Results, Meaning, Importance, Power of, Effects, Object of, Predicted or Prophesied, Proof of, Necessity of, Sign of, Fact, etc.

For as Jonah was three days and three nights in the belly of a huge fish, so the Son of Man will be three days and three nights in the heart of the earth. (Mat 12:40)

From that time on Jesus began to explain to his disciples that he must go to Jerusalem and suffer many things at the hands of the elders, chief priests and teachers of the law, and that he must be killed and on the third day be raised to life. (Mat 16:21; cp. Mt.17:23; Lk.9:22, 31; 24:7)

And will turn him over to the Gentiles to be mocked and flogged and crucified. On the third day he will be raised to life!" (Mat 20:19; cp. Mk.10:34)

But after I have risen, I will go ahead of you into Galilee." (Mat 26:32; cp. Mk. 14:28)

As they were coming down the mountain, Jesus gave them orders not to tell anyone what they had seen until the Son of Man had risen from the dead. They kept the matter to themselves, discussing what "rising from the dead" meant. (Mark 9:9-10)

On the third day he will rise again." (Luke 18:33)

He told them, "This is what is written: The Christ will suffer and rise from the dead on the third day, (Luke 24:46)

Jesus answered them, "Destroy this temple, and I will raise it again in three days." But the temple he had spoken of was his body. (John 2:19,21; cp. Mk.14:58)

"In a little while you will see me no more, and then after a little while you will see me." (John 16:16)

After his suffering, he showed himself to these men and gave many convincing proofs that he was alive. He appeared to them over a period of forty days and spoke about the kingdom of God. (Acts 1:3)

Beginning from John's baptism to the time when Jesus was taken up from us. For one of these must become a witness with us of his resurrection." (Acts 1:22)

But God raised him from the dead, freeing him from the agony of death, because it was impossible for death to keep its hold on him. David said about him: "'I saw the Lord always before me. Because he is at my right hand, I will not be shaken. Therefore my heart is glad and my tongue rejoices; my body also will live in hope, because you will not abandon me to the grave, nor will you let your Holy One see decay. You have made known to me the paths of life; you will fill me with joy in your presence.' (Acts 2:24-28)

God has raised this Jesus to life, and we are all witnesses of the fact. Exalted to the right hand of God, he has received from the Father the promised Holy Spirit and has poured out what you now see and hear. "Therefore let all Israel be assured of this: God has made this Jesus, whom you crucified, both Lord and Christ." Peter replied, "Repent and be baptized, every one of you, in the name of Jesus Christ for the forgiveness of your sins. And you will receive the gift of the Holy Spirit. (Acts 2:32-33, 36, 38)

You killed the author of life, but God raised him from the dead. We are witnesses of this. (Acts 3:15)

Then know this, you and all the people of Israel: It is by the name of Jesus Christ of Nazareth, whom you crucified but whom God raised from the dead, that this man stands before you healed. (Acts 4:10)

With great power the apostles continued to testify to the resurrection of the Lord Jesus, and much grace was upon them all. (Acts 4:33)

The God of our fathers raised Jesus from the dead—whom you had killed by hanging him on a tree. God exalted him to his own right hand as Prince and Savior that he might give repentance and forgiveness of sins to Israel. We are witnesses of these things, and so is the Holy Spirit, whom God has given to those who obey him." (Acts 5:30-32)

But God raised him from the dead on the third day and caused him to be seen. He was not seen by all the people, but by witnesses whom God had already chosen—by us who ate and drank with him after he rose from the dead. (Acts 10:40-41)

But God raised him from the dead, and for many days he was seen by those who had traveled with him from Galilee to Jerusalem. They are now his witnesses to our people. "We tell you the good news: What God promised our fathers he has fulfilled for us, their children, by raising up Jesus. As it is written in the second Psalm: "'You are my Son; today I have become your Fa-

ther.' The fact that God raised him from the dead, never to decay, is stated in these words: "'I will give you the holy and sure blessings promised to David.' So it is stated elsewhere: "'You will not let your Holy One see decay.' "For when David had served God's purpose in his own generation, he fell asleep; he was buried with his fathers and his body decayed. But the one whom God raised from the dead did not see decay. (Acts 13:30-37)

As his custom was, Paul went into the synagogue, and on three Sabbath days he reasoned with them from the Scriptures, explaining and proving that the Christ had to suffer and rise from the dead. "This Jesus I am proclaiming to you is the Christ," he said. For he has set a day when he will judge the world with justice by the man he has appointed. He has given proof of this to all men by raising him from the dead." (Acts 17:2-3, 31)

But I have had God's help to this very day, and so I stand here and testify to small and great alike. I am saying nothing beyond what the prophets and Moses said would happen— that the Christ would suffer and, as the first to rise from the dead, would proclaim light to his own people and to the Gentiles." At this point Festus interrupted Paul's defense. "You are out of your mind, Paul!" he shouted. "Your great learning is driving you insane." "I am not insane, most excellent Festus," Paul replied. "What I am saying is true and reasonable. (Acts 26:22-25)

And who through the Spirit of holiness was declared with power to be the Son of God by his resurrection from the dead: Jesus Christ our Lord. (Rom 1:4)

But also for us, to whom God will credit righteousness—for us who believe in him who raised Jesus our Lord from the dead. He was delivered over to death for our sins and was raised to life for our justification. (Rom 4:24-25)

For if, when we were God's enemies, we were reconciled to him through the death of his Son, how much more, having been reconciled, shall we be saved through his life! (Rom 5:10)

We were therefore buried with him through baptism into death in order that, just as Christ was raised from the dead through the glory of the Father, we too may live a new life. If we have been united with him like this in his death, we will certainly also be united with him in his resurrection. For we know that since Christ was raised from the dead, he cannot die again; death no longer has mastery over him. The death he died, he died to sin once for all; but the life he lives, he lives to God. (Rom 6:4-5, 9-10)

And if the Spirit of him who raised Jesus from the dead is living in you, he who raised Christ from the dead will also give life to your mortal bodies through his Spirit, who lives in you. (Rom 8:11)

Who is he that condemns? Christ Jesus, who died—more than that, who was raised to life—is at the right hand of God and is also interceding for us. (Rom 8:34)

That if you confess with your mouth, "Jesus is Lord," and believe in your heart that God raised him from the dead, you will be saved. (Rom 10:9)

By his power God raised the Lord from the dead, and he will raise us also. (1 Cor 6:14)

For what I received I passed on to you as of first importance : that Christ died for our sins according to the Scriptures, that he was buried, that he was raised on the third day according to the Scriptures, (1 Cor 15:3-4)

But Christ has indeed been raised from the dead, the firstfruits of those who have fallen asleep. For since death came through a man, the resurrection of the dead comes also through a man. For as in Adam all die, so in Christ all will be made alive. But each in his own turn: Christ, the firstfruits; then, when he comes, those who belong to him. (1 Cor 15:20-23)

We always carry around in our body the death of Jesus, so that the life of Jesus may also be revealed in our body. For we who are alive are always being given over to death for Jesus' sake, so that his life may be revealed in our mortal body. (2 Cor 4:10-11)

Because we know that the one who raised the Lord Jesus from the dead will also raise us with Jesus and present us with you in his presence. (2 Cor 4:14)

And he died for all, that those who live should no longer live for themselves but for him who died for them and was raised again. (2 Cor 5:15)

For to be sure, he was crucified in weakness, yet he lives by God's power. Likewise, we are weak in him, yet by God's power we will live with him to serve you. (2 Cor 13:4)

Paul, an apostle—sent not from men nor by man, but by Jesus Christ and God the Father, who raised him from the dead— (Gal 1:1)
which he exerted in Christ when he raised him from the dead and seated him at his right hand in the heavenly realms, (Eph 1:20)

I want to know Christ and the power of his resurrection and the fellowship of sharing in his sufferings, becoming like him in his death, (Phil 3:10)

And he is the head of the body, the church; he is the beginning and the firstborn from among the dead, so that in everything he might have the supremacy. (Col 1:18)

Having been buried with him in baptism and raised with him through your faith in the power of God, who raised him from the dead. (Col 2:12)

And to wait for his Son from heaven, whom he raised from the dead—Jesus, who rescues us from the coming wrath. (1 Th 1:10)

We believe that Jesus died and rose again and so we believe that God will bring with Jesus those who have fallen asleep in him. (1 Th 4:14)

Remember Jesus Christ, raised from the dead, descended from David. This is my gospel, (2 Tim 2:8)

Therefore he is able to save completely those who come to God through him, because he always lives to intercede for them. (Heb 7:25)

For Christ did not enter a man-made sanctuary that was only a copy of the true one; he entered heaven itself, now to appear for us in God's presence. (Heb 9:24)

Then Christ would have had to suffer many times since the creation of the world. But now he has appeared once for all at the end of the ages to do away with sin by the sacrifice of himself. Just as man is destined to die once, and after that to face judgment, so Christ was sacrificed once to take away the sins of many people; and he will appear a second time, not to bear sin, but to bring salvation to those who are waiting for him. (Heb 9:26-28)

But when this priest had offered for all time one sacrifice for sins, he sat down at the right hand of God. (Heb 10:12)

Abraham reasoned that God could raise the dead, and figuratively speaking, he did receive Isaac back from death. (Heb 11:19)

May the God of peace, who through the blood of the eternal covenant brought back from the dead our Lord Jesus, that great Shepherd of the sheep, (Heb 13:20)

Praise be to the God and Father of our Lord Jesus Christ! In his great mercy he has given us new birth into a living hope through the resurrection of Jesus Christ from the dead, and into an inheritance that can never perish, spoil or fade—kept in heaven for you, (1 Pet 1:3-4)

Through him you believe in God, who raised him from the dead and glorified him, and so your faith and hope are in God. (1 Pet 1:21)

For Christ died for sins once for all, the righteous for the unrighteous, to bring you to God. He was put to death in the body but made alive by the Spirit, (1 Pet 3:18)

And this water symbolizes baptism that now saves you also—not the removal of dirt from the body but the pledge of a good conscience toward God. It saves you by the resurrection of Jesus Christ, who has gone into heaven and is at God's right hand—with angels, authorities and powers in submission to him. (1 Pet 3:21-22)

And from Jesus Christ, who is the faithful witness, the firstborn from the dead, and the ruler of the kings of the earth. To him who loves us and has freed us from our sins by his blood, I am the Living One; I was dead, and behold I am alive for ever and ever! And I hold the keys of death and Hades. (Rev 1:5, 18)

1 Jesus was visited by tax collectors a. They questioned Peter instead of Jesus b. They asked if Jesus was a tax-dodger **2 Jesus demonstrated good citizenship: He paid taxes** **3 Jesus made a unique claim about His own citizenship**	**F. The Messiah Reveals Himself Through Good Citizenship, 17:24-27** (cp. Mk.12:13-17) 24 After Jesus and his disci- ples arrived in Capernaum, the collectors of the two- drachma tax came to Peter and asked, "Doesn't your teacher pay the temple tax?" 25 "Yes, he does," he re- plied. When Peter came into the house, Jesus was the first to speak. "What do you think,	Simon?" he asked. "From whom do the kings of the earth collect duty and taxes— from their own sons or from others? 26 "From others," Peter an- swered. "Then the sons are exempt," Jesus said to him. 27 "But so that we may not offend them, go to the lake and throw out your line. Take the first fish you catch; open its mouth and you will find a four-drachma coin. Take it and give it to them for my tax and yours."	a. He is the Son of a King, of God b. He is of another Kingdom, of heaven c. He is free of the earthly kingdom **4 Jesus set the standard for citizenship: To keep others from stumbling** **5 Jesus demonstrated His citizenship & Messiahship: He paid the tax miraculously**

DIVISION XI

THE MESSIAH'S DRAMATIC REVELATION: HIS MESSIAHSHIP HIS CHURCH, AND HIS CROSS, 16:13-17:27

F. The Messiah Reveals Himself Through Good Citizenship, 17:24-27

(17:24-27) **Introduction**: Jesus had been carrying His disciples through intensive training for some time now. He had been zeroing in on His death and resurrection (see notes—Mt.16:21-28; 17:1-13; 17:22-23). In this passage Jesus showed just how capable a teacher He really was. He was able to take a visit by a tax collector and continue to make the unique claims of Messiahship, and at the same time teach the importance of good citizenship. He is God's Son, and every believer is responsible to be a good citizen.

1. Jesus was visited by tax collectors (v.24).
2. Jesus demonstrated good citizenship: He paid taxes (v.25).
3. Jesus made a unique claim about His citizenship (v.25-26).
4. Jesus set the standard for citizenship: to keep others from stumbling (v.27).
5. Jesus demonstrated His citizenship and Messiahship: He paid the tax miraculously (v.27).

1 (17:24) **Tax, Temple**: Jesus was visited by a tax collector. Perhaps Jesus was behind in His tax payments because He had been away for so long. The tax collectors approached Peter instead of Jesus because it was Jesus' habit to lodge in Peter's house when in Capernaum or perhaps because they feared Jesus.

The tax spoken of is the temple tax. The temple was an extremely expensive building to maintain just as any large building is. Time deteriorates furnishings, even stone and mortar, and all has to be replaced. In addition, there was the upkeep of the priests, their shelter, food, and clothing. There was the provision of the animals, incense, wine, flour, and oil used in the sacrifices which had to be offered every day—and the list could go on and on. Upkeep of the temple was so expensive that a nation-wide tax had to be imposed upon every male Jew over twenty years old. It was just a small tax (one half-shekel) for each man, amounting to about two days work; nevertheless, it had to be paid. It was collected annually by the tax collectors setting up their *tax collecting* booths in strategic locations throughout the country. (Cp. Exodus 30:13-16.)

2 (17:25) **Citizenship—Taxes**: Jesus demonstrated good citizenship. He paid taxes. It was His practice to pay taxes, and Peter knew this. Therefore, Peter was able to answer, "Yes, he does pay taxes."

Note a point which really strikes out at those who say they do not attend church because the church has too many hypocrites in it. In Christ's day, the temple was *a den of thieves* and much of its worship was hypocritical and corrupt; yet Christ supported it (Mt.21:13; Mk.11:17). Why? There are at least three reasons.

1. Despite its corruptions, the temple was still the house of God and the house of prayer.

2. Christ benefited from the temple. When He entered the temple, His spirit was right with God, so He was able to worship and minister within its walls despite the hypocrisy of so many and the corruption of so much.

3. The temple was where God's people were thought and expected to be. The world expected God's people to be in the temple and not somewhere else when it was time for worship. Christ could be nowhere else "so that he might not offend them" (v.27). (See outlines and notes—Mt.22:15-22; Mk.12:13-17; Lk.20:19-26 for more discussion.)

> **Let us not give up meeting together, as some are in the habit of doing, but let us encourage one another—and all the more as you see the Day approaching. (Heb 10:25)**

3 (17:25-26) **Jesus Christ, Deity**: Jesus made a unique claim by sharing an illustration. The illustration is brief and yet forceful. Jesus asked Peter a simple question: "From whom do kings collect their taxes? from their own sons or from the citizens?" The answer is obvious: "He collects duties and taxes from the citizens, not from his own sons." And then Jesus made the phenomenal claim: "Then the sons are exempt."

The tax was the temple tax. The temple was God's, and Jesus was the Son of God. As the Son of God, He was free from the tax. He did not owe the tax.

Christ was not trying to keep from paying taxes. His point was to make a unique claim, a threefold claim.

1. He was the Son of a King, the Son of God Himself. (See notes—Jn.1:1-2; 1:34. Cp. DEEPER STUDY # 1—Jn.1:39; note—3:16-18; DEEPER STUDY # 1—5:25; notes 6:38-40, 44, 57;

DEEPER STUDY # 1—8:32; notes—9:35; 10:32-33, 36-38; 1 Jn.5:5, 9-12.)

2. He was of another kingdom—the Kingdom of Heaven (see note and DEEPER STUDY # 1—Jn.3:31; notes—6:33; 6:38; 6:41-51; DEEPER STUDY # 2—8:23; 16:28).

3. He was free of the earthly kingdom. He had no obligation to pay taxes. If He paid them, it was because He willingly and voluntarily paid them.

There is more than meets the eye to the fact that Christ is free of the earthly kingdom. He is free of it because He is of God. His citizenship is of heaven; therefore, He has no obligation to the earth. The world and man neither merit nor deserve any attention from God. Man has forfeited his right to God's attention by his sin—by his degradation, depravity, evil, rebellion, and treason—all manifesting themselves in daily acts ranging from thoughts of selfishness to the slaughter of human life. Whatever God does for man and the world is of grace and mercy; it is because He loves man and the world. It is not because He is obligated or in bondage to serve man by meeting his need.

The above truth, however, is not true of the believer. When the believer trusts Christ as his Savior, he receives the divine nature of God. He becomes a new man and a new citizen of heaven; however, he is still of the earth. He is a new creature born from heaven above, but he is still flesh—still of the earth as well (2 Pt.1:1; see DEEPER STUDY # 3—Eph.4:24; note—Ph.3:20). Therefore, he has an obligation not only to be a good citizen of heaven but also of the earth. God expects him to live for heaven by living a pure life and to live for the earth by sharing the good news of salvation with the rest of the world.

Thought 1. The three claims made by Christ are eye catching (glance at the outline points). There is a sense in which the same claims become the claims of the believer.

1) Even as Christ is the Son of a King, the Son of God, so the believer is adopted as a child of the King (see DEEPER STUDY # 2—Gal.4:5-6).
2) Even as Christ is of another kingdom and of another world—of heaven itself—so the believer is made a citizen of heaven (Ph.3:20; 1 Pt.1:4; cp. Lk.22:30).
3) Even as Christ is free of the earthly kingdom, so the believer is made free of the earthly kingdom. But remember: he is free only in a very special sense (Ro.6:18, 22; 8:2; Gal.5:1). He is free of the sin, bondage and death of this world, not free of the responsibility for this world. Even after being saved and made a citizen of heaven, he is still a citizen of this earth. He is a citizen of both earth and heaven, and as such he is obligated to care for the earth (cp. Mt.22:15-22; Mk.12:13-18; Lk.20:19-26. See outline and notes—Ro.13:1-7; 1 Tim.2:1-4; Tit.3:1-2; 1 Pt.2:13-17. Cp. 1 Cor.9:19; 1 Pt.2:16.)

"Caesar's," they replied. Then he said to them, "Give to Caesar what is Caesar's, and to God what is God's." (Mat 22:21)

Everyone must submit himself to the governing authorities, for there is no authority except that which God has established. The authorities that exist have been established by God. (Rom 13:1)

Remind the people to be subject to rulers and authorities, to be obedient, to be ready to do whatever is good, (Titus 3:1)

Submit yourselves for the Lord's sake to every authority instituted among men: whether to the king, as the supreme authority, or to governors, who are sent by him to punish those who do wrong and to commend those who do right. (1 Pet 2:13-14)

4 (17:27) **Citizenship**: Jesus set the standard for citizenship—to keep others from stumbling. Note the word offend (skandalizo, verb; or skandalon, noun). When used as a verb the word *offend* means to put a snare or stumbling block in someone's way; to cause someone to trip or fall. When used as a noun the word *offend* means something that causes someone to stumble, trip, fall, or slip back. It is anything that arouses prejudice within others; anything that is a roadblock or a hindrance to others; anything that causes others to fall by the wayside. It is important to note that the stumbling block is sometimes good, and those who stumble are the ones in the wrong. For example, Christ is said to be a "rock that makes them fall" (Ro.9:33) and His cross is said to "make some fall"; that is, it is a stumbling block to some (Gal.5:11).

Christ was saying that He must not set a bad example by not paying His taxes. He was not obligated to pay them, but if He refused, then He would be encouraging poor citizenship. Therefore, He would forego His freedom in order to keep from causing others to stumble. He must not offend others, cause them to slip, stumble, or fall—under any circumstances.

Note two things.

1. Christ *never did* anything that would cause others to minimize or think less of their duty toward others (whether individuals, groups, or government). He did the very opposite. He always encouraged others to fulfill their duty so long as the duty was a legitimate act.

2. Christ never did anything that would cause others to stumble. Even when He was allowed or had the right to do something, He refused to do it if it would offend or hurt someone.

Thought 1. Many things may be lawful for us, but they may cause others to fall. In such cases, abstinence is our Lord's command.

Therefore let us stop passing judgment on one another. Instead, make up your mind not to put any stumbling block or obstacle in your brother's way. As one who is in the Lord Jesus, I am fully convinced that no food is unclean in itself. But if anyone regards something as unclean, then for him it is unclean. If your brother is distressed because of what you eat, you are no longer acting in love. Do not by your eating destroy your brother for whom Christ died. Do not allow what you consider good to be spoken of as evil. (Rom 14:13-16)

We who are strong ought to bear with the failings of the weak and not to please ourselves. Each of us should please his neighbor for his good, to build him up. For even Christ did not please himself but, as it is written: "The insults of those who insult you have fallen on me." (Rom 15:1-3)

5 (17:27) **Citizenship**: Jesus demonstrated His citizenship and Messiahship. He paid the tax miraculously. This miracle demonstrated beyond question the three claims Christ had just made. His knowing (omniscience) that a coin was in the mouth of a fish showed Peter that He...

- was of royalty, the Son of God.
- was of another kingdom that was superior to this earth and its seas.
- was free of the earth and its restrictions and obligations. How could Christ better demonstrate His Messiahship and Deity?

Why would Jesus Christ pay taxes if He were really of heaven? Why would He who did not belong to this earth subject Himself to civil and religious law?

There seem to be several reasons.

1. Christ was born under the law (Gal.4:4). He was exactly who Peter had confessed Him to be: "the Christ, the Son of the living God" (Mt.16:16). Yet, He had deliberately subjected His glory and humbled Himself to become a man. He was the God-Man. As God, He was not obligated to the earth, but as Man, He was willingly subjecting Himself to the laws of men. The disciples needed to know this. What He and the Father were doing for man was not out of obligation but out of love and care.

2. Christ wished to foreshadow the atonement that He was soon to make for man. The temple tax was called "an atonement for your lives" (Ex.30:15. Cp. Ex.30:13-16.) Atonement means *a covering* for a person's sins, a covering that makes reconciliation between man and God possible. The tax was paid as an atonement for a person's sin. It was to be paid in an act of faith, believing that one's sins would be covered and forgiven and that one would be reconciled and accepted by God anew and afresh. It was intended by God to be a renewed dedication of life.

Christ was made "in the likeness of sinful man" (Ro.8:3), and He became sin for us (2 Cor.5:21). But Christ was not sinful. He had no sins for which to atone. Therefore, He had to declare to the disciples that He was free of the tax; for He was truly the Son of God, and He was truly free of sin. His payment of the tax was an entirely willing and voluntary act. As such it foreshadowed the *voluntary atonement* He was to bear for man.

3. Christ wished to reinforce that He was the Son of God. He could have paid the taxes without comment, but by declaring that He was free of the tax because He was God's Son, He reinforced who He was to the disciples.

4. Christ wished to set an example for man. Every person is to "fulfill all righteousness" (Mt.3:15). Since Christ proved to be a good citizen, so must all who follow Him.

5. Christ held both the temple and government in high regard (see outline and notes—Ro.13:1-7). While on earth He had benefited from the temple: He had worshipped and ministered there, and He had reaped benefits from the temple. Therefore, He was now setting an example of how man is to return a portion of his income to help in the temple's (church's) support.

6. Christ did not wish to make anyone fall or to be a stumbling block to anyone. If He refused to pay the taxes, He would cause some to fall. They would feel He was not carrying His load, and He would be a stumbling block to others. He would be setting an example of rebellion and lawlessness. If He refused to support the government and temple and everyone followed His example, then all governments and temples would collapse and cease to exist. Therefore, Christ demonstrated good citizenship for a very solid reason.

Thought 1. What is it that makes us pay attention to Christ and do what He taught? The fact that He proved His Messiahship and that He is truly the Son of the living God. It is because of who He is that we are driven to trust Him and to be the very best citizens we can.

"A new command I give you: Love one another. As I have loved you, so you must love one another. By this all men will know that you are my disciples, if you love one another." (John 13:34-35)

The entire law is summed up in a single command: "Love your neighbor as yourself." (Gal 5:14)

If you really keep the royal law found in Scripture, "Love your neighbor as yourself," you are doing right. (James 2:8)

And this is his command: to believe in the name of his Son, Jesus Christ, and to love one another as he commanded us. (1 John 3:23)

Outline	Heading	Scripture	Outline
1 **Two assumptions** a. A person is great if he	**CHAPTER 18** **XII. THE MESSIAH'S DISCIPLES & THEIR BEHAVIOR TOWARD ONE ANOTHER, 18:1-35** **A. The Conditions for Greatness, 18:1-4** (Mk.9:33-37;Lk.9:46-48) **A**t that time the disciples came to Jesus and asked,	"Who is the greatest in the kingdom of heaven?" 2 He called a little child and had him stand among them. 3 And he said: "I tell you the truth, unless you change and become like little children, you will never enter the kingdom of heaven. 4 Therefore, whoever humbles himself like this child is the greatest in the kingdom of heaven.	is in the Kingdom b. There are degrees of greatness c. Jesus gave a living demonstration: A child 2 **Condition 1: Conversion** a. How: By turning & becoming as a child b. Why: Non-conversion brings rejection 3 **Condition 2: Humility** a. How: Live as a child b. Result: Will be the greatest in heaven

DIVISION XII

THE MESSIAH'S DISCIPLES AND THEIR BEHAVIOR TOWARD ONE ANOTHER, 18:1-35

A. The Conditions for Greatness, 18:1-4

(18:1-4) **Introduction—Greatness**: the disciples argued over who should hold the highest positions in the kingdom of God. This conflict arose on several occasions (see outlines and notes—Mt.20:20-28; Mk.9:33-37; Lk.22:24-30). Their desire was for recognition and honor in an earthly kingdom. Jesus had to reeducate their thinking. The disciples' struggle for position and power should not surprise us, for all men have the same needs, the needs for...

- some recognition • some authority
- some position • some esteem
- some prestige • some challenge
- some money • some physical sastisfaction

There is nothing wrong with these needs. They are human and legitimate needs and they must be met. But men allow their hearts to be overtaken with *selfishness* and begin to want more and more to the point of lusting and consuming and hoarding. They become prideful, covetous, worldly, ambitious, envious, and hurtful even to the point of destroying and killing.

What Christ sets out to do is to change the lives of men and reeducate men in their concept of greatness.

1. Two assumptions (v.1-2).
2. Condition 1: conversion, change (v.3).
3. Condition 2: humility (v.4).

1 (18:1-2) **Children—Jesus Christ, Nature—Greatness**: note the two assumptions in the question of the disciples. First, a person is great if he is in the Kingdom of Heaven. Second, there are degrees of greatness.

Christ did not refute or deny these assumptions. On the contrary, He taught both: a person is great if he is in the Kingdom of Heaven. Everything and everyone in heaven is great, even perfected. As Christ says, a person can be *the greatest* in the Kingdom of Heaven (v.4. See scripture and notes—Mt.13:8, 23; 25:20-30; Lk.12:41-48; 16:10-12; 19:15-23). The question is not "who is the greatest" but how does one become *great* in God's kingdom? How does one prove that he is trustworthy and responsible before God? How does one show God that he can be trusted and depended upon and should be rewarded with responsibility in heaven (see notes—Mt.25:20; Lk.19:15; 22:28-29)?

Note several things about the question asked by the disciples.

1. Note what they meant. By "the greatest in the kingdom of heaven" they did not mean the greatest in quality or character, but in name and position. They were thinking in terms of power, fame, wealth, position, and name (see notes—Mt.1:1; DEEPER STUDY # 2—1:18; DEEPER STUDY # 3—3:11; notes—11:1-6; 11:2-3; DEEPER STUDY # 1—11:5; DEEPER STUDY # 2—11:6; DEEPER STUDY # 1—12:16; note—Lk.7:21-23 for a picture of their concept of the Messiah).
2. Note the reasons why they asked the question.
    a. They sensed that Christ was about to set up His kingdom, that He was about to assume His throne. They were looking forward to becoming chiefs of state in His kingdom.
    b. They had seen three of them honored in special ways (Peter, James, and John—Mt.17:1-13), and one of them in particular had been distinguished (Peter, Mt.16:17-19). Who were the leaders to be in the Lord's kingdom? They were apparently gripped with jealousy, envy, ambition, and some rivalry.
    c. They had just been arguing among themselves about who the greatest was going to be. Mark says that the argument had begun immediately after Christ began to intensify His teaching on His death and resurrection (Mk.9:33-34; cp. 9:30-37). They misinterpreted what He was saying, spiritualizing it instead of taking His Word at face value (see note—Mt.17:22). Apparently they connected the thought of *rising from the dead* with the setting up of His kingdom, and began to argue over the top positions of leadership.
3. Note: they did not yet understand what the Kingdom of Heaven is. They still saw an earthly, temporal kingdom and not a spiritual, eternal kingdom. It is interesting what Christ said in v.3. He was speaking to the disciples, and He *actually said* that they would not enter the kingdom of heaven unless they became as little children.

Christ gave a living demonstration of greatness. He "called a little child and had him stand among them." The child was not an infant, for he was personally *called* to come to Christ. Note how the child immediately demonstrated several traits of children. He *trusted* Christ enough to respond (trustfulness) and did what Christ requested (submission, humility, and obedience).

This says something about the nature and character of Christ as well. He demonstrated enough warmth and openness for the child to feel free to respond and to enter a group of adults who were sitting together in a formal session.

> **Thought 1**. The thoughts of the average person focus upon appearance, personal image, self-esteem, possessions, privileges, position, and glory, and he spends much time in thinking of these things. He imagines and fancies himself to be the center of attention, the *hero* of the game or play, the main attraction, the one considered most honorable and esteemed. It is such thoughts and ambitions that Christ wants to change. Our thoughts and minds are to be centered on Christ and others and upon things that are true, not on self (Ro.12:2; 2 Cor.10:5; Ph.4:8).

> **Thought 2.** How often we think in terms of *earthly and fleshly greatness*. If we are asked who are the *greatest* people in a city or country, we answer by naming the famous, the prestigious, the wealthy, the powerful, and the educated. We think little, if any, of those who serve and minister.

2 (18:3) **Greatness—Conversion**: the first condition for greatness is conversion. The word "conversion or change" (straphete) means to turn, to turn around; to be converted; to turn from one thing to something else (1 Th.1:9, "how you turned to God from idols"). (Cp. repentance for the same idea.)

The meaning here is that the disciples must *turn*; they must turn completely around. Christ warned them: "Unless you turn." Turn from what? Their sins were many, sins that are so common to men as they walk in selfishness day by day.

Note that they were possessed by a selfish desire for...

- position
- power
- prestige
- fame
- wealth
- fleshly stimulation

Note that they were possessed by a spirit of...

- pride
- covetousness
- ambition
- jealousy
- worldliness
- envy
- rivalry

Conversion or change is one of the great subjects of the Bible. The reason is made clear by Christ: "Unless you change [be converted]...you will never enter the kingdom of heaven" (v.3). Whether or not a person is changed (converted) determines his eternal destiny.

1. How is a person converted or changed? By turning and becoming as a little child. What does it mean "to become like a little child"? When Christ *called* the child to Him, the child demonstrated exactly what Christ meant.
    a. The child *trusted Christ*. The child responded to the call of Christ. He sensed the openness, warmth, tenderness, care, and love of Christ; so he felt free to respond and to trust Christ's call.
    b. The child *surrendered* himself to Christ. He was willing to give up what he was doing and go to Christ, willing to surrender whatever it was that was occupying his thoughts and behavior.
    c. The child was *obedient* to Christ. He obeyed and did exactly what Christ requested, and it was probably difficult to do so. There were at least thirteen adult men standing or sitting there, and the child was being asked to walk into the midst of these men. Note that he obeyed despite the difficulty and obeyed simply because Christ asked him.
    d. The child was *humble* before Christ. All the above traits show humility. However, there is something often overlooked and abused by the adult world. Little children do not push themselves forward. They are not interested in prominence, fame, power, wealth, or position. They do not want to be placed in the midst of a group of adults, for they prefer to be in the background, away from staring, gawking eyes. Such embarrasses them and makes them feel self-conscious. Therefore, they prefer to be left in their obscure world. They are by nature humble, knowing little if anything of the competitive world that surrounds them; that is, they know little of it until they are brought into it by adults.

2. Why is a person to be converted or changed? Because not changing brings rejection and loss of greatness. Note that the warning is severe: "Unless you change [be converted]...you will never enter the kingdom of heaven." And Christ is speaking to the disciples. "Unless they are converted and become as little children, they will never enter the kingdom of heaven."

If the disciples were warned, how much more are we and everyone else warned! The absolute necessity of conversion or change is hereby stressed.

> **And he said: "I tell you the truth, unless you change and become like little children, you will never enter the kingdom of heaven. (Mat 18:3)**
>
> **Repent, then, and turn to God, so that your sins may be wiped out, that times of refreshing may come from the Lord, (Acts 3:19)**
>
> **My brothers, if one of you should wander from the truth and someone should bring him back, remember this: Whoever turns a sinner from the error of his way will save him from death and cover over a multitude of sins. (James 5:19-20)**
>
> **The law of the LORD is perfect, reviving the soul. The statutes of the LORD are trustworthy, making wise the simple. (Psa 19:7)**
>
> **Restore to me the joy of your salvation and grant me a willing spirit, to sustain me. Then I will teach transgressors your ways, and sinners will turn back to you. (Psa 51:12-13)**
>
> **Let the wicked forsake his way and the evil man his thoughts. Let him turn to the LORD, and he will have mercy on him, and to our God, for he will freely pardon. (Isa 55:7)**
>
> **"But if a wicked man turns away from all the sins he has committed and keeps all my decrees and does what is just and right, he will surely live; he will not die. (Ezek 18:21)**

Thought 1. Note that the very traits possessed by a child are the essentials for conversion or salvation: trust, surrender, obedience, and humility.

Thought 2. What Christ is after is the total conversion or change of a person, a change that is complete and thorough: a change of heart, life, and thoughts. Our thoughts make us what we are. And, oh, how they are centered on self, making ourselves the center of attention.

> **A song of ascents. Of David. My heart is not proud, O LORD, my eyes are not haughty; I do not concern myself with great matters or things too wonderful for me. But I have stilled and quieted my soul; like a weaned child with its mother, like a weaned child is my soul within me. (Psa 131:1-2)**
>
> **Repent of this wickedness and pray to the Lord. Perhaps he will forgive you for having such a thought in your heart. (Acts 8:22)**
>
> **We demolish arguments and every pretension that sets itself up against the knowledge of God, and we take captive every thought to make it obedient to Christ. (2 Cor 10:5)**

3 (18:4) **Humility**: the second condition for greatness is humility.

1. How does a person become humble? By living as a child. The child had humbled himself to come to Christ. Christ said so.
   a. The child had given up what he was doing. Whatever it was that was occupying his thought and time, he walked away from it. He humbled himself in order to come to Christ.
   b. The child had obeyed Christ. He went to Christ. Obedience always demands humility, a humbling of oneself (thoughts, energy, time, effort) in order to do whatever another asks.
   c. The child overcame feelings he had in order to respond to Christ. Because of the twelve men surrounding Christ, there was bound to be some hesitation, dread, apprehension, or fear; yet he humbled himself and went to Christ despite all. Humility has always been one of the most *insignificant* traits among men, yet it determines whether a man enters heaven or not. It is of critical importance.

2. The result of humility is greatness. The greatest persons in the Kingdom of Heaven will be the persons who have been converted (changed) and walked the humblest among men. 1 Cor.13 says exactly what Christ is demonstrating.

> **Love is patient, love is kind. It does not envy, it does not boast, it is not proud. It is not rude, it is not self-seeking, it is not easily angered, it keeps no record of wrongs. Love does not delight in evil but rejoices with the truth. It always protects, always trusts, always hopes, always perseveres. And now these three remain: faith, hope and love. But the greatest of these is love. (1 Cor 13:4-7, 13)**

Thought 1. Men fear humility. They feel that *humility* is a sign of weakness and cowardice. They fear humility will make them the object of contempt and abuse. They fear humility may cause them to be passed over, but the very opposite is true. Humility leads a person to Christ and to conversion. It leads a person to realize his full potential. It causes a person to evaluate himself and to work at improving himself. It leads a person to become all that he can and should be. It also leads to better and more healthy relationships and to a stronger and more productive community and world.

When men consider others (humble themselves), they win friends and influence people. They build and strengthen everyone and everything involved.

> **Therefore, whoever humbles himself like this child is the greatest in the kingdom of heaven. (Mat 18:4)**
>
> **But you are not to be like that. Instead, the greatest among you should be like the youngest, and the one who rules like the one who serves. (Luke 22:26)**
>
> **For by the grace given me I say to every one of you: Do not think of yourself more highly than you ought, but rather think of yourself with sober judgment, in accordance with the measure of faith God has given you. (Rom 12:3)**
>
> **Do nothing out of selfish ambition or vain conceit, but in humility consider others better than yourselves. Each of you should look not only to your own interests, but also to the interests of others. (Phil 2:3-4)**
>
> **Humble yourselves before the Lord, and he will lift you up. (James 4:10)**
>
> **Young men, in the same way be submissive to those who are older. All of you, clothe yourselves with humility toward one another, because, "God opposes the proud but gives grace to the humble." (1 Pet 5:5)**

	B. The Warning against Causing a Child to Sin, 18:5-10 (Mk.9:42-48)	8 If your hand or your foot causes you to sin cut it off and throw it away. It is better for you to enter life maimed or crippled than to have two hands or two feet and be thrown into eternal fire.	c. The way to handle the sin of being a stumblingblock 1) Cut off the hand that sins 2) Cut off the foot that sins 3) Pluck out the eye that sins
1 The child represents Christ	5 "And whoever welcomes a little child like this in my name welcomes me.		
2 Offense 1: Leading a child astray a. A child who believes b. The worst conceivable sin	6 But if anyone causes one of these little ones who believe in me to sin, it would be better for him to have a large millstone hung around his neck and to be drowned in the depths of the sea.	9 And if your eye causes you to sin, gouge it out and throw it away. It is better for you to enter life with one eye than to have two eyes and be thrown into the fire of hell.	d. The escaping of the punishment is worth any price 1) It will be eternal fire[DS1] 2) It will be the fire of hell
3 Offense 2: Being a stumbling block a. The certainty of sin in a sinful world b. The warning to the sinner	7 "Woe to the world because of the things that cause people to sin! Such things must come, but woe to the man through whom they come!	10 "See that you do not look down on one of these little ones. For I tell you that their angels in heaven always see the face of my Father in heaven.	**4 Offense 3: Looking down upon a child** a. A caution: Take heed b. The reason: Children have direct access to God[DS2]

DIVISION XII

THE MESSIAH'S DISCIPLES AND THEIR BEHAVIOR TOWARD ONE ANOTHER, 18:1-35

B. The Warning against Causing a Child to Sin, 18:5-10

(18:5-10) **Introduction—Christians—Responsibility**: Christ used *the child* (cp. Mt.18:1-4) as an object lesson to teach that believers have an awesome responsibility for watching over one another. The Jews used the word *child* in two ways. It referred either to a small child or to a disciple of some teacher, a beginner in the faith. In this passage, Jesus used the word *child* to refer to three persons (see note and DEEPER STUDY # 1,2—Mk.9:42).

1. It means a small child.
2. It means a beginner in the faith, someone who has just been converted and become a newborn child of God. This person is a new Christian; therefore, he knows little about the Lord and about how he is to live. Hence he is very impressionable, and he can be easily misled or confused.
3. It means any believer who has a childlike spirit and character. This childlike spirit is the very spirit about which Christ has just spoken (Mt.18:3-4). It is the spirit He desires and expects in every follower of His.

Christ cares deeply for children, for all who have the childlike spirit and character. He calls those who follow Him "little ones" (18:6; 10:42). The depth of His care is clearly seen in this passage, a passage that lays a terrible responsibility upon all men—a responsibility that is unmistakably clear and so desperately needed. Christ gives three terrible warnings against causing a child to sin, and He spells out the three terrible offenses against a child, "little ones who believe in" Him (v.6).

1. The child represents Christ (v.5).
2. Offense 1: leading a child astray (v.6).
3. Offense 2: being a stumbling block (v.7-9).
4. Offense 3: looking down upon a child (v.10).

1 (18:5) **Children**: the child represented Christ. The word for "welcomes" (dechetai) means to receive a child in every way possible.

⇒ It means to welcome the child as a *person*: with tenderness, warmth, care, affection and love—no matter how low or unimportant or poor. Christ is contrasting *the child* with *the greatest person*, the person over whom the disciples had just been arguing (see notes—Mt.18:1-4; 18:1-2).

⇒ It means to welcome the child when he is in need *physically* or *materially*: to feed, cloth, shelter, visit, and help him (Mt.25:35f; Jas.1:27).

⇒ It means to welcome the child *spiritually*: to help him grow, build him up, encourage, and motivate him to follow Christ and to share his faith.

Note two reasons why we are to welcome the child.

1. The child represents Christ. To receive a child is to receive Christ. Whatever is done for the child is done for Christ.
2. Christ cared for each child, every single one. He said, "a little child"; that is, that single child is important to Christ. Christ does not want that child...

- left out, feeling like a non-person, uncared for and unloved.
- left in need physically or materially, having to scrap and scrounge around, surviving all alone.
- left alone, not knowing how to follow Christ and how to grow spiritually.

Christ clearly said: to welcome and help "a little child like this" is to receive and help Him (cp. Mt.25:35f).

> **Thought 1.** Welcoming and being receptive and open to people and their needs are of utmost importance to Christ (see outline and notes—Mt.10:40-42).
> **Thought 2.** There is an unbelievable lesson here, a lesson that is so often unheard of among men: to minister to people is much more important than "being the greatest" in an earthly kingdom (see notes—Mt.18:1-4; 18:1-2). The point is simply this: *to welcome another person is to welcome Christ*, and welcoming Christ is much more important than *being the greatest*.

2 (18:6) **Sin, Leading Others**: the first warning is against leading a child astray. Leading a child, a follower of

Christ, astray is the worst conceivable sin. There is nothing worse than leading another person into sin. In fact, it would be better to hang a millstone about one's neck and cast oneself into the depths of the sea than to lead another person astray. This sounds severe, very severe. And it is. But note: Christ meant what He said and said what He meant. How do we know this? From three facts.

1. The "millstone" (mulos) spoken of by Christ was the huge millstone, the one that the oxen or donkey pulled around to grind the grain. It was not the small hand millstone used by the women to grind a little grain at a time. The very fact that Christ chose the huge millstone to illustrate His point shows just how great this sin is. The person would be held at the bottom of the sea by the most awful and terrible weight. The sin of leading a child astray is the worst imaginable sin; therefore, its condemnation shall be the worst punishment imaginable.

2. Drowning was a form of criminal punishment used by the Romans, but never by the Jews. The Jews saw drowning as a symbol of *utter destruction and annihilation.* They feared it. Even the Romans reserved it only for the worst criminals.

3. Christ *added to the fear* of His audience. He painted the picture of a stone around the offender's neck so that the body could never rise to the top and be recovered for proper burial. And then He added even more to the fear. He pictured the huge millstone, not the small one. Why? Why did He strike fear into the hearts of His hearers? The answer is clear: the sin of leading another person astray is terrible, and the offender must know the fate that is awaiting him.

There are several ways we cause others to sin.

⇒ By leading them into sin and teaching them to sin: "Oh, come on, no one will know. It's not going to hurt you."
⇒ By example; by the things we do. Example is not a direct proposition, so we are not necessarily aware that *the child* sees or is observing us. Nevertheless, he sees and learns from what we do: "If it's all right for him, then it is bound to be all right for me." "If he can do it and still work and play and get by as well as he does, then I can too."
⇒ By overlooking or passing over wrong; by giving soft names to it; by considering some sins to be merely *white sins*: "Oh, that's all right. There's not that much to it. It isn't going to hurt anyone. Don't pay any attention to it. Just forget it."
⇒ By ridiculing and poking fun at, or joking and sneering at a person's attempt to do right: "Oh, don't be a fuddy-duddy. You're acting like a fanatic. You and your religion."
⇒ By looking, touching, and tasting some things that are socially acceptable but sinful to God. They are harmful and habit forming and physically stimulating when they should not be: "Wow, look at that." "Taste that." "Man! What a stir!"
⇒ By persecuting and threatening *a child* or a believer. The threat can range all the way from loss of promotion, job, friendship, or acceptance, to abuse, imprisonment, and death.

Thought 1. A genuine believer, no matter how young or immature as a Christian, has "received a faith as precious as ours" (2 Pt.1:1). Standing before God, a believer is on equal footing with all other believers. Of course, this does not mean they are to be given positions of leadership while they are young believers (1 Tim.3:6, 10). It simply means that they are to be focused upon and taught and developed in Christ, not ignored and overlooked because they cannot yet contribute much to the work of God's kingdom.

Thought 2. There are some things that seem innocent enough, yet they can lead others astray (1 Cor.8:10-11). A mature believer is not to abuse the young believer by his liberty (see outline and notes—Ro.14:1-23).

3 (18:7-9) **Stumbling Block—World, Sinful**: the second warning is against being a stumbling block. Note the outline points of the Scripture.

1. There is the certainty of sin in a sinful world. This is a sinful world, full of evil behavior. No one can walk out into the world without facing temptation after temptation and pull after pull to look, touch, and taste—to experience the *good life* of physical gratification and earthly comfort and personal fulfillment. We are tempted, seduced, and influenced by it at every turn. There is no escape (cp. Ro.3:9-18).

> **We know that we are children of God, and that the whole world is under the control of the evil one. (1 John 5:19)**
> **For all have sinned and fall short of the glory of God, (Rom 3:23)**

2. There is the warning to the sinner. Every man is personally responsible for his sin. The fact of a sinful world does not lessen a man's personal responsibility. He cannot blame the world, society, or others; for man...

- has free will.
- has the knowledge of much good.
- has the pull to do good (at least initially).
- usually has examples of goodness.
- can choose to do good.
- can work to overcome and strengthen his weakness.

Most of all, man has God who provides a way to escape temptation (1 Cor.10:13). The sinner is personally responsible. Every sin becomes a stumbling block to others! The man who sins becomes the stumbling block over which others can fall!

3. There is the way to handle the sin of being a stumbling block. Again, the severity of the language shows the severity of the sin. There is no greater sin than being a stumbling block to one of God's dear children.

a. Christ says "cut off the hand that causes you to sin": force the hand away, pull it back, push it aside. Let the hand that sins have no part of you. Deny the hand's presence, its existence.

> **"Therefore come out from them and be separate, says the Lord. Touch no unclean thing, and I will receive you." "I will be a Father to you, and you will be my sons and daughters, says the Lord Almighty." (2 Cor 6:17-18)**

b. Christ says "cut off the foot that causes you to sin": Remove it, take it away from the sin. Make the foot of no use and the body will be immobilized for you. Remove the foot and your body cannot go to the sin; take the foot far enough away that you will have time to think of the consequences. Deny the foot's presence, its existence.

> **Be very careful, then, how you live—not as unwise but as wise, (Eph 5:15)**
> **So then, just as you received Christ Jesus as Lord, continue to live in him, (Col 2:6)**
> **Whoever claims to live in him must walk as Jesus did. (1 John 2:6)**

c. Christ says "pluck out the eye": Turn away from the sight; leave it; don't look. In fact, make sure you cannot look upon sin. Deny the eye's presence, its existence.

> **But I tell you that anyone who looks at a woman lustfully has already committed adultery with her in his heart. (Mat 5:28)**
> **For everything in the world—the cravings of sinful man, the lust of his eyes and the boasting of what he has and does—comes not from the Father but from the world. (1 John 2:16)**
> **He who winks maliciously causes grief, and a chattering fool comes to ruin. (Prov 10:10)**
> **All things are wearisome, more than one can say. The eye never has enough of seeing, nor the ear its fill of hearing. (Eccl 1:8)**
> **There was a man all alone; he had neither son nor brother. There was no end to his toil, yet his eyes were not content with his wealth. "For whom am I toiling," he asked, "and why am I depriving myself of enjoyment?" This too is meaningless—a miserable business! (Eccl 4:8)**

Note that it is the *hand that touches* the sin, the *foot that takes* one to the sin or to the place of sin, and the *eye that looks* upon the sin and leads to the desire and lust for the sin. The way to escape is to deny self (see notes and DEEPER STUDY # 1—Lk.9:23; see outline—Ro.6:11-13) and to draw nigh to God (see outline—Jas.4:7-10).

4. There is the escaping of the punishment, which is worth any price. The most horrible death imaginable is death by fire. Just imagine burning and burning in everlasting fire. There is no more terrible punishment than that described by Christ. How horrible eternity apart from God must be. The severity of hell again stresses the severity of the sin in God's eyes.

> **Jesus said to his disciples: "Things that cause people to sin are bound to come, but woe to that person through whom they come. It would be better for him to be thrown into the sea with a millstone tied around his neck than for him to cause one of these little ones to sin. (Luke 17:1-2)**
> **Therefore let us stop passing judgment on one another. Instead, make up your mind not to put any stumbling block or obstacle in your brother's way. (Rom 14:13)**
> **If your brother is distressed because of what you eat, you are no longer acting in love. Do not by your eating destroy your brother for whom Christ died. (Rom 14:15)**
> **It is better not to eat meat or drink wine or to do anything else that will cause your brother to fall. (Rom 14:21)**
> **Do not cause anyone to stumble, whether Jews, Greeks or the church of God— (1 Cor 10:32)**
> **We put no stumbling block in anyone's path, so that our ministry will not be discredited. (2 Cor 6:3)**
> **Whoever loves his brother lives in the light, and there is nothing in him to make him stumble. (1 John 2:10)**

Thought 1. The world is full of people who are stumbling blocks, people who are...

- bad examples
- seducers
- tempters
- deceivers
- false guides
- persecutors

Thought 2. Note several logical facts.

1) *A righteous God* knows unmistakably who is a stumbling block to the *little child.*
2) *A righteous God* knows exactly at whose feet to lay the guilt for causing a *little child* to stumble.
3) *A righteous God* knows precisely who ruins the precious soul of a child, preventing the child from being saved.
4) *A righteous God* will reckon with the man who causes a *little child* to stumble—severely and eternally. He is righteous; therefore He has to deal severely, matching the punishment to the evil.

Thought 3. Note a critical fact: the hand, the foot, and the eye are the sinner's own hand, foot, and eye. He is sinning as well as causing another to sin. He is damaging and destroying his own life as well as the life of a child. He is dooming himself as well as the child to hell.

Thought 4. This is strong language, very descriptive and severe in its point. But honesty and thought are called for in seeing the point of Christ. What on earth is more horrible than leading a child astray and being a stumbling block to his salvation, dooming him to what Christ calls "the fire of hell" and "eternal fire." If God really loves the *little child* as Christ says, and if *the fire of hell* is real, then strong and severe language is needed to awaken the world to the truth.

DEEPER STUDY # 1

(18:8) **The Fire of Hell—Eternal Fire** (to pur to aionion): this is the first time the words *eternal fire* are used. The words point to an awful fate, a terrible and horrible eternity. Eternal means for the duration, on and on without end. The fact that the unforgiven sinner is to suffer so great a punishment should cause all sinners to cease being stumbling blocks. It should stir them to become stepping stones to God (see DEEPER STUDY # 2—Mt.5:22; DEEPER STUDY # 3—Lk.16:23; DEEPER STUDY # 4—16:24).

> **His winnowing fork is in his hand, and he will clear his threshing floor, gathering his wheat into the barn and burning up the chaff with unquenchable fire." (Mat 3:12)**
> **They will throw them into the fiery furnace, where there will be weeping and gnashing of teeth. (Mat 13:42)**
> **If your hand or your foot causes you to sin cut it off and throw it away. It is better for you to enter life maimed or crippled than to have two hands or two feet and be thrown into eternal fire. (Mat 18:8)**

"Then he will say to those on his left, 'Depart from me, you who are cursed, into the eternal fire prepared for the devil and his angels. (Mat 25:41)
But the cowardly, the unbelieving, the vile, the murderers, the sexually immoral, those who practice magic arts, the idolaters and all liars—their place will be in the fiery lake of burning sulfur. This is the second death." (Rev 21:8)
The sinners in Zion are terrified; trembling grips the godless: "Who of us can dwell with the consuming fire? Who of us can dwell with everlasting burning?" (Isa 33:14)
"And they will go out and look upon the dead bodies of those who rebelled against me; their worm will not die, nor will their fire be quenched, and they will be loathsome to all mankind." (Isa 66:24)

4 (18:10) **Children, Sins Against—Despite**: the third warning is against looking down upon a child. There are several ways that a child or a believer is looked down on or despised.

1. By considering the child unimportant. He is not considered as competent as others; therefore, he is neglected, ignored, or pushed aside. As a result, his growth and potential for life and service are untapped, or stiffled and stunted.

2. By doing unbecoming things in the child's presence; by disregarding the child's presence and going ahead with one's *off color* language and jokes, *little white lies*, and socially acceptable but sinful habits.

3. By twisting the child's mind or body into evil behavior and sin. This can range all the way from sinful ambition and self-seeking to child abuse through sexual deviation and murder.

"'Look, you scoffers, wonder and perish, for I am going to do something in your days that you would never believe, even if someone told you.'" (Acts 13:41)
Or do you show contempt for the riches of his kindness, tolerance and patience, not realizing that God's kindness leads you toward repentance? (Rom 2:4)
But mark this: There will be terrible times in the last days. People will be lovers of themselves, lovers of money, boastful, proud, abusive, disobedient to their parents, ungrateful, unholy, without love, unforgiving, slanderous, without self-control, brutal, not lovers of the good, (2 Tim 3:1-3)
Anyone who rejected the law of Moses died without mercy on the testimony of two or three witnesses. How much more severely do you think a man deserves to be punished who has trampled the Son of God under foot, who has treated as an unholy thing the blood of the covenant that sanctified him, and who has insulted the Spirit of grace? (Heb 10:28-29)
If this is so, then the Lord knows how to rescue godly men from trials and to hold the unrighteous for the day of judgment, while continuing their punishment. This is especially true of those who follow the corrupt desire of the sinful nature and despise authority. Bold and arrogant, these men are not afraid to slander celestial beings; (2 Pet 2:9-10)

Thought 1. Children have a most favored position before God. The fact that their guardian angels "always see the face" of God shows this. There could be no greater privilege than to be before God always "seeing His face." Children are very, very precious to God. For this reason alone, we should do all we can to rid ourselves and the world of evil.

DEEPER STUDY # 2

(18:10) **Angels**: see DEEPER STUDY # 1—Heb.1:4-14. We must always remember that Christ came from (ek, out of) the spiritual world, out of the dimension of heaven, to reveal heaven to us. He taught the reality of angels, that is, heavenly messengers. Here He teaches that children have "guardian angels" who have direct access to God. This fact is a warning to the offender: every sin and stumbling block placed before His children (believer, v.6) is brought before Him, so no offense will go unpunished. It is also an encouragement to every child of His: the child will be vindicated and can depend upon God Himself to vindicate Him.

Are not all angels ministering spirits sent to serve those who will inherit salvation? (Heb 1:14)
I tell you that in the same way there will be more rejoicing in heaven over one sinner who repents than over ninety-nine righteous persons who do not need to repent. In the same way, I tell you, there is rejoicing in the presence of the angels of God over one sinner who repents." (Luke 15:7, 10)
The angel of the LORD encamps around those who fear him, and he delivers them. (Psa 34:7)
For he will command his angels concerning you to guard you in all your ways; (Psa 91:11)

	C. The Parable of the Lost	go to look for the one that	c. The sheep was sought:
	Sheep: The Supreme	wandered off?	In the mountains[DS1]
	Example of Caring,	13 And if he finds it, I tell	**3 Jesus may or may not**
	18:11-14	you the truth, he is happier	**find the lost one**
	(Lk.15:1-7)	about that one sheep than	**4 Jesus forgives & rejoices**
		about the ninety-nine that did	**over the recovered one**
1 Jesus came to save the lost	12 "What do you think? If a	not wander off.	
2 Jesus seeks every single one	man owns a hundred sheep,	14 In the same way your	**5 God wills that not a**
a. The sheep wandered away	and one of them wanders	Father in heaven is not will-	**single one be lost**
b. The sheep was sought:	away, will he not leave the	ing that any of these little	
By the shepherd	ninety-nine on the hills and	ones should be lost.	

DIVISION XII

THE MESSIAH'S DISCIPLES AND THEIR BEHAVIOR TOWARD ONE ANOTHER, 18:1-35

C. The Parable of the Lost Sheep: The Supreme Example of Caring, 18:12-14

(18:11-14) **Introduction**: this is one of the most famous parables shared by Jesus—the parable of "The Lost Sheep" or the parable of "The Seeking Shepherd." It holds a great message for both the believer and the unbeliever, and Jesus applies it to both. Two things show this.

1. The words "these little ones" refer to genuine Christian believers, and the word "lost" refers to the unsaved person (see note—Mt.18:5-10).

2. On this particular occasion Jesus was speaking to His disciples (Mt.18:1). In Luke Jesus shared the same parable with a different audience and directed it more toward the lost.

Some believers are weak, never having grown in the Lord; others cool off and wander away; still others backslide into sin and shame. Some are stubborn toward the Lord, and some become self-centered because of hurt and neglect. Others allow the hurt and neglect to develop into bitterness and hostility against a person, and go out and sin in anger. There are innumerable reasons for sinning, but believers do sin, and some sin rather seriously.

The one who strays and the one who is lost are always with us. The thing to remember is this...

> **In the same way your Father in heaven is not willing that any of these little ones should be lost. (Mat 18:14)**

1. Jesus came to save the lost (v.11 [*see footnote*]).
2. Jesus seeks every single one that is lost (v.12).
3. Jesus may or may not find the lost one (v.13).
4. Jesus forgives and rejoices over the recovered one (v.13).
5. God wills that not a single one should be lost (v.14).

1 (18:11[1]) **Jesus Christ, Savior—Man, Lost**: Jesus came to save the lost. Note that the NIV eliminates verse 11 here. We are including the verse and discussion in the commentary for those who wish to use it. The verse reads, "The Son of Man came to save what was lost" (v.11).

This is the Messiah's great statement of purpose; this is why He came to earth. He came to save the lost. There is a world of meaning in this great statement.

1. It means that Christ willingly and deliberately *left* the glory of heaven and His equality with God and "made Himself nothing" of that glory and equality (see notes—Ph.2:6; 2:7).

2. It means that both the world as a whole and man as an individual have gone astray. Each person has strayed away from God, is lost, and is wandering about in a wilderness of sin; and each person is doomed to be destroyed by that wilderness unless he is reached and saved by Christ. Everyone needs to be saved (Ro.3:10-18, 23; 10:13; Jn.3:16; Acts 10:43; 1 Jn.5:1).

3. It means that *God lost man*. God lost man's worship and service and life. Not only has man *gone astray*, not only is man *not seeking* after God and gone out of the way—but he has become unprofitable, *lost to God* (Ro.3:11-12). While man remains lost *in the wilderness*, God has no hope of fellowship with man. Man's worship, service, and life are lost to God as long as man remains lost. The words "that which was lost" should be noted. They are in the Greek neuter participle. This means that the person lost is not only man (masculine) but woman (feminine) as well. "That [neuter] which was lost" and sought after is both man and woman. The point is to show the span of Jesus' love: He loves all who are lost, both man and woman. No one is outside the scope of His love and seeking. He loves and seeks after all.

> **Thought 1**. Note a striking truth: not only is man lost, but God has lost man and man has lost God. Both lose out and suffer when man chooses to wander out into the wilderness of the world and sin. Man has so much to gain from following God (Jn.5:24; Gal.5:22-23), and God has so much to gain by man's choosing to follow God (worship and service eternally).

2 (18:12) **Jesus Christ, Seeking—Shepherd**: Jesus seeks every single sheep that is lost. Christ made three significant points.

1. The sheep wandered off (see DEEPER STUDY # 1—Mt.18:12).

2. The sheep was sought by the shepherd. Note several facts.

a. The Shepherd takes care of the whole flock, the ninety-nine, in a very special way. While seeking the lost sheep, He leads the flock *into the mountains or hills* where the pasture is thick with grass and safe and secure. He makes sure that they are secure (Jn.10:27-29).

b. The Shepherd's concern is for the individual, no matter how large the flock. He loves the individual. He is unwilling to lose a single one.

---

[1] 11*The Son of Man came to save what was lost.*

c. The Shepherd is the One who does the seeking. He does not hire or send another person after the lost sheep. Neither does He wait for the sheep to return, and most interesting, He does not even allow the care of the ninety-nine to keep Him from going after the one lost sheep. The fact that the sheep is lost is so important a matter to Him that He personally goes after the sheep—no matter the cost.

d. The Shepherd is patient and enduring. He seeks and seeks after the sheep until He has either found it or else He knows there is no hope of the sheep's being alive.

e. The Shepherd seeks every path, ridge, and crevice; He uses every means at His disposal to find the lost sheep.

⇒ The Shepherd depends upon the hardness, danger, trials, and sufferings of the wilderness and the heart, conscience, and memory of the sheep to turn it around and begin seeking a way out.

⇒ The Shepherd depends upon his own knowledge of the sheep and wilderness to search for the sheep. The Shepherd knows every ridge and crevice of the wilderness. It is just a question of finding the sheep soon enough. Has the lost sheep gone too far out on a ridge, too far down into a crevice to be found? Has the lost sheep already been killed by enemies or the roughness of the wilderness?

⇒ The Shepherd depends rather heavily upon His voice to reach the ears and the heart of the lost sheep. By calling and calling, He hopes the lost sheep will hear Him. Whether He hears or not depends upon two things. (1) How far out into the wilderness the lost sheep has wandered? Can the sheep hear the voice of the Shepherd? (2) Does the sheep still have strength enough to answer (respond) even if he hears the voice of the Shepherd? Is the sheep so drained and sapped by the wilderness that he cannot answer? Or is the sheep injured or dying, unable to answer the call of the Shepherd?

"What do you think? If a man owns a hundred sheep, and one of them wanders away, will he not leave the ninety-nine on the hills and go to look for the one that wandered off? (Mat 18:12)

For the Son of Man came to seek and to save what was lost." (Luke 19:10)

Jesus heard that they had thrown him out, and when he found him, he said, "Do you believe in the Son of Man?" (John 9:35)

3. The sheep was sought in the mountains (see note 3—Lk.15:4 for the reasons a sheep wanders off. The reasons are simply stated here.)

⇒ The sheep is attracted by something "out in the open country or wilderness" away from the flock and shepherd.

⇒ The sheep is aimless, not paying attention to what is going on.

⇒ The sheep refuses to heed the shepherd's warnings and the other sheep's example.

⇒ The sheep is not attached enough to the shepherd or to the other sheep.

Thought 1. The Shepherd knew "the lost sheep." He had a large flock to tend, but He knew every single one. When "the lost sheep" got lost, the Shepherd knew it. He missed the sheep, and He went after it.

Thought 2. When a child is lost, a family stops everything to seek for the lost child. It does not matter how large the family is, the child is sought.

DEEPER STUDY # 1
(18:12) **World—Wilderness—Open Country**: see note 4—Lk.15:4 for a picture of the wilderness or open country.

3 (18:13) **Lost—Unsaved**: Jesus may or may not find the lost sheep. Finding the sheep is not a sure thing. It depends on so much…

- How far astray has the lost sheep wandered? Can the lost sheep hear the voice of the Shepherd? Or is it too far off?
- Is the lost sheep willing to respond when it hears the Shepherd's voice?
- Is the lost sheep *going on and on*, farther and farther into the wilderness or open country?
- Has the lost sheep been so careless and unconcerned that it has been injured by falling into a deep crevice?
- Is the mind of the lost sheep so numb that it is unconscious of the Shepherd's presence and voice?
- Is the lost sheep aware that it is lost? If so, how concerned is it over being lost?
- Is the lost sheep concerned enough to begin searching for a way out of the wilderness or open country?
- Has the patience of the Shepherd ended? Has he given up? Has so much time passed that He knows there is no longer any hope?

Thought 1. A person may resist the spirit of God so long and wander so far into the wilderness of the world that he can never be found (see thought 1—Mt.12:14-16).

Then the LORD said, "My Spirit will not contend with man forever, for he is mortal; his days will be a hundred and twenty years." (Gen 6:3)

A man who remains stiff-necked after many rebukes will suddenly be destroyed—without remedy. (Prov 29:1)

4 (18:13) **Joy—Salvation**: Jesus forgives and rejoices over the recovered sheep. The extreme joy is not because the lost sheep means more than the other sheep. The safe sheep have always filled the Shepherd with joy and peace, but there is a special moment of joy and celebration when a lost sheep is found. There are at least two reasons for this.

1. The lost sheep was almost *lost forever*, never to be known again or to share in and contribute to the life of the flock. All that the lost sheep meant and was capable of contributing was almost lost forever. There is bound to be great joy and glory over his being snatched out of the claws of danger and death.

2. The lost sheep cost so much of the Shepherd's life: His thoughts, energy, effort, time, and sufferings. There is great joy and glory when the trial is over and the task is successful. The effort was well worth the price.

Note the great appeal to the lost sheep to return to the Shepherd. There is...

- no grudging
- no contempt
- no lecture
- no rebuke
- no threat
- no punishment
- only love
- only concern
- only seeking

And goes home. Then he calls his friends and neighbors together and says, 'Rejoice with me; I have found my lost sheep.' I tell you that in the same way there will be more rejoicing in heaven over one sinner who repents than over ninety-nine righteous persons who do not need to repent. (Luke 15:6-7)

Even now the reaper draws his wages, even now he harvests the crop for eternal life, so that the sower and the reaper may be glad together. (John 4:36)

For what is our hope, our joy, or the crown in which we will glory in the presence of our Lord Jesus when he comes? Is it not you? Indeed, you are our glory and joy. (1 Th 2:19-20)

Let us fix our eyes on Jesus, the author and perfecter of our faith, who for the joy set before him endured the cross, scorning its shame, and sat down at the right hand of the throne of God. (Heb 12:2)

He who goes out weeping, carrying seed to sow, will return with songs of joy, carrying sheaves with him. (Psa 126:6)

5 (18:14) **God, Will of—Salvation**: God wills that not a single sheep should be lost. In verse ten Jesus had said "My Father," but here He switched to "your Father." This is significant: when the Savior *finds* each of us, we become a member of *our Father's* family. As a member, He expects our help in reaching the lost sheep and in caring for the flock. Being a member of the family carries with it the responsibilities of reaching the lost and of helping to care for the other members of the family.

Note two things.

1. The Father is not willing that any should be lost.

Who wants all men to be saved and to come to a knowledge of the truth. (1 Tim 2:4)

The Lord is not slow in keeping his promise, as some understand slowness. He is patient with you, not wanting anyone to perish, but everyone to come to repentance. (2 Pet 3:9)

2. Christ died for the weak brother as well as for the lost.

If your brother is distressed because of what you eat, you are no longer acting in love. Do not by your eating destroy your brother for whom Christ died. (Rom 14:15)

So this weak brother, for whom Christ died, is destroyed by your knowledge. (1 Cor 8:11)

Thought 1. This is critical: God cares for every single person. What a contrast with our lack of concern when just one or two wander off. What a lesson for us! The concern of God for a single soul!

	D. The Steps to Correcting Offending Brothers, 18:15-20 (Lk.17:3-4)	them, tell it to the church; and if he refuses to listen even to the church, treat him as you would a pagan or a tax collector.	**2 Step 2: Discipline the brother**[DS2] a. The earthly discipline b. The heavenly support of God
1 Step 1: Attempt reconciliation[DS1] a. Go to the brother alone	15 "If your brother sins against you, go and show him his fault, just between the two of you. If he listens to you, you have won your brother over.	18 "I tell you the truth, whatever you bind on earth will be bound in heaven, and whatever you loose on earth will be loosed in heaven.	
b. Go to the brother with witnesses	16 But if he will not listen, take one or two others along, so that 'every matter may be established by the testimony of two or three witnesses.'	19 "Again, I tell you that if two of you on earth agree about anything you ask for, it will be done for you by my Father in heaven.	**3 Step 3: The essential step—bathe the matter in prayer**[DS3] a. Seeking agreement b. Seeking God's will & approval
c. Go before the church	17 If he refuses to listen to	20 For where two or three come together in my name, there am I with them."	c. Seeking unity in His name d. Result: His presence

DIVISION XII

THE MESSIAH'S DISCIPLES AND THEIR BEHAVIOR TOWARD ONE ANOTHER, 18:1-35

D. The Steps to Correcting Offending Brothers, 18:15-20

(18:15-20) **Introduction—Division—Church Discipline**: sinning against a brother is a matter of great concern to God. It is so serious that if the offending brother refuses to rectify the matter, he is to be severely disciplined (v.17). However, when dealing with discipline, two critical points are to be noted.

1. The sinning brother *is a brother*, a *genuine* believer. He sins against another brother. The breach is between two genuine believers who are *in the church.*

2. The sin is a personal offense; that is, the wrong and harm are done against another person. A fellow Christian believer is injured, hurt, and damaged in some way.

God has one great concern: He wants peace restored. He wants peace between the brothers, and He wants peace within the church. The disturbance caused by two offending brothers is so damaging that God lays down very specific steps as to how the matter is to be handled; and if the sinning brother refuses to be reconciled and to rectify the wrong, God says the disturbance is not to be tolerated any longer.

1. Step 1: attempt reconciliation (v.15-16).
2. Step 2: discipline the brother (v.17-18).
3. Step 3: the essential step—bathe the matter in prayer (v.19-20).

1 (18:15-16) **Believers, Sin Against—Reconciliation**: the first step in correcting an offending brother is to attempt reconciliation (see DEEPER STUDY # 1—Mt.18:15). Note when a brother disturbs or offends us, we do not wait on the *offending brother* to come to us. We are to go immediately to him. There are three specific steps to be taken.

1. Go to the brother alone and "show him his fault." This seems to indicate that he may not know that he has done wrong and offended us. If we do not go to him, he may never know or be able to correct his behavior. If he does know he has offended us and we do not approach him, then the breach remains, and the guilt of the sin continues. The division and damaging effects of the division can only grow and deepen.

Something else can happen: our own heart and mind can brood, be poisoned, become resentful, even bitter and grudging and revengeful. We desperately need to do all we can to resolve the matter.

a. He is to be approached alone. We are not to share the matter with anyone else, nor are we to openly rebuke him. This only deepens and hardens the feelings and division, causing bitterness and hostility.

b. The words "just between the two of you" hint at how he is to be approached:
⇒ humbly; searching our own hearts (to see if we did anything to cause the offending behavior—knowing that we too can offend others ever so easily).
⇒ being soft spoken and gentle.
⇒ expressing our desire for understanding and straightening out the matter so that we may be reconciled.

Leave your gift there in front of the altar. First go and be reconciled to your brother; then come and offer your gift. (Mat 5:24)

Do nothing out of selfish ambition or vain conceit, but in humility consider others better than yourselves. (Phil 2:3)

Keep reminding them of these things. Warn them before God against quarreling about words; it is of no value, and only ruins those who listen. (2 Tim 2:14)

And the Lord's servant must not quarrel; instead, he must be kind to everyone, able to teach, not resentful. (2 Tim 2:24)

Thought 1. When a brother offends us, our response becomes critical to Christ. There are four responses common to human flesh that we are to guard against with all diligence.

1) *A self-centered response*: acting babyish, innocent, or as a martyr; brooding, hatching, and pondering the evil and hurt done to us; being consumed with

the wrong done; keeping our minds on the personal injury until the whole divisive affair poisons our hearts and minds. Remember: this is common to human flesh, a tendency among us all.

2) *A withdrawing response*: avoiding the brother; being apprehensive, perhaps even fearing to face or associate with him; showing displeasure or getting back at him by ignoring or neglecting him.

3) *A gossiping response*: a self-justifying sharing; a self-vindicating sharing; a tendency to share hurt and evil and wrong done, to share with close friends in order to picture ourselves as blameless. The problem with sharing the division with others is that Christ says we are to go to the person first. Then if he does not respond to our appeal, we are to seek loving and wise counsel.

4) *A retaliating response*: becoming embroiled in the divisiveness and wrongdoing ourselves; reacting and lowering ourselves to the level of the wrongdoer; getting back at the wrongdoer.

Thought 2. When a brother offends us, the most important response (after prayer, of course) is to go to the brother alone. There is great wisdom in this instruction, wisdom that teaches both brothers to subject the flesh and to give prominence to the spirit.

1) Wisdom for the *offended brother*. Human nature tends to react, brood, share the evil, and seek retaliation—whether simply withdrawing or attacking. Christ demands that we conquer the urges of the flesh to react and that we control the situation through the Spirit. We are to keep quiet and pray. Then we are to go to the brother and discuss the matter, seeking reconciliation. Simply put, we are to be spiritually minded.

2) Wisdom for the *offending brother*. Human nature avoids and is slow in admitting wrong. A humble, loving, and caring visit to seek reconciliation is *an encouragement* for a brother to confess, apologize, and be reconciled.

Thought 3. Note just how wise the Lord's instruction really is. Just think what enormous lessons and qualities are learned and developed by three brothers' sitting down to seek reconciliation, to seek the very qualities of the Spirit's fruit...

- Love
- Joy
- Peace
- Patience
- Kindness
- Goodness
- Faithfulness
- Gentleness
- Self-control

Thought 4. Think what a different world this would be if this step alone was practiced by all: the difference in human relationships personally, nationally, and internationally; the difference in health emotionally and physically (ulcers, blood pressure, heart attacks, etc.).

2. Go to the brother with witnesses. Some Christian brothers are stubborn; others are immature; still others are gripped by selfish and sinful motives and behavior. Therefore an offending brother may not be willing to be reconciled nor willing to admit his wrong. In such cases, one or two loving and wise brothers are to be taken with us to the offending brother. This act does several things.

a. It shows the brother that there is deep concern; a number of people do care and want to help.
b. It also shows that the offense is known by more than one or two people. At least several know.
c. It also provides objective and wise counsel between the two differing parties. Agreement and reconciliation are more likely to arise from this.
d. It helps to prevent bias, selfish reaction, and partial interest.

Thought 1. This step should never be taken until the brother has been approached alone. We are not to talk about or share a brother's wrong with anyone else—not ever—not until we have sat down with him personally in the love of Christ.

However, this step *is* to be taken if he persists in his divisiveness. But it is always to be done in a spirit of humility, love, care, and personal unworthiness.

Thought 2. There is sometimes a tendency to give up after a divisive brother refuses reconciliation—to let him suffer whatever punishment follows. However, Christ says, "Keep on; stay after him. Don't give up." Note: this is the demand of Christ throughout the whole course of discipline. Christ never gives up reaching out to the sinning brother. Therefore, the church is never to give up (see DEEPER STUDY # 2—Mt.18:17). The divisiveness of the Galatian church and its personal attack upon Paul are prime examples of this fact. Paul was constantly reaching out to those who were so imperfect and ever failing (cp. Gal.4:19f).

3. Go before the church (see DEEPER STUDY # 2—Mt.18:17 for discussion).

DEEPER STUDY # 1

(18:15) **Believers, Sin Against—Reconciliation**: how does a Christian brother sin against or offend another brother? There are many ways.

1. By his behavior and Christian liberty: doing that which is allowed but is offensive and misunderstood by a weaker brother. (Cp. Ro.14:1-23; 1 Cor.8:12.)

⇒ Offending his conscience
⇒ Grieving his spirit
⇒ Being a stumbling block
⇒ Being a bad example

2. By confronting him face to face.

⇒ Insulting
⇒ Abusing
⇒ Humiliating
⇒ Degrading
⇒ Arguing
⇒ Showing disrespect
⇒ Showing bitterness
⇒ Being angry
⇒ Being hostile

3. By tearing him down behind his back.

⇒ Talking about
⇒ Lying
⇒ Gossiping
⇒ Murmuring
⇒ Criticizing
⇒ Spreading rumors

4. By encroaching on his rights or property.

⇒ Deceiving
⇒ Cheating
⇒ Stealing
⇒ Lying
⇒ Envying
⇒ Bypassing

2 (18:17-18) **Church Discipline**: the second step in correcting an offending brother is to discipline the brother. Christ discusses two points in dealing with the actual disciplining of an offending brother.

1. The earthly discipline. If the offending brother refuses to be reconciled after the appeal by two or three believers, then the matter is to be carried to the church. Why would Christ say that personal offenses are to be taken before the church and made public?

a. The offending brother has already refused two humble and loving appeals: the first appeal of the offended person, and the second appeal by one or two loving and wise witnesses.

b. The offending brother's refusal to be reconciled is a serious threat and danger. If the breach continues unresolved, it will cause more division and harm both within and without the church. Other lives will be seriously affected, both among the saved and the lost. The testimony of the church and of those involved in the division will be weakened, and the interest of the almost saved will be soured and dampened, perhaps extinguished. The tongues of the carnal believers and of the lost will be set aflame. A brother who trespasses against another brother and causes division within the church (and who refuses to be reconciled) commits a serious offense that affects many lives. Because of this, the matter has to be dealt with step by step. It cannot be ignored and left unresolved.

Taking a person's behavior before the church, whether the church as a whole or some official committee of the church, is a very serious matter. It is as serious a matter as can be imagined. But what Christ is after must be kept in mind: Christ wants to keep the sin, division, and devastation from spreading and destroying the lives and testimonies of others.

c. Christ wants the two brothers to be reconciled with each other and with God, and He wants the offending brother to be restored into the care and fellowship of the church.

d. Christ wants to keep the sin, division, and devastation from spreading and destroying the interest of the *nearly saved*, perhaps causing them to be lost forever.

e. Christ wants to prevent giving the world a reason for setting their tongues on fire and spreading rumors that damage the image and work of His church.

f. Christ wants the two brothers and their close friends and fellow church members to build a strong witness, not a divisive witness. He is not willing for a single person to perish. He wants the world saved, every person in the world (2 Pt.3:9), and two things are essential for a church to reach the maximum number of people which it should be reaching:

⇒ Love—brother loving brother in the Lord (Jn.13:33-34).

⇒ A strong witness and testimony by the brothers of the church.

g. Christ wants differences and divisiveness settled among His people and not by the world's legal system of unspiritual (carnal) or godless philosophies and arguments. The atmosphere of law settles nothing; it only produces more trouble and deeper feelings and rifts. Among God's people, disputed relationships and differences are to be settled between the two involved persons *alone*. If that fails, then one or two loving and wise persons are to be called in. Then and only then, if these fail to settle the matter, is the matter to be taken before a number of official representatives from the church. This procedure is clearly the wish of our Lord (Mt.18:15-17. See outline and notes—1 Cor.6:1-8.)

h. Christ wants every member to work and build, not destroy the church. The church exists for worship, fellowship, ministry, and witness. Harmony, peace, love, and purpose build the church; sin and divisiveness destroy the church. For this reason alone, divisiveness must not be allowed to prevail within the church. It has to be dealt with if the church is to remain the church and be the Lord's.

What is said above bears repeating. Taking a person's behavior before the church is a very serious matter. It is as serious a matter as can be imagined. Several facts make it extremely serious.

a. A person's life is involved. The person can be damaged, turned off and pushed away from the Lord and God's people forever.

b. Public discussion of personal behavior is a very, very sensitive subject. It can easily arouse emotions and cause more division. It can even turn some of the spiritually minded away from the church.

c. Personal behavior and *juicy news* are what the *unspiritual or carnal nature* of man enjoys discussing. It is the subject of which rumors are made. It sets aflame the tongues and imaginations of most people. Few are spiritually free of the urge to talk about the faults and rumors surrounding others. The very nature of man enjoys knowing and sharing the faults of others with close friends. Why? It is the downing of others that elevates self and gives some justification (excuse) to sinful behavior and flesh-feeding habits. And most follow and revel in sinful flesh, not in God's Spirit. This is true even among many professing believers.

d. Few can keep confidences. Few can keep quiet. Even the most trusted and loving and wise do not keep confidences. A person who will keep confidences is more rare than a precious gem that takes many lifetimes to discover. Therefore, when a matter is shared, it must always be remembered and understood that it will be spread around. What will the effects be as it spreads around? The effects must always be measured as one considers sharing personal behavior and differences with others, whether with just another individual, or with the church as a whole.

e. The world—both the public and the lost within and without the local community—will hear about personal behavior being carried before the church. Again, the effect upon the world's thoughts, talk, attitudes, and openness of heart to the gospel must be carefully considered before rushing before the church with matters that concern personal behavior.

Now, when should a personal matter and difference be taken before the church? (Perhaps a more appropriate question would be, when should a personal matter concerning a brother ever be discussed with another individual?)

a. When we are *absolutely sure* that God does not want us to continue bearing the hurt and injury any longer as a learning experience. When we are absolutely sure there is no more need for us to be...
   - learning more trust
   - learning more patience
   - learning more endurance
   - learning more humility
   - learning more love
   - learning more experience
   - learning more hope
   - learning more conformity to His image (or suffering)
   - learning more glory

b. When we are *absolutely sure* that the Lord's Spirit is leading us to share the matter of personal behavior.

c. When we are *ready to acknowledge* our own failures and sinfulness and potential for failing (Ro.14:4; 1 Cor.10:12).

d. When we are gripped by a spirit of prayer, softness, tenderness, warmth, love, and humility.

e. When we are gripped by the spirit of "carrying each other's burdens" (Gal.6:1-3).

f. When we are *absolutely sure* that we have followed the steps spelled out by Christ (Mt.18:15-17).

2. The heavenly support of the discipline. Note that heaven's discipline of the divisive brother is the same as the earthly or church discipline. What does this mean? One thing is sure—it cannot mean that any man or any church has the power to forgive or not forgive sins. No man or church has the power to doom or save and set free a person.

What it probably means is this: when a brother chooses sin and refuses to be reconciled after the church reaches and reaches out after him, he is lost to the church. There is no relationship between him and the church. The church failed to reach him; therefore he is *bound to the earth* and to being treated as an outsider. Thus heaven—God Himself—will reckon him to be bound by sin as an outsider just as the church binds (reckons) him. Similarly, if he is ever reached by the church and "loosed" from the bondage of sin, heaven will reckon him loosed. God will receive him back as a redeemed brother, as an insider.

Thought 1. In the final analysis, divisiveness and those who cause divisiveness have to be confronted and handled. "A household divided against itself will not stand" (Mt.12:25).

Christ insists that a divisive brother be disciplined and treated as an outsider. (But we must *always* remember: this action is to be taken only after reconciliation has been attempted at least three times.) Why must divisiveness and the brother who caused the divisiveness be handled?

1) Divisiveness threatens survival. A body, an organization, even the church itself can stand only if it is unified and functioning in peace and harmony.
2) Divisiveness threatens purity and character. The church is seen as corrupt and weak if such things as divisiveness and grumbling are allowed.
3) Divisiveness threatens order and mission and ministry. Divisiveness can threaten and cause failure of any purpose, mission, or ministry. Disorder assures defeat and failure.

Thought 2. This passage is a wonderful thing: Christ Himself, our wonderful Lord, has given us the very procedure (steps) to take in dealing with divisive brothers. How much we need to follow His instructions!

Thought 3. Discipline of a divisive brother is necessary in order to preserve the church and all that it stands for.

DEEPER STUDY # 2

(18:17) **Discipline, Church**: the outlines and preceding notes of this Scripture should be read before reading this note in order to have a complete picture (Mt.18:15-20).

A brother who has a personal quarrel with another brother is to be disciplined if three things exist.

⇒ If he continues in open rebellion against the Lord.
⇒ If he continues to be gripped by the selfishness, covetousness, and worldliness of this earth.
⇒ If he refuses reconciliation with his brother after three attempts at reconciliation have been made as spelled out by Christ.

What is the discipline? The divisive brother is to be treated just as he is acting: as an outsider—just as a pagan and a tax collector. The pagans or sinners and tax collectors were the very people for whom Christ reached out. They were outside the fold, but they were reachable. The divisive brother is acting as an outsider: he will not listen and respond to the humble and loving appeals for reconciliation. Therefore, he is to be left alone and not bothered until he is ready to listen and be reconciled. He is refusing reconcilation and living as an outsider, just as the lost live. Accordingly, the church can do nothing but treat him as an outsider.

1. The offending brother himself made the choice not to be reconciled. He stood at the crossroads of reconciliation on three specific occasions. He is personally responsible for his decision.

2. The church reached and reached out for the dear brother. It made every attempt to lead the brother to stop the divisiveness and to be reconciled.

3. The life the brother has chosen to live is his discipline. It is his decision to be an outsider instead of being reconciled to his brother and his church. It is his decision to live in the world of "sinners and tax collectors" instead of living in the presence and reconciliation of God's people.

4. The discipline of the brother is a discipline which allows the church to continue to reach out for the backslidden brother. *Sinners and tax collectors* are the very people to whom Christ went and to whom the church is to go. The discipline of the brother is: "Treat him as you would a pagan or a tax collector." Apparently Christ is saying this: the church is to continue seeking after him *as it deems wise*, just as they seek after all outsiders. Realistically, however, the attempts at future reconcilation would probably be much less often. The dear brother's heart will have fewer opportunities to be stirred by those who love and care for him so deeply.

"And if anyone causes one of these little ones who believe in me to sin, it would be better for him to be thrown into the sea with a large millstone tied around his neck. (Mark 9:42)

> **Therefore let us stop passing judgment on one another. Instead, make up your mind not to put any stumbling block or obstacle in your brother's way. (Rom 14:13)**
>
> **If your brother is distressed because of what you eat, you are no longer acting in love. Do not by your eating destroy your brother for whom Christ died. (Rom 14:15)**
>
> **It is better not to eat meat or drink wine or to do anything else that will cause your brother to fall. (Rom 14:21)**
>
> **We put no stumbling block in anyone's path, so that our ministry will not be discredited. (2 Cor 6:3)**
>
> **Whoever loves his brother lives in the light, and there is nothing in him to make him stumble. (1 John 2:10)**

3 (18:19-20) **Prayer**: the third step in correcting an offending brother is the essential step—to bathe the matter in prayer. The words, "Again, I tell you," stress the importance of this step. The matter must be *bathed in prayer*, but how we go about praying is critical.

1. We must seek agreement about the matter of correcting a brother (v.19). The matter of correction is an awesome responsibility. It is not to be left in the hands of a single person. There are always to be at least two persons involved.

2. We must seek God's will and approval, making sure correction is His will (v.19). No correction should ever be attempted that is not God's will and is not according to the explicit statement of His Word. Any correction of an offending brother must demonstrate God's love, compassion, and mercy.

3. We must seek unity "in Jesus' name," not just human agreement, not just following human thoughts and rules governing discipline. The unity must be "in His name," brought about by His Spirit and in accordance with the whole counsel of God's Word (not just a section taken out of context or interpreted without considering all of God's teaching about a matter) (v.19).

If these steps are truly pursued, the Lord promises His presence in the decision made and in the correction of an offending brother.

> **"Ask and it will be given to you; seek and you will find; knock and the door will be opened to you. (Mat 7:7)**
>
> **If you believe, you will receive whatever you ask for in prayer." (Mat 21:22)**
>
> **And pray in the Spirit on all occasions with all kinds of prayers and requests. With this in mind, be alert and always keep on praying for all the saints. (Eph 6:18)**
>
> **Look to the LORD and his strength; seek his face always. (1 Chr 16:11)**

DEEPER STUDY # 3

(18:19-20) **Prayer**: this passage shows us the power of united prayer—even if the number praying is only two persons.

1. Christ says, "Anything you ask for, it will be done for you" (v.19).

2. Christ also says, "There I am with them" (v.20). Note: Christ did not say, "I will be there." He is already there. This is a very special presence, the real, actual presence of Christ. It is equivalent to the Shekinah glory, the very special presence of God that dwelt in the tabernacle and temple. It is a deep sense, a consciousness, an intense awareness of God's Spirit communing with our spirit. God manifests His presence in a very special way to the believer (see note—Jn.14:21-22; 2 Cor.3:17-18).

However, two things are absolutely essential to experience the power of united prayer.

1. "If two of you on earth <u>agree</u> [sumphonesosin] about anything": the word *agree* means to be in complete accord; to harmonize together like that of a symphony; to sound together; to act together in each other's nature. It is the very opposite of wandering thoughts, half-hearted commitment, disconnected purpose, disjointed and misplaced understanding, unsynchronized spirits, and imcomplete and piece-meal knowledge.

2. If "two or three come together <u>in my name</u> [eis to emon unoma]": literally this says "into my name." The idea is close and intimate union with Christ. It is a "getting into" the Spirit of Christ; a longing to be in union with Him and to act only for His glory. It is a depth of *spiritual union* demonstrated by so few. Note: it comes not only from private prayer but from prayer with others.

This says something of critical importance. We should never attempt to correct a brother unless we first have a deep spiritual union with Christ—a union so deep that we can act only for His glory. We must be free of all fleshly urges to *get at a brother*. We must act only for God's glory.

E. The Parable of the Unmerciful Servant: The Spirit of Forgiveness, 18:21-35

1 The spirit & practice of forgiveness
- a. Peter asked about forgiving a brother: Is forgiveness limited?
- b. Jesus answered: Forgiveness is unlimited[DS1]
- c. Jesus illustrated: Is like the K. of Heaven

2 There is God's spirit of forgiveness: Like a king who settles his accounts with his servants
- a. All must give account
- b. One is brought to Him
- c. The servant owes a huge debt
- d. The servant is bankrupt
  - 1) He is to be sold
  - 2) He is to lose all
- e. The servant faces Him
- f. The servant cries for mercy
  - 1) Worships the king
  - 2) Makes a commitment
- g. The servant experiences the compassion of a loving king: Is freed & forgiven

3 There is the servant's spirit of unforgiveness
- a. He faces a fellow servant who owes him: In comparison a very small sum
- b. He reacts severely
- c. He rejects the cry for mercy: Refuses to forgive
- d. He acts materialistically & selfishly—according to law & justice
- e. He grieves the other servants: They carry the matter to the Lord

4 There is the great day of accounting
- a. Two bases of judgment
  - 1) God's forgiveness: Offered in Christ
  - 2) The servant's wickedness: He lacks compassion & mercy
- b. The judgment
  - 1) The Lord's anger
  - 2) The Lord's justice: The man was condemned & punished

5 There is the point: An unforgiving person will be judged

21 Then Peter came to Jesus
and asked, "Lord, how
many times shall I forgive
my brother when he sins
against me? Up to seven
times?"
22 Jesus answered, "I tell
you, not seven times, but seventy-seven times.
23 "Therefore, the kingdom
of heaven is like a king who
wanted to settle accounts
with his servants.
24 As he began the settlement, a man who owed him
ten thousand talents was
brought to him.
25 Since he was not able to
pay, the master ordered that
he and his wife and his children and all that he had be
sold to repay the debt.
26 "The servant fell on his
knees before him. 'Be patient with me,' he begged,
'and I will pay back everything.'
27 The servant's master took
pity on him, canceled the
debt and let him go.
28 "But when that servant
went out, he found one of his
fellow servants who owed
him a hundred denarii. He
grabbed him and began to
choke him. 'Pay back what
you owe me!' he demanded.
29 "His fellow servant fell to
his knees and begged him,
'Be patient with me, and I
will pay you back.'
30 "But he refused. Instead,
he went off and had the man
thrown into prison until he
could pay the debt.
31 When the other servants
saw what had happened, they
were greatly distressed and
went and told their master
everything that had happened.
32 "Then the master called
the servant in. 'You wicked
servant,' he said, 'I canceled
all that debt of yours because
you begged me to.
33 Shouldn't you have had
mercy on your fellow servant
just as I had on you?'
34 In anger his master
turned him over to the
jailers to be tortured, until
he should pay back all he
owed.
35 "This is how my heavenly
Father will treat each of you
unless you forgive your
brother from your heart."

DIVISION XII

THE MESSIAH'S DISCIPLES AND THEIR BEHAVIOR TOWARD ONE ANOTHER, 18:1-35

E. The Parable of the Unmerciful Servant: The Spirit of Forgiveness, 18:21-35

(18:21-35) **Introduction**: How often are we to forgive a person? Does God expect us to forgive and forgive—no matter the abuse and number of times the wrong is done? Christ answered these and many other questions in this discussion.

1. The spirit and practice of forgiveness (v.21-22).
2. There is God's spirit of forgivensss: like a king who settles his accounts with his servants (v.23-27).
3. There is the servant's spirit of unforgiveness (v.28-31).
4. There is *the great day* of accounting (v.32-34).
5. There is the point: an unforgiving person will be judged (v.35).

1 (18:21-22) **Forgiveness**: there is the spirit and practice of forgiveness. Note exactly what happened between Peter and Jesus.

1. Peter asked about forgiving a brother. Is forgiveness limited? Peter's concern was forgiving another Christian brother, a fellow disciple (see notes—Mt.18:5-10; 18:5). Christ also placed the discussion in the context of "the kingdom of heaven," that is, the Christian community or church (see DEEPER STUDY # 3—Mt.19:23-24). Peter was very generous in his concept of forgiveness. To forgive a person seven times for having wronged oneself is very generous, far more generous than what most do.

2. Jesus answered that forgiveness is unlimited (see DEEPER STUDY # 1—Mt.18:22).

3. Jesus illustrated the spirit of forgiveness by referring to the kingdom of heaven. The kingdom of heaven in its present form includes some people who are servants of God, but they are servants in profession only. The servant in this parable professes faith in God, but his profession is false. He is in the church walking among God's people. In a desperate moment of dire need, God has met him and offered mercy and forgiveness but he has not personally learned anything about God's compassion and forgiveness (see note—Mt.18:35).

DEEPER STUDY # 1

(18:22) **Forgiveness—Relationship—Brotherhood—Unity**: The question is how often should we forgive a brother?

⇒ Peter: "Up to seven times?"

⇒ Jesus: "No. Seventy-seven times."

What Jesus meant is seventy-seven times and on and on through eternity. Forgiveness is a matter of the heart, not of the mind. The mind will only keep a record of wrongs. A spirit of forgiveness does not measure and limit the number of times it will forgive. A spirit of forgiveness will tolerate being wronged and hurt time after time. Why?

There are several reasons why the spirit of forgiveness knows no limit, no measure, no number of times that it will forgive.

1. Forgiveness is a thing of the spirit, a quality of the spirit. All spiritual things, substances and realities—such as love, mercy, grace, joy, forgiveness—cannot be measured or limited. They are by their very nature spiritual and not physical. Therefore they are without measure or limit, so they are to be known and practiced without limit or measure. We are to experience and practice love at every opportunity. We are to experience and practice forgiveness at every opportunity. Forgiveness is a reality of the spirit; therefore it is to be a spirit of life. The spirit of forgiveness is to forgive seventy times seven—*ad infinitum*.

2. Good human relationships are impossible without a forgiving spirit. Offending others is common to all. We are all sinful and we all offend—offend much too often. No one walks perfectly or anywhere close to what he should. If we kept score, there would be little time to do anything else. To keep relationships healthy, we need to know at least four things.

a. Coming short and sinning, failing and offending are common to us all. We all offend by failing…

- to smile
- to greet
- to love
- to be gentle
- be believe
- to recognize
- to speak
- to acknowledge
- to be joyful
- to be good
- to be humble
- to be controlled
- to word things properly
- to be unselfish
- to be non-irritable
- to be unprovoked
- to be long-suffering
- to be victorious

b. Offending others is usually unintentional and unknown. All of us offend others, but we are often unaware that we have offended them. The reasons we fail others are innumerable, but common causes are preoccupation of thought, heavy hearts and minds, and trials and problems that consume our thoughts. Keeping this in mind will help us to forgive others when they offend us.

c. We offend others as much as they offend us. We are as human as the next person, and we need forgiveness as much as the next person. Remembering this will do as much to maintain healthy relationships as any other single fact.

d. The common response to being offended is to react: react by withdrawing, taking vengeance, or wallowing around in self-pity and in a spirit of unforgiveness. Many revel in the attention secured by being the subject of abuse instead of handling the matter quietly in a true spirit of reconciliation.

3. An unforgiving spirit shows that a person is basically ill-natured, self-centered, and spiritually immature. Unforgiveness reveals that a person has not grown to be like Christ in his nature of understanding, compassion, and love. A forgiving spirit understands the nature of man (sinful and offending) and the nature of God (spiritual and forgiving, pt. 1 above).

4. Peace and health can be preserved only through a forgiving spirit. An unforgiving spirit causes as much disturbance and division as the offender. An unforgiving spirit has stooped to the level of the offender and has, in fact, become an offender. Think: as long as there is an unforgiving spirit, there can never be peace. Disturbance, conflict, and division prevail. An unforgiving spirit also affects a person's emotions and mind and body. It is the lack of peace, the lack of a good relationship with God and man, that disturbs the normal functioning of the body, mind, and emotions. Ulcers, high blood pressure, disturbed thoughts and emotions, and on and on—all can and often do come from an unforgiving spirit.

Above all, love each other deeply, because love covers over a multitude of sins. (1 Pet 4:8)

Peace I leave with you; my peace I give you. I do not give to you as the world gives. Do not let your hearts be troubled and do not be afraid. (John 14:27)

2 (18:23-27) **Forgiveness**: there is God's spirit of forgiveness. He is just like a king who settles the accounts of his servants. The parable is simple, yet very descriptive and full of meaning. God is the King, but He is a very unusual King. He is a King who rules justly as all kings should. But He is more. He is loving, compassionate, and forgiving; and He is even more than these. He is consumed with love and compassion—so much so that He forgives enormous debts, debts so enormous that they are inconceivable.

The king settles the accounts of his servants. He settles the accounts at varying times. An accounting is required at conversion and on those occasions when God leads us to evaluate our lives. Note how the seven steps related by Christ can be applied to either of these times.

1. All must give an account (v.24). The words "began the settlement" (sunairein) means to take account; to make a reckoning; to settle accounts. This is the same word that is translated "to settle accounts" in v.23. The king began to check the province and the ledgers of his province: receipts and expenditures and the capital improvements. The king had a critical interest in what his servant had received through gifts and what he had used in the ministry.

2. We are all brought to the King by the Spirit, the Word, or some Christian witness (v.24).

3. We are all led to see our huge debt of sin and service that we owe God (v.24. Cp. Ps.19:12; 40:12.) The debt of the servant was huge. It was millions of dollars. It was probably the gross revenues of a province or state in that day. The servant was the high official placed over the province who was held responsible for its administration. The point is that God has given us life and made us overseer of that life. To sin is to mismanage that life and to cause loss; therefore, sin puts us in debt to God. The debt is infinite, beyond anything we can ever pay.

4. We are all bankrupt (unable to pay) before God (v.25). Sin bankrupts man and puts him in debt to God. We are so bankrupt by sin that nothing can pay our debt.

⇒ Silver and gold, no amount of wealth, can pay our debt.

⇒ Neither a brother nor any other family member can pay our debt.

Those who trust in their wealth and boast of their great riches? No man can redeem the life of another or give to God a ransom for him— (Psa 49:6-7)

⇒ Good works cannot pay our debt.

He saved us, not because of righteous things we had done, but because of his mercy. He saved us through the washing of

rebirth and renewal by the Holy Spirit, whom he poured out on us generously through Jesus Christ our Savior, (Titus 3:5-6)

⇒ Making sacrifice and giving offerings cannot pay our debt.

But Samuel replied: "Does the LORD delight in burnt offerings and sacrifices as much as in obeying the voice of the LORD? To obey is better than sacrifice, and to heed is better than the fat of rams. (1 Sam 15:22)

Note that the man's debts affected his family. His enslavement and loss would have meant their enslavement and loss. A man's sins always affect both him and his family (see note—Ro.1:24; note and DEEPER STUDY # 1—Eph.1:7. Cp. Ro.7:14-20.)

5. We face the justice of a just God (v.25).

6. We cry for mercy (v.26). Our only hope is that God loves us enough that He will simply forgive us in compassion and mercy.

But because of his great love for us, God, who is rich in mercy, made us alive with Christ even when we were dead in transgressions—it is by grace you have been saved. (Eph 2:4-5)

7. We hear the love and forgiveness of a loving God (v.27).

Thought 1. Some of the things that bring us to God and cause us to evaluate and take account of our lives are trials, trouble, sickness, disease, a sermon or witness, tragedy, parents, friends, or special days or occasions (for example, the New Year).

Thought 2. Note that the false servant had not cried out for mercy until he was brought face to face with the king. We are often careless about sin until we are called to account. How fewer trials, sufferings, and temptations we would face if we turned from sin immediately.

3 (18:28-31) **Unforgiveness**: there was the servant's spirit of unforgiveness. The very steps taken by the servant are the steps involved in an unforgiving spirit.

1. He faced a person who owed him, that is, who *had offended* him in some way (v.28). In comparison, the debt or offense was very small. It was not a millionth of the debt owed by the unforgiving servant. The proportion was over 1 to 1,250,000—an enormous difference (A. Lukyn Williams. *St. Matthew*. "The Pulpit Commentary," Vol. 15, ed. by HDM Spense and Joseph S. Exell. Grand Rapids, MI: Eerdmans, 1950, p.215). This shows the enormous difference between our sin against a brother and our brother's sin against us. When we really see this, an unforgiving spirit toward a brother is inexcusable. We can forgive anything.

2. He reacted severely (v.28). He attacked the debtor; that is, he exercised his authority over the debtor and attempted to squeeze the payment out of him. He got angry and showed malice. There was no need for this kind of behavior; it was inexcusable. Remember the king's mercy to him. The king had not pressed charges against him; the king had even forgiven his debt. How we need to remember the love and forgiveness of God! God's love and forgiveness need to become the controlling factors of all our relationships.

3. He rejected the cry for mercy and refused to forgive (v.29).

4. He acted selfishly and worldly, according to law and justice (v.30). The man really owed the servant. The debt was a just and legal debt. The servant had every right to demand and force payment. Such was justice, but again, remember the point Christ was making. The King, God, does not act toward us legally, executing justice. He has compassion and mercy upon us and forgives us, wiping out all our debts.

The question is, how often should we forgive our brother? "Seventy-seven times," Christ said. "Have compassion and mercy; do not demand justice. Do not execute the law against a man. Do not trample him underfoot. Do not act cruelly, swallowing him up and destroying his spirit. Love him and forgive him 'just as Christ in God forgave you'" (Eph.4:32).

Thought 1. Note what it is that made this servant go to law and demand justice: money. He was materialistic and worldly minded. The debt was owed, so it was a true debt. It was money that made him selfish. How often money, materialism, and worldlinss destroy a person!

Thought 2. Note another point: he had just gone through a frightening experience himself—an experience that had carried him into the depths of insecurity. Such an experience was bound to affect him. He would thereafter want to make sure he had enough to care for himself and his family. Humanly speaking, he had every right to demand payment of those who owed him. No man would object to his demand in light of his experience. However, there was something objectionable, something missing in his heart and life. He was hard, not soft. He was exacting, not understanding. He was just, not compassionate. He was legal, not loving; He was the very opposite of God. God is loving, compassionate, merciful, and forgiving; and God expects His servants to be as He is.

5. He grieved others (v.31). Note the words "they were greatly distressed." God's true servants are always grieved to see people mistreated, abused, and trampled upon. Cruel and mean treatment always troubles God's people. Suffering, pain, hurt, and death cut the heart of God's people.

a. They feel for the afflicted: their suffering, pain, and hurt.
b. They feel for the just but sinful man: sinful in that he is unmerciful and uncompassionate. His strict justice causes more and more trouble and disturbance and oppression of people. God's people took the only recourse; they did the only thing they could. They took the matter to God. They could not remain silent and allow the license of oppression and legalism to destroy a human spirit.

4 (18:32-34) **Death—Judgment—Wickedness**: there was the great day of accounting. This is a day that lies out in the future for every man. It is both the summons of death and the summons to stand before God to be judged. It is the death and the day of judgment that every man must face (Heb.9:27).

Note the two bases for judgment.

1. The first basis of judgment is God's forgiveness. God's forgiveness is provided in Christ and is always available. Christ "is the atoning sacrifice for our sins, and not only for ours, but also for the sins of the whole world" (1 Jn.2:2).

> **"For God so loved the world that he gave his one and only Son, that whoever believes in him shall not perish but have eternal life. Whoever believes in him is not condemned, but whoever does not believe stands condemned already because he has not believed in the name of God's one and only Son. (John 3:16, 18)**

2. The second basis of judgment is man's wickedness. It is important to understand what wickedness and sin are. Wickedness and sin are primarily coming "short of God's glory," coming short of what God is. This is clearly illustrated by this wicked servant (church member). He was a just and lawful man. He was a high official in government and politics, serving directly under the king. He was well respected and honored, an outstanding citizen, but he was not like God. He was not compassionate and merciful, loving and forgiving in his dealings with others. There are two great commandments that a servant of the king must obey. This servant tried to obey the first one, "Love the Lord God...."; but he ignored the second one, "Love your neighbor as yourself" (Mt.22:39).

Very simply put, a wicked man is a man who does not honestly believe God nor diligently seek to live as God lives (Heb.11:6). He is a man who does not believe that God exists, does not believe to the point that it changes his life. His life is not compassionate, merciful, and forgiving. Because of this, he shall face the judgment of the King and be condemned.

> **Or do you show contempt for the riches of his kindness, tolerance and patience, not realizing that God's kindness leads you toward repentance? (Rom 2:4)**

Note the judgment and condemnation that man is to experience.

1. Man shall experience the Lord's anger. Two things are extremely detestable to God and arouse His anger: not believing Him and not being compassionate and merciful nor loving and forgiving toward others.

> **If we deliberately keep on sinning after we have received the knowledge of the truth, no sacrifice for sins is left, but only a fearful expectation of judgment and of raging fire that will consume the enemies of God. (Heb 10:26-27)**
>
> **But the LORD is the true God; he is the living God, the eternal King. When he is angry, the earth trembles; the nations cannot endure his wrath. (Jer 10:10)**

2. Man shall experience justice. Note two critical things about the justice executed.

a. The unmerciful servant received perfect justice. He received exactly what was due him. He had to *pay*; he was punished only for what he owed—no more, no less. He received the exact penalty, the exact punishment due him.

b. The King, God, was perfectly just. He merely executed perfect justice. He executed what the servant himself had chosen: due payment for due debt.

> **God is just: He will pay back trouble to those who trouble you (2 Th 1:6)**
>
> **For if the message spoken by angels was binding, and every violation and disobedience received its just punishment, how shall we escape if we ignore such a great salvation? This salvation, which was first announced by the Lord, was confirmed to us by those who heard him. (Heb 2:2-3)**
>
> **So I will not look on them with pity or spare them, but I will bring down on their own heads what they have done." (Ezek 9:10)**
>
> **But as for those whose hearts are devoted to their vile images and detestable idols, I will bring down on their own heads what they have done, declares the Sovereign LORD." (Ezek 11:21)**

5 (18:35) **Judgment**: this is the point—an unforgiving person will be judged. The point is clear and critical. It is critical because it determines our eternal destiny. We must not only forgive, we must live a life of forgiveness and mercy. We must develop a nature of forgiveness and compassion and mercy and love toward others. If we do not forgive *from our hearts*, neither will God forgive us. Note three things.

1. Forgiveness comes from the heart, from a new nature wrought in Christ.

2. Christ says "My Father," *not* "your Father." God was not the servant's Father. The servant was not a genuine follower of God. He only professed to be.

3. The person who does not forgive others does not know the forgiveness of God. Having a spirit of forgiveness is so important that Christ taught it time and again.

> **Blessed are the merciful, for they will be shown mercy. (Mat 5:7)**
>
> **But I tell you: Love your enemies and pray for those who persecute you, Be perfect, therefore, as your heavenly Father is perfect. (Mat 5:44, 48; cp. Lk.6:35-36)**
>
> **Forgive us our debts, as we also have forgiven our debtors. For if you forgive men when they sin against you, your heavenly Father will also forgive you. But if you do not forgive men their sins, your Father will not forgive your sins. (Mat 6:12, 14-15) because judgment without mercy will be shown to anyone who has not been merciful. Mercy triumphs over judgment! (James 2:13)**

CHAPTER 19

XIII. THE MESSIAH'S TEACHINGS ON THE WAY TO JERUSALEM 19:1-20:34

A. The Sanctity of Marriage[DS1] 19:1-12
(cp. Mt.5:31-32; Mk.10:1-12; Lk.16:18; 1 Cor.7:10-16)

When Jesus had finished
saying these things, he left
Galilee and went into the region of Judea to the other
side of the Jordan.
2 Large crowds followed
him, and he healed them
there.
3 Some Pharisees came to
him to test him. They asked,
"Is it lawful for a man to divorce his wife for any and
every reason?"
4 "Haven't you read," he
replied, "that at the beginning
the Creator 'made them male
and female,'
5 And said, 'For this reason a
man will leave his father and
mother and be united to his
wife, and the two will become one flesh'?
6 So they are no longer two,
but one. Therefore what God
has joined together, let man
not separate."
7 "Why then," they asked,
"did Moses command that a
man give his wife a certificate of divorce and send her
away?"
8 Jesus replied, "Moses
permitted you to divorce your
wives because your hearts
were hard. But it was not this
way from the beginning.
9 I tell you that anyone who
divorces his wife, except for
marital unfaithfulness, and
marries another woman
commits adultery."
10 The disciples said to him,
"If this is the situation between a husband and wife, it
is better not to marry."
11 Jesus replied, "Not everyone can accept this word, but
only those to whom it has
been given.
12 For some are eunuchs because they were born that
way; others were made that
way by men; and others have
renounced marriage because
of the kingdom of heaven.
The one who can accept this
should accept it."

1 A contrast between two attitudes toward Jesus
- a. Jesus left Galilee & entered Jordan
- b. Attitude 1: Seeking help by the large crowds
- c. Attitude 2: Testing & questioning by the religionists—questioned Him about marriage

2 There is the creation of male & female

3 There is the creation of a new family

4 There is the creation of one body[DS2]
- a. God joins the two bodies into one body
- b. Man is not to separate the body of marriage

5 There is the ideal of permanence in marriage
- a. The question of legal divorce[DS3]
- b. Divorce was only a concession
- c. The cause: Hard hearts[DS4]
- d. Divorce was never intended by God

6 There is the allowance for divorce: Marital unfaithfulness[DS5]

7 There is the supernatural power needed for marriage
- a. Disciples questioned the hard & fast rule
- b. Christ replied: Only believers can receive this truth[DS6]

8 There is the highest ideal in marriage: Total devotion to God's Kingdom

DIVISION XIII

THE MESSIAH'S TEACHINGS ON THE WAY TO JERUSALEM, 19:1-20:34

A. The Sanctity of Marriage, 19:1-12

(19:1-12) **Introduction—Marriage—Divorce**: the questions regarding marriage and divorce are always burning questions, extremely controversial within societies heavily influenced by Christian teaching. Opinions vary and interpretations differ. There is always the closed view that says divorce is never allowed by God no matter the cruelty and meanness that may exist. And there is always the more open view that says divorce is allowed if the rift between a couple is not reconciled and causes more damage than good.

⇒ The former view says that Christ gave a complete exposition on marriage and divorce; the latter says He gave guidelines.

⇒ The former view sometimes treats divorce in such a spirit that it appears to be the unpardonable sin; the latter view sometimes treats it in such a spirit that it appears to be the escape route to do as a person likes (ranging from minor selfish ends to licentious pleasures).

In Christ's day, the two schools of thought were the Shammai School (conservative) and the Hillel School (liberal). (See DEEPER STUDY # 1—Mt.19:1-12.) As in every generation, there were those within each school that would have nothing to do with anyone who held another opinion. A person's view was made a matter of fellowship.

It was because of these strong feelings that the religionists (Pharisees) thought they could entrap and discredit Jesus. No matter what He said, a great number of people would differ, and they would stop supporting His ministry. He would be discredited and His ministry destroyed.

Note several things.

1. There is always a reluctance to express a different opinion when a great number hold a particular position. Compare for example, slavery, smoking, over-eating, mixed bathing, gambling, playing cards, movies, television, and divorce.

2. It is wrong not to face the issues of marriage and divorce, no matter the different opinions and practices of society. Why?

a. There are always a large number of divorced people. Many of these need help, desperately need help. Their faith, hope, security, children, and whole lives have been drastically affected. If believers, God's people, do not open their hearts to them, then a great opportunity to reach out and help them grow in Christ is missed.

b. There are always a large number of marriages (perhaps most) experiencing difficulty, some serious difficulty. Hardness and cruelty, ranging from mild withdrawal to physical abuse, just tear and tear away at the marriage commitment. Sometimes it is the fault of one; sometimes it is the fault of both. In either case, great need exists. Again, if God's people do not reach out and help, a great opportunity is lost for Christ.

Note what Christ did: He spoke up and taught about the issue, and the issue was as controversial in His day as it has been in succeeding generations. (Also see outlines and notes—Mt.5:31-32; 1 Cor.7:1-7; 7:8-16.)

1. A contrast between two attitudes toward Jesus (v.1-3).
2. There is the creation of male and female (v.4).
3. There is the creation of a new family (v.5).
4. There is the creation of one body (v.5-6).
5. There is the ideal of permanence in marriage (v.7-8).
6. There is the allowance for divorce: marital unfaithfulness (v.9).
7. There is the supernatural power needed for marriage (v.10-11).
8. There is the highest ideal in marriage: total devotion to God's Kingdom (v.12).

DEEPER STUDY # 1

(19:1-12) **Marriage—Divorce—Shammai—Hillel**: the Pharisees came to Jesus tempting Him and saying, "Is it lawful for a man to divorce his wife for any and every reason?"

There is a background to this question. The society of Jesus' day was very lax in its morals. Marriage was considered nothing more than a piece of paper: if it worked, fine; if it did not work, fine. One could always divorce (see note—Mt.5:31).

There were two positions or schools of thought on divorce. Moses had said that any man could divorce his wife if "she becomes displeasing to him because he finds something indecent about her" (Dt.24:1).

1. The school of Shammai said that the words *some uncleanness* meant adultery only. A wife could be as loose and mean as Jezebel, but she was not to be divorced unless she committed adultery.

2. The school of Hillel said that the words *some uncleanness* meant anything that was not pleasing to the man. One should remember that women were counted as nothing but *property* to be possessed by men. They had no rights whatsoever except as a man might wish to give. Of course, this was the position followed by society, for it was the position that allowed human nature to run loose. Women were abused: used and discarded, neglected and violated. They were nothing but chattel property of men and were often considered of less value than property, whether animals or things. Therefore, divorce ran rampant in Christ's day.

The Pharisees wished to embroil Jesus in the controversy between the conservative (Shammai) and liberal view (Hillel). They were simply asking Jesus if He agreed with the school of Hillel: "Is it lawful for a man to divorce his wife for any and every reason?" (v.3). No matter which position He took, He would offend and stir up a large number of people, becoming embroiled in a mean controversy.

1 (19:1-3) **Divorce**: there are two attitudes toward Jesus, and there is a sharp contrast between the two attitudes. Christ was making His final journey toward Jerusalem where He was to be killed. He would not return to Galilee until after His resurrection (Mt.28:7).

The same two attitudes toward Christ prevail in every generation: there are those who sincerely seek the help of Christ; and there are those who are always testing and questioning Him, stretching every inch they can out of the world and the flesh. They question and question; and, by their questioning, they are able to create uncertainty and doubt over right and wrong. They are able to live as they wish.

Note the question asked, "Is it lawful for a man to divorce his wife for any and every cause?" The flesh or sinful nature says no matter how frivolous—if there is displeasure, disgust, dislike—then divorce is allowed. But is it? That is what Christ is answering.

2 (19:4) **Marriage—Divorce**: Christ said there is the creation of male and female: "The Creator made them [Adam and Eve] male and female" (v.4). He did not make them males and females, as He did animals, but He made one male and one female. Each one was made for the other. They were not made for anyone else, for there was no one else.

Thought 1. Creation is the root basis for marriage: one male for one female; one female for one male. There was no one else, just Adam and Eve. This was not so with the creation of other animals. They were created *en masse*; a large number were created simultaneously. There is also the added fact that male and female were created spiritual beings, created for much higher purposes. Since there were no others like them, they were sharing their purposes together in constant fellowship with God.

3 (19:5) **Marriage—Divorce**: Christ said there is the creation of a new family: "A man will leave his father and mother and be united to his wife" (v.5). One man shall cleave to his wife and create a new family distinct from the family of his parents. He says *a man*, not men, and *his wife*, not wives. Note that a man leaves his father and mother. The union between husband and wife is to gain primacy over the union between parent and child. The *act of uniting* is wrought by God and appointed by God. Therefore marriage is a divine institution. Just as parents and children are not to divorce one another, neither are the husband and wife to divorce each other.

Thought 1. Father, mother, and child comprise a unit, a family. However, Christ said father and mother are there when the child leaves. And the child (man) leaves to "be united to his wife." There is no thought, not even a hint of separation in this statement. It is unquestionably a statement of God's purpose for father, mother, and child. The structure of the family is the means by which man is to carry out the purposes of God on earth. Divorce, tearing down the structure of the family, is not the purpose of God. The structure of a family—father, mother, and child—is the purpose of God.

Thought 2. Note: Christ said the relation between father and mother is to be closer and more intimate, longer and more durable than that between parent and child. The day comes when the child (man) leaves the parent, and the parents are left with each other *all alone*. This says much to both husband and wife. They must not neglect their life together, for the day comes when they will be all alone and have the company *only of one another*.

4 (19:5-6) **Marriage—Divorce**: Christ said there is the creation of one body: "A man...will be united to his wife and the two will become one flesh" (v.5). There is the molding into one person. The man and the wife unite with each other: "So that they are no longer two, but one." What is it that makes them one flesh? *Being united.* They are one body, one flesh, one person. They are not joined to two or three or four other persons, but they unite only with one other person.

Christ also says that a marriage joined together by Him is not to be destroyed by any man. "A man...will be united to his wife, and the two will become one flesh [joined together by God]. Therefore what God has joined together, let no man separate" (v.5-6).

The points are clear.

a. The united husband and wife are joined together by God.
b. No one is to separate what God joins together. Neither the husband nor wife nor anyone else is to step in between the two and cause separation.

> **The man said, "This is now bone of my bones and flesh of my flesh; she shall be called 'woman, ' for she was taken out of man." For this reason a man will leave his father and mother and be united to his wife, and they will become one flesh. (Gen 2:23-24)**
>
> **May your fountain be blessed, and may you rejoice in the wife of your youth. (Prov 5:18)**
>
> **Enjoy life with your wife, whom you love, all the days of this meaningless life that God has given you under the sun— all your meaningless days. For this is your lot in life and in your toilsome labor under the sun. (Eccl 9:9)**
>
> **Husbands, love your wives, just as Christ loved the church and gave himself up for her (Eph 5:25)**
>
> **Husbands, in the same way be considerate as you live with your wives, and treat them with respect as the weaker partner and as heirs with you of the gracious gift of life, so that nothing will hinder your prayers. (1 Pet 3:7)**

Thought 1. Note something of critical importance. By *being united* Christ does not mean what is often thought or pictured: being united does not mean taking hold of a wife by civil contract, embracing, or sexual union.

Note the words...

- "united"
- "one flesh"
- "what God has joined together"

Spouses who are *obedient* to Christ by *uniting* to each other—in all of their being and life, not only physically, but also spiritually—are the ones who become one flesh. They are the ones whom God joins together. A civil contract does not bind people together, neither does embracing and neither does sex. Only God can bind a couple together *spiritually*, and He does so because a couple is obedient to Him. He rewards and blesses obedience, not disobedience.

Thought 2. Note how the power of God is infused into a couple who obeys Him. He causes their uniting to bind them so closely together they are as one person.

Thought 3. Note a significant point: "They are no longer two, but one." "No one ever hated his own body; but he feeds and cares for it"—he does not cut it off (Eph.5:29).

DEEPER STUDY # 2

(19:5) **Unite—Cleave** (kollao; proskollao): to join fast together; to glue together; to cement together; to be joined in the closest union possible; to be bound together; to be so totally united together that two become one. Therefore, to unite means a spiritual union. It is a union higher and stronger than the union of parent and child. It is a union that means more than living together, more than having sex and bearing offspring. Animals do this. It is a union that can be wrought by God alone (v.11). It is a spiritual union that places man above the physical plane of animals. It is a spiritual fulness, a spiritual sharing of life together: a dedication, a consecration, a completeness, a satisfaction that makes a person the exclusive possession of God and of the spouse. As said, such a uniting or spiritual union is wrought by God alone. Both husband and wife must be willing and submissive for God to bring about such a union in their lives. "Submit to one another out of reverence for Christ" (Eph.5:21; see outlines and notes—Eph.5:22-33).

There are three unions within a true marriage, that is, a marriage that *really unites* and is really *joined together* by God (Mt.19:6).

1. There is the physical union: the sharing of each other's body (1 Cor.7:2-5). But note: physical sharing cannot reach its ultimate fulness unless it is experienced while conscious of God's warm and tender mercies (Eph.5:25-33).
2. There is the mental union: the sharing of each other's life and dreams and hopes and the working together to realize those dreams and hopes. It is important to note that this union still deals only with the physical and material world.
3. There is the spiritual union: the sharing and melting and moulding of each other's spirit (see Eph.5:25-33). This can be wrought only by God. Therefore, there has to be a sharing together with God for there to be a *nourishing* and *nurturing* of the spirit.

Now here is the point: the greatest thing in the world is to know God personally and to be perfectly assured that we shall live now and eternally—to have life abundant with all the love, significance, meaning, and purpose humanly possible. But a man and a woman cannot experience abundant life of and by themselves. They can only nurture the mind and mesh themselves together mentally and physically. To be meshed together spiritually, the couple must share God and His saving grace together. When a couple shares God together day by day, God works supernaturally within their spirits, *melting* their beings and *moulding* them into what He calls *one flesh*. They actually become as *one person*. This is what is meant by "What God has joined together." The Greek word for "joined together" (sunzeugen) actually means to *yoke together*. It is God's yoking, God's joining, God's binding the couple together into a spiritual union that causes them to become one person.

A couple who is spiritually united does two very practical things.

1. The couple "submits themselves to one another out of reverence for Christ" (Eph.5:21). They submit, yield, surrender, sacrifice, give themselves up to the other as they live day by day in the fear (trust) of God. Day by day, they deliberately set out to nourish and cherish the other, even as the Lord feeds and cares for the church (Eph.5:29). They work to become part of each other—so deliberately that they seek to become part of each other's body, each other's flesh, each other's bones (Eph.5:30). They seek to be joined "as one flesh," no matter the surrender and sacrifice required. The meshing together is done by God. God takes such deliberate purpose and behavior, such a melting of one's being, and molds it into the flesh of the other—so much so the two actually become as one, not only physically and mentally but spiritually as well.

2. The couple shares the presence of God and His saving grace together. As a result, God gives them a spiritual assurance and strength which they share together throughout life. They share the knowledge and confidence...

- that God shall care for and look after them now and forever.
- that God shall carry them through the devastating trials of life that confront every human being every so often.
- that God shall bless them with all that is necessary as they walk through life together.
- that God shall give them an abundant entrance into the everlasting kingdom of the Lord Jesus Christ—forever and ever.

Again, the point is this: God takes such deliberate sharing of spiritual things and melts and molds the man and woman into *one flesh* spiritually—so much so that they actually become one. A man and a woman being spiritually united by God as one person is what being united means. Being united to one another in God's Spirit is true marriage—the glorious gift of God.

5 (19:7-8) **Marriage—Divorce**: there is the ideal of permanence in marriage. The Pharisees had entrapped Jesus, or so they thought. Jesus had given four reasons why there was to be no divorce. He was standing against Moses. In their view, Moses had given a commandment that allowed divorce (v.7). Jesus says three things about the ideal of marriage.

> **Jesus replied, "Moses permitted you to divorce your wives because your hearts were hard. But it was not this way from the beginning. (Mat 19:8)**

1. Moses made a concession.
2. The reason: man's hard, sinful hearts.
3. Divorce was never willed and was not the purpose of God.

Thought 1. Note three important facts.

1) God's will for marriage was permanence. Divorce was permitted under Moses, but it was not God's will. It was sin, short of God's will and purpose.
2) The cause for divorce is said to be *hardness of heart*—a very serious indictment.
3) The union of marriage is not brought about by a natural law but by God. Marriage is not a law of nature, inherent within man. It is not something that operates by nature, that just happens because two people agree to live together and sign a civil contract. A true union or marriage that is joined together by God is a blessing, a gift of God. It is brought about because a couple is obedient to God. They live in and for each other *under God* (acknowledging God in all things), just as He says to live *being united*. Therefore, God blesses them by joining them together in the most binding of spiritual unions.

It bears repeating: marriage is not a natural law; it is not a law of nature; it is a spiritual law that operates only if each spouse walks in the Spirit.

DEEPER STUDY # 3
(19:7) **Old Testament Reference**: cp. Dt.24:1-4.

DEEPER STUDY # 4
(19:8) **Hardness, of Heart—Marriage**: many are living together, both within and without marriage, who are not joined together by God. As Jesus said, "Not everyone can accept this word" (see DEEPER STUDY # 6—Mt.19:11). The world is corrupted; all are frail, selfish, and sinful. Many become hard of heart; and many, because of the hardness of heart, *wish* silently or vocally to divorce. Some do.

What is it that causes hardness of heart?

1. Many have not received God into their lives and marriages (Jn.1:12; Rev.3:20); therefore, God and His power are foreign, unknown to them (Eph.3:20).

2. Some are not *united* (see DEEPER STUDY # 2—Mt.19:5). One or both hearts are hard toward the other. Pride and hurt and barrier after barrier have grown between them. Therefore, one or both withdraw and have little to do with the other, avoiding daily contact and relationships as much as possible.

3. Some think sex is the basis for marriage. Many come short in thinking that the physical union is the unique feature that glues a marriage together. Sex is important, of course, as any well-adjusted couple knows. But when the newness of the experience passes and life settles into responsibility, there has to be more than the physical union to prevent barriers and hardness of heart. The unique feature is God, not sex (Mt.19:11; see outlines and DEEPER STUDY # 2—Mt.19:5; notes—Eph.5:22-24; 5:25-33).

4. Many are living only humanistic lives. They have no more than animals have: living together, being physically united, bearing offspring, and protecting and providing for each other. But that is all. They are not spiritually alive; they have not received God into their lives and marriage. They have *hard hearts* or *no heart* toward God. Therefore, some live on no higher plane than some animals live, and others do not even have the order and respect for one another that some animals have within their packs.

How do we prevent hardness of heart and divorce? There are four very basic essentials.

1. "Wives, submit to your husbands as to the Lord. For the husband is the head of the wife as Christ is the head of the church, his body, of which he is the Savior. Now as the church submits to Christ, so also wives should submit to their husbands in everything" (Eph.5:22-24).

2. "Husbands, love your wives, just as Christ loved the church and gave himself up for her....In this same way, husbands ought to love their wives as their own bodies. He who loves his wife loves himself. After all, no one ever hated his own body, but he feeds and cares for it, just as Christ does the church" (Eph.5:25, 28-29).

3. "However, each one of you also must love his wife as he loves himself, and the wife must respect her husband" (Eph.5:33).
4. "Be kind and compassionate to one another, forgiving each other, just as in Christ God forgave you" (Eph.4:32).

6 (19:9) **Marriage—Divorce**: there is the allowance for divorce—marital unfaithfulness. Christ says, "Anyone who divorces his wife except for marital unfaithfulness and marries another woman commits adultery...." (v.9).

- There is one clear reason for divorce: adultery.
- Remarriage commits adultery.

Before Christ came into the world, adultery was punishable by death. Since Christ has come, the penalty has been changed. Divorce itself is to be the punishment, not death. (What an impact this change of law has made on societies in the past! How much it is needed in some parts of the world even today! Compassion is the answer to sin, not anger and wrath.)

Note the importance and high esteem that Christ places upon sex within marriage. It is so intimate and meaningful and important an experience that if it is violated, divorce is allowed. Note however: Christ did not say that divorce must take place. It is only *allowed.* If the couple has been living in Him and blessed by Him and the violated spouse cannot emotionally accept the unfaithfulness, divorce can take place. But if the offended spouse can forgive—if he or she can be emotionally controlled and forgiving enough to forgive—then the spouse should forgive.

For this reason a man will leave his father and mother and be united to his wife, and they will become one flesh. (Gen 2:24)

"You have heard that it was said, 'Do not commit adultery.' But I tell you that anyone who looks at a woman lustfully has already committed adultery with her in his heart. (Mat 5:27-28)

But I tell you that anyone who divorces his wife, except for marital unfaithfulness, causes her to become an adulteress, and anyone who marries the divorced woman commits adultery. (Mat 5:32)

Therefore what God has joined together, let man not separate." (Mark 10:9)

For example, by law a married woman is bound to her husband as long as he is alive, but if her husband dies, she is released from the law of marriage. So then, if she marries another man while her husband is still alive, she is called an adulteress. But if her husband dies, she is released from that law and is not an adulteress, even though she marries another man. (Rom 7:2-3)

Do you not know that the wicked will not inherit the kingdom of God? Do not be deceived: Neither the sexually immoral nor idolaters nor adulterers nor male prostitutes nor homosexual offenders (1 Cor 6:9)

To the married I give this command (not I, but the Lord): A wife must not separate from her husband. (1 Cor 7:10)

They will be paid back with harm for the harm they have done. Their idea of pleasure is to carouse in broad daylight. They are blots and blemishes, reveling in their pleasures while they feast with you. With eyes full of adultery, they never stop sinning; they seduce the unstable; they are experts in greed—an accursed brood! (2 Pet 2:13-14)

DEEPER STUDY # 5

(19:9) **Unfaithfulness, Marital—Sexual Immorality—Adultery**: a person, especially a Christian believer, needs to think of the meaning of adultery here. Adultery is the turning away from a spouse to another person. Many a person would never think of turning away from their spouse to a third person, yet they readily and willingly turn toward self and toward other things. As God said of the nation Israel, "I gave faithless Israel her certificate of divorce and sent her away because of all her adulteries" (Jer.3:8). Many a person has done just as Israel did. They refused to surrender to God. They lived in a backslidden state, and day by day they turned more and more away from their spouse and, in many cases, from their children.

Day by day a person can take a spouse and children and...

- be mean and ugly.
- be nagging and mentally cruel.
- be neglectful and unthoughtful.
- be physically abusive and life-threatening.
- be deliberately withdrawn and separated.

And the truth of the matter is that many live selfishly that way.

⇒ Some are cruel; others sadistic.
⇒ Some are critical; others sarcastic; still others *demonic and hellish.*
⇒ Some are mentally abusive; others physically abusive, *even* to the point of murdering spouse and children—the unthinkable.

The truth of a marriage is known only to God. A husband or a wife can use his or her personality to present a front to the world. Yet within the heart, there can be such a hardness toward a spouse, such an unwillingness to be truly united together, that God just cannot join them together as one flesh. Hardness, very simply, wrecks a marriage. It wrecks a marriage by causing a person to turn away and separate from his or her spouse. If a spouse is not with the other spouse, then the two are separate, not truly united and joined together. There can be no true union if there are not *two* persons together; and as pointed out earlier, being united is the blessing and gift of God. Being united is only possible as each allows God to "join them together."

7 (19:10-11) **Marriage**: there is the supernatural power needed for marriage. The disciples were shocked, for Jesus was saying that divorce is not God's will: "It was not this way from the beginning," that is, not intended by God (v.8). Thus the disciples exclaimed: "It is better not to marry"—one can be caught in a bad situation.

"Jesus replied, 'Not everyone can accept this word, but only those to whom it has been given'" (v.11); that is, only a God-given power can make a marriage what it should be so that a person will not want out. It is necessary for God to be in the center of a marriage. God has to join the two together. (See outline and notes—Eph.5:22-24; 5:25-33.)

Thought 1. Men rebel at the strictness of Christ in marriage. The disciples rebelled to such an extent that they were ready to say that it is better not to marry. But note: they, as so many, had not yet grasped what Christ was saying. Marriage is to be a spiritual union joined together by God. It is to be a union ever so precious, tender, warm, supportive, meaningful, and significant—a union seldom heard of and known in experience, even among believers.

Thought 2. How many can truly *be united*, submitting wholly (100%, not 50-50). How many can truly love the other completely as oneself? Not everyone can receive this saying. Only they who will surrender to one another *under God* can receive a true marriage, a true joining together from God. It is not a matter of not marrying. It is a matter of obeying God and living as He wills.

Thought 3. There is *death to self* required in marriage in order to *be united* and to be *one flesh*. But there are also the blessings of *a new life*, the glory and excitement of two persons' living as *one flesh* and being joined together in all of life.

DEEPER STUDY # 6

(19:11) **Marriage, Essentials**: "Not everyone can accept this word." What word?

1. The word that a man and wife are "to be united to one another." They are to be (1) totally united together as *one flesh*: "So they are no longer two, but one" (v.5-6).

2. The word that it is God and God alone who can *join together* a man and a wife (v.6; cp. DEEPER STUDY # 2—Mt.19:5).

These two things, being united together and God Himself, are the two essentials for a true marriage. Many are living together who refuse *to be united* and refuse to let God join them together. They are not willing to be united, nor are they willing to let God make them as *one flesh*. They are not willing to let God join them together.

(Note: man and woman can only unite and join themselves together physically. God is not needed for a purely physical union. If a married couple wishes more than a physical union, they must turn to God. He alone can "join together" a couple spiritually.)

8 (19:12) **Marriage—Eunuchs**: there is the highest ideal in marriage—total devotion to God's Kingdom. The very highest ideal for a man is total concentration upon God and His Kingdom (cp. 1 Cor.7:1f). This is so whether a person is married or not married. Christ was not downgrading marriage nor was He saying that being unmarried is preferable to being married. He was simply answering the disciples' question, "Yes, some men have chosen not to marry and chosen to be eunuchs. Some are born eunuchs; others are enslaved and made eunuchs; and still others choose to devote themselves only to the Kingdom of Heaven." Then He said the very same thing He said in v.11, "Whoever is able to accept this word [be a eunuch], accept it." Christ spoke first to the married; then in answer to the disciples He spoke to the unmarried:

⇒ To the married, He said that it takes God in a person's life for the person to receive a true marriage, to be united and be joined together with a spouse (see DEEPER STUDY # 6—Mt.19:11).

⇒ To the unmarried, He said that it takes God to be a eunuch, to dedicate one's life to the Kingdom of Heaven (v.12).

Thought 1. Some can live more for God if they remain single. They should, therefore, commit themselves to remain single (see note—1 Cor.7:1).

Thought 2. Some choose to remain single in order to have the freedom to live lustful, sensual lives. Christ deals with sexual sins in other passages. He is not condoning such here by approving the single life. The single state is to be chosen for the purpose of serving God more diligently, and it is to be chosen for that purpose only.

	B. The Acceptance of Children 19:13-15 (Mk.10:13-16;Lk.18:15-17)
1 Children were brought for Jesus to touch & pray for **2 Parents cared & believed: Brought their children** **3 The disciples rebuked the parents: Jesus too busy**	13 Then little children were brought to Jesus for him to place his hands on them and pray for them. But the disciples rebuked those who brought them.
4 Jesus rebuked those who disregarded the children a. He received the children b. He said the Kingdom of Heaven belonged to children c. He touched the children	14 Jesus said, "Let the little children come to me, and do not hinder them, for the kingdom of heaven belongs to such as these." 15 When he had placed his hands on them, he went on from there.

DIVISION XIII

THE MESSIAH'S TEACHINGS ON THE WAY TO JERUSALEM, 19:1-20:34

B. The Acceptance of Children, 19:13-15

(19:13-15) **Introduction**: children are very dear to God. People in Jesus' day considered children to be insignificant and unimportant. It was this that Jesus was combating in this experience. Children are as important as any other persons to God, and they are not to be disregarded or discouraged from coming to God. They are to be welcomed and accepted with open arms.

1. Children were brought for Jesus to touch and to pray for (v.13).
2. Parents cared and believed: they brought their children to Jesus (v.13).
3. The disciples rebuked the parents: they felt that Jesus was too busy and that the children were too unimportant (v.13).
4. Jesus rebuked those who disregarded the children (v.14-15).

1 (19:13) **Children—Parents**: children were brought to Jesus for Him to touch and to pray for. Note four facts about the little children.

1. The children were so little that they had to be brought to Jesus. Luke called them *babies* (Lk.18:15).

2 The children were brought for Jesus to touch and to pray for. This was the purpose for their being brought to Him. The laying on of hands was a symbol of special blessing and dedication (Gen.48:14; Num.27:23). It demonstrated a belief in God, in His love and power to bless. Therefore, the laying on of hands during special moments has always been very meaningful to God's people.

3. The children were brought despite threatening opposition. At this particular time, Jesus was being greatly opposed by the religious and political leaders. They were seeking to kill Jesus (Mt.12:14; see note—Mt.12:7; note and DEEPER STUDY # 1—12:10). The parents knew this, but they still wanted Jesus to bless their children. His blessing was so important to the parents that they brought their children to Him despite the danger.

> **Their children, who do not know this law, must hear it and learn to fear the LORD your God as long as you live in the land you are crossing the Jordan to possess." (Deu 31:13)**

4. The children were too young to understand what was happening. They knew nothing about the importance of being blessed by Christ, but their age made no difference. They were brought to Him anyway.

> **Fathers, do not exasperate your children; instead, bring them up in the training and instruction of the Lord. (Eph 6:4)**
> **Impress them on your children. Talk about them when you sit at home and when you walk along the road, when you lie down and when you get up. (Deu 6:7)**
> **Train a child in the way he should go, and when he is old he will not turn from it. (Prov 22:6)**

Thought 1. Think of the children who are not brought to Christ. The result is tragic: they never come to know Christ and the life and security He brings to the human heart.

Thought 2. The benefits of bringing children to Christ are innumerable. Just a few major ones are as follows.

1) A child who is brought to Christ grows up learning love: that he is loved by God and by all who trust God. He matures year by year knowing that no matter how evil some people may act, he is to love even those who do wrong. He learns that he is to help sow the seed of love upon earth.
2) A child who is brought to Christ grows up learning power and triumph: that God will help His followers through all; that there is a supernatural power available to help, a power to help when mother and dad and loved ones have done all they can.
3) A child who is brought to Christ grows up learning hope and faith: that no matter what happens, no matter how great a trial, he can still trust God and hope in Him. God has provided a very special

strength to carry him through the trials of this life (no matter how painful). God has provided a very special place called heaven where He will carry him and his loved ones when he faces death.

4) A child who is brought to Christ grows up learning the truth of life and endurance (service): that God has given him the privilege of life and of living in a beautiful earth and universe; that the evil and bad which exist in the world are caused by evil and bad people; that despite such evil, he is to serve in appreciation for life and for the beautiful earth upon which God has placed him. He is to work and work diligently, making the greatest contribution he can.

5) A child who is brought to Christ grows up learning trust and endurance: that life is full of temptations and pitfalls which can easily rob him of joy and destroy his life and the fulfillment of his purposes; that the way to escape the temptations and pitfalls is to follow Christ and endure in his work and purpose.

6) A child who is brought to Christ grows up learning peace: that there is an inner peace despite the turbulent waters of this world; that peace is knowing and trusting Christ.

2 (19:13) **Parents—Children**: the parents cared for their children, and they believed Jesus could help them. Therefore, they brought their children to Jesus. Note three facts about the parents.

1. The parents cared for their children, cared enough that they wanted the very best for them. Jesus Christ was claiming to be the Messiah, the very Son of God; so they wanted their children to be blessed by Him instead of an ordinary religious leader.

2. The parents believed in Jesus, in His love and power to bless. They believed that Jesus' blessing was meaningful to their children—very, very meaningful. They also believed that He cared and loved enough that He would bless them.

3. The parents' concern for their children was strong and persistent. They brought their children to Jesus despite strong religious opposition and despite the disciples' public rebuke (see note—Mt.12:7; note and DEEPER STUDY # 1—12:10). They did not turn around and leave. They were determined to have their children blessed by Jesus.

Thought 1. Life is given by God, so children belong to God. In a very special sense, children are *bundles of trust* that God puts into the care of parents for a short time. Parents are *the trustees* of God's property, of the little lives that God has given. Parents are responsible for caring enough to trust God's power and blessing for their children.

Thought 2. Children should be presented to God as "living sacrifices" for His care and purposes.

Therefore, I urge you, brothers, in view of God's mercy, to offer your bodies as living sacrifices, holy and pleasing to God—this is your spiritual act of worship. Do not conform any longer to the pattern of this world, but be transformed by the renewing of your mind. Then you will be able to test and approve what God's will is—his good, pleasing and perfect will. (Rom 12:1-2)

Thought 3. Most parents have *the true love of a parent* for their children. The greatest gift of love they can show is to bring their children to Christ. They should also seek to bring other children to Christ.

Thought 4. There are several reasons why parents do not bring their children to Christ.

1) Some parents (in civilized as well as uncivilized parts of the world) are not aware of the only living and true God. Therefore, they are blind; they just do not know. Christians have failed to take the gospel to the whole world.
2) Some parents have heard the truth, but they have rejected Christ. They are agnostics or atheists or else they love the world and the things of the world more than they love the news of the living God who gives eternal life. They do not care about anything beyond comfort of self and the benefits of this world.
3) Some parents believe, at least mentally, but they are complacent and lethargic. They are not concerned enough to make the effort to come to Christ nor to bring their children to Christ.
4) Some parents are believers; but, unfortunately, they are immature and inconsistent in their religious lives. Their own Christian lives and worship are weak and neglected, sometimes up and sometimes down. Their children are thereby taught that Christ is not really all that important.
5) Some parents are liberal-minded. They are not willing to influence and mold their children's thinking spiritually. They want their children to make their own choices. They are willing to teach them what foods to eat and books to read, anything that will teach them how to care for themselves physically, but they leave the care of the spiritual up to them after they become adults.

Thought 5. There are two great errors committed by parents who do not bring their children to Christ.

1) Any parent who does not bring his child to Christ is following a false philosophy of life and reality.

And without faith it is impossible to please God, because anyone who comes to him must believe that he exists and that he rewards those who earnestly seek him. (Heb 11:6)

Jesus answered, "I am the way and the truth and the life. No one comes to the Father except through me. (John 14:6)

For there is one God and one mediator between God and men, the man Christ Jesus, (1 Tim 2:5)

2) A child's mind is molded by those with whom he associates. His mind is either molded by the loose and immoral or the disciplined and moral. If the child's mind is not molded by *godly parents*, it will be molded by the world and its selfish and corrupt ways.

3 (19:13) **Parents—Disciples**: the disciples rebuked the parents. Note several facts about the disciples.

1. The disciples thought they knew the mind of Christ. They were good men, and they were leaders among the followers of Christ. But they did not know the mind of Christ, not in this instance. They did not fully understand

the ways of God, but they were acting as though they did. They were determining who could and who could not approach to be blessed by Christ.

2. The disciples rebuked the parents for bringing the children to Jesus. There are several possible reasons for their action.

a. The parents' frivolous pride over their children. The disciples may have thought the parents just wanted to show off their children and have Jesus make over them.

b. A misunderstanding about the importance of children. The disciples may have thought the children were just not important or significant enough to merit the attention of so important a person as Jesus. He was just too busy, and His work was too important to be interrupted by those who really did not need Him.

c. An immature concept of the blessing and power of God. By rebuking the parents, the disciples definitely showed they were guilty of this. To them blessing and praying for little children were not important enough to merit the attention of Jesus. They could not understand how small infants, who were not yet old enough to believe, could receive any good from being blessed by Christ.

Thought 1. There are two attitudes toward children that are critical mistakes, both of which are sometimes adopted by parents and society.

1) There is the attitude that children are not as important as adults. They are, therefore, often neglected, ignored, bypassed, and pushed aside without much attention or training. Such, of course, leads to a *squashed*, weak personality, making the child shy, and instilling a sense of inferiority. To say that children are as important as adults does not mean that they are to be given the rights of an adult. Such would only indulge and pamper the child. But it does mean that they are to be treated as *real persons* with needs and rights—the needs and rights of a child, not of an adult.

2) There is the attitude that children are to be unrestrained and allowed to develop their own desires, urges, wills and personalities. The feeling is that few, if any, restrictions should be placed upon children. They are to have what they desire and go without nothing. Such an attitude, of course, leads to an indulged, pampered, and selfish personality. (See note—Eph.6:4.)

Thought 2. Children's questions about Jesus are often ignored or quickly and unthoughtfully answered. They are considered too young and too unimportant to merit much of our time. No one should ever be stopped from coming to Christ, no matter who they may be.

Thought 3. Too many *important persons* are unavailable to the small and less important persons of the world. The time of the *important* person is thought to be too valuable. There is some truth to this. Many of the less important could dominate the time of the more important to such an extent that the more important would not have time to function. But the demand of the important to be left alone is often a selfish and sinful demand.

4 (19:14-15) **Children**: Jesus rebuked those who stopped and disregarded the children. Note several things about Jesus.

1. Jesus rebuked those who stopped and disregarded the children. He said that such action was wrong. We are not to stop little children from coming to Him. Contrariwise, we are to bring them to Him. He is God; and as God, He is providential, doing as He wills. Therefore, He is the One who determines whom He will bless. No man determines for Him. No matter the tender age and lack of reason, children are not to be kept from coming to Him. No obstacle is to be put in their way.

2. Jesus called for and received the children. Children were welcomed even if they were so little they had to be brought. Children may be too little to understand, but Christ is big enough to bless them and to see that the blessing sticks all through eternity. He is, after all, God; and as God, He is omnipotent, all-powerful, and able to exercise His power as He wills. Children will in no way be rejected by Him.

3. Jesus said that the Kingdom of Heaven belongs to children. He was saying two things.

a. Children are citizens of His kingdom, at least until their minds mature enough to personally choose or reject Him. Such a time is usually referred to as the *age of accountability*.

b. Children demonstrate the traits needed to enter heaven (see outline and notes—Mt.18:3. This passage will help greatly in understanding just what Christ was saying.)

4. Jesus touched the children. He was not influenced by the objections. He went ahead and blessed the children. There is a great truth here that we often overlook. It is not so much that we come and touch God as it is that He comes and touches us. It is not so much that we apprehend God as it is that we are apprehended by Him (Ph.3:12-13).

> **Yet to all who received him, to those who believed in his name, he gave the right to become children of God— children born not of natural descent, nor of human decision or a husband's will, but born of God. (John 1:12-13)**

God's blessing is not so much due to how rational and capable we are as to His purpose and will. God can choose to touch and bless whom He wills, and He demonstrates beyond all question that He chooses to touch and bless the children brought to Him.

> **Jesus said, "Let the little children come to me, and do not hinder them, for the kingdom of heaven belongs to such as these." (Mat 19:14)**
>
> **Like arrows in the hands of a warrior are sons born in one's youth. Blessed is the man whose quiver is full of them. They will not be put to shame when they contend with their enemies in the gate. (Psa 127:4-5)**
>
> **Your wife will be like a fruitful vine within your house; your sons will be like olive shoots around your table. (Psa 128:3)**
>
> **Children's children are a crown to the aged, and parents are the pride of their children. (Prov 17:6)**

Thought 1. Jesus never refused to receive a person. We are…

- not to be too important to receive people.
- not to be too busy or tired to receive people.
- not to regard a person as too young or too old to receive.
- not to be unavailable to people.

	C. The Rich Young Ruler: How A Rich Man Enters the Kingdom of Heaven[DS1] **19:16-22** (Mk.10:17-22; Lk.18:18-23; cp. Lk.10:25-37)	inquired. Jesus replied, "'Do not murder, do not commit adultery, do not steal, do not give false testimony,	**commandments**
			a. The commandments dealing with our neighbor: Especially needed by the rulers & the rich of the world
		19 Honor your father and mother,' and 'love your neighbor as yourself.'"	
		20 "All these I have kept," the young man said. "What do I still lack?"	b. The wrong concept of God's law: A tragic sense of self-righteousness
1 **Step 1: Seek eternal life**[DS2]	16 Now a man came up to Jesus and asked, "Teacher, what good thing must I do to get eternal life?"		
a. Approach Christ			
b. Confess your need			
		21 Jesus answered, "If you want to be perfect, go, sell your possessions and give to the poor, and you will have treasure in heaven. Then come, follow me."	4 **Step 4: Give all you are & have to Christ**
			a. Results: We receive heaven & treasures in heaven
2 **Step 2: Know that God alone is good**	17 "Why do you ask me about what is good?" Jesus replied. "There is only One who is good. If you want to enter life, obey the commandments."		
a. The wrong concept of man's nature: Man is *good*			
b. The right concept: God alone is good		22 When the young man heard this, he went away sad, because he had great wealth.	b. Rejection
			1) Unbelief, v.17
			2) Self-righteousness, v.20
3 **Step 3: Obey the**	18 "Which ones?" the man		3) Love of world, v.21

DIVISION XIII

THE MESSIAH'S TEACHINGS ON THE WAY TO JERUSALEM, 19:1-20:34

C. The Rich Young Ruler: How a Rich Man Enters the Kingdom of Heaven, 19:16-22

(19:16-22) **Introduction**: the Lord's approach to this young man has often seemed perplexing. There are two reasons for the perplexity.

1. The young man asked how he might receive eternal life. Christ said nothing about believing but told the young man to keep certain laws.
2. The second perplexity is shocking. Christ told the young man that he had to sell all that he had and give it to the poor in order to receive eternal life. The question immediately arises, does Christ really demand that a person give all he is and has in order to be saved?

These three facts are puzzling. However, when we study the passage and understand what was happening, the puzzle fades. Christ led the young man through the steps that are needed to receive eternal life.

1. Step 1: seek eternal life (v.16).
2. Step 2: know that God alone is good (v.17).
3. Step 3: obey the commandments (v.18-20).
4. Step 4: give all you are and have to Christ (v.21-22).

DEEPER STUDY # 1

(19:16-22) **Young People**: this man is known as "the rich young ruler." He is so called because of the composite picture gleaned from all three gospels.

⇒ He was rich (Mt.19:22; Mk.10:22; Lk.18:23).
⇒ He was young (Mt.19:20).
⇒ He was a ruler (Lk.18:18).

He was a rare young man among the young people of his day. He was conscientious, responsible, dependable—so much so that he had already been placed in a responsible position and made a ruler.

1 (19:16) **Eternal Life**: the first step to entering God's kingdom is to seek eternal life. The rich young ruler demonstrated how we should seek eternal life. He did exactly what we must do when we wish anything: seek it. We are to seek eternal life just as the rich young ruler did. But in seeking, there is a critical step to be taken: we must go to the right source. This is exactly what the rich young ruler did: (a) he approached Christ, the Source of eternal life; and (b) he asked, that is, confessed his need.

Note two things about the rich young ruler's seeking eternal life.

1. He believed that eternal life existed, that there was a thing such as eternal life. He believed there was life in another world, and he was sincere and eager (perhaps desperate) to receive it. He "ran and fell on his knees" before Jesus (Mk.10:17).
2. He did a rare thing. He openly confessed his eager concern for eternal life. Few of the rich would ever confess an open concern as he did, and few of the young would ever consider it important enough at their stage of life. He lacked and had need, and he knew it and confessed it openly. He was seeking for inner peace and a sense of completeness, for a satisfaction which his wealth and position had not given him.

Thought 1. Note: a person does not secure eternal life; he receives it. And…

1) A man does not receive eternal life until he seeks it.

God did this so that men would seek him and perhaps reach out for him and find him, though he is not far from each one of us. (Acts 17:27)

Look to the LORD and his strength; seek his face always. (1 Chr 16:11)

The LORD is close to the brokenhearted and saves those who are crushed in spirit. (Psa 34:18)

For the director of music. To the tune of "Do Not Destroy." Of David. A miktam. When he had fled from Saul into the cave. Have mercy on me, O God, have mercy on me, for in you my soul takes refuge. I will

take refuge in the shadow of your wings until the disaster has passed. (Psa 57:1)

Look to the LORD and his strength; seek his face always. (Psa 105:4)

The LORD is near to all who call on him, to all who call on him in truth. (Psa 145:18)

Seek the LORD while he may be found; call on him while he is near. (Isa 55:6)

2) A man does not receive eternal life until he approaches Christ, the Source of life.

"Come to me, all you who are weary and burdened, and I will give you rest. (Mat 11:28)

The Spirit and the bride say, "Come!" And let him who hears say, "Come!" Whoever is thirsty, let him come; and whoever wishes, let him take the free gift of the water of life. (Rev 22:17)

"Come now, let us reason together," says the LORD. "Though your sins are like scarlet, they shall be as white as snow; though they are red as crimson, they shall be like wool. (Isa 1:18)

"Come, all you who are thirsty, come to the waters; and you who have no money, come, buy and eat! Come, buy wine and milk without money and without cost. (Isa 55:1)

3) A man does not receive eternal life until he confesses his need.

"Whoever acknowledges me before men, I will also acknowledge him before my Father in heaven. (Mat 10:32)

"I tell you, whoever acknowledges me before men, the Son of Man will also acknowledge him before the angels of God. (Luke 12:8)

That if you confess with your mouth, "Jesus is Lord," and believe in your heart that God raised him from the dead, you will be saved. (Rom 10:9)

No one who denies the Son has the Father; whoever acknowledges the Son has the Father also. (1 John 2:23)

If anyone acknowledges that Jesus is the Son of God, God lives in him and he in God. (1 John 4:15)

DEEPER STUDY # 2

(19:16) **Eternal Life**: note the different words that are used interchangeably throughout this passage. (Also see DEEPER STUDY # 3—Mt.19:23-24; DEEPER STUDY # 1—Jn.17:2-3; cp. DEEPER STUDY # 2—Jn.1:4; DEEPER STUDY # 1—10:10.)

⇒ Eternal life: "What good thing must I do to get eternal life" (v.16).

⇒ Life: "If you want to enter life" (v.17).

⇒ Heaven: "You will have treasure in heaven" (v.21).

The way Christ dealt with the subjects of eternal life, life, and heaven is meaningful. In essence, what He was saying is threefold.

1. He was making a distinction between life and existence. To receive eternal life is to enter life; to really live as one should live; to live just as God intended life to be lived; to live full of love, joy, and peace (Gal.5:22-23). He was saying what Scripture proclaims time and again—that man without Christ does not have life. He is not living; he is only existing. He is in a state of death (always dying) and is separated from God, the Source of real life (Eph.2:1; 1 Jn.5:12).

2. He was teaching eternal existence. Man does not cease to be; he continues on and on. The only question is, does he continue on in a state of life, living eternally, or of death, being separated from God eternally? To receive eternal life means that a man "enters life," a continuation of life. To remain as he is means that a person continues on just existing, existing in a state of death, that is, being without God in this world and existing without eternal life (see DEEPER STUDY # 1–Heb.9:27).

3. He was teaching that heaven is another world—a real world in another dimension of being, an eternal dimension. It is wholly different from the physical and temporal dimension of this world. Note: there is to be "treasure in heaven" for following Christ, eternal treasure.

2 (19:17) **Man, Misconceptions of**: the second step to entering God's kingdom is to know that God alone is good. The rich young ruler failed at one critical point: he lived a self-righteous life. He did not know that the only good person was God and God alone. This is what Christ was saying to him. The rich young ruler had a wrong concept about the nature of man and saw Christ only as a man. To him man could be good.

1. He called Jesus "Teacher." By "teacher" he meant "Master, Rabbi," acknowledging that Jesus was an honorable person to be highly regarded. But he saw Jesus only as a highly regarded teacher. He did not consider Jesus to be the Son of God. He perceived Jesus to be only a mere man, not God. He thought Jesus was a man who had achieved unusual moral goodness and by such had become a teacher capable of teaching the truths of God and life.

2. He asked, "What good thing must I do?" He had a religion of works not of faith. He thought he could secure eternal life by being good. If he could just keep some great rule and live a clean life, then God would accept him. He believed that his acts of morality and good works piled up a balance sheet, making him acceptable to God.

Christ had to correct these two errors. He attempted to do so by asking a pointed question, "Why do you ask me about what is good?...There is only One who is good." He was saying to the young man, "God alone is good. No man is good, not in comparison to God, not even good enough to stand before God in righteousness. If I am but a mere man, a good teacher, then I am not good and do not have the words to eternal life. But if I am God, then you can address me as good, and I do have the words to eternal life."

Note two things.

1. Christ told the young man how to enter life, that is, how to receive eternal life. Therefore, Christ was claiming to be God.

2. Christ was correcting the young man. He was speaking these words forcefully: "Why do you ask me about what is good? There is only One who is good". Christ would not have the young man's thinking of Him only as a man, no matter how preeminent a teacher the young man thought Him to be. He was God, God's very own Son, and He was to be called the Son of God. Therefore, Christ tried to lead the young man to

acknowledge Him as God. It was the only way the young man could ever receive eternal life.

> **"For God so loved the world that he gave his one and only Son, that whoever believes in him shall not perish but have eternal life. (John 3:16)**
> **Jesus answered, "I am the way and the truth and the life. No one comes to the Father except through me. If you really knew me, you would know my Father as well. From now on, you do know him and have seen him." (John 14:6-7)**
> **That if you confess with your mouth, "Jesus is Lord," and believe in your heart that God raised him from the dead, you will be saved. For it is with your heart that you believe and are justified, and it is with your mouth that you confess and are saved. (Rom 10:9-10)**
> **For, "Everyone who calls on the name of the Lord will be saved." (Rom 10:13)**
> **For there is one God and one mediator between God and men, the man Christ Jesus, (1 Tim 2:5)**

Thought 1. The great misconception of man is that man is good—that the basic core and the raw nature of man is good—that man…

- can be good enough to secure God's approval.
- can do enough good works to make himself acceptable to God.

There are at least two basic faults with the position of self-righteousness.

1) Self-righteousness lowers God, makes God less than perfect. It says that God will accept less than perfection. It almost makes man as high as God. In fact, theoretically and mathematically, if we can become better, gain more goodness, then we can work ourselves up to perfection. It says we can become as high as God, become as gods unto ourselves. Of course, such a theory or position is foolish. It fails to face up to the reality of the world, to the presence of evil and death and to the need to be transformed into a new creature capable of living eternally and perfectly.
2) Self-righteousness pollutes the area surrounding God with evil and imperfection. No matter how much good we do, we cannot make ourselves perfect. Bad and evil always lie in our background and roots. If God accepted us as bad and evil and wrong, then we would stand on the ground before Him imperfect, contaminating that ground and the atmosphere surrounding Him. Heaven would be contaminated and imperfect. Heaven would no longer be heaven, no longer perfect and free of sin.

There has to be a change, a complete and thorough change, of our being—a transformation, a new birth—before we can enter God's presence. Realistically, no man nor anything else can transform man so that his body becomes perfect and his acts become only good. No man has or ever will have the power to perfect his body and behavior to live perfectly, permanently and eternally. In our present bodies, we come short of God's glory and we die (Ro.3:23; 5:12; 6:23).

If we are going to be transformed, then God Himself will have to do it, and He will have to do it out of pure and perfect love. He will simply have to love us so much that he will transform us. And the glorious news is that He does love us that much. He loves us so much…

- that He gave His only Son to pay the penalty for our sins, which is death (1 Pt.2:24. This means, of course, that if the penalty has been paid, then we do not have to die.)
- that He gave His only Son to show us His great love and to lead us to believe in His love (Jn.5:24. This means, of course, that if we believe, then God will accept us and transform us.)

Thought 2. God alone is perfectly good. He is the Fountain, the Pattern, the Ideal of all goodness. All goodness is to be measured by Him.

The problem with the rich young ruler was that he had not thought deeply enough. His thinking was shallow. How could he ever measure up enough to become acceptable to God? Is God so low? If so, if God is less than perfect, then how could He be God?

Thought 3. Self-righteousness (a person who thinks that he can be good enough and do enough good to make God accept him) commits a terrible fault. It makes God's love less than perfect. How?

The person who walks in self-righteousness waters down God's love; he makes God's love less than perfect and disallows God the right to express His love perfectly.

⇒ A perfect love must express itself perfectly: it must, from its height of perfection, reach down to the lowest depth of imperfection and give itself for that imperfection. A perfect love reaches from the highest height to the lowest depth. And the lowest depth of imperfection is man, a being who (of all things) rebels against God Himself and lives a self-willed life instead of a God-centered life. (Just picture the terrible scene: a being, a man rebelling against the God of the universe, the Creator and Lord of all things.)

This is exactly what God did for man. He reached down from the highest height and gave His only Son, the highest and most perfect Being, for man who had reached the lowest depth in rebelling against God (Jn.3:16; 2 Cor.5:21; 1 Pt.2:24).

Thought 4. The rich young ruler failed in two areas.

1) He failed to face the reality of man's nature and the way of an imperfect world (Ro.3:10-20).
2) He failed to understand that Christ was more than a great and good man (see note—Mt.19:17).

3 (19:18-20) **Law—Commandments—Brotherhood**: the third step to entering God's kingdom is to obey the commandments. Once Christ had led the young man to trust Him as God, then Christ had to lead him to love his neighbor. This, too, was a critical weakness in the man. Because of his low concept of God and his inaccurate concept of man's nature, he would claim that he had loved his neighbor; that he had kept the commandments dealing with his neighbor. But Christ would prove that he had not loved his neighbor, not as he should. He had kept the commandments only in a superficial sense. He had not kept them within, not in his spirit. He had not loved his neighbor from the heart. If he had, he would have helped his neighbor more, much more (cp. v.21-22).

Christ told the young man very simply, "Obey the commandments." The young man asked, "Which ones?" By asking, the man revealed an inadequate concept of God's law. He thought some were more important than others. He wanted to know which ones would give him life.

Christ struck at the man's real problem. The man was failing to love his neighbor as himself, so Christ quoted five of the ten commandments, five that have to do with his duty toward his neighbor (Ex.20:12-16).

1. Murder: concerns our neighbor's life.

2. Adultery: concerns our neighbor's chastity and purity. To commit adultery does two things.

- ⇒ Adultery takes the body of our neighbor to ourselves and gives our body to another.
- ⇒ Adultery takes the body of our neighbor's spouse away from our neighbor and takes our own body away from our spouse.

3. Stealing: concerns our neighbor's property.

4. False witness: concerns our neighbor's name, reputation, and understanding of the truth.

5. Honoring parents: concerns our duty to the closest neighbors we have, our own family.

Note: Christ summed up all five commandments by saying, "Love your neighbor as yourself" (Lev.19:18). This is what James called the "royal law" (Jas.2:8). The person who loves his neighbor will have excellent relations with all and will experience love, joy, and peace—the abundance of life. He will experience exactly what Christ says: he will "enter life."

The man made the phenomenal claim that he had obeyed all five of the commandments that Christ quoted. Of course, as is true with all men, he had not obeyed them—not perfectly, not in God's eyes, not in the spirit in which God intended them to be kept. He was not generous enough with others, not giving and helping like he should. Christ was ready to show him this.

In essence, Christ had said to the rich young ruler: obey the commandments.

1. Obey the commandments dealing with your neighbor: the ones especially needed by the rulers and the rich of the world—the commandments which are so often misunderstood and neglected by rulers and the rich.

2. However, the rich young ruler misunderstood God's law: he had a tragic sense of self-righteousness.

a. He thought that some commandments were more important than others.

b. He thought that man could obey the commandments and build up a balance sheet against God, securing God's acceptance.

> **Everyone who believes that Jesus is the Christ is born of God, and everyone who loves the father loves his child as well.**
>
> **This is how we know that we love the children of God: by loving God and carrying out his commands. (1 John 5:1-2)**

Thought 1. Note two extremely important facts.

1) The first thing Jesus told the young man was the very commandment of God.

> **And this is his command: to believe in the name of his Son, Jesus Christ, and to love one another as he commanded us. (1 John 3:23)**

2) Christ summed up the law in two commandments. The first has to do with our love for God which sums up the first five commandments, and the second is the one He used to sum up the second group of commandments which He quoted to this young man.

> **And the second is like it: 'Love your neighbor as yourself.' (Mat 22:39)**

Thought 2. Note that the very commandments quoted by Christ are the commandments needed by the rich, the powerful, the famous, and the wise. They are the commandments so often ignored, neglected, and denied by the achiever. In fact, the achiever sometimes uses and steps upon his neighbor to secure what he seeks.

4 (19:21-22) **Self-Denial**: the fourth step to enter God's kingdom is to give all you are and have to Christ. Christ knew exactly what the young man needed. His rejection of Christ showed this. He was hoarding wealth instead of distributing it. God had given to him that he might have to give to others (Eph.4:28), but he was failing to love and help his neighbor anywhere close to what he should.

What the young man needed was just what Christ said: "If you want to be perfect [that is, really obey the commandments and receive heaven], then demonstrate to all publicly and without question that you love your neighbor: go and sell your possessions...and give to the poor...then come follow me."

In our struggle to protect the glorious truth that man is saved by grace and grace alone, we often forget and neglect another great truth: to follow Christ is to serve and minister to our neighbor. To follow Christ is to deny self completely, all that we are as well as all that we have (see note and DEEPER STUDY # 1—Lk.9:23). When we love our neighbor as ourselves, then we show that we truly love God. If we do not love and minister to our neighbor (above self), then we do not love God.

When we deny self by giving all we are and have (1 Jn.4:20), then and only then do we receive heaven and the treasures of heaven. To deny self, to give all we are and have, is a hard saying; but Christ demands it. Our attempts to soften it do not annul His demand (see note and DEEPER STUDY # 1—Lk.9:23; DEEPER STUDY # 1—Ro.3:3).

The young man rejected Christ for three reasons.

1. Unbelief: he was not willing to entrust his life to Christ. There was some lack of belief that Jesus Christ was really God's very own Son standing before him.

2. Self-righteousness and pride: his concept of religion was keeping laws and doing good in order to secure God's acceptance. He felt that he had the power and goodness to make God approve and accept him.

3. Love of the world: he was rich and was unwilling to give up the comfort and possessions he had obtained. He made the fatal mistake that so many make with wealth, power, and fame.

a. He loved the things of the world more than he loved people. He preferred hoarding and extravagance, preferred living sumptuously and comfortably to helping those who were so desperately in need: the hungry, thirsty, poor, diseased, suffering, orphans, widows, widowers, empty, lonely, and the lost.

b. He loved the things of the world more than he loved the hope of eternal life.

c. He loved the position and recognition and esteem and power of the earth more than he loved Christ.

Peter said to him, "We have left everything to follow you!" (Mark 10:28)

Then he said to them all: "If anyone would come after me, he must deny himself and take up his cross daily and follow me. (Luke 9:23)

"If anyone comes to me and does not hate his father and mother, his wife and children, his brothers and sisters—yes, even his own life—he cannot be my disciple. And anyone who does not carry his cross and follow me cannot be my disciple. (Luke 14:26-27)

In the same way, any of you who does not give up everything he has cannot be my disciple. (Luke 14:33)

	D. The Danger of Riches, 19:23-26	for a camel to go through the	**illustrated: It is easier**
	(Mk.10:23-27; Lk.	eye of a needle than for a rich	**for a camel to go thru the**
	18:24-27)	manto enter the kingdom of	**eye of a needle than for a**
		God."	**rich man to enter the**
		25 When the disciples heard	**Kingdom of God**
		this, they were greatly	**3 The shock: Who is saved**
1 The fact: Wealth pulls a	23 Then Jesus said to his	astonished and asked, "Who	**if wealth is not God's**
person from the K.[DS1,2,3]	disciples, "I tell you the truth,	then can be saved?"	**blessing & a blessing of**
a. Creates big "I," v.16,20	it is hard for a rich man to	26 Jesus looked at them	**righteousness?**
b. Makes one hoard, v.21	enter the kingdom of heav-	and said, "With man this	**4 The only hope for the rich**
c. Attaches to world, v.22	en.	is impossible, but with	a. To turn away from men
2 The great difficulty	24 Again I tell you, it is easier	God all things are possible."	b. To turn to God & His power[DS4]

DIVISION XIII

THE MESSIAH'S TEACHINGS ON THE WAY TO JERUSALEM, 19:1-20:34

D. The Danger of Riches, 19:23-26

(19:23-26) **Introduction**: the words "then Jesus said" connect this passage to the experience of the rich young ruler. Jesus took the rich young ruler's rejection and *warned* all men about the dangers of wealth. Wealth is fraught with dangers and pitfalls...

- for the man who is seeking to be rich.
- for the man who is already rich.

The dangers are many, and they are entangling and enslaving—so much so that Christ made the shocking statement that it was extremely difficult for a rich man to be saved.

The words are strong; the idea is shocking. However, Christ loves and cares for all men including the rich, so He had to be truthful. It is extremely difficult for a rich man to enter heaven. The dangers that face the rich are real and terrible, so the warning must be real and truthful.

1. The fact: wealth pulls a person from the Kingdom of Heaven (v.23).
2. The great difficulty illustrated: it is easier for a camel to go through the eye of a needle than for a rich man to enter the Kingdom of God (v.24).
3. The shock: who is saved if wealth is not God's blessing and a blessing of righteousness (v.25)?
4. The only hope for the rich (v.26).

1 (19:23) **Wealth—Materialism—Pride—Worldliness**: wealth pulls a person away from the Kingdom of Heaven. It is difficult for a rich person to enter heaven. Christ made this statement because of the things that *pulled* the rich young ruler away. Wealth does pull a person away from heaven. There is a lure, an attraction, a force, a power, a pull that reaches out to draw us when we look at or possess wealth. There are pulls so forceful that they will enslave and doom any rich man who fails to turn and embrace God.

1. *Wealth creates the big "I"* (cp. v.16, 20). The wealthy are usually esteemed, honored, and envied. Wealth brings comfort, possessions, position, power, and recognition. It boosts *ego* and makes a person self-sufficient and independent in this world. As a result, there is a tendency for the rich to feel independent and self-sufficient, to live as though they need nothing; and in such an atmosphere and world of thought, God is forgotten. A person forgets that there are things that money cannot buy and events from which money cannot save. Peace, love, joy—all that really matters within the spirit of man—can never be bought. Neither can money save a person from trouble, disaster, disease, accident, or death—the trials that are sure to come upon all.

2. *Wealth tends to make a person hoard* (cp. v.21). The Bible lays down the principle for handling money for all men, even for the poor:

> **He who has been stealing must steal no longer, but must work, doing something useful with his own hands, that he may have something to share with those in need. (Eph 4:28)**
>
> **Honor your father and mother,' and 'love your neighbor as yourself.'" (Mat 19:19; 22:39)**

The world reels in desperate need. People are starving, sick, unhoused, unclothed, and suffering by the millions; and teeming millions are spiritually lost and without God in this world and doomed to die without ever knowing Him. When any of us sit still and objectively look at the world in its desperate plight, we ask: "How in this world can any man hoard and not help—even to the last available penny? Why would any man keep more than what he needs for himself and his family?"

As God looks at the rich, He is bound to ask the same questions. In fact, His questions are bound to be more pointed and forceful. This is exactly what Christ said to the rich young ruler:

> **Jesus answered, "If you want to be perfect, go, sell your possessions and give to the poor, and you will have treasure in heaven. Then come, follow me." (Mat 19:21)**

3. *Riches tend to make a man selfish.* For some unexplainable reason, the more we get, the more we want. When we taste the things of this world and become comfortable, we tend to fear losing our possessions. We struggle to keep what we have and to get more. True, many are willing to make contributions—but only a certain amount, an amount that will not lower their overall estate, or standing, or level of comfort and possessions. There are few who give all they are and have to Christ in order to meet the needs of the world.

As Christ said, "It is difficult, very difficult for the rich [meaning those who have anything in comparison with most of the world] to enter heaven." If we do not have compassion and take care of our brothers (fellow-man) when they are in desperate need, how can we expect God to have compassion and take care of us when we face the desperate need for heaven? It is foolish for us to think that a loving and just God will meet our need for life when we would not meet the need of our fellow man for life. The rich (all of us who have anything in comparison with the rest of the world) have the means to help and to reach the world with the gospel if they just would.

4. *Wealth attaches a person to the world* (cp. v.22). Wealth enables a person to buy things that...

- make him comfortable
- please his taste
- stir his ego
- expand his experience
- challenge his mental pursuit
- stimulate his flesh
- stretch his self-image

If a man centers his life upon the things of the world, his attention is on the world and not on God. He tends to become wrapped up in securing more and in protecting what he has. Too often, he gives little if any time and thought to heavenly matters. Wealth and the things it can buy can and usually do consume the rich.

DEEPER STUDY # 1

(19:23) **Hard** (duskolos): the word means barely or with great difficulty. It is difficult, very difficult for a rich man to enter heaven. Why? In one simple sentence, it is difficult for a rich man to give all that he has to help the needy—to give all that has been so pleasing, so comfortable, so ego boosting, and so rewarding in possessions and position and self-esteem.

DEEPER STUDY # 2

(19:23) **Rich**: Who are the rich? This question desperately needs to be asked of every individual in light of the great and desperate needs of the world. Every one of us needs to compare what we have with what the vast majority of the world has. The rich are persons who have anything to put back beyond meeting the needs of their own family (and by needs is meant *real* needs). This is exactly what Christ and the Bible say time and again (cp. also Mk.12:41-44; Lk.21:1-4; Acts 4:34-35).

In a summary statement, who are the rich? The rich are any of us who have anything beyond what we need. What Christ demands is that we give all that we *are and have* to meet the needs of those in such desperate need, holding back nothing. This is often the great complaint against Christians, that we just do not believe, not to the point that we are willing to follow the sacrificial example of Christ. The evidence of our unbelief is seen in Christ's insistence that we give all we have to feed the starving and to meet the desperate needs of the world, and yet we do not do it. Gandhi, the great leader of India's independence, is said to have never embraced Christianity for this very reason. How many others have rejected Christ because of our hypocrisy?

Jesus answered, "If you want to be perfect, go, sell your possessions and give to the poor, and you will have treasure in heaven. Then come, follow me." (Mat 19:21)

And everyone who has left houses or brothers or sisters or father or mother or children or fields for my sake will receive a hundred times as much and will inherit eternal life. (Mat 19:29)

For where your treasure is, there your heart will be also. (Mat 6:21)

And the second is like it: 'Love your neighbor as yourself.' (Mat 22:39)

But seek his kingdom, and these things will be given to you as well. "Do not be afraid, little flock, for your Father has been pleased to give you the kingdom. Sell your possessions and give to the poor. Provide purses for yourselves that will not wear out, a treasure in heaven that will not be exhausted, where no thief comes near and no moth destroys. For where your treasure is, there your heart will be also. (Luke 12:31-34)

But Zacchaeus stood up and said to the Lord, "Look, Lord! Here and now I give half of my possessions to the poor, and if I have cheated anybody out of anything, I will pay back four times the amount." (Luke 19:8)

By this all men will know that you are my disciples, if you love one another." (John 13:35)

If you obey my commands, you will remain in my love, just as I have obeyed my Father's commands and remain in his love. (John 15:10)

Love must be sincere. Hate what is evil; cling to what is good. (Rom 12:9)

Even as I try to please everybody in every way. For I am not seeking my own good but the good of many, so that they may be saved. (1 Cor 10:33)

For you know the grace of our Lord Jesus Christ, that though he was rich, yet for your sakes he became poor, so that you through his poverty might become rich. (2 Cor 8:9)

He who has been stealing must steal no longer, but must work, doing something useful with his own hands, that he may have something to share with those in need. (Eph 4:28)

May the Lord make your love increase and overflow for each other and for everyone else, just as ours does for you. (1 Th 3:12)

Keep your lives free from the love of money and be content with what you have, because God has said, "Never will I leave you; never will I forsake you." (Heb 13:5)

DEEPER STUDY # 3

(19:23-24) **Kingdom of Heaven**: the Kingdom of Heaven evidently means the same thing as the Kingdom of God, eternal life, and salvation. The Kingdom of Heaven and the Kingdom of God are interchanged when Jesus says, "it is hard for a rich man to enter the Kingdom of Heaven" (Mt.19:23) or "Kingdom of God" (Mt.19:24). Eternal life

(Mt.19:26) and salvation (Mt.19:25) belong to the very same concept. Eternity and salvation, the Kingdom of God and the Kingdom of Heaven, is the very subject being discussed in Mt.19:16-30. Having eternal life, being saved, or entering into the Kingdom of God or of Heaven is more difficult for a rich man than for a camel to go through the eye of a needle.

The Kingdom of Heaven and of God is revealed in four different stages throughout history.

1. There is the spiritual kingdom that is at hand; it is present right now (Mt.4:17; 12:28).

a. The present kingdom refers to *God's rule and reign and authority in the lives of believers.*

> **I pray also that the eyes of your heart may be enlightened in order that you may know the hope to which he has called you, the riches of his glorious inheritance in the saints, and his incomparably great power for us who believe. That power is like the working of his mighty strength, which he exerted in Christ when he raised him from the dead and seated him at his right hand in the heavenly realms, far above all rule and authority, power and dominion, and every title that can be given, not only in the present age but also in the one to come. And God placed all things under his feet and appointed him to be head over everything for the church, which is his body, the fullness of him who fills everything in every way. (Eph 1:18-23)**
>
> **Your attitude should be the same as that of Christ Jesus: Who, being in very nature God, did not consider equality with God something to be grasped, but made himself nothing, taking the very nature of a servant, being made in human likeness. And being found in appearance as a man, he humbled himself and became obedient to death— even death on a cross! Therefore God exalted him to the highest place and gave him the name that is above every name, that at the name of Jesus every knee should bow, in heaven and on earth and under the earth, and every tongue confess that Jesus Christ is Lord, to the glory of God the Father. (Phil 2:5-11)**
>
> **For he has rescued us from the dominion of darkness and brought us into the kingdom of the Son he loves, (Col 1:13)**

b. The present kingdom is offered to the world and to men in the person of Jesus Christ.

c. The present kingdom must be received as a little child.

> **When Jesus saw this, he was indignant. He said to them, "Let the little children come to me, and do not hinder them, for the kingdom of God belongs to such as these. I tell you the truth, anyone who will not receive the kingdom of God like a little child will never enter it." (Mark 10:14-15)**

d. The present kingdom is experienced only by the new birth.

> **In reply Jesus declared, "I tell you the truth, no one can see the kingdom of God unless he is born again." (John 3:3)**

e. The present kingdom is entered now and must be received now.

> **"Which of the two did what his father wanted?" "The first," they answered. Jesus said to them, "I tell you the truth, the tax collectors and the prostitutes are entering the kingdom of God ahead of you. (Mat 21:31)**
>
> **I tell you the truth, anyone who will not receive the kingdom of God like a little child will never enter it." (Mark 10:15)**

f. The present kingdom is a spiritual, life-changing blessing.

> **For the kingdom of God is not a matter of eating and drinking, but of righteousness, peace and joy in the Holy Spirit, (Rom 14:17)**

g. The present kingdom is to be the first thing sought by believers.

> **But seek first his kingdom and his righteousness, and all these things will be given to you as well. (Mat 6:33)**

2. There is the professing kingdom that is also in this present age. It refers to modern-day Christianity in every generation. It pictures what the Kingdom of Heaven or professing Christianity is like and what professing Christianity will be like between Christ's first coming and His return. This imperfect state is what is called "the secrets of the kingdom of heaven" (Mt.13:1-52, esp.11).

> **Jesus told them another parable: "The kingdom of heaven is like a man who sowed good seed in his field. But while everyone was sleeping, his enemy came and sowed weeds among the wheat, and went away. (Mat 13:24-25)**

3. There is the millennial kingdom that is future. It is the actual rule of Christ or the government of Christ that is to come to this earth for a thousand years.

a. The millenial kingdom is the kingdom predicted by Daniel.

> **"In the time of those kings, the God of heaven will set up a kingdom that will never be destroyed, nor will it be left to another people. It will crush all those kingdoms and bring them to an end, but it will itself endure forever. (Dan 2:44)**
>
> **But the saints of the Most High will receive the kingdom and will possess it forever—yes, for ever and ever.' until the Ancient of Days came and pronounced judgment in favor of the saints of the Most High, and the time came when they possessed the kingdom. Then the sovereignty, power and greatness of the**

kingdoms under the whole heaven will be handed over to the saints, the people of the Most High. His kingdom will be an everlasting kingdom, and all rulers will worship and obey him.' (Dan 7:18, 22, 27)

b. The millenial kingdom is the kingdom promised to David.

When your days are over and you rest with your fathers, I will raise up your offspring to succeed you, who will come from your own body, and I will establish his kingdom. Your house and your kingdom will endure forever before me ; your throne will be established forever.'" (2 Sam 7:12, 16)

You said, "I have made a covenant with my chosen one, I have sworn to David my servant, 'I will establish your line forever and make your throne firm through all generations.'" Selah (Psa 89:3-4)

On that day the LORD will shield those who live in Jerusalem, so that the feeblest among them will be like David, and the house of David will be like God, like the Angel of the LORD going before them. (Zec 12:8)

c. The millenial kingdom is the kingdom pictured by John.

I saw thrones on which were seated those who had been given authority to judge. And I saw the souls of those who had been beheaded because of their testimony for Jesus and because of the word of God. They had not worshiped the beast or his image and had not received his mark on their foreheads or their hands. They came to life and reigned with Christ a thousand years. (The rest of the dead did not come to life until the thousand years were ended.) This is the first resurrection. Blessed and holy are those who have part in the first resurrection. The second death has no power over them, but they will be priests of God and of Christ and will reign with him for a thousand years. (Rev 20:4-6)

4. There is the perfect kingdom of the new heaven and earth that is future.

a. The eternal kingdom is the rule and reign of God in a perfect universe for all eternity.

"Do not let your hearts be troubled. Trust in God; trust also in me. In my Father's house are many rooms; if it were not so, I would have told you. I am going there to prepare a place for you. And if I go and prepare a place for you, I will come back and take you to be with me that you also may be where I am. (John 14:1-3)

Then the end will come, when he hands over the kingdom to God the Father after he has destroyed all dominion, authority and power. (1 Cor 15:24)

But the day of the Lord will come like a thief. The heavens will disappear with a roar; the elements will be destroyed by fire, and the earth and everything in it will be laid bare. Since everything will be destroyed in this way, what kind of people ought you to be? You ought to live holy and godly lives as you look forward to the day of God and speed its coming. That day will bring about the destruction of the heavens by fire, and the elements will melt in the heat. But in keeping with his promise we are looking forward to a new heaven and a new earth, the home of righteousness. (2 Pet 3:10-13)

Then I saw a new heaven and a new earth, for the first heaven and the first earth had passed away, and there was no longer any sea. (Rev 21:1)

b. The eternal kingdom is the perfect state of being for the believer in the future.

I declare to you, brothers, that flesh and blood cannot inherit the kingdom of God, nor does the perishable inherit the imperishable. (1 Cor 15:50)

He will wipe every tear from their eyes. There will be no more death or mourning or crying or pain, for the old order of things has passed away." He who was seated on the throne said, "I am making everything new!" Then he said, "Write this down, for these words are trustworthy and true." (Rev 21:4-5)

c. The eternal kingdom is an actual place into which believers are to enter sometime in the future.

I say to you that many will come from the east and the west, and will take their places at the feast with Abraham, Isaac and Jacob in the kingdom of heaven. (Mat 8:11)

d. The eternal kingdom is a gift of God that will be given in the future.

"Do not be afraid, little flock, for your Father has been pleased to give you the kingdom. (Luke 12:32)

2 (19:24) **Riches—Camel—Needle**: it is extremely difficult for a rich man to enter into the Kingdom of God. It is so difficult that Jesus says, "It is easier for a camel to go through the eye of a needle, than for a rich man to enter the kingdom of God."

There have been various interpretations of *camel* and *needle* in an attempt to soften the words of Jesus. For example, some have said that the "needle" was a small gate in the wall surrounding Jerusalem, a small gate which sat right beside the large gate. It is thought that the large gate was closed at night to protect the city from marauders and enemies, and the small gate was used by the travelling public. The small gate is said to have been called "the Needle's Eye" because it was so small that it was difficult for even a single person to pass through.

Others have said that the Greek word Christ used was *kamilos* (a ship's rope or cable) not *kamelos* (camel). Note:

the only difference between the two words is that the letter *i* is an *e* in the word for camel (kamelos).

Three things need to be noted about these interpreta-tions.

1. There is no doubt that Jesus means a literal *needle.* He as much as says so in v.26, "With man this is impossible." What He does is use a proverbial saying *for an impossibility.* Most countries have proverbs that express the impossibility of some things. The camel was the largest animal among the Jews, so Christ either used a well known proverb among the Jews or else created one. There is also this point, when Christ chose to speak in parables, He chose the most common and ordinary thing to express His meaning.

2. Attempts to soften the Lord's point are just that: attempts to soften. But nothing can be softened with v.26, "With man this is impossible." No man, not even the rich man himself, can save a rich man. The danger of riches is very real and terrible. Wealth entangles and enslaves a man so much that it is extremely difficult for a rich man to let go and give his wealth to help the desperate needs of the world. He just cannot accept the fact that he is to "work so that he may have to give to others" (Eph.4:28). If a man is rich, it is difficult not to live in personal luxury and to build large estates. Heavy and fancy meals, full and fashionable wardrobes, a fine and large house, recognition and attention, position and power—so much is so difficult to let go. It is the ego that refuses to let go.

3. It is just as difficult for the softening interpretations to be performed as it is for the literal interpretation. How does a camel's trying to get through a gate made only for a man soften anything? It would be impossible. And how does threading a needle with a ship's cable soften anything? Again, it is impossible.

Thought 1. In the illustration given by Christ, there are some comparisons between a camel and a rich man.

1) A camel is *too big* to go through the eye of a needle; a rich man is too big to go through the gate of heaven.

Command those who are rich in this present world not to be arrogant nor to put their hope in wealth, which is so uncertain, but to put their hope in God, who richly provides us with everything for our enjoyment. (1 Tim 6:17)

2) A camel *never thinks* about going through the eye of a needle; a rich man seldom, if ever, thinks about going into heaven.

And I'll say to myself, "You have plenty of good things laid up for many years. Take life easy; eat, drink and be merry." "But God said to him, 'You fool! This very night your life will be demanded from you. Then who will get what you have prepared for yourself?' (Luke 12:19-20)

The wealth of the rich is their fortified city; they imagine it an unscalable wall. (Prov 18:11)

And when your herds and flocks grow large and your silver and gold increase and all you have is multiplied, then your heart will become proud and you will forget the LORD your God, who brought you out of Egypt, out of the land of slavery. (Deu 8:13-14)

3) A camel was *not made* to go through the eye of a needle; a man was not made for wealth, not made to be possessed and enslaved by the *things* and *possessions* of this world.

But the worries of this life, the deceitfulness of wealth and the desires for other things come in and choke the word, making it unfruitful. (Mark 4:19)

People who want to get rich fall into temptation and a trap and into many foolish and harmful desires that plunge men into ruin and destruction. (1 Tim 6:9)

4) A camel *works* for its master; a man is to work for his Master (God).

"No one can serve two masters. Either he will hate the one and love the other, or he will be devoted to the one and despise the other. You cannot serve both God and Money. (Mat 6:24)

Slaves, obey your earthly masters in everything; and do it, not only when their eye is on you and to win their favor, but with sincerity of heart and reverence for the Lord. Whatever you do, work at it with all your heart, as working for the Lord, not for men, since you know that you will receive an inheritance from the Lord as a reward. It is the Lord Christ you are serving. (Col 3:22-24)

3 (19:25) **Wealth—Salvation**: the disciples were shocked, thoroughly dismayed. Christ was saying something diametrically opposed to what they and everyone else had always thought. They had been taught (as have succeeding generations, even the church)...

- that prosperity (wealth, comfort, and things) is God's blessing
- that a person receives and has because God is blessing him
- that prosperity is the reward of righteousness and obedience
- that God blesses a person with the things of this earth if they are righteous and obedient

However, Christ was saying the very opposite: that a prosperous person would most likely never enter heaven; that prosperity posed such a dangerous threat to a person that his eternal doom was almost assured. The disciples knew that God would never put a person in such a precarious and dangerous position. They knew that Christ was attacking the world's most cherished and ardent belief: be good (righteous) and you will be blessed by God (and the thought of blessing is always of material blessing. See note—Eph.1:3 for more discussion.)

They were shocked, thoroughly dismayed: Who then could be saved? The vast majority of people were threatening their own eternal destiny. They were dooming themselves. Since prosperity is not the reward (sign) for righteousness, and the rich are barred from heaven, that means that the poor, too, are barred; for they are spending most of their time dreaming and seeking prosperity!

The idea that prosperity is the reward for righteousness, that God blesses a person with the things of this earth if they are righteous and obedient, is so prevalent a view that a comment is needed at this point.

1. God's concern is spiritual blessings, not material blessings. God promises a man the necessities of life (food, clothing, shelter) if he seeks God first (Mt.6:33; cp. Mt.6:25-34). God can, if He chooses, bless any of us with whatever and however much He wishes for special purposes, for the purposes of having in order "to share with those in need." But just because a man is prosperous does not mean the man is righteous, and just because a person is righteous does not mean that he is going to be blessed materially. Righteousness and prosperity have nothing to do with each other. In fact, "It is hard for a rich man to enter the kingdom of heaven."

2. Wealth is seldom a good thing. As Christ taught in this passage, wealth is fraught with dangers that make it extremely difficult for the rich to enter heaven. Nevertheless the whole world, rich and poor alike, puts its primary attention upon securing more and more.

3. Wealth is secured by man himself, by his own energy and effort. Man secures wealth by dreaming how to make it (a vision, perspective) and having the initiative to make it (acting and timing). A man may trust God to help him secure wealth, but a man may have nothing to do with God and secure wealth on his own. There is a sense in which a man's strength and mind are from God, but that has nothing to do with a personal or active relationship with God. Most rich men control their own lives and go about securing their treasure on this earth *without God* (Mt.6:21).

On the other hand, a man may trust God to bless him so that he may help others, and God may choose to bless him. But God's choosing to bless him is for the purpose of helping others, not to hoard and live above what is needed (extravagantly and sumptuously). In fact what Christ teaches is that the rich are *to live just as sacrificially* as the poor. (See DEEPER STUDY # 1,2—Mt.19:23; Mk.12:42. See outline—Lk.21:1-4.)

> **Thought 1**. Something is usually forgotten: man was not made for things (money, wealth, possessions), but things were made for man. Yet man allows himself to become enslaved to things, ever lusting after more and more.
>
> Wealth (money, possessions, things) is only a commodity—a means, a tool—to help man carry out his purpose and service upon earth. At least, that is what wealth is supposed to be. But most men become the tool and the commodity of money. Few men know why God put them on earth.
>
> **It is better to take refuge in the LORD than to trust in princes. (Psa 118:9)**
>
> **Stop trusting in man, who has but a breath in his nostrils. Of what account is he? (Isa 2:22)**
>
> **This is what the LORD says: "Cursed is the one who trusts in man, who depends on flesh for his strength and whose heart turns away from the LORD. (Jer 17:5)**

4 (19:26) **Wealth—Salvation—Repentance**: there is one hope for the rich man—God.

1. A rich man must turn away from men. No man can save a rich man nor any other man for that matter.

a. No man has the strength or know-how to break the power of *seeking things* that hold sway over a rich man. The natural urge within man is to seek more and more comfort and ease and possessions. No man has the power to break that *natural urge*. The entanglements are too pleasing and enslaving

b. No man can recreate the soul of a man, change it so that he seeks "things above" and sets his "mind on things above, not on earthly things" (Col.3:1-2). No philosophy, no psychology, no medicine, no education, no politics, no social movement can change the soul of a man.

> **Then Jesus said to his disciples, "I tell you the truth, it is hard for a rich man to enter the kingdom of heaven. Jesus looked at them and said, "With man this is impossible, but with God all things are possible." (Mat 19:23, 26)**

2. A rich man must turn to God and His power. God is the only hope for a rich man. Only God can break a rich man's enslavement to this earth—only God can convert and change, turn and save the rich man from the danger and doom of wealth.

How? Very simply. The words of Christ to the rich young ruler tell the rich what to do: "...go, sell your possessions, and give to the poor, and you will have treasure in heaven, then come follow me" (Mt.19:21).

This is a hard saying, a difficult thing for any of us to do—so difficult that we try to escape from its stringent demand, softening it and explaining it away. *But it is what Christ said. The disciples understood it perfectly* (v.25-27).

In very practical terms, to receive eternal life, we must *give all we are and have*. Naturally, this is more difficult for the rich, for he has "great wealth" (v.22).

There are four practical steps that will help a rich man be saved.

1. He must listen and heed immediately the inner voice, the pricking of conscience to give his life and possessions to God. He must turn immediately to God and never turn away.

2. He must study God's Word daily for direction and talk to and trust God to keep his heart free from the lure and deceptions of possessions.

3. He must use his wealth to help the desperate needs of others. He must *realize, know, and acknowledge* that the vast majority of the world is hungry, hurting, and needing help—desperately so—and that God expects him to use all he has to meet those needs. He must not hoard and live extravagantly in the midst of so much need.

4. He must develop a strong desire for heaven, knowing that his sojourn on earth is ever so short, as brief as the lily of the field.

> **For nothing is impossible with God." (Luke 1:37)**
>
> **"I know that you can do all things; no plan of yours can be thwarted. (Job 42:2)**
>
> **Command those who are rich in this present world not to be arrogant nor to put their hope in wealth, which is so uncertain, but to put their hope in God, who richly provides us with everything for our enjoyment. Command them to do good, to be rich in good deeds, and to be generous and willing to share. In this way they will lay up treasure for themselves as a firm foundation for the coming age, so that they may take hold of the life that is truly life. (1 Tim 6:17-19)**

For no one can lay any foundation other than the one already laid, which is Jesus Christ. (1 Cor 3:11)

By faith Moses, when he had grown up, refused to be known as the son of Pharaoh's daughter. He chose to be mistreated along with the people of God rather than to enjoy the pleasures of sin for a short time. He regarded disgrace for the sake of Christ as of greater value than the treasures of Egypt, because he was looking ahead to his reward. (Heb 11:24-26)

DEEPER STUDY # 4
(19:26) **Rich, The**: some rich persons did turn to Christ. They serve as excellent examples for the rich to follow in turning to God (also see outline—Lk.8:2-3).

⇒ James and John (Mk.1:20; cp. note—Mk.10:36-37).
⇒ Matthew (see note and DEEPER STUDY # 1—Mt.9:9-13).
⇒ Zacchaeus (Lk.19:1-10).
⇒ Joseph of Arimathaea (Mt.27:57).
⇒ Nicodemus (Jn.20:39 cp. 3:1f. He may or may not have been saved.)
⇒ Lydia (Acts 16:14-15).
⇒ Manaen, a foster brother of Herod, who was probably wealthy (Acts 13:1).
⇒ Some women who supported Jesus (see outline and notes—Lk.8:2-3).

Outline	Scripture	Scripture	Outline
1 **The two essentials for reward** a. Must leave everything behind b. Must follow Christ 2 **The apostles' reward: Will reign & rule with Christ** a. When: In the new age b. Purpose: To judge—	**E. The Reward for Believers, 19:27-30** (Mk.10:28-31; Lk.18:28-30) 27 Peter answered him, "We have left everything to follow you! What then will there be for us?" 28 Jesus said to them, "I tell you the truth, at the renewal of all things, when the Son of Man sits on his glorious throne, you who have followed me will	also sit on twelve thrones, judging the twelve tribes of Israel. 29 And everyone who has left houses or brothers or sisters or father or mother or children or fields for my sake will receive a hundred times as much and will inherit eternal life. 30 But many who are first will be last, and many who are last will be first.	rule, govern, direct c. Judge, govern whom: Twelve tribes of Israel*DS1* 3 **The believer's reward: Will receive great reward** a. Reason: Left all—supreme allegiance b. The present reward: A hundred times as much c. The future reward: Eternal life 4 **The shocking surprise: The severe judgment of believers—perfect justice**

DIVISION XIII

THE MESSIAH'S TEACHINGS ON THE WAY TO JERUSALEM, 19:1-20:34

E. The Reward for Believers, 19:27-30

(19:27-30) **Introduction**: Peter's question is often misunderstood. Peter was not being mercenary; he needed assurance. He wanted to make sure that he and the other disciples were *really saved*. Anyone would need assurance after what Jesus had just said: "If you want to be perfect, go, sell your possessions and give to the poor, and you will have treasure in heaven. Then come, follow me" (Mt.19:21).

Few sell everything and give it all away (v.21), and few, whether rich or poor, control their dreams and urges to have more (see note—Mk.10:25). The disciples, as all honest men, knew this. They also knew the extreme demands Christ was making to be a true follower of Christ. They, unlike so many of us in our attempts to soften His words, understood exactly what He was saying. The extremity of His words was shocking. They could not see how anyone could be saved, and the answer Christ gave to their question about salvation said nothing to give them *personal* assurance: "With man this is impossible, but with God all things are possible" (v.26).

The disciples sensed a deep need for assurance. Had they done enough and given up enough? They thought so and were almost sure they had, but had they?

Somewhat meekly Peter said, "Lord, we have left everything to follow you! We have surrendered all to you. What then will there be for us? Shall we receive eternal life?" Christ used Peter's question to teach a wonderful truth. They and all who followed Him could rest assured—they would be enormously rewarded.

Note the Lord's assuring words: "I tell you the truth, that you will also sit on twelve thrones....And everyone who has left [all]...will inherit eternal life" (v.28-29).

1. The two essentials for reward (v.27).
2. The apostle's reward: will reign and rule with Christ (v.28).
3. The believer's reward: will receive great reward (v.29).
4. The shocking surprise: the severe judgment of believers—perfect justice (v.30).

1 (19:27) **Rewards—Believers—Self-Denial**: there are two essentials for reward.

1. A person must leave or forsake all. What is meant by this? Peter and some of the other disciples had families, and they readily met the needs of their families (Mt.8:14). Therefore, *leaving or forsaking all* does not mean deserting and shirking our day-to-day responsibilities to our families. What *leaving all* means is to renounce and to relinquish all—to give up all unreservedly. It means that a person takes care of his family, yes; but beyond that, he uses what he has to meet the needs of a desperate world. It means that a person serves and puts Christ before all, including family and friends. It means that a person *leaves behind all sinful behavior* such as dirty habits, evil associations, crooked ways, off colored jokes and curse words. It means that we allow nothing to interfere with serving Christ. It means to put *following Christ* first. When we put Him first, we discover a wonderful truth: life becomes balanced. All other things, including family, fall into their proper place; and life becomes a most enriching experience (even if a person's family rejects him).

2. A person must follow Christ (see note and DEEPER STUDY # 1—Lk.9:23). A person who really follows Christ has no sense of regret and no desire to complain. He is truly a new creation: "the old has gone, the new has come!" (2 Cor.5:17). He is satisfied and complete (Col.2:10).

> **Peter said to him, "We have left everything to follow you!" (Mark 10:28)**
>
> **After this, Jesus went out and saw a tax collector by the name of Levi sitting at his tax booth. "Follow me," Jesus said to him, (Luke 5:27)**
>
> **Then he said to them all: "If anyone would come after me, he must deny himself and take up his cross daily and follow me. For whoever wants to save his life will lose it, but whoever loses his life for me will save it. (Luke 9:23-24)**
>
> **In the same way, any of you who does not give up everything he has cannot be my disciple. (Luke 14:33)**
>
> **"I tell you the truth," Jesus said to them, "no one who has left home or wife or brothers or parents or children for the sake of the kingdom of God will fail to receive many times as much in this age and, in the age to come, eternal life." (Luke 18:29-30)**
>
> **What is more, I consider everything a loss compared to the surpassing greatness of knowing Christ Jesus my Lord, for whose sake I have lost all things. I consider them rubbish, that I may gain Christ (Phil 3:8)**

Thought 1. We face two great dangers that can lower our reward.
1) Not leaving or forsaking all for Christ: hanging on to some things whether behavior, habit, relationship, or possession.
2) Super-spirituality: after forsaking all for Christ, there is always the danger of thinking that we have given up and sacrificed more than others. Several areas in particular lend themselves to spiritual pride...
- suffering
- service & works
- financial and benevolent gifts
- talents and spitirual gifts
- ministry and ministerial position
- being saved from the depth of sin

Thought 2. Some attempt to bargain with God. This is not to be. We are to go ahead and leave all, trusting and following Christ (2 Cor.6:17-18; 1 Jn.2:15-16).

2 (19:28) **Reward—Apostles—Renewal**: the apostles were to be wonderfully rewarded. They were to receive a great honor—the honor of ruling and reigning with Christ Himself. Note that Christ told them three things. (See DEEPER STUDY # 1—Mt.19:28 for a discussion of these three points.)

⇒ When they would reign with Him.
⇒ Why they would reign with Him.
⇒ Whom they would govern and direct in their reign.

The word "renewal" (paliggenesia) means recreation, restoration, renovation, new birth. The word is used one other time in the New Testament referring to the new birth of an individual (Tit.3:5). Here Christ uses the word to refer to the "restoration of everything" (Acts 3:21), a period of time in the future when He will set up the new order of things under His personal rule and reign (cp. Ro.8:19-23; Is.11:6-9). That day is often called the day of redemption or referred to as the Kingdom of God. (See note and DEEPER STUDY # 1—Eph.1:7; DEEPER STUDY # 3—Mt.19:23-24.)

Note several things.

1. The "The renewal of all things" is in the future. Christ did not say "you who have followed me in the renewal," but "you who have followed me, in the renewal when the Son of Man sits on his glorious throne." The period of time is "when the Son of man shall sit in the throne of His glory"—a time out in the future.

2. Christ said that the apostles would be rewarded with twelve thrones, each one governing one of the twelve tribes of Israel. When were they to govern? "In the renewal," when the new order of things shall be set up under the rule and reign of Christ. But when is the new order of things to be? There are two possible answers: either during the milenial reign of Christ (see DEEPER STUDY # 3—Mt.19:23-24; DEEPER STUDY # 2—Rev.20:4-6) or during the new heavens and earth (Rev.21:1f; cp. 1 Cor.15:23-28).

There are three passages in which Christ deals with the renewal as predicted here.

> **Jesus said to them, "I tell you the truth, at the renewal of all things, when the Son of Man sits on his glorious throne, you who have followed me will also sit on twelve thrones, judging the twelve tribes of Israel. (Mat 19:28)**

> **"What is it you want?" he asked. She said, "Grant that one of these two sons of mine may sit at your right and the other at your left in your kingdom." Jesus said to them, "You will indeed drink from my cup, but to sit at my right or left is not for me to grant. These places belong to those for whom they have been prepared by my Father." (Mat 20:21, 23)**
>
> **You are those who have stood by me in my trials. And I confer on you a kingdom, just as my Father conferred one on me, so that you may eat and drink at my table in my kingdom and sit on thrones, judging the twelve tribes of Israel. (Luke 22:28-30)**

The fulfillment of this promise seems to be the Messianic kingdom or millenial reign of Christ on earth. This seems to be the way Christ's promise to Israel will be fulfilled.

> **I will restore your judges as in days of old, your counselors as at the beginning. Afterward you will be called the City of Righteousness, the Faithful City." (Isa 1:26)**

3. It should be noted, however, that some find great difficulty in saying there is *ever again to be a distinction between Jew and Gentile*. They say that Christ came to bring peace to all men and between all men, breaking down the wall of partition between all. They say that the great weight of Scripture is opposed to there ever again being a distinction between Jew and Gentile. This interpretation simply says that when Christ returns, that is it; the end of time will be at hand. When He returns, He sets up His *eternal* reign and rules forever. Therefore, the apostles' rule and reign refers to the church, that is, to spiritual Israel or to the true Israel of God (Gal.6:15-16; cp. Ro.2:28-29).

4. Christ said He would reward the apostles with *a particualar honor*. Why? The apostles believed and followed Christ in the embryonic or beginning stage of Christianity. They clung to their belief and endured in the face of unbelievable odds. Just imagine!

⇒ Imagine standing before a man who looks just like all other men, merely a man, and believing that man to really be the *Son of God*.
⇒ Imagine clinging to and continuing to follow Christ when everyone else had turned away from Him (cp. Jn.6:67).
⇒ Imagine following immediately upon the heels of the risen Lord and being instantly responsible for reaching the world. (No wonder God had to plan for His Spirit to infill the disciples as He did on Pentecost and to live within our bodies as He does. See notes—1 Cor.3:16; 6:19-20.)
⇒ Imagine continuing on and on, trying to be obedient and to reach more and more despite unbelievable odds and having to constantly face the harassment of their fellow citizens, the Judaizers or religionists.
⇒ Imagine confronting and enduring through unbelievable threats and persecution launched from both an immoral government and a man-corrupted religion that reacted fiercely against those who differed with it.

The apostles not only were responsible for more and faced more than most of us will ever know but they also were responsible for and faced more than we can ever imagine (cp. 1 Cor.4:9-13; 2 Cor.11:24-28).

Thought 1. There are two renewals.

1) The renewal of a person's life: a rebirth, a recreation of a person's nature and life (see Deeper Study # 1—Jn.3:1-15).
2) The renewal of the universe: a remaking of heaven and earth (Ro.8:21-23; 2 Pt.3:10-13; 21:1).

DEEPER STUDY # 1

(19:28) **Judging (Krino)—Eternal Life**: to judge, govern, direct; to administer affairs, supervise, and oversee. The assignment of responsibilitiy, of duties, of work to be done is being taught here. There is to be *judging*, that is, governing, giving direction and supervision and oversight throughout eternity. Christ told the apostles that they would govern and oversee Israel. Paul said that believers would direct and oversee the world and angels (1 Cor.6:2-3). All this activity and responsibility, of course, is under the direction of Christ.

For some unknown reason we so often picture *eternal life* as some dreamy sleep or semi-conscious type of existence. We think of it as some future existence that puts us on a fluffy cloud upon which we float in an eternal state of inactivity. Why man cannot accept the simple statement of Christ that life is to be eternal is difficult to understand. Eternal life is life that goes on and on. There is, however, one basic difference: life shall be perfected—perfected in body, mind, and spirit. It is life lived in the midst of a new heavens and earth (perfected)—life lived before Christ and responsible to Christ in all that it is assigned (Jn.3:16; 5:24; Ro.8:19-23; 2 Pt.3:9-18; 1 Jn.5:11-13; Rev.21:1).

3 (19:29) **Reward**: the apostles are not the only ones to be rewarded. Every true follower of *Christ* shall be greatly rewarded. Christ said three things about the reward of the believer in this verse.

1. The reason for the reward: the believer is to be rewarded because he has left all; he has given his supreme allegiance to Jesus Christ (see note—Mt.19:27, the two essentials for reward).

Note that the two closest things to a man are named by Christ: his immediate family and his possessions (honor and lands). These are by far the most difficult things to surrender to Christ. Hobbies, habits, pleasures, friends—all can be given up (subjected to Christ) quicker than family or possessions. Note also that Christ began and ended the list with material possessions. How enslaving they are, even more so than family for some persons!

2. The present reward: a hundred times as much. The Gospel of Mark makes it clear that Christ was speaking of present reward (Mk.10:21). No true follower of Christ has ever forsaken anyone or anything and been left alone and destitute by Christ. Christ rewards His true follower many times over. Note: the reward is both human and material.

a. The human reward is a real and true fellowship among genuine believers. Christ knows when a follower of His has been turned against by those whom Christ loves ever so deeply. Christ knows when to send someone into the life of His own, when to meet the aching need of His follower for true friendship. He more than abundantly meets the need.

We proclaim to you what we have seen and heard, so that you also may have fellowship with us. And our fellowship is with the Father and with his Son, Jesus Christ. (1 John 1:3)

But if we walk in the light, as he is in the light, we have fellowship with one another, and the blood of Jesus, his Son, purifies us from all sin. (1 John 1:7)

They devoted themselves to the apostles' teaching and to the fellowship, to the breaking of bread and to prayer. (Acts 2:42)

For where two or three come together in my name, there am I with them." (Mat 18:20)

So in Christ we who are many form one body, and each member belongs to all the others. (Rom 12:5)

I am a friend to all who fear you, to all who follow your precepts. (Psa 119:63)

Then those who feared the LORD talked with each other, and the LORD listened and heard. A scroll of remembrance was written in his presence concerning those who feared the LORD and honored his name. (Mal 3:16)

b. The material reward is the meeting of necessities and whatever else God wants us to have left over so that we can help meet the needs of others.

The idea Christ was conveying is that of perfect material care and security. The very reason we seek and seek is because we are basically insecure and have a basic urge to crave more and more. Craving, greediness, fear, and insecurity are most unhealthy and destabilizing. When we forsake all, genuinely following Christ, He gives us the greatest peace and security possible: Himself and His power to provide for our necessities. We never have to worry or be anxious again (see notes—Mt.6:25-34; Lk.16:10-12. Cp. Mk.10:29-30; Lk.18:28-30; Eph.4:28.) There is much more happiness, joy, peace, security, assurance, confidence, satisfaction, completeness, and fulfillment in Christ than in any amount of possessions or worldly companionship and friendship.

But seek first his kingdom and his righteousness, and all these things will be given to you as well. (Mat 6:33; cp. Mt.6:25-34)

The thief comes only to steal and kill and destroy; I have come that they may have life, and have it to the full. (John 10:10)

And God is able to make all grace abound to you, so that in all things at all times, having all that you need, you will abound in every good work. (2 Cor 9:8)

Now to him who is able to do immeasurably more than all we ask or imagine, according to his power that is at work within us, (Eph 3:20)

And my God will meet all your needs according to his glorious riches in Christ Jesus. (Phil 4:19)

And you will receive a rich welcome into the eternal kingdom of our Lord and

Savior Jesus Christ. (2 Pet 1:11)

You prepare a table before me in the presence of my enemies. You anoint my head with oil; my cup overflows. (Psa 23:5; cp. Ps.36:8)

Praise be to the Lord, to God our Savior, who daily bears our burdens. Selah (Psa 68:19)

He will also send you rain for the seed you sow in the ground, and the food that comes from the land will be rich and plentiful. In that day your cattle will graze in broad meadows. (Isa 30:23)

You will have plenty to eat, until you are full, and you will praise the name of the LORD your God, who has worked wonders for you; never again will my people be shamed. (Joel 2:26)

Bring the whole tithe into the storehouse, that there may be food in my house. Test me in this," says the LORD Almighty, "and see if I will not throw open the floodgates of heaven and pour out so much blessing that you will not have room enough for it. (Mal 3:10)

3. The future reward is eternal life (see DEEPER STUDY # 1—Jn.17:2-3; cp. DEEPER STUDY # 2—Jn.1:4; note and DEEPER STUDY # 1—Mt.19:28. Cp. Ro.8:16-18.)

Jesus looked at him and loved him. "One thing you lack," he said. "Go, sell everything you have and give to the poor, and you will have treasure in heaven. Then come, follow me." (Mark 10:21)

That everyone who believes in him may have eternal life. (John 3:15)

Whoever believes in the Son has eternal life, but whoever rejects the Son will not see life, for God's wrath remains on him." (John 3:36)

Even now the reaper draws his wages, even now he harvests the crop for eternal life, so that the sower and the reaper may be glad together. (John 4:36)

"I tell you the truth, whoever hears my word and believes him who sent me has eternal life and will not be condemned; he has crossed over from death to life. (John 5:24)

Now this is eternal life: that they may know you, the only true God, and Jesus Christ, whom you have sent. (John 17:3)

The one who sows to please his sinful nature, from that nature will reap destruction; the one who sows to please the Spirit, from the Spirit will reap eternal life. (Gal 6:8)

Thought 1. Christ promises to reward His followers presently, reward them with an unbelievable Christian community, fellowship, and security. He founded the church to fulfill this promise. The church has a high calling. Imagine, the local church and its genuine believers are to be as close to one another as families are. The church is to provide a precious fellowship for the alienated, lonely, shy, friendless, and stranger. It is to meet the needs where families fail.

A pointed question: how many churches provide a true fellowship (see Deeper Study # 3—Acts 2:42)? How often does God have to turn away from local congregations to others in order to meet the needs of a disciple of His?

4 (19:30) **Reward—Judgment**: the Lord's words are clear. There is to be a severe judgment of believers—the execution of perfect justice. Our judgment, human judgment, is often inaccurate. *Many persons* shall be switched around: many whom we esteemed and rewarded the highest shall be placed last, and many whom we thought weakest and lowest shall be placed first. Only God knows the true heart of His servants. We judge and reward...

- by visible works
- by visible morality
- by age and seniority
- by friendliness
- by years as a Christian
- by recognition
- by esteem or influence
- by ability and skill
- by position

However, God sees into the heart of His dear followers, into the heart of every single one; and He shall straighten out the misjudgments of all our dear brothers and sisters in Christ. Christ leaves no doubt: the most humble on earth shall be elevated to be the greatest in heaven. It may be a shocking surprise, but there is to be judgment, a just realignment and positioning of believers (see DEEPER STUDY # 1—2 Cor.5:10; note—1 Jn.3:1-2).

For we must all appear before the judgment seat of Christ, that each one may receive what is due him for the things done while in the body, whether good or bad. (2 Cor 5:10)

His work will be shown for what it is, because the Day will bring it to light. It will be revealed with fire, and the fire will test the quality of each man's work. If what he has built survives, he will receive his reward. If it is burned up, he will suffer loss; he himself will be saved, but only as one escaping through the flames. (1 Cor 3:13-15)

He has brought down rulers from their thrones but has lifted up the humble. (Luke 1:52)

Woe to you who are well fed now, for you will go hungry. Woe to you who laugh now, for you will mourn and weep. (Luke 6:25)

"But Abraham replied, 'Son, remember that in your lifetime you received your good things, while Lazarus received bad things, but now he is comforted here and you are in agony. (Luke 16:25)

Outline	Scripture	Scripture (cont.)	Outline (cont.)
	CHAPTER 20 **F. The Parable of Workers in the Vineyard: God's Glorious Grace, 20:1-16**	his foreman, 'Call the workers and pay them their wages, beginning with the last ones hired and going on to the first.'	**appointed time, at the end of the day** a. Paid through His foreman
1 God's grace provides work for man—a field to tend[DS1] **2 God's grace seeks & calls men to work**[DS2,3,4,5] a. The early call: To the willing & eager 1) Shown grace: Promised a full wage 2) Sent into the field	"For the kingdom of heaven is like a landowner who went out early in the morning to hire men to work in his vineyard. 2 He agreed to pay them a denarius for the day and sent them into his vineyard.	9 "The workers who were hired about the eleventh hour came and each received a denarius. 10 So when those came who were hired first, they expected to receive more. But each one of them also received a denarius.	b. Paid out of a heart of care & grace 1) Cared & showed grace to the late comers: A full wage 2) Cared & showed grace to the eager workers: A full wage
b. The late-comer call: To the idle—slothful—self-seeking—complacent 1) Shown grace: A forceful challenge & the promise of a just wage 2) Some responded	3 "About the third hour he went out and saw others standing in the marketplace doing nothing. 4 He told them, 'You also go and work in my vineyard, and I will pay you whatever is right.'	11 When they received it, they began to grumble against the landowner. 12 'These men who were hired last worked only one hour,' they said, 'and you have made them equal to us who have borne the burden of the work and the heat of the day.'	c. Pay is not based on works & energy: Illustrated by the eager workers who murmured over the same pay
c. The constant call: To all—shows constant grace	5 So they went. "He went out again about the sixth hour and the ninth hour and did the same thing.	13 "But he answered one of them, 'Friend, I am not being unfair to you. Didn't you agree to work for a denarius?	1) Pay is gracious & just: A full wage as promised
d. The final call: The eleventh hour call—to the idle 1) He strongly rebuked 2) They excuse themselves 3) He showed grace: A forceful challenge & the promise of a just wage	6 About the eleventh hour he went out and found still others standing around. He asked them, 'Why have you been standing here all day long doing nothing?' 7 "'Because no one has hired us,' they answered. "He said to them, 'You also go and work in my vineyard.	14 Take your pay and go. I want to give the man who was hired last the same as I gave you. 15 Don't I have the right to do what I want with my own money? Or are you envious because I am generous?'	2) Pay is based on God's care for all: For the last as well as for the first d. Pay is not as man sees (evil, selfish eyes): Pay is as God wills—He is good
3 God's grace pays the promised wages: At the	8 "When evening came, the owner of the vineyard said to	16 "So the last will be first, and the first will be last."	**4 God's justice will reign in paying what He promised**[DS6]

DIVISION XIII

THE MESSIAH'S TEACHINGS ON THE WAY TO JERUSALEM, 19:1-20:34

F. The Parable of Workers in the Vineyard: God's Glorious Grace, 20:1-16

(20:1-16) **Introduction**: this is one of the most meaningful parables in Scripture, yet the meaning is sometimes missed. Christ was continuing His discussion of salvation (Mt. 19:25) and eternal life (Mt.19:29). (See note—Mt.19:27-30.) What He now wished to do was show *the marvelous grace of God* in salvation, in giving eternal life. This He did by sharing a parable—a parable which demonstrates God's marvelous grace as few other lessons do.

1. God's grace provides work for man—a field to tend (v.1).
2. God's grace seeks and calls men to work (v.1-7).
3. God's grace pays the promised wages: at the appointed time, at the end of the day (v.8-15).
4. God's justice will reign in paying what He has promised (v.16).

1 (20:1) **Work—Labor—Grace—Purpose**: God's grace provides work for man, a field to tend. Two significant facts are being stressed.

1. It is God who provides work for man, who gives a field to be tended. The great Landowner is God. The vineyard or field can be either the world or the church. The world, the church, and man himself are all due to God's grace. It is God's grace that has created man. It is God's grace that has provided the field (the world and church) for man to work in. Without God there would be nothing (Ro.11:36; Col.1:16f).

2. It is God who goes out to seek and call men to work. It is not the workers who come to Him. God's going out after man is grace, marvelous grace (Lk.19:10; Jn.3:16; 15:16). Every step involved in the call of God is of grace: the call itself, the challange to go and labor, the promise of wages (reward), the acceptance of the responses, and the sending forth into the field. God did not have to issue a call or take any of the steps taken. Each step is a marvelous demonstraton of God's care and grace.

Note another matter: the soul of man serves something. It either serves self and sin or God and righteousness. Man either works for the world and its end or for heaven and its end (Ro.6:16-22). It is for this reason that God issues call after call (see outline above and notes for each of the calls).

> **Then he said to his disciples, "The harvest is plentiful but the workers are few. Ask the Lord of the harvest, therefore, to send out workers into his harvest field." (Mat 9:37-38)**

Do you not say, 'Four months more and then the harvest'? I tell you, open your eyes and look at the fields! They are ripe for harvest. Even now the reaper draws his wages, even now he harvests the crop for eternal life, so that the sower and the reaper may be glad together. (John 4:35-36)

The Lord answered, "Who then is the faithful and wise manager, whom the master puts in charge of his servants to give them their food allowance at the proper time? It will be good for that servant whom the master finds doing so when he returns. (Luke 12:42-43)

He said: "A man of noble birth went to a distant country to have himself appointed king and then to return. So he called ten of his servants and gave them ten minas. 'Put this money to work,' he said, 'until I come back.' (Luke 19:12-13)

DEEPER STUDY # 1
(20:1) **Kingdom of Heaven**: see DEEPER STUDY # 3—Mt.19:23-24.

2 (20:2) **Call—Purpose—Reward**: the early call is God's very first call to a person. It is directed at a person when there is a special willingness and eagerness to serve God. The first call is God's beginning to speak to the heart of a person. There is a tug, a pull, a voice, a thought, a movement in one's heart to listen and turn to God.

Note two things.

1. The landowner promised the workers a full wage. If the willing workers believed his promise, they would go into the fields and work. If they did not believe his promise, they would not go. Their belief preceded their work. He promised, and they believed and served.

God's call is by grace, not by works. The fact that Christ speaks of work and wages does not in any sense mean that salvation is earned, that it is of works. We are saved by God's grace through faith (Ro.4:3-5; Eph.2:8-10).

2. The time of service was a day, which symbolizes a lifetime. When the day (life) ended, the willing workers would receive the promise of the landowner. They would be rewarded with exactly what he had promised, and the reward would be theirs forever. The day was but a brief period of time in comparison with having their needs met. They could withstand any trial (burden or heat, v.12) for just a day, for it would soon end.

They had two things to encourage them to remain with the work: they had only a short period of time to work, only one day, and they had the presence of the landowner himself. He was constantly encouraging them, fellowshipping with them and reminding them of his promise.

Go to the street corners and invite to the banquet anyone you find.' (Mat 22:9)

Who wants all men to be saved and to come to a knowledge of the truth. (1 Tim 2:4)

See, I set before you today life and prosperity, death and destruction. (Deu 30:15)

DEEPER STUDY # 2
(20:3-4) **Call—Purpose**: the late-comer's call is a later call to a person. Every city has its labor market hang-out. Any of us who have dealt with the labor market know that an employer often finds that he needs more workers as the day progresses. So he returns to call for more workers. Each time he returns it is, so to speak, an act of grace—he meets the need of more men.

An employer who asks workers to join his working force meets all kinds of responses.

1. There are the *willing and eager* workers. These are always out early, needing and looking for work. They realize and know their need, and they are extremely responsible in doing all they can to provide for their needs. Often they are men who want purpose, meaning, and significance as much as they want physical provision.

2. There are what Christ calls *the idle*. They have little if any interest in work at all. They are there simply because it is a gathering place where they can find company and pass time away.

3. There are the *self-seeking* or *pleasure workers*. These move around questioning each employer about what kind of work is to be done. If the work sounds too difficult or not enjoyable and pleasing, they refuse, choosing to wait for something more pleasing and enjoyable. However, later on in the day, after nothing else more satisfying has come along, they are willing to heed the call of the earlier employer.

4. There are the *slothful workers*. These are just lazy, not interested in a full-day's work. They prefer lying around, being loose and unobligated rather than exerting the energy and effort required by work. They choose to live with less rather than to work a full day. Thus, they show up at the marketplace only when they need a little work.

5. There are the *complacent workers*, the slow-movers. They sleep late, move slow, and are always late in getting to the marketplace. They could care less if they miss the better opportunities, just so they are able to get enough to meet their immediate needs.

6. There are the workers who are *weak failures*. These go to work at jobs that appeal to them, but they discover the jobs are hard and difficult. So they walk away from their commitment and return to the marketplace for something easier.

The parallel with God's late-comer call is easily seen. Note two things about the late-comer call that is different from the early call.

1. The call to work is more forceful: "You also go." It has to be more forceful. All of these have already rejected the early call or else were not present to hear the call. Some of the day (of their life) has already passed and can never be recovered. It takes more force and more convincing to stir most of the late-comers.

2. The promise of a wage (reward) is promised but not an amount. The Lord merely said, "I will pay you whatever is right." A late-comer, the person who does not respond to God until later in life, must simply trust God to be fair and just. The promise is that He will give *a just reward*.

We hear that some among you are idle. They are not busy; they are busybodies. (2 Th 3:11)

We do not want you to become lazy, but to imitate those who through faith and patience inherit what has been promised. (Heb 6:12)

One who is slack in his work is brother to one who destroys. (Prov 18:9)

I went past the field of the sluggard, past the vineyard of the man who lacks judgment; thorns had come up everywhere, the ground was covered with weeds, and the stone wall was in ruins. (Prov 24:30-31)

DEEPER STUDY # 3

(20:5) **Call—Purpose**: the constant call is the occasional movement of God in the heart of man. There is nothing so tragic as a person who is unemployed, that is, not serving God in this world and in the church. God cares and God has plenty of work for every man to do. Therefore, He tries and tries to reach the heart of man, calling at every hour He can. Note three things about the constant call of God.

1. It is God's great compassion for all of us that keeps His calling to us.

2. The calls of God are limited; they are only periodic. In the parable, only four calls have been issued up to this point. There is only one more call to go, only five calls in a day and in a life. God's movement, His Spirit does not always contend with us (Gen.6:3). We know this by experience. When *the contending* begins in our heart or mind (whether through reading, hearing a message, or whatever) and we ignore it and do not make a decision immediately, it diminishes and finally quits. It leaves us, and we continue on just as we always have.

3. The calls of God become dimmer and dimmer and less forceful with the rejection of each call.

⇒ Our conscience becomes harder; our minds less impressionable.
⇒ Our hearts become less sensitive; our ego more self-centered.
⇒ Our thoughts become more worldly; our lives more encumbered.
⇒ Our wills become more sluggish (Pr.29:1).

But if serving the LORD seems undesirable to you, then choose for yourselves this day whom you will serve, whether the gods your forefathers served beyond the River, or the gods of the Amorites, in whose land you are living. But as for me and my household, we will serve the LORD." (Josh 24:15)

Elijah went before the people and said, "How long will you waver between two opinions? If the LORD is God, follow him; but if Baal is God, follow him." But the people said nothing. (1 Ki 18:21)

Again and again I sent all my servants the prophets to you. They said, "Each of you must turn from your wicked ways and reform your actions; do not follow other gods to serve them. Then you will live in the land I have given to you and your fathers." But you have not paid attention or listened to me. (Jer 35:15)

Say to them, 'As surely as I live, declares the Sovereign LORD, I take no pleasure in the death of the wicked, but rather that they turn from their ways and live. Turn! Turn from your evil ways! Why will you die, O house of Israel?' (Ezek 33:11)

"Come, let us return to the LORD. He has torn us to pieces but he will heal us; he has injured us but he will bind up our wounds. (Hosea 6:1)

DEEPER STUDY # 4

(20:5) **Time, Jewish**: a Jewish day began at 6 a.m. and ended at 6 p.m. The early call was issued before 6 a.m., the hour that work would begin. The late-comer call would have been issued at 9 a.m. when a fourth of the day (a life) had already passed. The sixth hour was 12 noon; the ninth hour was 3 p.m., and the eleventh hour was 5 p.m.

DEEPER STUDY # 5

(20:6-7) **Call—Purpose—Decision**: the final call is the last call of God to a man—it is the eleventh-hour call. Note what happens with the persons who wait until the eleventh hour.

1. God strongly rebukes them, much more forcibly than any of the others: "Why have you been standing here *all day* long doing nothing?" There is no excuse for such behavior.

2. They excuse themselves: no one has hired us. Such is not the case; they lie, deceiving their own hearts.

3. God shows grace despite their deceptive excuse: He issues a forceful call and a promise of a just wage.

But note something: nothing is said about how many responded. Just think. How many actually would respond to go out for just one hour's work? How many would be willing to trust after rejecting four other offers during a single day? Realistically, not many would respond.

Three very practical things militate against a person who waits until the eleventh hour to accept God's call.

1. A man does not often know when the eleventh hour is. Few know when they are to die, much less when God shall call for the last time.

2. A man in the eleventh hour has little time to serve. A man who has failed to capture an opportunity that has passed tends to accuse and condemn himself. He senses unworthiness. There is little likelihood that he will sense God's call to the point of responding.

3. A man in the eleventh hour who has rejected call after call is hard, very hard. There is little softness and sensitivity left to respond to God's call—no matter how forceful.

He sent his servants to those who had been invited to the banquet to tell them to come, but they refused to come. (Mat 22:3)

Yet you refuse to come to me to have life. (John 5:40)

But concerning Israel he says, "All day long I have held out my hands to a disobedient and obstinate people." (Rom 10:21)

While you were doing all these things, declares the LORD, I spoke to you again and again, but you did not listen; I called you, but you did not answer. (Jer 7:13)

My God will reject them because they have not obeyed him; they will be wanderers among the nations. (Hosea 9:17)

3 (20:8-15) **Reward—Grace—Death**: God's grace pays the promised wages to those who have worked for Him. He will pay at the appointed time. When is the appointed time? In the evening, at death, when all work ends. This is the meaning of *the evening*, of *the appointed time*. There are two *evenings*, two appointed times for the servant of God.

First, there is the evening or the time of death when the servant passes from this life into God's presence. He receives his reward of eternal life. God transports him into the Lord's presence, and the believer is transformed into the image of Christ (see note—1 Jn.3:2). This is the reward of wages referred to in this parable.

Second, there is the evening or the appointed time of judgment when the servants' works are to be judged (see DEEPER STUDY # 1—2 Cor.5:10). This evening of judgment *is not* what this parable is about.

1. The foreman is Christ, God's Son, to whom God has committed all judgment (Jn.5:22; 2 Cor.5:10).

2. God pays everyone out of a heart of grace and care. This is so cricital to understand: God is love and He cares. He cares for all servants, no matter how old or how long they have been serving Him. He cares, wanting the workers to have enough to meet their needs. A day's wage (the reward of eternal life) was necessary to meet their need. He would have no servant go away without at least that much. Therefore, He pays *even the late-comers* a full wage (eternal life).

Note another point: when we speak of eternal life and perfection, that is, of being conformed to the nature and image of Christ, God shows no preference. We shall all be made just like Christ, perfected in nature.

⇒ We shall have different responsibilities and, apparently, varying degrees of glory; but we shall all be perfected in nature.

⇒ We shall all face the Judgment Seat of Christ. We shall all receive different duties in heaven because of good and bad service here on earth, but we shall all be perfectly happy and joyful in what we do.

⇒ We shall all be judged for our faithfulness on this earth. Some shall be set up as large articles and others as smaller instruments, but we shall all be perfectly complete and filled to the brim (2 Tim. 2:20-21).

⇒ We shall all give an account for the trust and gifts put into our keeping. We shall all be rewarded accordingly, but we shall all be perfectly fulfilled.

⇒ We shall all stand before Christ for what fruit we have borne on earth, but we shall all be perfectly satisfied and fruitful.

> **"Then the master told his servant, 'Go out to the roads and country lanes and make them come in, so that my house will be full. (Luke 14:23)**
>
> **I say to you that many will come from the east and the west, and will take their places at the feast with Abraham, Isaac and Jacob in the kingdom of heaven. (Mat 8:11)**

3. God's pay (reward) is not based on works and energy. It is based on God's grace and justice, and it is based on God's concern and care for all.

a. Note that God is gracious and just and caring. God's grace and care do not annul or erase His justice. God is not unjust (cp. Ro.4:5-6).

⇒ When God gives work to a man who is desperate for work, it is a caring and gracious act. Such was the case with the early call to the eager worker. Not to take advantage of the man's desperation is an act of grace. To offer and pay a full wage and not take advantage of the man is not unjust but the very opposite. It is a just and gracious act, a very caring act.

⇒ Similarly, when God pays a man more than what he earned because God cares that the man has enough to live, it is a gracious and caring act. It is not an unjust act against the first or earlier worker. It is simply a gracious act that reveals God to be an enormously caring Person.

⇒ If God gives us what He promised us, He is not unjust if He gives something to someone else. He is not even unjust to us if He gives an enormous gift to another person. He is just, and He is enormously caring and gracious by keeping His Word and giving to us *and to the other person.*

b. Note that the complaining by the earlier workers causes some to apply the parable to the relationship between God and the Jews and the Gentiles. The earlier workers, representing the Jews, complain because God gives an equal pay (reward and position in His kingdom) to the Gentiles. Almost any commentary will give insight into this interpretation if the reader wishes to pursue it.

4. God's pay (reward) is not as man sees but as God knows and wills. Our eyes are evil because we are of an evil world. Therefore, we judge and understand from an imperfect and selfish stance. God is good; He cares and is full of mercy and grace. Therefore, He gives eternal life to all who come, no matter when they come, at the early call or the eleventh-hour call.

> **No! We believe it is through the grace of our Lord Jesus that we are saved, just as they are." (Acts 15:11)**
>
> **And are justified freely by his grace through the redemption that came by Christ Jesus. (Rom 3:24)**
>
> **For it is by grace you have been saved, through faith—and this not from yourselves, it is the gift of God— not by works, so that no one can boast. (Eph 2:8-9)**
>
> **For the grace of God that brings salvation has appeared to all men. (Titus 2:11)**
>
> **So that, having been justified by his grace, we might become heirs having the hope of eternal life. (Titus 3:7)**

4 (20:16) **Justice—Reward**: this is the very statement that caused Christ to share the parable—"So the last will be first, and the first will be last" (cp. Mt.19:30; 20:16). Remember that the disciples needed assurance of their salvation. Christ gave them assurance and promised the reward of ruling and reigning with Him and living forever (cp. Mt.19:27-30. See note—Mt.19:27-30.) But Christ wanted them to know that they could not judge others, for they could not tell what was within a man, not for sure. They did not know who was to be highly rewarded and who was not.

For example, who would have ever thought that the willing and eager workers who immediately responded to the Lord would expose a grumbling, jealous spirit? To prevent His servants from judging and showing preference among themselves, Christ closes His discussion of eternal life and salvation with a strong warning: the last will be first. That is, many of the last (late-comers) will outstrip us unless we are fervent and zealous in serving God. We may have professed and served Christ for years before others did; yet we may...

- fail to worship Christ day by day as consistently as the later workers.
- fail to grow in the knowledge of Christ as eagerly as the later workers.
- fail to study the Scriptures and pray as much as the later workers.
- fail to use our gifts as faithfully as the later workers.
- fail to witness as boldly as the later workers.
- fail to give all that we are and have as willingly and sacrificially as the later workers.
- fail to love as meekly as the later workers.
- fail to respond as kindly as the later workers.
- fail to live as unselfishly as the later workers.
- fail to relate as lovingly as the later workers.
- fail to endure as patiently as the later workers.
- fail to look for the return of Christ as hopefully as the later workers.

Note: Christ seems to switch from discussing the gift of eternal life to warning His servant that there will be a judgment of works—a judgment that will determine degrees of glory and position and responsibility (See DEEPER STUDY # 1, Judgment Seat of Christ—2 Cor.5:10).

He has brought down rulers from their thrones but has lifted up the humble. (Luke 1:52)

Woe to you who are well fed now, for you will go hungry. Woe to you who laugh now, for you will mourn and weep. (Luke 6:25)

"But Abraham replied, 'Son, remember that in your lifetime you received your good things, while Lazarus received bad things, but now he is comforted here and you are in agony. (Luke 16:25)

But it is God who judges: He brings one down, he exalts another. (Psa 75:7)

The LORD sustains the humble but casts the wicked to the ground. (Psa 147:6)

DEEPER STUDY # 6

(20:16) **Justice**: this footnote is placed last because it deals with a different subject than the outline above. *Is God unjust in His treatment of men*? This is the charge levelled against God by the willing and eager servant (v.10-15). Men often question and charge God with being unjust. Such an unholy charge is caused by religious and theological discussions and by wrong belief and unbelief. The charge is also levelled against God when a crisis arises and we question, "How could God do that or let that happen?"

The New Testament discusses the question of God's being unjust in three passages (see note, pts. 3 and 4—Mt.20:8-15; also see notes—Ro.3:5-8; Ro.9:14-33).

	G. The Messiah Foretells His Death and Resurrection (3rd Time), 20:17-19 (Mk.10:32-34; Lk.18:31-34)
1 Jesus took the disciples aside a. While on the way b. To prepare for death	17 Now as Jesus was going up to Jerusalem, he took the twelve disciples aside and said to them,
2 He was to be betrayed & delivered for prosecutionDS1 a. The betrayer or deliverer was not named b. The prosecutors: The Jews or religionists	18 "We are going up to Jerusalem, and the Son of Man will be betrayed to the chief priests and the teachers of the law. They will condemn him to death
3 He was to be delivered for execution a. To the Gentiles b. By crucifixion **4 He was to be raised from the dead**	19 And will turn him over to the Gentiles to be mocked and flogged and crucified. On the third day he will be raised to life!"

DIVISION XIII

THE MESSIAH'S TEACHINGS ON THE WAY TO JERUSALEM, 19:1-20:34

G. The Messiah Foretells His Death and Resurrection (3rd Time), 20:17-19

(20:17-19) **Introduction**: this is the third time that Matthew stresses the death and resurrection of Jesus Christ. Christ had warned His disciples time and again that He was to die and be raised on the third day (see outline and notes—Mt.16:21-23; 17:22-23; Mk.8:31-33; 9:30-32; 10:32-34. These passages should be studied with this passage. Matthew 17:22-23 includes most, if not all, of the New Testament passages on the death and resurrection of Christ. There is an abundance of material in these references.)

Jesus Christ had to get three facts across to His disciples.

1. Jesus took His disciples aside (v.17)
2. He was to be betrayed and delivered for *prosecution* (v.18).
3. He was to be delivered for *execution* (v.19).
4. He was to be raised from the dead (v.19).

1 (20:17) **Jesus Christ, Death**: Jesus took the disciples aside to get all alone. The word "took" (parelaben) means that He took His disciples "aside." There is great meaning in these words.

1. There is tenderness and warmth and intimacy. He needed and wanted them close to Him, right by His side. He needed to feel and know their presence, in particular that they were with Him as He *went up to Jerusalem* to face death. They also needed His presence, to have Him right beside them and to feel what He felt. Such memories would help them as they faced the trials that lay ahead of them.

2. There is tremendous pressure and tension (also see note—20:19). The very aire surrounding them was tight. There seemed to be a heavy weight hanging over the Lord's head. He seemed to be consumed in deep thought—the kind of thought that quickens a person's pace, tightens the muscles of the body, and strains the expressions of the face. The pressure and tension cannot be overstated. Mark expressed it well: "They were on their way up to Jerusalem, with Jesus leading the way, and the disciples were astonished [bewildered, perplexed], while those who followed were afraid [seized with alarm]" (Mk.10:32).

Two events show just how much the pressure must have been building at this time:

⇒ The experience in the garden of Gethsemane where the pressure was so great that Christ sweated great drops of blood (Lk.22:44)

⇒ The experience of the cross where Christ was to suffer for the sins of the world, bearing to the ultimate degree all the pain possible for a heart, mind, and body to bear (1 Pt.2:24; cp. Mt.27:46; 2 Cor.5:21)

3. There is purpose and encouragement. This is seen in two facts.

a. Jesus was deliberately "going up to Jerusalem." He did not have to go. He was fully Man, and as Man, He could choose what to do (Heb.2:16-18; 4:15). He knew what lay ahead, yet He would not shirk God's purpose.
b. Jesus deliberately took the disciples apart to prepare them for His coming death. They were to face the most shocking event of their lives—an event so shocking that it could potentially devastate their lives and hinder God's plan for the ages. Christ had to prepare them to withstand the shock of His death (see note—Mt.16:21-28).

There are at least two reasons why Jesus could not reveal His death by crucifixion to the public.

1. Many would have become discouraged from following Him. They would have feared the Romans who were to be the executioners of Christ. The fervor of the crowds would have cooled, and they would have forsaken Him. Seeing great crowds desert Christ could have discouraged the disciples tremendously, and this was not what they needed at this time. They needed encouragement and preparation for facing the cross.

2. Some of the people would be tempted to defend Christ, perhaps striking first. Some of the disciples, perhaps all, could be caught up in the fervor of such an ill-advised reaction.

Thought 1. Christ wants to draw all of us "aside."
1) He wants moments of tenderness and warmth with us, many such moments (Rev.3:20; cp. Ps.145:18; Lk.18:1; 1 Jn.1:3).
2) He wants us to draw near to Him in times of pressure and tension (Ph.4:6-7; Heb.4:15-16; Ps.34:18).
3) He wants us to draw near to Him for purpose and encouragement (Is.43:10; Mt.11:28-30; Jas.4:8-10). He wants us to guard against *shirking* God's purpose and to be more and more prepared to proclaim His death. He wants us fortified against the shock of being rejected, ridiculed, abused, and even persecuted as we go about fulfilling the purpose of God.

Thought 2. There are times to minister to the great crowds and times not to minister to them. The crowd was not yet ready to hear about the death of Christ. People have to be fed progressively. All have not reached the same level of spiritual growth and spiritual maturity.
1) Some are new in Christ. They are not yet grounded in the basics. They are not ready for the *meat* of the Word (1 Pt.2:2-3).
2) Some live carnal lives. They are not spiritually minded. They would not have the interest nor would they understand (1 Cor.3:1-2; Heb.5:11-14).
3) Some are unregenerate. They are in the church but are not followers of Christ. They have no interest in Christ and would be offended by the cross of Christ.

2 (20:18) **Jesus Christ, Death**: Christ was to be betrayed and delivered for prosecution.

1. The betrayer is not named. However, note the words "will be betrayed" (paradothesetai). The phrase means *will be turned over*. It is the same Greek word translated *will turn over* in the next verse. Who turned Jesus over to be prosecuted and executed? Jesus did not name the person. Scripture teaches that three persons delivered Jesus to be crucified (see note—Mt.17:22 for discussion).

2. The prosecutors of Jesus are named. They were the Jews, in particular the leaders among the Jews, the chief priests and Scribes and elders (see DEEPER STUDY # 1,2—Mt.16:21; note—1 Th.2:15-16). But note: they were to be only the prosecutors not the executioners. They were forbidden by law to execute anyone (Jn.18:31). They had to turn Him over to the Gentiles for execution. There is symbolism seen in this fact:
a. Both Jew and Gentile (the world) are guilty of the death of God's Son.
b. Christ was to bear the sin of both Jew and Gentile in His death. He was to reconcile both, that is, reconcile the whole world to God. (See outline and notes—Eph.2:14-18.)

"For God so loved the world that he gave his one and only Son, that whoever believes in him shall not perish but have eternal life. (John 3:16)
And in this one body to reconcile both of them to God through the cross, by which he put to death their hostility. (Eph 2:16)
And through him to reconcile to himself all things, whether things on earth or things in heaven, by making peace through his blood, shed on the cross. (Col 1:20)
He is the atoning sacrifice for our sins, and not only for ours but also for the sins of the whole world. (1 John 2:2)

Thought 1. There is a truth that is seldom thought about: we are to *think often about death* even as Christ was obsessed with His death. There are three reasons we are not to shun and deny the thought.
1) Death is an eternal matter even as life is an eternal matter (2 Cor.10:5).
2) Death is no longer to be feared (Heb.2:14-15; 2 Tim.1:7).
3) We are to live—dying daily, constantly denying self (see note and DEEPER STUDY # 1—Lk.9:23; cp. Ro.8:36; Tit.3:12-15).

DEEPER STUDY # 1
(20:18) **Jesus Christ, Death**: the pain of suffering reached its summit in the sufferings of Jesus Christ. He suffered pain to the ultimate degree, in an absolute sense. Yet in the midst of such terrible suffering, there is something that is very precious—a thought, a truth that should be very, very precious to us. It is this: *Jesus' death was dear to His own heart*—dear despite the terrible suffering He was to endure. In a way unknown to man and which can never be understood by man, Jesus set His heart and face toward the cross. He was consumed and obsessed with the cross. Why? Because the cross was the focus of God's purpose throughout all eternity.

1. The cross was dear to His heart because it was His Father's will. In dying, He could please His Father, and pleasing His Father was the supreme objective of His life (see note—Eph.5:2).

2. The cross was dear to His heart because it was the means by which He was to gain many brothers (see note—Ro.8:29).

3. The cross was dear to His heart because through death He was to be made *the author* of man's salvation (Heb.2:9-10).

4. The cross was dear to His heart because by death He was to destroy the power of the devil over man, that is, death (Heb.2:14-15).

5. The cross was dear to His heart because by the cross He was to reconcile all men, reconcile them both to God and to one another (see outline and notes—Eph.2:13-18).

6. The cross was dear to His heart because through death He was to return to His former glory which He had possessed with the Father before the foundation of the world (Jn.17:1-5).

3 (20:19) **Jesus Christ, Death**: Christ was to be delivered to the Gentiles for torture and execution. Note the three forms of torture mentioned.

⇒ Mockery: to ridicule, scorn, insult, humiliate, defy, jeer.
⇒ Flogging: to beat with a rod or a whip weighted with either jagged metal or bone chips. Thirty nine or forty lashes were inflicted. The whole purpose of scourging was to inflict severe pain.
⇒ Crucifixion (see DEEPER STUDY # 1—Mt.27:26-44 for the terrible suffering of the cross).

Jesus bore the sins of man, suffering the ultimate degree of pain. He suffered pain in an absolute sense.

1. Mentally: while He was being tortured, His mind was bound to be upon why He was suffering. He was thinking about the sin of man and the problem sin had caused God. Imagine the world's sin, all of it, the enormity and awfulness of it consuming His mind. He was suffering mentally to the ultimate degree.

> **God made him who had no sin to be sin for us, so that in him we might become the righteousness of God. (2 Cor 5:21)**
> **He is the atoning sacrifice for our sins, and not only for ours but also for the sins of the whole world. (1 John 2:2)**

2. Spiritually: His heart was being broken. Those whom He loved so much were committing a sin so horrendous it defied imagination. They were rebelling against God so much that they were killing God's own Son.

In addition and even more terrible, His own Father, God Himself, was to turn His back upon Him. God was to separate Himself from His very own Son (see notes—Mt.27:46-49; Mk.15:34). He was beginning to bear, and was going to bear, the judgment, condemnation, and punishment due man—He was going to bear spiritual pain in an absolute sense. The wrath of God's holiness against sin was to be cast against Him.

> **We all, like sheep, have gone astray, each of us has turned to his own way; and the LORD has laid on him the iniquity of us all. (Isa 53:6)**
> **And at the ninth hour Jesus cried out in a loud voice, "Eloi, Eloi, lama sabachthani?"—which means, "My God, my God, why have you forsaken me?" (Mark 15:34)**
> **And being in anguish, he prayed more earnestly, and his sweat was like drops of blood falling to the ground. (Luke 22:44)**
> **In bringing many sons to glory, it was fitting that God, for whom and through whom everything exists, should make the author of their salvation perfect through suffering. (Heb 2:10)**
> **Although he was a son, he learned obedience from what he suffered (Heb 5:8)**
> **And so Jesus also suffered outside the city gate to make the people holy through his own blood. (Heb 13:12)**
> **He himself bore our sins in his body on the tree, so that we might die to sins and live for righteousness; by his wounds you have been healed. (1 Pet 2:24)**
> **For Christ died for sins once for all, the righteous for the unrighteous, to bring you to God. He was put to death in the body but made alive by the Spirit, (1 Pet 3:18)**

3. Physically: His pain was to be more severe because of the mental and spiritual pressure He was having to bear at the same time. There is also truth to the fact that the more ridicule within a persecutor's heart, the more he tortures his victim (cp. the crown of thorns, royal robe, and excessive mockery of the soldiers). The fact that Christ claimed to be the Son of God aroused the persecutors to inflict more scorn and torture. (Cp. Mt.27:1f.)

> **I offered my back to those who beat me, my cheeks to those who pulled out my beard; I did not hide my face from mocking and spitting. (Isa 50:6)**
> **If someone asks him, 'What are these wounds on your body?' he will answer, 'The wounds I was given at the house of my friends.' (Zec 13:6)**
> **And then twisted together a crown of thorns and set it on his head. They put a staff in his right hand and knelt in front of him and mocked him. "Hail, king of the Jews!" they said. (Mat 27:29)**
> **When they had crucified him, they divided up his clothes by casting lots. (Mat 27:35)**
> **Those who passed by hurled insults at him, shaking their heads (Mat 27:39)**
> **Those who passed by hurled insults at him, shaking their heads and saying, "So! You who are going to destroy the temple and build it in three days, (Mark 15:29)**

Thought 1. Jesus suffered the ultimate degree of pain, and He did it *for us*. This fact should break our hearts, yet it seldom does. Why? Because so few of us spend time meditating upon His death—and, among us who do, an even smaller percentage spend anywhere close to the time that should be spent.

4 (20:19) **Jesus Christ, Resurrection**: Christ was to be raised from the dead. Covering the resurrection in the same discussion with His death does three major things.

1. The prediction of the resurrection drove the point of the resurrection into the mind of the disciples again. They must forever remember the resurrection. The death of Christ was not the final word.

> **Remember Jesus Christ, raised from the dead, descended from David. This is my gospel, (2 Tim 2:8)**

2. The prediction of the resurrection foreshadowed the power of God. After the Lord's resurrection, the disciples would remember, and the glorious truth of God's power would be reinforced in their minds and hearts forever.

a. The power of God is victorious.

> **"Where, O death, is your victory? Where, O death, is your sting?" But thanks be to God! He gives us the victory through our Lord Jesus Christ. (1 Cor 15:55, 57)**

b. The power of God does triumph.

> **And having disarmed the powers and authorities, he made a public spectacle of them, triumphing over them by the cross. (Col 2:15)**

c. The power of God does conquer.

> **No, in all these things we are more than conquerors through him who loved us. For I am convinced that neither death nor life, neither angels nor demons, neither the present nor the future, nor any powers,**

neither height nor depth, nor anything else in all creation, will be able to separate us from the love of God that is in Christ Jesus our Lord. (Rom 8:37-39)

Since the children have flesh and blood, he too shared in their humanity so that by his death he might destroy him who holds the power of death—that is, the devil— and free those who all their lives were held in slavery by their fear of death. (Heb 2:14-15)

3. The prediction of the resurrection foreshadowed the stirring that God's power was going to work in their lives.

a. The power to encourage and motivate.

I pray also that the eyes of your heart may be enlightened in order that you may know the hope to which he has called you, the riches of his glorious inheritance in the saints, and his incomparably great power for us who believe. That power is like the working of his mighty strength, (Eph 1:18-19)

For God did not give us a spirit of timidity, but a spirit of power, of love and of self-discipline. (2 Tim 1:7)

b. The power to assure and build confidence.

A week later his disciples were in the house again, and Thomas was with them. Though the doors were locked, Jesus came and stood among them and said, "Peace be with you!" Then he said to Thomas, "Put your finger here; see my hands. Reach out your hand and put it into my side. Stop doubting and believe." Thomas said to him, "My Lord and my God!" Then Jesus told him, "Because you have seen me, you have believed; blessed are those who have not seen and yet have believed." (John 20:26-29)

c. The power to give courage and boldness.

On their release, Peter and John went back to their own people and reported all that the chief priests and elders had said to them. When they heard this, they raised their voices together in prayer to God. "Sovereign Lord," they said, "you made the heaven and the earth and the sea, and everything in them. (Acts 4:23-24)

So do not be ashamed to testify about our Lord, or ashamed of me his prisoner. But join with me in suffering for the gospel, by the power of God, who has saved us and called us to a holy life—not because of anything we have done but because of his own purpose and grace. This grace was given us in Christ Jesus before the beginning of time, (2 Tim 1:8-9)

Outline	Scripture	Outline
	H. The Price & Meaning of Greatness, 20:20-28 (Mk.10:35-45; cp. Lk.22:24-27)	
1 The sin of false ambition—seeking personal greatness[DS1] a. Is self-seeking b. Is deceptive & uses people c. Misuses influence, position, & power d. Arises from pride & contempt e. Misunderstands true greatness	20 Then the mother of Zebedee's sons came to Jesus with her sons and, kneeling down, asked a favor of him. 21 "What is it you want?" he asked. She said, "Grant that one of these two sons of mine may sit at your right and the other at your left in your kingdom."	
2 What greatness requires: Is a person willing to pay the price? a. The price of contemplation: Understanding greatness b. The price of suffering: The cup[DS2] c. The price of determination: "We can" (v.22) d. The price of unshakeable loyalty: To Christ[DS3,4]	22 "You don't know what you are asking," Jesus said to them. "Can you drink the cup I am going to drink?" "We can," they answered. 23 Jesus said to them, "You will indeed drink from my cup, but to sit at my right or left is not for me to grant. These places belong to those for whom they have been prepared by my Father."	
	24 When the ten heard about this, they were indignant with the two brothers. 25 Jesus called them together and said, "You know that the rulers of the Gentiles lord it over them, and their high officials exercise authority over them.	**3 What greatness is** a. Eternal greatness is of God b. Greatness is not dominion over people 1) The disciples' misconception 2) The world's characteristics
	26 Not so with you. Instead, whoever wants to become great among you must be your servant, 27 And whoever wants to be first must be your slave—	c. Greatness is serving others 1) The great: Are servants 2) The greatest: Are slaves
	28 Just as the Son of Man did not come to be served, but to serve, and to give his life as a ransom for many."	d. True greatness is demonstrated by Christ[DS5]

DIVISION XIII

THE MESSIAH'S TEACHINGS ON THE WAY TO JERUSALEM, 19:1-20:34

H. The Price and Meaning of Greatness, 20:20-28

(20:20-28) **Introduction**: Jesus was on His way to Jerusalem. This was to be a momentous visit to the capital. This was the visit when the crisis was to take place, the crisis of His death and resurrection. He had just shared the fact of the crisis again (v.17-19). For months His death and resurrection had consumed His attention and private messages to the disciples (Mt.16:13-20; 16:21-28; 17:1-13; 17:22; 17:24-27; 20:17). There was no question in the disciples' minds: this visit to Jerusalem was the momentous event for which they had long looked. Jesus was about to free Israel and set up His kingdom on earth.

We who live today know what Christ meant by His death and resurrection. He was to die for our sins, and He was to be raised again to impart new life to us, but the disciples did not know this. Christ had not yet died nor been raised from the dead. To them, He was speaking of an earthly and material kingdom. If He were about to set up His kingdom, now was the time to seize the promise of position and power in His kingdom. Now was the time to secure the positions of rule and authority. (See notes—Mt.1:1; DEEPER STUDY # 2—1:18; DEEPER STUDY # 3—3:11; notes—11:1-6; 11:2-3; DEEPER STUDY # 1—11:5; DEEPER STUDY # 2—11:6; DEEPER STUDY # 1—12:16; note—Lk.7:21-23.)

This is what James and John were doing. They were assuring themselves of key positions in Christ's government. (See outlines and notes—Mt.18:1-4; Lk.22:24-30.)

1. The sins of false ambition—seeking personal greatness (v.20-21).
2. What greatness requires: Is a person willing to pay the price (v.22-23)?
3. What greatness is (v.23-28).

1 (20:20-21) **Ambition, False—Greatness**: note the sins of false ambition and of seeking personal greatness. They are fivefold.

1. False ambition is self-seeking. James and John were interested in position for honor only, not for the purpose of serving. Pomp and ceremony, position and recognition, power and authority were on their minds, not ministering to and serving people.

2. False ambition is deceptive and uses people. Note how deceptively James and John and their mother came to Jesus. The sons persuaded their mother to use her influence with Jesus. She was a tool for their ambition. By her having taken the lead, they hoped Christ would think the request originated with her and not with them. He had already rebuked them for self-ambition (see outline and notes—Mt.18:1-4). Ambition often causes us to use people. Too often we put desire for things, position, power, and influence before and over people. Some even deceive and use others to achieve their ends.

3. False ambition misuses influence, position, and power. James and John along with Peter formed the inner circle around Christ. Christ gave them opportunities to witness several events the others were not permitted to see. They felt more favored and felt that their position was superior to the other disciples (see DEEPER STUDY # 1—Mk.9:2). This became especially true when James and John used their family's position to influence Jesus (see DEEPER STUDY # 1—Mt.20:20-21).

4. False ambition arises from pride. They felt more honored, more special, more preferred; and they were showing their conceit. They fully expected their request to be granted. Their kneeling with their mother (probably behind their mother) showed this. There is always contempt for others in pride. Feeling more honored and more preferred elevates one over others and treats them as inferior.

5. False ambition misunderstands the facts. James and John did not understand Jesus' death and resurrection. They misinterpreted it. They made the same mistake that man so often makes: they spiritualized God's Word.

When Christ said that He was to die, they probably thought He was referring to the conflict that was going to take place as He overthrew Roman domination. When Christ said that He was to arise, they probably thought it referred to the rising of God's kingdom to power. They thought only in terms of an earthly or temporal power. They missed the point entirely—missed the literal death and resurrection of God's Son which was to save man spiritually and eternally. The point is this: false ambition centers attention on securing things now, not eternally. It interprets life and the values of life only in terms of earthly power, position, recognition, and wealth. It fails to see that such is ever so brief and does not last. It misunderstands the facts entirely.

Thought 1. There is good, healthy ambition; and there is bad, unhealthy ambition. Good ambition gives purpose, meaning, and significance to life; it builds drive, initiative, self-esteem and much, much more. All such qualities are healthy and needed by every human being. We must all feel worthwhile, yet true inner health comes only from serving others, not from position and power. This is what James and John were missing.

Bad ambition is false ambition. It is deceptive in every conceivable way. It may lead to exaltation and power, but it corrupts and destroys. It eats away at a person's body as well as a person's spirit and consumes and misuses people. Sin corrupts and destroys, so false ambition is sin.

Thought 2. There is nothing wrong with high positions of responsibility and authority. Leadership and organization, government and law, teachers and learners, parent and child—all are essential. However, all positions should exist not to *lord it over people* but to serve people. We are to seek to serve people, not seek to rule people. Our ambition should not be to *lead* but to serve. This was James' and John's error. It is often ours. There is a tremendous difference between leading and serving.

Thought 3. There is something very commendable about James and John in this experience: their strong faith in Jesus and His kingdom. They were wrong in their ambition, but they were right about Jesus Himself. He was the true Messiah who had come to rule over the works and lives of men. They were just wrong about His method. He was going to do it spiritually not militarily.

Thought 4. James and John had left all for Christ (Mt.19:27-29). They had travelled about the country and suffered with Him for three years. Now they thought their trials were about over. Christ was going to change things and raise them up above the sufferings, and He was to reward their trust. They were so wrong. Like so many of us, they misunderstood what following Christ really meant. Christ does not remove our trials; He carries us through them. He does not take suffering away; He delivers us through suffering. Our rest from labor and trials and our crown come in the next world, not this world.

DEEPER STUDY # 1

(20:20-21) **Salome**: the mother of James and John was named Salome (Mt.27:56; cp. Mk.15:40; 16:1). An interesting fact is that Salome was probably the sister of Mary, the mother of Jesus, which means that James and John were first cousins of Jesus. We see this in Mark's and John's accounts of the crucifixion. Mark says that Salome was at the cross with Mary, Jesus' mother (Mk.15:40). John simply says, "[Jesus'] mother... his mother's sister...." (John 17:25).

2 (20:22-23) **Greatness**: What does greatness require, and, is a person willing to pay the price? Christ told James and John how to become great; greatness in His kingdom requires four things.

1. The price of contemplating suffering and death. A person must understand that greatness involves the suffering of discipline and obedience and the death of self and comfort, of indulgence and extravagance. The person must think about, contemplate, and understand what he is seeking. Thinking takes time; it takes concentration, energy, and effort. It means many long and tiring hours and days of concentration in study and learning. It means knowing and understanding what one asks. It means knowing where one is, has been, and should be going in life.

2. The price of bearing the cup of suffering. It means a willingness to die to self daily and to give one's life in bearing whatever has to be borne in order to serve Christ (see DEEPER STUDY # 2, Cup—Mt.20:22-23; note and DEEPER STUDY # 1—LK.9:23).

3. The price of determination. James and John answered Christ: "We can." Greatness is accepting the challenge because one loves the Lord and is willing to share in His sufferings and death no matter the cost.

4. The price of unshakable loyalty to Christ. Greatness is enduring and persevering no matter the suffering or denial demanded. James and John both drank the cup (see DEEPER STUDY # 3,4—Mt.20:23).

In the same way, any of you who does not give up everything he has cannot be my disciple. (Luke 14:33)

Then he said to them all: "If anyone would come after me, he must deny himself and take up his cross daily and follow me. For whoever wants to save his life will lose it, but whoever loses his life for me will save it. (Luke 9:23-24)

"If anyone comes to me and does not hate his father and mother, his wife and children, his brothers and sisters—yes, even his own life—he cannot be my disciple. And anyone who does not carry his cross and follow me cannot be my disciple. (Luke 14:26-27)

For if you live according to the sinful nature, you will die; but if by the Spirit you put to death the misdeeds of the body, you will live, (Rom 8:13)

Those who belong to Christ Jesus have crucified the sinful nature with its passions and desires. (Gal 5:24)

What is more, I consider everything a loss compared to the surpassing greatness of knowing Christ Jesus my Lord, for whose sake I have lost all things. I consider them rubbish, that I may gain Christ (Phil 3:8)

Thought 1. Christ pulls no punches. If we desire greatness, there is a price to pay, a tremendous price. If we wish to have the crown He gives, there is a bitter cup to be drunk (see note—Mt.20:22).

Thought 2. When we say "yes" to Christ, we have to mean it. There has to be an iron determination to follow Him. We must be able to say with James and John, "We can"—no matter the cup. However, we must always remember that *we are able* only through the strength of His resurrected power.

Thought 3. Note that Christ did not write James and John off because they were wrong and had committed a terrible sin. He did not give up on them, cast them aside as useless. He simply corrected them, taught them the truth, and continued to use them. Note something else: Christ trusted them. He knew their hearts deep within, knew they would come through and, in the final analysis, pay any price for Him.

There is a tremendous lesson here. Christ believes in us and counts us trustworthy (1 Tim.1:12; cp. Ro.8:28f). Even when we fail and begin to dislike and hate ourselves, He loves and cares for us, wanting to correct us, teach us, and set us back on our feet on the path of usefulness.

DEEPER STUDY # 2
20:23) **James**: was killed by Herod. He was the first apostle to drink the cup of martyrdom.

DEEPER STUDY # 3
(20:23) **John**: lived to be around one hundred years old and died in bed as far as we know. However, he drank the cup of suffering in a most distressful way:
⇒ He witnessed the sufferings of Christ's death.
⇒ He lived through the murder and deaths of all the other apostles.
⇒ He lived a long life of banishment and exile on the island of Patmos (see Introduction, Revelation—Date).

3 (20:23-28) **Greatness**: What is true greatness? It is four things.

1. Greatness that is eternal is of God. There is no greatness other than that of God, not a greatness that brings eternal position and honor. The greatness conceived by men is superficial; it fades away. Note two things Christ seemed to be saying.

a. Christ said that some will sit on His right hand and some on His left hand. God is preparing to bestow such honor upon some. This seems to point toward degrees of glory in heaven (cp. v.26-27).
b. Christ was saying that the right to reign with Him was to be determined by God alone (that is, His absolute justice). He also made a distinction between *the great* who only commit themselves to serve, and the *first* (greatest) who commit themselves to be *bond-slaves* (v.26; cp. v.27).

What I tell you in the dark, speak in the daylight; what is whispered in your ear, proclaim from the roofs. (Mat 10:27)

Whoever serves me must follow me; and where I am, my servant also will be. My Father will honor the one who serves me. (John 12:26)

Now that I, your Lord and Teacher, have washed your feet, you also should wash one another's feet. (John 13:14)

Again Jesus said, "Simon son of John, do you truly love me?" He answered, "Yes, Lord, you know that I love you." Jesus said, "Take care of my sheep." (John 21:16)

You were bought at a price. Therefore honor God with your body. (1 Cor 6:20)

For he who was a slave when he was called by the Lord is the Lord's freedman; similarly, he who was a free man when he was called is Christ's slave. (1 Cor 7:22)

Since you know that you will receive an inheritance from the Lord as a reward. It is the Lord Christ you are serving. (Col 3:24)

2. Greatness is not dominion over people. The disciples still thought the Messiah's kingdom would be the restoration of Israel as an earthly nation and power. The ten other disciples were indignant because they desired the highest positions themselves. They would have been worried, not angered, by such evil and selfish behavior if they had not had the same feelings. The world's view of greatness is twofold.

a. The external view is measured by power, fame, recognition, influence, authority, dominion, and position.
b. The internal view is measured by wealth, buildings, vehicles, and machines, and the ability to work and achieve goals. The world seeks after these things; individuals as well as nations seek after them. In fact, most men are caught up to some degree in *worldly greatness*, seeking some recognition, position, influence, fame, and wealth. Few are void of *worldly greatness*.

He who loves a quarrel loves sin; he who builds a high gate invites destruction. (Prov 17:19)

It is not good to eat too much honey, nor is it honorable to seek one's own honor. (Prov 25:27)

For whoever exalts himself will be humbled, and whoever humbles himself will be exalted. (Mat 23:12)

How can you believe if you accept praise from one another, yet make no effort to obtain the praise that comes from the only God ? (John 5:44)

3. Greatness is serving others. The great are they who minister. The greatest, the first among all, are they who are bond-slaves (see note—Ro.1:1). Note the two words *first* (protos) and *slave* (doulos, bond slave). Christ made a significant distinction between what He said in v.26 and v.27. The difference is striking and challenging. There is...

- the *great* (v.26) vs. the *first* (v.27).
- the *minister* (v.26) vs. the *slave* (v.27).

Another way to see the difference is...

- the *great* are they who *are servants*.
- the *first* are they who are *slaves*.

What Christ was saying is this: among His disciples, the person who serves is great, but the person who is a slave is the first. The idea of the person who serves is that of occasional service; whereas the slave is a person who is bound to the Lord every moment of life, always serving, regardless of the hour or call or difficulty.

The idea that there are degrees of service is unquestionably in mind. Not every believer serves with the same fervor or commitment. The idea of *degrees of reward* for work is conveyed by our Lord time and again (see note, Reward—Lk.16:10-12 for a complete list).

> **And if anyone gives even a cup of cold water to one of these little ones because he is my disciple, I tell you the truth, he will certainly not lose his reward." (Mat 10:42)**
> **In the same way your Father in heaven is not willing that any of these little ones should be lost. (Mat 18:14)**
> **But you are not to be like that. Instead, the greatest among you should be like the youngest, and the one who rules like the one who serves. (Luke 22:26)**
> **Now that I, your Lord and Teacher, have washed your feet, you also should wash one another's feet. (John 13:14)**
> **Serve wholeheartedly, as if you were serving the Lord, not men, (Eph 6:7)**
> **Therefore, since we are receiving a kingdom that cannot be shaken, let us be thankful, and so worship God acceptably with reverence and awe, (Heb 12:28)**
> **Humility and the fear of the LORD bring wealth and honor and life. (Prov 22:4)**
> **He has showed you, O man, what is good. And what does the LORD require of you? To act justly and to love mercy and to walk humbly with your God. (Micah 6:8)**

4. True greatness was demonstrated by Christ in three supreme acts.
   a. The act of coming to earth: "The Son of Man came." The incarnation is the Son of God becoming man. Most men look upon mankind as the summit of creation on this earth. But within the span and scope of the universe and the dimension of the spiritual world, and in particular before God, man is nothing—not to an honest and thinking man. He is only as a speck of sand on the beach or a drop of water in the ocean. At most, he lasts only about seventy years *if he can*.
   In all reality, for God to become a member of so low a race of beings is unimaginable. It is the most humiliating act possible.
   b. The act of ministering: "[He] came not to be served, but to serve." Furthermore, He was treated as the lowest of creatures by the men to whom He came. Impossible, yet true! They gave Him no place to lay His head (Mt.8:20; Lk.9:58) and, only three years after publicly announcing that He had come to save them, they killed Him. Now note: Jesus is the King of kings and Lord of lords, yet He secured His kingdom by becoming a minister and a slave to all. He did not *lord it* over men. He ministered to and served men, and because He became the slave to all, God has now highly exalted Him (Ph.2:8).
   c. The act of giving His life "a ransom for many" (see note—Mt.20:28).

DEEPER STUDY # 4

(20:28) **Ransom for many** (lutron anti pollon): a ransom in exchange (anti) for many; a ransom for many; a ransom instead of many.

Ransom is a means of setting loose in the Old Testament. It is the setting loose of a life or the ransom for a life (Ex.21:30). It is the setting loose, the ransom price, the redemptive price for something, for example...

- it is the price paid for the setting loose or freeing of a slave (Lev.19:20).
- it is the redemptive price paid for land (Lev.25:24).
- it is the ransom price paid for a captive (Is.45:13).

The Greek word for ransom (lutron) is significant. There is no question that the idea of *exchange* is present. Christ gave His life in *exchange*, that is, in the place of or as a substitute for many. (See DEEPER STUDY # 2, Justification—Ro.4:22; note—5:1.)

The word is used two other times in the New Testament (Mk. 10:45; 1 Tim.2:6). In 1 Tim.2:6, the words are "a substitutionary ransom for all" (antilutron huper panton). *Huper* is the preposition for the idea of substitution. It is a substitution in behalf of all. However, note two things.

1. All do not receive the offer. Paul said, "[Christ] gave Himself as a ransom for all" (1 Tim.2:6). John said, "He is the atoning sacrifice [propitiation]...for the sins of the whole world" (1 Jn.2:2). And He is—potentially. Christ has met the need and provided the ransom price for every man and woman, but everyone has to accept the offer of the ransom in their own behalf. Christ has made provision, but anyone can reject the offer of ransom. And some do. Therefore, Scripture speaks of Christ's dying "for all" and also "for many." He died for *all* in that He has made *provision* for all to be saved, but He died for *many* in that only some receive the offer of the ransom.

2. There is the idea of sacrifice in the word ransom. In fact, that is just what *ransom* is. It is the exchange, the sacrifice, the giving up of something for something else. Something is substituted and sacrificed for something else. This is exactly what Christ did for us. He sacrificed and gave Himself up as a ransom for us (Eph.1:7; 1 Jn.2:1-2). (Cp. the Old Testament sacrifices; they were a picture of what Christ was to do for us.)

> **And from Jesus Christ, who is the faithful witness, the firstborn from the dead, and the ruler of the kings of the earth. To him who loves us and has freed us from our sins by his blood, (Rev 1:5)**
> **For you know that it was not with perishable things such as silver or gold that you were redeemed from the empty way of life handed down to you from your forefathers, but with the precious blood of Christ, a lamb without blemish or defect. (1 Pet 1:18-19)**
> **Christ redeemed us from the curse of the law by becoming a curse for us, for it is written: "Cursed is everyone who is hung on a tree." (Gal 3:13)**
> **And he died for all, that those who live should no longer live for themselves but for him who died for them and was raised again. (2 Cor 5:15)**

God made him who had no sin to be sin for us, so that in him we might become the righteousness of God. (2 Cor 5:21)

Unlike the other high priests, he does not need to offer sacrifices day after day, first for his own sins, and then for the sins of the people. He sacrificed for their sins once for all when he offered himself. (Heb 7:27)

The blood of goats and bulls and the ashes of a heifer sprinkled on those who are ceremonially unclean sanctify them so that they are outwardly clean. How much more, then, will the blood of Christ, who through the eternal Spirit offered himself unblemished to God, cleanse our consciences from acts that lead to death, so that we may serve the living God! (Heb 9:13-14)

Nor did he enter heaven to offer himself again and again, the way the high priest enters the Most Holy Place every year with blood that is not his own. Then Christ would have had to suffer many times since the creation of the world. But now he has appeared once for all at the end of the ages to do away with sin by the sacrifice of himself. (Heb 9:25-26)

And by that will, we have been made holy through the sacrifice of the body of Jesus Christ once for all. (Heb 10:10)

But when this priest had offered for all time one sacrifice for sins, he sat down at the right hand of God. because by one sacrifice he has made perfect forever those who are being made holy. (Heb 10:12, 14)

He himself bore our sins in his body on the tree, so that we might die to sins and live for righteousness; by his wounds you have been healed. (1 Pet 2:24; cp. 1 Cor.5:7; Eph.5:2)

	I. The Two Blind Men Healed: How the Desperate Can Be Saved, 20:29-34 (Mk.10:46-52; cp. Lk.18:35-43)	mercy on us!"	
		31 The crowd rebuked them and told them to be quiet, but they shouted all the louder, "Lord, Son of David, have mercy on us!"	a. In the face of opposition
		32 Jesus stopped and called them. "What do you want me to do for you?" he asked.	b. Until Jesus responds
1 Jesus left Jericho a. The crowd followed Him b. Two blind men sat nearby	29 As Jesus and his disciples were leaving Jericho, a large crowd followed him.	33 "Lord," they answered, "we want our sight."	**5 Step 4: Asking great things of Christ**
2 Step 1: Seizing the chance when Jesus passes by **3 Step 2: Crying for mercy**[DS1] **4 Step 3: Persisting in crying for mercy**	30 Two blind men were sitting by the roadside, and when they heard that Jesus was going by, they shouted, "Lord, Son of David, have	34 Jesus had compassion on them and touched their eyes. Immediately they received their sight and followed him.	**6 Step 5: Receiving the compassion & touch of Jesus** **7 Step 6: Following Jesus**

DIVISION XIII

THE MESSIAH'S TEACHINGS ON THE WAY TO JERUSALEM, 19:1-20:34

I. The Two Blind Men Healed: How the Desperate Can be Saved, 20:29-34

(20:29-34) **Introduction**: we live in a desperate world full of desperate people. Many hurt because of emptiness, loneliness, disease, death, accidents, problems, conflicts, difficulties, poverty, hunger, no purpose, no meaning, no significance, hopelessness, and helplessness. The two blind men show how the desperate can be saved and helped.

1. Jesus left Jericho (v.29-30).
2. Step 1: seizing the chance when Jesus passes by (v.30).
3. Step 2: crying for mercy (v.30).
4. Step 3: persisting in crying for mercy (v.31-32).
5. Step 4: asking great things of Christ (v.33).
6. Step 5: receiving the compassion and touch of Jesus(v.34).
7. Step 6: following Jesus (v.34).

1 (20:29-30) **Multitudes—Jesus Christ**: as Jesus left Jericho there was also a host of pilgrims on their way to Jerusalem to celebrate the passover feast. The famous Jewish historian Josephus estimated that two to three million attended this feast every year. An enormous crowd would have been following Christ at this time.

There were several reasons why the crowds followed Christ in such numbers throughout His ministry.

1. Some followed Christ because they had great need. They truly believed He could help them.

2. Some followed Christ for what they could get out of Him. Following Him met, to some degree, their material and physical desires (Jn.6:26).

3. Some followed Christ out of curiosity.

4. Some followed Christ because they thought He was the answer to utopia, to personal and national fulfillment. They thought He might possibly be the Messiah who was to free Israel and meet the needs of its people forever (see DEEPER STUDY # 2—Mt.1:18).

5. Some few followed Christ because they honestly believed He was the true Messiah and had the words of eternal life. They desired to be a true disciple of His (Jn.6:67-68; cp. Jn.1:29, 34, 40-41, 45, 49; Mt.16:16).

As Jesus was walking out of the city, two blind men were sitting on the side of the road. There are three things said about these two men.

⇒ They were desperate. They were both blind and suffering the same physical infirmity.

⇒ They were together. They were companions who found some fellowship together. They sat and talked together, and as this event shows, acted together.

⇒ They were sitting where Christ passed by. Some may call it fate or chance, others destiny, and still others purpose; but the fact is, they were exactly where Christ passed by.

Thought 1. The two men suffered together and acted together. There is great benefit in our sharing together with someone who has a common experience, not to moan over our common plight but to encourage one another.

Note another fact: Christ encourages praying together. Every friendship among Christians should include praying together. These two men approached Christ together, and they could not even see. Christ should be made a significant part of our fellowship (Mt.18:20).

Thought 2. Note two things.

1) The needy and desperate need to put themselves where Christ is. They need to go and sit where they know they can hear Christ.
2) The needy and desperate can have great hope, but there is a condition. They must be where they can hear Christ. If these two had been elsewhere, they would have missed Christ. It is critical to find out where Christ can be heard.

2 (20:30) **Salvation—Need**: first, the desperate can be saved by seizing the chance when Christ passes by, but alertness and sensitivity are essential. These two men were both alert and sensitive. They heard the feet and the conversation of the crowd as they passed by. Hearing the feet of the crowd alerted them, and hearing the conversation told them exactly what was going on.

Thought 1. The desperate can find where Jesus is by being alert to where God's people go and by listening to where God's people say He is. The feet and voice of the followers of Christ will direct the desperate to Christ.

Thought 2. One thing is critical for the desperate: to seize the opportunity. They must not let it pass. When we see or hear where Jesus is we must go to Him. If we do not put ourselves where He is, we increase the chance that we will miss Him forever. There are three reasons why our chances diminish.

1) We become more dull, hardened, insensitive, unconcerned, and inactive; and we begin to accept conditions as they are.
2) A more convenient time will never present itself. Intentions are good, but an immediate decision is needed. Paul preached and many listened. A few said, "We want to hear you again on this matter" (Acts 17:32). But they never did.
3) Christ may never come our way again. If He does, He may not return with such force.

God did this so that men would seek him and perhaps reach out for him and find him, though he is not far from each one of us. (Acts 17:27)

Look to the LORD and his strength; seek his face always. (Psa 105:4)

Seek the LORD, all you humble of the land, you who do what he commands. Seek righteousness, seek humility; perhaps you will be sheltered on the day of the Lord's anger. (Zep 2:3)

Seek the LORD while he may be found; call on him while he is near. (Isa 55:6)

3 (20:30) **Salvation—Mercy**: second, the desperate can be saved by crying for mercy. Three things need to be noted about the two blind men's crying out for mercy.

1. They had an imperfect knowledge of Christ. They were blind; therefore, they could not travel about and learn of Him. Their knowledge of Him was based upon what they had heard *about* Him.

2. They believed what they had heard: that He was the Messiah, the promised Son of David. They believed in His power to help and deliver them.

3. They stirred themselves up and cried out for mercy. Imagine the obstacles: the crowd was large, the noise was loud. They were blind, and their chance of getting to Christ and being heard by Him was slim. But two things made the difference. They were desperate, and they believed. So they stirred themselves up, and cried out. *They acted on what knowledge and faith* they had.

There are two important facts about their cry for mercy.

⇒ They cried out for mercy themselves. They did not ask someone else to approach Christ for them.

⇒ They asked for mercy and only mercy. They did not ask for anything else. They were poor and they were beggars, but they did not ask for housing or clothing or even for food. They asked for their most basic need to be met—for mercy.

His mercy extends to those who fear him, from generation to generation. (Luke 1:50)

"But the tax collector stood at a distance. He would not even look up to heaven, but beat his breast and said, 'God, have mercy on me, a sinner.' "I tell you that this man, rather than the other, went home justified before God. For everyone who exalts himself will be humbled, and he who humbles himself will be exalted." (Luke 18:13-14)

But because of his great love for us, God, who is rich in mercy, made us alive with Christ even when we were dead in transgressions—it is by grace you have been saved. (Eph 2:4-5)

Be merciful to me, LORD, for I am faint; O LORD, heal me, for my bones are in agony. My soul is in anguish. How long, O LORD, how long? (Psa 6:2-3)

Hear my voice when I call, O LORD; be merciful to me and answer me. (Psa 27:7)

For the director of music. A psalm of David. When the prophet Nathan came to him after David had committed adultery with Bathsheba. Have mercy on me, O God, according to your unfailing love; according to your great compassion blot out my transgressions. (Psa 51:1)

Show us your unfailing love, O LORD, and grant us your salvation. (Psa 85:7)

Let your compassion come to me that I may live, for your law is my delight. (Psa 119:77)

Rend your heart and not your garments. Return to the LORD your God, for he is gracious and compassionate, slow to anger and abounding in love, and he relents from sending calamity. (Joel 2:13)

Do not gloat over me, my enemy! Though I have fallen, I will rise. Though I sit in darkness, the LORD will be my light. (Micah 7:8)

DEEPER STUDY # 1

(20:30) **Son of David**: see notes—Mt.1:1; DEEPER STUDY # 2—1:18; DEEPER STUDY # 3—3:11; notes—11:1-6; 11:2-3; DEEPER STUDY # 1—11:5; DEEPER STUDY # 2—11:6; DEEPER STUDY # 1—12:16; note—Lk.7:21-23.

4 (20:31-32) **Salvation—Persistence**: third, the desperate can be saved by persisting in their cry for mercy.

1. The desperate must persist even in the face of opposition. A person who really wants Christ is to persevere; he is to fight against all obstacles until Christ responds.

These two men teach us perseverance. The crowd rebuked and tried to stop them from reaching Christ, but they would not be stopped. Note the Scripture: "They shouted all the louder." A stream of fervency and sensation vibrated through their bodies. They were in dead earnest; nothing was going to keep them back. They were desperate—this opportunity might never come again—so they struggled, wrestled, and fought against the crowd, crying at the top of their voices, "Lord, Son of David, have mercy on us."

Thought 1. Note two things.

1) There are many hindrances to our seeking after Christ—hindrances within and without. Sometimes we stand in the way, sometimes another person, sometimes circumstances. The hindrances are always there.
2) Hindrances are to be struggled against and overcome. We are not to give in to hindrances, but we

are to use them to learn endurance and experience (victorious living) and hope. Trials are to be used to sharpen, to increase, and to grow our faith. It is for this reason that we not only "rejoice in the hope of the glory of God....but we also rejoice in our sufferings" (Ro.5:2-4).

2. The desperate are to persist until Jesus responds. Persistence always grabs the Lord's attention (see outline and notes—Mt.7:7-11. Cp. Lk.18:1.) Note the question Jesus asked. He already knew what the blind men wanted. He had probably heard their crying out as well, but He wanted them to experience persistence. Why? Why does Christ teach persistence and perseveThere are at least five reasons.

⇒ Having to persevere sharpens and grows our faith. It teaches endurance, character (victorious living), and hope (Ro.5:2-4).
⇒ Having to persevere sharpens and makes us more aware of our minds. It gives us more time for thought, meditation, and searching for the truth of ourselves and our needs. It zeros in on real needs.
⇒ Having to persevere teaches us to pray and to seek God more and more. It creates more awareness of our helplessness and our need for His presence and help. It necessitates more fellowship and deep communion with Him.
⇒ Having to persevere gives us more part in His work and worship. It creates a sense within us of having a greater part. This is not a need on God's part, but a need on our part. Serving Him is a great privilege which He allows us.
⇒ Having to persevere allows more time for a greater number of people to be reached with God's power. Perseverance is a greater witness for God. When God answers and moves, more people are aroused to observe God's working.

"Ask and it will be given to you; seek and you will find; knock and the door will be opened to you. (Mat 7:7)

But if from there you seek the LORD your God, you will find him if you look for him with all your heart and with all your soul. (Deu 4:29)

This is what the LORD says to the house of Israel: "Seek me and live; (Amos 5:4)

Thought 1. This is an important lesson for the church. Often the poor and most needful are pushed back, ignored, neglected, rebuked, and not wanted by the church. They are thought to be lazy or lacking in initiative or unable to contribute much. The church rationalizes that the poor and needy would feel uncomfortable and not want to be a part of the fellowship anyway.

Our Lord never rejected a person. He never planned for the church to meet the needs only of a certain class. What is class anyway? Is it a certain amount of money? Is is a certain *number* of dresses? Of suits? Of shoes? Of watches? Is it a certain *size* of house? Of car? Of office? Of desk? Of chair? Is it stature? Hairstyle? Is it a certain location in town? In a suburb? Beside a golf course? A lake? How foolish can we be? How long will we play the fool while the world around us cries out in desperation? Is there anyone anywhere who will think and see and feel as God thinks and sees and feels? Where is the person who will stand in the gap for God and reach out to help the lost and poor of this world?

5 (20:33) **Prayer**: fourth, the desperate can be saved by asking great things of Christ. Note what a great request they asked of Christ.

1. They were beggars, ever so poor. There was nothing appealing about them at all.

2. Society rejected them. Even the crowd surrounding Jesus pushed them away and tried to silence their search for God.

3. They had never followed Christ. They had never heard Him preach even once. They knew very little about Him.

4. They had an unbelievable request to make: for Christ to heal their blindness.

If you believe, you will receive whatever you ask for in prayer." (Mat 21:22)

And I will do whatever you ask in my name, so that the Son may bring glory to the Father. (John 14:13)

If you remain in me and my words remain in you, ask whatever you wish, and it will be given you. (John 15:7)

Until now you have not asked for anything in my name. Ask and you will receive, and your joy will be complete. (John 16:24)

This is the confidence we have in approaching God: that if we ask anything according to his will, he hears us. And if we know that he hears us—whatever we ask—we know that we have what we asked of him. (1 John 5:14-15)

Before they call I will answer; while they are still speaking I will hear. (Isa 65:24)

'Call to me and I will answer you and tell you great and unsearchable things you do not know.' (Jer 33:3)

Thought 1. Many come to Christ only when they are in physical trouble (blindness). However, their real problem is spiritual blindness. They are spiritually blind and do not know it (Jn.9:41).

Thought 2. There is a lesson here on being specific in our requests. At first, the blind men asked for mercy without identifying just where they needed mercy. Christ asked for them to be specific: "What do you want me to do for you?"

6 (20:34) **Decision**: fifth, the desperate can be saved by receiving the compassion and touch of Jesus. Note what happens.

1. Jesus had compassion. They no sooner asked than Jesus' compassion was immediately aroused. He cared and felt for them.

2. Jesus touched their eyes. He did more than express compassion and feelings; He reached out to them and touched them. He let them feel His touch and care. He reached out and gave Himself to them. What a lesson for ministry!

3. Jesus healed them. They *immediately* experienced the love and power of God. They were healed.

Therefore he is able to save completely those who come to God through him, because he always lives to intercede for them. (Heb 7:25)

And without faith it is impossible to please God, because anyone who comes to him must believe that he exists and that he rewards those who earnestly seek him. (Heb 11:6)

Commit your way to the LORD; trust in him and he will do this: (Psa 37:5)

Trust in the LORD with all your heart and lean not on your own understanding; (Prov 3:5)

Trust in the LORD forever, for the LORD, the LORD, is the Rock eternal. (Isa 26:4)

Thought 1. The men had their prayer and cry answered; they had their need met for two reasons.
1) They believed in Christ, the Messiah, and His power to meet their need.
2) They persisted in that belief. They were not quitters. They did not allow other people and circumstances to prevent them from seeking Jesus.

7 (20:34) **Discipleship**: sixth, the desperate can be saved by following Jesus. Note the simple words: "And [they] followed Him." He had shown mercy, and they became His disciples. Being a disciple meant two things.

1. They followed Him to learn of Him.

Then he said to them all: "If anyone would come after me, he must deny himself and take up his cross daily and follow me. (Luke 9:23)

My sheep listen to my voice; I know them, and they follow me. (John 10:27)

Whoever serves me must follow me; and where I am, my servant also will be. My Father will honor the one who serves me. (John 12:26)

Be imitators of God, therefore, as dearly loved children (Eph 5:1)

So then, just as you received Christ Jesus as Lord, continue to live in him, (Col 2:6)

To this you were called, because Christ suffered for you, leaving you an example, that you should follow in his steps. (1 Pet 2:21)

Whoever claims to live in him must walk as Jesus did. (1 John 2:6)

2. They followed Him to be witnesses to Him and His power.

In the same way, let your light shine before men, that they may see your good deeds and praise your Father in heaven. (Mat 5:16)

So that with one heart and mouth you may glorify the God and Father of our Lord Jesus Christ. (Rom 15:6)

You were bought at a price. Therefore honor God with your body. (1 Cor 6:20)

We pray this so that the name of our Lord Jesus may be glorified in you, and you in him, according to the grace of our God and the Lord Jesus Christ. (2 Th 1:12)

Through Jesus, therefore, let us continually offer to God a sacrifice of praise—the fruit of lips that confess his name. (Heb 13:15)

But you are a chosen people, a royal priesthood, a holy nation, a people belonging to God, that you may declare the praises of him who called you out of darkness into his wonderful light. (1 Pet 2:9)

Sing praises to the LORD, enthroned in Zion; proclaim among the nations what he has done. (Psa 9:11)

May the peoples praise you, O God; may all the peoples praise you. (Psa 67:3)

Thought 1. There is a lesson here on gratitude. The men expressed their appreciation in the greatest way possible. They became witnesses to His benevolence, love, mercy, and power. Many never express gratitude at all. Too many get what they want then soon forget that it came from God.

Outline	Scripture	Scripture (cont.)	Outline (cont.)
	CHAPTER 21 **XIV. THE MESSIAH'S LAST WEEK: HIS CLAIM CHALLENGED AND REJECTED, 21:1-23:39** **A. The Triumphal Entry: Jesus Deliberately Claimed to Be the Messiah**[DS1] **21:1-11** (Mk.11:1-11; Lk.19: 28-40; Jn.12:12-19)	prophet: 5 "Say to the Daughter of Zion, 'See, your king comes to you, gentle and riding on a donkey, on a colt, the foal of a donkey.'"	a picture of Zech.9:9 1) A warning to Jerusalem 2) The King comes 3) He comes gently 4) He comes upon a colt[DS3]
		6 The disciples went and did as Jesus had instructed them. 7 They brought the donkey and the colt, placed their cloaks on them, and Jesus sat on them.	**3 He deliberately received the homage of the disciples** a. They did as He requested b. They used their own clothes for a saddle
1 Jesus' last week began in Jerusalem a. In suburb: Bethphage[DS2] b. Sent two disciples on a special mission	As they approached Jerusalem and came to Bethphage on the Mount of Olives, Jesus sent two disciples,	8 A very large crowd spread their cloaks on the road, while others cut branches from the trees and spread them on the road.	**4 He deliberately received the homage of the people** a. Many received Him as King: Spread cloaks & branches before Him
2 He deliberately fulfilled prophecy a. The disciples' special mission: To secure a donkey & her colt	2 Saying to them, "Go to the village ahead of you, and at once you will find a donkey tied there, with her colt by her. Untie them and bring them to me.	9 The crowds that went ahead of him and those that followed shouted, "Hosanna to the Son of David!" "Blessed is he who comes in the name of the Lord!" "Hosanna in the highest!"	b. Many received Him as Messiah: Hosanna 1) As the Son of David 2) As the Lord 3) As the Highest
	3 If anyone says anything to you, tell him that the Lord needs them, and he will send them right away."	10 When Jesus entered Jerusalem, the whole city was stirred and asked, "Who is this?"	**5 Conclusion: The question of the people in Jerusalem** a. Question: Who is this?
b. The point: A deliberate fulfillment of prophecy—	4 This took place to fulfill what was spoken through the	11 The crowds answered, "This is Jesus, the prophet from Nazareth in Galilee."	b. Answer: Jesus the prophet of Nazareth[DS4]

DIVISION XIV

THE MESSIAH'S LAST WEEK: HIS CLAIM CHALLENGED AND REJECTED, 21:1-23:39

A. The Triumphal Entry: Jesus Deliberately Claimed to Be the Messiah, 21:1-11

(21:1-11) **Jesus Christ, Last Week:** Jesus began the last week of His life. He had spent the night before (the Sabbath evening) in Bethany with Lazarus, Mary, and Martha (Jn.12:1f). He was now going to deliberately demonstrate that He was the Messiah, the One prophesied to be the Savior of the world. He pictured without question that He was the fulfillment of prophecy, the One for whom all righteous men had longed and looked.

1. Jesus' last week began in Jerusalem (v.1).
2. He deliberately fulfilled prophecy (v.2-5).
3. He deliberately received the homage of the disciples (v.6-7).
4. He deliberately received the homage of the people (v.8-9).
5. Conclusion: the question of the people in Jerusalem (v.10-11).

DEEPER STUDY # 1
(21:1-11) **Holy Week—Palm Sunday**: the last week of our Lord's life has been known as Holy Week since the earliest of times. The Triumphal Entry was the first event of the week, taking place on the first day. It was and still is called Palm Sunday.

1 (21:1) **Jesus Christ, Poverty**: Jesus' last week began in Jerusalem. Note the lowliness of Jesus. He had to depend upon friends for lodging. Up to the very end "the Son of Man [had] no place to lay His head" (Mt.8:20; Lk.9:58).

He also "approached Jerusalem" by foot. He had no stallion, no donkey, no camel—no means of transportation. He had only what God had given Him as He entered the world, His feet, to get Him where He wished to go. How God's heart must be cut to the core by our concern for material comfort and ease. Jesus' face was always set toward saving and helping the world. Up to the very end, He went about His purpose untainted and unswerved by the world. What a lesson for us!

1. Christ began His last week in Bethphage (see DEEPER STUDY # 2—Mt.21:1).
2. Christ sent two disciples on a special mission.

DEEPER STUDY # 2
(21:1) **Bethphage**: the name of the city means "House of figs." It was a suburb of Jerusalem, lying toward the Mount of Olives. Note that Jesus arrived in Bethphage by foot, indicating that He had no means of travel except walking.

2 (21:2-5) **Prophecy**: the Lord deliberately fulfilled prophecy.

1. Christ sent two disciples into the city to secure a donkey and her young colt. He borrowed the two animals from another man, probably another disciple. One of three things happened that led the man to loan the animals.

a. The man was a disciple who would allow *the Lord* to borrow his animals. The emphasis, "The Lord needs them," points rather strongly to this fact's being at least part of what happened. The Lord (o kurios) would be a strong expression to use with an unbeliever. It was equivalent to Jehovah.
b. The Lord had made previous arrangements with the owner to borrow the animals. This was, or course, possible; but the possibility that the disciples would be questioned about borrowing the animals makes this unlikely.
c. The Lord demonstrated His Divine omniscience to further validate His claim of Messiahship. As God, He knew exactly where the animals would be, the questioning about loaning them, and the fact that the owner would loan them. This could easily be part of what happened.

The important thing to note is the strength and authority of Christ throughout this whole event. He assumed the position of Messiah, the Lord God (Jehovah) of all men, of their will and their property, even of their animals.

Thought 1. Every mission of the Lord—every task, no matter how small—is important. Going to fetch the animals was a small task, yet it was critically important in the proclamation of Christ as King. No task should ever be thought too small in the service of our Lord.

Thought 2. Note two things.
1) Jesus encourages and comforts us with the presence of others. He seldom sends us out alone.
2) How often has Christ had a mission to be done and there was no one present to do it, especially the small and insignificant missions such as this one?

Thought 3. The colt was borrowed. Again, Jesus had nothing of this world's goods. In order to fulfill the Scripture that the Messiah was to enter the city riding a colt, Jesus had to borrow the colt. How materialistic we become, thinking we must have things in order to live! We even think we *cannot minister* effectively without the latest *material things* of the world (machines, equipment, methods). How unlike Christ!

For you know the grace of our Lord Jesus Christ, that though he was rich, yet for your sakes he became poor, so that you through his poverty might become rich. (2 Cor 8:9)

Thought 4. Note a significant fact: when the proclamation of His Messiahship was at stake, Christ let nothing stand in the way. It was essential that the people know that He was the Messiah. He did not own a donkey to fulfill the prophecy, so He went out to find one. Such determination and unswerving purpose should grip us in proclaiming that He is the Messiah.

2. Christ had a reason for making such detailed preparations to enter Jerusalem. He was deliberately fulfilling the prophecy of Zech. 9:9. The prophecy said four things.

a. "Rejoice greatly, O Daughter of Zion! [that is, Jerusalem]": Jerusalem was to be told, given a threefold warning. Why must she be warned? Because what she expected was not going to happen, not like she anticipated.
b. "See, your King comes to you": this was the first warning. Jerusalem's King was coming, coming just as Jerusalem had expected. The people were correct in this part of their expectation. But there is danger in expectation, the danger of being so fervent in our own ideas that we miss what really happens. Fervent expectation can miss the event when the event occurs a little differently than what was expected. "Your King cometh," but He comes somewhat differently than expected.
c. "Your King comes...gently": this was the second warning. The Messiah was coming in gentleness not as a reigning monarch. He was coming to win men's hearts and lives spiritually and eternally, not physically and materially (see notes—Mk.11:1-11; Eph.1:3; cp. Mt.11:29).
d. "Your King comes...riding on a donkey, on a colt...": this was the third warning. The Messiah was coming not as a conqueror riding a white stallion but as a King of peace riding a donkey. He was coming to save the world through peace, to reconcile the world to the God of love, not to the God of hate and retaliation and war. He was not going to kill men and overthrow their governments (the Romans and Gentiles). He was coming to win men's hearts and lives through the glorious news (gospel) that God loves and reconciles (see outline and notes—Eph.2:13-18).

Note the prophecy and the careful preparation Christ made to fulfill the prophecy. This is significant, for it means that Christ was dramatizing His Messiahship—dramatizing it so clearly that men could not fail to see that He was God's Messiah. This was God's will prophesied generations before Christ came. God wanted His Son to proclaim His Messiahship so clearly that the people could not mistake what He was doing.

Thought 1. Jesus claimed to be the Messiah, God's very own Son. The great pains He took to fulfill this prophecy clearly showed what He was claiming. He was deliberately working out God's will. He was doing exactly what God said He wanted His Son to do centuries before (Zech.9:9). He was making the claim to be God's Messiah in a dramatic way. He was painting a picture so clearly that man could not fail to see what He was claiming. A deliberate decision is now required of us. We either accept His claim or not. As He *deliberately* fulfilled the prophecy, so we now *deliberately accept or deliberately reject* His claim.

Because of the tender mercy of our God, by which the rising sun will come to us from heaven to shine on those living in darkness and in the shadow of death, to guide our feet into the path of peace." (Luke 1:78-79)

Suddenly a great company of the heavenly host appeared with the angel, praising God and saying, "Glory to God in the highest, and on earth peace to men on whom his favor rests." (Luke 2:13-14)

Peace I leave with you; my peace I give you. I do not give to you as the world gives. Do not let your hearts be troubled and do not be afraid. (John 14:27)

"I have told you these things, so that in me you may have peace. In this world you

will have trouble. But take heart! I have overcome the world." (John 16:33)

You know the message God sent to the people of Israel, telling the good news of peace through Jesus Christ, who is Lord of all. (Acts 10:36)

Therefore, since we have been justified through faith, we have peace with God through our Lord Jesus Christ, (Rom 5:1)

For the kingdom of God is not a matter of eating and drinking, but of righteousness, peace and joy in the Holy Spirit, (Rom 14:17)

For he himself is our peace, who has made the two one and has destroyed the barrier, the dividing wall of hostility, (Eph 2:14)

And through him to reconcile to himself all things, whether things on earth or things in heaven, by making peace through his blood, shed on the cross. (Col 1:20)

The LORD gives strength to his people; the LORD blesses his people with peace. (Psa 29:11)

Thought 2. Note two very significant things.

1) Christ did not come to execute justice but to save men spiritually through the forgiveness of sin. Christ came not as a judge to judge men for ignoring, neglecting, rejecting, and misinterpreting God; but He came as the Messenger of Peace to reconcile men to God by the cross (see outline and notes—Eph.2:13-18; Col.1:20).
2) Christ is coming again, coming as Judge to execute justice among all men, both the saved and unsaved (DEEPER STUDY # 1—Heb.9:27; cp. Mt.25:31-46; 2 Cor.5:10).

DEEPER STUDY # 3
(21:5) **Donkey—Colt**: see DEEPER STUDY # 4—Mk.11:7.

3 (21:6-7) **Homage—Obedience**: Christ deliberately received the homage of the disciples. The disciples paid Him homage (reverence, recognition). They did exactly what He asked despite the uncertainty of the matter. They had no money to buy or rent the animals, and they were to be questioned about why they wanted the animals. Yet they obeyed—not questioning, not doubting.

Note the other act of homage: there was no saddle for their Lord. They cared about Him and His comfort, so they took their own cloaks and threw them across the animals. Again, this was an act of homage (reverence and recognition). In following Christ, the two men had lived a life of poverty, so they had little clothing. It cost them to use their clothing for such a humble act. The clothing would be soiled and smelly, but they cared and they worshipped through this act.

The point is that Christ was now unmistakably claiming the dignity and rights of a King. He was not washing feet now; He was deliberately accepting their homage and reverence.

But note something of critical importance. In claiming the dignity and rights of a King, He was doing it in the most humble practice of His day: entering the city as a King of Peace. This was symbolized by riding a young colt, instead of riding the conqueror's stallion. He was disclaiming all ideas of an earthly and material kingdom. He had come to save Jerusalem and the world through peace, not war.

Thought 1. There are three clear lessons in this event.

1) We are to give homage to the Lord by obeying His commands. They may sometimes be difficult to understand and somewhat embarrassing, yet we are to trust and obey just as the two disciples did—not doubting or questioning.

Whoever has my commands and obeys them, he is the one who loves me. He who loves me will be loved by my Father, and I too will love him and show myself to him." (John 14:21)

If you obey my commands, you will remain in my love, just as I have obeyed my Father's commands and remain in his love. You are my friends if you do what I command. (John 15:10, 14)

And receive from him anything we ask, because we obey his commands and do what pleases him. (1 John 3:22)

But Samuel replied: "Does the LORD delight in burnt offerings and sacrifices as much as in obeying the voice of the LORD? To obey is better than sacrifice, and to heed is better than the fat of rams. (1 Sam 15:22)

2) We are to give homage to the Lord by giving Him the best we have. He is worthy of all and due all, so we are to do as the disciples did, give Him all—even the very best of our clothing if needed.

Jesus answered, "If you want to be perfect, go, sell your possessions and give to the poor, and you will have treasure in heaven. Then come, follow me." (Mat 19:21)

Peter said to him, "We have left everything to follow you!" (Mark 10:28)

After this, Jesus went out and saw a tax collector by the name of Levi sitting at his tax booth. "Follow me," Jesus said to him, and Levi got up, left everything and followed him. (Luke 5:27-28)

In the same way, any of you who does not give up everything he has cannot be my disciple. (Luke 14:33)

What is more, I consider everything a loss compared to the surpassing greatness of knowing Christ Jesus my Lord, for whose sake I have lost all things. I consider them rubbish, that I may gain Christ (Phil 3:8)

3) We worship and pay homage to Christ when we give the clothes off our back. Such is a most noble ministry and assures great reward.

"Then the King will say to those on his right, 'Come, you who are blessed by my Father; take your inheritance, the kingdom prepared for you since the creation of the world. For I was hungry and you gave me something to eat, I was thirsty and you gave me something to drink, I was a

stranger and you invited me in, I needed clothes and you clothed me, I was sick and you looked after me, I was in prison and you came to visit me.' (Mat 25:34-36. Cp.25:31-46)

But note: there is a difference in giving old unusable clothes and in buying new clothes, or else giving the clothes off our backs. In order to minister, the disciples gave what they had to minister. They gave the clothes they were wearing (cp. the widow's mite, Lk.21:1-4).

4 (21:8-9) **Homage—Messiah**: Christ deliberately received the homage of the people. And note: it was a "very large crowd" (v.8). Apparently what happened was this. The crowd had begun to gather since early morning, excitedly looking for Him who had raised Lazarus from the dead. John told us this. In fact, he said there were so many people that the Pharisees said, "the whole world has gone after Him" (Jn.12:17-19). There was the crowd of disciples already accompanying Him and the pilgrims on their way to the Passover Feast who had joined His caravan. There were also the residents of Bethany and Bethphage who had heard of His presence and the miracles, and those who were already in Jerusalem, citizens and pilgrims who were rushing out to search for Him.

We are led to imagine an enormous crowd of teeming thousands lining the roadway as Christ was helped atop the donkey to begin His triumphal entry into Jerusalem. There are several facts that point toward this conclusion.

1. Two or more million pilgrims gathered in Jerusalem every year for the Passover Feast (see DEEPER STUDY # 1—Mt.26:2). Thousands upon thousands were strict religionists, believing in the Jewish Messiah.

2. The news being spread throughout the city and surrounding area concerned the miracles Christ had performed, a concentration of miracles for some days now which included the raising of Lazarus from the dead (Jn.11:1f; 11:55-56). The very atmosphere was electric with the exciting news that Jesus was God's promised Messiah. Multitudes had heard that He was in Bethany and Bethphage (Mk.14:1-9). As said above, there was the crowd who had turned around from Jerusalem to meet Him (Jn.12:17-19); there was the crowd already travelling with Him (Mt.21:29); and there was the crowd of citizens in Bethany and Bethphage who had begun gathering around Him (Mk.14:1-9; Jn.12:1f). The whole thrust of the picture points to teeming thousands searching for Him and rushing out to welcome Him when they heard He was coming. (Note the words of Matthew, "the crowds that went ahead of him and those that followed shouted" v.9.)

The crowds did two things.

1. They received Him as King. This is shown by two acts which were always done for Kings' entering a city. They stripped off their cloaks and cut down tree branches, and they spread both out on the roadway before Him. They wished to honor and pay Him the homage of a King. They wished to show Him that they received Him as the promised King of Israel.

2. They received Him as Messiah. This is seen in what they shouted about Christ.

⇒ They shouted out, "Hosanna," which means save now, or save, we pray.

⇒ They called Him "the Son of David," which was the title of the Messiah (see notes—Mt.1:1; DEEPER STUDY # 2—1:18; DEEPER STUDY # 3—3:11; notes—11:1-6; 11:2-3; DEEPER STUDY # 1—11:5; DEEPER STUDY # 2—11:6; DEEPER STUDY # 1—12:16; note—Lk.7:21-23).

⇒ They shouted out, "Blessed is He who comes in the name of the Lord." This means blessed is He who is sent by God to save His people; blessed is He who is sent with the authority of God.

⇒ They shouted out, "Hosanna in the Highest" which means "God save, we pray. Thou who art in the Highest, save now through Him whom You have sent."

Thought 1. There are several critical lessons in this point.

1) We must proclaim Christ as our King. He is to be the King of our hearts and lives, to rule and reign over us. But note the critical question: What do we mean by King? The people of Christ's day were willing to accept him as an earthly King; that is, they were willing to accept what authority and power He would use in their behalf. The farthest thought from their minds was the spiritual rule and reign of their lives. They wanted earthly and material benefits. How much like so many of us! We want His kingly power when in need (physically or materially), but we want nothing to do with His kingly authority over our lives.
2) We must welcome Christ as God's true Messiah, the One who has come to truly save us. But again, what we mean by *save* is critical. We should not presume upon His earthly care and deliverance unless we are first willing to receive His spiritual care and deliverance (salvation and rebirth, the surrendering of all we are and have).
3) Every man should cry out, "Hosanna, save now, I pray O Lord."

For he says, "In the time of my favor I heard you, and in the day of salvation I helped you." I tell you, now is the time of God's favor, now is the day of salvation. (2 Cor 6:2)

4) We must make two confessions.
   ⇒ Christ is *the Blessed* (who) comes in the name of the Lord.
   ⇒ "Hosanna in the highest": salvation is "in the highest"; it is in Christ whom God has sent.

Then Nathanael declared, "Rabbi, you are the Son of God; you are the King of Israel." (John 1:49)

"For God so loved the world that he gave his one and only Son, that whoever believes in him shall not perish but have eternal life. (John 3:16)

"You are a king, then!" said Pilate. Jesus answered, "You are right in saying I am a king. In fact, for this reason I was born, and for this I came into the world, to testify to the truth. Everyone on the side of truth listens to me." (John 18:37)

For he says, "In the time of my favor I heard you, and in the day of salvation I helped you." I tell you, now is the time of God's favor, now is the day of salvation. (2 Cor 6:2)

Which God will bring about in his own time—God, the blessed and only Ruler, the

King of kings and Lord of lords, (1 Tim 6:15)
For the grace of God that brings salvation has appeared to all men. It teaches us to say "No" to ungodliness and worldly passions, and to live self-controlled, upright and godly lives in this present age, (Titus 2:11-12)

5) We must lay all that we are and have before Christ, not only our clothes.

5 (21:10-11) **Jesus Christ, Response to**: there was the question of the people in Jerusalem. All the city was stirred (eseisthe), that is, shaken. John reported that "the whole world has gone after him" (Jn.12:19).

⇒ The Romans sensed that a popular uprising might be in the making.
⇒ The Herodians, who were the Jewish ruling party, feared they would be overthrown, losing their power.
⇒ The Pharisees were stirred to new depths of envy and malice.
⇒ The common people were convinced that their day of liberation had finally arrived in Jesus of Nazareth.

DEEPER STUDY # 4
(21:11) **Prophet**: this was definitely a reference to the Messiah, the One who was sent from God (cp. Jn.1:21; 6:14; 9:17).

	B. The Temple Cleansed: Authority over God's House,[DS1] 21:12-16 (Mk.11:15-19; Lk.19: 45-46; cp. Jn.2:13-16)	14 The blind and the lame came to him at the temple, and he healed them.	**3 The temple (church) is to be a place for ministry**
		15 But when the chief priests and the teachers of the law saw the wonderful things	**4 The temple (church) is to be a place where wonderful things are done**
1 The temple (church) is to be a place where people are not exploited	12 Jesus entered the temple area and drove out all who were buying and selling there. He overturned the tables of the money changers and the benches of those selling doves.	he did and the children shouting in the temple area, "Hosanna to the Son of David," they were indignant.	**5 The temple (church) is to be a place where Christ is praised** a. Children praised Him b. Some objected
2 The temple (church) is to be a house of prayer	13 "It is written," he said to them, "'My house will be called a house of prayer,' but you are making it a 'den of robbers.'"	16 "Do you hear what these children are saying?" they asked him. "Yes," replied Jesus, "have you never read, "'From the lips of children and infants you have ordained praise'?"	c. Christ insisted[DS2]

DIVISION XIV

THE MESSIAH'S LAST WEEK: HIS CLAIM CHALLENGED AND REJECTED, 21:1-23:39

B. The Temple Cleansed: Authority over God's House, 21:12-16

(21:12-16) **Introduction**: the cleansing of the temple took place on Monday, the day after the triumphal entry into Jerusalem. Mark told us this.

> **Jesus entered Jerusalem and went to the temple. He looked around at everything, but since it was already late, he went out to Bethany with the Twelve. (Mark 11:11)**

The scene was this: teeming thousands had lined the roadway for Jesus' triumphal entry. As He rode along to the shouts of welcome from the crowds, He was led right up to the steps of the temple. He entered the temple, as Mark said, "looked around at everything," and observed all that was going on. He stood off to the side observing all the corruption. After some time, heartbroken and weary, He left and returned to Bethany to spend Sunday night. When He arose on Monday morning, He returned to the temple to cleanse it of those who profaned its sacredness.

Four things should be noted about the temple during the last week of our Lord's life.

1. Jesus was ending His ministry in the temple, His Father's house of prayer, the place where God's presence dwelt in a very, very special way. He is about to complete His life upon earth, a glorious ministry fulfilling the will of God perfectly. The night before, as He stood off by Himself in the temple observing all that was taking place, His thoughts are very contemplative: thoughts that were meditating upon His Father; upon His life now about completed; upon the great sacrifice He was to pay for man's sins; upon the corruption of the temple taking place all around Him; upon the worshipping that should be taking place; and upon so much more. His heart was drawn ever so close to God, yet it was broken and weeping within. Right before Him was a picture of the terrible sin for which He was to die. The temple itself, the place where men should be able to draw close to God, was corrupted by men. It had become anything but a house of prayer. It was a place for commercialism, for man's greed.

2. Jesus was revealing who He was by cleansing the temple. He was proclaiming to all generations that He had the right to determine how the temple was to be used and to purge it of corruptions. As God's Son, the temple was His dwelling place, the place where the worship of God was to be especially known.

3. Jesus was revealing how men were to treat and use the temple of God.

4. Jesus began and ended His ministry by cleansing the temple. The two cleansings were separate events which marked the opening and closing of His ministry. The importance of the temple as God's house of prayer and worship was thereby demonstrated.

When our Lord entered Jerusalem, He did not go up to the palace of the King nor to the courts of the rulers, but He went up to the temple, the House of God. His kingdom was not of this world, not physical, but of heaven and spiritual. His authority and rule were in the temple of God and in the hearts of men. Therefore, He went up to the temple of God to cleanse it and to teach men how the temple was and is to be used.

1. The temple is to be a place where people are not exploited (v.12).
2. The temple is to be a house of prayer (v.13).
3. The temple is to be a place for ministry (v.14).
4. The temple is to be a place where wonderful things are done (v.15).
5. The temple is to be a place where Christ is praised (v.15-16).

DEEPER STUDY # 1

(21:12-16) **Temple**: one must understand the layout of the temple in order to see what was happening in this event. The temple sat on top of Mt. Zion and was thought to have covered about thirty acres of land. It consisted of two parts, the temple building itself and the temple precincts or courtyards. The Greek language has two different words to distinguish which is meant.

1. *The temple building* (naos) was a small ornate structure which sat in the center of the temple property. It was called the Holy Place or Holy of Holies, and only the High

Priest could enter its walls, and he could enter only once during the year, on the Day of Atonement.

2. *The temple precincts* (hieron) were four courtyards which surrounded the temple building, each decreasing in their importance to the Jewish mind. It is critical to remember that great walls separated the courts from each other.

a. First, there was the Inner Court of the Priests. Only the priests were allowed to enter this court. Within the courtyard stood the great furnishings of worship: the Altar of Burnt Offering, the Brazen Laver, the Seven Branched lampstand, the Altar of Incense, and the Table of Showbread.

b. The Court of the Israelites was next. This was a huge courtyard where Jewish worshippers met together for joint services on the great feast days. It was also where worshippers handed over their sacrifices to the priests.

c. The Court of the Women was the third Courtyard. Women were usually limited to this area except for worship. They could, however, enter the Court of the Israelites when they came to make sacrifice or worship in a joint assembly on a great feast day.

d. The Court of the Gentiles was the last courtyard. It covered a vast space, surrounding all the other courtyards, and was the place of worship for all Gentile converts to Judaism.

Three facts need to be noted about the Court of the Gentiles.

1. It was the courtyard farthest removed from the center of worship, the Holy of Holies which represented God's very presence (see note—Eph.2:14).

2. A high wall separated the Court of the Gentiles from the other courts, disallowing any Gentile a closer approach into God's presence. There were, in fact, tablets hanging all around the wall threatening death to any Gentile who went beyond his own courtyard.

3. It was in the Court of the Gentiles where so much commercialism took place. There was a regular commercial market within its walls. How did a commercial market ever get into the temple of God? Very simply, greed. Worshippers needed animals, (oxen, sheep, doves), incense, meal, wine, oil, salt, and other items for their sacrifices and offerings. Pilgrims from foreign nations needed money exchanged. At some point in the history of the temple, the priests had decided to take advantage of the market themselves instead of letting retailers on the outside reap all the profits. So the priests began to set up booths within the court of the Gentiles and to lease out space to *outside* retailers. These often turned out to be family members. The owner of the booths or space was the High Priest or Annas. The courtyard was filled with booth-like spaces where worshippers could find any kind of service they needed. The atmosphere was one of commercial traffic and commotion, not of worship and prayer.

Remembering the teeming thousands who attended the great feasts, we can imagine the loudest commotion and our picture would still come short of the actual scene. Who can picture thousands of animals with their peculiar noises, wastes, and smells within the temple of God? And for what? What would cause men to so abuse the worshipping center of God? As said above, money, the greed of men. It is no wonder Christ did what He did. He could not do otherwise, for He was the Son of God, the Messiah sent into the world to bring about a true worship of God. And there was no hope of worship within the Court of the Gentiles. Prayer and worship were impossible.

1 (21:12) **Temple—Church**: the temple or church is to be a place where people are not exploited. Note what Jesus did to show this.

1. He went into the temple (Court of the Gentiles) where God's presence was to be and where He and others should be able to worship in quietness and meditation. But what He found was the very opposite: commotion, commercial selling, and buying.

2. He reacted in the power and cleansing judgment of God—the kind of power and cleansing judgment that causes men to tremble before God (Ph.2:9-11).

3. He ran through the temple doing three things: (a) He chased out *all* who were buying and selling; (b) He threw over the tables of the moneychangers; and (c) He threw over the chairs of the dove dealers.

> **To those who sold doves he said, "Get these out of here! How dare you turn my Father's house into a market!" (John 2:16)**
>
> **Don't you have homes to eat and drink in? Or do you despise the church of God and humiliate those who have nothing? What shall I say to you? Shall I praise you for this? Certainly not! (1 Cor 11:22)**
>
> **"'Observe my Sabbaths and have reverence for my sanctuary. I am the LORD. (Lev 19:30)**
>
> **Guard your steps when you go to the house of God. Go near to listen rather than to offer the sacrifice of fools, who do not know that they do wrong. (Eccl 5:1)**
>
> **"'The people of Judah have done evil in my eyes, declares the LORD. They have set up their detestable idols in the house that bears my Name and have defiled it. (Jer 7:30)**
>
> **Her prophets are arrogant; they are treacherous men. Her priests profane the sanctuary and do violence to the law. (Zep 3:4)**

Thought 1. There is serious warning here. The temple was corrupted for money; the church can be. People who came to worship were taken advantage of; they were used for material gain. Note something that should really speak to the church. The people were sold items that were necessary for their worship. They were not just items that would help them in their spiritual growth and their worship; they were essential items. Without them, the people were not able to worship.

Now think for a moment. If the items were necessary for their worship and growth, what was wrong with what they did? The words of v.12 tell us: "Jesus...drove out all who were buying and selling there." The buying and selling of the items for worship and growth were necessary and good, but not within the temple. They were to be done outside the temple walls, off the temple grounds. The temple and church are not the place for commercialism.

Thought 2. People's desire for worship and spiritual growth is not to be used for material gain, not by the church nor within the church. Church leadership has to be responsible for protecting its worshippers from abusing the hallowed ground set apart for the worship of God.

Thought 3. Legitimate things, such as buying and selling items that help us grow, can be used wrongly. *Where* something is done is critical. Buying and selling is not to take place in God's church. The point is: worship should be the preoccupation of a person's mind when he is within the church.

Thought 4. Jesus' anger can be fierce. Note who aroused such fierce anger in Him.
1) Those who abused God's temple (church).
2) Those who exploited others.
3) Those who made it impossible for others to truly worship God.

Thought 5. Note what happens to the man who abuses God's temple and exploits others: he is "driven out."

2 (21:13) **Temple—Church**: Jesus proclaimed the temple to be a house of prayer. This was an Old Testament quotation from two passages.

> **These I will bring to my holy mountain and give them joy in my house of prayer. Their burnt offerings and sacrifices will be accepted on my altar; for my house will be called a house of prayer for all nations." (Isa 56:7)**
>
> **Has this house, which bears my Name, become a den of robbers to you? But I have been watching! declares the LORD. (Jer 7:11)**

Christ made two points.

1. The temple was to be a house of prayer *for all people*. This included the Gentiles as well as the Jews. All people should have been able to worship in quietness and peace within God's temple. No one should have been barred, separated, or discouraged from worshipping God in His temple. All should have been welcomed.

Note something else. The temple (church) was called a house of prayer, not a house of sacrifice, offerings, teaching, prophecy, or preaching. Everything done within the House of God was to lead to prayer, the *worship and communion* of the Father.

2. The temple was not to be used for commercial purposes. It was not to be a place of buying and selling, marketing and retailing, stealing, and cheating. It was not to be profaned. The temple was the House of God, God's House of prayer. It was to be a place of sanctity, refined and purified by God Himself. It was to be a place of quietness and meditation, a place set aside for worship, not for buying and selling where man gets gain.

> **Surely goodness and love will follow me all the days of my life, and I will dwell in the house of the LORD forever. (Psa 23:6)**
> **Better is one day in your courts than a thousand elsewhere; I would rather be a doorkeeper in the house of my God than dwell in the tents of the wicked. (Psa 84:10)**
>
> **A song of ascents. Of David. I rejoiced with those who said to me, "Let us go to the house of the LORD." (Psa 122:1)**

Thought 1. The temple or church is a piece of ground and a structure that is set apart for the worship of God. This is the very difference between it and all other grounds and structures. It is specifically set apart and dedicated for the sole purpose of worshipping God. It should, therefore, be used for that purpose. Once it is set apart for Him and His worship, God expects it to be His and to be used for that purpose alone.

Thought 2. There are plenty of markets surrounding the church, places where all services involving buying and selling can take place. The church is to be the house of prayer, not a market place, not a place where man is to get gain. It is not to be profaned, either to a minor degree or to a major degree, by becoming a "den for robbers."

Thought 3. A person's thoughts are to be centered upon God when he first steps on the hallowed ground of God's temple. While he is on the grounds of God's temple, He is to be praying and meditating upon His Lord. There should be nothing to distract his thoughts until he steps off God's property. Just think! How revered would God's temple, our churches, be if we really brought them back to God's original purpose? How far away have we really gotten from true worship centers, from the house of prayer?

3 (21:14) **Church—Ministry**: the temple or church is to be a place for ministry. Jesus used the temple as a place for ministry, and by such, He demonstrated that it was to be a place of ministry for all men.

Two wonderful things happened when the temple was cleansed of its corruptions.

1. The worshippers, those in need (symbolized by the blind and lame), were able to come to Christ to worship and have their needs met quietly.

2. Christ was able to take His rightful position within the temple. He was able to become the prominent figure and to receive the worshippers and to minister to those who had need.

Thought 1. People are barred, kept away from the church, when corruption is within its walls. It may not be only buying and selling; it may be divisiveness, grumbling, complaining, gossiping, and a host of other sins. But nothing will keep people away from the church quicker than sin within the church.

When such sins are removed and the church is purified, then Christ can and will be known to have His rightful place in the church. People can then come and be helped. They can worship and have their needs met.

Thought 2. The needy are often barred, cut off, and unwelcomed by society. Such is not to be true of the church. The church is to have open arms and a pure heart, welcoming all, no matter how poor and needy. In fact, the church is to be the very worship center for ministry.

4 (21:15) **Temple, Purpose:** the temple is to be a place where wonderful things are done. The term "wonderful things" (thaumasios) means wonders, wonderful things, wonderful works. It refers to all the things Christ was doing in the temple. This is the only time the word is used in the New Testament. What a beautiful description of what the church is to be: a place where wonderful things are to be done for God.

> **Now to him who is able to do immeasurably more than all we ask or imagine,**

according to his power that is at work within us, (Eph 3:20)

5 (21:15-16) **Temple—Church:** The temple is to be a place where Christ is praised. Note three things that happen in this scene.

1. Children are in the temple (Court of the Gentiles) crying, "Hosanna to the Son of David." Apparently, these children had participated with their parents in the Triumphal Entry the day before and were now witnessing the ministry of Christ to the lame and blind. They pick up the chorus which they had either sung along with their parents or heard sung the day before. The chorus, of course, proclaims Jesus to be the Messiah. It is most unlikely that the children were playing, as some suggest. Two facts suggest a seriousness in what the children were saying: Christ's clearing out all the commotion and noise and the extreme seriousness and hallowedness of His ministry to the people coming to Him. It is very difficult to picture too much commotion allowed by Christ in His serious moments of ministry; and He certainly would not have allowed the commotion and disturbance of His meeting by a group of children playing around. He would have dismissed them along with the others if they had not been serious in their worship and praise. It would be particularly difficult to picture Christ's allowing commotion after what He had just been through.

2. The religionists (chief priests and scribes) are displeased and object to what they see and hear. They do not like the "wonderful things" being done in the temple, nor do they like Jesus' being praised in the temple. They object for at least three reasons.

   a. They are angered. Their own establishment and procedures for handling things have been disrupted and, in their minds, declared "no good" or else "less good" than what they should be.
   b. They do not like Jesus' being proclaimed the Messiah of God.
   c. They do not like the unseemly behavior occurring: ministering to the needs of common men, healing the lame and blind (v.14), and teaching (cp. Mk.11:18; Lk.19:47).

Note that these are the very reasons people often become disturbed in the church today.

3. Christ insists that He is to be praised. He simply replies to the objections, "God Himself has taken the mouths of these children and provided (brought forth) the praise you hear. And it is perfect praise because it is brought forth by God Himself and heaped upon His Son. The church is to be a place where God's Son is to be praised."

Thought 1. Self-examination is called for. Is Christ really praised in our church? Really acknowledged and proclaimed as the Messiah, the Son of God?

Thought 2. Children should be encouraged to praise God.
1) Note how the children were in attendance when Christ taught and ministered (Mk.11:18; Lk.19:47). They were welcomed by Him and felt comfortable around Him.
2) Note how Christ stood up for the children against the leadership (priests).

Thought 3. The children follow the example of their parents. They had seen and participated with their parents in praising Christ the day before. Now they praise Him on their own as they witness His ministry and teaching.

Thought 4. Some leaders make the same three tragic objections in churches today.
1) They object to the old way being changed, especially if it affects one's position, recognition, or authority.
2) They object to Christ's being proclaimed the Messiah, the Son of God. Some are willing to acknowledge Him as a great teacher and only as a great teacher.They deny Him as the Savior of the world who died for the sins of men.
3) They object to a public praising of God and to a ministry that helps the needy within the church walls.

Thought 5. Note something. Christ says that God Himself raised up these children to praise Him and His ministry within the church. If a church ceases to praise Him, the likelihood is that God will raise up another to fill its voices with the praise and ministry of His Son.

DEEPER STUDY # 2
(21:16) **Old Testament Reference** Cp. Ps.8:2.

Outline	Scripture
	C. The Fig Tree Cursed: The Source of Power, 21:17-22 (Mk.11:12-14, 20-26)
1 Jesus lodged in Bethany	17 And he left them and went out of the city to Bethany, where he spent the night.
a. He returned to Jerusalem[DS1] b. He was hungry	18 Early in the morning, as he was on his way back to the city, he was hungry.
2 Jesus' great power over the physical world[DS2] a. His expectation: Fruit[DS3] b. His disappointment:No fruit c. His absolute power over the physical world demonstrated	19 Seeing a fig tree by the road, he went up to it but found nothing on it except leaves. Then he said to it, "May you never bear fruit again!" Immediately the tree withered.
3 Jesus' great source of power: Faith, not doubting a. The power of Christ stirred marvel, wonder, & questioning b. The great source of power 1) Faith 2) Not doubting at all 3) God's authority: Given to those who speak the Word	20 When the disciples saw this, they were amazed. "How did the fig tree wither so quickly?" they asked. 21 Jesus replied, "I tell you the truth, if you have faith and do not doubt, not only can you do what was done to the fig tree, but also you can say to this mountain, 'Go, throw yourself into the sea,' and it will be done.
4 Jesus' promise of power to the disciples: Through prayer & faith	22 If you believe, you will receive whatever you ask for in prayer."

DIVISION XIV

THE MESSIAH'S LAST WEEK: HIS CLAIM CHALLENGED AND REJECTED, 21:1-23:39

C. The Fig Tree Cursed: The Source of Power, 21:17-22

(21:17-22) **Introduction—Power—Judgment**: Jesus destroyed the fig tree. Why? Some have said such destruction is out of character for Christ. He would never destroy a tree for not bearing fruit.

Why did Jesus destroy the tree?

⇒ He destroyed it for the same reason that He angrily ran through the temple casting out all who bought and sold (Mt.21:12-16).

⇒ He destroyed it for the same reason that He lashed out at the Pharisees for being hypocritical (Mt.23:13-39).

⇒ He destroyed it for the same reason that He cast the evil spirits into a herd of pigs, killing them (Mt.8:28-34).

⇒ He destroyed it for the same reasons that He became indignant (angry) with the disciples for keeping little children from coming to Him (see DEEPER STUDY # 4—Mk.10:14).

⇒ He destroyed it for the same reason that He deliberately demanded uncompromising loyalty despite family or personal needs (Mt.8:18-22; 10:34-39).

Why did Jesus act with such force in destroying the tree? For the same reason He acted with such force in all of the above. Jesus always acted either to teach man or to save and help man. In destroying the fig tree, He was teaching man a much needed lesson.

The lesson: the Messiah has absolute power over all the physical universe. The unfruitful among men (symbolized in the fig tree) do not have such power. Contrariwise, He alone has such enormous power. He alone has the power to judge and to determine fruitfulness and unfruitfulness, life and death, salvation and condemnation. He alone laid down His life; no man took it from Him (Jn.10:11, 15-18, esp.18).

Remember this was Jesus' last week. It was Tuesday, just three days before He was to be killed by unfruitful men. Jesus had to do all He could to prepare His disciples for His onrushing death and for all they were to bear through the ensuing years. He had only two days left, so He had to undergird them all He could. He was hungry, and He saw a fig tree full of leaves. He walked up to pluck some fruit, but He found no fruit. He saw an object lesson in the event—a lesson that could be uniquely used in teaching and preparing the disciples.

In destroying the tree, Jesus was showing the disciples (in an unmistakable way) that He had absolute power over all the physical world, even the power to keep from being killed. He was not dying out of weakness, not dying because He was not the Messiah, not dying because of the plots and intrigues of men. Men may be judging Him to be unfruitful and unworthy of life, but He was not dying because of them. He was dying because the death of God's Son was the way of salvation (Jn.3:16; 2 Cor.5:19-20; 1 Pt.2:24). He was not being judged by unfruitful men or events; rather, unfruitful men and events were being judged by Him upon the cross (1 Pt.2:24; cp. Eph.2:13-22).

Very simply put, Jesus was picturing that He was truly God's Son with omnipotent power, picturing it in a way that we can never forget. He had the power to save Himself and to destroy the unfruitful men who would take His life. But He of course could not—not then. Right then He was sent into the world to die for men and to save men, including the very ones who were judging and condemning Him to be unfruitful and unworthy of life. However, the day is coming when He will judge the unfruitful just as He judged the fig tree. But that day is out in the future, for the present He was to save men.

Note: the lesson of *power through prayer and faith* was the lesson Christ drew from His action (v.20-22).

1. Jesus lodged in Bethany (v.17-18).
2. Jesus' great power over the physical world (v.19).
3. Jesus' great source of power: faith, not doubting (v.20-21).
4. Jesus' promise of power to the disciples (v.22).

Thought 1. Jesus returned to Jerusalem despite the threat to His life. He returned because it was God's will. He would not be stopped from doing God's will. So it should be with us. We should never allow opposition and threats to stop us from doing God's will. Note that like Christ, Paul did not shirk from God's will, from setting his face toward Jerusalem despite the bonds and trials that awaited him there (Acts 21:13-15).

1 (21:17-18) **Bethany**: Jesus lodged in Bethany, which was a suburb of Jerusalem. It lay about two miles east of the great city. Bethany was the home of Lazarus, Mary, and Martha. Jesus stayed with the family when ministering in and around Jerusalem. We must remember that Jesus apparently had no home of His own, which was partly due to the fact that His immediate family did not believe in Him (Jn.7:1-5, esp.5). He Himself had said, "Foxes have holes and birds of the air have nests, but the Son of man has no place to lay his head" (Mt.8:20). The only housing He had was the homes of others such as Mary and Martha (Jn.11:1f; cp. Lk.11:1f; Lk.10:38-42; 19:29f; Jn.12:1f).

DEEPER STUDY # 1
(21:18) **Early in the morning** (proias): means very early in the morning, the fourth or last watch of the previous night (Mk.1:35). Jesus began the events of Tuesday so early it was in the wee hours of the morning, or according to Jewish time, in the last hours of the previous day.

2 (21:19) **Jesus Christ, Power**: Jesus had great power over the physical world. He demonstrates His great power by three acts. These same acts are applicable to a human life.

1. His expectation: fruit. The tree looked healthy and full of leaves. It was time for Him to feast, and He had the right to expect fruit on such a *mature* looking fruit tree. It professed fruit.

2. His disappointment: no fruit. The tree had life; it was living. It had the sap to produce a rich foliage of leaves and it was professing fruit, but it had none. Its very purpose was to bear fruit, but it did not. It failed at three points.
   a. It had an empty profession.
   b. It had an unfulfilled purpose.
   c. It deceived instead of served.

3. His absolute power over the physical world demonstrated. Christ demonstrated that He has the right and the power to execute judgment as He wills. He can deliver or He can destroy. His disciples needed to have this lesson fresh on their minds. His omnipotent power, the enormous power available to them, would encourage them as they experienced His death and as they faced the trials that lay ahead of their own witness. (See note—Mt.21:17-22.)

Thought 1. The fig tree is a clear picture of hypocrisy, of false profession (see DEEPER STUDY # 2—Mt.21:19).

Thought 2. If a tree is living, it is expected to bear fruit. That is its purpose for living. If it does not bear fruit, it is useless and good for nothing but to be cut down and burned (cp. Lk.13:7). Note another fact: the more alive a tree is, the fuller it appears and the more fruit it is expected to bear. If we give the appearance of righteousness, then God expects us to bear righteousness.

Thought 3. There are two times in particular when Christ looks for fruit within a person.
1) There are the times of deep sensitivity wrought by life's great trials and great opportunities. These times cause a person to think of God, of his need for God, and of his obligation to use his life for good (for example, feeding, clothing, and giving to others). Christ expects us to bear fruit in a very special way during these times: to turn to Him in trial and to help and bear witness when great opportunities arise.
2) There will be the time of eternal judgment. There is a day coming at the end of the world when Christ will judge all men, both believers and unbelievers. Fruit will be expected (see DEEPER STUDY # 1—2 Cor.5:10; cp. Gal.5:22-23).

Thought 4. Christ has absolute power over the universe. He did not die at the hands of men. He died purposefully for the sins of the world just as God willed. He had the power to keep from dying, but He chose to lay down His life for the sake of men (Ro.5:8).

Thought 5. There is no question, the cursing of the fig tree shows the enormous power of Christ to do three things. (1) It shows the power of Christ to deliver His disciples out of great trial. (2) It shows the power of Christ to determine when His disciples should depart out of this world (cp. 2 Tim.4:6-8). (3) It shows the power of Christ to judge and condemn. The great day of His wrath is not yet come (Rev.6:17), but the day will come. When the day does come, then all unfruitfulness of men shall be judged by His absolute power. (Cp. the parable of the fig tree, Lk.13:6-9.)

Thought 6. Some things will doom us: hypocrisy, false profession, uselessness, purposelessness, and no fruit. The cursed fig tree symbolizes all this.

DEEPER STUDY # 2
(21:19) **Fig Tree Cursed**: there are some who say the fig tree represented Israel. The fig tree was full of leaves, appearing fruitful; but it had no fruit. So Israel appeared to be full, that is, to be religious. The nation professed spiritual fruit, yet the nation bore no fruit. Its religion was barren, legalistic, and fruitless ceremony. Thus, the tree was a sign of God's disappointment and of the justice and punishment to be executed upon Israel.

We must note, however, that this is not the lesson drawn by Christ. There may be many lessons drawn from the event, including Israel's experience; but the application made by Christ is clearly power, power that comes through faith and prayer (v.20-22).

DEEPER STUDY # 3
(21:19) **Fig Tree**: some claim that late-bearing fruit would bear late in the fall and remain on the tree until the next spring. When the sap returned to the tree and began producing its leaves, the fruit would ripen. A tree in full leaf would therefore be expected to have some early fruit. Whatever the case, this much is known: the fig tree is unusual in that its fruit *appears* before the leaves. Therefore, when the tree is full of developed foliage, a person could expect the earliest fruit to be either ripe or close to ripening. Perhaps at least some fruit would be tasty enough to be edible to a hungry traveller.

Remember also that the word *Bethphage* means "House of Figs." It is possible that the latest methods of fruit growing had grafted an early developing variety. Who knows? Early, mid, and late varieties are a common practice today. There are certainly indications that the people of old were astonishingly advanced in some areas.

3 (21:20-21) **Power—Faith**: the demonstration of Jesus' great power did just what He had wanted. It stirred the disciples to marvel and question. In amazement they asked, "How did the fig tree immediately wither so quickly?" (This is a better understanding of the Greek.)

Jesus had them just where He wanted them: they were asking about His great power. He wanted to teach them that He had absolute power over the physical world and that the same power was available to them in the future as they served Him. He had demonstrated His absolute power; now they were asking about the source of that power.

Note how Jesus shared the source of His power. He said in essence, "Here is the source of my power, and the same power source is available to you." He was explaining the source of His power in the *second person* which makes it applicable to all His disciples. He was answering their question about His power, but He was doing it in such a way that they would know the same power was available to them.

What is the source of Christ's great power? Or, we may ask, what is the source of great power for the disciple of Christ? It is three things. (All the notes referred to in the following points give an excellent study on faith. Also see complete outline and notes—Mt.17:14-21.)

1. Faith (see notes—Mk.11:22-23; Heb.11:1; note and DEEPER STUDY # 1—11:6).

2. Not doubting at all. This means never having a thought as to whether a thing can be done or not. It means not hesitating, not wondering, not questioning, not considering, not being concerned at all. Realistically, only God Himself could ever know whether or not something would happen—know so perfectly that no wondering thought would ever cross His mind. What Christ is after is that we grow in belief and trust. He wants us to believe that all things are possible through Christ who strengthens us (Ph.4:13). (See outlines and notes—Mt.17:15-16; 17:17-18; 17:19-20; Mk.9:18.)

3. God's authority: given to those who speak the Word. Note the phrase "Can say" (see note—Mt.17:20). The power of Christ came from the authority of God. All He had to do was *say*, that is, speak the Word, and it was done. That is the very point He is making to us. If we believe, not doubting, then we stand in the authority of God. We may *say*, that is, speak the Word, and it shall be done.

> **Then the disciples came to Jesus in private and asked, "Why couldn't we drive it out?" He replied, "Because you have so little faith. I tell you the truth, if you have faith as small as a mustard seed, you can say to this mountain, 'Move from here to there' and it will move. Nothing will be impossible for you." (Mat 17:19-20)**
>
> **If you believe, you will receive whatever you ask for in prayer." (Mat 21:22)**
>
> **"I tell you the truth, if anyone says to this mountain, 'Go, throw yourself into the sea,' and does not doubt in his heart but believes that what he says will happen, it will be done for him. Therefore I tell you, whatever you ask for in prayer, believe that you have received it, and it will be yours. (Mark 11:23-24)**
>
> **If you remain in me and my words remain in you, ask whatever you wish, and it will be given you. (John 15:7)**
>
> **Now faith is being sure of what we hope for and certain of what we do not see. (Heb 11:1)**
>
> **And without faith it is impossible to please God, because anyone who comes to him must believe that he exists and that he rewards those who earnestly seek him. (Heb 11:6)**
>
> **In the same way, faith by itself, if it is not accompanied by action, is dead. (James 2:17)**

4 (21:22) **Prayer**: Jesus' promise of power to us is through prayer and faith. Christ drives home two striking points.

1. His promise is comprehensive: "you will receive whatever you ask for in prayer." It is all inclusive, much beyond the sphere of what we can ask or even think (Eph.3:20).

2. His promise is conditional: "If you believe." We have to *pray and believe* to receive.

a. Prayer is to be constant. The person who receives answers from God knows God personally. He is in constant, unbroken fellowship and sharing with God. A person cannot come every now and then to God and expect answers. This is not what Christ means.

> **They all joined together constantly in prayer, along with the women and Mary the mother of Jesus, and with his brothers. (Acts 1:14)**
>
> **Be joyful in hope, patient in affliction, faithful in prayer. (Rom 12:12)**
>
> **Do not deprive each other except by mutual consent and for a time, so that you may devote yourselves to prayer. Then come together again so that Satan will not tempt you because of your lack of self-control. (1 Cor 7:5. refer to this whole verse for a graphic picture.)**
>
> **And pray in the Spirit on all occasions with all kinds of prayers and requests. With this in mind, be alert and always keep on praying for all the saints. (Eph 6:18)**
>
> **Devote yourselves to prayer, being watchful and thankful. (Col 4:2)**

b. Believing is, of course, essential. Mark says it well: "If anyone says...and does not doubt in his heart but believes that what he says will happen, it will be done for him" (Mk.11:23). (See note—Heb.11:1.)

Thought 1. see note—Mt.21:22. See outline and notes—Mt.7:7-11.

Thought 2. God's supernatural power is available to us, but it is conditional. We do not possess supernatural power within ourselves. God's power comes only through prayer and faith.

Thought 3. Prayer is the vehicle; faith is the energy. It takes both to reach the desired destination.

Thought 4. Faith stirs prayer and communion with God. A person who really *believes*, who has real faith in God, is driven to pray and commune with God.

Thought 5. This great promise should stir us to pray and believe God, to ask and ask.

Outline	Scripture
	D. The Questioning of the Messiah's Power: The Problem with Obstinate Unbelief, 21:23-27 (Mk.11:27-33; Lk.20:1-8)
1 The obstinate unbelief of leaders	23 Jesus entered the temple courts, and, while he was
2 Unbelief treats Christ with disdain: They disturbed the people's teaching & worship	teaching, the chief priests and the elders of the people came to him.
3 Unbelief questions the authority of Christ	"By what authority are you doing these things?" they asked. "And who gave you this authority?"
4 Unbelief must face the personal interrogation of Christ a. Must face His right to question	24 Jesus replied, "I will also ask you one question. If you answer me, I will tell you by what authority I am doing these things.
b. The question: Was John's ministry from heaven or from men?	25 John's baptism—where did it come from? Was it from heaven, or from men?"
5 Unbelief causes a threefold sin & guilt a. A deliberate denial by men	They discussed it among themselves and said, "If we say, 'From heaven,' he will ask, 'Then why didn't you believe him?'
b. A deliberate cowardice by men c. A deliberate ignorance or expediency of men	26 But if we say, 'From men'—we are afraid of the people, for they all hold that John was a prophet."
6 Unbelief results in Christ's silence: He refuses to reveal Himself	27 So they answered Jesus, "We don't know." Then he said, "Neither will I tell you by what authority I am doing these things."

DIVISION XIV

THE MESSIAH'S LAST WEEK: HIS CLAIM CHALLENGED AND REJECTED, 21:1-23:39

D. The Questioning of the Messiah's Power: The Problem with Obstinate Unbelief, 21:23-27

(21:23-27) **Introduction—Jesus Christ, Opposition**: from this passage to the end of chapter 23, Jesus deals with His opponents, self-righteous religionists and civil leaders (the elders). All the events of this section as well as the Olivet discourse (Mt. 24-25) seem to have taken place on Tuesday (cp. Mt.22:23; 25:1; 26:1-2). A quick reading of this section is an eye-opener into the great tragedy and problem with self-righteousness and unbelief. Christ was forceful, very forceful, in attacking self-righteousness and unbelief. He delivered a *sustained attack*, leaving no doubt that a person who continues in self-righteousness, even a religionist, is unworthy of God's kingdom. Obstinate unbelief is doomed.

1. The obstinate unbelief of leaders (v.23).
2. Unbelief treats Christ with disdain (v.23).
3. Unbelief questions the authority of Christ (v.23).
4. Unbelief must face the personal interrogation of Christ (v.24-25).
5. Unbelief causes a threefold sin and guilt (v.25-27).
6. Unbelief results in Christ's silence: He refuses to reveal Himself (v.27).

1 (21:23) **Unbelief, Obstinate—Sanhedrin**: the obstinate unbelief of leaders. This event continues the Lord's final ministry in the courtyards of the temple. Pilgrims from all over the world were in Jerusalem. A large number had gathered in the temple and were surrounding Christ. They were listening to Him teach. Matthew said, "the chief priests and elders" became extremely upset and confronted Christ. Mark and Luke tell us that the Scribes were also present. This indicates that the leaders were an official delegation representing the ruling body of the Jews, the Sanhedrin (see notes—Mt.26:57; 26:59). All that had happened naturally created a crisis for the ruling body: the triumphal entry, Christ's acceptance of the people's homage, the cleansing of the temple, the disruption of the priests' profits from those who sold and bought, the healing of the blind and lame, and the worship of the children. What Christ was doing simply infuriated them, sending them into a rage. It aroused them to question: "Who does Jesus of Nazareth think He is?" (Mt.21:10-11).

But note: the question was one of contempt, not of seeking. The question was an attempt to discredit, not to learn the truth. The question was aroused because their own position, esteem, and gain were disturbed, not because they wanted to really know if He were the Messiah. Their minds were closed or shut to His claims. They had many claims and many proofs of His Messiahship, but they wilfully ignored and denied His divine mission. They had plenty of opportunities to learn the truth, yet they allowed nothing to change them (see note—Jn.3:2). They were gripped with obstinate unbelief (see notes—Mt.12:1-8; note and DEEPER STUDY # 1—12:10; note—15:1-20; DEEPER STUDY # 2—15:6-9. These notes will give some background to the opposition against Christ.)

> **Thought 1.** See notes—Mt.21:23. Cp. DEEPER STUDY # 4—Mt.12:24; note—12:31-32.

> **Thought 2.** These things often happen to a person who has position, esteem, and wealth and who seeks more gain.
> 1) He fears the truth lest it threaten what he has.
> 2) He is forced to continue in unbelief and denial. The person fears facing the issue honestly lest he has to confess he has been wrong. Such would be too embarrassing and humiliating, causing more ridicule than he is willing to bear.

2 (21:23) **Unbelief**: unbelief treats Christ with disdain. Christ was teaching and people were worshipping. Nevertheless, in utter rudeness, the unbelievers walked right in, interrupting His teaching and the people's worship.

> **Thought 1.** Unbelief treats Christ with contempt. Unbelief pays no attention to what Christ says and does. Imagine how serious the contempt is. Christ, the Son of God…
> - has left the glory of heaven and come to earth.
> - has spoken, revealing the truth about God, man, and the world.

- has secured salvation and everlasting life for man.

Yet despite all that Christ has done, man denies Christ. He prefers a few years of human esteem and pleasure to believing and committing his hope upon the fact that life continues on forever. Speaking of contempt—there is no greater contempt than to deny the Son of God. Unbelief definitely treats Christ with disdain.

Thought 2. Unbelief always interrupts. What God wants is a free flow for the spirit of belief. When one unbelieving person is present, he disrupts the spirit of belief. There is not a free flow of the spirit of belief. The more unbelief present, the more the free flow is hindered. Unbelief hinders, hampers, disrupts, and disturbs belief.

> **Those who passed by hurled insults at him, shaking their heads and saying, "You who are going to destroy the temple and build it in three days, save yourself! Come down from the cross, if you are the Son of God!" (Mat 27:39-40)**
>
> **In the same way the chief priests and the teachers of the law mocked him among themselves. "He saved others," they said, "but he can't save himself! Let this Christ, this King of Israel, come down now from the cross, that we may see and believe." Those crucified with him also heaped insults on him. (Mark 15:31-32)**
>
> **The people stood watching, and the rulers even sneered at him. They said, "He saved others; let him save himself if he is the Christ of God, the Chosen One." (Luke 23:35)**
>
> **The Pharisees and the teachers of the law began thinking to themselves, "Who is this fellow who speaks blasphemy? Who can forgive sins but God alone?" (Luke 5:21)**
>
> **For this reason the Jews tried all the harder to kill him; not only was he breaking the Sabbath, but he was even calling God his own Father, making himself equal with God. (John 5:18)**
>
> **Are you greater than our father Abraham? He died, and so did the prophets. Who do you think you are?" (John 8:53)**
>
> **"We are not stoning you for any of these," replied the Jews, "but for blasphemy, because you, a mere man, claim to be God." (John 10:33)**

3 (21:23) **Unbelief**: unbelief strikes at the very core of Christ's nature; it questions His authority, who He really is.

The Sanhedrin (chief priests, elders and Scribes) were the leaders of the nation and the chief priests were the guardians and rulers of the temple. They wanted to know who gave Christ the right to do what He was doing. He was interfering with their management and had no right to interfere.

They asked two questions: "By what authority are you doing these things? And who gave you this authority?" They were questioning the authority for His works (first question) and for His person (second question). Unbelief always questions both works and person: *by what* authority "these things are done" and "who gave you" such authority. Christ can give one of three possible answers: by the authority of Himself, of God, or of one of the temple authorities. His questioners knew that no temple authority had given Him authorization to do what He was doing; thus, by the questioning, they hoped to discredit Him.

If He said His authority came from God, they could demand a sign from heaven and accuse Him of blasphemy (see note—Mt.12:38-40; cp. Mt.26:65). If He said His authority was of Himself, the people would probably turn away from Him.

> **Thought 1.** Unbelief strikes at the very core of Christ's nature. A man may say He believes in Christ but show no sign that he has committed his life to Him. Such belief is not biblical, not what the Bible means by belief. Such belief is only mental acceptance of an historical person. Belief that does not commit one's life is nothing more than thoughtless, mental acceptance. If a person really knows that Jesus is God's Son, that person will commit His life to Christ. Unbelief, whatever its claim or thoughts, questions and denies that Christ is truly the Son of God.
>
> **Thought 2.** Unbelief always questions a person's genuineness and works. Unbelievers are always around watching for a chance to justify their position when a believer falls into sin. Therefore, every believer should know by whose authority he acts. Is he acting because of self or because of God? Minister and congregation alike need to be sure their action and behavior are of God and not of self. Living a life of righteousness is acting under God's authority. Righteousness is the only thing that will silence unbelief.

4 (21:24-25) **Unbelief**: unbelief must face the personal interrogation of Christ. Christ has as much right to question unbelievers as unbelievers do Him. He asked only one question: "Is John's ministry from heaven or from men?"

If John's ministry were from heaven, then Christ was God's Son. Why? Because John bore testimony: "Look, the Lamb of God who takes away the sin of the world...I have seen and *I testify* that this is the Son of God" (Jn.1:29, 34).

If John's ministry were from men, then how can we account for so many changed lives and marvelous works? This one question shows the absurdity and sin of unbelief, not only of unbelievers in Jesus' day but of unbelievers in our day as well. (See outline and notes—Mt.3:1-17; Lk.7:29-31.)

> **Thought 1.** Is John's ministry from heaven or from men? The very same question is applicable to our day. The question forces confession or denial, and denial is totally absurd and ridiculous. How can so many changed lives and wonderful works throughout the world and history be accounted for apart from Christ? There is an abundance of witnesses.
>
> **Thought 2.** Think for a moment. Was John's ministry really of himself, from his own mind? How could so many down through history minister from their own minds? Imagine—an unbeliever has to say unbelievable things:

1) That every believer who has ever ministered created his own ministry (works) out of his own mind.
2) That every believer who has ever ministered was mistaken about Christ (knowing Him personally as the Son of God and being called and gifted by Him).

(All the people, even the tax collectors, when they heard Jesus' words, acknowledged that God's way was right, because they had been baptized by John. (Luke 7:29)

Jesus answered, "I did tell you, but you do not believe. The miracles I do in my Father's name speak for me, (John 10:25)

What about the one whom the Father set apart as his very own and sent into the world? Why then do you accuse me of blasphemy because I said, 'I am God's Son'? Do not believe me unless I do what my Father does. But if I do it, even though you do not believe me, believe the miracles, that you may know and understand that the Father is in me, and I in the Father." (John 10:36-38)

And many people came to him. They said, "Though John never performed a miraculous sign, all that John said about this man was true." And in that place many believed in Jesus. (John 10:41-42)

Don't you believe that I am in the Father, and that the Father is in me? The words I say to you are not just my own. Rather, it is the Father, living in me, who is doing his work. (John 14:10)

5 (21:25-27) **Unbelief**: unbelief causes a threefold sin and guilt. The words "they discussed it among themselves" (par eantois). They did not just reason in (en) themselves, each left to his own thoughts. This was a planned attack against Christ, a deliberate rejection of Christ.

The Lord's questioners immediately knew their predicament. If they replied that John's ministry was of God, then Christ would ask them why they did not believe John's testimony about the Messiah. If they replied that John's ministry was from men, they would arouse the people against themselves, for the people believed strongly that John was a true prophet from God.

Note how the questioners discussed it among themselves. Their concern was not to discover the truth but to save face and protect their position, esteem, and security. They committed a threefold sin.

1. They deliberately denied Christ. To confess that John was of God would force them to acknowledge Christ, and they just were not willing to confess Him. They feared the loss of all they possessed (position, power, wealth, esteem, image, security).

If we endure, we will also reign with him. If we disown him, he will also disown us; (2 Tim 2:12)

But there were also false prophets among the people, just as there will be false teachers among you. They will secretly introduce destructive heresies, even denying the sovereign Lord who bought them—bringing swift destruction on themselves. (2 Pet 2:1)

Who is the liar? It is the man who denies that Jesus is the Christ. Such a man is the antichrist—he denies the Father and the Son. (1 John 2:22)

2. They feared men; they were deliberately cowardly. They feared the reactions of men (abuse, ridicule, persecution).

If anyone is ashamed of me and my words in this adulterous and sinful generation, the Son of Man will be ashamed of him when he comes in his Father's glory with the holy angels." (Mark 8:38)

3. They chose expediency, to deliberately be ignorant. They feared being shamed, embarrassed, and ridiculed. To confess Christ would mean confessing they had been wrong all along. It would mean denying self completely and doing so publicly. Most men...

- choose expediency rather than principle.
- choose to play it safe rather than to stand up for the truth.
- choose to say, "I don't know," rather than to speak the truth.

Jesus answered, "I did tell you, but you do not believe. The miracles I do in my Father's name speak for me, (John 10:25)

What about the one whom the Father set apart as his very own and sent into the world? Why then do you accuse me of blasphemy because I said, 'I am God's Son'? Do not believe me unless I do what my Father does. But if I do it, even though you do not believe me, believe the miracles, that you may know and understand that the Father is in me, and I in the Father." (John 10:36-38)

Don't you believe that I am in the Father, and that the Father is in me? The words I say to you are not just my own. Rather, it is the Father, living in me, who is doing his work. (John 14:10)

Thought 1. It is the duty of every thinking man to know whether or not Christ is true. For a thinking man to say, "I do not know," is unacceptable. A *thinking man* ought to know, for he has the capability to know. He is to think, determining the true from the false. If he fails to do this, he condemns himself.

Thought 2. Two things are absurd.
1) It is absurd to acknowledge a truth and then reject it. An unbeliever cannot acknowledge that John and Christ *are from God* and then not confess them. To say that they are *from God* and then deny them is the height of absurdity.
2) It is absurd not to confess Christ. Denial is the height of absurdity. The evidence is overwhelming.

Thought 3. At least two things cause a man to reject and oppose the truth.
1) Sin: a man loves sin too much to give it up. His sin may be such things as the flesh, pride, fame, power, wealth, self will, position, property. He is just too possessed to turn to Christ.

2) Fear: men fear two things.
   a) They fear God. If they confess Christ, they fear God will make demands upon them and they will have to give some things up. They fear the loss of whatever they have and enjoy: position, wealth, pleasure.
   b) They fear men. If they confess Christ, they fear ridicule, embarrassment, persecution, shame, abuse, rejection, being passed over. These things and so many more cause men to commit the threefold sins of unbelief.

6 (21:27) **Decision—Unbelief**: unbelief results in Christ's silence. His questioners said, "We don't know." They lied. They knew perfectly well that John's baptism was from God. They just were not willing to run the risk of losing their position, livelihood and security. They loved the world more than God and the hope He extended toward them. Thus they denied, acted cowardly, and chose the route of expediency.

Thought 1. The point is this: these unbelievers would not be convinced of the truth. It is not that they *could not* be convinced, but they *would not*. Such obstinate unbelief seldom, if ever, sees the truth of Christ. Even if Christ openly revealed the truth to them, they would reject it.

"He said to him, 'If they do not listen to Moses and the Prophets, they will not be convinced even if someone rises from the dead.'" (Luke 16:31)

Thought 2. When the sins of unbelief are pointed out, men are often provoked and retaliate. They act with malice, often legally and legitimately within society's rules. Sometimes they attempt to denounce and discredit, sometimes persecute.

Thought 3. The judgment of Christ stands against obstinate unbelief. What judgment? The judgment of silence; Christ will honor unbelief, honor it by not revealing Himself to the unbeliever. Unbelief is doomed.

"He said to him, 'If they do not listen to Moses and the Prophets, they will not be convinced even if someone rises from the dead.'" (Luke 16:31)

Yet you refuse to come to me to have life. (John 5:40)

He sent his servants to those who had been invited to the banquet to tell them to come, but they refused to come. (Mat 22:3)

While you were doing all these things, declares the LORD, I spoke to you again and again, but you did not listen; I called you, but you did not answer. I will thrust you from my presence, just as I did all your brothers, the people of Ephraim.' (Jer 7: 13, 15)

This day I call heaven and earth as witnesses against you that I have set before you life and death, blessings and curses. Now choose life, so that you and your children may live and that you may love the LORD your God, listen to his voice, and hold fast to him. For the LORD is your life, and he will give you many years in the land he swore to give to your fathers, Abraham, Isaac and Jacob. (Deu 30:19-20)

For he says, "In the time of my favor I heard you, and in the day of salvation I helped you." I tell you, now is the time of God's favor, now is the day of salvation. (2 Cor 6:2)

Outline	Heading	Scripture	Scripture (cont.)	Outline
	E. The Parable of Two Sons: What It Takes to Enter God's Kingdom, 21:28-32		'I will, sir,' but he did not go.	c. The first son did what his father wanted
1 The parable: A man & two sons a. Commands first son to go work in his vineyard 1) He says "I will not" 2) He later changes his mind &goes		28 "What do you think? There was a man who had two sons. He went to the first and said, 'Son, go and work today in the vineyard.' 29 "'I will not,' he answered, but later he changed his mind and went.	31 "Which of the two did what his father wanted?" "The first," they answered. Jesus said to them, "I tell you the truth, the tax collectors and the prostitutes are entering the kingdom of God ahead of you.	**2 The point: Sinners enter the kingdom before religionists (the self-righteous & those who make a false profession)**
b. Commands second son 1) He says "I will, sir" 2) He never goes		30 "Then the father went to the other son and said the same ting. He answered,	32 For John came to you to show you the way of righteousness, and you did not believe him, but the tax collectors and the prostitutes did. And even after you saw this, you did not repent and believe him.	**3 The reason: Religionists do not believe John—that Jesus is the Son of God** a. Yet John was righteous b. Sinners believe John c. The religionists' problem: See changed lives but still do not repent & believe

DIVISION XIV

THE MESSIAH'S LAST WEEK: HIS CLAIM CHALLENGED AND REJECTED, 21:1-23:39

E. The Parable of Two Sons: What It Takes to Enter God's Kingdom, 21:28-32

(21:28-32) **Introduction**: the words "what do you think?" tie this parable to the Jewish leaders who had just confronted Christ and tried to discredit Him. The Lord wanted to convey a critical message to them, a message that would determine their eternal destiny.

What does it take to enter God's Kingdom? Not only profession and righteousness, but also repentance and belief.

1. The parable: a man and two sons (v.28-31).
2. The point: sinners enter the kingdom before religionists (the self-righteous and those who make a false profession) (v.31).
3. The reason: religionists do not believe John's message—that Jesus is the Christ, the Son of God (v.32).

1 (21:28-31) **Parable—Work—Service**: the parable is simple and clear. It concerns a man who had two sons. Note several facts.

1. The command "go and work" is an emphatic imperative. The father meant what he said: "You go! You work!" There is no other choice in the father's mind; no other alternative. The sons were to work and serve their father.

2. Note the word "today." Today is the day to go. Today is the day to work, not tomorrow. Tomorrow may be too late. The harvest will rot in the field. The night will come when no man can work (Jn.9:4). The sons could also die (Heb.9:27). They had to go today while they had a chance to help their father.

> **For he says, "In the time of my favor I heard you, and in the day of salvation I helped you." I tell you, now is the time of God's favor, now is the day of salvation. (2 Cor 6:2)**
>
> **For he is our God and we are the people of his pasture, the flock under his care. Today, if you hear his voice, do not harden your hearts as you did at Meribah, as you did that day at Massah in the desert, (Psa 95:7-8)**

3. The first son said, "I will not." This was disrespectful rebellion. It was the refusal of a son who wished to go his own way in life, who rebelled at being told what to do. He was selfish, worldly, carnal, fleshly, materialistic, and prideful. He would have his own way and do his own thing regardless. However, note that the first son *later changed his mind and went.* The word *change* means to repent, to turn. (See note and DEEPER STUDY # 1, Repent—Acts 17:29-30.) The first son changed and turned from his self-chosen life of rebellion and worldliness—turned back to his father and went into his father's vineyard to work. He did exactly what his father commanded him to do.

4. The second son said "I will, sir." Note: his response indicates that he will go immediately and serve zealously in the father's work. He said I go to work *for you.* But he failed; he *never* did go to work for his father. He went to work, but not for his father. He was just like the first son: selfish, disregarding the father and his needs. He went about his own life, living and working for *himself.* The only difference between the two sons is that the second son *professed* respect for the father and *professed* to work for the father, but he *never* went into the father's vineyard. He never did the father's work. (This implies that what he did day by day was his own work, his own labor. He worked and lived as he wished, disregarding the father entirely. It was a life of religion and moral strictness as we shall see.)

5. Christ asked the religionists standing around which of the two sons did the father's will. The religionists did not see the point of the parable yet, so they gave the obvious answer: the first son did the father's will.

Their immediate response to Christ is interesting. They demonstrated just how much religion and self-righteousness can blind a person, giving a sense of false security. A person, clergyman and layman alike, who sincerely lives a life of religion and moral purity has great difficulty understanding why he is not acceptable to God and cannot enter God's kingdom.

2 (21:31) **Salvation—Self-righteousness—Labor**: Jesus gave the point of the parable. Sinners enter the kingdom before religionists (the self-righteous and professors only). Note what Jesus did.

1. Jesus identified the man and the two sons in the parable.
   a. The man who owned the vineyard was God. God is the Person who possesses the kingdom (see DEEPER STUDY # 3—Mt.19:23-24).
   b. The first son represents the non-religious and worldly of this earth. These do not profess religion, and they do not know they are lost. They desire to go their own way, wanting nothing to do with God. The tax collectors represented the rejected and worldly-minded, those more interested in money and in the things of this world than in God. The prostitutes represented the immoral and sensual, those more interested in pleasure than God.
   c. The second son represents the religious of this earth (the self-righteous and those who make a false profession). These were either reared in church from earliest childhood or else came into the church sometime in later life. They professed religion and righteousness to be the way a person should live.
2. Jesus identified the vineyard and work that was to be done. The vineyard is the Kingdom of God and the work is "entering the kingdom of God"—serve God within His kingdom (see DEEPER STUDY # 3—Mt.19:23-24). Note two things:
   a. Both sons (all men) receive the same command and obligation: "Go into the vineyard."
   b. God respects both sons. He does not force either son to work, neither the son who rebels nor the son who makes a commitment but fails to work in God's vineyard. The sons' wills are honored. They may go and work wherever they wish.
3. Jesus clearly stressed the point of the parable.
   a. He said emphatically "I tell you the truth." The word "I" means the Messiah, the Son of God Himself. The Messiah is revealing a critical truth.
   b. He said in unmistakable terms: sinners "are entering the kingdom of God ahead of you," before the self-righteous and false religionist and false professor. It is important to pay close attention to the Lord's words. He said, "ahead of you." He was not shutting the door of heaven to the religionists. They just could not enter as they presently were. As Christ said in the next verse, they lacked one thing, and they must do that thing in order to enter God's kingdom.
4. Jesus shocked His audience. He declared that man's idea of religion is wrong. Religion and righteousness are not enough to enter God's kingdom. It takes more. Religion is not enough (worship services, ceremony, ritual, profession, and ordinance). Righteousness is not enough (morality, virtue, law, rules and regulations, good works, and commitment). Christ shockingly declared to the religionist and to the righteous: "Sinners are entering the kingdom *ahead of you*. What *you* have is not enough; it takes more. Something else is needed."

> **For I tell you that unless your righteousness surpasses that of the Pharisees and the teachers of the law, you will certainly not enter the kingdom of heaven. (Mat 5:20)**
>
> **Since they did not know the righteousness that comes from God and sought to establish their own, they did not submit to God's righteousness. (Rom 10:3)**
>
> **Come back to your senses as you ought, and stop sinning; for there are some who are ignorant of God—I say this to your shame. (1 Cor 15:34)**

3 (21:32) **Salvation—Rejection**: the reason sinners enter God's kingdom and religionists do not is clearly stated: religionists do not believe John's message that Jesus is the Messiah, the Son of God. Note that Christ said three things.

1. John was righteous. John came "to show you the way of righteousness," the very righteousness that religionists say is necessary to live for God. John was godly and lived just like religionists said he should live, yet religionists did not believe John; that is, they did not believe his ministry and witness—that Jesus was the Messiah, the Son of God.

Christ said to the religionists standing around Him: "You are contradictory. John came to show you 'the way of righteousness' which you profess. He was godly, yet you did not receive his ministry and witness":

> **The next day John saw Jesus coming toward him and said, "Look, the Lamb of God, who takes away the sin of the world! (John 1:29; cp. Jn1:29-36)**
>
> **I have seen and I testify that this is the Son of God." (John 1:34)**
>
> **But the Pharisees and experts in the law rejected God's purpose for themselves, because they had not been baptized by (John) (Luke 7:30)**

Thought 1. The great tragedy of religionists is this: they stand aloof. They reject the counsel of God; they do not go and work in His vineyard.

2. Sinners believed John's witness: "The tax collectors and prostitutes believed him." The first son did exactly what John said to do: he repented of his loose life and believed that Jesus was the Son of God (see note—Mt.21:31).
3. Religionists saw the evidence, but they rejected it. They saw the evidence of John's righteousness and of the changed lives of sinners ("even after you saw this"). But the religionists still denied the facts. Note: a religionist commits two gross errors that are seen in this passage.
   a. The religionist lives a strict religious life, but he does not repent of coming short. He tells God he will *go and work in His vineyard,* that is, *His kingdom*, but he does not go into *God's* vineyard. However, note: he does work. In fact, he is very strict in his work, but he works in the vineyard of his own *religion* and righteousness and rules. He never enters God's vineyard (kingdom) to serve the Father.

      What happened is what Jesus said. The religionists rejected the Scriptural witness which began with John's ministry and witness. This witness said that the only way to get into God's vineyard is through faith in Christ, and the only way to serve God adequately is through the indwelling power of Christ (Jn.14:6; 1 Tim.2:5).

> **"I am the vine; you are the branches. If a man remains in me and I in him, he will bear much fruit; apart from me you can do nothing. (John 15:5)**
>
> **Now to him who is able to do immeasurably more than all we ask or imagine,**

according to his power that is at work within us, (Eph 3:20)

b. The religionist does not believe John's personal witness: that Jesus is the Messiah, the Son of God. The religionist most likely accepts Jesus as a great teacher, but not as the Lamb of God who sacrificed Himself for the sins of the world (1 Pt.2:24).

No one takes it from me, but I lay it down of my own accord. I have authority to lay it down and authority to take it up again. This command I received from my Father." (John 10:18)

He himself bore our sins in his body on the tree, so that we might die to sins and live for righteousness; by his wounds you have been healed. (1 Pet 2:24)

For Christ died for sins once for all, the righteous for the unrighteous, to bring you to God. He was put to death in the body but made alive by the Spirit, (1 Pet 3:18)

Thought 1. John's witness is the standard by which Jesus is measuring religionists. It is not enough to be religious and righteous, that is, a good, moral, outstanding citizen. A person has to do more.

1) He has to repent for not going into *God's* vineyard or God's kingdom. The religionist created his own vineyard of religion and righteousness, but his vineyard was not God's vineyard. God's vineyard is the vineyard of faith.
2) He has to believe in God's Son, Jesus Christ. He has to enter the vineyard of faith, and he has to work within the vineyard of faith.

For it is by grace you have been saved, through faith—and this not from yourselves, it is the gift of God— not by works, so that no one can boast. For we are God's workmanship, created in Christ Jesus to do good works, which God prepared in advance for us to do. (Eph 2:8-10)

Outline	Scripture	Scripture	Outline
	F. The Parable of the Wicked Tenants: Israel's Rejection of Jesus' Messiahship, 21:33-46 (Mk.12:1-12;Lk.20:9-19; cp. Is.5:1-7)	threw him out of the vineyard and killed him.	f. God is to judge the tenants[DS6]
		40 "Therefore, when the owner of the vineyard comes, what will he do to those tenants?"	1) God is coming
		41 "He will bring those wretches to a wretched end," they replied,	2) God will miserably destroy the wicked
1 The parable: Israel's history as God sees it		"and he will rent the vineyard to other tenants, who will give him his share of the crop at harvest time."	3) God will trust His vineyard to others (to the Gentiles, v.43)
a. God planted a vineyard (the nation of Israel)[DS1]	33 "Listen to another parable: There was a landowner who planted a vineyard. He put a wall around it, dug a winepress in it and built a watchtower.	42 Jesus said to them, "Have you never read in the Scriptures: "'The stone the builders rejected has become the capstone ; the Lord has done this, and it is marvelous in our eyes'?	**2 The three claims of Jesus**
b. God entrusted His vineyard to the cultivators[DS2]	Then he rented the vineyard to some farmers and went away on a journey.		a. He is the Head cornerstone[DS7]
			1) At first, He is rejected
			2) But He becomes the Head cornerstone
c. God sent messengers to gather the fruit[DS3]	34 When the harvest time approached,	43 "Therefore I tell you that the kingdom of God will be taken away from you and given to a people who will produce its fruit.	b. God shall take His kingdom away from Israel & give it to another people[DS8]
1) Fruit was expected	he sent his servants to the tenants to collect his fruit.		c. Some are doomed[DS9,10]
2) The tenants rebelled & rejected God's messengers	35 "The tenants seized his servants; they beat one, killed another, and stoned a third.	44 He who falls on this stone will be broken to pieces,	1) Those who stumble over the stone
d. God showed patience—He continued to send messengers[DS4]	36 Then he sent other servants to them, more than the first time, and the tenants treated them the same way.	but he on whom it falls will be crushed."	2) Those who oppose the stone
e. God finally sent His Son[DS5]	37 Last of all, he sent his son to them.	45 When the chief priests and the Pharisees heard Jesus' parables,	**3 The results of the parable**
1) Christ claimed to be God's Son	'They will respect my son,' he said.	they knew he was talking about them.	a. The religionists saw that Christ spoke to them
2) They saw God's Son	38 "But when the tenants saw the son,	46 They looked for a way to arrest him,	b. The religionists reacted instead of repenting
3) They plotted His death	they said to each other, 'This is the heir. Come, let's kill him	but they were afraid of the crowd because the people held that he was a prophet.	c. The people saw Christ as a prophet, not as the Messiah
4) They planned to seize His inheritance	and take his inheritance.'		
5) They murdered the Son	39 So they took him and		

DIVISION XIV

THE MESSIAH'S LAST WEEK: HIS CLAIM CHALLENGED AND REJECTED, 21:1-23:39

F. The Parable of the Wicked Tenants: Israel's Rejection of Jesus' Messiahship, 21:33-46

(21:33-46) **Introduction**: this is one of the most interesting parables ever told by Christ. It is interesting because it is both historical and predictive. Christ covered the history of Israel from God's perspective, just as God sees it (v.33-36). Then He predicted or revealed exactly what was going to happen to Israel: they were going to reject God's own Son (v.37-39, 42); and because of their rejection and cruelty, God was going to reject them by giving the Kingdom of God to another people (v.43).

What is said throughout this passage is applicable to all nations as well as to Israel. God has entrusted the vineyard of the church and of the world to us (Mt.28:19-20), the new nation, the new creation of God (see notes—Eph.2:11-18; pt.4, 2:14-15; 4:17-19). Every point covered in Israel's history should, therefore, be a dynamic message speaking loudly and clearly to our hearts.

There are three major points in this passage.

1. The parable: Israel's history as God sees it (v.33-41).
2. The three claims of Jesus (v.42-44).
3. The results of the parable (v.45-46).

1 (21:33-41) **Israel**: Israel's history as God sees it. The landowner is God. The vineyard is Israel, true Israel, the people of God. The tenants are the religious leaders of Israel; the servants are the prophets; and the Son is Jesus Christ, the Messiah (cp. Is.5:1-7). (The sub-points of this point are so important they are discussed in separate notes. See DEEPER STUDY # 1,2,3,4,5,6—Mt.21:33-41.)

DEEPER STUDY # 1

(21:33) **God—Care—Provision—World—Church—Israel**: God planted a vineyard. The vineyard can be looked upon in several ways.

1. The vineyard is Israel, that is, true Israel, a people for God (Is.5:7).

2. The vineyard is the Kingdom of God which Israel was to look after. This is probably the most accurate understanding of what Christ meant and what actually happens in God's dealing with men. He entrusts His kingdom or church (vineyard) into our hands and expects us to culti-

vate it (cp. v.43. See DEEPER STUDY # 3—Mt.19:23-24.)

3. The vineyard can also be applied to the earth itself, to which Israel was to minister (see DEEPER STUDY # 1—Jn.4:22).

Note three marvelous things that God did for His vineyard. He provided every conceivable thing needed to take care of His vineyard and the tenants. Everything was provided to assure growth and fruitfulness. The tenants had no excuse for not producing.

1. God "put a wall around it." This was a wall built around the vineyard to keep the animals away from the grapes. The hedge or wall *assured* growth and fruitfulness.

> **You did not choose me, but I chose you and appointed you to go and bear fruit—fruit that will last. Then the Father will give you whatever you ask in my name. (John 15:16)**
>
> **Filled with the fruit of righteousness that comes through Jesus Christ—to the glory and praise of God. (Phil 1:11)**
>
> **And we pray this in order that you may live a life worthy of the Lord and may lease him in every way: bearing fruit in every good work, growing in the knowledge of God, being strengthened with all power according to his glorious might so that you may have great endurance and patience, and joyfully (Col 1:10-11)**

2. God dug a winepress. This was a trough or vat into which the wine was pressed. The trough was sometimes dug in rock, sometime built out of wood. The trough stands for the equipment which God provides to get His work done.

> **To one he gave five talents of money, to another two talents, and to another one talent, each according to his ability. Then he went on his journey. (Mat 25:15)**
>
> **But you will receive power when the Holy Spirit comes on you; and you will be my witnesses in Jerusalem, and in all Judea and Samaria, and to the ends of the earth." (Acts 1:8)**
>
> **We have different gifts, according to the grace given us. If a man's gift is prophesying, let him use it in proportion to his faith. (Rom 12:6)**
>
> **There are different kinds of gifts, but the same Spirit. (1 Cor 12:4)**

3. God built a watchtower. This was a watchtower used to guard and protect the vineyard from thieves. The tower stands for the assurance and security of God's care which He gives to His tenants (cp. Mt.6:25-34).

> **So do not worry, saying, 'What shall we eat?' or 'What shall we drink?' or 'What shall we wear?' For the pagans run after all these things, and your heavenly Father knows that you need them. Mat 6:31-32)**
>
> **Indeed, the very hairs of your head are all numbered. Don't be afraid; you are worth more than many sparrows. (Luke 12:7)**
>
> **Cast all your anxiety on him because he cares for you. (1 Pet 5:7)**
>
> **And my God will meet all your needs according to his glorious riches in Christ Jesus. (Phil 4:19)**

DEEPER STUDY # 2

(21:33) **Labor—Responsibility—Ministry**: God entrusted His vineyard to tenants. The tenants were the nation and people of Israel, in particular the leaders (both religious and civil). Everyone was responsible to take care of the whole nation, looking after everyone else, thereby contributing to the welfare and provision of all. (Cp. the whole body of the church and every member's responsibility to labor in the vineyard, 1 Cor.12:12f.)

Note two things.

1. God puts trust in men. Think what a glorious privilege it is to be trusted by God! Imagine how dear God's vineyard is to Him, and then think about how He entrusts its care to us and not to angels nor to some other higher form of being. What a wonderful and marvelous thing that God would trust us with His most precious vineyard!

2. God gives freedom to man. God left the tenants to care for His vineyard as they wished. They were to exercise their will and energy in caring for the vineyard. They had the glorious privilege of freedom, of being free to use their own ingenuity and ideas and not have someone looking over their shoulders forcing behavior.

> **So God created man in his own image, in the image of God he created him; male and female he created them. God blessed them and said to them, "Be fruitful and increase in number; fill the earth and subdue it. Rule over the fish of the sea and the birds of the air and over every living creature that moves on the ground." (Gen 1:27-28)**
>
> **You made him ruler over the works of your hands; you put everything under his feet: (Psa 8:6)**
>
> **"Again, it will be like a man going on a journey, who called his servants and entrusted his property to them. (Mat 25:14)**
>
> **Now it is required that those who have been given a trust must prove faithful. (1 Cor 4:2)**
>
> **Timothy, guard what has been entrusted to your care. Turn away from godless chatter and the opposing ideas of what is falsely called knowledge, (1 Tim 6:20)**
>
> **So he called ten of his servants and gave them ten minas. 'Put this money to work,' he said, 'until I come back.' (Luke 19:13)**

DEEPER STUDY # 3

(21:34-35) **Man—Rebellion—Rejection—Persecution**: God sent messengers to gather the fruits of His vineyard. The messengers would be the prophets and the good and godly leaders throughout Israel's history (judges, kings, and priests).

Note three things.

1. Fruit was expected. Every tenant, that is, every person was responsible for the vineyard; everyone was expected to labor and produce.

2. A day of accountability came. Every man was expected to pay his dues and to make his contribution for the

wonderful privilege of living in the beautiful vineyard and being blessed by it. (The Kingdom of God, the world, the church—however one applies this passage—all are wonderful vineyards for which we are responsible to contribute what fruit we can.)

> **Then he told this parable: "A man had a fig tree, planted in his vineyard, and he went to look for fruit on it, but did not find any. (Luke 13:6)**
>
> **He cuts off every branch in me that bears no fruit, while every branch that does bear fruit he prunes so that it will be even more fruitful. (John 15:2)**
>
> **"I am the vine; you are the branches. If a man remains in me and I in him, he will bear much fruit; apart from me you can do nothing. If anyone does not remain in me, he is like a branch that is thrown away and withers; such branches are picked up, thrown into the fire and burned. (John 15:5-6)**

3. The tenants rebelled and refused to pay the Master. In fact, their rebellion led to the persecution and murder of God's servants.
   a. Man deliberately rebels against God. Man wants to rule the vineyard himself. He wants to be the king of the kingdom, the ruler of the earth, and even the head of the church. He wants things to go his way, to rule and reign as he desires and wills. He wants no authority above himself; he wants to live as he wishes and do things as he wishes. He wants to claim the fruit for himself.
   b. Man wants his own way so much that he ridicules, slanders, persecutes, and even murders the true servants of God.

> **Was there ever a prophet your fathers did not persecute? They even killed those who predicted the coming of the Righteous One. And now you have betrayed and murdered him— (Acts 7:52; cp. Mt.23:34-37; Heb.11:36-38)**

   c. The servant of God must understand that he is called to suffer (see DEEPER STUDY # 4—Mt.21:36. Cp. note and DEEPER STUDY # 2—Mt.20:22-23.)

DEEPER STUDY # 4

(21:36) **Persecution**: God showed patience—He continued to send messengers. All through Israel's history God loved and showed His loving-kindness by not reacting and rejecting the nation. God has given us chance after chance. He sends messengers across our path time after time. He loves us and longs for us to pay our dues. He longs for us to bear fruit and live as we should.

Tragically, most tenants continue as always: rebelling and claiming all rights to the vineyard and to their own lives. Therefore, they continue to react against God's messengers.

Thought 1. How many believers, laymen and ministers alike, are mistreated by the world!

> **For it has been granted to you on behalf of Christ not only to believe on him, but also to suffer for him, (Phil 1:29)**
>
> **In fact, everyone who wants to live a godly life in Christ Jesus will be persecuted, (2 Tim 3:12)**
>
> **Dear friends, do not be surprised at the painful trial you are suffering, as though something strange were happening to you. But rejoice that you participate in the sufferings of Christ, so that you may be overjoyed when his glory is revealed. (1 Pet 4:12-13; cp. 1 Pet. 2:21; 4:5-6; Mt.19:29; Ro.8:16-17)**

DEEPER STUDY # 5

(21:37-39) **Jesus Christ, Deity—Death**: God finally sent His Son. God wanted to speak to man Himself. Perhaps they would listen to His voice and reverence His rights. He condescended and asked His Son to leave the glory of eternity and to bring His Word to earth, speaking face to face with man.

Note five facts.

1. Christ claimed to be God's Son. He was different from all the servants sent before. He was more than another man-servant; He was God's very own Son. There is no question that Christ was making this unique claim for Himself.
2. The tenants saw God's Son. There were all kinds of evidence: Old Testament prophecies; the testimony of John the Baptist; Jesus' own claim and the miraculous works; the signs of the times (Gal.4:4); the feeling that He was the promised Messiah, even among those who now opposed Him (see note—Jn.3:1-2; cp. Jn.11:47-52). This is the tragic indictment against the Jews. Down deep within they had a sense that Jesus really was the Messiah, but sin and greed for position, esteem, power, and security kept them from acknowledging Him. Their unbelief was deliberate and obstinate (see outline and notes—Mt.21:23-27).
3. The tenants plotted His death (cp. Mt.12:14; Jn.11:53).
4. The tenants planned to seize His inheritance. Man wants to possess the kingdom, nation, property, power, rule, reign, position, esteem, fame, recognition, and wealth. Whatever the possession is, man wants the possession himself; and he will deny, deceive, lie, cheat, steal, and even kill to get it. (See notes—Mt.12:1-8; note and DEEPER STUDY # 1—12:10; note—15:1-20; DEEPER STUDY # 2—15:6-9.)
5. The tenants murdered the Son. They committed the worst crime in human history. They killed the Son of God Himself. Note that Christ's death was being prophesied. He was predicting His death Himself, and His death was to be a willing act on His part. He knew death lay ahead and could have escaped, but He chose to die. It was in "God's set purpose and foreknowledge" (Acts 2:23).

> **"For God so loved the world that he gave his one and only Son, that whoever believes in him shall not perish but have eternal life. (John 3:16)**
>
> **But God demonstrates his own love for us in this: While we were still sinners, Christ died for us. (Rom 5:8)**
>
> **But because of his great love for us, God, who is rich in mercy, made us alive with Christ even when we were dead in transgressions—it is by grace you have been saved. (Eph 2:4-5)**

DEEPER STUDY # 6

(21:40-41) **Judgment—Church**: God is to judge the tenants. There are three important points here.

1. Christ said that the Lord of the vineyard is coming. He is coming to revenge the death of His only Son.

2. God is coming to destroy the wicked. The destruction is to be wretched (kakos) and terrible. Note: it was both the rulers and the people who said that justice would be executed. Man, by his very nature, expects injustice to be punished.

3. God is going to trust His vineyard to others. Again, it was the crowd who said this. Even man knows that a vineyard will not lie unkept. It will be cultivated by someone. God will raise up a new people to care for it (the church, the new creation of God. See DEEPER STUDY # 8—Mt.21:43; notes—Eph.2:11-18; pt.4, 2:14-15; 4:17-19.)

> **The ax is already at the root of the trees, and every tree that does not produce good fruit will be cut down and thrown into the fire. (Mat 3:10)**
>
> **If anyone does not remain in me, he is like a branch that is thrown away and withers; such branches are picked up, thrown into the fire and burned. (John 15:6)**
>
> **But land that produces thorns and thistles is worthless and is in danger of being cursed. In the end it will be burned. (Heb 6:8)**

2 (21:42-44) **Jesus Christ, Cornerstone—Capstone**: Christ made three astounding claims in these verses, claims that affect both world history and the personal destiny of everyone who ever lives in the world.

1. He is the Head Cornerstone or Capstone. (See DEEPER STUDY # 7—Mt.21:42 for discussion.)

2. God shall turn away from Israel to another nation. (See DEEPER STUDY # 8—Mt.21:43 for discussion.)

3. A man's rejection of Christ will cause that man to be crushed.

DEEPER STUDY # 7

(21:42) **Jesus Christ, Head Cornerstone**: Christ is the Head cornerstone (see note—Lk.2:34). This is a quotation from Ps.118:22-23 which was recognized as a Messianic prophecy. The Messiah was to be the Head Cornerstone who was to begin building the Kingdom of God and who was to support all other stones or leaders who came later. The religious leaders standing around Christ would know that He was referring to the Messiah (Is.28:16; Dan.2:34; Zech.3:9).

But note the prophecy: the stone is to be rejected at first. It is considered unsuitable, useless for the building, so the builders do not allow the stone to be a part of the building. It is cast aside and treated as undesirable.

However, the great Architect overrules the builders. He raises the stone from the graveyard of rejected stones and exalts it to the position of Head cornerstone, the stone which supports all other stones and which holds the building of God's kingdom together (cp. Ph.2:9-11. See notes—Eph.2:20.)

The symbolism of the Head cornerstone says at least two significant things.

1. The cornerstone is the first stone laid. All other stones are placed after it. It is the *preeminent* stone in time. So it is with Christ; He is *the first* of God's new movement.

⇒ Christ is the *Author* of salvation. All others are the readers of the story.

> **In bringing many sons to glory, it was fitting that God, for whom and through whom everything exists, should make the author of their salvation perfect through suffering. (Heb 2:10)**

⇒ Christ is the *Source* of eternal salvation, of our faith. All who trust and obey Him are partakers of that Source.

> **And, once made perfect, he became the source of eternal salvation for all who obey him (Heb 5:9)**
>
> **Let us fix our eyes on Jesus, the author and perfecter of our faith, who for the joy set before him endured the cross, scorning its shame, and sat down at the right hand of the throne of God. (Heb 12:2)**

⇒ Christ is the *Alpha and Omega—the beginning and the ending*. All others come after Him and are in between Him.

> **"I am the Alpha and the Omega," says the Lord God, "who is, and who was, and who is to come, the Almighty." (Rev 1:8; cp. 21:6; 22:13)**

⇒ Christ is the *Forerunner, the One who went before us* into the very presence of God. All others enter God's presence after Him.

> **We have this hope as an anchor for the soul, firm and secure. It enters the inner sanctuary behind the curtain, where Jesus, who went before us, has entered on our behalf. He has become a high priest forever, in the order of Melchizedek. (Heb 6:19-20)**

2. The cornerstone is the supportive stone. All other stones are placed upon it and held up by it. They all rest upon it. It is the preeminent stone in position and power. So it is with Christ; He is the support and power, the Foundation of God's new movement.

⇒ Christ is *the Head Cornerstone (Capstone)*, the only true foundation upon which man can build. All who are not laid upon Him will crumble.

> **For no one can lay any foundation other than the one already laid, which is Jesus Christ. (1 Cor 3:11)**

⇒ Christ is *the Chief Cornerstone* upon which all others are fitly formed together. All who wish to be fitly formed together have to be laid upon Him.

> **Built on the foundation of the apostles and prophets, with Christ Jesus himself as the chief cornerstone. In him the whole building is joined together and rises to become a holy temple in the Lord. And in him you too are being built together to be**

come a dwelling in which God lives by his Spirit. (Eph 2:20-22)

⇒ Christ is *the Living Stone* upon which all others are built. It is upon Him that we are built up into a spiritual house. All others have to be built upon Him if they wish to live and have their spiritual sacrifice accepted by God.

As you come to him, the living Stone—rejected by men but chosen by God and precious to him— you also, like living stones, are being built into a spiritual house to be a holy priesthood, offering spiritual sacrifices acceptable to God through Jesus Christ. (1 Pet 2:4-5)

DEEPER STUDY # 8
(21:43) **Israel—Gentiles—Church—New Creation**: God shall take away His kingdom and give it to another nation. Christ gave a prophecy that dramatically affects world history: His vineyard or kingdom is going to be taken away from Israel and given to another people.

There are several important facts that need to be understood at this point in order to grasp the significance of the Lord's prophecy.

1. Israel was the nation of people raised up by God to be His witness to the world (see DEEPER STUDY # 1—Jn.4:22).

a. Israel bore up the name of God in the world.

For the director of music. With stringed instruments. A psalm of Asaph. A song. In Judah God is known; his name is great in Israel. His tent is in Salem, his dwelling place in Zion. (Psa 76:1-2)

b. Israel was given the very words of God, that is, the Word of God, the revelation of God to the world.

What advantage, then, is there in being a Jew, or what value is there in circumcision? Much in every way! First of all, they have been entrusted with the very words of God. (Rom 3:1-2)

c. Israel was a greatly privileged people in spiritual things.

The people of Israel. Theirs is the adoption as sons; theirs the divine glory, the covenants, the receiving of the law, the temple worship and the promises. Theirs are the patriarchs, and from them is traced the human ancestry of Christ, who is God over all, forever praised! Amen. (Rom 9:4-5. See notes—Ro.9:3-5 for a discussion of their great privileges.)

d. Israel was given the glorious plan of salvation.

You Samaritans worship what you do not know; we worship what we do know, for salvation is from the Jews. (John 4:22)

e. Israel was given the glorious privilege of being God's witnesses upon the earth.

"You are my witnesses," declares the LORD, "and my servant whom I have chosen, so that you may know and believe me and understand that I am he. Before me no god was formed, nor will there be one after me. (Isa 43:10)

2. Israel failed God in its God-given mission and failed God miserably. Therefore, God took His kingdom away from them. As Christ points out in this parable, they "took [God's] servants, they beat one, killed another, and stoned a third" (v.35-36). Then they committed the most atrocious crime of history: they rejected and killed God's very own Son (v.39). All through its history Israel was unfruitful except for a bright spot here and there. They opposed the reins of God upon their lives, and in the final step of rebellion, they rejected and opposed the gospel of Christ. Therefore, they forfeited their Godly privileges. The Kingdom of God was taken from them and given to another nation.

a. God turned from Israel because they killed His Son.

So they took him and threw him out of the vineyard and killed him. "He will bring those wretches to a wretched end," they replied, "and he will rent the vineyard to other tenants, who will give him his share of the crop at harvest time." (Mat 21:39, 41)

b. God turned from Israel because they were unfruitful.

"Therefore I tell you that the kingdom of God will be taken away from you and given to a people who will produce its fruit. (Mat 21:43)

c. God turned from Israel because they sought after righteousness by law and not by faith.

But Israel, who pursued a law of righteousness, has not attained it. Why not? Because they pursued it not by faith but as if it were by works. They stumbled over the "stumbling stone." As it is written: "See, I lay in Zion a stone that causes men to stumble and a rock that makes them fall, and the one who trusts in him will never be put to shame." (Rom 9:31-33)

d. God turned from Israel because they would not submit themselves to the righteousness of God.

For I can testify about them that they are zealous for God, but their zeal is not based on knowledge. Since they did not know the righteousness that comes from God and sought to establish their own, they did not submit to God's righteousness. (Rom 10:2-3)

e. God turned from Israel because they did not obey the gospel.

But not all the Israelites accepted the good news. For Isaiah says, "Lord, who has believed our message?" (Rom 10:16)

f. God turned from Israel because they were a disobedient and obstinate people.

But concerning Israel he says, "All day long I have held out my hands to a disobedient and obstinate people." (Rom 10:21)

g. God turned from Israel because of unbelief.

Granted. But they were broken off because of unbelief, and you stand by faith. Do not be arrogant, but be afraid. For if God did not spare the natural branches, he will not spare you either. Consider therefore the kindness and sternness of God: sternness to those who fell, but kindness to you, provided that you continue in his kindness. Otherwise, you also will be cut off. (Rom 11:20-22)

3. Israel as a nation was never saved. Not all citizens believed in God. When God chose Israel to be His people, He did not mean *national salvation.* God knew that not all the citizens of Israel would believe. Not all citizens of any nation believe. What God meant, very simply, was that Israel as a nation was to be the *primary recipient and messenger* of His Kingdom and gospel (see the special privileges of Israel above—point 1). Salvation was never a national matter, not a matter of race or heritage. It was always a matter of personal belief. There was never a moment in Israel's history when every Jew believed in the promises of God.

It is not as though God's word had failed. For not all who are descended from Israel are Israel. Nor because they are his descendants are they all Abraham's children. On the contrary, "It is through Isaac that your offspring will be reckoned." In other words, it is not the natural children who are God's children, but it is the children of the promise who are regarded as Abraham's offspring. (Rom 9:6-8)

Isaiah cries out concerning Israel: "Though the number of the Israelites be like the sand by the sea, only the remnant will be saved. It is just as Isaiah said previously: "Unless the Lord Almighty had left us descendants, we would have become like Sodom, we would have been like Gomorrah." (Rom 9:27, 29)

A man is not a Jew if he is only one outwardly, nor is circumcision merely outward and physical. No, a man is a Jew if he is one inwardly; and circumcision is circumcision of the heart, by the Spirit, not by the written code. Such a man's praise is not from men, but from God. (Rom 2:28-29)

It was not through law that Abraham and his offspring received the promise that he would be heir of the world, but through the righteousness that comes by faith. (Rom 4:13)

What does the Scripture say? "Abraham believed God, and it was credited to him as righteousness." Now when a man works, his wages are not credited to him as a gift, but as an obligation. However, to the man who does not work but trusts God who justifies the wicked, his faith is credited as righteousness. David says the same thing when he speaks of the blessedness of the man to whom God credits righteousness apart from works: "Blessed are they whose transgressions are forgiven, whose sins are covered. Blessed is the man whose sin the Lord will never count against him." (Rom 4:3-8)

4. Israel did, however, always have a remnant, a small number of genuine believers (see outline and notes—Ro.11:1-10; cp. 9:27-29).

Isaiah cries out concerning Israel: "Though the number of the Israelites be like the sand by the sea, only the remnant will be saved. It is just as Isaiah said previously: "Unless the Lord Almighty had left us descendants, we would have become like Sodom, we would have been like Gomorrah." (Rom 9:27, 29)

I ask then: Did God reject his people? By no means! I am an Israelite myself, a descendant of Abraham, from the tribe of Benjamin. God did not reject his people, whom he foreknew. Don't you know what the Scripture says in the passage about Elijah—how he appealed to God against Israel: "Lord, they have killed your prophets and torn down your altars; I am the only one left, and they are trying to kill me"? And what was God's answer to him? "I have reserved for myself seven thousand who have not bowed the knee to Baal." So too, at the present time there is a remnant chosen by grace. (Rom 11:1-5)

5. God turned to a new nation and gave His kingdom to them.

"Therefore I tell you that the kingdom of God will be taken away from you and given to a people who will produce its fruit. (Mat 21:43)

As he says in Hosea: "I will call them 'my people' who are not my people; and I will call her 'my loved one' who is not my loved one," and, "It will happen that in the very place where it was said to them, 'You are not my people,' they will be called 'sons of the living God.'" (Rom 9:25-26)

What then shall we say? That the Gentiles, who did not pursue righteousness, have obtained it, a righteousness that is by faith; but Israel, who pursued a law of righteousness, has not attained it. Why not? Because they pursued it not by faith but as if it were by works. They stumbled over the "stumbling stone." As it is written: "See, I lay in Zion a stone that causes men to stumble and a rock that makes them fall, and the one who trusts in him will never be put to shame." (Rom 9:30-33)

And Isaiah boldly says, "I was found by those who did not seek me; I revealed myself to those who did not ask for me." (Rom 10:20)

Just as you who were at one time disobedient to God have now received mercy as a result of their disobedience, (Rom 11:30)

6. God's new people or nation was to be a new creation; that is, it was not to be an existing people or nation. Just as God had created Israel to be a new nation through one man, Abraham, so God was to create another new people through one Man, Jesus Christ.

Two things need to be noted about God's new people or nation.

a. The land or inheritance of this new nation is not of this earth but of heaven. The inheritance is of the spiritual dimension of being; it is heavenly and eternal. It is not of the physical dimension of being; it is not worldly and temporal.
b. The citizens of this new nation are people from all earthly nations who truly believe in the Lord Jesus Christ. When a person from any nation of the earth believes in Christ, God takes that person and gives him a new birth spiritually, (Jn.3:3-17; 1 Pt. 1:23; 1 Jn.5:1, 4-5). The person becomes a new creature and a new man (2 Cor.5:17; Eph.4:24; Col.3:10).

All believers counted together are said to comprise...

- the citizens of the new people or nation (Eph.2:19; 1 Pt.2:9).
- the family and household of God (Eph.2:19; 5:1, 8; cp. Ro.8:16-17).
- a new body of believers (1 Cor.12:12-14; Eph.2:16).
- a holy temple (Eph.2:21-22).
- a new race (Eph.4:17).
- a spiritual house (1 Pt.2:5).
- a holy priesthood (1 Pt.2:5).
- a chosen people (1 Pt.2:9).
- a royal priesthood (1 Pt.2:9).
- a peculiar people, a people belonging to God (1 Pt.2:9).
- the people of God (1 Pt.2:10).
- strangers, aliens, and pilgrims on earth (1 Pt.2:11).

7. God is going to restore Israel; that is, He is going to have mercy upon Israel and turn them from ungodliness. Why? That He might have mercy upon all, both Gentile and Jew (Ro.11:32). (See outlines and notes—Ro.11:25-36. Cp. Ro.11:11-16. God's historical dealings with the Jews and Gentiles are covered in detail in Romans, chapters 9, 10, and 11. Also see outline and notes—Rev.11:3-13 for more discussion.)

DEEPER STUDY # 9

(21:44) **Judgment—Stone, Stumbling—Stone, Crushing**: Christ said two types of people are doomed.

1. The people who stumble over Christ, the Head cornerstone of God, are doomed. Many who stood around Christ in that day stumbled and many stumble today. Many cannot believe that God actually sent His Son into the world. The idea that God would humiliate Himself that much is beyond understanding, so they refuse to believe. The belief that Christ was a great teacher is acceptable to them; but acknowledging Him to be more than a man, to be the Son of God who was to die for the sins of the world, is beyond them. Therefore, they stumble over the cornerstone, the very foundation which God has laid for the salvation of man. They stumble and fall over who He is, and they are shattered and broken (see note—Lk.2:34).

2. The men who oppose Christ over His being the Head cornerstone are doomed. Some actively oppose Christ and His kingdom. They say and teach that He is not really the Son of God. Neither He nor any other human being could ever be the Son of God. A good man, yes, but never the Son of God who has been exalted to the right hand of God. Christ says the Son (He Himself) will crush those who oppose Him, those who lead others astray trying to stamp out belief in Him and His kingdom. Severe judgment, holy vengeance shall straighten out all the injustices and sins of men.

DEEPER STUDY # 10

(21:44) **Jesus Christ, Names—Titles**: there are four pictures of Christ as the Stone given in Scripture. Each shows how the coming of Christ affects the world (see note—Lk.2:34).

1. Christ is the Head or Chief Cornerstone, the Foundation Stone. He is the Foundation and Cornerstone upon which every man must build his life. There is no other Foundation upon which man can build and be secure. In addition, Christ is the Foundation and Cornerstone of the church (see DEEPER STUDY # 7—Mt.21:42. Cp. 1 Cor.3:11; Eph.2:20-22; 1 Pt.2:4-5.)

2. Christ is the Stumbling Stone and the Rock of Offense. Some cannot understand the fact that Jesus is the Son of God. Others are repulsed by the cross and His blood. They stumble and are offended by His deity and death for sins. Israel was the first to stumble and multitudes have stumbled ever since (see DEEPER STUDY # 9—Mt.21:44. Cp. Is.8:14-15; Ro.9:32-33; 1 Cor.1:23; 1 Pt.2:8.)

3. Christ is the Crushing Stone or the Striking Stone of Destruction (Mt.21:44; Dan.2:34). Christ rules and reigns at the right hand of God now. However, with so much evil and destruction in the world, it may appear as though He is not ruling; but He is. He is just waiting until more and more persons believe, not willing that any should perish. But the day of redemption for the believer and of destruction for the unbeliever is coming. He shall become the Crushing Stone, the Smiting Stone of Destruction to all who *oppose* Him. He shall crush and smite, destroying all who stand in opposition to Him. This apparently refers both to individuals and to world powers who oppose Him (DEEPER STUDY # 9—Mt.21:44. Cp. Dan.2:34; Rev.16:13; 19:17.)

4. Christ is the Living Stone (1 Pt.2:4-5). He was disallowed by men but chosen by the Chief Architect, God Himself, and counted as the most Precious of Stones. All men who come to Him are laid upon Him, and they are built up into a spiritual house to offer up spiritual sacrifices (see DEEPER STUDY # 7—Mt.21:42).

3 (21:45-46) **Jesus Christ, Response**: the results of the parable are threefold.

1. The religionists saw that Christ was speaking directly to them, but their consciences were seared by obstinate unbelief (1 Tim.4:2). They were insensitive to His warnings (Mt.21:41-44).

2. The religionists reacted instead of repenting. They should have heeded the Lord's warning, but they did not. They were set against Him, seeking to destroy Him and to silence His claim.

3. The people saw Christ only as a prophet (a great teacher) and not as the Messiah. This too is tragic, but God was able to use their respect to protect Christ until the appointed time of His death.

	CHAPTER 22 **G. The Parable of the Marriage Feast: Israel's Rejection of God's Great Invitation, 22:1-14** (Lk.14:15-24)	7 The king was enraged. He sent his army and destroyed those murderers and burned their city. 8 "Then he said to his servants, 'The wedding banquet is ready, but those I invited did not deserve to come. 9 Go to the street corners and invite to the banquet anyone you find.'	1) Destroyed the abusers & murderers 2) Rejected the rejectors **3 God's invitation to any & all** a. God then invited all 1) Those who were out on the street corners
1 Jesus again shared a parable a. Of the Kingdom of Heaven b. Of a marriage prepared by God for His Son	Jesus spoke to them again in parables, saying: 2 "The kingdom of heaven is like a king who prepared a wedding banquet for his son.	10 So the servants went out into the streets and gathered all the people they could find, both good and bad, and the wedding hall was filled with guests.	2) Those who were both good & bad b. God's invitation was accepted
2 God's invitation to Israel a. God invited Israel, but they rejected	3 He sent his servants to those who had been invited to the banquet to tell them to come, but they refused to come.	11 "But when the king came in to see the guests, he noticed a man there who was not wearing wedding clothes.	**4 God's confrontation with the guests** a. God entered to see the guests 1) He saw a man without wedding clothes
b. God showed great mercy 1) Extended a second invitation 2) Prepared an abundance	4 "Then he sent some more servants and said, 'Tell those who have been invited that I have prepared my dinner: My oxen and fattened cattle have been butchered, and everything is ready. Come to the wedding banquet.'	12 'Friend,' he asked, 'how did you get in here without wedding clothes?' The man was speechless.	2) He asked only one question 3) The man was speechless
c. God saw His second invitation rejected 1) By a busy farmer 2) By a busy businessman 3) By the rel. & worldly: Who denied, scoffed, abused, & persecuted	5 "But they paid no attention and went off—one to his field, another to his business.	13 "Then the king told the attendants, 'Tie him hand and foot, and throw him outside, into the darkness, where there will be weeping and gnashing of teeth.'	b. God judged the man who was not clothed properly 1) Was bound 2) Was taken away 3) Was cast into the darkness[DS1,2,3]
d. God judged Israel for rejecting His invitation	6 The rest seized his servants, mistreated them and killed them.	14 "For many are invited, but few are chosen."	c. God calls & invites many, but few are chosen

DIVISION XIV

THE MESSIAH'S LAST WEEK: HIS CLAIM CHALLENGED AND REJECTED, 21:1-23:39

G. The Parable of the Marriage Feast: Israel's Rejection of God's Great Invitation, 22:1-14

(22:1-14) **Introduction—Lord's Great Marriage Feast**: several things need to be noted about this parable.

1. This parable should be compared with the parable in Luke 14:15-24. There are many similarities, but they do differ. Matthew's parable is *The Great Marriage Feast*; Luke's parable is *The Great Supper*. Luke's parable was told at a much earlier date. Matthew's parable was shared during the last week of Christ's life. Each parable had a different purpose and was shared in a different place. Some details also differ.

It is important not to confuse the two parables with each other. Each has its own lesson and truths. Christ is bound to have repeated His parables and teachings often, for all trials are common to all men (1 Cor. 10:13). All men need the same lessons and the same truth. Christ just varied the details to apply to various congregations and their particular needs.

2. This parable, the Great Marriage Feast, deals with the *Kingdom of Heaven* (v.2). This is important. Although the parable tells how God dealt with Israel and turned from Israel, its major point is God's dealings with His new people, the church (the new nation. See DEEPER STUDY # 8—Mt.21:43; esp. pt.6.)

3. The meaning of the various points of the parable is clear.

⇒ The King is God.

⇒ The Son is Christ Himself. Note that He again claims to be the Son of God, distinctive from the servants of the King. This is a critical point to see. There is no question about Christ's understanding just who He is (see DEEPER STUDY # 5—Mt.21:37-39).

⇒ The Great Marriage Feast is the glorious day of redemption. It is the glorious day when the church will see Christ for the very first time and be joined with Him forever (cp. 1 Th.4:13-18).

⇒ Those "who have been invited" to the marriage refers to Israel. They were called by God from the very first, beginning with Abraham. However, this point can be applied to any of us—the farmer, the businessman, the religionist, the worldly—any who scoff, abuse, persecute and deny that Christ is the Son of God.

⇒ Those "on the street corners" are the Gentiles, people from all other nations who are willing to accept God's glorious invitation to His dear Son's wedding.

⇒ The wedding clothes represent righteousness. No guest is acceptable for the wedding unless he is properly clothed, and the only proper clothing is righteousness, the righteousness of the Lord Jesus Christ.

The parable has both an historical and personal meaning. That is to say, its points can be applied to any of us. A quick glance at its points, both major and minor, will show this.

1. Jesus again shared a parable (v.1-2).
2. God's invitation to Israel (v.3-7).
3. God's invitation to any and all (v.8-10).
4. God's confrontation with the guests (11-14).

1 (22:1-2) **The Great Marriage Feast**: Jesus again shared a parable about the Kingdom of Heaven. God has prepared a Great Marriage Feast for His Son and His true followers. The intimate relationship between Christ and His Church are often compared to a marriage (cp. Mt.9:15; Jn.3:29; 2 Cor.11:2; Eph.5:23-32).

> **Let us rejoice and be glad and give him glory! For the wedding of the Lamb has come, and his bride has made herself ready. (Rev 19:7)**
>
> **One of the seven angels who had the seven bowls full of the seven last plagues came and said to me, "Come, I will show you the bride, the wife of the Lamb." (Rev 21:9)**

The covenant of faith is like a covenant of marriage. When a person believes, Christ promises an eternal relationship with Himself. The relationship or union is forever, once and for all.

2 (22:3-7) **Israel—Invitation**: God's invitation to Israel is both historical and prophetic. This is clearly seen as we see the various events covered by Christ in verses 3-7. The various invitations sent out by the King were the practice of Jewish custom. The King would announce the upcoming occasion and then send out reminders as the day approached (cp. Esth.5:8 with 6:14). Note four points.

1. God invited Israel, but they rejected.
   a. The words "who have been invited" refer to the fact that Israel had *already* been invited. From the very first, beginning with Abraham himself (Gen.12:1f), God had invited Israel to the great feast of His Son.
   b. The servants "sent" with this particular invitation were those living during the life of Christ. In relation to time, this parable picks up the story of God's dealing with Israel during the life of Christ. The servants would, therefore, be John the Baptist, the twelve apostles (Mt.10:5f), and the seventy who were sent out into every city to prepare the people for the coming of Christ (Lk.10:1f).
   c. "They [Israel] refused to come." The words are few and simply stated, yet the fact is so tragic. This was the first invitation, and they would not accept it. Why would anyone not accept the first invitation of a King to the marriage celebration of His only Son? (Cp. Lk.13:34-35.) A person...
      - can be too busy
      - can set aside the invitation to accept later
      - can be committed to something else
      - can not care enough for the King
      - can prefer some other festivity
      - can wish to show personal dislike
      - can not trust, not believe, that the King will actually have a feast
      - can not believe in the Son
      - can dislike the Son

> **For I can testify about them that they are zealous for God, but their zeal is not based on knowledge. Since they did not know the righteousness that comes from God and sought to establish their own, they did not submit to God's righteousness. (Rom 10:2-3)**
>
> **But concerning Israel he says, "All day long I have held out my hands to a disobedient and obstinate people." (Rom 10:21)**
>
> **"But my people would not listen to me; Israel would not submit to me. (Psa 81:11)**
>
> **While you were doing all these things, declares the LORD, I spoke to you again and again, but you did not listen; I called you, but you did not answer. (Jer 7:13)**

2. God showed great mercy. He had been spurned and rejected with all the disrespect and disgrace imaginable. Yet He did not react—despite the people's disregarding the invitation of the King the way they had. He acted with mercy and grace, still asking the people to attend the Great Marriage Feast of His only Son.
   a. God extended a second invitation. The servants who carried this invitation were the witnesses who went forth immediately after the Lord's resurrection and the coming of the Holy Spirit.

      Note that the dinner was now said to be ready: "everything is [now] ready." The great sacrifice necessary to prepare the meal had taken place. They were to come now, come immediately to the feast that *preceded* the marriage itself. Everyone was still invited (2 Cor.5:11, 20; 2 Cor. 6:1).
   b. God prepared an abundance.
      ⇒ It was time for all dislikes and differences to be laid aside. The day for the King's only Son to be married had arrived.
      ⇒ It was time for joy: the only Son of the King was about to be married. The Feast was to be the greatest feast ever held. It was to be the most joyful of all occasions.
      ⇒ It was time for feasting.

Thought 1. The very fact that God calls and calls reveals how His heart is *ready* to receive us. He longs for us to be present and prepared for His Son's Great Marriage.

3. God saw His second invitation rejected. The people treated it lightly. The word for "paid no attention" (amelesantes) means to care little if any; to be careless. In the Greek, this is an aorist participle: they were *making light of it*. They were *definite* in their decision not to attend the Great Marriage Feast. They were *careless and negligent* about it. They were *too busy* to be concerned with the King's invitation, too busy with the world and making a living and getting more and more for pleasure and comfort (cp. Jas.4:13).
   a. Some were busy farmers. Property and crops needed to be looked after. Note the words "His field" (ton idion agron). It was his *own* farm or property. The idea seems to be that of selfish enjoyment. The man went to the selfish enjoyment of his own property. He was *wrapped up* in the possessions of this world.

What good will it be for a man if he gains the whole world, yet forfeits his soul? Or what can a man give in exchange for his soul? (Mat 16:26)

The seed that fell among thorns stands for those who hear, but as they go on their way they are choked by life's worries, riches and pleasures, and they do not mature. (Luke 8:14)

And do not set your heart on what you will eat or drink; do not worry about it. (Luke 12:29)

Man is a mere phantom as he goes to and fro: He bustles about, but only in vain; he heaps up wealth, not knowing who will get it. (Psa 39:6)

So my heart began to despair over all my toilsome labor under the sun. (Eccl 2:20)

b. Some were busy businessmen (city dwellers). They were engaged in commerce, business, trade. They were wrapped up in the business of the world.

Now listen, you who say, "Today or tomorrow we will go to this or that city, spend a year there, carry on business and make money." (James 4:13)

No one serving as a soldier gets involved in civilian affairs—he wants to please his commanding officer. (2 Tim 2:4)

"But they all alike began to make excuses. The first said, 'I have just bought a field, and I must go and see it. Please excuse me.' "Another said, 'I have just bought five yoke of oxen, and I'm on my way to try them out. Please excuse me.' (Luke 14:18-19)

c. Some were worldly-minded and religious. They were so attached to the world that they wanted nothing to do with the King. He disturbed their interests and their lives. He was a threat to their position, prestige, wealth, and security. Therefore, they were hostile to Him. In fact, they would have overthrown His reign and taken His kingdom for themselves. They persecuted and killed His servants, anyone who reminded them of their obligation to keep the Marriage Feast of the King (cp. Acts 4:3; 5:40; 7:58; 9:2; 12:2f; 14:19; 16:23; 2 Cor.11:23-25).

Thought 1. Men are always rejecting God's invitation. Why? *Not because* they *have* to but because they *want* to.

Yet you refuse to come to me to have life. (John 5:40)

Thought 2. What a paradox! If anyone should ever be received with open arms, it is the messenger who brings the invitation to the King's Great Marriage Feast for His Son. Yet, the very opposite is too often true. The King's messengers are often unwelcomed, ridiculed, criticized, mistreated, abused, cursed, persecuted, murmured against, and sometimes killed.

When we are slandered, we answer kindly. Up to this moment we have become the scum of the earth, the refuse of the world. (1 Cor 4:13)

4. God judged Israel for rejecting His invitation. Some interpret this verse to refer to the destruction of Jerusalem in 70 A.D. by Titus. Perhaps such an application can be made, but it would mean that the death referred to is only physical death and destruction. Such an interpretation comes far short of what Christ meant. He was primarily referring to the eternal judgment which will take place in the future. Wrath will come upon all rejectors to the uttermost (1 Th.2:15-16). This is a parable, so the reference to armies and the burned city is parabolic language. Israel had the privilege of attending the Great Marriage Feast of God's only Son, but the people of Israel abused their privilege by rejecting the invitation and killing the messengers of the King. They have, therefore, lost their witness as God's people and are to be judged eternally just as all rejectors of God's invitation are to be judged.

Note the words, "Those I invited did not deserve to come." They were not worthy to attend the Feast and wedding. And they shall not attend.

Thought 1. Note the two sins that bring the judgment of God upon our heads.

1) Ridiculing and abusing God's servants. Note that God "destroyed those murderers" (v.7), the people who had persecuted His messengers.
2) Rejecting God's invitation. Note the words: "did not deserve." The thing that made them unworthy was rejecting God's most gracious invitation. It is the rejection of the invitation that caused their judgment, not the act of God. When we reject God, it is our rejection that causes us to be condemned. Rejection equals condemnation.

Whoever believes in him is not condemned, but whoever does not believe stands condemned already because he has not believed in the name of God's one and only Son. (John 3:18)

The ax is already at the root of the trees, and every tree that does not produce good fruit will be cut down and thrown into the fire." (Luke 3:9)

And give relief to you who are troubled, and to us as well. This will happen when the Lord Jesus is revealed from heaven in blazing fire with his powerful angels. He will punish those who do not know God and do not obey the gospel of our Lord Jesus. They will be punished with everlasting destruction and shut out from the presence of the Lord and from the majesty of his power (2 Th 1:7-9)

3 (22:8-10) **Invitation—Gentiles—Man**: God's invitation is now given to any and all. This is what is meant by the word "street corners." God's servants are to go out on the street corners of the world, inviting any and all to the Great Wedding Feast of His Son.

Note several things.

1. God's servants are to invite as many as they can find. The invitaton is no longer just to the few. It is universal: to the Jew and Gentile, the rich and poor, the high and low,

the free and slave, the moral and immoral, the religious and irreligious. Note an important point. Few, if any, on the street corners would ever expect an invitation to a King's wedding.

> **Then Peter began to speak: "I now realize how true it is that God does not show favoritism but accepts men from every nation who fear him and do what is right. (Acts 10:34-35)**
>
> **For there is no difference between Jew and Gentile—the same Lord is Lord of all and richly blesses all who call on him, (Rom 10:12)**
>
> **Who wants all men to be saved and to come to a knowledge of the truth. (1 Tim 2:4)**

2. God's servants are to invite both good and bad, that is, both the moral and thoughtful (for example, Cornelius, Acts 10:1f; the devout Greeks, Acts 17:4), and the immoral and irreligious (1 Cor.6:9-11). This could also mean that some bad do presently accept the invitation, but never really dress for the occasion (v.11-14). The visible church contains both bad and good (cp. Mt.13:1f).

> **But go and learn what this means: 'I desire mercy, not sacrifice.' For I have not come to call the righteous, but sinners." (Mat 9:13)**
>
> **For the Son of Man came to seek and to save what was lost." (Luke 19:10)**

3. God's servants are to fill the wedding with guests *from the street corners*. God assures His Son: His wedding will have guests; but note, only as many as they can "find" (v.9).

> **"Come to me, all you who are weary and burdened, and I will give you rest. (Mat 11:28)**
>
> **The Spirit and the bride say, "Come!" And let him who hears say, "Come!" Whoever is thirsty, let him come; and whoever wishes, let him take the free gift of the water of life. (Rev 22:17)**
>
> **"Come, all you who are thirsty, come to the waters; and you who have no money, come, buy and eat! Come, buy wine and milk without money and without cost. (Isa 55:1)**

4 (22:11-14) **Judgment—Great Wedding Feast**: God's confrontation with the guests was a momentous occasion. However, note the emphasis of this parable. The emphasis was not on the joy and festivity of the Marriage Feast but on a guest who came improperly dressed for the occasion. A man tried to attend the wedding without the proper clothing. He was not clothed in the righteousness of Jesus Christ.

Christ said three things.

1. God entered the Feast to see the guests. Upon entering, He immediately saw the man without wedding clothes. The words "to see" (theasasthai) mean to view attentively; to carefully look over; to closely look upon and contemplate and inspect. The stress is upon the person who is seeing. He beholds and inspects. The idea is that God entered the banqueting feast *for the purpose* of looking over and inspecting the guests. He wanted to make sure everyone and everything was in order for His Son's great celebration. Noone can be allowed to detract from His Son by being improperly dressed or clothed. (See notes and DEEPER STUDY # 2—Righteousness, Ro.13:14; note—2 Cor.5:21. See DEEPER STUDY # 2, Justification—Ro.4:22; note—5:1.)

a. The guests did not know that the man lacked the proper clothes, but the King did. The man deceived the other guests, but the King knew the kind of dress He had spelled out for all His guests to wear. And observe: the man was showing disrespect and dishonor by not following the King's request for proper dress.

b. He asked only one question, and He asked the question before the feast began: "Friend, why have you come not wearing wedding clothes?" He could not allow an eyesore to detract from the joyful occasion. He had to deal with the detraction. The man had been invited, and he was responsible for wearing *proper* and *clean* clothes (cp. Eph.4:24f; cp. Eph.4:1; Ph.1:27).

> **For I tell you that unless your righteousness surpasses that of the Pharisees and the teachers of the law, you will certainly not enter the kingdom of heaven. (Mat 5:20)**
>
> **And to put on the new self, created to be like God in true righteousness and holiness. (Eph 4:24)**
>
> **Filled with the fruit of righteousness that comes through Jesus Christ—to the glory and praise of God. (Phil 1:11)**
>
> **and have put on the new self, which is being renewed in knowledge in the image of its Creator. (Col 3:10)**

c. The man was speechless (ephimothe). The word means muzzled, muted, silenced, tongue-tied, closed-mouthed. He had no excuse. He stood guilty of disrespect and dishonor for wearing the wrong clothes, clothes that were not right for a kingly occasion. The garment was unclean.

2. God judged the man who was not clothed properly. Note that God called His servants together. The servants (diakonois) were not the same servants who delivered the invitations. They were not the disciples (v.3, 4) and preachers (v.8, 10) of the Lord. They were the angelic guardians of heaven who minister to the Godhead (cp. Mt.13:41-43, 49-50). Three things were done.

a. The man was bound hand and foot. The hand and foot are usually the bodily parts used by man to sin. The hands are bound so there is no resistence. The feet are bound so there is no escape. Whatever the King says is done in the Great Day of the Feast. No man can resist or flee.

b. The man was taken away, out of the King's presence and out of the presence of His Son and of the other guests. He was not allowed to share in the joy and bounty of the occasion.

c. He was cast into outer darkness, far, far away from everyone else. He was not only cut off from the sharing of the occasion but from ever seeing the occasion. Whatever light and brilliance there was in the Great Wedding Feast, he was cast into the darkness, never to glimpse the light.

3. God calls and invites many, but few are chosen. Christ had said this before (Mt.20:16). In the context of

this parable, there were several calls of God to the Great Wedding Feast of His Son.

a. There was God's call to the Jews, but few responded.
b. There is God's call to the Gentiles, but few are responding.
c. There is God's call to all those who enter in, but few wear the wedding clothes. The only clothes they have is that of hypocrisy and false profession.

What Christ was saying becomes clear if we look at the church and consider all who are in the church...

- There are those within the church who care more for the things and possessions of this world than they do for Christ.

And do not set your heart on what you will eat or drink; do not worry about it. For the pagan world runs after all such things, and your Father knows that you need them. (Luke 12:29-30)

For we brought nothing into the world, and we can take nothing out of it. But if we have food and clothing, we will be content with that. People who want to get rich fall into temptation and a trap and into many foolish and harmful desires that plunge men into ruin and destruction. For the love of money is a root of all kinds of evil. Some people, eager for money, have wandered from the faith and pierced themselves with many griefs. Command those who are rich in this present world not to be arrogant nor to put their hope in wealth, which is so uncertain, but to put their hope in God, who richly provides us with everything for our enjoyment. Command them to do good, to be rich in good deeds, and to be generous and willing to share. (1 Tim 6:7-10, 17-18)

- There are those within the church who do not deny self nor sacrifice all they are and have to follow Christ (see note and DEEPER STUDY # 1—Lk.9:23).

Then he said to them all: "If anyone would come after me, he must deny himself and take up his cross daily and follow me. (Luke 9:23)

- There are those within the church who are still conformed to the world.

Do not conform any longer to the pattern of this world, but be transformed by the renewing of your mind. Then you will be able to test and approve what God's will is—his good, pleasing and perfect will. (Rom 12:2)

- There are those within the church who are careless in their conversation.

Nor should there be obscenity, foolish talk or coarse joking, which are out of place, but rather thanksgiving. (Eph 5:4)

Avoid godless chatter, because those who indulge in it will become more and more ungodly. Their teaching will spread like gangrene. Among them are Hymenaeus and Philetus, who have wandered away from the truth. They say that the resurrection has already taken place, and they destroy the faith of some. (2 Tim 2:16-18)

We all stumble in many ways. If anyone is never at fault in what he says, he is a perfect man, able to keep his whole body in check. Likewise the tongue is a small part of the body, but it makes great boasts. Consider what a great forest is set on fire by a small spark. The tongue also is a fire, a world of evil among the parts of the body. It corrupts the whole person, sets the whole course of his life on fire, and is itself set on fire by hell. All kinds of animals, birds, reptiles and creatures of the sea are being tamed and have been tamed by man, but no man can tame the tongue. It is a restless evil, full of deadly poison. With the tongue we praise our Lord and Father, and with it we curse men, who have been made in God's likeness. (James 3:2, 5-9)

- There are those within the church who demonstrate spirits other than the spirit of love.

"My children, I will be with you only a little longer. You will look for me, and just as I told the Jews, so I tell you now: Where I am going, you cannot come. "A new command I give you: Love one another. As I have loved you, so you must love one another. (John 13:33-34)

- There are those within the church who live after the flesh or sinful nature instead of living for Christ.

Do not love the world or anything in the world. If anyone loves the world, the love of the Father is not in him. For everything in the world—the cravings of sinful man, the lust of his eyes and the boasting of what he has and does—comes not from the Father but from the world. (1 John 2:15-16)

- There are those within the church who do not worship God consistently, either daily or weekly.

Let us not give up meeting together, as some are in the habit of doing, but let us encourage one another—and all the more as you see the Day approaching. (Heb 10:25)

- There are those within the church who profess Christ, but live hypocritical lives.

"So when you give to the needy, do not announce it with trumpets, as the hypocrites do in the synagogues and on the streets, to be honored by men. I tell you the truth, they have received their reward in full. (Mat 6:2)

The warning of Christ was clear and should cause thought and concern.

"For many are invited, but few are chosen." (Mat 22:14; 20:16)

"Make every effort to enter through the narrow door, because many, I tell you, will try to enter and will not be able to. (Luke 13:24)

But small is the gate and narrow the road that leads to life, and only a few find it. (Mat 7:14)

"Not everyone who says to me, 'Lord, Lord,' will enter the kingdom of heaven, but only he who does the will of my Father who is in heaven. (Mat 7:21)

Thought 1. The Lord walks among the churches. He knows how much or how little we work, labor, endure, and love (Rev.2:1-2).

Thought 2. Note that God in particular sees the hypocrite. The hypocrite stands out like a cancerous sore in God's eyes, and God is forced to treat the hypocrite as the master physician treats a cancerous sore.

Thought 3. The Great Feast Day is first of all a Great Inspection Day. Before God presents us to Christ, He is going to cast out all who do not wear the garment of righteousness (see outline and notes—1 Cor.3:10-17).

Thought 4. The wedding clothes which the man lacked represented righteousness. The man did not possess the righteousness of Christ nor did he live righteously (see note—Mt.5:6).

1) The man had not trusted the righteousness of Christ to make him acceptable to God. (See note, Justification—Ro.5:1 for more discussion.)

Since they did not know the righteousness that comes from God and sought to establish their own, they did not submit to God's righteousness. Christ is the end of the law so that there may be righteousness for everyone who believes. (Rom 10:3-4)

God made him who had no sin to be sin for us, so that in him we might become the righteousness of God. (2 Cor 5:21)

2) The man had not lived a moral and self-denying life (see note—Lk.9:23). He was not what he had professed to be.

Then he said to them all: "If anyone would come after me, he must deny himself and take up his cross daily and follow me. (Luke 9:23)

DEEPER STUDY # 1
(22:13) **Outer darkness**: see note—Mt.8:12 for discussion.

DEEPER STUDY # 2
(22:13) **Weeping**: see note—Mt.8:12 for discussion.

DEEPER STUDY # 3
(22:13) **Gnashing of Teeth**: see note—Mt.8:12 for discussion.

H. The Question about God & Caesar: The Two Citizenships, 22:15-22
(Mk.12:13-17; Lk. 20:20-26)

1 The false concepts of citizenship
a. Religion is supreme: The Pharisees[DS1]
b. The state is supreme: The Herodians[DS2]
2 The sins common to false concepts of citizenship
a. Selfish ambition: Leads to compromise
b. Deception: Leads to false flattery & destruction
c. Close-minded & obstinate unbelief: Leads to the rejection of truth & self-condemnation[DS3]
3 The truth about citizenship: There are two citizenships
a. Christ sees through false concepts & evil motives
b. There are things which belong to Caesar: An earthly citizenship
c. There are things which belong to God: A heavenly citizenship

15 Then the Pharisees went
out and laid plans to trap him
in his words.
16 They sent their disciples
to him along with the Herodians. "Teacher," they said,
"we know you are a man of
integrity and that you teach
the way of God in accordance
with the truth. You aren't
swayed by men, because you
pay no attention to who they
are.
17 Tell us then, what is your
opinion? Is it right to pay
taxes to Caesar or not?"
18 But Jesus, knowing their
evil intent, said, "You hypocrites, why are you trying to
trap me?
19 Show me the coin used
for paying the tax." They
brought him a denarius,
20 and he asked them,
"Whose portrait is this? And
whose inscription?"
21 "Caesar's," they replied.
Then he said to them, "Give
to Caesar what is Caesar's,
and to God what is
God's."
22 When they heard this,
they were amazed. So they
left him and went away.

DIVISION XIV

THE MESSIAH'S LAST WEEK: HIS CLAIM CHALLENGED AND REJECTED, 21:1-23:39

H. The Question about God and Caesar: The Two Citizenships, 22:15-22

(22:15-22) **Introduction**: this is the second challenge or attack by the leaders against Christ. The words "laid plans" indicate that the ruling body of the Jews, the Sanhedrin, held an official meeting. They plotted how they might deal with this man who was claiming to be the Messiah. They feared Christ, for He was gathering the loyalty of the people so strongly around Himself.

Their plot was to ask Him a question about a person's citizenship. The question was supposed to "trap him in his words" (v.15); that is, it was supposed to be impossible for Christ to answer without discrediting Himself either with the people or with the Roman authorities. If He discredited Himself with the people, they would react and desert Him; if He discredited Himself with the Romans, they would arrest Him.

Christ *is* the Messiah, the Son of God Himself; therefore, He saw through their plot. Christ used the occasion to teach the truth about citizenship, a truth which was both astounding and earth-shaking to the people of that day—earth-shaking because the Jews believed that the loyalty of a citizen belonged only to God, and the rest of the world believed that loyalty belonged to the ruling monarch of their territory.

Christ astounded the world of His day by declaring there was an earthly, physical citizenship to which some things are to be given; and there was a spiritual, heavenly citizenship to which some things are to be given.

1. The false concepts of citizenship (v.15-16).
   a. Religion is supreme: the Pharisees.
   b. The state is supreme: the Herodians.
2. The sins common to the false concepts of citizenship (v.16-17).
   a. Selfish ambition: leads to compromise.
   b. Deception: leads to false flattery and destruction.
   c. Close-minded, obstinate unbelief: leads to rejection of the truth and self-condemnation.
3. The truth about citizenship: there are two citizenships (v.18-22).
   a. Christ sees through false concepts and evil motives.
   b. There is something which belongs to Caesar: an earthly citizenship.
   c. There is something which belongs to God: a heavenly citizenship.

1 (22:15-16) **Citizenship**: these two false concepts of citizenship are seen in the Pharisees and Herodians. However, it must be remembered, the world did not know the concepts were false until this experience.

1. The first false concept is that *religion is supreme.* This is seen in the view of the Pharisees (see DEEPER STUDY # 3—Acts 23:8). They believed strongly in the heavenly world, so much so they believed that all obedience and loyalty were due God and God alone. In fact, all things on earth were due God. The state and all other power and authority were to be subject to religious rule. Therefore, they were strongly against paying taxes to a foreign king. Such was an infringement upon God's right.

2. The second false concept is that *the state is supreme.* This is seen in the view of the Herodians (see DEEPER STUDY # 2—Mt.22:16 for discussion).

Picture the scene and how strange it was. The Pharisees held that religion was dominant over government, and they despised Roman authority and taxation. The Herodians held that government was dominant over religion; consequently, they would agree that taxes must be paid to Caesar rather than to God. The Herodians and the Pharisees were bitter enemies. To find them together was strange indeed, but their hatred of Jesus brought them together against One whom they considered a common enemy. (See notes—Mk.3:6; DEEPER STUDY # 3—Acts 23:8.)

> **Thought 1.** The world's concept of citizenship is still the same as it was in Christ's day, despite His teaching. The vast majority of the world would be humanists and secularists, that is, worldly-minded citizens and unbelieving politicians. They would hold that the state is supreme. On the other hand, there would be some who would hold that religion is supreme and is to dominate the state. However, the position of religious supremacy is very difficult to practice in an educated and industrialized society. To a large degree, it can be held only theoretically.

For, "All men are like grass, and all their glory is like the flowers of the field; the grass withers and the flowers fall, (1 Pet 1:24)

For he will take nothing with him when he dies, his splendor will not descend with him. (Psa 49:17)

Therefore the grave enlarges its appetite and opens its mouth without limit; into it will descend their nobles and masses with all their brawlers and revelers. (Isa 5:14)

Hear the word of the LORD, you who tremble at his word: "Your brothers who hate you, and exclude you because of my name, have said, 'Let the LORD be glorified, that we may see your joy!' Yet they will be put to shame. (Isa 66:5)

"And you, son of man, on the day I take away their stronghold, their joy and glory, the delight of their eyes, their heart's desire, and their sons and daughters as well— (Ezek 24:25)

The more the priests increased, the more they sinned against me; they exchanged their Glory for something disgraceful. (Hosea 4:7)

DEEPER STUDY # 1
(22:15) **Pharisees**: see DEEPER STUDY # 3—Acts 23:8.

DEEPER STUDY # 2
(22:16) **Herodians**: the Herodians were not a religious party but a political party of Herod, the King of Galilee. They were supportive of Rome, compromising wherever they could in order to preserve their own power and influence. They had compromised to such a point that they gave some degree of consent to pagan temples. Religiously, they were mainly Sadducees who gave their first loyalty to the state (see DEEPER STUDY # 2—Acts 23:8). Thus, they opposed all Messianic claims because of the disturbance the claims caused among the people. They would agree that taxes must be paid to Caesar rather than to God.

2 (22:16-17) **Citizenship**: there are sins that are often committed by those who hold false concepts of citizenship. Some of these sins are seen in the plot of the Pharisees and Herodians against Christ.

1. There is *selfish ambition* which often leads to compromise and intrigue. Nothing could have been more surprising than to see the Pharisees and Herodians working together. They stood diametrically opposed to one another. The Pharisees thought the Herodians no better than the heathen doomed for hell, yet they were seen working with the Herodians against Christ. What was it that brought them together? Selfish ambition. They feared the loss of their position, influence, power, wealth, and security (see notes—Mt.12:1-8; note and DEEPER STUDY # 1—12:10; note—15:1-20; DEEPER STUDY # 2—15:6-9. These notes will help considerably in understanding why the rulers feared Christ so much.) A man who lives for this world will become a bedfellow with almost anyone to protect his security. The degree or strange appearance of the compromise will seldom matter.

The depth of the sin in selfish ambition is also seen here. The primary plotters were religious leaders; and they were not only willing to plot evil, they were trying to cause a man, Christ Himself, to be put to death. Just how evil government and religion can be in their ambition is clearly seen in this passage.

2. There is *deception* which usually leads to flattery and destruction. The deception is seen in two facts.

a. Deception is seen in that the Pharisees themselves did not go to Christ. They sent "their disciples along with the Herodians." The disciples were learners or students who would actually be seeking the answer to such a question themselves. The Herodians were along to give the appearance that the disciples had asked them first, but the disciples were not satisfied with their answer. It would seem that the disciples of the Pharisees wanted to know what Christ, One who claimed to be the Messiah, would answer. Thus, Christ would think the question was the legitimate question of a student, never suspecting a plot to entrap Him.

b. Deception, the lowest kind of deception, is seen in the words of flattery which were used in approaching Christ.

⇒ "Teacher...
⇒ "We know you are a man of integrity...
⇒ "And that you teach the way of God in accordance with the truth...
⇒ "You aren't swayed by men...
⇒ "...because you pay no attention to who they are."

Note that everything they said about Christ was true.

⇒ He was Teacher: a rabbi, a teacher. He was even more: He was the Master and Lord of the universe.
⇒ He was a man of integrity: a teacher from God. (Contrast their hypocritical approach with the sincerity of Nicodemus, Jn.3:2.)
⇒ He did teach the way of God: how a man is to live and behave if he wishes to please God.
⇒ He did not care what men said about Him: it did not influence Him or His action.
⇒ He did not pay attention to who men were: show partiality or favoritism.

The problem is that they did not mean what they were professing not in their hearts. What they were professing about Him was coming from an evil motive. They wanted to use Him and to secure their own selfish purposes. In the end they were successful; they were able to do what they were plotting and to have Him destroyed. As always, deception destroys that which is truthful and strong and lovely.

Your sin prompts your mouth; you adopt the tongue of the crafty. (Job 15:5)

Not a word from their mouth can be trusted; their heart is filled with destruction. Their throat is an open grave; with their tongue they speak deceit. (Psa 5:9)

A man cannot be established through wickedness, but the righteous cannot be uprooted. (Prov 12:3)

Whoever flatters his neighbor is spreading a net for his feet. (Prov 29:5)

3. There is *close-mindedness and obstinate unbelief* which leads to rejection of the truth and self-condemnation. The question asked of Christ was simple: "Is it right to pay taxes to Caesar or not?"

⇒ The Pharisees, sincere Jewish religionists, would shout, "No."
⇒ The Herodians (and those securing position and wealth by Roman rule) would say, "Yes."

Standing there, the questioners thought they had entrapped Christ. If He said, "No, taxes should not be paid to Caesar," then the authorities would arrest and remove Him. The people would then know that His claim to Messiahship was false.

If He said, "Yes, taxes should be paid to Caesar," then He would be denying the Sovereignty of God; and the people, who strongly opposed Roman rule and taxes, would rise up against Him. Both the Pharisees and Herodians were close-minded. They saw nothing beyond themselves and the threat to their position and wealth. They were steeped in obstinate unbelief. Thus, they rejected the truth; and, as results from all rejection of the truth, they condemned themselves (cp. Jn.3:18-21).

Thought 1. Selfish ambition can, and too often does, penetrate the very heart of those who are called to serve. The halls of government and the sanctity of religion are not exempt. Regardless of who a man is, he can crave and be corrupted by position, influence, power, wealth, and security.

Thought 2. Too many will compromise anything to hang on to their earthly possessions.

Thought 3. Any man who loves the things of this world will turn away from Jesus, and any man who feels threatened by Jesus and His claims will react against Jesus (1 Jn.2:15-16).

Thought 4. Note the testimony Jesus had even among His enemies. He was true, teaching the way of God, self-denying and courageous, and completely impartial toward others. Knowing and professing the truth about Jesus is not enough. Those who opposed Christ knew the truth about Him. They were just not willing to surrender to the truth.

Thought 5. Obstinate unbelief, pride, and haughtiness will cause us to be condemned by the Lord. (See DEEPER STUDY # 4—Mt.12:24; note—12:31-32 for a discussion of their obstinate unbelief.)

DEEPER STUDY # 3
(22:17) **Tribute—Tax**: the tax asked about is the poll tax. It was a tax that had to be paid by every person between the ages of twelve or fourteen to sixty-five. The poll tax amounted to about one day's wage in that time (see DEEPER STUDY # 1—Ro.13:6).

3 (22:18-22) **Citizenship**: the truth about citizenship. A man has two citizenships. A man is a citizen of this world; this is clearly evident. Therefore, he owes to the earthly powers what belongs to them. But a man is also a citizen of heaven, of the spiritual world; therefore, he owes to God what belongs to Him.

Note three things.

1. Christ saw through the false concepts of these men. He was the Son of God, so He naturally knew that they held a false concept of citizenship. Moreover, as the Son of God, He also saw that they had an evil motive.

Christ was pointed and forceful: "You hypocrites, why are you trying to trap me?" He knew their hearts...

- their selfish ambition with every act of compromise and intrigue.
- their deception with all the flattery and destructive poison of their tongues.
- their close-mindedness and obstinate unbelief that led them to reject Him and to condemn themselves.

Note the words "their evil intent" and "you hypocrites" (v.18). They were evil and they were hypocrites. They were pretending something that was not so.

⇒ They were pretending to be something they were not.
⇒ They were pretending to seek the truth when they were not really after the truth.
⇒ They were pretending to honor Him when they really did not.

2. There is something which belongs to Caesar: an earthly citizenship. Christ was brilliant and brief as He dealt with the Pharisees and their false concept of citizenship. "Show me the coin used for paying the tax...Whose portrait is this? And whose inscription?" He simply asked.

Note two things.

a. He forced the Pharisees (religion is supreme concept) to admit that some things belonged to an earthly power. The portrait was Caesar's; the inscription was Caesar's; and the coin had been made or coined by Caesar's government. Therefore, the coin was Caesar's if Caesar said it was due him. The point was clear:since the religionists, as citizens, *used what was owned and provided by Caesar*, then they owed to Caesar what was due him. Christ said strikingly, "Give to Caesar what is Caesar's."
b. He revealed a very important truth for believers of all time: they *have a double citizenship*. They are citizens of heaven, yes, but they are also citizens of this world. They have an obligation to the government under which they live. They receive the benefits of government just as *the worldly-minded* do: for example, roads, sewage, water, protection, public transportation, and on and on. Therefore, believers are to pay their due share. (See note—Ro.13:1-7. This note is a thorough discussion of citizenship.)

Everyone must submit himself to the governing authorities, for there is no authority except that which God has established. The authorities that exist have been established by God. (Rom 13:1)

"But so that we may not offend them, go to the lake and throw out your line. Take the first fish you catch; open its mouth and you will find a four-drachma coin. Take it and give it to them for my tax and yours." (Mat 17:27)

Remind the people to be subject to rulers and authorities, to be obedient, to be ready to do whatever is good, (Titus 3:1)

Submit yourselves for the Lord's sake to every authority instituted among men: whether to the king, as the supreme authority, or to governors, who are sent by him to punish those who do wrong and to commend those who do right. For it is God's will that by doing good you should silence the ignorant talk of foolish men. (1 Pet 2:13-15; cp. 1 Pet.2:17)

Whoever does not obey the law of your God and the law of the king must surely be punished by death, banishment, confiscation of property, or imprisonment. (Ezra 7:26)

Obey the king's command, I say, because you took an oath before God. (Eccl 8:2)

3. There is something which belongs to God: an heavenly citizenship. Christ was just as brilliant in dealing with the Herodians and their false concept of citizenship as He had been with the Pharisees. The Herodians not only subjected religion to the state, but they were worldly minded and denied much of the supernatural, including life after death and the spiritual dimension of being.

Note two things.

a. Christ declared unequivocally to the Herodians: there is a spiritual world. God is; God exists, and there are some things which belong to God. "Give to God what is God's." Again, the point is clear. Since the Herodians (the state is supreme concept) as citizens of the world and of life itself, used what was owned and provided by God, then they owed God what was due Him.

b. Christ revealed a very important truth to all men. They are beings of God as well as of this world, spiritual as well as physical beings. Therefore, they are responsible to live as citizens of God as well as citizens of this world. All men have received much from God:

⇒ life that was made to exist with God forever; therefore man owes God his life.

⇒ a spirit that can be "born again" and live a self-denying life of love, joy, and peace for the sake of all men everywhere (Gal.5:22-23).

⇒ a mind and body that have the power to enjoy the aesthetic beauty of the earth, learning to reason and produce for the betterment and service of all mankind.

All men receive these benefits and many more from God. Therefore, they are to pay their due share to God.

But seek first his kingdom and his righteousness, and all these things will be given to you as well. (Mat 6:33)

Then he said to them all: "If anyone would come after me, he must deny himself and take up his cross daily and follow me. (Luke 9:23)

Therefore, I urge you, brothers, in view of God's mercy, to offer your bodies as living sacrifices, holy and pleasing to God—this is your spiritual act of worship. Do not conform any longer to the pattern of this world, but be transformed by the renewing of your mind. Then you will be able to test and approve what God's will is—his good, pleasing and perfect will. (Rom 12:1-2)

Do you not know that your body is a temple of the Holy Spirit, who is in you, whom you have received from God? You are not your own; you were bought at a price. Therefore honor God with your body. (1 Cor 6:19-20)

Worship the LORD your God, and his blessing will be on your food and water. I will take away sickness from among you, (Exo 23:25)

But remember the LORD your God, for it is he who gives you the ability to produce wealth, and so confirms his covenant, which he swore to your forefathers, as it is today. (Deu 8:18)

So if you faithfully obey the commands I am giving you today—to love the LORD your God and to serve him with all your heart and with all your soul— then I will send rain on your land in its season, both autumn and spring rains, so that you may gather in your grain, new wine and oil. I will provide grass in the fields for your cattle, and you will eat and be satisfied. (Deu 11:13-15)

Thought 1. See notes—Ro.13:1-7; 13:8-10; 1 Pt. 2:13-17. These notes are sufficient to stir thoughts for application. One may also wish to refer to the Master Subject Index for a complete study on citizenship.

Thought 2. The truth that Christ covers in this passage is just what He says: there are two citizenships—an earthly and a heavenly citizenship. A man is to be a good citizen of both.

Show proper respect to everyone: Love the brotherhood of believers, fear God, honor the king. (1 Pet 2:17)

I. The Question about the Resurrection: The Resurrection Denied, yet Proven, 22:23-33
(Mk.12:18-27; Lk.20:27-38)

1 The Sadducees tried to discredit Christ
2 The resurrection was scoffed at and denied
a. Moses' law: The levirate law or law of the brother-in-law
1) To carry on family
2) To protect property
b. The logical situation: A childless widow marries seven brothers

23 That same day the Sad-
ducees, who say there is no
resurrection, came to him
with a question.
24 "Teacher," they said,
"Moses told us that if a man
dies without having children,
his brother must marry the
widow and have children for
him.
25 Now there were seven
brothers among us. The first
one married and died,
and since he had no children,
he left his wife to his
brother.
26 The same thing happened
to the second and third
brother, right on down to the
seventh.
27 Finally, the woman died.
28 Now then, at the resurrection, whose wife will she
be of the seven, since all
of them were married to
her?"
29 Jesus replied, "You are
in error because you
do not know the Scrip
tures or the power of
God.
30 At the resurrection people
will neither marry nor be given
in marriage; they will be like
the angels in heaven.
31 But about the resurrection
of the dead—have you
not read what God said to
you,
32 'I am the God of Abra-
ham, the God of Isaac, and
the God of Jacob' ? He is not
the God of the dead but of the
living."
33 When the crowds heard
this, they were astonished at
his teaching.

c. The logical question supposedly shows the absurdity of the resurrection: Whose wife is she in eternity?
3 The resurrection was denied for two reasons
a. Did not know Scripture
b. Did not know the power of God
4 The resurrection exceeds earthly relationships
a. Exceeds marital relationships
b. Equal to angels & God
5 The resurrection has four basic proofs
a. God has spoken & revealed the resurrection in His Word
b. God is; God exists
c. God is the God of Abraham, Isaac, Jacob
d. God is not the God of the dead, but of the living
6 The resurrection causes astonishment

DIVISION XIV

THE MESSIAH'S LAST WEEK: HIS CLAIM CHALLENGED AND REJECTED, 21:1-23:39

I. The Question about The Resurrection: The Resurrection Denied, yet Proven, 22:23-33

(22:23-33) **Introduction**: it was still Tuesday of the Lord's last week. (Note the statement, "that same day.") On this day, the challenges to His authority had been pressing in ever so heavily upon Him.

First, the chief priests and lay leaders (elders) had challenged His authority (see outline and notes—Mt.21:23-27). Christ had met the challengers head on and routed them. In so doing, His mind had been focused upon His death and Israel's rejection. The very thought that Israel, in whom God had put so much trust, was failing God by putting His Son to death was bound to be ripping out the heart of Christ (see outline and notes—Mt.21:33-46; 22:1-14).

Second, the Pharisees and Herodians (Herod's political party) had attempted to discredit Christ by pitting Him either against the government or the people (see outlines and notes—Mt.22:15-22). Again, Christ had met and routed His challengers; but again, the struggle had been tiring and pressuring, hard and heavy.

Now, for a third time, the Lord was confronted and challenged; and again, it was a different group who tried to out-argue and discredit Him. His challengers were the Sadducees, the religious and political liberals of the day. As Matthew pointed out, "[They] say that there is no resurrection" (v.23). Luke added, "The Sadducees say that there is no resurrection, and that there are neither angels, nor spirits" (see DEEPER STUDY # 3—Mt.16:12; DEEPER STUDY # 2—Acts 23:8). Their liberal position caused two things.

1. It caused them to stumble at the spiritual and supernatural. They ridiculed and scorned both. In their minds, the teachings of Christ lacked philosophical analysis and natural or scientific proof; therefore, they were the teachings of an unthinking and illogical man.

2. Their liberal position caused them to feel threatened and to oppose Christ. The people were flocking to Christ and soaking up His teachings. This meant the Sadducees were losing their grip on the people; their position and wealth were being jeopardized. Therefore, they were compelled to attack and discredit Him before the people.

It was their liberal belief—their denial of the spirit and of a spiritual world, of life after death and of the resurrection—that they used to attack Christ.

1. The Sadducees tried to discredit Christ (v.23).
2. The resurrection was scoffed at and denied (v.23-28).
3. The resurrection was denied for two reasons (v.29).
4. The resurrection exceeds earthly relationships (v.30).
5. The resurrection has four basic proofs (v.31-32).
6. The resurrection caused astonishment (v.33).

1 (22:23) **Sadducees**: this sect had already been seen on two other occasions. They had already opposed John the Baptist (Mt.3:7f) and Christ (Mt.16:1-12. See DEEPER STUDY # 3—Mt.16:12; DEEPER STUDY # 2—Acts 23:8.)

2 (22:23-28) **Resurrection—Sadducees**: the resurrection was denied and scoffed at by the Sadducees. Down through the centuries many liberal-minded men have continued in their steps (cp. 1 Cor.15:12-58; 2 Pt.3:3-18). Note the argument of the Sadducees.

1. They used Moses' law, the levirate law, as the basis of their argument (Dt.25:5-6). When a husband died without a son, the levirate law said that his brother was to marry his wife and bear a son. By law, the son was considered the first-born son of the deceased brother. This as-

sured two things: (a) that the family name continued, and (b) that the property holdings were kept in the family. This was a law that had been given to help preserve and to enlarge the nation of Israel (cp. Ruth 4:5).

2. The Sadducees then suggested a logical situation that could have arisen. Note the words, "Now there were seven brothers among us." The first brother married, but he died before bearing children. Each of the other brothers obeyed the law, but each died before bearing a child. Finally, the woman died also.

3. The logical question was now asked, the question which in the Sadducees' mind showed the absurdity of the resurrection. They asked, "Whose wife will she be?" Note three things by reading through verses 23-28 several times.

a. The situation was logical; but the spirit of questioning was cold and coarse, egotistical and unbelieving, regrettable and revolting. The unbelievers's spirit is often self-incriminating and self-condemning.

b. The argument was thought to be irrefutable by the Sadducees. They believed it pointed out just how foolish the idea of another world was to the thinking person.

c. The Sadducees were thinking that the spiritual world would be just like the physical world, that it would be nothing more than a continuation of this world, both in *its nature and in its relationships*.

As this point is closed, a picture of what the Scripture says about the natural man, the man without the Spirit, is clearly seen.

The man without the Spirit does not accept the things that come from the Spirit of God, for they are foolishness to him, and he cannot understand them, because they are spiritually discerned. (1 Cor 2:14)

Thought 1. Every generation has its Sadducees, those who are liberal minded and who scoff at the idea of the resurrection and of a spiritual world. God knows this. He has always known that many would scoff and ridicule, so He has dealt with the issue in at least two extensive passages of Scripture (1 Cor. 15:12-58; 2 Pt.3:3-18).

But if it is preached that Christ has been raised from the dead, how can some of you say that there is no resurrection of the dead? (1 Cor 15:12)

First of all, you must understand that in the last days scoffers will come, scoffing and following their own evil desires. They will say, "Where is this 'coming' he promised? Ever since our fathers died, everything goes on as it has since the beginning of creation." (2 Pet 3:3-4)

Thought 2. Today's arguments against the existence of a spiritual world and resurrection arise from...

- logical and rational thought
- philosophical positions
- a natural and scientific hypothesis
- humanistic beliefs
- an unwillingness to change one's lifestyle
- a fear of rejection and ridicule by one's peers
- a refusal to admit that one's former position was wrong

Thought 3. Most unbelief in the spiritual world arises not from a thinking position, but from a worldly position. Few study through both the natural and spiritual positions. Most just love the world and the things of the world so much that they wish to reject the restraints which the spiritual world puts upon them.

3 (22:29) **Resurrection—Spiritual World—Scripture—God, Power of**: Christ said very pointedly to the Sadducees and to all who followed their liberal position: "You are in error. You deny the resurrection for two erroneous reasons."

1. "You do not know the Scriptures." The Scriptures are plain and clear. They leave no doubt that there is a spiritual world—that there is to be a resurrection into the spiritual world or spiritual dimension of being.

I know that my Redeemer lives, and that in the end he will stand upon the earth. And after my skin has been destroyed, yet in my flesh I will see God; I myself will see him with my own eyes—I, and not another. How my heart yearns within me! (Job 19:25-27)

But your dead will live; their bodies will rise. You who dwell in the dust, wake up and shout for joy. Your dew is like the dew of the morning; the earth will give birth to her dead. (Isa 26:19)

Multitudes who sleep in the dust of the earth will awake: some to everlasting life, others to shame and everlasting contempt. (Dan 12:2)

I tell you the truth, a time is coming and has now come when the dead will hear the voice of the Son of God and those who hear will live. (John 5:25)

"Do not be amazed at this, for a time is coming when all who are in their graves will hear his voice and come out—those who have done good will rise to live, and those who have done evil will rise to be condemned. (John 5:28-29)

For my Father's will is that everyone who looks to the Son and believes in him shall have eternal life, and I will raise him up at the last day." (John 6:40)

Jesus said to her, "I am the resurrection and the life. He who believes in me will live, even though he dies; (John 11:25)

And I have the same hope in God as these men, that there will be a resurrection of both the righteous and the wicked. (Acts 24:15)

And if the Spirit of him who raised Jesus from the dead is living in you, he who raised Christ from the dead will also give life to your mortal bodies through his Spirit, who lives in you. (Rom 8:11)

For as in Adam all die, so in Christ all will be made alive. (1 Cor 15:22)

Because we know that the one who raised the Lord Jesus from the dead will also raise us with Jesus and present us with you in his presence. (2 Cor 4:14)

For the Lord himself will come down from heaven, with a loud command, with

the voice of the archangel and with the trumpet call of God, and the dead in Christ will rise first. (1 Th 4:16)

But God will redeem my life from the grave; he will surely take me to himself. Selah (Psa 49:15; cp. Ps.71:20; Hos.13:14)

Thought 1. There are three reasons why a person may not know the Scriptures.

1) He simply has not *studied* the Scriptures, not *really studied.*
2) He does not believe the Scriptures. He rejects the Scripture as God's Word.
3) He does not take the Scriptures for what they say. He spiritualizes or allegorizes them.

2. "You do not know the power of God." There are three reasons why a person does not know the power of God.

a. He is ignorant of God. He knows nothing about God and seldom, if ever, gives any thought to God and His power.
b. He does not believe in God or His power. He refuses to acknowledge God's eternal power and Godhead seen in creation and goes about *creating* gods of his own (both mental and physical images). (Cp. Ro.1:20-32.) He refuses to acknowledge the picture of nature that clearly illustrates the resurrection:

How foolish! What you sow does not come to life unless it dies. When you sow, you do not plant the body that will be, but just a seed, perhaps of wheat or of something else. But God gives it a body as he has determined, and to each kind of seed he gives its own body. (1 Cor 15:36-38)

c. He believes, but his belief in God and His power is weak. He cannot picture much happening beyond the physical world and the power of natural laws.

Thought 1. The idea of a spiritual world is perplexing to the natural man. Just imagine! While we are sitting here surrounded by all that we see...

- there is another world, a spiritual world, an unseen spiritual dimension of being that actually exists.
- there is a spirit, the real life within our bodies, that is destined to exist forever.
- there is to be a resurrection of all the dead bodies that have been lying scattered and decaying in the graves for ages and ages. God shall *call* all the parts of decayed bodies back together again, no matter where they are scattered, and these bodies shall be perfected and glorified to live and work again. How can He do such a thing? By the Word of His power *as God.*

Thought 2. When we really think about the facts of the resurrection, two confessions have to be made by every man, believer and unbeliever.

1) The natural man, that is man within himself and his world, *can never know* about a spiritual world. He is bound by the physical and material world of which he is a part. He can only think and guess and theorize that a spiritual world exists and speculate on details such as a resurrection. Man cannot, while living in this world, penetrate the spiritual world with his body to scientifically prove the existence of the spiritual world.
2) God alone can reveal the reality of the spiritual dimension and the fact that a resurrection will take place. Such can be known and experienced only by the power of God. No man has the power to bring it about. If a resurrection is to take place, God's power will have to do it.

Thought 3. By its very nature of permanence, the spiritual world supersedes and becomes much more important than the physical and dying world. Therefore, the spiritual world demands that man give preeminence to it. It is these demands that man rebels against. Therefore...

- a scientific society questions what it cannot prove.
- a materialistic society questions what it cannot use to satisfy its lust for more.
- an immoral society questions what it fears will correct its behavior.
- a worldly society questions what it fears will restrain its pleasure.
- a power society questions what it fears will loosen its grip and lessen its authority.

4 (22:30) **Resurrection—Spiritual Dimension**: Christ said that the resurrection exceeded earthly relationships. The Sadducees did not know the Scriptures nor the power of God. When they thought of being resurrected into another world, they simply saw life continuing on as it does now. They pictured heaven as being just a continuation of this world. Very simply, they could not conceive that the qualities of life would be changed and that man would be given a totally new environment in which to live.

Christ said two things.

1. Future life and relationships shall exceed earthly relationships—even the bond of marital relationships. The strong union and bond of marriage will not be less, it will be greater and stronger.

2. Future life and relationships shall be equal to that experienced by the angels and God. This means at least two things. (Note: Christ had just admitted the existence of angels, refuting the disbelief of the liberal minded Sadducces.)

a. Heavenly life and relationships will be perfect. In heaven our relationships will not cease to be. They will be changed in that selfishness and sin will not affect our love and lives. Our love will be perfected; thus, we shall love everyone perfectly. A wife on this earth will not be loved as she was on this earth—imperfectly. She shall be loved more and loved perfectly. Everyone will love everyone else perfectly. God will change all relationships into perfection, even as the relationships between angels and God are perfected.
b. Heavenly life and relationships shall be eternal. There will be no ending of relationships. A man and wife will always have the other to love. One shall not cease to be (die) before the other (as is the case now). Everyone will always have everyone else to love. God will change the brief time we have with each other now into an eternal relationship. We shall enjoy the presence of each other eternally, even as the relationship between angels and God is enjoyed eternally.

Thought 1. Two warnings must always be issued when thinking of heaven and eternal life.

1) A person can *materialize* heaven and *humanize* eternal life; that is, we can conceive heaven to be nothing more than a *glorified* world and eternal life to be nothing more than physical life plus a little more. This was the mistake of the Sadducees and is often the concept pictured by liberal thinkers when they hear about the resurrection.
2) A person can *idealize* heaven and *allegorize* eternal life. We can think of heaven as little more than an ideal land for which we should seek and toward which we should direct our lives. And we can think of eternal life as little more than a utopian state of being, a utopian dream of an indefinite quality, or of floating around and being free of trouble and trials.

The teaching of Scripture or of God's revelation must always be kept in mind when thinking of heaven and eternal life. Scripture teaches that the very nature of things will be changed.

1. Heaven is said to be a spiritual dimension, a real world of being, and Scripture declares that the heavens and earth shall one day be transformed into that spiritual dimension of being. There will be a new heavens and earth, a perfect and eternal heavens and earth (2 Pt.3:3-13; Rev.21:1, 5).

2. Eternal life is said to be life that shall exist forever in the spiritual dimension of being. The Scripture says:

> **So will it be with the resurrection of the dead. The body that is sown is perishable, it is raised imperishable; it is sown in dishonor, it is raised in glory; it is sown in weakness, it is raised in power; it is sown a natural body, it is raised a spiritual body. If there is a natural body, there is also a spiritual body. (1 Cor 15:42-44; cp. 1 Th. 5:13-18)**
>
> **And just as we have borne the likeness of the earthly man, so shall we bear the likeness of the man from heaven. I declare to you, brothers, that flesh and blood cannot inherit the kingdom of God, nor does the perishable inherit the imperishable. Listen, I tell you a mystery: We will not all sleep, but we will all be changed— in a flash, in the twinkling of an eye, at the last trumpet. For the trumpet will sound, the dead will be raised imperishable, and we will be changed. For the perishable must clothe itself with the imperishable, and the mortal with immortality. When the perishable has been clothed with the imperishable, and the mortal with immortality, then the saying that is written will come true: "Death has been swallowed up in victory." (1 Cor 15:49-54)**

(See notes and DEEPER STUDY # 1—Mt.19:28; DEEPER STUDY # 1—Jn.17:2-3; DEEPER STUDY # 1—2 Tim.4:18. Cp. Jn.1:4.)

5 (22:31-32) **Resurrection**: Jesus said the resurrection had four basic proofs.

1. God had spoken and revealed the truth of the resurrection in His Word (cp. Job 19:26; Ezk.37:1f; Daniel 12:2). The Sadducees held only to the first five books of Moses as God's Word, that is, Genesis through Deuteronomy (see DEEPER STUDY # 2—Acts 23:8). Therefore, Christ used this Scripture to prove the resurrection.

Note three facts about what Christ said: "Have you not read what God said to you?" (v.31).

a. Christ said that God had spoken to man; God had revealed the truth to man in the Scripture.
b. Christ said the Scripture *is* God's Word.
c. Christ questioned why they had not read what God had spoken. "Have you not read" hints that they were without excuse. They should have read and understood; therefore, they should have known the truth of the resurrection (and all other truths) as God had revealed it.

2. God is; God exists. The fact that *God is* proves the resurrection. The Greek (ego eimi) means the self-existent, eternal One (see DEEPER STUDY # 1—Jn.6:20; 18:4-6).

> **'I am the God of Abraham, the God of Isaac, and the God of Jacob' ? He is not the God of the dead but of the living." (Mat 22:32)**
>
> **And without faith it is impossible to please God, because anyone who comes to him must believe that he exists and that he rewards those who earnestly seek him. (Heb 11:6)**

Since God is, He possesses omnipotent power—power that is perfect and eternal. God can do anything, and He can do it perfectly and eternally. He can call the elements of a decayed body back together again and raise it up to live in the spiritual world both perfectly and eternally.

Note carefully: the argument for *God's being* (living) is irrefutable. Note carefully the great passage in Ephesians dealing with the spiritual blessings that are ours in Christ: "In whom we were also chosen...in order that we...might be" (Eph.1:11-12).

The resurrection is a fact. It will be experienced by all men of all ages because *God is*. God has willed to give us an inheritance to *be*, that is, to live eternally with Him. We shall undergo a transformation of nature, a transformation of perfection and permanency. For this reason, we need to pay close attention to what Scripture says: "And without faith it is impossible to please God, because anyone who comes to him must believe that he [God] exists and that he rewards those who earnestly seek him" (Heb.11:6).

We must believe that God is, and that He is a rewarder of those who earnestly seek after Him; that is, He rewards all who seek to live eternally with Him.

> **And so, somehow, to attain to the resurrection from the dead. (Phil 3:11)**

3. God is the God of Abraham, Isaac, and Jacob. Christ meant at least two things in this point.

a. God's relationships are active relationships not inactive. God says, "I am the God of...," not "I was the God of...." His relationships with His people are continuous. They are maintained. God is eternal; therefore, He creates and maintains eternal, active relationships. God's people enter into the spiritual realm of His presence and actively relate to Him. The resurrection is a fact.
b. God's relationships are good and rewarding. The patriarchs of old were promised rewards, personal rewards (cp. Heb.11:13-16). There has to be a resurrection if our relationship with God is good

and rewarding. To die and be left dead as a decayed corpse is not good nor rewarding. Abraham, Isaac, and Jacob have a good and rewarding relationship with God. They are alive, more alive than they were while on earth, for they are now perfected and eternal. They are with God Himself. And so shall we be. The resurrection is a fact.

4. God is not the God of the dead, but of the living. God is the God of Abraham, Isaac, and Jacob, not the God of dead, decayed corpses. When Moses wrote these words, the three patriarchs had been dead for many years. If they were dead, God was not their God. Since He was their God, they were alive, living in God's presence and living in relationship to Him, perfect and eternal. There is to be a resurrection.

For none of us lives to himself alone and none of us dies to himself alone. If we live, we live to the Lord; and if we die, we die to the Lord. So, whether we live or die, we belong to the Lord. For this very reason, Christ died and returned to life so that he might be the Lord of both the dead and the living. (Rom 14:7-9)

Christ makes one point, and makes it very clearly: *since God exists*, God is not the God of the dead, but of the living.

Why should any of you consider it incredible that God raises the dead? (Acts 26:8)

And I have the same hope in God as these men, that there will be a resurrection of both the righteous and the wicked. (Acts 24:15)

Note what Scripture says about the resurrection (see notes—Mt.17:23; Acts 2:29-31; Col.3:1-4. See Related Subjects, General Subject Index.)

1. Note the emphatic statements of Christ:

And come out—those who have done good will rise to live, and those who have done evil will rise to be condemned. (John 5:29)

And this is the will of him who sent me, that I shall lose none of all that he has given me, but raise them up at the last day. For my Father's will is that everyone who looks to the Son and believes in him shall have eternal life, and I will raise him up at the last day." "No one can come to me unless the Father who sent me draws him, and I will raise him up at the last day. Whoever eats my flesh and drinks my blood has eternal life, and I will raise him up at the last day. (John 6:39-40, 44, 54)

Jesus said to her, "I am the resurrection and the life. He who believes in me will live, even though he dies; and whoever lives and believes in me will never die. Do you believe this?" (John 11:25-26)

2. Note the personal testimony of Paul.

Then Paul, knowing that some of them were Sadducees and the others Pharisees, called out in the Sanhedrin, "My brothers, I am a Pharisee, the son of a Pharisee. I stand on trial because of my hope in the resurrection of the dead." (Acts 23:6)

However, I admit that I worship the God of our fathers as a follower of the Way, which they call a sect. I believe everything that agrees with the Law and that is written in the Prophets, and I have the same hope in God as these men, that there will be a resurrection of both the righteous and the wicked. unless it was this one thing I shouted as I stood in their presence: 'It is concerning the resurrection of the dead that I am on trial before you today.'" (Acts 24:14-15, 21)

3. Note the unquestionable teaching of Scripture.

If we have been united with him like this in his death, we will certainly also be united with him in his resurrection. (Rom 6:5)

And if the Spirit of him who raised Jesus from the dead is living in you, he who raised Christ from the dead will also give life to your mortal bodies through his Spirit, who lives in you. (Rom 8:11)

By his power God raised the Lord from the dead, and he will raise us also. (1 Cor 6:14)

But if it is preached that Christ has been raised from the dead, how can some of you say that there is no resurrection of the dead? If there is no resurrection of the dead, then not even Christ has been raised. And if Christ has not been raised, our preaching is useless and so is your faith. (1 Cor 15:12-14; cp. 1 Cor.15:12-58)

Because we know that the one who raised the Lord Jesus from the dead will also raise us with Jesus and present us with you in his presence. (2 Cor 4:14)

And so, somehow, to attain to the resurrection from the dead. (Phil 3:11)

For the Lord himself will come down from heaven, with a loud command, with the voice of the archangel and with the trumpet call of God, and the dead in Christ will rise first. After that, we who are still alive and are left will be caught up together with them in the clouds to meet the Lord in the air. And so we will be with the Lord forever. Therefore encourage each other with these words. (1 Th 4:16-18)

Women received back their dead, raised to life again. Others were tortured and refused to be released, so that they might gain a better resurrection. (Heb 11:35)

(The rest of the dead did not come to life until the thousand years were ended.) This is the first resurrection. Blessed and holy are those who have part in the first resurrection. The second death has no power over them, but they will be priests of God and of Christ and will reign with him for a thousand years. (Rev 20:5-6)

4. Note the reactions of men to the resurrection (cp. 2 Pt.3:3-18).

> **The priests and the captain of the temple guard and the Sadducees came up to Peter and John while they were speaking to the people. They were greatly disturbed because the apostles were teaching the people and proclaiming in Jesus the resurrection of the dead. (Acts 4:1-2)**
>
> **A group of Epicurean and Stoic philosophers began to dispute with him. Some of them asked, "What is this babbler trying to say?" Others remarked, "He seems to be advocating foreign gods." They said this because Paul was preaching the good news about Jesus and the resurrection. (Acts 17:18)**
>
> **But if it is preached that Christ has been raised from the dead, how can some of you say that there is no resurrection of the dead? (1 Cor 15:12)**
>
> **But whatever was to my profit I now consider loss for the sake of Christ. and so, somehow, to attain to the resurrection from the dead. (Phil 3:7, 11)**

6 (22:33) **Resurrection**: the glorious hope of the resurrection not only caused amazement in Christ's day, it causes amazement today.

1. The believer is amazed that God would love him so much.
2. The unbeliever is amazed at such an idea as the resurrection, that anyone could believe such a thing.

	J. The Question about the Great Commandment: A Study of Love, 22:34-40 (Mk.12:28-34; cp. Lk.10:25-37)	greatest commandment in the Law?” 37 Jesus replied: “‘Love the Lord your God with all your heart and with all your soul and with all your mind.’	the greatest commandment?[DS2] **2 First: Love God**[DS3] a. Love as *your own God* b. Love with *all your being*: Your heart, soul, & mind[DS4,5,6]
1 The Pharisees plotted a. They gathered together	34 Hearing that Jesus had silenced the Sadducees, the Pharisees got together.	38 This is the first and greatest commandment.	c. Love is man’s chief duty
b. They appointed a brilliant lawyer, an expert in the law, to challenge Christ[DS1] c. The question: Which is	35 One of them, an expert in the law, tested him with this question: 36 “Teacher, which is the	39 And the second is like it: ‘Love your neighbor as yourself.’ 40 All the Law and the Prophets hang on these two commandments.”	**3 Second: Love your neighbor**[DS7] a. Love self b. Love neighbor as self **4 The conclusion: Love includes & embraces all the commandments**

DIVISION XIV

THE MESSIAH’S LAST WEEK: HIS CLAIM CHALLENGED AND REJECTED, 21:1-23:39

J. The Question about the Great Commandment: A Study of Love, 22:34-40

(22:34-40) **Introduction—Jesus Christ, Challenged**: Jesus had just met His third group of challengers, the Sadducees. He had *silenced* and routed them. The Pharisees, the strict religionists of that day, heard about Christ’s conquering His challengers again. In their minds, His threat to their security had increased. All three attempts to discredit Him had failed. They felt that they must somehow discredit Him before the people in order to break His hold on them. There was a very live possibility that the people might follow through with their proclaiming Him to be the Messiah by rising up against the Roman authorities. The responsibility for such action, of course, would lie at their feet as Jewish leaders; and they would be replaced as the ruling body of the Sanhedrin, losing their position, authority, esteem, and livelihood.

They met together to plan and plot again. This time they took a different approach. They had, over the last few hours, challenged Christ as a body of questioners; now they chose from among their body one who was most brilliant and versed in the law, a lawyer or a Scribe.

However, there was something about this brilliant lawyer that the others did not know. Apparently, his heart had been touched by Christ. There are two indications of this. First, Mark tells us that the man was present when Christ was “debating” with the Sadducees (Mk.12:28), and he noticed “that Jesus had given them a good answer.” Second, at the conclusion of his own discussion with Christ, Christ said to the man, “You are not far from the kingdom of God” (Mk.12:34). This indicates that the lawyer had been in deep thought about Christ and was under conviction.

Something about Christ struck a chord within this man. His heart was touched and stirred rather deeply. True, he was being put forward by the official body to challenge Christ; but personally, the spirit, the wisdom, the self-consciousness, the authority—something about Christ when He was answering the Sadducees—had stirred his heart to wonder and to want to search more into Christ.

Christ used the occasion to teach man the greatest *provision* and *duty* of human life: love. Love will provide for every need man has; therefore, love is the greatest duty of man.

1. The Pharisees plotted (v.34-36).
2. First: love God (v.37-38).
3. Second: love your neighbor (v.39).
4. The conclusion: love includes and embraces all the commandments (v.40).

1 (22:34-36) **Religionists**: the Pharisees plotted against Jesus. The Pharisees and Sadducees obviously met together when the Pharisees heard about the Sadducees being *silenced* or routed by Christ. They met together in the council (Sanhedrin) to determine the next step to take (see note—Mt.22:34-40).

DEEPER STUDY # 1

(22:35) **Lawyer—An Expert in the Law** (nomikos): a profession of laymen who studied, taught, interpreted, and dealt with the practical questions of Jewish law. They were a special group within the profession commonly called Scribes (cp. Mark 12:28). They functioned both in the court and synagogues (cp. Lk.7:30; 10:25; 11:45, 46, 52; 14:3; Tit.3:13). They apparently dealt more with the study and interpretation of the law.

DEEPER STUDY # 2

(22:36) **Commandment**: note the question, “Which is the greatest commandment in the law?” Through the years, Jewish teachers had set up six hundred commandments. No person could keep them all, so the question was often asked and discussed: Which commandment or commandments must be absolutely obeyed? Which ones are important and which ones are not? Can the failure to obey some be condoned or not? Which commandments are heavy and which are light? If a person keeps the greatest of the precepts, can he be excused for his failure to keep others (cp. Mt.19:16f)?

Note two things about the tendency to count some of God’s laws important and some not.

1. This was the sin which James attacked.

> **For whoever keeps the whole law and yet stumbles at just one point is guilty of breaking all of it. (James 2:10)**

2. Christ taught that some laws are all inclusive and broader than others.

> **“Woe to you, teachers of the law and Pharisees, you hypocrites! You give a tenth of your spices—mint, dill and cummin. But you have neglected the more important matters of the law—justice, mercy and**

faithfulness. You should have practiced the latter, without neglecting the former. (Mat 23:23)

The Pharisees were trying to turn the people against Jesus. People differed as to what the greatest commandment was. Some believed that it had to do with circumcision, others with sacrifices, and still others with the Sabbath. The Pharisees hoped that by stating His opinion, Christ would disturb the people who held a position different from His. He would thereby lose their following. There was the strong possibility that a man's giving his judgment would seem to be lessening the weight of other very important commandments.

Thought 1. All of God's laws are important—equally important. One is first and *weightier* only because it includes and embraces other laws. This means several things.

1) We may think in terms of supreme laws and lesser laws—that if we keep the greater laws, we do not have to pay much attention to the lesser. We may think that if we break the lesser laws we can be excused, but such thinking is false.

For whoever keeps the whole law and yet stumbles at just one point is guilty of breaking all of it. (James 2:10)

2) Just because we may deny the importance of some laws does not make them unimportant. Our unbelief and denial do not void the law, not a single one. They still condemn us. Each law, in the force of its pronouncement, strikes out at our violation. It condemns us—no matter how little value we may place upon it.

This is a common deception of man: unbelief makes a thing ineffective and voids it. A man thinks, "If I deny something, ignore it, refuse to accept it, push it out of my mind, it will not be, nor will it come to pass." Many treat God's Word and some commandments in this way, especially if they wish some sensual or stimulating pleasure. Too many conform their religion and their principles, their beliefs and the laws they obey to their behavior. They want the right to do as they wish, so they make all things fit their wishes, including their principles. They follow only the commandments that allow them to satisfy their desires, and because they obey some standards, they feel acceptable and secure.

Thought 2. This passage is a profitable passage for lawyers and for other professionals, in particular if they are open and honest as this man seems to have been. Just a passing thought—in the day of judgment it will be interesting to see if this lawyer is one of the converts mentioned in Acts 6:9.

2 (22:37-38) **Commandment**: first, love God. Which is the greatest commandment in the law? (Cp. Dt.6:5.) Christ's answer was powerful; it is an eye opener to people steeped in man-made religions.

1. Love God: "Love the Lord your God." Love God as *your* very own God. The word *your* is a personal relationship, not a distant relationship. God is not impersonal, far out in space someplace, distant and removed. God is personal, ever so close, and we are to be personally involved with God on a face-to-face basis. Note another fact: the command is to "love the Lord your God." *Loving* God is an act that is alive and active, not dead and inactive. We are, therefore, to maintain a personal relationship with God that is alive and active.

2. Love God with all your being. Christ breaks our being into three parts: the heart, the soul, and the mind (see DEEPER STUDY # 4,5,6—Mt.22:37).

3. Love is man's chief duty. Man is responsible to maintain a loving relationship with God. Very practically, loving God involves the very same factors that loving a person involves (see outlines and notes—Eph.5:22-33).

a. A loving relationship involves *commitment and loyalty*. True love does not allow lustful behavior with others. True love does not covet; it does not care for a carnal definition of love that allows fleshly acts and sensual relationships with others.

True love is commitment and loyalty to one another. This is very significant. The first commandment deals with *commitment and loyalty*. God strikes out at the very core of man's carnal and fleshly behavior, at his tendency to define love in terms that allow him to satisfy his lust. God irrevocably says, "You shall have no other gods" (Ex.20:3). God demands our total commitment and loyalty.

b. A loving relationship involves *trust and respect* for the person loved. It is loving the person just for who he is. So it is when we love God. We love God because of Himself, because He is who He is. We love Him because...

- He is the Creator and Sustainer of life.
- He is the Savior and Redeemer of our souls.
- He is the Lord and Owner of our lives.

c. A loving relationship involves the *giving and surrendering* of oneself. The drive is to give oneself, to surrender oneself to the other, not to take and conquer. We are to so love God, to give and surrender ourselves to Him.

d. A loving relationship involves *knowing and sharing*. The desire is to know and to share, learning, growing, working, and serving ever so closely together. We are to know and share with God, learning, growing, working, and serving ever so closely with Him

Thought 1. The importance of a personal relationship with God cannot be overstated.

1) It is the greatest, the sum and substance of all commandments.
2) God demands that He be loved. It is His first commandment, and to love is both personal and active.
3) The commandment to love God is given by Christ, the Son of God Himself.

Thought 2. A personal relationship can be maintained only through communication: we must talk to God and allow God to talk to us through prayer, His Word, and the presence of His Spirit.

Thought 3. A person's heart, soul, and mind are focused upon something: self, possessions, the world, the flesh or sinful nature, power, fame, a person. God demands that we focus our whole being upon Him.

DEEPER STUDY # 3
(22:37) **Love**: cp. Dt.6:5. See note—Jn.21:15-17.

DEEPER STUDY # 4
(22:37) **Heart**: the *seat* of man's affection and will (devotion). The heart attaches and focuses our will and devotion. The heart causes us to give either good things or bad things. The heart causes us to devote ourselves to either good or bad. Therefore, Christ says we are to love God "with all our heart." We are to focus our heart, our affection, and our will (devotion) upon God. We are to love God supremely.

> **For where your treasure is, there your heart will be also. (Mat 6:21)**
> **You brood of vipers, how can you who are evil say anything good? For out of the overflow of the heart the mouth speaks. The good man brings good things out of the good stored up in him, and the evil man brings evil things out of the evil stored up in him. (Mat 12:34-35; cp. Mat. 15:18-19)**

DEEPER STUDY # 5
(22:37) **Soul** (psuche): the seat of man's breath and life or consciousness. The soul is the life of a man, the consciousness, the breath, the essence, the being of a man. The soul is the *animal life* of a man. The soul is the breath and consciousness that distinguishes man and other animals from vegetation. The world of vegetation lives and man and animals live, but there is a difference in their living. Man and animals are *breathing* and *conscious* beings. The essence of their being is breath and consciousness. They are living souls. This is clearly pointed out in the Hebrew language of Gen.1:20: "Let the waters teem with 'living souls' [nephesh]." The "living souls" that God created were different from the vegetation He had just created. The "living souls" were creatures (fish) that breathed and possessed consciousness.

Christ said we are to love God "with all our soul," that is, with all our life, our breath, our consciousness. We are to love God with all the breath and consciousness, all the life and awareness, we have.

DEEPER STUDY # 6
(22:37) **Mind**: the seat of reasoning and understanding. God has given intellectual powers to man. Man thinks, reasons, and understands. Christ says that our minds and thoughts are to be centered upon God. We are to love God "with all our mind."

> **Do not conform any longer to the pattern of this world, but be transformed by the renewing of your mind. Then you will be able to test and approve what God's will is—his good, pleasing and perfect will. (Rom 12:2)**
> **And to put on the new self, created to be like God in true righteousness and holiness. (Eph 4:24)**
> **Finally, brothers, whatever is true, whatever is noble, whatever is right, whatever is pure, whatever is lovely, whatever is admirable—if anything is excellent or praiseworthy—think about such things. (Phil 4:8)**
> **And have put on the new self, which is being renewed in knowledge in the image of its Creator. (Col 3:10)**
> **We demolish arguments and every pretension that sets itself up against the knowledge of God, and we take captive every thought to make it obedient to Christ. (2 Cor 10:5)**

3 (22:39) **Love—Brotherhood—Neighbor**: Christ gave a second commandment: "Love your neighor as yourself." (Cp. Lev.19:18.) The lawyer had not asked for the second greatest commandment, but the first commandment is abstract. It cannot be seen or understood standing by itself. There has to be a *demonstration, an act, something done* for love to be seen and understood. A profession of love without demonstration is empty. It is profession only. Love is not known without showing it.

Several important things need to be said about love at this point.

1. Love is an active experience, not inactive and dormant. That is what Christ is pointing out. Love for God *acts*. Love acts by showing and demonstrating itself. It is inaccurate and foolish for a man to say, "I love God," and then be inactive and dormant, doing nothing for God. If he truly loves God, he will *do things* for God. Any person who loves does things for the one loved.

2. The primary *thing* God wants from us is love for our neighbors, not the doing of *religious things*. Doing *religious things* is good, but it is not the first thing God wants. God wants us to make loving our neighbor the first order of our lives. To do *religious things* is only dealing with things such as rituals, observances, ordinances, and laws. Such things are lifeless, unfeeling, and unresponsive. They are immaterial. They are not helped by our doing them; we alone are helped. They make us feel good and religious which is beneficial to our growth, but *religious things* are not what demonstrates our love for God. Loving our neighbor is what proves our love for God. A man may say he loves God, but if he hates and acts unkindly and spitefully toward his neighbor, everyone knows his religion is profession only.

> **"A new command I give you: Love one another. As I have loved you, so you must love one another. By this all men will know that you are my disciples, if you love one another." (John 13:34-35)**
> **If anyone says, "I love God," yet hates his brother, he is a liar. For anyone who does not love his brother, whom he has seen, cannot love God, whom he has not seen. And he has given us this command: Whoever loves God must also love his brother. (1 John 4:20-21)**

3. The great commandment to love God flows downward into another great commandment—to love our neighbor as ourselves. The fact is inescapable.

> **But God demonstrates his own love for us in this: While we were still sinners, Christ died for us. (Rom 5:8)**

When a man really sees the love of God for him, he cannot help but love God and share the love of God with his neighbors. It is the love of Christ for us, His death and sacrifice, that compels us to go and love all men everywhere.

> **We love because he first loved us. And he has given us this command: Whoever loves God must also love his brother. (1 John 4:19, 21)**
>
> **For Christ's love compels us, because we are convinced that one died for all, and therefore all died. And he died for all, that those who live should no longer live for themselves but for him who died for them and was raised again. (2 Cor 5:14-15)**

4. We are to love ourselves.
   a. There is a corrupt love of self that feels the world should center around oneself. This self-love...
      - wants all attention centered around oneself.
      - pushes self forward.
      - insists on one's own way.
      - demands and revels in recognition.
      - shows conceit and ignores others.

   b. However, there is a godly love for self that is natural and pleasing to God. It is a love that stirs a strong self-image, confidence, and assurance. It is a love that even helps in preventing some illnesses such as ulcers, tension, and high blood pressure. The godly love of self comes from knowing three things.
      ⇒ That one is actually the creation of God: the highest creation possible.
      ⇒ That one is actually the object of God's love: the most supreme love possible.
      ⇒ That one is actually the trustee of God's gifts: the greatest gifts possible.

   c. The godly love of self has three traits that are clearly seen.
      ⇒ It considers others better than yourself. It does esteem self ever so highly as God's glorious creation, but it esteems others more highly.

> **Do nothing out of selfish ambition or vain conceit, but in humility consider others better than yourselves. (Phil 2:3)**

⇒ It looks to the interests of others. It looks to one's own interests as a trustee of God's gifts, but it also looks to the interests of others.

> **Each of you should look not only to your own interests, but also to the interests of others. (Phil 2:4)**

⇒ It walks humbly before others.

> **The greatest among you will be your servant. For whoever exalts himself will be humbled, and whoever humbles himself will be exalted. (Mat 23:11-12)**
>
> **Young men, in the same way be submissive to those who are older. All of you, clothe yourselves with humility toward one another, because, "God opposes the proud but gives grace to the humble." (1 Pet 5:5)**

5. We are to love our neighbor as ourselves. Note three very specific things about this second great commandment.
   a. To love our neighbor is a command, not an option. If the commandment is not obeyed, God is displeased and we stand guilty of having broken the law of God.
   b. To love our neighbor arouses the question: Who is our neighbor? Christ answers the question Himself in the Parable of the Good Samaritan.
      ⇒ A good neighbor is *he that shows mercy on any who need mercy*—even if the needy person is socially despised (Lk.10:25-37, esp. 36-37).

      Therefore our neighbor is everyone in the world, no matter his status, condition, or circumstances. Every man is to be esteemed ever so highly and helped no matter who he is. No man is to be injured or wronged. Every man is to be esteemed better than oneself (Ph.2:3).
   c. To love our neighbor is a very practical command. It involves some very practical acts that are spelled out in Scripture.
      ⇒ Love is patient (endures long).
      ⇒ Love is kind.
      ⇒ Love does not envy (is not jealous).
      ⇒ Love does not boast (does not brag).
      ⇒ Love is not proud (vainglorious, arrogant).
      ⇒ Love is not rude (unbecoming, indecent, unmannerly).
      ⇒ Love is not self-seeking (is not selfish; does not insist on one's own right and way).
      ⇒ Love is not easily angered (not easily provoked, touchy, angry, fretful, resentful).
      ⇒ Love keeps no record of wrongs (harbors and plans no evil thought; takes no account of a wrong done it).
      ⇒ Love does not delight in evil (wrong, sin, evil, injustice) but rejoices in the truth (justice and righteousness).
      ⇒ Love always protects.
      ⇒ Love always trusts (exercises faith in everything; is ready to believe the best in everyone).
      ⇒ Love always hopes (keeps up hope in everything, under all circumstances).
      ⇒ Love always perseveres (without weakening; it gives power to endure).

Thought 1. *Religious things* can enslave a person. A person can be so engrossed in religion, buildings, ritual, ceremony, rules, and regulations that he neglects and ignores people, in particular the poor and downtrodden.

Thought 2. The church and *religious things* are the picture of religion among men. Therefore, a man feels *good* and *religious* when he attends church and does *religious things*.

Thought 3. A man loves God when he loves his neighbor. In fact, a man loves God only if he truly loves his neighbor (1 Jn.4:20-21; cp. Jn.13:34-35).

DEEPER STUDY # 7
(22:39) **Love**: cp. Lev.19:18. See note—1 Cor.13:4-7.

4 (22:40) **Love**: Christ says that love includes and embraces all the commandments. In fact, the term "the law and the prophets" is a term often used to refer to all Scripture. What Christ really says is that all Scripture hangs on love for God and love for one's neighbor. Christ actually paints a picture by using the word "hang." He says that love for God is a *hanger* and love for neighbor is a *hanger*. Upon these two hangers hang all that God has ever said, whether commandments or revelation of truth or practice of ceremony and ritual. The sum and substance of all that God has said and done is love. And the sum and substance of all that God wants of man is love: love of God and love of neighbor.

Love does no harm to its neighbor. Therefore love is the fulfillment of the law. (Rom 13:10)

The goal of this command is love, which comes from a pure heart and a good conscience and a sincere faith. (1 Tim 1:5)

So in everything, do to others what you would have them do to you, for this sums up the Law and the Prophets. (Mat 7:12)

Outline		Scripture	Outline
	K. The Question Asked by Jesus: What Do You Think About the Messiah? 22:41-46 (Mk.12:35-37; Lk.20: 39-44)	43 He said to them, "How is it then that David, speaking by the Spirit, calls him 'Lord'? For he says, 44 "'The Lord said to my Lord: "Sit at my right hand until I put your enemies under your feet."'	**4 Scripture's claim: He is Lord—Lord of David**DS1 a. Fact: David called Him Lord—by the *Spirit* 1) Is exalted with God 2) Will have enemies subjected to Him b. Question: How can He be David's Lord & Son?
1 Jesus questioned men	41 While the Pharisees were gathered together, Jesus asked them,	45 If then David calls him 'Lord,' how can he be his son?"	
2 The critical question: What do you think about the Messiah? **3 Man's idea: He is the Son of a man—of David**	42 "What do you think about the Christ ? Whose son is he?" "The son of David,"they replied.	46 No one could say a word in reply, and from that day on no one dared to ask him any more questions.	**5 Conclusion: The question silenced the critics of Jesus**

DIVISION XIV

THE MESSIAH'S LAST WEEK: HIS CLAIM CHALLENGED AND REJECTED, 21:1-23:39

K. The Question Asked by Jesus: What Do You Think About the Messiah? 22:41-46

(22:41-46) **Introduction**: it was still Tuesday of the Lord's last week on earth. He had just been challenged four different times by four different opponents. He had met each group and questioner in a unique way. He had answered the questions and turned them around to teach a much needed truth (cp. 21:23f; 22:15f; 22:23f; 22:34f). Christ had silenced those who opposed His claim to be the Messiah.

Now it was His turn; He questioned His opponents. But Christ did not stand against them as an opponent. Christ questioned them as men who were in error and needed to see the truth. He was reaching out to them in hope. He hoped that some would receive the truth of His Messiahship and accept Him as the Son of God. The spirit of His questioning is seen in the discussion He had with them. Note the question He asked: it is the all important question which He asks of every man: "What do you think about the Messiah?"

1. Jesus questioned men (v.41).
2. The critical question: What do you think about the Messiah (v.41-42)?
3. Man's idea: He is the son of a man—of David (v.42).
4. Scripture's claim: He is Lord—the Lord of David (v.43-45).
5. Conclusion: The question silenced the critics of Jesus (v.46).

1 (22:41) **Jesus Christ, Questions**: Jesus questioned and questioned men, and there are reasons why He questioned them. These are clearly seen in His dealing with these men.

1. Christ is long-suffering and tender. These men had challenged Christ time and again trying to discredit and embarrass Him before the crowd, yet He never reacted once. He answered their questions honestly and in such a way that He opened up new truths which they desperately needed to know. He questioned them because He was patient and long-suffering. He wanted to open up further truth to them. He longed for them to see and surrender to His Messiahship.

2. Christ questioned and questioned in order to reach people *with* the truth. In the case of these men, Christ was making a last-ditch effort, a last appeal to them. They had rejected and rejected until there was little hope. But Christ was still hoping, still reaching out to them. He questioned them in order to lead them to see that He is the Messiah, the Lord, the Son of God Himself.

While considering the Lord's questioning, there is another fact to consider, a critical fact. There is an end to His questioning, a time when He knows there is no hope and no chance that a man will repent and believe. There is a time when He begins to pronounce judgment. This question of Christ was His last question; after asking it, He began to pronounce judgment. Christ discussed and questioned the truth with these men time and again, but after they continually rejected it and became steeped in their unbelief, Christ ceased the discussion and began to pronounce judgment (cp. Mt.23:1-39).

> **Thought 1.** Most people, at one time or another, think and wonder who Christ is. God uses such things as preaching, teaching, events, circumstances, situations, and tragedies to cause us to think about Christ and who He is. He tries to stir us to reason with Him so that we might be led to believe.

> **Thought 2.** Man can become obstinate in unbelief, reject and reject until he becomes so hardened that he will not believe. These men (leaders) demonstrate such obstinate unbelief (cp. Gen.6:3; Pr.29:1).

2 (22:41-42) **Messiah**: Jesus asked the critical question. "What do you think about the Messiah?" This is the critical question for all men. Note two things about the question.

1. The Greek uses the definite article "the Christ or Messiah" (tou Christou). Jesus was trying to stir these men to think about the Messiah. He did not ask them what they thought of Him but what they thought about *the Messiah*. A man's destiny is determined by what he thinks about the Messiah.

2. Jesus asked a specific question about the Messiah: "Whose son is he?" Think about the Messiah. What is His origin? Who is to give birth to Him? In practical day-to-day terms, Jesus was asking three things.

a. Where does your deliverance come from? The Messiah is to deliver man from all the evil and enslavements of the world. Where will such a One come from?
b. Where does your Lord come from—the person you are to follow? The Messiah is to be the Lord

who is to rule and reign and govern all lives, executing perfect justice and care. Where will He come from—from earthly parents or from God?
c. Where does your utopia come from—the person who is to bring about the perfect world and all that is good and beneficial? Where will the One come from who is to bring utopia, the Kingdom of God to earth? Will He come from earth or heaven?

Thought 1. It is not enough to ask this question: "What do you think about the Messiah?" True, it must be asked; but standing alone, the question will not lead a man to the truth. This is clearly seen in the experience of these religionists. Jesus asked them the critical question, yet they did not come to the truth. Two things are necessary before answering the question.
1) A man must think. He must be willing to study and think through the question of the Messiah.
2) A man must be honest. He must rid himself of bias and presuppositions. He must approach the subject of the Messiah with a willingness to see and confess the truth.

Thought 2. There are three critical questions which need to be asked by each of us.
1) Where does my deliverance come from? From the son of a mere man like myself or from God?
2) Where does my Lord come from—the person I am willing to follow as long as I exist? From the son of a mere man like myself or from God?
3) Where does my utopia come from—the person who is to bring about the perfect world and all that is good and beneficial? From a man who is like myself or from God?

Thought 3. In all honesty, are there parents anywhere who can give birth to a son...
- who can deliver us?
- who can be a true Lord to us?
- who can bring about a world that is nothing but good and beneficial to all?

3 (22:42) **Messiah**: the Pharisees answered Jesus' question by giving the common idea of man—the Messiah is the son of a man, the son of David.

Note two facts about their answer.

1. The common title for the Messiah was "the Son of David." The Old Testament definitely said the Messiah was to come from the line of David. It was from such passages as these that the Messiah was known as "the Son of David." (See note—Lk.3:24-31 for the Davidic promises and their fulfillment.)

Once for all, I have sworn by my holiness— and I will not lie to David— that his line will continue forever and his throne endure before me like the sun; (Psa 89: 35-36)

For to us a child is born, to us a son is given, and the government will be on his shoulders. And he will be called Wonderful Counselor, Mighty God, Everlasting Father, Prince of Peace. Of the increase of his government and peace there will be no end. He will reign on David's throne and over his kingdom, establishing and upholding it with justice and righteousness from that time on and forever. The zeal of the LORD Almighty will accomplish this. (Isa 9:6-7)

A shoot will come up from the stump of Jesse; from his roots a Branch will bear fruit. The Spirit of the LORD will rest on him— the Spirit of wisdom and of understanding, the Spirit of counsel and of power, the Spirit of knowledge and of the fear of the LORD— and he will delight in the fear of the LORD. He will not judge by what he sees with his eyes, or decide by what he hears with his ears; but with righteousness he will judge the needy, with justice he will give decisions for the poor of the earth. He will strike the earth with the rod of his mouth; with the breath of his lips he will slay the wicked. Righteousness will be his belt and faithfulness the sash around his waist. (Isa 11:1-5)

The Messiah was to do four specific things. (See notes—Mt.1:1; DEEPER STUDY # 2—1:18; DEEPER STUDY # 3—3:11; notes—11:1-6; 11:2-3; DEEPER STUDY # 1—11:5; DEEPER STUDY # 2—11:6; DEEPER STUDY # 1—12:16; notes—22:42; Lk.7:21-23. These notes are important for the full concept of the Messiah.)
a. He was to free Israel from all enslavement. Enslavement was to be abolished and all men set free under God's domain.
b. He was to give victory over all enemies, and Israel was to be established as the seat of His rule. This, of course, meant Israel was to be the leading nation of the world.
c. He was to bring peace to earth. All people were to serve God under the government established by the Messiah.
d. He was to provide plenty for all. The Messiah was to see that all men had the benefits of God's rule and care.

2. The common idea of the Messiah's origin was that He was to be human, born of a man. The idea that he might be of divine origin, of God Himself, was just unacceptable to men.

Thought 1. Note two striking points about man's common concept of the Messiah.
1) Man thinks of deliverance and plenty in terms of power.
   - national power
   - political power
   - military power
   - institutional power
   - personal power
   - monetary power
2) Man thinks that deliverance and plenty come from human ability and fame, from...
   - a national leader
   - a political leader
   - a military leader
   - an institutional leader
   - a business leader

4 (22:43-45) **Messiah**: Jesus then pointed out the claim of Scripture—the Messiah is Lord, the Lord of David. Scripture says that the Messiah is the Son of David, but it also says that He is the *Lord* of David.

The Scripture is strong in its statement.

1. David called the Messiah Lord, speaking *by the Spirit*; that is, David's words were spoken under the inspiration of the Holy Spirit. God was directing Him (cp. 2 Pt.1:21 and 1 Cor.12:3).

2. David said that "the Lord [Jehovah God] said to my Lord [the Messiah]." David unquestionably called the Messiah, "My Lord."

3. David said that *my* Lord sits on the right hand of God. The Messiah is *Lord*, for He is *exalted* by God.

> **Which he exerted in Christ when he raised him from the dead and seated him at his right hand in the heavenly realms, (Eph 1:20)**
>
> **Therefore God exalted him to the highest place and gave him the name that is above every name, (Phil 2:9)**
>
> **The point of what we are saying is this: We do have such a high priest, who sat down at the right hand of the throne of the Majesty in heaven, (Heb 8:1)**

4. David said that my Lord's "enemies are to be put under His feet." The Messiah is Lord, for all His enemies are to be subjected under Him.

> **That at the name of Jesus every knee should bow, in heaven and on earth and under the earth, and every tongue confess that Jesus Christ is Lord, to the glory of God the Father. (Phil 2:10-11)**

After quoting the Scripture, Jesus asked the pointed question: How can the Messiah be both David's Lord and Son? Jesus is doing at least two things in this question.

1. Jesus was saying this: man's concept of the Messiah as being only human is inadequate—totally inadequate. It is not enough to think in terms of earthly power, of national and political, military and institutional leadership. There is no way a mere man can bring *perfect* deliverance, leadership, and utopia to this earth. The Messiah is not only man, He is the Lord from heaven.

2. Jesus was claiming to be the Son of God Himself. Man's concept has to *go beyond* the mere human and physical. Man's idea has to *stretch upward* into God's very own heart. God loves this earth; therefore, God sent His Son to earth, sacrificing Him in order to save the earth and all those within it (Jn.3:16).

> **"For God so loved the world that he gave his one and only Son, that whoever believes in him shall not perish but have eternal life. (John 3:16)**
>
> **Simon Peter answered, "You are the Christ, the Son of the living God." (Mat 16:16)**
>
> **The woman said, "I know that Messiah" (called Christ) "is coming. When he comes, he will explain everything to us." Then Jesus declared, "I who speak to you am he." (John 4:25-26)**
>
> **"You do not want to leave too, do you?" Jesus asked the Twelve. Simon Peter answered him, "Lord, to whom shall we go? You have the words of eternal life. We believe and know that you are the Holy One of God." (John 6:67-69)**
>
> **I told you that you would die in your sins; if you do not believe that I am the one I claim to be, you will indeed die in your sins." (John 8:24)**
>
> **So Jesus said, "When you have lifted up the Son of Man, then you will know that I am the one I claim to be and that I do nothing on my own but speak just what the Father has taught me. (John 8:28)**
>
> **Jesus said to her, "I am the resurrection and the life. He who believes in me will live, even though he dies; and whoever lives and believes in me will never die. Do you believe this?" "Yes, Lord," she told him, "I believe that you are the Christ, the Son of God, who was to come into the world." (John 11:25-27)**
>
> **As his custom was, Paul went into the synagogue, and on three Sabbath days he reasoned with them from the Scriptures, explaining and proving that the Christ had to suffer and rise from the dead. "This Jesus I am proclaiming to you is the Christ," he said. (Acts 17:2-3)**
>
> **Everyone who believes that Jesus is the Christ is born of God, and everyone who loves the father loves his child as well. (1 John 5:1)**

Thought 1. Jesus' emphasis upon the inspiration of Scripture was very important. He was unmistakably declaring the authority of the Old Testament. We should note the attention and reverence Jesus gave to Scripture—a striking lesson for us.

Thought 2. The Messiah is the Son of David. He is Man, but He is more: He is both God's Son, the Lord from heaven, as well as man.

Thought 3. Man's concept of an earthly deliverer or Messiah is foolish. There is no way permanent peace and perfect utopia can be brought to a corruptible world *apart from God.* If permanency of anything is ever to be known, it has to come through Him who is permanent. (See notes—Jn.8:21-22; Ro.10:6-7. These notes discuss the very practical and spiritual needs of man for the Messiah and/or utopia.)

DEEPER STUDY # 1
(22:43) **Old Testament Reference**: cp. Ps.110:1.

5 (22:46) **Jesus Christ, Response to**: Jesus' question silenced His critics. A heart that is truly honest and a mind that is willing to study and think has to confess the truth. If either is missing, the honest heart or the thinking mind, then a man will turn from Christ and be silent. He will be silent in belief and act in unbelief.

1 Jesus spoke to the crowds & to the disciples
2 False religion is a religion that claims to "sit" in the truth, Moses' seat
3 False religion is a religion of hypocrisy
a. It is good to obey their preaching
b. It is not good to follow their practice
4 False religion is a religion of heavy burdens
a. Leaders imposed heavy burdens upon others
b. Leaders did not impose the burdens upon themselves
5 False religion is a religion of show, of display

CHAPTER 23

L. The Warning against False Religion 23:1-12 (Mk.12:38-40; Lk.20:45-47)

Then Jesus said to the
crowds and to his disciples:
2 "The teachers of the law
and the Pharisees sit in
Moses' seat.
3 So you must obey them
and do everything they
tell you. But do not do
what they do, for they do
not practice what they
preach.
4 They tie up heavy loads
and put them on men's
shoulders, but they them-
selves are not willing to
lift a finger to move
them.
5 "Everything they do is
done for men to see: They
make their phylacteries wide
and the tassels on their garments long;
6 They love the place of
honor at banquets and the
most important seats in the
synagogues;
7 They love to be greeted in
the marketplaces and to have
men call them 'Rabbi.'
8 "But you are not to be
called 'Rabbi,' for you have
only one Master and you are
all brothers.
9 And do not call anyone on
earth 'father,' for you have
one Father, and he is in
heaven.
10 Nor are you to be called
'teacher,' for you have one
Teacher, the Christ.
11 The greatest among you
will be your servant.
12 For whoever exalts himself will be humbled, and
whoever humbles himself
will be exalted.

a. A religion of appearance: Dress, clothing
b. A religion of position: Positions that honor & exalt men
c. A religion of titles: Titles that honor & exalt men
6 False religion is a religion to be guarded against
a. Because position & relationships are already established
1) God is your Father
2) Christ is your Teacher
3) You are brothers
b. Because greatness is measured by service
c. Because judgment is coming

DIVISION XIV

THE MESSIAH'S LAST WEEK: HIS CLAIM CHALLENGED AND REJECTED, 21:1-23:39

L. The Warning against False Religion, 23:1-12

(23:1-12) **Introduction**: in order to understand what is happening in this passage, it is helpful to recall the events which led up to it. It was still Tuesday of Jesus' last week on earth. On Sunday, just two days before, He had been escorted into the city by teeming thousands proclaiming Him to be the Messiah. On Monday, He had cast out the money changers and those who were doing business within the temple walls. Following these two dramatic events, He had taken upon Himself the right and authority to teach and heal within the temple. Naturally the governing leaders, both religious and civil, were upset and angered by what was happening. More to the point, the leaders felt threatened by Christ, fearing the people might rally around Him as the Messiah and rise up against the Romans. Such action, of course, would cause the Romans to march against Jerusalem and blame the Jewish leadership for not maintaining order. Then after putting the insurrection down, Rome would remove the present Jewish leadership from office. In the minds of the leaders, Christ was a threat to their position, power, wealth, and security (see notes—Mt.12:1-8; note and DEEPER STUDY # 1—12:10; note—15:1-20; DEEPER STUDY # 2—15:6-9; DEEPER STUDY # 3—16:12). They were forced to discredit Jesus before the people.

They sent group after group to challenge Christ, attempting to trip Him up. Each time He answered brilliantly, teaching a much needed lesson not only to those standing around, but to men of all generations. Finally, the leaders were baffled and silenced. But Christ did not give up trying to reach them. He reached out once more, trying to lead them to the truth: the Messiah is not only Man, He is also Lord, the Son of God Himself (cp. Mt.22:41-46). The result? Again, the leaders refused to open their minds and hearts. They remained closed to the truth, obstinately so. They rejected Christ and turned and walked away. They began the final plot—not to challenge Christ in argument again but to kill Him.

As the present passage is studied, it is helpful to keep in mind the major reason these leaders opposed Jesus so violently: they feared the loss of all they held dear and possessed in this world: position, power, livelihood, wealth, and security. In their minds, as long as Christ was alive, He was a threat to them and to their nation (see notes—Mt.12:1-8; note and DEEPER STUDY # 1—12:10).

The great tragedy was that they were supposed to be the godly teachers and leaders, God's very own representatives and messengers to the people. Yet, they were so far removed from God that they were unable to recognize God's very own Son. Despite appeal after appeal and proof after proof by Christ Himself, they still refused to believe and follow Him. They deliberately chose to be obstinate in their unbelief and chose to follow the way of the world by plotting to kill Him.

This background lies behind the present chapter—the most severe attack Christ ever spoke against a people. The true nature of these religionists, the Scribes and Pharisees, is clearly seen as Christ opened up the hypocrisy of their lives and religion point by point. In this particular passage, Christ warned against their religion—a religion which stands as a symbol of the false religions of the world. (Also see outline, note, and DEEPER STUDY # 1—Ro.2:17-29.)

1. Jesus spoke to the crowds and the disciples (v.1).
2. False religion is a religion that claims to "sit" in the truth, in Moses' seat (v.2).
3. False religion is a religion of hypocrisy (v.3).
4. False religion is a religion of heavy burdens (v.4).
5. False religion is a religion of show, of display (v.5-7).
6. False religion is a religion to be guarded against (8-12).

1 (23:1) **Religion, False—Scripture**: in this particular passage, Jesus spoke to the crowd and to the disciples, not to the religionists, not to the Pharisees and Scribes. There are at least four reasons why Christ warned the crowd and disciples at this point. These same reasons make this passage extremely applicable to every generation.

1. Everyone needs to know what is true and what is false in religion. Man-made religion always includes some truth and some error. And unfortunately even the true religion, God's revealed religion, is sometimes added to or taken away from by men. This is what had happened to the Pharisees and Scribes, the religionists of Jesus' day. They were staunch followers of God's Word, the Old Testament Scriptures, but they added to the Scripture. Therefore, Christ needed to teach what was true and what was false in the present religion (cp. v.2-3).

2. Everyone needs to have the hypocrisy and sin of religion exposed. When men add to or take away from God's revealed truth, it creates and causes hypocrisy and sin within religion. When men *add* rules and regulations to Scripture, self-discipline is demanded and super-spirituality results. When men deny or *take away* certain portions of Scripture, it creates and causes the exaltation of man and his rationality, making *gods* out of man and his ability. Again, pride and vain glory result.

3. Everyone needs to be warned against following the error of religion. Just being religious is not enough (cp. Mt.5:20). A person must follow the truth. If a person follows false religion, he is doomed (v.8-12).

4. Everyone needs to have his false ideas about Christ corrected. The false teaching and attacks of the religionists had influenced the people. Unbelief and false ideas about the Messiah were running rampant. Christ needed to declare the truth (v.7-10).

> **Thought 1.** The warning concerning false religion was directed primarily to the public and the disciples because there is always more hope for them. It is always difficult for a leader who teaches error to repent and change.
> 1) He fears embarrassment in admitting that he has held to error and taught error.
> 2) He fears the ridicule and rejection of his peers.
> 3) He fears the loss of position, power, and security.

2 (23:2) **Religion, False—Minister—Teaching**: false religion is a religion that claims to "sit" in the truth, that is, in Moses' seat. Moses was the great teacher and interpreter of God's law and Word. Christ said that the Scribes (the teachers of the law) and Pharisees "sit in Moses' seat." They were responsible for teaching and interpreting God's Word just as Moses had been. The application is clear: all religions, false and true, "sit in Moses' seat"—all religion is responsible for teaching the truth of God's Word. As shall be seen, all teachers shall be held accountable for how they "sit in Moses' seat," how they *sit* in their position as teachers and interpreters of God's Word.

> **"Why do you call me, 'Lord, Lord,' and do not do what I say? (Luke 6:46)**
> **You, therefore, have no excuse, you who pass judgment on someone else, for at whatever point you judge the other, you are condemning yourself, because you who pass judgment do the same things. (Rom 2:1)**
> **You who brag about the law, do you dishonor God by breaking the law? As it is written: "God's name is blasphemed among the Gentiles because of you." (Rom 2:23-24)**

> **Thought 1.** The place of religion in the world has been *set* and *ordained* by God. Just because bad men may sit in places of leadership does not mean that all religion is bad nor that all religion is to be invalidated or ignored. Hypocrites within the church, even within positions of leadership, do not mean that the church is evil and can be neglected and avoided. We are to *test the spirits*, distinguish between the true and the false, and we are to go on worshipping God and edifying those who follow the truth.

> **Thought 2.** It is a terrible thing for a false teacher to "sit in Moses' seat." The most severe judgment awaits those who teach error (cp. Mt.23:12; 23:13-36, esp. 14, 15, 33).

> **"You snakes! You brood of vipers! How will you escape being condemned to hell? (Mat 23:33)**

3 (23:3) **Religion, False**: false religion is a religion of hypocrisy (v.3). However, there is a fact that must be noted: not all religion is false, even when it is taught by a false teacher. Christ says, "Observe, obey the truth of what they say, in so far as it is God's Word; but do not follow after their works" (v.3). Note several things.

1. Jesus is condemning false religion and teachers, but not the truth. False teachers can and do teach some truth. The truth is to be obeyed, no matter who teaches it. The truth and our duty to obey it are not invalidated just because a hypocrite teaches it.

2. Jesus is saying that teaching the truth does not mean that a person is acceptable to God. Being acceptable to God depends upon one thing and one thing alone: living the truth. A man may teach the truth yet be unacceptable to God. He is unacceptable because he is a hypocrite and does not obey the Lord. He simply does not live the truth. A man is not acceptable just because he proclaims and professes the truth—even if he is a teacher. He is acceptable because he walks in the truth day by day.

> **You, then, who teach others, do you not teach yourself? You who preach against stealing, do you steal? You who say that people should not commit adultery, do you commit adultery? You who abhor idols, do you rob temples? You who brag about the law, do you dishonor God by breaking the law? (Rom 2:21-23)**

3. We must separate the office from the officer, the ministry from the minister, the church from the people, the truth from the teaching, the doctrine from the practice. The spirits must be tried.

> **Dear friends, do not believe every spirit, but test the spirits to see whether they are from God, because many false prophets have gone out into the world. (1 John 4:1)**

4. Jesus is saying that the claims of religion and of men must not be allowed to lead us. The doctrine, morality, and discipline of religion and men may be commendable; on the other hand, both religion and men may be false.

They claim to know God, but by their actions they deny him. They are detestable, disobedient and unfit for doing anything good. (Titus 1:16)

Dear children, let us not love with words or tongue but with actions and in truth. (1 John 3:18)

Thought 1. Preaching and practice must always be separated. There is always some difference. Every man is human, and every man comes short, but God's Word is perfect.

4 (23:4) **Religion, False**: false religion is a religion of heavy burdens or loads. Jesus said that false religion and teachers impose heavy burdens upon men.

There are four ways heavy burdens or loads are laid upon the shoulders of men.

1. God's Word and law can be imposed upon men in such a strict and severe way that mercy is lacking.

2. Religion and men can add to God's Word through rules, regulations, rituals, observances, and traditions. Such tends to become more important than the truth.

3. Religion and men can deny and take away from God's Word, leaving men to stumble around searching for the truth within themselves and other imperfect and frail men.

4. Religion and men can exercise undue authority, lording it over people, insisting that tradition and ritual and other man-made burdens or loads be kept.

In discussing rules and regulations, many are willing to impose the rules upon others, but not upon themselves. There are two particular failures with such hypocrisy.

1. Some teachers and laymen fail to lift a finger to practice the burden or load themselves. They are strict in laying the burden upon others but lax in bearing the weight themselves. They will not be bound by such rules themselves, at least not strictly, but they will preach and teach the rules to others and bind them to keep the rules. The shoulders of others are weighed down ever so heavily, yet they will not lift their own fingers to carry the weight of the rule or restriction.

2. Some teachers and laymen fail to lift a finger to ease the burden for the weak and heavy laden. This is another possible interpretation of what Christ is saying. Some just will not show mercy; they will not help those who need help in practicing the burden. Some teachers are so strict and assuming that they know little of the love and mercy of God. They know little about Christian liberty (cp. Acts 15:28. See outline and notes—Ro.14:1-23.)

But now that you know God—or rather are known by God—how is it that you are turning back to those weak and miserable principles? Do you wish to be enslaved by them all over again? (Gal 4:9)

It is for freedom that Christ has set us free. Stand firm, then, and do not let yourselves be burdened again by a yoke of slavery. (Gal 5:1)

Since you died with Christ to the basic principles of this world, why, as though you still belonged to it, do you submit to its rules: (Col 2:20)

Thought 1. There is the possibility of terrible pride in imposing burdens or loads upon men. The right to impose burdens sets a person up as *lord* over others. Of course, there is a place for authority in proclaiming and exercising God's Word, but not for imposing man-made rules (legalistic conservatism) and human rationalizations (liberalism). Both weigh man down ever so heavily. Both force man to secure the approval of God by keeping rules through a person's own strength. Both know little if any of the mercy and discipline of God's Spirit. God's Word is fully adequate for both faith and practice. God's Word is all man needs to direct and govern his life. We do not have to add to or take away from God's Word.

5 (23:5-7) **Religion, False—Pride**: false religion is a religion of show and display. Christ points out three things these teachers did to be seen by men.

1. They changed their appearance, dress, and clothing to draw attention to themselves.

a. They wore phylacteries. These were little leather type boxes which contained a piece of parchment with four passages of Scripture written on it. The Scriptures were Ex.13:1-10; 13:11-16; Dt.6:4-9; and Dt.11:13-21.

   The use of the phylacteries seems to have arisen from a literal translation of Ex.13:9 and Pr.7:3. The true meaning of these two passages seems to be that we are to have the word of God in our minds just as clearly as if we had them before our eyes.

   The great fault of the religionists was that they interpreted these passages literally, and they enlarged the little leather boxes to draw attention to themselves as being religious.

b. They also made the tassels on their clothing long. God had instructed the Jews to make fringes or tassels on the borders of their outer robe. When a person noticed them, he was to be reminded to keep God's commandments. Again, the error was that the religionist changed his appearance from others; he enlarged his tassels, drawing attention to the fact that he was more religious than others.

Thought 1. A person can wear clothes that expose the body, that actually attract attention to certain parts of the body. A person can wear clothes that are too tight, too low cut, too high cut, too thin. A person can wear too little clothing and clothing that fails to cover enough of the body.

Jesus said to beware of dressing to attract attention. The religionists did it to appear righteous. Others do it to appear worldly (appealing).

Do not offer the parts of your body to sin, as instruments of wickedness, but rather offer yourselves to God, as those who have been brought from death to life; and offer the parts of your body to him as instruments of righteousness. (Rom 6:13)

I also want women to dress modestly, with decency and propriety, not with braided hair or gold or pearls or expensive clothes, but with good deeds, appropriate for women who profess to worship God. (1 Tim 2:9-10)

Your beauty should not come from outward adornment, such as braided hair and the wearing of gold jewelry and fine clothes. Instead, it should be that of your

inner self, the unfading beauty of a gentle and quiet spirit, which is of great worth in God's sight. For this is the way the holy women of the past who put their hope in God used to make themselves beautiful. They were submissive to their own husbands, (1 Pet 3:3-5)

2. They loved the positions of honor, special seats, and places of recognition. There are those who love the restricted neighborhoods and clubs and the preferred lists. They love the preeminence, the recognition (3 Jn.9). Note what is condemned: not being in these positions and places, but the *love* of them. Someone has to hold the upper positions and fill the major places of responsibility. It is the *love* of such, the love and the feeling of pride because of the place and position that is wrong.

How can you believe if you accept praise from one another, yet make no effort to obtain the praise that comes from the only God? (John 5:44)

But man, despite his riches, does not endure; he is like the beasts that perish. (Psa 49:12)

3. They loved the titles that honored and exalted them. The title was simply "Rabbi" which meant teacher or master. It carried with it the modern idea of *Doctor* or *My lord*. It was a title that took a man who was supposed to be God's messenger and said, "Here he is; this is he." It honored the man and not the Lord.

For whoever exalts himself will be humbled, and whoever humbles himself will be exalted. (Mat 23:12)

For he will take nothing with him when he dies, his splendor will not descend with him. (Psa 49:17)

Thought 1. Too often men change their clothing and seek the upper places, positions, and titles to draw attention to themselves and their abilities. They are honored and not the Lord (cp. Mt.6:1-7, 16-18).

Thought 2. There is nothing wrong with living holy and godly lives, with being religious. But it is wrong to draw attention to oneself instead of to the Lord. We should not *overdo* or *remake* our outward being (appearance, position, titles) to draw attention to ourselves. We should always walk humbly among men, walk as one of them, walk pointing them to Christ by our lives.

Thought 3. God has no favorites among men. Why should we seek to appear as a favorite? Why should we seek *appearance*, *position*, and *honor* that would point toward us as being special?

Thought 4. If there is anyone who should walk humbly before men and point them toward God, it is the man who professes to serve God. He, of all men, should not love the appearance and positions and titles and honor that point toward him instead of his Lord.

6 (23:8-12) **Religion, False**: false religion is a religion to be guarded against. There are three strong reasons why we are to guard against false religion.

1. All positions and relationships are already set in the Kingdom of God. There is no position and no relationship left to be determined. All have already been determined.

a. God is the Father of our faith, of the true religion. No earthly founder or teacher is *Father*. Therefore no man is to be acknowledged as such. God alone is to be proclaimed *Father*.

One God and Father of all, who is over all and through all and in all. (Eph 4:6)

Every good and perfect gift is from above, coming down from the Father of the heavenly lights, who does not change like shifting shadows. (James 1:17)

b. Christ is our Teacher. One alone is Teacher, even Christ. We are not to be called teachers (kathegetes, leaders, guides, v.10. Cp. Ro.2:19-20.) We are servants of the Teacher. Note that Jesus is claiming to be the Messiah.

c. Believers are brothers. One is not above or more exalted than another. Each stands as an equal before God and one another. Each is to serve and help the other.

2. Greatness is measured by service, not by earthly honor. (See outline and notes—Mt.20:20-28. This is a good discussion on "The Price of Greatness.") When religion is conceived by man or influenced by man, that religion focuses upon ritual, ceremony, rules, and regulations and upon honor, recognition, position, and influence.

Not so with you. Instead, whoever wants to become great among you must be your servant, whoever wants to be first must be your slave— (Mat 20:26-27)

But you are not to be like that. Instead, the greatest among you should be like the youngest, and the one who rules like the one who serves. (Luke 22:26)

For by the grace given me I say to every one of you: Do not think of yourself more highly than you ought, but rather think of yourself with sober judgment, in accordance with the measure of faith God has given you. (Rom 12:3)

Young men, in the same way be submissive to those who are older. All of you, clothe yourselves with humility toward one another, because, "God opposes the proud but gives grace to the humble." (1 Pet 5:5)

3. Judgment is coming. It is what a person does himself that determines his fate: he exalts himself or humbles himself. Again, someone has to fill positions of leadership; but if a person pushes himself forward for the honor of the position and not for the purpose of serving, he is to be judged by God. The rule is: we are called to serve, not to rule.

Anyone who breaks one of the least of these commandments and teaches others to do the same will be called least in the kingdom of heaven, but whoever practices and

teaches these commands will be called great in the kingdom of heaven. (Mat 5:19)

He has brought down rulers from their thrones but has lifted up the humble. (Luke 1:52)

Look at every proud man and humble him, crush the wicked where they stand. (Job 40:12)

Those who trust in their wealth and boast of their great riches? No man can redeem the life of another or give to God a ransom for him— (Psa 49:6-7)

A man's pride brings him low, but a man of lowly spirit gains honor. (Prov 29:23)

The LORD Almighty has a day in store for all the proud and lofty, for all that is exalted (and they will be humbled), (Isa 2:12)

"Surely the day is coming; it will burn like a furnace. All the arrogant and every evildoer will be stubble, and that day that is coming will set them on fire," says the LORD Almighty. "Not a root or a branch will be left to them. (Mal 4:1)

Thought 1. One thing that can be said of the Christian faith is this: Christian faith is a faith of *oneness* (Eph.4:1-6, esp. 4-6; 1 Cor.12:4-13). There is no room for pride or divisiveness, neither for the love of position, honor, or title.

M. The Eight Accusations against False Religionists, 23:13-36
(Lk.11:39-50)

1 False religionists shut the door to heaven against seekers[DS1,2,3]
a. They do not enter themselves
b. They do not allow seekers to enter

2 False religionists are missionaries who double the corruption of new followers[DS4]

3 False religionists mislead others: They are blind guides in oaths & commitments[DS5]
a. Their blindness: They stress the secondary over the primary (two examples)
1) They stress the temple gold over the temple
2) They stress the gift over the altar
b. Their folly: They try to evade commitments & responsibility, v.17,19
c. The raw facts
1) All commitments & oaths are heard by God—there is no evasion
2) All commitments & oaths are binding & are accountable to God

4 False religionists stress the lighter commandments & neglect the more important ones[DS6]
a. They stress the lighter duties *& neglect* the more important duties
b. They avoid the lesser sins & commit the greater sins

13 "Woe to you, teachers of
the law and Pharisees, you
hypocrites! You shut the
kingdom of heaven in men's
faces. You yourselves do not
enter, nor will you let those
enter who are trying to.*
15 "Woe to you, teachers of
the law and Pharisees, you
hypocrites! You travel over
land and sea to win a single
convert, and when he be-
comes one, you make him
twice as much a son of hell as
you are.
16 "Woe to you, blind
guides! You say, 'If anyone
swears by the temple, it
means nothing; but if anyone
swears by the gold of the
temple, he is bound by his
oath.'
17 You blind fools! Which is
greater: the gold, or the temple that makes the gold sacred?
18 You also say, 'If anyone
swears by the altar, it means
nothing; but if anyone swears
by the gift on it, he is bound
by his oath.'
19 You blind men! Which
is greater: the gift, or the altar
that makes the gift sacred?
20 Therefore, he who swears
by the altar swears by it
and by everything on
it.
21 And he who swears by the
temple swears by it and by
the one who dwells in it.
22 And he who swears by
heaven swears by God's
throne and by the one who
sits on it.
23 "Woe to you, teachers of
the law and Pharisees, you
hypocrites! You give a tenth
of your spices—mint, dill and
cummin. But you have ne-
glected the more important
matters of the law—justice,
mercy and faithfulness. You
should have practiced the
latter, without neglecting the
former.
24 You blind guides! You
strain out a gnat but swallow
a camel.
25 "Woe to you, teachers of
the law and Pharisees, you
hypocrites! You clean the
outside of the cup and dish,
but inside they are full of
greed and self-indulgence.
26 Blind Pharisee! First
clean the inside of the cup
and dish, and then the outside
also will be clean.
27 "Woe to you, teachers of
the law and Pharisees, you
hypocrites! You are like
whitewashed tombs, which
look beautiful on the outside
but on the inside are full of
dead men's bones and everything unclean.
28 In the same way, on the
outside you appear to people
as righteous but on the inside
you are full of hypocrisy and
wickedness.
29 "Woe to you, teachers of
the law and Pharisees, you
hypocrites! You build tombs
for the prophets and decorate
the graves of the right-
eous.
30 And you say, 'If we had
lived in the days of our forefathers, we would not have
taken part with them in
shedding the blood of the
prophets.'
31 So you testify against
yourselves that you are the
descendants of those who
murdered the prophets.
32 Fill up, then, the measure
of the sin of your forefathers!
33 "You snakes! You brood
of vipers! How will you escape being condemned to
hell?
34 Therefore I am sending
you prophets and wise men
and teachers. Some of them
you will kill and crucify; others you will flog in your
synagogues and pursue from
town to town.
35 And so upon you will
come all the righteous blood
that has been shed on earth,
from the blood of righteous
Abel to the blood of
Zechariah son of Berekiah,
whom you murdered between
the temple and the altar.
36 I tell you the truth, all this
will come upon this generation.

5 False religionists are blind to real cleanness
a. Their outside appears clean
b. Their insides are full of greed & self-indulgence
c. Their need: First clean the inside; then the outside will be clean

6 False religionists disguise inner decay
a. Illustration: They are like white tombs
1) Outward: Appear clean & beautiful
2) Inward: Full of death & uncleanness
b. Their wrong
1) Outward: Appear righteous
2) Inward: Full of Hypocrisy & wickedness

7 False religionists pride themselves in a godly heritage
a. Honor the relics of the past
b. Denounce the former abuses
c. Pride themselves in being better: Would not have committed such sins
d. Testify against themselves (by rejecting Christ)
1) Show themselves to be descendants of murderers
2) Fill up the father's cup of murder
e. Result: Have become snakes, vipers—doomed to hell

8 False religionists reject & abuse many of God's present-day messengers[DS7,8,9]
a. Their abuse: They persecute & kill
b. Their judgment
1) They shall have imputed to them the sins of all the righteous blood shed throughout history[DS10,11]
2) All these things shall come upon this generation[DS12]

* [14] *Woe to you, teachers of the law and Pharisees, you hypocrites! You devour widow's houses and for a show make lengthy prayers. Therefore you will be punished more severely.*

DIVISION XIV

THE MESSIAH'S LAST WEEK: HIS CLAIM CHALLENGED AND REJECTED, 21:1-23:39

M. The Eight Accusations Against False Religionists, 23:13-36

(23:13-36) **Introduction—Religion, False**: this is probably the most stern and sustained denunciation in all history. It is beyond doubt the most tragic because it involves the souls of men, and it is pronounced by the Judge of all the earth, the Lord Himself. But it was deserved, and it stands as a dramatic warning to all men, in particular religionists of every generation.

Four things need to be seen before studying this passage.

1. The sin of these religionists (Pharisees) was great: it was hypocrisy.
   a. They professed religion, but they did not really follow God. They never entered heaven themselves, and by their lives and teaching, they misled others and kept them out of heaven.
   b. They used religion for their own ends, to advance themselves professionally and materially (cp. v.14-15).
2. Christ was angry, but He was also sorrowful. He was harsh and condemning, but He was also broken-hearted and full of pity. Two facts show this.
   a. The Greek word *woe* includes both wrath and pity (see DEEPER STUDY # 1—Mt.23:13).
   b. Jesus expressed great lament over Jerusalem (v.37-39).
3. Christ was attacking and denouncing the religionists, but He was also warning them. Their sin was a great and terrible sin, but it was not unpardonable. They were shutting the door of heaven against themselves and others, and they were close to never being able to enter themselves. But all was not hopeless, not yet. Those *who will* hear this warning of Christ can respond by fearing and shaking under its denunciation, and they can repent and turn to God with a believing heart.
4. Some Scribes and Pharisees did repent and accept Christ and begin to follow Him (cp Lk.13:31; Acts 6:7; 15:5; 18:8, 17).

Christ levelled His denunciation against the religionists of His day. He dealt frankly and openly with them. He exposed the truth of their human hearts: they were full of hypocrisy. Nothing thereafter would be hid; all would be exposed. They had to look at themselves and see the corruption of their hearts; and they had to repent, believe, and follow Christ or else be doomed to hell (v.33).

Christ, frankly and openly, levelled eight accusations against the religionists.

1. False religionists shut the door to heaven against seekers (v.13).
2. False religionists are missionaries who double the corruption of new followers (v.15).
3. False religionists mislead others; they are blind guides in oaths and commitments (v.16-22).
4. False religionists stress the lighter commandments and neglect the more important ones (v.23-24).
5. False religionists are blind to real cleanness (v.25-26).
6. False religionists disguise inner decay (v.27-28).
7. False religionists pride themselves in a godly heritage (v.29-33).
8. False religionists reject and abuse many of God's present-day messengers (v.34-36).

1 (23:13) **Religionists—False Teachers**: false religionists shut the door to heaven against seekers. The picture is that of men's standing right at the door desperately needing to enter, but the false religionist shuts the door of heaven against them. The Greek word is "em prosthen" which means *in the face of.*

Christ said two things in this point.

1. The false religionists did not enter heaven themselves. There are three reasons why they did not enter. (These reasons are pointed out in the preceding Scriptures.)
   a. They rejected God as Messiah, as being the Lord from heaven, the very Son of God (cp. Mt.22:41-45; Jn.10:31-39).
   b. They preferred their own ideas of religion rather than God's ideas. They preferred a religion that honored man's ability to do religious things rather than a religion that honored God's mercy for man (see outline and notes—Mt.23:1-12).
   c. They chose the world over God's demand for self-denial. They chose the things of the world such as position, honor, recognition, esteem, wealth, power, authority, and security (see notes—Mt.12:1-8; note and DEEPER STUDY # 1—12:10).

2. The false religionists not only did not enter heaven themselves, they did not allow *seekers* to enter. They shut the door by misleading people, and thereby doomed them to an eternity apart from God.
   a. They tried to discredit Jesus Christ, denying that He was the Son of God incarnated in human flesh (Mt.21:23-22:46).
   b. They twisted the Scriptures, falsely interpreting them (cp. Mt.22:41-46).

Jesus replied, "You are in error because you do not know the Scriptures or the power of God. (Mat 22:29)

Unlike so many, we do not peddle the word of God for profit. On the contrary, in Christ we speak before God with sincerity, like men sent from God. (2 Cor 2:17)

Rather, we have renounced secret and shameful ways; we do not use deception, nor do we distort the word of God. On the contrary, by setting forth the truth plainly we commend ourselves to every man's conscience in the sight of God. (2 Cor 4:2)

He writes the same way in all his letters, speaking in them of these matters. His letters contain some things that are hard to understand, which ignorant and unstable people distort, as they do the other Scriptures, to their own destruction. (2 Pet 3:16)

   c. They ridiculed and threatened anyone who confessed Christ (Jn.9:22, 34).

"Woe to you experts in the law, because you have taken away the key to

knowledge. You yourselves have not entered, and you have hindered those who were entering." (Luke 11:52)

"For the lips of a priest ought to preserve knowledge, and from his mouth men should seek instruction—because he is the messenger of the LORD Almighty. But you have turned from the way and by your teaching have caused many to stumble; you have violated the covenant with Levi," says the LORD Almighty. (Mal 2:7-8)

Thought 1. The fields are white unto harvest. Many seek to enter heaven, yet the door is often shut in their faces. By whom? By false religionists.

1) False religionists deny Christ: they do not teach and preach that Jesus is the true Savior of men, the Son of God. Therefore, the seeker never knows the salvation of Christ. He never knows that Christ died for his sins and that he must trust Christ, giving all he is and has to Christ.

   But there were also false prophets among the people, just as there will be false teachers among you. They will secretly introduce destructive heresies, even denying the sovereign Lord who bought them—bringing swift destruction on themselves. (2 Pet 2:1)

   Who is the liar? It is the man who denies that Jesus is the Christ. Such a man is the antichrist—he denies the Father and the Son. (1 John 2:22)

2) False religionists have their own thoughts about religion and how to be right with God. They teach their own thoughts on religion and righteousness. Therefore, the seeker never knows God's true righteousness and religion.

   For I tell you that unless your righteousness surpasses that of the Pharisees and the teachers of the law, you will certainly not enter the kingdom of heaven. (Mat 5:20)

   Therefore no one will be declared righteous in his sight by observing the law; rather, through the law we become conscious of sin. (Rom 3:20)

   Since they did not know the righteousness that comes from God and sought to establish their own, they did not submit to God's righteousness. Christ is the end of the law so that there may be righteousness for everyone who believes. (Rom 10:3-4)

3) False religionists often choose the world over the denial of self. They choose place, position, honor, and security over sacrifice and true service.

   For you know that it was not with perishable things such as silver or gold that you were redeemed from the empty way of life handed down to you from your forefathers, but with the precious blood of Christ, a lamb without blemish or defect. (1 Pet 1:18-19)

Thought 2. Many religionists mislead people. They prefer their own ideas of religion rather than God's ideas. They prefer their own ideas that exalt self and honor their own abilities.

Thought 3. A man must guard against his own ideas and prejudices. Personal ideas and prejudice must not replace what God has revealed to be the truth. Personal ideas and prejudices shut the door of heaven to everyone who accepts and believes them.

DEEPER STUDY # 1

(23:13) **Woe** (ouai): means both wrath and sorrow, anger and pity. There is no single English word to express what it means. It is a grieving denunciation; a sorrowful wrath; a pitying anger. It is a godly threat.

DEEPER STUDY # 2

(23:13) **Hypocrites** (hupokrites): one who pretends, puts on a show, acts out something he is not. At first the word simply meant one who replied or answered. Then it came to mean acting, as actors play-acted the lines of a scene. Finally, the word was used in the worst sense: play-acting; pretending; one who wore a mask to hide his real self; one who acted one way but who was really another way; one who put on an outward show.

The religionists, the Scribes and Pharisees, were hypocrites.

⇒ They acted as though they believed and loved God, yet they did not accept God's Son.

⇒ They pretended to be seeking God; but they were really seeking profession, esteem, recognition, honor, position, power, and security (see notes—Mt.12:1-8; note and DEEPER STUDY # 1—12:10).

⇒ They showed a concern for the things of God, but they were really concerned with the things of this world.

⇒ They acted humble and helpful; but they were really full of pride, envy, possessiveness, selfishness, and covetousness.

⇒ They claimed to be ministers of God's religion; but they were really ministers of a man-made religion, a religion that honored man's ability to *be good* and to do enough good to become acceptable to God.

⇒ They professed God's Word, but they added to and took away from His Word.

What Christ had to say about hypocrites is very serious. His words are a warning to every pretender and deceiver.

⇒ Hypocrites will receive the greater damnation (v.14).

⇒ Hypocrites are sons of hell (v.15).

⇒ Hypocrites are fools and they are blind (v.17, 19).

⇒ Hypocrites are blind guides (v.24).

⇒ Hypocrites are full of greed and selfishness (v.25).

⇒ Hypocrites are full of everything unclean(v.27).

⇒ Hypocrites are snakes, a generation of vipers (v.33).

⇒ Hypocrites shall not escape being condemned to hell (v.33).

DEEPER STUDY # 3

(23:13) **Kingdom of Heaven**: see DEEPER STUDY # 3—Mt.19:23-24.

2 (23:15) **Evangelism—Proselytes**: false religionists are missionaries who double the corruption of new followers. Note that Christ said two significant things.

1. False religionists seek converts.
2. False religionists are very zealous in evangelism; they brave the world to make a single convert.

But there were problems with the zeal of these false religionists, and the problems were serious.

1. They were missionaries of a false religion. They were not reaching people for God, but for a man-made religion (see DEEPER STUDY # 2—Mt.23:13). They were not bringing people to a personal relationship with God but to their own ideas of religion.
2. They were doubling the damnation of these converts. The primary people they went after were the God-fearing and devout people who had already shown interest in religion (Judaism). Some of these people were so pleased with what Judaism offered them that when one really became a convert, he became extremely zealous for Judaism. He was so indoctrinated that he was made into a fanatic, more devoted than many of the Jews themselves. Thus the false teachers caused these converts to heap damnation upon themselves.

Thought 1. One of the strongest lessons to be learned from the Scribes and Pharisees is zeal in evangelism.

1) They had a willingness to go. They who held to a false religion were so willing to go. Why are we, who know the truth, so unwilling to go? Where is our zeal to reach people?
2) They were willing to go anyplace. They travelled worldwide to reach just one convert. Where is our willingness to go as missionaries? As witnesses? Where is our willingness to go even around the corner?

For the Son of Man came to seek and to save what was lost." (Luke 19:10)

Again Jesus said, "Peace be with you! As the Father has sent me, I am sending you." (John 20:21)

But you will receive power when the Holy Spirit comes on you; and you will be my witnesses in Jerusalem, and in all Judea and Samaria, and to the ends of the earth." (Acts 1:8)

He said to them, "Go into all the world and preach the good news to all creation. (Mark 16:15)

Thought 2. The Pharisees should also cause us to search and evaluate our hearts and our religion. Are we teaching the truth? Are we adding to or taking away from God's revelation, that is, from His Word? Are we actually doing just what God has called us to do: to live and work as servants and messengers of God and not as lords of religion and saviors of the world?

DEEPER STUDY # 4

(23:15) **Convert** (proselutos): a stranger, a sojourner (Ex.12:48-49; 22:21; 23:9; Dt.10:19). It is a person who has actually approached and drawn near religion, that is, adopted the beliefs of religion.

There were many converts to Judaism. Two things in particular attracted Gentiles.

1. The concept of one God (monotheism). The idea of many gods ran rampant throughout the world. A thinking man often had difficulty with the idea of a multitude of gods (polytheism). The corrupt worship and divisive demands insisted upon by so many religious gods did not make sense. It left the human soul empty.

Judaism worshipped one God alone, and He was proclaimed to be moral in an absolute sense. God's commandments were consistent with that for which the human soul cried; therefore, many turned to Judaism.

2. The concept of morality. The ancient world ran rampant in injustice and immorality, all sorts of sexual perversion. Weak women and men were abused and used as the strong willed to use them. Judaism's idea of purity and justice appealed to many. Women, who were treated as nothing more than pieces of property for the pleasure of men, were especially attracted to Judaism and its doctrine of morality.

Something needs to be noted about these Gentile worshippers, however. Not all were full-fledged converts or proselytes. They did attend the synagogues throughout the world wherever Jews met, but they were not circumcised nor did they participate in all the ceremonies and observances. They were known as *devout* and *God-fearing* converts or proselytes (Acts 10:2; 17:4).

3 (23:16-22) **Religionists, False**: false religionists mislead others; they are blind guides in oaths and commitments. Note: Christ said that they were blind guides; they misled people. How? They stressed the secondary over the primary. They took the least important and made it more meaningful than the essential. Christ gave two examples.

1. They stressed the gold of the temple over the temple itself. Anyone who swore by the temple did not have to keep his commitment nor was he held responsible for his oath. But if he swore by the gold of the temple, he was held responsible and did have to keep his commitment.
2. They stressed the gift over the altar upon which the gift lay. Making a commitment or swearing by the altar was not binding, whereas a commitment or swearing by the gift was binding.

Christ used strong words against the religionists at this point. They were "blind fools." Christ meant two things by these words.

1. What they were doing and saying was absurd and irrational. Common sense should tell anyone that the temple is greater than what is within it and the altar is greater than the gift that is laid upon it.
2. What they were doing and saying was full of folly and sin. They were merely trying to evade commitments and responsibility for swearing. They wanted the right to make promises and to swear, but they also wanted the right to break their promises if it benefited them later.

Christ pointed out the raw facts about commitments and oaths.

1. All commitments and oaths are heard by God. There is no evasion of commitments made or of things sworn to.
   ⇒ God is the One to whom sacrifices are made upon the altar (implied) (v.20).
   ⇒ God dwells in the temple (v.21).
   ⇒ God sits upon His throne in heaven (v.22).

2. All commitments and oaths are binding and accountable to God.

"Again, you have heard that it was said to the people long ago, 'Do not break your oath, but keep the oaths you have made to the Lord.' But I tell you, Do not swear at

all: either by heaven, for it is God's throne; or by the earth, for it is his footstool; or by Jerusalem, for it is the city of the Great King. And do not swear by your head, for you cannot make even one hair white or black. Simply let your 'Yes' be 'Yes,' and your 'No,' 'No'; anything beyond this comes from the evil one. (Mat 5:33-37)

Thought 1. There are at least four sins seen in what the religionists were saying and doing.
1) The sin of stressing the secondary over the primary.
2) The sin of evading commitments.
3) The sin of covetousness. By stressing the gold over the temple, they were centering the people's minds upon the gold, the wealth, and the gifts instead of upon the God who dwelt in the temple.
4) The sin of self-righteousness. By stressing man's gift over the altar, they were saying in essence that man's gift was more important than God's altar which sanctified the gift. The gift honored the altar instead of the altar's honoring the gift. Such, of course, was ridiculous; for symbolically God stood behind the altar. And no gift is ever greater than God.

Thought 2. The very same sins are committed today.
1) Ritual, ceremony, programs—commitment to practically every phase of church life is often stressed over God. Commitment to the various phases of church life is even said to be commitment to God.
2) The gift is stressed more than the altar. A commitment to give and to make sacrifice often takes precedence over the altar (commitment to God). Stewardship of money (the gift and the gold) is even said to be an equal part with the stewardship of life to God.
3) The motive is often to make the institution stronger instead of making people stronger by centering their lives upon God.

DEEPER STUDY # 5
(23:16-22) **Oath—Swearing—Cursing**: a discussion of oaths can be enlarged to include negative oaths and swearing or what is commonly called *cursing*. It can be broadened on the basis of its definition. An oath is an appeal that something is to be cursed or sworn. (Also see outline and notes—Mt.5:33-37 for more discussion.)

⇒ Sometimes the appeal is for God to do something (damn something); sometimes the appeal (damning) is just declared by the person.
⇒ Sometimes a man swears an oath to God (a commitment); sometimes he swears an oath against something (curses).
⇒ Sometimes a man curses by using words that are distasteful or base; sometimes he chooses words thought to be more socially acceptable such as *rats*, *dog-gone it*, *darn*, etc..

There are at least three things wrong with oaths, swearing, and cursing.

1. Oaths reveal a weak character and lack of trustworthiness. The reason an oath is needed is because a person's word and character are sometimes suspicious and questionable. Therefore, he feels he must enforce his word with an oath. A trustful and trustworthy person only needs to say "yes" or "no." He will stand behind his word (Mt.5:37).

2. All oaths, swearing, and cursing come from the same spirit of emotion and feelings. Just because some words may be more acceptable to society does not mean they are more acceptable to God. It is the heart of emotion and feeling that causes the mouth to speak the words. God judges the heart, not the softness or harshness, tastefulness or distastefulness of the words. It is what is within that God condemns: the untruthfulness, distrustfulness, or willingness to curse because of a self-centered desire to *fit in*.

3. All swearing and cursing makes a person his *own* god. It puts oneself in the place of God. It claims the *right*, the prerogative to act and to curse something. No man has such a right himself. Only God possesses the right and power to speak and act against, to curse and condemn a person.

4 (23:23-24) **Religionists, False**: false religionists stress the lighter commandments and neglect the more important ones. Christ said two things.

1. Religionists stress the lighter duties and neglect the greater duties. They pick and choose what they want and are willing to do and omit the rest. They stress *outward* duties such as tithing, observances, rituals, ceremonies, and works; they minimize the change and *inward* duties of the heart. Christ mentions three duties of the human heart that are omitted.

a. There is justice: treating our neighbor as we should; doing and saying nothing that would hurt another person; showing honor and respect to all men; never being guilty of injustice.
b. There is mercy: showing care, concern, kindness, and tenderness to all who are weak, bad, and needy; and not being hard, distant, demanding, or cruel.
c. There is faithfulness: believing God and trusting Him to fulfill His promises.

Christ said that the more important matters of the law are these: justice and mercy and faithfulness. But the false religionists minimize and omit these matters. They talk about and stress the lighter or outward matters of religion such as tithing. Outward matters such as observances, rituals, and works just do not carry the weight that inward matters of the heart carry. Why? Because, if the heart is right, then outward behavior will follow. All outward behavior will be changed and not just certain areas that have been picked out to show that a person is religious. Note what Christ says: stress the more important matters and do not leave the other undone. Do the lighter, yes, but major upon the more important matters.

2. Religionists avoid the lesser sins but commit the greater sins. They strain at a gnat and swallow a camel. This was a humorous proverb in Christ's day. Wine was carefully strained through a piece of linen cloth to catch gnats and other impurities before drinking. This was to avoid violating the law of purity (Lev.11:20-23; 17:10-14).

The false religionists strained to keep the lighter matters of religion but failed to keep the weightier matters. They did not sin by straining to keep the lighter matters; they sinned by neglecting the more important matters.

"This is what the LORD Almighty says: 'Administer true justice; show mercy and compassion to one another. Do not oppress the widow or the fatherless, the alien

or the poor. In your hearts do not think evil of each other.' (Zec 7:9-10)

Jesus answered, "If you want to be perfect, go, sell your possessions and give to the poor, and you will have treasure in heaven. Then come, follow me." (Mat 19:21)

And the second is like it: 'Love your neighbor as yourself.' (Mat 22:39)

Love must be sincere. Hate what is evil; cling to what is good. (Rom 12:9)

Let no debt remain outstanding, except the continuing debt to love one another, for he who loves his fellowman has fulfilled the law. (Rom 13:8)

Thought 1. Many have a form of religion, but few pay much attention to the more important matters of godliness. How many attend church regularly, give of their money, pray, and take part in church affairs; but they…

- do not give an honest day's work to an employer (justice)?
- do not humble themselves, showing mercy toward the weak and less disciplined?
- do not sacrifice, showing mercy toward the needy and less fortunate?
- do not act responsibly and lovingly toward others, even toward their own family (justice and mercy)?

Having a form of godliness but denying its power. Have nothing to do with them. (2 Tim 3:5)

Thought 2. Think about it. How easy it is to keep up an outward appearance of religion, but how difficult it is to be godly within. Yet inward godliness is what Christ demands. We are to treat all people with pure justice and mercy and to believe God in all things.

Thought 3. One of the great failures of false religionists is this: they emphasize and stress the wrong matters. They stress the lighter matters and omit the more important matters. What they stress is important and should be done, but they are not the major matters.

Thought 4. The false religionist fails at both points of sin. He sins both by omission and commission. He *neglects* the more important duties, and he *commits* the greater sins.

Thought 5. Christ called false religionists "blind guides." Note three things.

1) Some are blind to what Christ was saying. They *do not know* they are stressing the lighter matters. The lighter matters are all they have ever known and been taught. Therefore, they are steeped in the lighter matters, knowing very little about the more important matters of religion.
2) Some *do know* they are stressing the lighter matters; and they deliberately continue in their error, refusing to change lest they face ridicule, loss of position, security, and all they count dear in this world.
3) Religionists are guides, teaching the lighter matters of religion and omitting the weightier matters.

DEEPER STUDY # 6

(23:23) **Tithe—Mint—Dill—Cummin**: the tithe was always important to Jewish religion. The tithe was used to keep up the temple and to provide for the priests who served God and the people.

Be sure to set aside a tenth of all that your fields produce each year. Eat the tithe of your grain, new wine and oil, and the firstborn of your herds and flocks in the presence of the LORD your God at the place he will choose as a dwelling for his Name, so that you may learn to revere the LORD your God always. (Deu 14:22-23)

"'A tithe of everything from the land, whether grain from the soil or fruit from the trees, belongs to the LORD; it is holy to the LORD. (Lev 27:30)

Note that the tithe was to be corn, wine, and oil. The Pharisees expanded the tithe to include all crops, including the smallest potted and garden plants, such as mint, dill, and cummin. Such plants were grown only in small patches for a family's use and never in large quantities. All three were used in cooking. Dill and cummin were also used as medicines. The religionists even included the leaves and stalks of the plants in their tithes. Imagine such strictness that would tithe a certain number of leaves and a small portion of stalk. But note something: Christ says such a spirit of strictness in tithing should be true of our lives. We should never fail to tithe (see note—Mt.23:23-24).

5 (23:25-26) **Religionists, False—Heart—Purity**: false religionists are blind to real cleanness. Christ used an illustration to show just how blind a religionist can be. Religionists are like cups and dishes which have been washed on the outside but left dirty on the inside.

Christ made three points about the illustration.

1. The outside of the cup and dish of the religionists appeared clean. It was the outside that concerned them, for it was the outside that was seen. So they washed and cleaned the outside. The point is well taken. They guarded against scandalous sins, sins that would damage their image and reputation among neighbors and the public. Publicly they walked uprightly, just as the public thought they should. Their concern was what people thought, not what God thought.

2. The inside of the cup and dish of the religionists was dirty. The inside was not seen by men, so they paid little or no attention to it. They took what they wanted and lived as they wished. They were full of extortion and self-indulgence, that is, greed and selfishness, robbery and indulgence, lusting and consuming, taking and seldom sharing, getting and seldom giving. Such is what is on the inside of the religionists: a selfishness and greed for a following, for security, position, influence, attention, recognition, and acknowledgment. The religionists would never commit a gross visible sin, yet they would hold selfish greed and excessive desires within, living self-centered and indulgent lives.

3. The religionists needed to clean up the inside of their hearts. Once the inside was clean, then the outside would be automatically clean. If their spirits were clean, their outside behavior would be clean. A clean heart will lead to a clean life. Christ teaches that it is the inside of a man that determines his behavior. It is the heart that determines what a man does.

Above all else, guard your heart, for it is the wellspring of life. (Prov 4:23)

The good man brings good things out of the good stored up in him, and the evil man brings evil things out of the evil stored up in him. (Mat 12:35)

For out of the heart come evil thoughts, murder, adultery, sexual immorality, theft, false testimony, slander. These are what make a man 'unclean'; but eating with unwashed hands does not make him 'unclean.'" (Mat 15:19-20)

Note: Christ called the false religionist *blind*. The false religionist does not know that the inside of a man can be cleansed. He does not know that it is a cleansed heart than changes behavior.

Thought 1. The whole approach of man and society is to change the outside of a man in order to change him inside. Change his environment, situation, circumstances, education, housing, nourishment, job, beliefs, philosophy, and self-image and he will become *good*.

Christ's point is that all of the above are determined by man's heart. A bad environment is due to evil within men. A poor education is due to evil short-comings within men. A man can have the very best environment and education yet still be evil. It is not the environment and education that changes the evil within men. It is God. Let God change the heart; then a man will be clean on the outside. He will live justly and mercifully toward all men, doing all he can to build the right environment and educational opportunities for all men.

6 (23:27-28) **Religionists, False—Spiritual Death**: false religionists disguise inner decay. Christ again used an illustration to make His point. He said that religionists are like tombs that have been washed white and freshly cleansed. Outwardly they appear clean and white, but within they are full of dead men's bones.

The picture of the freshly cleansed tombs was taken from the countryside of Jesus' day. Tombs dotting the roadways and countryside were a common sight. Jewish law said that anyone who touched a dead body became unclean (Num.19:16). Therefore, tombs had to be clearly marked and kept up, not only to show respect for the family and deceased but also to prevent travellers from becoming *religiously* unclean.

There was one particular time during the year when the danger of touching a tomb became a serious threat. That was during the Passover season when teeming thousands of pilgrims swarmed over the roads and countryside leading to Jerusalem. One of the preparations made for the feast was the cleansing or washing of the tombs in order to make them clearly visible. It was probably these newly whited tombs, sparkling in the sunlight as they dotted the countryside, that Jesus was picturing.

The great wrong with the false religionist is this: outwardly, he appears righteous; but inwardly, he is full of hypocrisy and wickedness.

The Lord's contrast between outward appearance and inward truth is thought-provoking.

⇒ Outwardly we may attend church regularly, but what is the inward truth during the week?

⇒ Outwardly we may profess religion, but what is the inward truth out in the market place?

⇒ Outwardly we may give thanks as a family at meals, but what is the inward truth toward the hungry of the world?

⇒ Outwardly we may agree with justice and mercy, but what is the inward truth in dealing with money?

⇒ Outwardly we may bow our heads in a prayer of thanksgiving, but what is the inward truth toward other sinners?

⇒ Outwardly we may walk humbly before our peers, but what is the inward truth toward the derelict and those down and out?

Something is often forgotten. Christ preached against the outward sins of passion which society often considers the gross sins, but He condemned much more strongly the inward sins of the spirit such as pride and greed. Sinners and harlots enter heaven much more quickly than *religionists* who do not surrender their lives to Jesus Christ. This is exactly what Jesus Christ said (Mt.21:31-32). The world's concept is that a person is acceptable to God if he does not commit a gross sin. What he is within his heart and what he is behind the scene and closed doors matter little. He is an acceptable member of the community if he is...

- respectable
- successful
- wealthy
- money-shrewd
- nice-looking
- famous
- powerful
- gainfully employed

Note: Christ said the false religionist is "full of dead men's bones." This is most likely referring to spiritual death. The false religionist goes through life *living acceptably* in the eyes of men, but he is spiritually dead to God. His acts are the acts of a man-made morality and religion, not the acts of true morality and religion as revealed by God in Christ.

In the same way, on the outside you appear to people as righteous but on the inside you are full of hypocrisy and wickedness. (Mat 23:28)

"Woe to you, because you are like unmarked graves, which men walk over without knowing it." (Luke 11:44)

Meanwhile, when a crowd of many thousands had gathered, so that they were trampling on one another, Jesus began to speak first to his disciples, saying: "Be on your guard against the yeast of the Pharisees, which is hypocrisy. There is nothing concealed that will not be disclosed, or hidden that will not be made known. (Luke 12:1-2)

For it is shameful even to mention what the disobedient do in secret. (Eph 5:12)

The Spirit clearly says that in later times some will abandon the faith and follow deceiving spirits and things taught by demons. Such teachings come through hypocritical liars, whose consciences have been seared as with a hot iron. (1 Tim 4:1-2)

They claim to know God, but by their actions they deny him. They are detestable, disobedient and unfit for doing anything good. (Titus 1:16)

Thought 1. False religion is the most beautiful and deadly tomb among men. It leads to the eternal death of man's spirit. It makes him insensitive to the danger of eternal death by instilling a sense...

- of confidence in being religious.
- of security in being religious.
- of acceptability in being religious.
- of pride in being religious.
- of righteousness in being religious.

Thought 2. Others may not know the truth—the truth of the closed doors and the dark—the sinful secrets of the heart. We may appear respectable to men. The heart can be full of secrets and full of sin; the life can appear free of blame. But God knows all secrets, and God knows what fills the heart.

The point is clear: God shall judge the secrets of men. Then the sinful heart will be in hell, and it will find no comfort in remembering that it appeared respectable to men (Ro.2:16; Lk.16:23).

7 (23:29-33) **Religionists, False—Heritage—Roots**: false religionists pride themselves in a godly heritage. Christ said four significant things about this point.

1. False religionists honor the relics of the past. They show great respect for former prophets. They build, renovate, adorn and look after the tombs of the great men of the past. But note: Christ says they pay honor to their tombs and memory, not to their teaching and godly lives.

2. False religionists denounce former abuses. Their forefathers had rejected, abused, and killed many of the prophets. The false religionists denounced such evil behavior. They preached and taught against murder.

3. False religionists are prideful, claiming that they are better than the religious people of former years. They feel they are beyond such sins and would never have rejected and abused the prophets of God. They believe they would have gladly heard the preachers of the past and done exactly what they said.

4. False religionists testify against themselves. They reverence the prophets of old but reject the prophets who are living. They reverence Abraham, Moses, Jeremiah, and Zechariah; but they reject God's very own Son. In rejecting Him, they prove that they are just as their fathers were: murderers. They are children of their fathers, following in the very steps of their fathers, rejecting the messengers of God. Like father, like son.

Note what Christ said: they were filling up the measure or cup of murder which was begun by their fathers. Christ was probably saying that His death was the last drop. The cup was about to reach the *filled* point; the cup would not be able to take another drop. There would be no chance to turn to God after they killed *the Prophet*, Christ Himself (see outline and notes—Mt.22:1-14).

> **But because of your stubbornness and your unrepentant heart, you are storing up wrath against yourself for the day of God's wrath, when his righteous judgment will be revealed. God "will give to each person according to what he has done." (Rom 2:5-6)**
> **And I saw the dead, great and small, standing before the throne, and books were opened. Another book was opened, which is the book of life. The dead were judged according to what they had done as recorded in the books. (Rev 20:12; cp. Rev.22:12)**
> **And that you, O Lord, are loving. Surely you will reward each person according to what he has done. (Psa 62:12)**
> **If you say, "But we knew nothing about this," does not he who weighs the heart perceive it? Does not he who guards your life know it? Will he not repay each person according to what he has done? (Prov 24:12)**
> **"I the LORD search the heart and examine the mind, to reward a man according to his conduct, according to what his deeds deserve." (Jer 17:10)**

Thought 1. It is easy to honor great men of the past. They are not present to speak the truth and demand that we follow the truth. A dead man cannot disturb us with his warnings.

Thought 2. Every generation has *this one* great deception: since they are more educated and technologically advanced, they think they are stronger and better off than the former generation. They think...

- if they had been given the opportunities of the past, they would have done more with them.
- if they had faced the temptations of the past, they would have withstood them better.

8 (23:34-36) **Religionists, False**: false religionists reject and abuse many of God's present-day prophets. Christ said He was going to send forth messengers with the message of God, but false religionists were going to beat (flog, scourge), persecute, and kill them. They were going to be dogged in their persecution, following after God's messenger from city to city.

Note: Christ said something else, something of terrible consequence to false religionists. All the abuse and all the righteous blood shed throughout human history is to be laid to the account of false religionists. Why? Because they of all people had the greatest opportunity.

> **The people of Israel. Theirs is the adoption as sons; theirs the divine glory, the covenants, the receiving of the law, the temple worship and the promises. (Rom 9:4)**

Thought 1. There is one question that every man needs to face: When I am gone, what will the verdict be? What kind of legacy will I leave behind? Did I hinder or help God?

> **And I saw the dead, great and small, standing before the throne, and books were opened. Another book was opened, which is the book of life. The dead were judged according to what they had done as recorded in the books. (Rev 20:12)**

DEEPER STUDY # 7
(23:34) **Prophets**: see DEEPER STUDY # 1—1 Cor.14:3; note—Eph.4:11.

DEEPER STUDY # 8
(23:34) **Wise men**: the wise servants of God who are especially gifted by the Holy Spirit with godly wisdom.

DEEPER STUDY # 9
(23:34) **Scribes—Teachers**: not the Judaistic Scribe, but men who would be gifted by the Holy Spirit to teach the New Testament, the great Covenant of Christ Himself, of God's very own Son.

DEEPER STUDY # 10
(23:35) **Abel**: cp. Gen.4:8-10; Heb.12:24.

DEEPER STUDY # 11
(23:35) **Zechariah**: there is some doubt as to who this is. It is probably not Zechariah the prophet, but the Zechariah who was stoned and killed in the court of the Lord's house (2 Chron.24:20-21). His father, called Jehoiada in the Old Testament and Barachias in the New Testament, was probably known by both names. It was common for Jews to have two names. The main support for this explanation is based upon the Jewish Bible. The books of the Jewish Bible are arranged differently from the Christian Bible. Second Chronicles is the *last book* of the Jewish Bible. Jesus is simply saying (referring to the arrangement of the Jewish Scriptures) that the false religionists are guilty of all the righteous blood throughout history, from the first murder, Abel, to the last murder, Zechariah.

DEEPER STUDY # 12
(23:36) **Generation, This**: "all this" will come in a terrible judgment upon the generation of Christ's day. They stand especially guilty because they had such a unique opportunity: they had the very presence of God's Son visibly among them (Jn.20:29).

However, does this mean they are to bear a special judgment in eternity because of their special privileges (Ro.9:1-5)? Or is the reference to the destruction of Jerusalem and the nation under Titus in 70 A.D.? Both positions are held by various commentators.

	N. The Great Lament of Jesus: Jesus' Love Rejected, 23:37-39 (Lk.13:34-35)
1 The past sin of Jerusalem: Persecuted God's messengers **2 The great love of Christ for Jerusalem**DS1 a. Patient: "How often" b. Cared & protected: "Gather" **3 The great sin of Jerusalem: Rejected the Messiah**	37 "O Jerusalem, Jerusalem, you who kill the prophets and stone those sent to you, how often I have longed to gather your children together, as a hen gathers her chicks under her wings, but you were not willing.
4 The terrifying judgment upon Jerusalem a. Deserted & desolateDS2	38 Look, your house is left to you desolate.
c. Blinded to the Messiah **5 The glorious prediction: Jerusalem & Israel will proclaim the Messiah**	39 For I tell you, you will not see me again until you say, 'Blessed is he who comes in the name of the Lord.'"

DIVISION XIV

THE MESSIAH'S LAST WEEK: HIS CLAIM CHALLENGED AND REJECTED, 21:1-23:39

N. The Great Lament of Jesus: Jesus' Love Rejected, 23:37-39

(23:37-39) **Introduction—Jerusalem—Israel**: God's great love for Jerusalem and for Israel is seen in this passage. This is Christ's great lament for Jerusalem, the city of God, and for Israel, the people of God. God's love, which was demonstrated perfectly by giving His one and only Son, was rejected. Christ sighed from the depth of His heart and wept. He cried out with intense groanings:

> **"O Jerusalem, Jerusalem, you who kill the prophets and stone those sent to you, how often I have longed to gather your children together, as a hen gathers her chicks under her wings, but you were not willing. (Mat 23:37)**

The depth of the Lord's emotion and broken heart can never be known by man. Why? Because Christ knew that God's loving appeal had been in vain. The people who were chosen to be God's witness upon earth, that is, Jerusalem, "[had] sinned greatly" (Lam.1:8). They had rejected the only begotten Son of God, their very own Messiah and Savior.

However, God's great love for Jerusalem is not all that is seen in the Lord's words. God's justice is seen upbraiding Jerusalem.

> **"O Jerusalem, Jerusalem, you who kill the prophets and stone those sent to you, how often I have longed to gather your children together, as a hen gathers her chicks under her wings, but you were not willing. Look, your house is left to you desolate. For I tell you, you will not see me again until you say, 'Blessed is he who comes in the name of the Lord.'" (Mat 23:37-39)**

The depth of the city's sin, being stored up over the centuries, could never be known by man (Ro.2:5). The measure of the cup had been filled. The time had now come…

> **God "will give to each person according to what he has done." To those who by persistence in doing good seek glory, honor and immortality, he will give eternal life. But for those who are self-seeking and who reject the truth and follow evil, there will be wrath and anger. There will be trouble and distress for every human being who does evil: first for the Jew, then for the Gentile; (Rom 2:6-9)**

The place of Jerusalem in God's heart is seen in this great passage, but the terrifying judgment of God's heart is also seen. All those who reject His Son shall be judged and condemned—no matter who they are, both Jew and Gentile. The passage is applicable to all of us (add vs. 10 and 11 to Ro.2:6-9 quoted above and see outline and notes—Ro.11:11-16; 11:17-24 for more discussion).

1. The past sin of Jerusalem: they persecuted God's messengers (v.37).
2. The great love of Christ for Jerusalem (v.37).
3. The great sin of Jerusalem: they rejected the Messiah (v.37).
4. The terrifying judgment upon Jerusalem (v.38-39).
5. The glorious prediction: Jerusalem and Israel will proclaim the Messiah (v.39).

1 (23:37) **Jews, Sins of**: the great sin of Jerusalem is that they persecuted God's messengers. They ridiculed, abused, and killed the messengers of God. Christ, of course, was speaking to all unbelieving Israelites; but He specified Jerusalem because it was the capital, the place where the Sanhedrin (the ruling court of the Jews) sat. Some examples of Israel's rejecting and abusing the messengers of God would be…

- the reaction against and imprisonment of Hanani (2 Chron.16:7-10, esp. 10).
- the stoning of Zacharias (2 Chron.24:20-21; Mt.23:35).
- the hatred and imprisonment of Micaiah (1 Ki.22:7-27, esp. 27).
- the casting of Jeremiah into a dungeon (Jer.38:6).
- the attempt to silence Amos (Amos 7:11-13).

Some examples of persecution by the Sanhedrin after Christ would be...

- the issuing of warrants for the arrest of early believers (Acts 9:2).
- the orders to round up and persecute early believers (Acts 8:1).
- the stoning of Stephen (Acts 7:57-60).

The ridicule and persecution of God's messengers were so common down through the centuries that Christ was led to say on another occasion: "For surely no prophet can die outside Jerusalem" (Lk.13:33).

God holds His messengers very dear to His heart, and He is extremely protective of them. To ridicule and abuse one of His servants is a very serious offense. Jerusalem and the people of Israel were guilty of many sins, but it is this sin that is the *most condemning*. In conjunction with this thought is this fact: it was primarily the grumbling of Israel in the wilderness against God that caused God to judge that generation so severely.

Scripture says:

> **Who are you to judge someone else's servant? To his own master he stands or falls. And he will stand, for the Lord is able to make him stand. (Rom 14:4)**

Thought 1. The true messenger of God is often ridiculed, abused and persecuted. Two facts need to be noted about this.

1) The reason for their persecution: God's concern is the correcting of an unjust world; the changing of a self-righteous heart; the purifying of a lustful mind; the sacrificing of a selfish life. Men oppose God's correction and His demand for change and purity. They oppose the sacrifice of oneself—oppose such restraint by nature. Therefore, men often oppose the messenger who *truly* proclaims God's Word.
2) The leaders of the persecution are often false religionists who are wrapped up in the world and its institutional religions. They feel threatened by a message that proclaims there is *truth* beyond man himself. Such a positive message endangers their own humanistic beliefs and threatens them with loss of security, livelihood, prestige, and all that this world offers.

2 (23:37) **Jesus Christ, Love**: the great love of Christ is strongly pictured in this passage (see note—Mt.23:37-39)—both His patience and His great desire to care for and protect people.

1. His patience is seen in the words, "How often I have longed...." He personally would have saved the people. He would have saved them often. He desired their salvation, not their condemnation (cp. Jn.3:17). Jerusalem had abused and even killed many of His messengers, yet God had not turned away from them. He continued to send messengers, and finally, He sent His Son. Time and again He reached out to the people through men of God; and each time Jerusalem rejected, abused, and sometimes killed His servants. The patience of God endured and endured with man's sin in the knowledge that some would be saved (see outline—Ro.9:22-24; cp. 2 Pt.3:8-9).

2. His care and protection are seen in the word "gather." The picture of a hen's gathering her chickens under her wings is the picture of care and protection. The very purpose of Christ is to gather and keep a person from wandering around and facing the dangers of the world all alone.

> **He will cover you with his feathers, and under his wings you will find refuge; his faithfulness will be your shield and rampart. (Psa 91:4)**

Thought 1. Christ longs to gather us to Himself *often*. Every time we hear the gospel and sense a pull within our hearts to draw near Him, He is reaching out to gather us unto Himself.

> **But I, when I am lifted up from the earth, will draw all men to myself." (John 12:32)**
>
> **But concerning Israel he says, "All day long I have held out my hands to a disobedient and obstinate people." (Rom 10:21)**
>
> **We are therefore Christ's ambassadors, as though God were making his appeal through us. We implore you on Christ's behalf: Be reconciled to God. (2 Cor 5:20)**
>
> **Here I am! I stand at the door and knock. If anyone hears my voice and opens the door, I will come in and eat with him, and he with me. (Rev 3:20)**
>
> **The LORD appeared to us in the past, saying: "I have loved you with an everlasting love; I have drawn you with loving-kindness. (Jer 31:3)**

DEEPER STUDY # 1

(23:37) **Jesus Christ, Deity**: the words "How often I have longed to gather your children together" point backward to all the history of Israel. Christ was saying He was One with God. He was the One who was overseeing Israel throughout its history, the One who would have gathered Israel under His care and protection.

3 (23:37) **Jews, Sins of**: the *great* sin of Jerusalem was this: the people rejected God's one and only Son. Note the words "you were not willing." He would have saved them, but they would not be saved. They heard Christ; they saw Christ; they were even able to touch Christ (1 Jn.1:1), but they rejected Him. And their rejection was *deliberate*.

⇒ They rejected the love of God which was demonstrated to them in Christ. God demonstrated His love by giving His one and only Son.

⇒ They rejected the terms of God's demand. God demanded that they live for Him. How? By believing in God's Son and by living holy lives day by day. Then they were to go forth and proclaim the message of sal-vation in God's Son.

⇒ They rejected God's righteousness (faith in Christ) and trusted their own righteousness (see DEEPER STUDY # 2—Ro.4:22).

Thought 1. Men reject Christ for the very same reasons.
1) They reject the revelation of God to man.

"For God so loved the world that he gave his one and only Son, that whoever believes in him shall not perish but have eternal life. (John 3:16)

But God demonstrates his own love for us in this: While we were still sinners, Christ died for us. (Rom 5:8)

2) They reject Christ's claim to be the revelation of God, to be the Son of God.

Jesus heard that they had thrown him out, and when he found him, he said, "Do you believe in the Son of Man?" "Who is he, sir?" the man asked. "Tell me so that I may believe in him." Jesus said, "You have now seen him; in fact, he is the one speaking with you." (John 9:35-37)

"We are not stoning you for any of these," replied the Jews, "but for blasphemy, because you, a mere man, claim to be God." (John 10:33)

What about the one whom the Father set apart as his very own and sent into the world? Why then do you accuse me of blasphemy because I said, 'I am God's Son'? (John 10:36)

Then Jesus cried out, "When a man believes in me, he does not believe in me only, but in the one who sent me. When he looks at me, he sees the one who sent me. (John 12:44-45)

Jesus answered: "Don't you know me, Philip, even after I have been among you such a long time? Anyone who has seen me has seen the Father. How can you say, 'Show us the Father'? (John 14:9)

3) They reject God's righteousness and trust their own righteousness.

Since they did not know the righteousness that comes from God and sought to establish their own, they did not submit to God's righteousness. Christ is the end of the law so that there may be righteousness for everyone who believes. (Rom 10:3-4)

Those who are pure in their own eyes and yet are not cleansed of their filth; (Prov 30:12)

4 (23:38-39) **Judgment—Jesus, Judgment of**: the terrifying judgment upon Jerusalem was threefold.

1. Their house was to be deserted by God, "left in their own hands." The word "house" refers to their temple, their nation and their lives. They wanted control of all; to do as they willed with their lives and possessions. Christ said that God would grant their wish. God's presence was going to depart their temple, their nation, and their lives; and He was going to leave all in their hands (see DEEPER STUDY # 2—Mt.23:38).

2. Their house was to be desolated. It was to be destroyed. This would be a reference both to earthly judgment (the lack of God's presence) when Jerusalem was devastated by Titus in 70 A.D. and to eternal judgment (Heb.9:27). It should be noted, however, that many ancient manuscripts do not have the word "desolate" in their text.

3. They would thereafter be unable to see Christ. This meant two things.

a. They would not be able to see Him soon. He was departing the world, dying, and ascending into God's presence. They would not see Him again until He returned.
b. They would continue to be blind and obstinate in their unbelief. They would not submit to Christ as the Messiah, the very Son of God. Therefore, they would be blinded as part of the judgment of God (Ro.11:7-10, 25).

Thought 1. The same three judgments are applicable to every man and nation who walk in obstinate unbelief.
1) God will desert them.

Therefore God gave them over in the sinful desires of their hearts to sexual impurity for the degrading of their bodies with one another. (Rom 1:24)

Because of this, God gave them over to shameful lusts. Even their women exchanged natural relations for unnatural ones. In the same way the men also abandoned natural relations with women and were inflamed with lust for one another. Men committed indecent acts with other men, and received in themselves the due penalty for their perversion. Furthermore, since they did not think it worthwhile to retain the knowledge of God, he gave them over to a depraved mind, to do what ought not to be done. (Rom 1:26-28)

2) God will destroy them.

The ax is already at the root of the trees, and every tree that does not produce good fruit will be cut down and thrown into the fire." (Luke 3:9)

And give relief to you who are troubled, and to us as well. This will happen when the Lord Jesus is revealed from heaven in blazing fire with his powerful angels. He will punish those who do not know God and do not obey the gospel of our Lord Jesus. They will be punished with everlasting destruction and shut out from the presence of the Lord and from the majesty of his power (2 Th 1:7-9)

If this is so, then the Lord knows how to rescue godly men from trials and to hold the unrighteous for the day of judg-ment, while continuing their punishment. (2 Pet 2:9)

By the same word the present heavens and earth are reserved for fire, being kept for the day of judgment and destruction of ungodly men. (2 Pet 3:7)

Enoch, the seventh from Adam, prophesied about these men: "See, the Lord is coming with thousands upon thousands of his holy ones to judge everyone, and to convict all the ungodly of all the

ungodly acts they have done in the ungodly way, and of all the harsh words ungodly sinners have spoken against him." (Jude 1:14-15)

3) They will be unable to see Christ.

"Then he will say to those on his left, 'Depart from me, you who are cursed, into the eternal fire prepared for the devil and his angels. (Mat 25:41)

"But he will reply, 'I don't know you or where you come from. Away from me, all you evildoers!' (Luke 13:27)

For the wages of sin is death, but the gift of God is eternal life in Christ Jesus our Lord. (Rom 6:23)

Just as man is destined to die once, and after that to face judgment, (Heb 9:27)

DEEPER STUDY # 2
(23:38) **Desolate** (eremos): to lay waste and make into a wilderness; to desert. Without the presence of God a place and person are like a wilderness, deserted and left all alone. They are left to waste away.

5 (23:39) **Jews, Restoration**: Jesus shares the glorious prediction that Jerusalem and Israel will proclaim the Messiah. Israel will not be blinded to Jesus as the true Messiah forever; Israel will profess and proclaim Jesus to be the Messiah.

Note two things.

1. The words "until you say" look to the future. Israel will not be blinded forever. Israel will profess Jesus to the Messiah. That day is coming.

2. The words "blessed is He who comes" look to the return of Jesus. Israel is going to proclaim Jesus to be the Messiah when He returns in great glory "in the name of the Lord" (Jehovah) (cp. Ph.2:9-11). (See outline and notes—Ro.11:25-36. Cp. outline and notes—Ro.9:1-11:36.)

I do not want you to be ignorant of this mystery, brothers, so that you may not be conceited: Israel has experienced a hardening in part until the full number of the Gentiles has come in. And so all Israel will be saved, as it is written: "The deliverer will come from Zion; he will turn godlessness away from Jacob. And this is my covenant with them when I take away their sins." (Rom 11:25-27)

For the Israelites will live many days without king or prince, without sacrifice or sacred stones, without ephod or idol. Afterward the Israelites will return and seek the LORD their God and David their king. They will come trembling to the LORD and to his blessings in the last days. (Hosea 3:4-5)

"And I will pour out on the house of David and the inhabitants of Jerusalem a spirit of grace and supplication. They will look on me, the one they have pierced, and they will mourn for him as one mourns for an only child, and grieve bitterly for him as one grieves for a firstborn son. (Zec 12:10)

Thought 1. One of the most glorious moments of life is when a person turns to Christ and proclaims Him to be the Messiah. It is a *turning* that every person should experience. Israel will experience this one day.

Outline	Scripture
	CHAPTER 24 **XV. THE MESSIAH'S PROPHECY OF HIS RETURN AND THE END OF THE AGE: THE OLIVET DISCOURSE,[DS1,2] 24:1-25:46** **A. The Signs of the Last Days,[DS3] 24:1-14** (Mk.13:1-13; Lk.21:5-11)
1 Events that led to the great prophecies a. Disciples admired the temple's magnificence & showed it to Jesus	Jesus left the temple and was walking away when his disciples came up to him to call his attention to its buildings.
b. Jesus used the occasion to arouse interest in prophecy: Predicted the temple's utter destruction[DS4]	2 "Do you see all these things?" he asked. "I tell you the truth, not one stone here will be left on another; every one will be thrown down."
c. Disciples were aroused: Asked two questions 1) When would the temple be destroyed 2) What signs would precede Christ's return & the world's end	3 As Jesus was sitting on the Mount of Olives, the disciples came to him privately. "Tell us," they said, "when will this happen, and what will be the sign of your coming and of the end of the age?"
d. Jesus warned: Must guard against deception	4 Jesus answered: "Watch out that no one deceives you.
2 Sign 1: False messiahs	5 For many will come in my name, claiming, 'I am the Christ,' and will deceive many.
3 Sign 2: World violence	6 You will hear of wars and rumors of wars, but see to it that you are not alarmed. Such things must happen, but the end is still to come.
4 Sign 3: Natural disasters (Note: These signs are the beginning of sorrows or birth pains)[DS5]	7 Nation will rise against nation, and kingdom against kingdom. There will be famines and earthquakes in various places. 8 All these are the beginning of birth pains.
5 Sign 4: Severe religious persecution	9 "Then you will be handed over to be persecuted and put to death, and you will be hated by all nations because of me.
6 Sign 5: Terrible apostasy—betrayal & division	10 At that time many will turn away from the faith and will betray and hate each other,
7 Sign 6: The rising of many false leaders—offering false hope	11 And many false prophets will appear and deceive many people.
8 Sign 7: A great falling away—sin's increasing & love's growing cold[DS6,7]	12 Because of the increase of wickedness, the love of most will grow cold,
9 Sign 8: Some enduring & being saved	13 But he who stands firm to the end will be saved.
10 Sign 9: World evangelism	14 And this gospel of the kingdom will be preached in the whole world as a testimony to all nations, and then the end will come.

DIVISION XV

THE MESSIAH'S PROPHECY OF HIS RETURN AND THE END OF THE AGE: THE OLIVET DISCOURSE, 24:1-25:46

A. The Signs of the Last Days, 24:1-14

(24:1-25:46) DIVISION OVERVIEW: End Time: these two chapters, Mt.24-25, deal with three great subjects. All three subjects lay out in the future as Christ discussed them.

1. The destruction of Jerusalem (v.3; cp. v.2).
2. The Lord's return (v.3).
3. The end of the world (v.3).

A quick glance at the first four verses will show the events that led Jesus to deal with the great prophecies covered by these chapters.

1. The disciples admire the temple's magnificence and draw Jesus' attention to its beauty (v.1). The temple was magnificent. It sat upon the towering summit of Mount Sion. It was built of white marble plated with gold. The temple was a massive structure that could hold thousands of people (cp. Acts 4:4 where five thousand men were saved among a crowd which probably numbered many thousands more). The temple had several porches such as Solomon's Porch and the Royal Porch. Each porch was supported with huge towering pillars, each one so large that it took three to four men reaching arm to arm to reach around it. The temple was a striking sight, one of the building wonders of the world. The disciples apparently stood some place where the temple in all its magnificent beauty struck them with awe, and they wanted Christ to see the beautiful sight.

2. Jesus uses the occasion to arouse the disciples' interest in coming events. He predicts the temple's utter destruction (v.2).

3. The disciples are aroused to ask two questions of the Lord. When will the temple be destroyed and what will be the sign of His return and of the end of the world (v.3) (see note—Lk.21:5-7).

4. Jesus warns His disciples. They must guard against being deceived (v.4). This can mean one or two things. A person can be easily deceived when dealing with end-time prophecies, or a person can be easily deceived when facing the end-time events. He can be deceived into thinking that certain cataclysmic events are infallible signs that the end is at hand (v.6, 14). Such too often results...

- in wild guesses about the end time.
- in universal predictions.
- in the deceiving of others.
- in discouragement of one's faith when the end does not come.

DEEPER STUDY # 1

(24:1-31) **End Time**: noting the exact words of Christ will help in understanding this passage.

1. Christ says, "All these are the beginning of birth pains" (v.8) or of sorrows. The words "the beginning of birth pains" indicate that Christ is dealing with "the beginning" of a terrible period of trial for the believer ("you," v.9). He is not *just* referring to the normal trials that occur upon earth or the regular persecutions that are launched against believers over the centuries (see DEEPER STUDY # 2—Mt.24:1-31). World trouble and persecutions against God's people have always existed, even from the beginning of time. The great sorrow He now speaks about refers to some terrible period which is so terrible that it can be said to be the "*the beginning* of birth pains" or "woes," a time which is to be distinguished from all other trouble the world and believers have suffered throughout history.

2. Christ says, "When you see standing in the holy place 'the abomination that causes desolation'...then...flee...for then there will be great distress, unequaled from the beginning of the world until now" (v.15-16, 21). There is no question about this sign. It launches the worst period of distress [tribulation] the world has ever seen. This sign definitely points to a specific period of human history. As to what the period should be called, it is probably best to simply use the words of Scripture and title it "great distress" (v.21).

3. Now, note what Christ has said in the above verses.

> **"All these are the beginning of birth pains" (v.8).**
>
> **"So when you see standing in the holy place 'the abomination that causes desolation,' spoken of through the prophet Daniel—let the reader understand— then let those who are in Judea flee to the mountains. For then there will be great distress, unequaled from the beginning of the world until now—and never to be equaled again. (Mat 24:15-16, 21)**

Christ seems to be giving a list of signs, *one of which* is "the abomination that causes desolation." In verses 5-14, He gives nine signs, the ninth's being world evangelism (v.14). He closes this ninth sign with the words, "Then the end will come" (v.14). But note in verse 15 how He seems to pick up the signs again, giving what seems to be the most visible and terrible sign for which to watch. Note His words, reading verses 14, 15, and 21 together.

> **And this gospel of the kingdom will be preached in the whole world as a testimony to all nations, and then the end will come. "So when you see standing in the holy place 'the abomination that causes desolation,' spoken of through the prophet Daniel—let the reader understand—then let those who are in Judea flee to the mountains. For then there will be great distress, unequaled from the beginning of the world until now—and never to be equaled again. (Mat 24:14-16, 21)**

Christ is saying there is a difference between the signs that precede "the abomination" and the unparalleled trials that follow. When "the abomination that causes desolation" stands in the holy place, the trials that follow are much, much worse—unparalleled in human history.

"The abomination that causes desolation" is the sign that launches the worst distress [tribulations] the world has ever known. Just when this abomination will appear, Christ does not say. But His appearance is one of the ten signs Christ gives; and His appearance will signal the worst devastation ever known by the world.

A chart diagramming Christ's own words will perhaps help in understanding what He says.

1. His words are: "All these (signs) are the beginning of birth pains" (v.8).

2. "When you see standing in the holy place...the abomination that causes desolation...*then there will be great distress*" (v.15, 21).

3. "Immediately after the distress of those days... all...*will see* the Son of Man coming" (v.29-31).

THE END OF THE WORLD

Signs which are "The beginning of birth pains" (v.8).	*Seeing the Sign of theAbomination that causes Desolation In the Middle of the Time or Years* (v.15)	Unparalleled trials of "the great distress" (v.21)	*Seeing the Son of Man Coming* (v.29-30) "His angels...will gather His elect" (v.31)

Another way to express what Christ is saying in these chapters, which may be of help as we seek to understand His words, is as follows.

1. Christ is asked two questions by the disciples: When shall the temple be destroyed, and what shall be the sign of thy coming and of the end of the world?

2. Christ answers by giving nine signs (v.5-14). When He gives the ninth sign, world evangelism, He says, "And then the end will come" (v.14).

3. Christ then says in essence, "But there is a tenth sign, a sign that you should see and for which you should watch. And this tenth sign He discusses at some length. He says: "When you see the abomination that causes desolation..." (v.15-28).

   a. It shall launch the worst tribulation or distress the world has ever seen (v.15-22).
   b. It shall cause a frantic search for the Messiah and false prophets, that is, for a great deliverer (v.23-26).
   c. But know this: the return of Christ will not be in an isolated place or done in secret (v.26). His return will be as lightning: it will be quick, stretching across the sky and visible to all (v.27-28).

4. Christ then says, "Immediately after the distress [tribulation] of those days" He will return (v.29-31).

Many Biblical scholars point out great similarities between what Christ says about the end time and sections of Revelation (Mt.24; Mk.13; Lk.21. See notes—Rev.6:1-7:1; 7:1; 8:1; 11:15; 16:1-21.)

1. There seems to be a similarity between the structure of what Christ says and the book of Revelation in dealing with the end time (see notes given in paragraph above).

• The beginning of sorrow or birth pains: preliminary sorrows, trouble and evil in society and nature; yet world evangelism continues (Mt.24:5-14).	....corresponds to	...The Seven Seals (Rev.6:1-17)
• "The Great Distress [Tribulation]": unparalleled...trials (Mt.24:15-28).	....corresponds to	...The Seven Trumpets, the bowls, and the beast (Rev.8:1-18:24).
• "The Son of Man coming"	....corresponds to	...The Final Triumph of Christ (Rev.19:1-22:21).

2. There seems to be similarity between "the beginning of birth pains" or sorrows (Mt.24:5-14) and the seals of Revelation (Rev.6:1-17). The end of the world *will not come all at once*. The future will be filled with wars, natural disasters, persecutions, and the claims of false deliverers (messiahs). And at the very end, there will be an increase and intensification of the signs. But this is not all. There is to be a terrible sign: the appearance of the rider on the white horse (see note—Rev.6:2); "the abomination of desolation" (AV), "the desolating sacrilege" (RSV), "the man of lawlessness" (2 Th.2:3); the "little horn" (Dan.7); the Antichrist. This person will afflict the people of God beyond imagination.(See DEEPER STUDY # 1—Rev.11:7.)

3. There seems to be a similarity between "the great distress [tribulation]" spoken of by Christ and the seven trumpets, the seven bowl judgments, and the beast covered by Revelation.

4. Others point to a great similarity between "the beast" (Antichrist) pictured time and again in Revelation and "the abomination that causes desolation" spoken of by Christ (see DEEPER STUDY # 2—Mt.24:1-31; DEEPER STUDY # 1—Rev.11:7).

DEEPER STUDY # 2

(24:1-31) **End Time**: three other things will help in understanding what Christ is doing in this passage.

1. It will help to remember that Jesus is preparing His disciples for His death and departure from this world and preparing them to carry on after He is gone. His immediate disciples were to face some terrible times, ranging all the way from personal trials brought on by their witness for Christ to national trials involving the utter destruction of their nation. And it would be generations stretching into centuries before He returned to earth. No one knew this at that time—But He did. So He needed to prepare His future disciples as well. They, too, were going to face all kinds of trials; and there was always the danger that His disciples might tire waiting for His return. They were to see and experience so much trouble in the world their faith might falter. They, along with many in the world, might begin to ask:

> **They will say, "Where is this 'coming' he promised? Ever since our fathers died, everything goes on as it has since the beginning of creation." (2 Pet 3:4)**

What Christ does is use this occasion to reveal some of the events that are to take place upon the earth during "these last days," the days of the church (Acts 2:16-17; 1 Jn.2:18). By knowing some of the events, His disciples will be better prepared to endure and to keep alive their hope for His return.

⇒ They will know that God is not caught off guard. God is still on the throne and still in control of the events.

⇒ They will not be caught off guard themselves. They will know what to expect in this corruptible and sinful world. When the events happen, they will not be as likely to become discouraged.

⇒ They will be challenged to *keep themselves* ever so close to God in order to be as strong as possible in facing the trials coming upon earth.

⇒ They will be encouraged to place their hope in God and in the new heavens and earth and not in this corruptible world. They will be looking for "the glorious appearing of our great God and Savior, Jesus Christ" (Tit.2:13).

2. Remembering that Jesus is dealing with two questions will also help in understanding what is being said. He is answering the questions: When will the temple be destroyed and what shall be the sign of His return and of the end of the world?

Note something. Christ is dealing with the end of the temple and with the end of the world, the destruction of the temple and the destruction of the world. He is covering the signs, the events that both cause the judgment and occur during the judgment of the temple and the world. What is the point? Simply this. The Scripture teaches that the same signs and events cause the judgment of anything. That is, the events (sins) that cause judgment upon one thing are the same events that will bring judgment upon everything else. Thus, the signs that surround the destruction of Jerusalem are much the same as the signs that shall surround the end of the world. Therefore, what Christ is saying has a double meaning and application (see DEEPER STUDY # 3—Mt.24:1-14; 24:15-28. Both notes will help to see the double application.)

The Lord's words apply both to the disciples of His day and to all disciples who were to follow in succeeding generations. As long as the earth stands, the disciples of "the last days" (or ages) will face many of the same signs faced by those who experienced the destruction of Jerusalem. But there is to be one difference. At the end of the world the signs will increase and intensify. So terrible a day is coming that it can be called, "the beginning of birth pains [sorrows]" (Mt.24:8) and "the great distress [tribulation]" (Mt.24:21). (See DEEPER STUDY # 1,2—Mt.24:1-28; note—24:15-28.)

3. A quick overview of the passages dealing with the signs also help in understanding the chapters.

a. The nine signs of the last days (that is, the last days before both Jerusalem's destruction and the world's end) (Mt.24:1-14).

b. The tenth and most terrible sign: "the abomination that causes desolation" and the Great Distress [Tribulation] (Mt.24:15-28).

c. The Coming of the Son of Man (Mt.24:29-31).

The rest of what Christ covers deals with the actual time of the Lord's return (Mt.24:32-41) and the believer's duty to watch and be prepared (Mt.24:42-25:46).

DEEPER STUDY # 3

(24:1-14) **End Time:** in Mt.24:1-29 Christ gives at least ten signs of the last days. Several things need to be noted as this passage is studied.

1. Christ is answering two or three very specific questions. When will the temple be destroyed? And what shall be the sign of Christ's return and of the end of the world?

2. The signs given by Christ are to some extent present in every generation. A quick review of world history shows this. In light of this fact, a question has to be asked: why, then, is Christ spelling out every day happenings as signs of the last days? The next point, point three, answers this question.

3. There is to be an intensification of the signs right before the fall of Jerusalem and right before the end of the world. The intensification of the signs is clearly seen by the following.

a. The emphasis upon the possibility of being deceived.

> **"Watch out that no one deceives you" (v.5).**
>
> **"Many will...deceive many" (v.5).**
>
> **"False prophets...will deceive many people" (v.11).**

b. Christ uses both the word and the idea of "many" time and again, indicating an increase over what had been (the word is used in v.5, 10, 11; and the idea is used in v.6, 7, 9).

c. Christ makes three significant statements that definitely point toward an intensification of the signs.

> **"All these are the beginning of birth pains [sorrows]" (v.8).**
>
> **"But he that shall endure unto the end, the same shall be saved" (v.13).**
>
> **"And this gospel of the kingdom will be preached in the whole world as a testimony unto all nations; and then the end will come" (v.14).**

d. Other Scriptures say there is to be an intensification of evil in the last days.

> **But mark this: There will be terrible times in the last days. (2 Tim 3:1)**
>
> **First of all, you must understand that in the last days scoffers will come, scoffing and following their own evil desires. (2 Pet 3:3)**
>
> **They said to you, "In the last times there will be scoffers who will follow their own ungodly desires." (Jude 1:18)**

4. The present age is considered by God to be "the age of the last days" or "the last time." According to God's time-table, the history of the church, its presence on earth, takes place in "the last days" or during "the last times."

> **No, this is what was spoken by the prophet Joel: "'In the last days, God says, I will pour out my Spirit on all people. Your sons and daughters will prophesy, your young men will see visions, your old men will dream dreams. (Acts 2:16-17)**
>
> **But in these last days he has spoken to us by his Son, whom he appointed heir of all things, and through whom he made the universe. (Heb 1:2)**
>
> **Dear children, this is the last hour; and as you have heard that the antichrist is coming, even now many antichrists have come. This is how we know it is the last hour. (1 John 2:18)**

5. Christ gives these signs for a very specific purpose. He is preparing His disciples to endure and to keep their hope for His return alive. He is strengthening their faith in God and in the world to come, the new heavens and earth (see note, pt. 1—Mt.24:1-31, the three things that help in understanding the passage).

(24:1-14) **Introduction:** in understanding this passage, we have to be very careful not to read into the passage more than Christ was saying, nor to miss what He was saying. Both mistakes were made by religionists concerning Christ's first coming (Mt.2:4-6).

A major fact to keep in mind is this. The disciples did think that all three events (Jerusalem's destruction, the Lord's return, and the world's end) would happen at about the same time. They did think in terms of the Messianic kingdom of God (Acts 1:6 compared with the Jewish concept of the Messiah shows this. See notes—Mt.1:1; DEEPER STUDY # 2—1:18; DEEPER STUDY # 3—3:11; notes—11:1-6; 11:2-3; DEEPER STUDY # 1—11:5; DEEPER STUDY # 2—11:6; DEEPER STUDY # 1—12:16; notes—22:42; Lk.7:21-23). When Christ said that the temple would be destroyed, they assumed it would happen at the same time that He returned and ended the world, thereby restoring the kingdom to Israel.

Christ, however, gave no time-table. He did not say when the three events would occur. What He did was give signs that will occur before the events, signs that point toward His return, toward the end of Jerusalem, and the end of the world.

It is important to keep in mind that most of the signs happen all through history. But there is this difference: the signs increase and intensify right before the end of Jerusalem and of the world. There will be a period known as "the beginning of birth pains [sorrows]" (v.8), and a period launched by "the abomination of desolation" known as the "great distress [tribulation], such as was not since the beginning of the world" (v.21).

1. Events that lead to the great prophecies (v.1-4).
2. Sign 1: false messiahs (v.5).
3. Sign 2: world violence (v.6).
4. Sign 3: natural disasters (v.7).
5. Sign 4: severe religious persecution (v.9).
6. Sign 5: terrible apostasy—betrayal and division (v.10).
7. Sign 6: the rising of many false leaders—offering false hope (v.11).
8. Sign 7: a great falling away—sin's increasing and love's growing cold (v.12).
9. Sign 8: some's enduring and being saved (v.13).
10. Sign 9: world evangelism (v.14).

(24:1-14) **Another Outline:** Christ gives at least nine signs of the last days in these fourteen verses. But He divides them into three sections.

1. The beginning signs: the beginning of birth pains [sorrows] (v.5-8). Verse 8 makes this division. "All these (the signs just given in v.5-7) are the beginning of birth pains [sorrows]."

2. The succeeding signs: personal threats and birth pains [sorrows] (v.9-12). Note the word "then" in verse 9. After the beginning of birth pains [sorrows], "then" these birth pains [sorrows] will happen. At this point, Luke says, "But before all this (the above signs) they will...persecute you..." (Lk.21:12). The word "before" (pro) should probably be taken in the sense of "more important" than of time. That is, Luke is saying, "But before (more important than) all this...." (see note—Lk.21:12).

3. The promising signs: the result of faithfulness (v.13-14). The word "but" in verse thirteen points toward two signs that offer all the promise and hope a believer could ever desire. In fact, his salvation and witness are what he lives for. And the fulfillment of both is promised in the last days.

1 (24:1-4) **Prophecy**: The events that lead to the great prophecies (see note above—Mt.24:1-25:46 for discussion).

> **Thought 1.** It is not the outward appearance that makes an object acceptable; it is what is within. The temple showed that this principle is even true with buildings. The glory of a building can be tarnished by what goes on within it. The corruption of the priests within the temple stained its glory, greatly so.

> **Thought 2.** Man's perspective must be kept right. Being honest and remembering two things will help tremendously.
> 1) All the glory and magnificence of buildings will lie as dust not too many years hence. If they are not destroyed by war or catastrophe, they shall deteriorate and waste away.
> 2) Within a short, short time the human body itself, even the most beautiful, will decay, becoming nothing more than dirt.

> **Thought 3.** Note the words of Christ: "I tell you the truth" (v.2). What Christ said happens (see DEEPER STUDY # 3—Mt.24:2). Thus, all nine signs are bound to take place. But, note a critical point. The signs happen not because God destines them but because man sins. They come to pass because of the passion and evil within man.

> **Thought 4.** The world and every single man should know by now what Jesus knew. The way of God is the only way. Every nation who walks its own way without God is doomed (Ps.9:17; Prov.14:34). And every politician and man who walks their own way without God is also doomed (Ro.6:23; Heb.9:27).

> **Thought 5.** We must be very, very careful when looking into the secret things of God, into the prophecies of the end time. Christ gives us a special warning: "Watch out that *no one* deceives you" (v.4). Note 2 Th.2:3: "Don't let anyone deceive you in any way" (cp. Mt.24:11).

DEEPER STUDY # 4
(24:2) **Temple**: the prophecy of Jesus was graphically fulfilled. Just a few years after Jesus' words, Rome grew tried of the hard rebellious spirit of the Jews who refused to submit to Roman rule. In 70 A.D., Rome sent Titus to march against the city of Jerusalem. The city and temple were utterly destroyed, so much so that Josephus, the great Jewish historian of that day, said that a passer-by would not have known the place was ever inhabited. Not a stone was left upon another.

2 (24:5) **Messiah, False**: the first sign of the last days is that of false messiahs. Note what Christ said.

1. "Many will come." There will not be a few but *many* false messiahs.

2. The false messiahs actually claim, "I am Christ," the Messiah. They will not be the false prophets and teachers mentioned later. They will be persons who claim to be *the Messiah*, the Messenger of God to the world. They will be "pseudo-Christs" or "anti-Christs."

3. The false messiahs "will deceive many." Not a few, but many will believe and follow the false messiahs, believing they are the way, the truth, and the life of God (cp. Jn.14:6).

Right after Jesus' death, several men arose who claimed to be the Messiah. Josephus, the Jewish historian, said many were led astray by them. Scripture also mentions two who apparently claimed to be the Messiah or at least the deliverer of the Jews: Theudas and Judas of Galilee (Acts 5:36-37). Simon Magus claimed to "the great power of God" (Acts 8:9-10). Every generation has its false messiahs, each one claiming to be the special messenger of God, the deliverer of the human race. Every false religion and sect of every generation has its false messiahs, but there shall be *many* as the last days approach.

> **Thought 1.** Men seek utopia, inward peace and outward security. Unfortunately, too many churches and believers do not demonstrate enough trust in Christ to show that peace and security are found in Him alone. Therefore, they turn to other messiahs.

3 (24:6-7) **World Violence—War:** the second sign of the end time is world violence. Note several things.

1. Believers "*will hear*" of so much violence it will sound as though the world is coming apart. Believers can be troubled, extremely troubled over the news.

2. Christ said, "See to it that you are not alarmed" (me throeithe), disturbed, frightened, confused. Do not be put into confusion or commotion. World violence can disturb and frighten. It can lead us into confusion and commotion. But Christ says such is not to be the case of His disciples. Our hearts are to be fixed upon God, trusting His presence, care, and security eternally (Mt.10:28; Lk.12:4).

3. World violence "must happen." Violence does not happen because God wills or destines it to be but because of the passions and evil of men's hearts (Mt.18:7; cp. Jas.4:1-3).

4. World violence can so dominate the news that man is led to believe the end is at hand. But Christ warned, "The end is still to come." He had just said, "Watch out that no one deceives you" (v.4).

Now note something. All the violence mentioned thus far deals with the violence that men hear about. The fact of the violence is given in verse 7: "Nation will rise against nation, and kingdom against kingdom."

A descriptive picture of the violence that gripped the world during the days immediately following our Lord is given by Tacitus, the Roman historian (55? - after 117). In the opening statements of his Histories of the Roman empire, he says:

> "I enter upon a work fertile in vicissitudes, stained with the blood of battles, embroiled with dissensions, horrible even in the intervals of peace. Four princes slain by the sword; three civil wars, more with foreign enemies, and sometimes both at once; prosperity in the East; disasters in the West; Illyricum disturbed; the Gauls ready to revolt; Britain conquered, and again lost; Sarmatians and Suevians conspiring against us; the Dacians renowned for defeats given and sustained; the Parthians almost aroused to arms by a counterfeit Nero. Italy afflicted with calamities unheard of, or recurring only after a long interval; cities overwhelmed or swallowed up in the fertile region of Campania; Rome itself laid waste by fire, the most ancient temples destroyed, the very capital burned by its own citizens: etc." ('Hist.,' 1.2).

Remember however, despite the bleakness of world events within a particular generation, the words of our Lord stretch over the centuries covering all of history and point toward an intensification of violence toward the end of the world.

> **Thought 1.** A critical point. God does not cause violence. It is the passion and evil of men that causes violence.
>
> **Thought 2.** The believer's hope is not in this world; neither is his real citizenship. His hope and his life are in God and in heaven (Ph.3:21). Therefore, we are not to fear men and world events. Men and world events can only take our lives, not our souls. Our lives are in God's hands, even to the end of the world (Mt.28:20; Heb.13:5).

4 (24:7) **Nature—Famine—Earthquake:** the third sign of the last days is natural disasters. Three disasters of nature are mentioned in particular.

1. Famines. Scripture speaks of a "great famine" throughout all the world that "happened during the reign of Claudius" (Acts 11:28-30). Josephus described the famine as being so terrible that when flour "was brought into the temple...not one of the priests was so hardy as to eat one crumb of it...while so great a distress was upon the land" (Josephus, Ant. 3. 15:3). He said in another place, "A famine did oppress them (Jerusalem)...and many people died for want of what was necessary to procure food" (Ibid. 20. 2:5).

In the very last days before Jerusalem's fall, Josephus spoke of another terrible famine:

> "It was now a miserable case, and a sight that would justly bring tears into our eyes, how men stood to their food, while the more powerful had more than enough, and the weaker were lamenting (for want of it)"(Josephus, Wars. 5. 10:3).
>
> "Then did the famine widen its progress, and devoured the people by whole houses and families; the upper rooms were full of women and children that were dying by famine; and the lanes of the city were full of the dead bodies of the aged; the children also and the young men wandered about the market-places like shadows, all swelled with famine, and fell down dead wheresoever their misery seized them" (Ibid. 5. 12:3).

There is evidently to be terrible famine in the last days. The black horse of the four horsemen of the Apocalypse indicates terrible famine (see note—Rev.6:5-6). The unbearable pain and terrible evil that hunger can cause is graphically described by Scripture.

> **Those killed by the sword are better off than those who die of famine; racked with hunger, they waste away for lack of food from the field. With their own hands compassionate women have cooked their own children, who became their food when my people were destroyed. (Lam 4:9-10)**

2. Earthquakes. Unbelievable destruction and death are sometimes caused by earthquakes. Again, Josephus recorded the fulfillment of Jesus' prophecy. He even hinted that the natural disasters which happened were a sign of coming destruction.

> "...there broke out a prodigious storm in the night, with the utmost violence, and very strong winds, with the largest showers of rain, and continual lightnings, terrible thunderings, and amazing concussions and bellowings of the earth, that was in an earthquake. These things were a manifest indication that some destruction was coming upon men, when the system of the world was put into this disorder; and any one would guess that these wonders foreshowed some grand calamities that were coming" (Josephus, Wars. 4. 4:5).

Earthquakes will occur in many places during the last days of the earth.

> **I watched as he opened the sixth seal. There was a great earthquake. The sun turned black like sackcloth made of goat hair, the whole moon turned blood red, (Rev 6:12)**
>
> **Then they heard a loud voice from heaven saying to them, "Come up here." And they went up to heaven in a cloud, while their enemies looked on. (Rev 11:12)**
>
> **At that very hour there was a severe earthquake and a tenth of the city collapsed. Seven thousand people were killed in the earthquake, and the survivors were terrified and gave glory to the God of heaven. (Rev 11:13)**
>
> **Then God's temple in heaven was opened, and within his temple was seen the ark of his covenant. And there came flashes of lightning, rumblings, peals of thunder, an earthquake and a great hailstorm. (Rev 11:19)**
>
> **The seventh angel poured out his bowl into the air, and out of the temple came a loud voice from the throne, saying, "It is done!" (Rev 16:17)**

Then there came flashes of lightning, rumblings, peals of thunder and a severe earthquake. No earthquake like it has ever occurred since man has been on earth, so tremendous was the quake. (Rev 16:18)

The great city split into three parts, and the cities of the nations collapsed. God remembered Babylon the Great and gave her the cup filled with the wine of the fury of his wrath. (Rev 16:19)

DEEPER STUDY # 5
(24:8) **Birth Pains [Sorrows]** (odinon): birth-pains; labor-pains; travailings; intolerable anguish. Quick, sharp, violent travailing pain.

5 (24:9) **Persecution:** the fourth sign of the end time is that of severe religious persecution. Christ says two things.

1. What the persecution will be:
   a. Affliction (Acts 4:3; 8:1; 12:4; 13:50; 14:19; 2 Cor.11:23-25).
   b. Killing (Acts 7:59; 12:2).
   c. Hatred by all nations.

But we want to hear what your views are, for we know that people everywhere are talking against this sect." (Acts 28:22) (See outline notes--Mt.10:16-23. Cp. Jn. 15:20;16:2)

2. Why believers are persecuted: "Because of me" (cp. Mt.10:22). "Because of me" means at least three things. Or to say it another way, there are at least three reasons why the world often tries to silence and stamp out the believer.
   a. The world opposes the believer's standard of true godliness. The believer sets before the world a different standard. Neither the world nor its standard are godly. Therefore, any man who lives for the world and does not wish to change his behavior opposes believers. He opposes believers by his very nature (1 Jn.2:14-15).
   b. The world opposes the believer's life of purity and justice. The genuine believer lives such a life. He controls his mind, dresses modestly, converses respectfully, and behaves justly. The world lives to fulfill the lust of the flesh and to have what one wishes. Thus, the believer is opposed by any person who does not wish to live a pure and just life (Gal.5:19-21).
   c. The world opposes the believer's message of repentance and self-denial. The genuine believer proclaims the message of Christ which is repentance and self-denial. Few men are willing to change (repent) to the degree that self is totally denied. Most, even the religious, oppose the idea of giving all one is and has, even if it does mean saving a starving and dying world. (See outline and notes—Mt.19:21-22; 19:23-26.)

Note the words "hated by all nations." This definitely points to persecution all around the world. Christ is again looking well beyond the last days before Jerusalem's fall. He is looking to the persecution that shall be launched against His followers across the centuries and be intensified in the end time. He had even foretold such persecution before.

"Be on your guard against men; they will hand you over to the local councils and flog you in their synagogues. On my account you will be brought before governors and kings as witnesses to them and to the Gentiles. (Mat 10:17-18)

6 (24:10) **Apostasy:** The fifth sign is terrible apostasy—betrayal and division. Christ says three things about the apostasy.

1. "Many will turn away from the faith (fall away)." Persecution shall cause droves to turn from professing Christ. They do not know Him: not really, not personally, not inwardly. They have only professed Him with their lips. They have neither trusted Him with their hearts nor denied self, nor lived sacrificially, nor given, nor served to meet the needs of a needy and dying world. They know only the comfort and benefits that rub off from being in the church and associating with genuine believers. They know nothing about the call of God to share in the sufferings of Christ (Ph.1:29; 2 Cor.4:11).

Consequently, when the fiery trial comes, they have no idea what denying self and dying daily for Christ is all about. They have no inward desire or strength, actually no real reason, to stand firm. They are offended; therefore, they fall away (cp. Mt.13:21).

Note something. Every generation has some apostasy. Some who have professed Christ do turn away (2 Tim.4:10; 1 Jn.2:18-19). What Christ is saying is that apostasy is to increase, be intensified in the end time. Many will be offended by the persecution to come, and they will fall away.

2. "(Many) will betray each other." Again, informing on others, betraying them is to intensify in the end time. Neighbor will turn against neighbor, friend against friend, family against family.

A reading of The War of the Jews by Josephus graphically pictures just how inhuman man can become when his survival is threatened. And, of course, the Gospels show rather graphically how greed and power and selfishness can cause men to mistreat, abuse, threaten, plot and kill others (see notes—Mt.12:1-8; note and DEEPER STUDY # 1—12:10).

Both survival and selfishness are seen in the last days of Jerusalem when Titus besieged the city: the wealthy saw to their needs and neglected the poor, and the powerful took what they wanted. As the siege wore on, famine and pestilence struck. The strong took from the weak and the weak informed on his neighbor's hidden supplies, no matter how little, in order to receive a morsel from the strong. Within the city walls, betrayal and murder ran rampant in order to survive. Others just outrightly betrayed their nation and went over to the side of the Romans in order to save their lives.

"The people, they had a great inclination to desert to the Romans...the main reasons why they were so ready to desert were these: that now they should be freed from those miseries which they had endured in that city...the robbers came running into, and searched men's private houses; and if they found none [food], they tormented them worse, because they supposed they had more carefully concealed it. The indication they made use of whether they had any or not, was taken from the bodies of these miserable wretches; which, if they were in good case, they supposed they were in no want at all of food; but

> if they were wasted away, they walked off without searching any further...children pulled the very morsels that their fathers were eating, out of their very mouths, and what was still more to be pitied, so did the mothers do as to their infants: and when those that were most dear were perishing under their hands, they were not ashamed to take from them the very last drops that might preserve their lives...the seditious everywhere came upon them immediately, and snatched away from them what they had gotten from others; for when they saw any house shut up, this was to them a signal that the people within had gotten some food; whereupon they broke upon the doors, and ran in, and took pieces of what they were eating, almost up out of their very throats and this by force; the old men, who held their food fast, were beaten; and if the women hid what they had within their hands, their hair was torn for so doing; nor was there any commiseration shown either to the aged or to infants, but they lifted up children from the ground as they hung upon the morsels they had gotten, and shook them down upon the floor; but still were they more barbarously cruel to those that had prevented their coming in, and had actually swallowed down what they were going to seize upon, as if they had been unjustly defrauded of their right. They also invented terrible methods of torment to discover where any food was" (Josephus, Wars. 5. 10:1).

Tacitus, the great Roman historian, summarizes the betrayal of some in the early church.

> "First those were seized who confessed that they were Christians; and then on their information a vast multitude was convicted" (Tacitus, Annuals. 15:44).

Christ had already warned His followers of terrible persecution and even betrayal by one's own family (see outline and DEEPER STUDY # 2—Mt.10:21). The difference in what He is saying now is His stress upon the end time. The persecution and betrayal will increase and intensify in the end time.

Several things cause a person to betray others. All will evidently be involved in the end time, as they were in the last days of Jerusalem.

⇒ to escape persecution
⇒ to save life
⇒ to secure some favor
⇒ to get what one wants
⇒ to get back at someone (vengeance)
⇒ to escape embarrassment
⇒ to escape fear
⇒ to preserve selfish honor

3. "(Many) will hate each other." So few will be kind, tender, and loving. Dissension and division will prevail in the last days. Most will begrudge what another has or is doing or is not doing. Such has been the case down through the centuries. Too often the church has experienced one person's disliking and opposing another person. Envy, greed, concern for security and recognition—all the sins of selfishness—have caused too many to stand against another's position, beliefs, abilities, leadership, and on and on. Unfortunately, criticism and judging, dissension and division among believers has been and is one of the most visible traits of the church, both locally and universally. Christ says that such hatred will increase and intensify in the end times.

Thought 1. Why are professing Christians sometimes *turned off* or *offended* by Christ? Some of the reasons would be...

- fear of ridicule
- fear of abuse
- fear of being ignored
- fear of not fitting in
- fear of persecution
- fear of not having
- fear of losing position, security, wealth, and power

All these, and many other reasons, will be taking their toll in the last days.

Thought 2. The two things that God and Christ desire above all others from the believer are love and unity.

1) Love is basic.

> **And this is his command: to believe in the name of his Son, Jesus Christ, and to love one another as he commanded us. (1 John 3:23)**
>
> **"A new command I give you: Love one another. As I have loved you, so you must love one another. By this all men will know that you are my disciples, if you love one another." (John 13:34-35)**
>
> **My command is this: Love each other as I have loved you. (John 15:12)**
>
> **This is my command: Love each other. (John 15:17)**

2) Unity is basic.

> **I will remain in the world no longer, but they are still in the world, and I am coming to you. Holy Father, protect them by the power of your name—the name you gave me—so that they may be one as we are one. (John 17:11)**
>
> **"My prayer is not for them alone. I pray also for those who will believe in me through their message, that all of them may be one, Father, just as you are in me and I am in you. May they also be in us so that the world may believe that you have sent me. I have given them the glory that you gave me, that they may be one as we are one: I in them and you in me. May they be brought to complete unity to let the world know that you sent me and have loved them even as you have loved me. (John 17:20-23)**

7 (24:11) **Leaders, False—Teachers, False:** The sixth sign is the rise of false leaders offering false hope. Christ makes two points.

1. "Many false prophets will appear." They will be prophets; that is, they will claim to preach and teach the

message of God. Jerusalem, facing the crises of its last days, experienced a great number of false prophets arising; and each had his own message about how the people could be saved.

> "Now, there was then a great number of false prophets suborned by the tyrants to impose upon the people, who denounced this to them, that they should wait for deliverance from God; and this was in order to keep them from deserting, and that they might be buoyed up above fear and care by such hopes. Now, a man that is in adveristy does easily comply with such promises; for when such a seducer makes him believe that he shall be delivered from those miseries which oppress him, then it is that the patient is full of hopes of such deliverance" (Josephus, Wars. 6. 5:2).

A false teacher is one who develops his own way, truth, and life for people to follow rather than follow Jesus as the way, the truth, and the life. The church has always had its false teachers: teachers who presented what they wished instead of what Christ said; teachers who taught their own ideas instead of the truth of Christ; teachers who attached people to themselves instead of attaching them to Christ.

2. "Many will be deceived." There are several reasons why a person is deceived.

⇒ A person's frantic hope for deliverance causes him to search for a savior and to grasp at almost anyone who appears on the scene.

⇒ The humanistic desire to better and strengthen oneself and to impose and control one's destiny causes a person to look to leaders who offer hope and a better world.

⇒ The evidence of signs, wonders, power, reasonableness, logic, knowledge, and help causes a person to follow leaders who demonstrate unusual abilities.

False teachers are both within and without the church, and they shall increase as the last days of the world approach (cp. 2 Cor.11:13; 2 Th.2:1f; 1 Tim.6:3).

> **Dear children, this is the last hour; and as you have heard that the antichrist is coming, even now many antichrists have come. This is how we know it is the last hour. They went out from us, but they did not really belong to us. For if they had belonged to us, they would have remained with us; but their going showed that none of them belonged to us. (1 John 2:18-19)**
>
> **Dear friends, do not believe every spirit, but test the spirits to see whether they are from God, because many false prophets have gone out into the world. This is how you can recognize the Spirit of God: Every spirit that acknowledges that Jesus Christ has come in the flesh is from God, but every spirit that does not acknowledge Jesus is not from God. This is the spirit of the antichrist, which you have heard is coming and even now is already in the world. (1 John 4:1-3)**

Thought 1. The genuine believer knows how to pray and commune with God. He knows how to receive strength from God, to conquer and live above the most difficult circumstances (Ph.4:4, 6-7, 11-14, 19. Cp. 1 Cor.10:13; Acts 16:25f.)

Thought 2. Discouragement is a terrible thing. It defeats life. However, there is one sure way to live above discouragement: learn to live and walk in an unbroken communion with God every day. Study His Word and pray without ceasing, learning and claiming His promises (Is.26:3; Ph.4:6-9).

8 (24:12) **Apostasy:** the seventh sign is a great falling away. Sin shall increase and love shall grow cold.

1. "Increase of wickedness." Lawlessness [sin and wickedness] is always present, but there are times when it seems to multiply and overflow (see note—Iniquity—Mt.24:12). It ran rampant in the last days of Jerusalem as the quotations from Josephus clearly show. It shall also run wild in the last days of world history (2 Tim.3:1-5; 2 Th.2:1-12).

2. "The love of most will grow cold." At least four things can dampen one's love for God. Each of these shall be greatly intensified toward the end of the world.

a. Self-seeking and worldliness. Men will seek what they want and what the world offers instead of sacrificing and serving. They just choose to satisfy their own desires and worldly urges instead of seeking diligently after God.

b. Dissension and division. Both discourage, dishearten, and cause confusion and the desire to flee. Many just cool off and back away, desiring to have no part of anything that is divisive. Even if the truth is under attack, some will withdraw rather than take a stand for the truth.

c. Persecution. Unless a person truly believes and trusts in Christ, whatever affection he has is soon dampened when he is questioned and opposed. Only a *real belief and conviction* will stand up under ridicule and the threat of death.

d. Ignorance and weak faith. Some go through a dampening of spirit and affection simply because they cannot understand why God would let such trials happen. There is no true understanding of man's sin and death, of the world's corruption and destined end, of God's righteousness and promise of life. Therefore, there is little within to stir a fervent love for God when things are going bad and the world seems to be caving in.

e. Lawlessness and immorality. Being around a crowd that lives lawless and immoral lives causes many to lose their love for Christ and turn away.

Christ warns the believer who lets his love grow cold.

> **So, because you are lukewarm—neither hot nor cold—I am about to spit you out of my mouth. (Rev 3:16)**
>
> **The Spirit clearly says that in later times some will abandon the faith and follow deceiving spirits and things taught by demons. Such teachings come through hypocritical liars, whose consciences have been seared as with a hot iron. (1 Tim 4:1-2)**
>
> **So, because you are lukewarm--neither hot nor cold--I am about to spit you out of my mouth. (Rev 3:16)**

DEEPER STUDY # 6
(24:12) **Wickedness** (anomia): lawlessness, iniquity, unrighteousness; transgression of the law. It is taking license with the law and righteousness, with morality and discipline.

DEEPER STUDY # 7
(24:12) **Increase** (plethunthenai): to multiply, to abound.

9 (24:13) **Endurance—Salvation**: the eighth sign is that of some's enduring and being saved. It must be remembered Christ is talking to His disciples. His promise, "Being saved," is bound to mean the soul's salvation in the last days. It could not mean the safety of human life. He had already said some will be killed (v.9). Thus, the believer who stands firm through persecution and hatred, betrayal and division, false teaching and deception, lawlessness and immorality, and keeps fervent love will be saved.

> **Do not be afraid of what you are about to suffer. I tell you, the devil will put some of you in prison to test you, and you will suffer persecution for ten days. Be faithful, even to the point of death, and I will give you the crown of life. (Rev 2:10)**
> **To those who by persistence in doing good seek glory, honor and immortality, he will give eternal life. But for those who are self-seeking and who reject the truth and follow evil, there will be wrath and anger. There will be trouble and distress for every human being who does evil: first for the Jew, then for the Gentile; (Rom 2:7-9)**

Thought 1. The believer can find great encouragement to endure in such passages as the following. (Scan quickly some of the books that deal heavily with suffering, such as First Peter. See General Subject Index, related subjects.)

> **For it has been granted to you on behalf of Christ not only to believe on him, but also to suffer for him, (Phil 1:29)**
> **Consider him who endured such opposition from sinful men, so that you will not grow weary and lose heart. (Heb 12:3)**
> **If anyone speaks, he should do it as one speaking the very words of God. If anyone serves, he should do it with the strength God provides, so that in all things God may be praised through Jesus Christ. To him be the glory and the power for ever and ever. Amen. Dear friends, do not be surprised at the painful trial you are suffering, as though something strange were happening to you. (1 Pet 4:11-12)**

10 (24:14) **Evangelism—Witnessing**: the ninth sign is world evangelism. Christ says five very significant things.

1. His gospel is of the Kingdom. What Kingdom? The Kingdom of God that is spiritual and eternal (see DEEPER STUDY # 3—Mt.19:23-24; note—Eph.1:3. Cp. 2 Cor.5:19.)

2. His gospel is unstoppable: "This gospel of the kingdom *will* be preached." No amount of trouble and failure can stop it from being preached: neither severe persecution (v.9), nor terrible apostasy (v.10), nor many false teachers (v.11), nor multiplied lawlessness (v.12), nor the love of many growing cold (v.12). God's glorious Word of grace will force its way over land and sea, no matter the strength of the storms and bodies that oppose it.

3. His gospel will be triumphant: "This gospel...will be preached in the whole world." Amazingly, in just a brief span of time during the first century, the gospel was evidently carried to all parts of the known world.

> **But I ask: Did they not hear? Of course they did: "Their voice has gone out into all the earth, their words to the ends of the world." (Rom 10:18)**
> **That has come to you. All over the world this gospel is bearing fruit and growing, just as it has been doing among you since the day you heard it and understood God's grace in all its truth. (Col 1:6)**
> **If you continue in your faith, established and firm, not moved from the hope held out in the gospel. This is the gospel that you heard and that has been proclaimed to every creature under heaven, and of which I, Paul, have become a servant. (Col 1:23)**

The very tone of Christ's words point to the same sign of world evangelism toward the end of the world. The uttermost part of the earth will be privileged to hear the gospel before the final appearance of Christ (Acts 1:8; cp. Mt.28:19-20. Cp. Mt.24:3, 14 with Mt.28:19 noting the word "age." Then see Acts 8:12; 28:23, 28, 30-31 for examples of preaching the Kingdom.)

4. His gospel is a testimony: "This gospel...will be preached...as a testimony to all nations." The gospel as a *testimony* means at least two things.

a. The gospel is a testimony, proclaiming the truth and the will of God for man. It reveals the truth about man and his world. It tells man where he has come from, why he is here, and where he is going. It tells man what he has done, what he is doing, and what he should do. It tells man why he is as he is, why he does what he does, and why he should do as God says.
b. The gospel is a testimony, bearing record either for man or against man.
   ⇒ The gospel is called a "testimony."

> **And this is the testimony: God has given us eternal life, and this life is in his Son. He who has the Son has life; he who does not have the Son of God does not have life. (1 John 5:11-12)**

⇒ The gospel testifies for a man, that he believes and is saved; or it testifies against a man, that he does not believe and is condemned.

> **Whoever believes and is baptized will be saved, but whoever does not believe will be condemned. (Mark 16:16)**

5. His gospel will be preached in all the world before the end comes. The term "the end" refers to both the end of Jerusalem and the end of the world. As Scripture states, the gospel had been preached to all the known world right

before the fall of Jerusalem (Ro.10:18; Col.1:6, 23) and will be preached to the uttermost part of the earth before the end time (Acts 1:8; cp. Mt.28:19-20).

However, something needs to be noted that is sometimes overlooked. Christ does not say the gospel will *convert* the world, but rather the gospel will be *preached* to the world before the end comes. All the world will not respond to the gospel, but all the world will hear the gospel. Christ does, however, give some indication of the results to expect from preaching the gospel.

"So the last will be first, and the first will be last." (Mat 20:16; 22:14)

"Make every effort to enter through the narrow door, because many, I tell you, will try to enter and will not be able to. (Luke 13:24)

I tell you, he will see that they get justice, and quickly. However, when the Son of Man comes, will he find faith on the earth?" (Luke 18:8)

B. The Most Terrible Sign: The Abomination of Desolation & The Great Distress [Tribulation], 24:15-28
(Mk.13:14-27; Lk.21: 20-28)

Outline	Scripture
1 There is the appearance of the abomination that causes desolation[DS1] a. Will be seen b. Prophesied by Daniel c. Stands in Holy Place d. To read & understand	15 "So when you see standing in the holy place 'the abomination that causes desolation,' spoken of through the prophet Daniel—let the reader understand—
2 There is the warning to flee immediately a. To forget all comfort of home[DS2] b. To forget all personal possessions c. To grieve for those who cannot flee rapidly d. To pray for good conditions in fleeing	16 Then let those who are in Judea flee to the mountains. 17 Let no one on the roof of his house go down to take anything out of the house. 18 Let no one in the field go back to get his cloak. 19 How dreadful it will be in those days for pregnant women and nursing mothers! 20 Pray that your flight will not take place in winter or on the Sabbath.
3 There is the great distress [tribulation]: Unparalleled in history	21 For then there will be great distress, unequaled from the beginning of the world until now—and never to be equaled again.
4 There is the promise: The days shall be shortened for the elect's sake	22 If those days had not been cut short, no one would survive, but for the sake of the elect those days will be shortened.
5 There is the frantic search for a deliverer, for an earthly messiah (one who is false) a. They will arise b. They will show great signs & miracles c. They will be convincing, threatening to deceive even the elect	23 At that time if anyone says to you, 'Look, here is the Christ!' or, 'There he is!' do not believe it. 24 For false Christs and false prophets will appear and perform great signs and miracles to deceive even the elect—if that were possible. 25 See, I have told you ahead of time.
6 There is the truth about deliverance, about Messiah's coming a. Comes not from the desert: An unknown or remote spot b. Comes not in secret: Unseen, quietly c. Comes as lightning 1) From heaven 2) Suddenly—surprising 3) Visibly—seen east to west d. Comes to execute judgment	26 "So if anyone tells you, 'There he is, out in the desert,' do not go out; or, 'Here he is, in the inner rooms,' do not believe it. 27 For as lightning that comes from the east is visible even in the west, so will be the coming of the Son of Man. 28 Wherever there is a carcass, there the vultures will gather.

DIVISION XV

THE MESSIAH'S PROPHECY OF HIS RETURN AND THE END OF THE AGE: THE OLIVET DISCOURSE, 24:1-25:46

B. The Most Terrible Sign: The Abomination That Causes Desolation and The Great Distress [Tribulation], 24:15-28

(24:15-28) **Introduction—End Time—The Great Distress [Tribulation]**: the disciples had asked two questions. First, when was Jerusalem to be destroyed; and second, what was to be the sign of His coming and of the end of the world (Mt.24:3)? This passage evidently has a double meaning. It refers both to the destruction of Jerusalem by Titus in 70 A.D. and to the end time when Christ will return. The passage has to be severely strained to make it refer to only one of these events. It should be remembered that Christ was experiencing the most severe emotions during these days. Death was only hours away, and He was the only One aware of it. He had just gone through the triumphal entry (Mt.21), the cleansing of the temple (Mt.21), the savage attacks by the religionists (Mt.21-22), His severe denunciation of the religionists (Mt.23), and His lament over Jerusalem (Mt.23). No ordinary man could possibly bear so many pressuring and diverse emotions in so short a time. Jesus loved Jerusalem; He had just wept and wept bitterly over the city. They had been a people of sin and were to commit the most heinous sin of human history—killing the Messiah, the Son of God Himself. They were to experience two judgments for their sinful rejection. They were to be immediately judged in 70 A.D. Then at the end of the world, they, along with the rest of the world, were to be finally judged.

Simply stated the situation was this: Jesus, filled with so wide a range of emotions, began to answer the two questions the disciples had asked. He gave the signs of the coming destruction of Jerusalem and of the end of the world. He said, in essence, that the fall of Jerusalem was judgment upon sin, and the fall of the world would be judgment upon sin. The questions asked refer to similar conditions that bring about judgment. Thus, the signs of both the fall of Jerusalem and of the end of the world are similar. (See notes and DEEPER STUDY # 3—Mt.24:1-14; note and DEEPER STUDY # 1—Mk.13:14; note—Lk.21:5-38.)

As a person studies this passage, two things need to be kept in mind.

1. The overall outline of *Christ's answer*, His actual words (see DEEPER STUDY # 1,2—Mt.24:1-31).

2. The fact that Christ *was answering* two questions dealing with the end of Jerusalem and with the end of the world, and that the end of both is due to judgment upon sin. Thus, the signs that point to the end of both Jerusalem and of the world are bound to be similar, for both are *ending* and being judged because of sin. The only difference is that in the end of the world there is to be an increase and intensification of the signs. (See DEEPER STUDY # 1,2—Mt.24:1-31.)

A quick glance at the overall outline of Matthew 24-25 will show the following:

1. The Nine Signs of the Last Days, Mt.24:1-14.
2. The Tenth and Most Terrible Sign: The Abomination That Causes Desolation and The Great Distress [Tribulation], Mt.24:15-28.
3. The Coming of Messiah, the Son of Man, Mt.24:29-31.

4. The Time of the Lord's Return, Mt.24:32-41.
5. The Lord's Return & The Believer's Duty: Watch—Be Ready—Be Faithful, Mt.24:42-51.
6. The Warning to Watch & Be Wise, Not Foolish, Mt.25:1-13.
7. The Believer's Duty to Work Anticipating the Lord's Return, Mt.25:14-30.
8. The Final Judgment of the Nations, Mt.25:31-46.

Note the Lord's words: "the abomination that causes desolation" and "great distress [tribulation], such as was not since the beginning of the world." It is for this reason that the title given to this tenth sign is, "The Most Terrible Sign: The Abomination That Causes Desolation and the Great Distress [Tribulation]."

1. There is the appearance of the abomination that causes desolation (v.15).
2. There is the warning to flee immediately (v.16-20).
3. There is the great distress [tribulation]: unparalleled in history (v.21).
4. There is the promise: the days will be shortened for the elect's sake (v.22).
5. There is the frantic search for a deliverer, for an earthly Messiah (v.23-24).
6. There is the truth about deliverance, about Messiah's coming (v.25-28).

1 (24:15) **Abomination That Causes Desolation—Antichrist—End Times**: there is the appearance of the abomination that causes desolation. Christ said four things about this sign.

1. It (He) will be seen. Believers can see it take place and prepare for the terrible trials which will follow it (see DEEPER STUDY # 2—Mt. 24:1-31).

2. It (He) was also prophesied by Daniel (see DEEPER STUDY # 1—Mt. 24:15).

3. It (He) will stand in the Holy Place. The sign will take place and be seen in the temple. Some hold that the sign will be repeated in the end time and literally fulfilled within the temple, just as it was literally fulfilled twice in the past when Antiochus and Titus stood within the temple. Others hold the words "the temple" to be representative of all religion. They believe the abomination will be the desolation of all religion, in particular genuine Christianity.

4. Whosoever reads about the sign, as revealed by Christ, is to understand it. Daniel had said, "Know and understand" (Dan. 9:25; cp. Dan.12:10). Believers are to study the sign and gain an understanding of it, so that they can be better prepared to "stand firm to the end...[and] be saved" (Mt.24:13). There is the idea that a person is to know and understand the *times*, to watch and observe the happenings of the times in which he lives.

Thought 1. The terrible desolation that took place upon Jerusalem and that is to take place at the end of the world is due to sin. Jerusalem *cut off the Messiah*, that is, killed Him. They committed the most heinous of sins: they rejected God for centuries and eventually killed God's very own Son. Therefore, Jerusalem was desolated. There is a critical warning here for believers: sin results in desolation.

Thought 2. Note two significant facts.
1) Christ predicted the terrible desolation of Jerusalem. His words were spoken somewhere around 30 A.D. The desolation occurred just forty years later in 70 A.D.
2) Christ has predicted the "abomination that causes desolation" at the end of the world (cp. the questions of the disciples, v.3 and v.15). The sign *will occur* at the appointed time.

Thought 3. Something is of critical importance.
1) If we interpret "the abomination that causes desolation" only as historical and Christ meant it to be future as well as historical, we are more likely to miss the sign.
2) If we interpret the sign only as future and Christ meant it to be historical as well as future, we will have already missed a significant part of the sign and will not be looking at the past to help us understand the future.

Making sure we are accurate in our understanding of the sign is important. It involves the Lord's words and the Lord's people and their testimony. There may be different interpretations, but each one must humbly secure his understanding bowed in prayer before the Lord.

Thought 4. God's Word is not a secret; it is a revelation. It is to be searched out and understood.

DEEPER STUDY # 1

(24:15) **End Times—Antichrist—Abomination That Causes Desolation** (To Bdelugma Tes eremoseos): the abomination that makes desolate. Note Christ's words, "the abomination that causes desolation, spoken through the prophet Daniel." There are three passages in Daniel that speak of "the abomination that causes desolation."

> **"Seventy 'sevens' are decreed for your people and your holy city to finish transgression, to put an end to sin, to atone for wickedness, to bring in everlasting righteousness, to seal up vision and prophecy and to anoint the most holy. "Know and understand this: From the issuing of the decree to restore and rebuild Jerusalem until the Anointed One, the ruler, comes, there will be seven 'sevens,' and sixty-two 'sevens.' It will be rebuilt with streets and a trench, but in times of trouble. After the sixty-two 'sevens,' the Anointed One will be cut off and will have nothing. The people of the ruler who will come will destroy the city and the sanctuary. The end will come like a flood: War will continue until the end, and desolations have been decreed. He will confirm a covenant with many for one 'seven.' In the middle of the 'seven' he will put an end to sacrifice and offering. And on a wing of the temple he will set up an abomination that causes desolation, until the end that is decreed is poured out on him." (Dan 9:24-27)**
>
> **"His armed forces will rise up to desecrate the temple fortress and will abolish the daily sacrifice. Then they will set up the abomination that causes desolation. (Dan 11:31)**
>
> **"From the time that the daily sacrifice is abolished and the abomination that causes desolation is set up, there will be 1,290 days. (Dan 12:11)**

In Daniel 9:27, the term is *delugma ton eremoseon.* The Hebrew says, "Upon the wing [or pinnacle] of abominations [will come] the desolater" or "upon wings as a desolater [will come] abomination."

In Daniel 11:31, the Hebrew says, "they will put [place] the abomination that desolates."

In Daniel 12:11, the Hebrew says, "and from the time the daily [sacrifice] will be taken away, and the abomination that makes desolate set up, [will be]...."

Several matters need to be discussed about the "abomination that causes desolation" spoken of by Christ and Daniel.

1. When was Daniel's prophecy fulfilled?
   a. There was a past fulfillment; that is, there was a fulfillment before the time of Christ about 170 B.C. This is clear. Antiochus Epiphanes, the king of Syria, conquered Jerusalem and tried to force Grecian society upon the Jews. He wanted the Jews to become full-fledged Greeks both in custom and religion. He knew that to be successful he had to destroy the Jewish religion. He therefore did three of the most horrible things that could ever be done in the mind of the Jewish people. He desecrated the temple (1) by taking the great altar of the burnt offering and turning it into an altar for the Greek Olympian god Zeus, (2) by sacrificing swines' flesh upon it, and (3) by setting up a trade of prostitution in the temple chambers (cp. 1 Maccabees 1:20-62; cp. also Josephus, Ant. 12. 5:3-4; Wars. 1. 1:2).
   b. Christ said there is a future fulfillment: "When you see standing in the holy place the abomination that causes desolation, spoken through the prophet Daniel...." There are primarily four views of the future fulfillment of Daniel's prophecy.
      ⇒ One view says there is no future fulfillment; all the signs were fulfilled in the destruction of Jerusalem in 70 A.D. by Titus.
      ⇒ Others see Christ's referring to the church age and to the trials which the church has to go through before Christ returns.
      ⇒ Still others view the prophecy as referring exclusively to the end time, having nothing to do with the destruction of Jerusalem in 70 A.D.
      ⇒ Others believe Christ is answering the very questions the disciples asked. He predicts both the destruction of Jerusalem and the end of the world.

In looking at what Christ was saying, it is best to let Him speak for Himself without *adding to* or *taking away* from His words. An attempt to let Him speak for Himself has been made in the former notes (see all notes—Mt.24:1-25:46; DEEPER STUDY # 1,2—24:1-31; 24:1-14; 24:15-28). The conclusion of the notes is that the prophecy is *fulfilled* in both Jerusalem's destruction and the end of the world. The Lord is answering the disciples' questions.

Christ was saying this: the same thing that happened under Antiochus Epiphanes will happen again to the Holy Place. In fact, Christ was saying that the temple would be so destroyed that not one stone would be left upon another. This destruction did happen: what Christ said took place in a most literal sense under Titus in 70 A.D. (See outline and notes—Mt. 24:1-14, especially the notes that quote Josephus, the Jewish historian. Reading Josephus' record of Jerusalem's desolation reveals just how terrible the temple, the city, and the people were devastated.)

However, as discussed in the former notes, Christ was not only answering the disciples' question about when the destruction of Jerusalem would take place, He was *also answering* their question about His return and the end of the world. Daniel's prophecy and the Lord's elaboration on Daniel's prophecy are to have a double fulfillment. The signs that point toward one who had sinned so terribly (Jerusalem) are much the same as the signs that point toward another who is guilty of terrible sin (the world in the end time). The sin of Jerusalem was the most heinous sin that could be committed: the killing of God's own Son. And the sin of the world at the end of time will be just as terrible by following "the abomination that causes desolation." Therefore, the world will witness an increase, an intensification of the signs at the end of time. As a result, there will be *great trial* such as the world has never seen (v.21). (Again, see the outline and notes—Mt. 24:1f.)

2. A second matter that needs to be discussed about "the abomination that causes desolation" is the division of time that Christ and Daniel both seem to give. Christ says that the abomination that causes desolation launches the worst tribulation the world has ever known (Mt. 24:15, 21). In His own words, the signs that occur up until the abomination that causes desolation are called "the beginning of birth pains [sorrows]" (Mt. 24:8); and the trials that take place after the abomination that causes desolation are called "great distresses [tribulations]," distresses so great that they are unparalleled in history (Mt.24:21). Daniel also gives a division of time just as Christ does.

> **He will confirm a covenant with many for one 'seven.' In the middle of the 'seven' he will put an end to sacrifice and offering. And on a wing of the temple he will set up an abomination that causes desolation, until the end that is decreed is poured out on him." (Dan 9:27)**

"In the middle of the 'seven'" (Daniel's seventieth week) definitely points to a period of time (one week) that is divided into two parts. Now note these factors.

   a. Daniel was dealing with the "seventieth week," the *end* of his prophecy. Two facts tell us that Daniel was also dealing with the *end time* just as Christ was: (1) the fact that Christ was dealing with the end of Jerusalem and the end of the world and, (2) the fact that Christ said He was elaborating on Daniel's prophecy.
   b. Daniel said that what begins the second half of his seventieth week is "the abomination [that causes] desolation" or the prince who causes "abominable idols."

The words of Christ should be carefully noted: "When you see standing in the holy place 'the abomination that causes desolation,' spoken through the prophet Daniel...." (Mt.24:15). Christ was about to explain in more detail what Daniel had prophesied. Thus Christ explained that the first half of Daniel's week would consist of signs which were "the beginning of birth pains [sorrows]" (Mt.24:8; cp. Mt.24:5-14), and the last half of Daniel's week would consist of unparalleled trials of "great distress [tribulation]." The second half of the week would be launched by "the abomination that causes desolation standing in the holy place" (Mt. 24:15, 21).

3. A third matter that needs to be looked at is the time frame of the end time (the seventieth week) as predicted by Christ and Daniel.

Scripture does refer to the length in these words (see notes—Rev.11:2; 12:6).

> **Time, times and half a time. (Dan 7:25; 12:7)**
> **1,260 days. (Rev 12:6)**
> **42 months. (Rev 11:2; 13:5-6)**

Based upon the days and months given in the Book of Revelation, if Daniel's time equals one year, then his words, "Time [1 year], times [2 years], and half a time [1/2 year]" are equal to 3 1/2 years. Daniel stated that the abomination that causes desolation will be executed "in the midst of the week," that is, after three and one half years. It is assumed that Christ's words "the beginning of birth pains [sorrows]" (that is, the first half of the week) are also three and one-half years. Thus in combining the two periods of time (3 1/2 years each), the length of the last days or end time is said to be a literal seven years. Based upon the words of Revelation the prophecy of Christ can be charted as follows.

THE END OF THE WORLD

Seeing the Sign of the Abomination That Causes Desolation In the Middle of the Time or Years (v.15)		Seeing the Son of Man Coming (v.29-30)
3 1/2 years Signs which are "The beginning of birth pains [sorrows]" (v.8)	3 1/2 years Unparalleled trials of "the great distress [tribulation] (v.21)	"His angels...will gather His elect" (v.31)

However, it should be noted that many Biblical scholars say that the words "times" in Dasniel and "days" and "months" in Revelation (in fact, throughout all Scripture) are often used to refer to blocks of time, that is, to longer periods or indefinite periods of time.

4. A fourth matter that needs to be looked at is this: What or who is meant by "the abomination that causes desolation"? As has already been discussed, many excellent commentators hold that the prophecy refers to the destruction of Jerusalem under both Antiochus Epiphenes (170 B.C.) and under Titus (70 A.D.). There is strong historical evidence, as well as the fact that Christ was answering a specific question of the disciples (Mt. 24:3), to support a past fulfillment of the prophecy. But, what about the future fulfillment? What or who is meant by "the abomination that causes desolation" at the end of the world? (See DEEPER STUDY # 1—Rev.11:7; cp. 2 Th.2:3-4; Rev.13:1; 13:3 13:5-6. See Master Subject Index.)

a. Some indication is perhaps given by the phrase itself. In the Old Testament the word *abomination* is connected with idolatry or sacrilege. In this case, it is *the abomination* that causes *desolation.* That is, the abomination acts upon the Holy Place and personally causes the desolation. This, of course, points toward a person's fulfilling the prophecy in the future just as there were two literal persons who fulfilled it in the past, Antiochus and Titus.

b. Mark 13:14 actually uses the *masculine* participle which indicates strongly that the abomination that causes desolation is a person.

c. Daniel 9:27 speaks of a prince who causes the desolation. Leupold, the great Lutheran theologian, translates the prince as *the destroyer.* (Leupold. *Exposition of Daniel,* p.433. Because of his extraordinary scholarship and simplicity of writing, Leupold should be referred to in studying Daniel.)

d. Second Thessalonians and Revelation identify an *antichrist* who is to arise in the last days and cause unparalleled havoc upon the world and God's people.

> **Don't let anyone deceive you in any way, for that day will not come until the rebellion occurs and the man of lawlessness is revealed, the man doomed to destruction. He will oppose and will exalt himself over everything that is called God or is worshiped, so that he sets himself up in God's temple, proclaiming himself to be God. Don't you remember that when I was with you I used to tell you these things? (2 Th 2:3-5). (See notes and DEEPER STUDY # 1—Mk.13:14; notes—2 Th.2:4-9; Rev.6:2-7; DEEPER STUDY # 1—11:7; notes—13:1-10; 13:11-18; 17:7-14. Cp. Dan.9:20-27; 11:31; 12:11.)**

2 (24:16-20) **Antichrist—Abomination That Causes Desolation**: there is the warning to flee "the abomination that causes desolation"—immediately. No believer will be able to stand up against the abomination, not even the strongest. The imminent danger and urgency is stressed by Christ in four statements.

1. A person is to forget all comfort of home: pictured by arising from his roof and immediately fleeing (see DEEPER STUDY # 2—Mt.24:17).

2. A person is to forget all personal possessions: pictured by not returning from his work to get his clothes (or possessions).

3. A person is to grieve for those who cannot flee rapidly: pictured by pregnant women who are responsible for small children.

4. A person is to pray for good conditions in fleeing: pictured by both winter and the sabbath day. The sabbath day represented certain religious rules that would forbid fleeing (travel) for the religiously strong.

> **But when he saw many of the Pharisees and Sadducees coming to where he was baptizing, he said to them: "You brood of vipers! Who warned you to flee from the coming wrath? Produce fruit in keeping with repentance. (Mat 3:7-8)**

Thought 1. The danger is so imminent that Christ said, "Remember Lot's wife" (Lk.17:32).

Thought 2. There is a great stress here: when life is threatened, our minds need to be focused upon doing what we can to save our lives. As we walk day by day, what we should really be thankful for is our lives and not things.

Thought 3. Note to whom Christ speaks, who are the ones to forget worldly possessions and comforts of home: His disciples, His followers. Was He thinking of the materialistic comforts that characterize so many of His followers?

DEEPER STUDY # 2
(24:17) **House—Rooftop**: in ancient days, the rooftops of houses were flat; they were used for rest, meditation, and neighborly visits. Most houses had steps both inside and outside that led up to the roof. When the abomination is seen, the danger is so imminent that a person should flee from his roof immediately, using the outside stairs.

3 (24:21) **Great Distress—Great Tribulation**: there is the great distress [tribulation] that will be unparalleled in history.

1. In 66-70 A.D., Jerusalem experienced one of the most terrible sieges in all of history. In 66 A.D. the Jews revolted, and the Roman army was swift to attack. However, the city was difficult to take, primarily for two reasons. It sat upon a hill, well protected by the terrain, and the leaders of the revolt were religious fanatics. Well over a million people had fled into the city behind its protective walls.

As the siege wore on, the predictions of Christ were literally fulfilled. Outside the walls was the Roman army and all the maiming and killing of war. Inside the walls, neighbor after neighbor faced famine, pestilence, false deliverers (messiahs), betrayal, murder, revolt, rebellion, and hatred. And all took their toll. Josephus says over 1,000,000 people died and 97,000 were taken captive. The horrors of the siege are well described by him (see notes—Mt.24:7; 24:10; 24:11. See Josephus, Wars. 5. 12:3; 6. 3:4; 6. 8:5.)

> "It appears to me that the misfortunes of all men, from the beginning of the world, if they be compared to these of the Jews, are not so considerable as they were" (Josephus, Wars. Preface 4).

2. In the end time, the world will experience great distresses [tribulations] unparalleled in history. Note that Christ does not describe the great trials beyond what He has already said in v.5-12. A quick glance at the great distress [tribulation] period covered in Revelation will give some idea of the trials (see outlines and notes—all of the following. Cp. Dan.12:1-2.)

⇒ Thunderings, lightnings, and an earthquake Rev.8:1-5).
⇒ Natural catastrophes (Rev.8:6-12).
⇒ Demonic-like locusts or plagues (Rev.8:13-9:11).
⇒ Demonic-like army (Rev.9:12-21).
⇒ Angry nations who destroy the earth (Rev.11:18; cp. Rev.11:14-19).
⇒ An evil political ruler (Rev.13:1-10).
⇒ A false and evil religious ruler (Rev.13:11-18).
⇒ Terrible destruction and suffering, both upon nature and men (Rev.16:1-21).
⇒ An evil, deceptive world power (Rev.17:1-18:24).

4 (24:22) **End Time—Great Distress—Great Tribulation**: there is the promise that the days will be shortened for the elect's sake. Note that Christ said two things.

1. The days of "the great distress [tribulation]" will be shortened. What is meant by shortened?

⇒ Shorter than what God would usually allow for such great sinfulness.
⇒ Shorter than what the enemy expected.
⇒ Shorter than what others would expect of a ruling government against such revolting fanatics.

In dealing with Jerusalem, God in His providence used His power to shorten the days for Israel's sake. In the midst of judgment, He was merciful—Israel was not totally annihilated. The siege was shorter than expected. Many have listed *the natural causes* that led to the shorter siege.

⇒ Division and factions. The Jewish leaders were divided from the first. They never could form a cohesive policy.
⇒ A disastrous fire. The fire destroyed too many weapons and provisions for the city to continue fighting.
⇒ Rampaging gangs. These were set on self-preservation by any means: stealing, assaulting and killing. They are well documented by Josephus.
⇒ Treason and betrayal. Some even surrendered their fortifications without a fight.
⇒ The quick attack by Rome. Rome sent the armed force under Titus much quicker than expected.
⇒ Weak fortifications. Herod Agrippa had intended to strengthen the walls of Jerusalem, but he never did.

The believer, of course, sees God's hand in these natural causes. God *worked all things out for good* in order to shorten the days and to fulfill His Word. Despite *the terrible distress or tribulation*, some lives were saved—saved because God was compassionate (2 Pt.3:9).

In dealing with the end time, the distresses or tribulations upon the earth and its inhabitants will also be shortened.

> **Therefore rejoice, you heavens and you who dwell in them! But woe to the earth and the sea, because the devil has gone down to you! He is filled with fury, because he knows that his time is short." (Rev 12:12)**
>
> **They are also seven kings. Five have fallen, one is, the other has not yet come; but when he does come, he must remain for a little while. (Rev 17:10)**
>
> **And then the lawless one will be revealed, whom the Lord Jesus will overthrow with the breath of his mouth and destroy by the splendor of his coming. (2 Th 2:8)**

2. God will shorten the days of the great distress or tribulation for the elect's sake. From the historical perspective, some of the Christians remembered the Lord's warning and fled Jerusalem before the attack, sometime around 66 A.D. They fled to a smaller town called Pella in the district of Decapolis. These believers prayed for their neighbors and their beloved city, and God heard their intercessions. He shortened the days of terrible trials—shortened them because of the prayers of the elect.

God's mercy toward the lost—even toward civilizations and cities—and His willingness to save the lost in answer to the believers' intercessory prayer are clearly illustrated in Scripture. Abraham's prayer for Sodom and Gomorrah is an example. If just ten righteous people could have been found, the cities would have been spared despite their terrible sin (Gen.18:23f). Lot's prayer for Zoar is another example (Gen.19:20-22).

> **Therefore confess your sins to each other and pray for each other so that you may be healed. The prayer of a righteous man is powerful and effective. (James 5:16)**
>
> **"Go up and down the streets of Jerusalem, look around and consider, search through her squares. If you can find but one person who deals honestly and seeks the truth, I will forgive this city. (Jer 5:1)**
>
> **Last night an angel of the God whose I am and whom I serve stood beside me and said, 'Do not be afraid, Paul. You must stand trial before Caesar; and God has graciously given you the lives of all who sail with you.' Altogether there were 276 of us on board. but the centurion wanted to spare Paul's life and kept them from carrying out their plan. He ordered those who could swim to jump overboard first and get to land. The rest were to get there on planks or on pieces of the ship. In this way everyone reached land in safety. (Acts 27:23-24, 37, 43-44)**

Thought 1. God will honor the prayers of His *true followers*, even to the point of overriding natural disasters. How much change could occur in the evil of the world, both natural and human, if God's people really believed in intercessory prayer and became real intercessors for this corruptible world?

Thought 2. Too many of us are complainers, not intercessors. Too many of us complain over our affliction or else the length of our affliction. It is beyond us how God could ever allow such suffering. Three things are needed.

1) We must realize that God does not cause evil and suffering. God does not afflict; He delivers.
2) We must realize that we never suffer as much as we deserve. We are ever so sinful and have so polluted the earth with evil that we deserve the worst.
3) We must realize that God is merciful. What is needed is not complaining, but prayer—intercessory prayer. We need to pray, thanking God that the evil is not worse. Then in unceasing prayer, we need to ask Him to correct and shorten the evil.

5 (24:23-24) **False Messiahs—End Times**: there is the frantic search for a deliverer, for an earthly Messiah. Christ says three things.

1. False messiahs and prophets will appear. When men are oppressed and oppressed, witnessing scene after scene of death by hunger, pestilence, murder, and war, they cry for deliverance. They are ever so open to *a deliverer's* appearing on the scene, and some are always ready to assume the power and leadership for which men cry. In the siege of Jerusalem, such men (deliverers) arose who promised deliverance from both the Romans and the natural disasters. Apparently there had been the constant belief and rumors that the Messiah had returned, and He was either out in the desert or in some secret room within the city. He was just awaiting the hour to strike. The scene in Jerusalem was somewhat like Jeremiah's day.

> **But I said, "Ah, Sovereign LORD, the prophets keep telling them, 'You will not see the sword or suffer famine. Indeed, I will give you lasting peace in this place.'" Then the LORD said to me, "The prophets are prophesying lies in my name. I have not sent them or appointed them or spoken to them. They are prophesying to you false visions, divinations, idolatries and the delusions of their own minds. (Jer 14:13-14)**

The same kind of scene will repeat itself in the last days. The antichrist, the false deliverer of the earth, will arise to deceive the whole earth (see outlines and note—Rev.13:1-18 and related passages). Note that Christ simply says, "Do not believe it"—believe neither the rumors nor the false deliverer.

2. False deliverers will show great signs and miracles. Deliverers, local and national, always claim to be destined. They point to signs and miracles. This has always been true—and always will be true—through all times. The end time will witness an increase and intensification of signs and miracles that will stretch across the whole world.

> **And then the lawless one will be revealed, whom the Lord Jesus will overthrow with the breath of his mouth and destroy by the splendor of his coming. The coming of the lawless one will be in accordance with the work of Satan displayed in all kinds of counterfeit miracles, signs and wonders, and in every sort of evil that deceives those who are perishing. They perish because they refused to love the truth and so be saved. (2 Th 2:8-10)**
>
> **And he performed great and miraculous signs, even causing fire to come down from heaven to earth in full view of men. Because of the signs he was given power to do on behalf of the first beast, he deceived the inhabitants of the earth. He ordered them to set up an image in honor of the beast who was wounded by the sword and yet lived. (Rev 13:13-14)**

3. False deliverers will be so convincing they will even threaten the elect. The elect, of course, are genuine believers who stick with Christ regardless of the temptation, trials, threat and danger. An excellent passage that describes much of the same picture is seen in 2 Th.2:1-17. The way the elect are able to stand is clearly stated.

> **So then, brothers, stand firm and hold to the teachings we passed on to you, whether by word of mouth or by letter. May our Lord Jesus Christ himself and God our Father, who loved us and by his grace gave us eternal encouragement and good hope, encourage your hearts and strengthen you in every good deed and word. (2 Th 2:15-17)**

6 (24:25-28) **Jesus Christ, Return**: there is the truth about deliverance and about the Messiah's coming. Christ said four things about His return.

1. He will not come from the desert, that is, from some unknown and remote spot. When people proclaim that the great deliverer has appeared in a certain place, the message or rumor is not to be believed: "do not go out."

2. He will not come from an inner room, that is, in secret, unseen, quietly. Again, when such a message or rumor is proclaimed, "Do not believe it."

3. He will come "as lightning."
   a. His coming will be out of heaven (out of the spiritual world and dimension)—just as lightning.
   b. His coming will be sudden and surprising—just as lightning.
   c. His coming will be visible to all, seen from east to west—just as lightning (cp. Rev.1:7).

> **"At that time the sign of the Son of Man will appear in the sky, and all the nations of the earth will mourn. They will see the Son of Man coming on the clouds of the sky, with power and great glory. (Mat 24:30)**
>
> **After he said this, he was taken up before their very eyes, and a cloud hid him from their sight. They were looking intently up into the sky as he was going, when suddenly two men dressed in white stood beside them. "Men of Galilee," they said, "why do you stand here looking into the sky? This same Jesus, who has been taken from you into heaven, will come back in the same way you have seen him go into heaven." (Acts 1:9-11)**
>
> **For the Lord himself will come down from heaven, with a loud command, with the voice of the archangel and with the trumpet call of God, and the dead in Christ will rise first. After that, we who are still alive and are left will be caught up together with them in the clouds to meet the Lord in the air. And so we will be with the Lord forever. Therefore encourage each other with these words. (1 Th 4:16-18)**
>
> **Look, he is coming with the clouds, and every eye will see him, even those who pierced him; and all the peoples of the earth will mourn because of him. So shall it be! Amen. (Rev 1:7; cp. Rev.19:11-19)**

4. He will come to execute judgment (v.28. Cp. Is.30:30; Rev.19:20-21.) The eagles, birds of prey, always gather where the carcass is. There are at least two meanings to this verse.
   a. The carcass is the Jewish people, and the eagles are the Roman armies under Titus who gathered around Jerusalem to consume the prey.
   b. The carcass is the world, the spiritually dead, and the eagles are Christ and His holy angels and saints. They come to gather around the dead world, executing judgment.

   The point of this passage is that the coming of Christ will be to execute universal judgment. He will come for the carcase, for all the spiritually dead in order to execute judgment upon them. Christ will execute judgment upon the whole world.

> **And I saw an angel standing in the sun, who cried in a loud voice to all the birds flying in midair, "Come, gather together for the great supper of God, so that you may eat the flesh of kings, generals, and mighty men, of horses and their riders, and the flesh of all people, free and slave, small and great." (Rev 19:17-18)**
>
> **"When the Son of Man comes in his glory, and all the angels with him, he will sit on his throne in heavenly glory. All the nations will be gathered before him, and he will separate the people one from another as a shepherd separates the sheep from the goats. (Mat 25:31-32)**
>
> **Just as man is destined to die once, and after that to face judgment, (Heb 9:27)**
> **if this is so, then the Lord knows how to rescue godly men from trials and to hold the unrighteous for the day of judgment, while continuing their punishment. (2 Pet 2:9)**
>
> **By the same word the present heavens and earth are reserved for fire, being kept for the day of judgment and destruction of ungodly men. (2 Pet 3:7)**
>
> **Enoch, the seventh from Adam, prophesied about these men: "See, the Lord is coming with thousands upon thousands of his holy ones to judge everyone, and to convict all the ungodly of all the ungodly acts they have done in the ungodly way, and of all the harsh words ungodly sinners have spoken against him." (Jude 1:14-15)**

	C. The Coming of the Son of Man: Five Events, 24:29-31
1 Immediately after the distress or tribulation **2 Event 1: There will be astronomical happenings**	29 "Immediately after the distress of those days "'the sun will be darkened, and the moon will not give its light; the stars will fall from the sky, and the heavenly bodies will be shaken.'
3 Event 2: The sign of Christ will appear **4 Event 3: All the nations will see Christ's coming in the clouds** **5 Event 4: All the nations of the earth will mourn**	30 "At that time the sign of the Son of Man will appear in the sky, and all the nations of the earth will mourn. They will see the Son of Man coming on the clouds of the sky, with power and great glory.
6 Event 5: The angels will be sent forth to gather the elect	31 And he will send his angels with a loud trumpet call, and they will gather his elect from the four winds, from one end of the heavens to the other.

DIVISION XV

THE MESSIAH'S PROPHECY OF HIS RETURN AND THE END OF THE AGE: THE OLIVET DISCOURSE, 24:1-25:46

C. The Coming of the Son of Man: Five Events, 24:29-31

(24:29-31) **Jesus Christ, Return—Distress—Tribulation—Israel**: Christ revealed exactly when He was to return—"immediately after the distress [tribulation] of those days." The great distress [tribulation] occurs, then our Lord returns—"immediately." (See outline and notes—Mt.24:1-28 for background to this passage.)

1. Now note: Christ did not return immediately after the downfall of Jerusalem; therefore, what did He mean? Luke explains:

> **How dreadful it will be in those days for pregnant women and nursing mothers! There will be great distress in the land and wrath against this people. They will fall by the sword and will be taken as prisoners to all the nations. Jerusalem will be trampled on by the Gentiles until the times of the Gentiles are fulfilled. (Luke 21:23-24)**

Very simply, Christ said that the fall of Jerusalem was only the beginning of the distress or tribulation of the Jews. Their distress or tribulation continues until "the times of the Gentiles are fulfilled." The accuracy of the Lord's words is clearly seen by simply breaking down the verses of Luke and thinking through world history since Christ.

⇒ There is still "great distress in the land" of Israel.
⇒ There is still "great wrath against this people."
⇒ Many Jews still "fall by the sword."
⇒ Many are still "prisoners [dispersed] in all nations."
⇒ Jerusalem is still "trampled on by the Gentiles."

No people have ever gone through such great distress or tribulation as the Jews. They are still suffering at the hands of the Gentiles (for example, World War II, where over 5,000,000 were slaughtered in less than eight years); and they shall suffer great distress or tribulation "until the times of the Gentiles be fulfilled." It is *immediately after the great distress or tribulation of the Jews* and after *the great distress or tribulation* coming at the end of the world that the coming of Christ shall take place.

Note a very significant fact: Luke's prophecy definitely points toward the double meaning of Christ's words. Since the *great distress or tribulation* of the Jews in 70 A.D. (cp. v.20), they have continued to suffer *great distress [tribulation]* through the present age, and they shall suffer right on through the great distress [tribulation] that is to occur at the end of the world.

2. Also note it is immediately after the "great distress [tribulation]" of the world (v.21) that Christ returns (see DEEPER STUDY # 1,2—Mt. 24:1-31; notes—24:1-14; 24:15-28).

1. Immediately after the distress or tribulation (v.29).
2. Event 1: there will be astronomical happenings (v.29).
3. Event 2: the sign of Christ will appear (v.30).
4. Event 3: all the nations will see Christ coming in the clouds (v.30).
5. Event 4: all the nations of the earth will mourn (v.30).
6. Event 5: the angels will be sent forth to gather the elect (v.31).

1 (24:29) **Jesus Christ, Return—Distress—Tribulation**: the scene is immediately after the distress or tribulation (see note—Mt. 24:29-31 for discussion).

> **Thought 1.** There are several lessons in the words "after the distress [tribulation]"—lessons for us as

well as for those who will follow Christ through the tribulation.

1) God is in control. He can, does, and will end the trials. Note the word "after the distress [tribulation]." There *shall* be an end to all the trials of the distress or tribulation.
2) God's people are to look to Him and hope in Him. The end of all trials is coming.
3) God's people are always to be waiting and watching for the Lord's return.

2 (24:29) **Jesus Christ, Return—End Times—Astronomical Bodies—Outer Space**: the very first event to occur when Christ returns in glory will be astronomical happenings. The heavenly bodies—the sun, moon, stars, and "the heavenly bodies"—will be affected.

Note the exact words of the astronomical happenings.

⇒ "The sun will be darkened."
⇒ "The moon will not give her light."
⇒ "The stars will fall from heaven."
⇒ "The heavenly bodies will be shaken."

Very practically, such astronomical happenings occur now. The earth is sometimes darkened by dust from earthly catastrophes such as volcanic eruptions, wind storms, and smoke from huge fires. Of course, whatever darkens the sun hides the light of the moon from earth. Stars or meteorites of varying sizes fall throughout space often. "The heavenly bodies" being shaken could be the heavenly bodies outside our solar system that are called by the Bible "all the heavenly array" (Dt.4:19).

Is this what Christ meant? There is no way to know for sure; however, it is likely that this is the meaning. *But note*: His coming is going to trigger astronomical happenings worldwide and universally. The whole universe is going to be affected, or to word it in a much more meaningful way: the whole universe is going to open up and receive Him, including the astronomical bodies; and every man is going to know beyond any doubt that He is coming in all the power and the glory of God Himself. Christ says He is coming "with power and great glory." He is coming that "at the name of Jesus every knee should bow, in heaven and on earth and under the earth, and every tongue confess that Jesus Christ is Lord, to the glory of God the Father" (Ph.2:10-11).

He is coming, and "all the nations of the earth will [know it] and mourn [for] they will see the Son of Man coming in the clouds of the sky with power and great glory." The words "power and great glory" convey the idea that He is coming to subject all men, to rule and reign over all the nations or nations of the earth.

Scripture definitely reveals that astronomical happenings will precede and accompany the coming of the Lord.

The stars of heaven and their constellations will not show their light. The rising sun will be darkened and the moon will not give its light. I will punish the world for its evil, the wicked for their sins. I will put an end to the arrogance of the haughty and will humble the pride of the ruthless. I will make man scarcer than pure gold, more rare than the gold of Ophir. Therefore I will make the heavens tremble; and the earth will shake from its place at the wrath of the LORD Almighty, in the day of his burning anger. (Isa 13:10-13)

Terror and pit and snare await you, O people of the earth. Whoever flees at the sound of terror will fall into a pit; whoever climbs out of the pit will be caught in a snare. The floodgates of the heavens are opened, the foundations of the earth shake. The earth is broken up, the earth is split asunder, the earth is thoroughly shaken. The earth reels like a drunkard, it sways like a hut in the wind; so heavy upon it is the guilt of its rebellion that it falls—never to rise again. In that day the LORD will punish the powers in the heavens above and the kings on the earth below. They will be herded together like prisoners bound in a dungeon; they will be shut up in prison and be punished after many days. (Isa 24:17-22)

I will show wonders in the heavens and on the earth, blood and fire and billows of smoke. The sun will be turned to darkness and the moon to blood before the coming of the great and dreadful day of the LORD. (Joel 2:30-31)

The sun and moon will be darkened, and the stars no longer shine. The LORD will roar from Zion and thunder from Jerusalem; the earth and the sky will tremble. But the LORD will be a refuge for his people, a stronghold for the people of Israel. (Joel 3:15-16)

"But in those days, following that distress, "'the sun will be darkened, and the moon will not give its light; the stars will fall from the sky, and the heavenly bodies will be shaken.' (Mark 13:24-25)

But the day Lot left Sodom, fire and sulfur rained down from heaven and destroyed them all. "It will be just like this on the day the Son of Man is revealed. (Luke 17:29-30)

"There will be signs in the sun, moon and stars. On the earth, nations will be in anguish and perplexity at the roaring and tossing of the sea. Men will faint from terror, apprehensive of what is coming on the world, for the heavenly bodies will be shaken. (Luke 21:25-26)

I will show wonders in the heaven above and signs on the earth below, blood and fire and billows of smoke. The sun will be turned to darkness and the moon to blood before the coming of the great and glorious day of the Lord. (Acts 2:19-20)

I watched as he opened the sixth seal. There was a great earthquake. The sun turned black like sackcloth made of goat hair, the whole moon turned blood red, and the stars in the sky fell to earth, as late figs drop from a fig tree when shaken by a strong wind. The sky receded like a scroll, rolling up, and every mountain and island was removed from its place. Then the kings of the earth, the princes, the generals, the rich, the mighty, and every slave and every free man hid in caves and among the rocks of the mountains. They called to the mountains and the rocks, "Fall on us and hide us from the face of him who sits on the throne

> **and from the wrath of the Lamb! For the great day of their wrath has come, and who can stand?" (Rev 6:12-17). (See outline and notes—Rev.6:12-17)**

Note the exact words of the verses in Revelation above, for they are referring to the same event as Christ (v.30; cp. Rev.6:17). Christ triggers a great earthquake on earth and astronomical happenings in the heavens above (v.12-14). Men, great and small, are terrified and hide themselves (v.15) and cry for immediate death instead of having to face Christ (v.16). Why? Because they know something: "The great day of God's wrath has come; and who can stand?" (v.17).

The disciples had asked, "What will be the sign of your coming, and of the end of the age?" And Christ is answering them. Terrifying astronomical happenings will be a sign.

> **Thought 1.** Happenings in nature should cause us to turn our attention toward God. They are reminders of the *stressful* events that are to occur in the end time. As Christ said: "Stand up, and lift up your heads; because your redemption is drawing near" (Lk.21:28). If we look up and trust Him *now*, catastrophes and circumstances can be borne much better. His presence with us assures us of strength and endurance and victory (Heb.12:3; cp. 1 Cor.10:13; Mt.28:20; cp. Heb.13:5-6).

3 (24:30) **Jesus Christ, Return—End Times**: when Christ returns, there will be a second event to occur—there will be *the* sign of Christ's appearing in the heavens. What is the sign? Christ does not specifically say. There are four different thoughts.

- ⇒ Some say the sign will be a star, just like the star that proclaimed His birth.
- ⇒ Others say it will be the Shekinah glory, His glory shining forth in all the splendor and brightness of God Himself. His glory will, of course, shine forth as described; but again, Christ does not say specifically that this is the sign.
- ⇒ Some, including many of the early church fathers, believe the sign will be the cross of Christ. There is no question that seeing the cross appear in the sky universally would attract attention and signal that something is about to happen. The cross is the symbol of Christianity and points toward the purpose of God in the world more than any other single thing.
- ⇒ Many believe the sign to be simply the appearance of the Son of Man Himself (Mt.26:64; Dan.7:13-14).

Note four points.

1. When the sign appears, "all the nations of the earth will mourn." They know exactly what the sign is and what it means: the judgment and rule and reign of Christ. The nations (people) do not have to guess and interpret what it means.

2. When the sign appears, "all the nations of the earth mourn...they will see the Son of Man coming on the clouds of the sky."

3. The Lord says that His coming will be as lightning, quick and sudden (v.27). Will there be time for a sign other than His personal appearance?

4. The disciples had asked about the *sign*: "What will be the sign of your coming...?" (v.3). Christ gives them a number of signs. Perhaps He is simply saying, "At that time the sign of the Son of Man will appear" This would, of course, be a fulfillment of Daniel's well-known sign of the Son of Man and His coming (Dan.7:13-14).

Whatever the sign, there is one important thing to note: everyone knows exactly what it means. God's Son is coming to judge and to rule and reign over all the earth.

> **"When the Son of Man comes in his glory, and all the angels with him, he will sit on his throne in heavenly glory. All the nations will be gathered before him, and he will separate the people one from another as a shepherd separates the sheep from the goats. (Mat.25:31-32)**
>
> **If this is so, then the Lord knows how to rescue godly men from trials and to hold the unrighteous for the day of judgment, while continuing their punishment. (2 Pet 2:9)**
>
> **By the same word the present heavens and earth are reserved for fire, being kept for the day of judgment and destruction of ungodly men. (2 Pet 3:7)**
>
> **Enoch, the seventh from Adam, prophesied about these men: "See, the Lord is coming with thousands upon thousands of his holy ones to judge everyone, and to convict all the ungodly of all the ungodly acts they have done in the ungodly way, and of all the harsh words ungodly sinners have spoken against him." (Jude 1:14-15)**
>
> **Then I saw a great white throne and him who was seated on it. Earth and sky fled from his presence, and there was no place for them. And I saw the dead, great and small, standing before the throne, and books were opened. Another book was opened, which is the book of life. The dead were judged according to what they had done as recorded in the books. The sea gave up the dead that were in it, and death and Hades gave up the dead that were in them, and each person was judged according to what he had done. Then death and Hades were thrown into the lake of fire. The lake of fire is the second death. If anyone's name was not found written in the book of life, he was thrown into the lake of fire. (Rev 20:11-15)**

Thought 1. There will be a sign that triggers the coming of the Son of Man. Whatever the sign is, four things are certain.

1) *Now* the stars point toward the eternal power and Godhead and love of God in a beautiful creation. *Then* the stars shall point toward the wrath of God.
2) *Now* the Shekinah glory, the glory of God, shines before men calling them to righteousness. *Then* the Shekinah glory shall shine before men consuming them for their unrighteousness.
3) *Now* the cross stands before the world attracting the world to God. *Then* the cross shall stand before the world condemning the world.
4) *Now* Christ stands before the world as its Savior. *Then* Christ shall stand before the world as its Judge.

Thought 2. There are sign(s) of Christ's presence *now*. There are also signs that His return is ever so near. How much better to *mourn* and repent now than to be left with nothing but *mourning* then. The day is coming when it will be too late to turn to Christ.

Thought 3. Today, every man is without excuse. There are sign(s) and evidence(s) that He is the Savior of the world, God's very own Son. Much better to have the Son of Man appear now, in a person's heart and life by faith, than to have Him appear in the skies as a person's Judge (Heb.9:27; cp. Jn.3:18).

4 (24:30) **Jesus Christ, Return**: the third event of the Lord's return is that it will be visible to all—all the nations of the earth will see Christ's coming in the clouds with power and great glory. There are four things said in this brief prophecy.

1. It is the Son of Man who will come. Christ claims He is the Son of Man, God's very own Son, the Ideal Man, the Perfect Man, the Son of God incarnate in human flesh (see DEEPER STUDY # 3—Mt.8:20). In that day, there will be no doubt about who He is (cp. Mk.14:61-62). Right now He is recognized only by believers, but then He will be recognized by all men. It will be unmistakable: He is the Son of Man.

2. All the nations of the earth will see His coming—visibly. How will everyone on earth, a round planet, see Him all at once? It is useless to speculate how God's power *works* (effects) any miracle. The point Christ is making is that His return will be visible and that every man on earth will see Him and acknowledge Him to be the Son of Man (cp. Rev.1:7). (Note: the light—the great splendor and brightness—of the Lord's glory can easily be manifested throughout the universe and surround the earth when He returns.)

3. Christ will come in the clouds of the sky. In Scripture, clouds are often associated with God.

> **He mounted the cherubim and flew; he soared on the wings of the wind. He made darkness his covering, his canopy around him— the dark rain clouds of the sky. Out of the brightness of his presence clouds advanced, with hailstones and bolts of lightning. (Psa 18:10-12)**
>
> **And lays the beams of his upper chambers on their waters. He makes the clouds his chariot and rides on the wings of the wind. (Psa 104:3)**
>
> **An oracle concerning Egypt: See, the LORD rides on a swift cloud and is coming to Egypt. The idols of Egypt tremble before him, and the hearts of the Egyptians melt within them. (Isa 19:1)**
>
> **"In my vision at night I looked, and there before me was one like a son of man, coming with the clouds of heaven. He approached the Ancient of Days and was led into his presence. (Dan 7:13)**

When Jesus departed this earth after His resurrection, He departed in a cloud, and it was foretold that He would return in a cloud (Acts 1:9-11). Christ clearly says that He is going to return in a cloud and every eye will see Him come in the clouds of heaven. There is a strong claim here, a claim to be the God of the clouds.

4. Christ will come with power and great glory. There are at least two points being stressed in this fact.

a. Christ will come in the full dignity of His person. He will not come as a babe in a manger who lives through the stages of life to secure salvation for man. He will come with power and great glory. He will come in all the omnipotence and glory of God, revealing just who He is.

b. Christ will come as a Judge to execute justice upon the earth. He will come to rule and reign in His rightful position as Sovereign Lord over the earth.

Thought 1. Every man will acknowledge Christ to be the Son of Man. There will not be a single exception.

⇒ Now, there is *voluntary* acknowledgement; then, there will be *involuntary* acknowledgement.

⇒ Now, there is *wilful* confession; then, there will be *enforced* confession.

⇒ Now, there is a *loving* appeal; then, there will be the *condemning* judgment.

> **For he has set a day when he will judge the world with justice by the man he has appointed. He has given proof of this to all men by raising him from the dead." (Acts 17:31)**
>
> **This will take place on the day when God will judge men's secrets through Jesus Christ, as my gospel declares. (Rom 2:16)**
>
> **Therefore God exalted him to the highest place and gave him the name that is above every name, that at the name of Jesus every knee should bow, in heaven and on earth and under the earth, and every tongue confess that Jesus Christ is Lord, to the glory of God the Father. (Phil 2:9-11)**
>
> **Since you call on a Father who judges each man's work impartially, live your lives as strangers here in reverent fear. (1 Pet 1:17)**

5 (24:30) **Jesus Christ, Return**: the fourth event is that all the nations of the earth will mourn when Christ returns in power and great glory. Why? Because they will see beyond any question that Christ is the Son of Man. They will realize that they ignored, neglected, rejected, abused, and cursed Him. They will know that they have missed His salvation and that they are now to be judged. There is a picture of this great mourning in Revelation where "all the peoples of the earth...will mourn because of Him" (Rev.1:7). They wail and mourn because of the terrible judgment which is to be inflicted upon them.

Very simply, Christ is going to return, and every eye will see Him and know beyond any question that He is the Son of Man. The worldly will mourn because He comes as Judge; the elect will rejoice because they are to be gathered together with Him.

Thought 1. Every man has a choice. He mourns now, or he shall mourn when Christ returns. A man experiences a godly sorrow that leads to repentance *now*, or he shall experience a worldly sorrow that leads to eternal sorrow when Christ returns (see DEEPER STUDY # 1—2 Cor.7:10).

Peter replied, "Repent and be baptized, every one of you, in the name of Jesus Christ for the forgiveness of your sins. And you will receive the gift of the Holy Spirit. (Acts 2:38)

Repent of this wickedness and pray to the Lord. Perhaps he will forgive you for having such a thought in your heart. (Acts 8:22)

Godly sorrow brings repentance that leads to salvation and leaves no regret, but worldly sorrow brings death. (2 Cor 7:10)

Rid yourselves of all the offenses you have committed, and get a new heart and a new spirit. Why will you die, O house of Israel? (Ezek 18:31)

6 (24:31) **Jesus Christ, Return**: the fifth event of the Lord's coming is that the angels will be sent forth to gather the elect. There are four points made in this verse.

1. Christ will send forth *His* angels. He is God, the Lord of the angels. They are His; He is over them. They are at His beck and call to carry out His sovereign will. This again is a claim to deity.

2. Christ will send forth His angels with "a loud trumpet call." The trumpet was used to call an assembly of the people together. This is probably the meaning here. (Cp. 1 Cor.15:52; 1 Th.4:16.)

3. The angels will gather together the Lord's elect. Only the elect will be gathered at this point. The elect may be but a few when compared to the mass of humanity. But there will be a remnant of genuine believers scattered all over the earth, a remnant who will have endured to the end. They will be saved (v.13. Cp. Mt.20:16; 22:14.)

As Christ said:

I tell you, on that night two people will be in one bed; one will be taken and the other left. Two women will be grinding grain together; one will be taken and the other left." (Luke 17:34-35; cp.Mt.24:40-41)

4. The elect will be gathered from the four winds, from one end of heaven to the other. The meaning is this: the elect will be scattered all over the world; they will be everywhere, in all nations of the world (cp. Dt.4:32; Rev.7:9). As Christ had just said:

And this gospel of the kingdom will be preached in the whole world as a testimony to all nations, and then the end will come. (Mat 24:14)

Thought 1. There is one glorious hope for every believer, whatever his generation and the trials of it:

While we wait for the blessed hope—the glorious appearing of our great God and Savior, Jesus Christ, who gave himself for us to redeem us from all wickedness and to purify for himself a people that are his very own, eager to do what is good. (Titus 2:13-14)

Thought 2. The angels are subject to Christ; we, too, should be subject to Him. The angels do His sovereign will; we, too, should do His sovereign will. If we administer His will now, we shall be in that select company in that glorious day.

Thought 3. Not a single believer will be missed when Jesus returns. No matter where we are or how isolated and lonely and forgotten we may feel, He is coming for us.

	D. The Time of the Lord's Return, 24:32-41 (Mk.13:28-34; Lk.21:29-35)	angels in heaven, nor the Son, but only the Father.	
		37 As it was in the days of Noah, so it will be at the coming of the Son of Man.	**3 The day shall come suddenly—unexpectedly—shattering to the world of unbelievers**[DS2]
1 The time can be generally discerned	32 "Now learn this lesson from the fig tree: As soon as its twigs get tender and its leaves come out, you know that summer is near.	38 For in the days before the flood, people were eating and drinking, marrying and giving in marriage, up to the day Noah entered the ark;	a. Its counterpart is Noah's day: A day of sensuality & of refusing to heed the message of coming judgment[DS3,4]
a. Its events are compared to a fig tree[DS1]	33 Even so, when you see all these things, you know that it is near, right at the door.	39 And they knew nothing about what would happen until the flood came and took them all away. That is how it will be at the coming of the Son of Man.	b. Its shock: "Knew noth ing"—were unbelieving, close-minded, ignorant c. Its certainty: "How it will be"
b. Its events will be witnessed by one generation	34 I tell you the truth, this generation will certainly not pass away until all these things have happened.	40 Two men will be in the field; one will be taken and the other left.	**4 The day shall be a time of separation & judgment**
c. Its events are certain	35 Heaven and earth will pass away, but my words will never pass away.	41 Two women will be grinding with a hand mill; one will be taken and the other left.	
2 The actual day & hour are known only by God	36 "No one knows about that day or hour, not even the		

DIVISION XV

THE MESSIAH'S PROPHECY OF HIS RETURN AND THE END OF THE AGE: THE OLIVET DISCOURSE, 24:1-25:46

D. The Time of the Lord's Return, 24:32-41

(24:32-41) **Introduction—End Time**: the disciples had asked, "When will this happen?" At this point of His discussion, Christ said, "*Now* learn this lesson from the fig tree: As soon as...." Note the words "will this happen." He was beginning to discuss the end time and His return. It should be noted that the first part of His discussion can apply to the fall of Jerusalem in 70 A.D. as well as to the end time (v.32-35). However, Christ definitely said this passage had to do with the end time only, with the coming of the Son of Man (v.37, 39). When will Christ return? He revealed four significant points.

1. The time can be generally discerned (v.32-35).
2. The actual day and hour are known only by God (v.36).
3. The day shall come suddenly—unexpectedly—shattering to the world of unbelievers (v.37-39).
4. The day will be a time of separation and judgment (v.40-41).

1 (24:32-35) **Jesus Christ, Return**: Christ said that the time of His return can be generally discerned.

1. The events (signs) that point to His return are compared to a fig tree. When the fig tree begins to put forth its leaves, it is known that summer is near. So when we see "all these things," the signs He has been sharing, "know that it [His coming] is near, right at the door." His coming is at the very threshold; He is about to enter into the world again (cp. Jas.5:9).

Note what Christ said:

a. When the leaves on a fig tree are seen, summer is not yet. But we *know* summer is near, at hand.
b. "Even so, when you see all these things you know that it [His coming, His kingdom] is near." He definitely says we can "know that it is near."

2. The events (signs) will be witnessed by one generation. The disciples had asked two questions—one about Jerusalem's destruction and one about the end of the world. In answering their questions, Christ nowhere drew a definite line between the two questions. The signs and events that precede one shall precede the other. The implication is clear: just as the signs and destruction of Jerusalem took place within a generation, the signs and destruction of the world will also occur within a generation. (See DEEPER STUDY # 2, pt.2—Mt.24:1-31.)

3. The events (signs) are certain. Christ was definite about what He had said. "Heaven and earth will pass away, but my words will never pass away."

Note two things.

a. Heaven and earth will pass away. Christ was saying they are actually going to be done away with (2 Pt.3:10-11).
b. All that He had said about the great distress (tribulation) and His return will happen. The great distress (tribulation) and His return are more sure than heaven and earth.

Thought 1. *Expectation* is a key word when dealing with the Lord's return. When we see a fig tree's putting forth its leaves, we *expect* summer to be near. "Even so" we should expect two things.

1) We should expect the signs, "all these things" that Christ has been mentioning (v.33[a]).
2) We should expect and "know that it [His coming] is near" (v.33[b]).

Thought 2. In the eyes of men, it has been a long time since Christ spoke these words, and an innumerable list of events have happened. Therefore, men assume that the second coming is a fable, the figment of hopeful imagination. God knew this would happen.

First of all, you must understand that

in the last days scoffers will come, scoffing and following their own evil desires. They will say, "Where is this 'coming' he promised? Ever since our fathers died, everything goes on as it has since the beginning of creation." But do not forget this one thing, dear friends: With the Lord a day is like a thousand years, and a thousand years are like a day. The Lord is not slow in keeping his promise, as some understand slowness. He is patient with you, not wanting anyone to perish, but everyone to come to repentance. But the day of the Lord will come like a thief. The heavens will disappear with a roar; the elements will be destroyed by fire, and the earth and everything in it will be laid bare. Since everything will be destroyed in this way, what kind of people ought you to be? You ought to live holy and godly lives as you look forward to the day of God and speed its coming. That day will bring about the destruction of the heavens by fire, and the elements will melt in the heat. But in keeping with his promise we are looking forward to a new heaven and a new earth, the home of righteousness. (2 Pet 3:3-4, 8-13)

Thought 3. Three things are certain to happen in human history: "the beginning of birth pains [sorrows]" (v.8); "the great distress [tribulation], unequaled from the beginning of the world" (v.21); and "the Son of Man coming on the clouds of the sky with power and great glory" (v.30). Heaven and earth shall pass away, but not the words He spoke, not what He said would happen. What He said would happen will happen. These three events are certain.

DEEPER STUDY # 1
(24:33-34) **Jesus Christ, Return**: note the time involved in these two verses—they agree. "When you see all these things...it is near" (v.33). All will happen in "one generation" (v.34).

2 (24:36) **End Time**: the actual day and hour that Christ will return are known only by God. Note two things.

1. The return of Christ is a real event that is yet to happen. There is "that day or hour." There is *a fixed day and a fixed hour* when Christ will return. It is an actual event.

2. The return of Christ is secret. "No one knows...but only the Father." Some have thought they knew, but Christ is explicit: "No one knows, not even the angels of heaven, but only the Father." (See note—2 Th.2:1-2.)

But no one in heaven or on earth or under the earth could open the scroll or even look inside it. (Rev 5:3)

The secret things belong to the LORD our God, but the things revealed belong to us and to our children forever, that we may follow all the words of this law. (Deu 29:29)

Thought 1. Some things are to be left entirely in God's hands. The exact day and hour of the Lord's return is one of these things. *Watchful* believers will be sensitive to the season (fig tree, v.32-33) and know the generation (v.34), but the exact hour and day are hid from men, even from the wisest and most spiritual men. *Only* God Himself knows when Christ will return. If a man claims to know the hour and day, he is the man from which we should flee. That man's word conflicts with the Lord's Word.

3 (24:37-39) **Jesus Christ, Return**: the coming of the Lord will be sudden—unexpected—shattering to the world of unbelievers. Christ says three things.

1. When will Christ return? His coming finds its counterpart in Noah's day. He will come when the world is living just as it was living in Noah's day:

⇒ Living sensual lives, eating, drinking, marrying, divorcing, and remarrying time after time (see DEEPER STUDY 3,4—Mt.24:38; cp. Lk.17:26-30).

⇒ Refusing to heed Noah's message of righteousness and coming judgment (2 Pt.2:5).

a. Note that eating, drinking (water), and marriage are all necessary to maintain life. It is the excessiveness, the lust for more and more, the extravagance that is sinful. It is setting one's mind upon the pleasure of the flesh and of the world and lusting for more and more. (See note—Jas.4:1; DEEPER STUDY # 1—4:1-3; note—4:2. Cp. Ro.1:24.)

b. Note another point: What is it that Christ says will characterize the age? Not stealing and murder and immorality, but eating and drinking and marrying time after time. When the earth was destroyed the first time, it was because "the earth was corrupt...and...full of violence" (Gen.6:11). However, the sins that bring the second destruction of the earth seem to be eating and drinking and marrying time after time. These are the sins stressed by Christ.

c. Note the words "up to the day that Noah entered the ark." While Noah was building the ark, he preached the righteousness of God and the coming judgment. The people had the testimony of Noah's life and his belief in God's Word as a warning, a warning that man was responsible to live righteously and that judgment was coming. They saw Noah building the ark. They saw the ark sitting there, yet they rejected Noah's message and testimony. They went on living in worldliness, in their eating and drinking and in pursuing their own lustful desires, and they did so right up until the very day that "Noah entered into the ark." Then suddenly, unexpectedly, their world was shattered.

2. When will Christ come? He will come just as He came in Noah's day: at a shocking time. Just as they "knew nothing about" the end that was coming, so He will come again when the world does not know.

a. They "knew nothing" means this: they did not expect the coming judgment. They *did not believe* the fact, the word, the message. They *were close-minded*; they did not bother too much about listening and studying the matter. Therefore, they *were ignorant* about the truth. They did not know the Word of God.

b. "They knew nothing" means this: they felt secure in themselves and in their world. As Scripture says in another place:

While people are saying, "Peace and safety," destruction will come on them suddenly, as labor pains on a pregnant

woman, and they will not escape. (1 Th 5:3)

c. They "knew nothing" means this: they were living worldly and materialistic lives, eating and drinking when they should have been sensible and clear-minded, listening and turning to God.
d. They "knew nothing" means this: their concern was "Let us eat and drink: for tomorrow we die" (Is.22:13); whereas their concern should have been *righteousness* (2 Cor.5:21).

3. When will Christ come? He will come when people are living just as they were living in the days of Noah: "As it was in the days of Noah, so it will be at the coming of the Son of Man" (v.37, 39). His coming is certain and assured.

> **For in the days before the flood, people were eating and drinking, marrying and giving in marriage, up to the day Noah entered the ark; and they knew nothing about what would happen until the flood came and took them all away. That is how it will be at the coming of the Son of Man. (Mat 24:38-39)**
>
> **"Be careful, or your hearts will be weighed down with dissipation, drunkenness and the anxieties of life, and that day will close on you unexpectedly like a trap. (Luke 21:34)**
>
> **It teaches us to say "No" to ungodliness and worldly passions, and to live self-controlled, upright and godly lives in this present age, while we wait for the blessed hope—the glorious appearing of our great God and Savior, Jesus Christ, (Titus 2:12-13)**
>
> **You adulterous people, don't you know that friendship with the world is hatred toward God? Anyone who chooses to be a friend of the world becomes an enemy of God. (James 4:4)**
>
> **Do not love the world or anything in the world. If anyone loves the world, the love of the Father is not in him. For everything in the world—the cravings of sinful man, the lust of his eyes and the boasting of what he has and does—comes not from the Father but from the world. (1 John 2:15-16)**

Thought 1. Note the words "knew nothing." They *knew nothing* because they were steeped in sensual living. A person can eat, drink, and be immoral until he is gripped and enslaved (see notes—Ro.1:24; Jas.4:1-6).
- ⇒ *Conscience* becomes dull, hardened, and insensitive to right.
- ⇒ *Will* becomes more craving.
- ⇒ *Spirit* becomes more selfish.
- ⇒ *Life* becomes more worldly.
- ⇒ *Hope* becomes more materialistic.
- ⇒ *Death* becomes more final.

Thought 2. Christ's return will shatter the world of the person...
- who eats and eats.
- who drinks and drinks.
- who marries and marries.
- who "knows nothing."
- who does not believe.
- who is close-minded.
- who is ignorant.

Thought 3. There are many genuine believers in the world. The testimony of righteousness should be right before the face of most people just as it was before the face of the people in Noah's day. We are without excuse. We should be prepared for His coming. His *sudden* coming should not catch us unexpectedly; it should not shock or shatter our world.

Thought 4. A man must not allow himself to be so immersed in worldliness that he forgets eternity (1 Jn.2:15-16; Ro.12:1-2; 2 Cor.6:17-18).

DEEPER STUDY # 2
(24:37) **Jesus Christ, Return**: it must be remembered that the righteous, that is, the only believers of Noah's day, were Noah himself and his family. They were not caught unaware. It was to the unbelieving world that the day came unexpectedly and with shattering suddenness. This is understandable: the true believer is ever looking "for the blessed hope—the glorious appearing of our great God and Savior, Jesus Christ" (Tit.2:13). When that day begins to approach, believers will see and discern the times through the power of the Holy Spirit. The Holy Spirit will be preparing the believer's heart for that day. But the unbelieving world will be mocking what it considers foolish belief. It will be going about its merry way and wantonness, paying no attention whatever to an event that it considers foolish. (Cp. Dan.12:10.)

DEEPER STUDY # 3
(24:38) **Eating** (trogontes): to gnaw; to chew. It has the idea of grabbing and gnawing greedily like a hungry dog. Here it means the habitual practice of eating with a gluttonous appetite, eating excessively.

DEEPER STUDY # 4
(24:38) **Drinking** (pinontes): to drink; to participate in the partying spirit of drink; to participate in the abomination of drinking. The idea is a habitual practice, drinking to excess (cp. Gal.5:21; cp. Eph.5:18).

> **"Be careful, or your hearts will be weighed down with dissipation, drunkenness and the anxieties of life, and that day will close on you unexpectedly like a trap. (Luke 21:34)**
>
> **Nor thieves nor the greedy nor drunkards nor slanderers nor swindlers will inherit the kingdom of God. (1 Cor 6:10)**
>
> **"Woe to him who gives drink to his neighbors, pouring it from the wineskin till they are drunk, so that he can gaze on their naked bodies. (Hab 2:15)**

4 (24:40-41) **Jesus Christ, Return**: the coming of the Lord will be a time of separation and judgment. Several things are seen in these two verses.

1. On the day when Jesus comes, no one knows He is coming, not even believers. All go about their affairs, their occupations as usual.

2. On the day when Jesus comes, while people are going about their affairs, all of a sudden one shall be taken and the other left.

3. On the day when Jesus comes, there will be separation from those nearest us—from those right by our side. The believer will be caught up to be with the Lord; the unbeliever will be left behind to face judgment (v.30-31, 50-51; cp. 2 Th.1:7-10).

> **Let both grow together until the harvest. At that time I will tell the harvesters: First collect the weeds and tie them in bundles to be burned; then gather the wheat and bring it into my barn.'" (Mat 13:30)**
>
> **This is how it will be at the end of the age. The angels will come and separate the wicked from the righteous (Mat 13:49)**
>
> **All the nations will be gathered before him, and he will separate the people one from another as a shepherd separates the sheep from the goats. (Mat 25:32)**
>
> **"Then they will go away to eternal punishment, but the righteous to eternal life." (Mat 25:46)**
>
> **And besides all this, between us and you a great chasm has been fixed, so that those who want to go from here to you cannot, nor can anyone cross over from there to us.' (Luke 16:26)**
>
> **I tell you, on that night two people will be in one bed; one will be taken and the other left. (Luke 17:34)**

Thought 1. The basis of separation and judgment is belief. In Noah's day no one believed the message of righteousness. Only the man who believes the message of righteousness and adheres to it will be taken (2 Cor.5:21 cp. Jn.3:16; Mt.24:13).

	E. The Lord's Return and the Believer's Duty: Watch—Be Ready—Be Faithful & Wise, 24:42-51 (Mk.13:35-37; Lk.21:36)	the servants in his household to give them their food at the proper time?	a. His responsibility: To oversee & feed
		46 It will be good for that servant whose master finds him doing so when he returns.	b. His accountability: Is faithful
		47 I tell you the truth, he will put him in charge of all his possessions.	c. His reward: Put in charge
1 The believer's duty: Watch a. The Lord does return b. Exact time unknown	42 "Therefore keep watch, because you do not know on what day your Lord will come.	48 But suppose that servant is wicked and says to himself, 'My master is staying away a long time,'	**4 Parable 3: A wicked servant** a. His attitude: Plenty of time
2 Parable 1: The owner of the house (a professing believer) a. He had a house to look after b. He lived without watchfulness c. He suffered disaster d. The point: Readiness is essential, for Christ comes unexpectedly	43 But understand this: If the owner of the house had known at what time of night the thief was coming, he would have kept watch and would not have let his house be broken into. 44 So you also must be ready, because the Son of Man will come at an hour when you do not expect him.	49 And he then begins to beat his fellow servants and to eat and drink with drunkards. 50 The master of that servant will come on a day when he does not expect him and at an hour he is not aware of.	b. His behavior: Acts unjustly & worldly c. His judgment: He is doomed 1) The Lord catches him unexpectedly
3 Parable 2: A faithful & wise servant (a genuine believer)	45 "Who then is the faithful and wise servant, whom the master has put in charge of	51 He will cut him to pieces and assign him a place with the hypocrites, where there will be weeping and gnashing of teeth.	2) The Lord condemns him to death—with the hypocrites

DIVISION XV

THE MESSIAH'S PROPHECY OF HIS RETURN AND THE END OF THE AGE: THE OLIVET DISCOURSE, 24:1-25:46

E. The Lord's Return and The Believer's Duty: Watch—Be Ready—Be Faithful and Wise, 24:42-51

(24:42-51) **Introduction**: it is most important to remember that this was Christ's last week on earth. This was His last chance to teach the disciples. All that He said was of critical importance and, out of necessity, must be clear and pointed. He had led the disciples to ask two intriguing questions: "When will the temple [or Jerusalem] be destroyed? and what will be the sign of your coming and of the end of the age?" (v.3). (See note—Mt.24:1-25:46.)

Christ had just answered the disciples' questions. Now He came to the all important point of application. Since He would be returning to earth and God wanted the hour to be kept secret, what was the believer to do? How was the believer to live? What was the believer's duty? Christ answered these questions in one forceful warning: "Keep watch!" Then He shared three parables to explain what He meant by the strong exhortation, "Keep watch!"

1. The believer's duty: keep watch (v.42).
2. Parable 1: the owner of the house (a professing believer) (v.43-44).
3. Parable 2: a faithful and wise servant (a genuine believer) (v.45-47).
4. Parable 3: a wicked servant (v.48-51).

1 (24:42) **Keep Watch** (gregoreo): to keep awake; to stay alert; to be watchful and sleepless; to be vigilent. It also includes the idea of being motivated, of keeping one's attention (mind) upon a thing. Watching also has the idea of being alert at the *right time*. It is at night that a person really needs to stay awake to watch for the thief (cp. 1 Th.5:4-9).

The Lord said, "Keep watch." What does it mean for a believer to *watch*? (Mt. 26:41; Mk.13:33, 34, 36; 14:38; cp. 1 Cor.16:13; 1 Th.5:6; 2 Tim.4:5; 1 Pt.4:7).

1. The believer *watches* and stays *ready* for the Lord's return. He does not know the exact hour of the Lord's return; therefore, he is to watch and stay ready at all times (v.42-44). He should be so ready that his eyes are open and watching for the signs of Christ's return.
2. The believer *watches* his ministry and his duty to God. He sees to it that he serves faithfully and wisely (v.45).
3. The believer *watches* his *attitude and behavior* (v.48-49). He stays his mind upon the Lord's return and walks soberly and godly among others.

> **For though we live in the world, we do not wage war as the world does. The weapons we fight with are not the weapons of the world. On the contrary, they have divine power to demolish strongholds. We demolish arguments and every pretension that sets itself up against the knowledge of God, and we take captive every thought to make it obedient to Christ. (2 Cor 10:3-5)**
>
> **It teaches us to say "No" to ungodliness and worldly passions, and to live self-controlled, upright and godly lives in this present age, while we wait for the blessed hope—the glorious appearing of our great God and Savior, Jesus Christ, (Titus 2:12-13)**

4. The believer *watches* by being ready to die and to meet the Lord through death (Heb.9:27). Christ does not

mention this point, but its truth is ever so clear to the maturing believer.

2 (24:43-44) **Jesus Christ, Return**: the first parable Christ shared concerned the owner of a house. He represents the professing believer. Christ shared four things.

1. The owner had a house to look after. He was blessed, for he owned a house, and it was full of possessions. The belongings were valuable enough to attract a thief.
2. The owner lived without watchfulness.
    a. The owner knew the thief was coming, and he knew he was coming that night. He just did not know what time he was coming.
    b. The owner began to watch. He had tried to protect his house; he had bolted the doors and closed the windows. He was staying up listening to every noise and was ready to try to protect his house.
    c. The owner failed to protect his house, and he failed in an area least expected. He simply did not watch *long enough*. As the hours wore on and on, he grew more and more drowsy and nodded more and more. The owner simply failed...
    - to stay awake long enough.
    - to keep his mind alert long enough.
    - to look and listen to the noises (signs) long enough.
    - to keep active long enough.
    - to stand guard long enough.
3. The owner suffered disaster. The thief came while the owner was asleep. The owner ceased watching, and the thief broke into his home, taking his most prized valuables.
4. Christ's point is clear: readiness is essential. By *readiness,* Christ meant diligence. We are to be diligently living a life of righteousness, looking for His return.

Since everything will be destroyed in this way, what kind of people ought you to be? You ought to live holy and godly lives But in keeping with his promise we are looking forward to a new heaven and a new earth, the home of righteousness. (2 Pet 3:11, 13)

Christ gave two reasons why we are to be ready: (a) He is definitely coming, and (b) He is coming in a hour when the unprepared will not expect Him (v.44, 50).

But understand this: If the owner of the house had known at what hour the thief was coming, he would not have let his house be broken into. (Luke 12:39)

In my Father's house are many rooms; if it were not so, I would have told you. I am going there to prepare a place for you. And if I go and prepare a place for you, I will come back and take you to be with me that you also may be where I am. (John 14:2-3)

For you know very well that the day of the Lord will come like a thief in the night. But you, brothers, are not in darkness so that this day should surprise you like a thief. (1 Th 5:42)

But the day of the Lord will come like a thief. The heavens will disappear with a roar; the elements will be destroyed by fire, and the earth and everything in it will be laid bare. (2 Pet 3:10)

Remember, therefore, what you have received and heard; obey it, and repent. But if you do not wake up, I will come like a thief, and you will not know at what time I will come to you. (Rev 3:3)

Then I heard the angel in charge of the waters say: "You are just in these judgments, you who are and who were, the Holy One, because you have so judged; (Rev 16:5)

Thought 1. The Lord's return is imminent. This is the point. We must stay alert and be diligent in looking for His return—today!

Thought 2. The owner's house can represent a man's life. Every man is responsible for taking care of his life. Christ says we keep our house (life) by "watching" and being ready for His return, for He may return at any moment.

3 (24:45-47) **Jesus Christ, Return**: the second parable Christ shared concerned the faithful and wise servant. He represents a genuine believer, a person who not only professes Christ but lives for Christ. The genuine believer may be a minister, a teacher, or a young learner in Christ. But note: the point is not the believer's position but his being faithful and wise. The simplest believer is to be faithful and wise, no matter who he is or what his calling is.

Christ put this parable in the form of a question: "Who then is the faithful and wise servant?" He does this to stir more thought about the issue at hand and to force a much more personal application. Christ covers three points about the faithful and wise servant.

1. His responsibility is twofold. He is *to oversee* the Master's household and he is *to feed* the Master's family.
    a. He is to oversee the Master's household. Note: it is the Master who sets him over His household. The servant does not appoint himself, nor is he appointed by other servants (or churches) of the household. The Master alone sets him over His family.

        He is given the responsibility to rule, to oversee, to look after the household and family of the Master. But he is under his Lord and he is to oversee primarily by example.

Be shepherds of God's flock that is under your care, serving as overseers—not because you must, but because you are willing, as God wants you to be; not greedy for money, but eager to serve; not lording it over those entrusted to you, but being examples to the flock. (1 Pet 5:2-3)

Obey your leaders and submit to their authority. They keep watch over you as men who must give an account. Obey them so that their work will be a joy, not a burden, for that would be of no advantage to you. (Heb 13:17)

b. He is to provide food for the Master's family, and he is to do it in due season. His family has to be fed. It is the servant's duty to provide food for them. Note that he gives; it is his duty to give, not to take (cp. Ezk.34:8; Acts 20:35). He gives food for their nourishment, and He gives the food "at the proper time," at the right time.

> **Be shepherds of God's flock that is under your care (1 Pet 5:2)**
> **"Feed my lambs....my sheep. (John 21:15-17)**

2. His accountability is clearly stated. The Lord is coming, and when He comes, He will judge what the faithful servant is doing. The servant will be looked at and observed to see if he is managing the household and feeding the family *faithfully and wisely.*

> **It will be good for that servant whose master finds him doing so when he returns. (Mat 24:46)**
> **Now it is required that those who have been given a trust must prove faithful. (1 Cor 4:2)**
> **Each one should use whatever gift he has received to serve others, faithfully administering God's grace in its various forms. (1 Pet 4:10)**
> **Therefore, my dear brothers, stand firm. Let nothing move you. Always give yourselves fully to the work of the Lord, because you know that your labor in the Lord is not in vain. (1 Cor 15:58)**
> **Watch your life and doctrine closely. Persevere in them, because if you do, you will save both yourself and your hearers. (1 Tim 4:16)**

3. His reward will be unbelievable. The Master will put the faithful servant in charge over all His goods. The idea is that he will be placed first: looked upon, loved, and considered first, as though he were the only one. He had been managing, looking after only a small portion for the Master. Now he will be given a much greater responsibility to oversee for his Lord.

> **"Whoever can be trusted with very little can also be trusted with much, and whoever is dishonest with very little will also be dishonest with much. (Luke 16:10)**
> **He who did not spare his own Son, but gave him up for us all—how will he not also, along with him, graciously give us all things? (Rom 8:32)**
> **However, as it is written: "No eye has seen, no ear has heard, no mind has conceived what God has prepared for those who love him"— (1 Cor 2:9; cp. Rev.2:26; 3:21)**

Thought 1. Who is faithful and wise? The believer who is found "doing so." This means he is enduring (v.13) and watching over the task the Lord has given him (v.42). (See note—Mt.24:42.)

Thought 2. This is a precious thought: to picture Christ's renting the skies above and returning, and to know that His first sight of us will be that of our laboring for Him. May the Lord grant just this: when He returns, may His first sight be to see us working for Him. Blessed is that servant "whose master finds him doing so." Note the word "doing" is continuous action.

This is a frightful thought: to picture Christ's appearing and His first sight of us is that of...

- sleeping late
- working half-heartedly
- mistreating someone
- arguing
- being engaged in an immoral act
- overeating

4 (4:48-51) **Servant, Unfaithful—Evil—Wicked—Untrustworthy**: the third parable Christ shared concerns the evil servant. He represents a professing believer. Some say he is even a professing minister. If so, he is not a genuine believer, despite his profession and ministerial position. He is *unfaithful* and *untrustworthy* (1 Tim.1:12). His life is tragic. Christ covers his attitude, his behavior, and his end or judgment.

1. His attitude. Note the word *heart*. The attitude of his heart is, "My master is staying away a long time; there is plenty of time." Several things can cause such an attitude.

⇒ Doubting the Lord's Word, that He is ever coming.
⇒ Misinterpreting the Lord's coming as being only symbolic, instead of accepting it as literal; symbolizing it to mean some spiritual truth such as the Lord's meeting a person when the person dies.
⇒ Ignoring the Lord's coming in order to allow the person to live as he wishes.
⇒ Thinking the Lord's coming is so far away that it has little meaning for today.

2. His behavior. Note that it is after the evil servant says there is plenty of time that he begins to live as he wishes. *His attitude* (his heart) *determines his behavior.*

a. He acts unjustly. He begins to "beat his fellow-servants." He seeks more and more materially, both power and things. He strikes and mistreats anyone who stands in his way. He seeks "money," and he seeks to *lord it over people* (1 Pt.5:2-3).
b. He lives carnally. He begins "to eat and drink with drunkards." He walks with them, sits with them, lies with them. He is their companion in sin. He is indulgent, living to please the flesh.

3. His end and his judgment are certain. There is no escape.

a. The Lord will catch the evil servant unexpectedly. Some deny that the Lord is coming to judge them; others ignore His coming; and still others put the thought out of their minds. But nothing will keep the Lord from coming: "the master of that servant will come." And He will come when the wicked man is not looking for Him. To the evil person, the Lord's coming will be the most frightful experience of human history (cp. v.21-22; Rev.6:15-17).

   In talking about meeting the Lord, it must be remembered that every man meets the Lord at death: "Just as man is destined to die once, and after that to face judgment" (Heb.9:27). The point Christ makes is that the evil man will face eternal doom at the end of the world. As other Scriptures point out, the Great White Throne of judgment is to take place at the end of the age.
b. The Lord will condemn the wicked servant to death—with the hypocrites. He will be "cut to pieces," cut off from among the living and from among believers; and most tragic, he will be "cut

to pieces" from God's presence. His position and place will be with hypocrites. Where are the hypocrites? Christ says "[Where] there will be weeping and gnashing of teeth" (see note—Mt.8:12).

The sin of the wicked servant, of a person who makes a false profession, does several terrible things.

1. He deceives himself and others. He deceives people into thinking that they will not have to face the judgment of the Lord's return, or if they do, it will be minimal.

2. He minimizes the truth of eternity, of heaven, of life with God, and of the judgment which every man must face.

3. He takes away from the message and effectiveness of the gospel.

4. He keeps people from the truth. He keeps them from watching and preparing, from protecting and guarding, from living and walking with their eyes upon the Lord's coming.

> **When these things begin to take place, stand up and lift up your heads, because your redemption is drawing near." (Luke 21:28)**
>
> **In my Father's house are many rooms; if it were not so, I would have told you. I am going there to prepare a place for you. And if I go and prepare a place for you, I will come back and take you to be with me that you also may be where I am. (John 14:2-3)**

Thought 1. Note that Christ still speaks of a servant. The difference is onefold: this is a wicked servant. He may be a minister, a teacher, or a layman. Christ says that he is an wicked servant and spells out what it is that makes him wicked.

Thought 2. The worst of all men is the man who professes, and while he professes, he is living in sin. As Christ says, "and assign him a place with the hypocrites" (v.51). His only hope is to confess his evil and repent, turning back to God, ever trusting His wonderful mercy and grace.

> **If we confess our sins, he is faithful and just and will forgive us our sins and purify us from all unrighteousness. (1 John 1:9)**

Thought 3. The man who walks ignoring, twisting, misinterpreting, or denying the Lord's return is walking by his *senses*—what he knows about the physical universe. He is walking as he *senses* things to be, not as God has revealed them to be.

Outline	Scripture	Scripture (cont.)	Outline (cont.)
	CHAPTER 25 **F. The Parable of the Ten Virgins: The Warning to Watch,**[DS1,2] **25:1-13** (cp. Lk.12:35-37)	Come out to meet him!' 7 "Then all the virgins woke up and trimmed their lamps. 8 The foolish ones said to the wise, 'Give us some of your oil; our lamps are going out.' 9 "'No,' they replied, 'there may not be enough for both us and you. Instead, go to those who sell oil and buy some for yourselves.'	a. A surprise: Midnight b. A cry: "Come—meet Him" c. The awakening: Prepare their lamps[DS5] d. The foolish discover their lamps are out: Frantic—beg for oil e. The wise scarcely have enough for themselves
1 Describes the Kingdom of Heaven **2 There are wise & foolish virgins (believers) who attend a wedding** a. Five are wise; five are foolish b. The foolish take no oil for their lamps: Provision & supply c. The wise take oil for their lamps: Provision & supply	"**A**t that time the kingdom of heaven will be like ten virgins who took their lamps and went out to meet the bridegroom. 2 Five of them were foolish and five were wise. 3 The foolish ones took their lamps but did not take any oil with them. 4 The wise, however, took oil in jars along with their lamps.	10 "But while they were on their way to buy the oil, the bridegroom arrived. The virgins who were ready went in with him to the wedding banquet. And the door was shut. 11 "Later the others also came. 'Sir! Sir!' they said. 'Open the door for us!'	**5 There is the bridegroom's return & the gathering of the wise** **6 There is a shut door to the foolish** a. The door was shut b. The foolish cry for entry
3 There is a long delay waiting for the bridegroom: All are drowsy & sleep[DS3,4]	5 The bridegroom was a long time in coming, and they all became drowsy and fell asleep.	12 "But he replied, 'I tell you the truth, I don't know you.'	c. The foolish will be rejected
4 There is a great summons when He comes	6 "At midnight the cry rang out: 'Here's the bridegroom!	13 "Therefore keep watch, because you do not know the day or the hour.	**7 The point: We must watch & expect the Lord's return at any moment**

DIVISION XV

THE MESSIAH'S PROPHECY OF HIS RETURN AND THE END OF THE AGE: THE OLIVET DISCOURSE, 24:1-25:46

F. The Parable of the Ten Virgins: The Warning to Watch, 25:1-13

(25:1-13) **Introduction**: the believer must *watch* for the Lord's return, and he must be wise and not foolish in watching (see note—Mt.24:42). This is the point of Jesus' parable in this passage (v.13): the parable of the ten virgins, five foolish and five wise.

⇒ The *bridegroom*, of course, is Christ Himself.
⇒ The *virgins* are believers, all professors of religion. The *five wise virgins* are genuine believers; the *five foolish virgins* are false believers, those who have a false profession.
⇒ The *lamps* represent the lives, that is, the testimony, the witness, the heart, and the profession of the virgins (professing believers).
⇒ The *oil* is the provision of righteousness, the supply of the Holy Spirit that is to fill the lamps (lives) of the professing believers.

The parable is a dramatic picture of just what will happen to all professing believers, both the wise and the foolish, when the Lord returns.

1. The parable describes the Kingdom of Heaven (v.1).
2. There are wise and foolish virgins (believers) who attend a wedding (v.1-4).
3. There is a long delay waiting for the bridegroom: all are drowsy and sleep (v.5).
4. There is a great summons when the bridegroom comes (v.6-9).
5. There is the bridegroom's return and the gathering of the wise (v.10).
6. There is a shut door to the foolish (v.10-12).
7. The point: we must watch and expect the Lord's return at any moment (v.13).

DEEPER STUDY # 1

(25:1-13) **Wedding, Jewish:** this event, so unlike what occurs in most countries, was a common custom among Jews. The wedding festivities, which lasted for a whole week, were centered in the home where the couple was to live. The bridegroom was allowed to show up at any moment and enter the house; but when he chose to come, he always sent a man ahead crying out, "Here's the bridegroom! Come out to meet him!." This enabled everyone to prepare for his arrival. The bride had ten young ladies (virgins) who were always to be prepared to rush out and meet the bridegroom. In the event that he came at night, they were to have lamps ready so they could go out to light his path along the streets. This is the picture Christ was painting of His return.

DEEPER STUDY # 2

(25:1-13) **Jesus Christ, Bridegroom—Great Marriage Feast**: throughout Scripture the symbolism lying behind this parable involves three pictures.

1. Christ is pictured as the bridegroom.

> **As a young man marries a maiden, so will your sons marry you; as a bridegroom rejoices over his bride, so will your God rejoice over you. (Isa 62:5)**
> **Jesus answered, "How can the guests of the bridegroom mourn while he is with them? The time will come when the bridegroom will be taken from them; then they will fast. (Mat 9:15)**

The bride belongs to the bridegroom. The friend who attends the bridegroom waits and listens for him, and is full of joy when he hears the bridegroom's voice. That joy is mine, and it is now complete. (John 3:29)

But in the days when the seventh angel is about to sound his trumpet, the mystery of God will be accomplished, just as he announced to his servants the prophets." So I went to the angel and asked him to give me the little scroll. He said to me, "Take it and eat it. It will turn your stomach sour, but in your mouth it will be as sweet as honey." (Rev 10:7, 9)

I saw the Holy City, the new Jerusalem, coming down out of heaven from God, prepared as a bride beautifully dressed for her husband. (Rev 21:2)

2. Believers and the church are pictured as the bride of Christ.

As a young man marries a maiden, so will your sons marry you; as a bridegroom rejoices over his bride, so will your God rejoice over you. (Isa 62:5)

I will betroth you to me forever; I will betroth you in righteousness and justice, in love and compassion. (Hosea 2:19)

So, my brothers, you also died to the law through the body of Christ, that you might belong to another, to him who was raised from the dead, in order that we might bear fruit to God. (Rom 7:4)

For we are members of his body. (Eph 5:30)

I am jealous for you with a godly jealousy. I promised you to one husband, to Christ, so that I might present you as a pure virgin to him. (2 Cor 11:2)

Let us rejoice and be glad and give him glory! For the wedding of the Lamb has come, and his bride has made herself ready. (Rev 19:7)

I saw the Holy City, the new Jerusalem, coming down out of heaven from God, prepared as a bride beautifully dressed for her husband. (Rev 21:2)

The Spirit and the bride say, "Come!" And let him who hears say, "Come!" Whoever is thirsty, let him come; and whoever wishes, let him take the free gift of the water of life. (Rev 22:17)

3. The return of the Lord is pictured as a great marriage feast.

Let us rejoice and be glad and give him glory! For the wedding of the Lamb has come, and his bride has made herself ready. Then the angel said to me, "Write: 'Blessed are those who are invited to the wedding supper of the Lamb!'" And he added, "These are the true words of God." (Rev 19:7,9)

One of the seven angels who had the seven bowls full of the seven last plagues came and said to me, "Come, I will show you the bride, the wife of the Lamb." (Rev 21:9; see outline and notes—Mat 22:1-14)

1 (25:1) **Kingdom of Heaven—Jesus Christ, Return**: the words *at that time* refer back to the Lord's return discussed in Chapter 24. He was saying, "At that time [when the Lord returns] the kingdom of heaven will be like ten virgins [believers]." Five are foolish and five are wise, and there is going to be a separation of the wise from the foolish. Note *the kingdom of heaven* does not refer only to the perfect state of being in the future; it also refers to the present imperfect state of religion in the church (see DEEPER STUDY # 3—Mt.19:23-24; cp. Mt.13:1-58).

When Christ returns, something will be clearly seen—the foolish within the kingdom, those who have a false profession within the church and religion, shall be separated from the wise, "Therefore keep watch" (v.13).

2 (25:1-4) **Parable**: there are wise and foolish virgins or believers who attend a wedding. Christ says three things about them.

1. The ten virgins (all professing believers) take their lamps (lives or testimonies) and go forth to meet the bridegroom. All believers take their lives and go forth, professing a testimony that they live for Christ and look to Christ. All professing believers (whether genuine or just religionists and church people) go forth to meet the Lord. However, as they "go forth" some (five) are wise and some (five) are foolish.

2. The *foolish* virgins (believers) take no oil *except what they already have in their lamps (lives).* They have *no provision of righteousness* beyond themselves, beyond their own righteousness. They have no supply of the Holy Spirit.

He replied, "Isaiah was right when he prophesied about you hypocrites; as it is written: "'These people honor me with their lips, but their hearts are far from me. (Mark 7:6)

For from within, out of men's hearts, come evil thoughts, sexual immorality, theft, murder, adultery, (Mark 7:21)

As it is written: "There is no one righteous, not even one; (Rom 3:10)

3. The *wise* virgins (believers) take oil; they do not depend upon what they have in their lamps (lives). As they go forth through life to meet the bridegroom (Christ), they lay hold of additional oil, the provision of righteousness, the supply of God's Spirit.

God made him who had no sin to be sin for us, so that in him we might become the righteousness of God. (2 Cor 5:21)

I am jealous for you with a godly jealousy. I promised you to one husband, to Christ, so that I might present you as a pure virgin to him. (2 Cor 11:2)

These are those who did not defile themselves with women, for they kept themselves pure. They follow the Lamb wherever he goes. They were purchased from among men and offered as firstfruits to God and the Lamb. (Rev 14:4)

Thought 1. The main duty of the virgins (believers) is to meet and light the path for the bridegroom.

Thought 2. Note: there was no visible difference between the virgins. They all had lamps, and they were all called to participate in the marriage feast. The lack of provision by the foolish could not be seen until the Bridegroom actually came.

Thought 3. How foolish! To depend only on the oil in one's lamp or life. No one has enough oil, enough righteousness, to make himself perfect, that is, to make himself acceptable to God.

Thought 4. When Christ comes, He must find righteousness in a person if that person is to be allowed in God's presence. A man must participate in the Divine nature by faith (2 Pt.1:4). (See DEEPER STUDY # 2, Justification—Ro.4:22; 5:1.)

3 (25:5) **Jesus Christ, Return**: Christ said an interesting thing. There is a long delay before the bridegroom came and *all* the virgins became drowsy and slept—not just the foolish virgins, but *all* the virgins became drowsy and slept.

1. The idea is that this bridegroom waited much longer than was expected. The virgins had lit their lamps expecting him any moment, but he never came. As they waited and waited, the night wore on and on.

In the eyes of many, the Lord's return *has* lingered and lingered, well beyond what many have thought and taught (cp. 2 Pt.3:3-4, 9-10).

2. All the virgins became drowsy and slept. Not just the foolish slept, but the wise slept as well (see DEEPER STUDY # 3,4—Mt.25:5). This is true throughout life. Even the wise grow weary and find it difficult to stay awake and alert, to stay at peak performance all the time. No believer, whoever he is, walks anywhere as close as he should. The world is too dark and the darkness too heavy for the believer to see enough light so that he can always be victorious over the pull of heavy eyelids.

⇒ His body is too weak to be *always laboring*.
⇒ His mind is too undeveloped to be *always concentrating*.
⇒ His energy is too limited to be *always driving*.
⇒ His spirit is too young to be *always sacrificing*.
⇒ His motives are too self-centered to be *always walking unselfishly*.

"Therefore keep watch because you do not know when the owner of the house will come back—whether in the evening, or at midnight, or when the rooster crows, or at dawn. If he comes suddenly, do not let him find you sleeping. What I say to you, I say to everyone: 'Watch!'" (Mk 13:35-37)

Do you not say, 'Four months more and then the harvest'? I tell you, open your eyes and look at the fields! They are ripe for harvest. (John 4:35)

And do this, understanding the present time. The hour has come for you to wake up from your slumber, because our salvation is nearer now than when we first believed. (Rom 13:11)

Therefore, my dear brothers, stand firm. Let nothing move you. Always give yourselves fully to the work of the Lord, because you know that your labor in the Lord is not in vain. (1 Cor 15:58)

Whatever you do, work at it with all your heart, as working for the Lord, not for men, (Col 3:23)

So then, let us not be like others, who are asleep, but let us be alert and self-controlled. (1 Th 5:6)

For this reason I remind you to fan into flame the gift of God, which is in you through the laying on of my hands. (2 Tim 1:6)

Whatever your hand finds to do, do it with all your might, for in the grave, where you are going, there is neither working nor planning nor knowledge nor wisdom. (Eccl 9:10)

Thought 1. Christ has delayed His coming longer than many thought He would. Why? Only God really knows, but Scripture does give some indication.

1) God's purposes have to be completely fulfilled.
2) "The times of the Gentiles" has to be completely fulfilled.
3) God's love must be fully demonstrated, apparently to a certain number of people. A certain number of people apparently have to be saved before Christ returns.
4) The gospel must first be preached "in the whole world for a testimony to all nations" (Mt.24:14).
5) The harvest must *be ripened* and then *fully gathered.*
6) The sufferings of Christ must be completely filled up (see note—Col.1:24).
7) God is patient, not wanting anyone to perish (2 Pt.3:9).

Thought 2. A pointed question needs to be answered. Remember the fervent zeal we had when we were first saved? Why does it die out as time passses by?

⇒ We have not lost all love for Christ, but we have left our first love (Rev.2:4).
⇒ We have not stopped all worship of God, but we have lost our first duty to worship.
⇒ We have not ceased all witness for Christ, but we have cooled our first passion.
⇒ We have not turned from all righteousness, but we have been diverted from our first attention.

Thought 3. Note that the virgins allowed themselves to become drowsy, then the drowsiness led to sleep. We must guard against becoming drowsy, against cooling off. A little drowsiness and a little cooling of ferver for just a little while may not seem too serious; but the first step, as small as it may seem, leads to heavy eyelids.

DEEPER STUDY # 3
(25:5) **Became Drowsy** (enustazan): to nod; to nap.

DEEPER STUDY # 4
(25:5) **Slept - Sleep** (katheudo): to go to sleep. This is a natural sleep of a person at night.

4 (25:6-9) **Jesus Christ, Return**: there is to be a great summons. Christ said several things.

1. The summons will be a great surprise, totally unexpected. It will come at a surprising hour: at midnight, the most surprising hour, the hour when sleep is most desired and unlikely to be disturbed. It is an hour when all are asleep. Christ is coming as a thief in the night.

2. The summons will be a cry, a shout: "Come out to meet Him: (cp. Mt.24:31; 1 Th.4:16). The word "cometh" is not in the oldest and best Greek manuscripts. The cry is simply, "Here's the bridegroom!" which makes the shout much more forceful. Note two things.
   a. What the shout is: "Come out to meet Him."
   b. What the shout does: it awakens; it shocks; it disturbs. It is totally unexpected. The shout awakens the sleeping and demands, "Come to meet Him."

3. All awaken and prepare their lamps. All the virgins (professing believers) awoke, for the shout pierces the air and shocks the virgins, demanding immediate arousal. *Not one remains asleep*. Each leaps up. The voice demands obedience, for the bridegroom comes. And all begin immediately to prepare their lamps (see DEEPER STUDY # 5—Mt. 25:7).

4. All the foolish discover a shocking fact: their lamps are burned out. The bridegroom had not come while their lamps were burning, and now their lamps had used up all the oil they had. They became frantic, for they saw that they were not prepared. They did not have the oil (righteousness) necessary to burn their lamps (lives) for the bridegroom's coming.

> **"Be careful, or your hearts will be weighed down with dissipation, drunkenness and the anxieties of life, and that day will close on you unexpectedly like a trap. For it will come upon all those who live on the face of the whole earth. (Luke 21:34-35)**
>
> **Since they did not know the righteousness that comes from God and sought to establish their own, they did not submit to God's righteousness. (Rom 10:3)**
>
> **They are darkened in their understanding and separated from the life of God because of the ignorance that is in them due to the hardening of their hearts. (Eph 4:18)**
>
> **But they do not know the thoughts of the LORD; they do not understand his plan, he who gathers them like sheaves to the threshing floor. (Micah 4:12)**

5. All the wise scarcely have enough for themselves. Note two things.
   ⇒ They had prepared. They had the oil (righteousness) necessary to burn the lamps (lives) for the bridegroom's coming
   ⇒ They had only enough, and barely enough, for their own lamps. They were not able to give any of their own oil to those who had none.

> **"Be dressed ready for service and keep your lamps burning, like men waiting for their master to return from a wedding banquet, so that when he comes and knocks they can immediately open the door for him. (Luke 12:35-36)**
>
> **Come back to your senses as you ought, and stop sinning; for there are some who are ignorant of God—I say this to your shame. (1 Cor 15:34)**
>
> **For it is light that makes everything visible. This is why it is said: "Wake up, O sleeper, rise from the dead, and Christ will shine on you." (Eph 5:14)**
>
> **You are all sons of the light and sons of the day. We do not belong to the night or to the darkness. So then, let us not be like others, who are asleep, but let us be alert and self-controlled. (1 Th 5:5-6)**
>
> **"Behold, I come like a thief! Blessed is he who stays awake and keeps his clothes with him, so that he may not go naked and be shamefully exposed." (Rev 16:15)**
>
> **Let us rejoice and be glad and give him glory! For the wedding of the Lamb has come, and his bride has made herself ready. (Rev 19:7)**

Thought 1. Death is usually a surprise, yet it comes to every one of us. The same fact is true with the Lord's return. His return is as certain as death, and it will be as surprising as most deaths are.

Thought 2. When the summons comes, all will arise. Not a person—whether in the grave, in the sea, or scattered all over the world—shall remain. Shockingly, surprisingly, all will arise when the shout comes. Both the dead and the living will arise to meet the Lord in the air (1 Th.4:14f).

Thought 3. When Christ first came to earth, no announcement to the world was made. Only a few knew when He came as a babe in Bethlehem. But when He returns, the world—all men—will know. A universal shout, the voice of the archangel, will summon all to arise and to prepare for the coming of the Bridegroom.

Thought 4. *The righteousness of Christ* is the only oil that lights the lamp of life. *The righteousness of Christ* is the only oil that is acceptable to God. A person who depends only upon the oil in his lamp or life, who does not secure additional oil, is foolish—as foolish as the foolish virgins—for the bridegroom shall come. It will be at midnight, yes, but midnight is coming. In fact, our watches tell us it is almost midnight now.

Thought 5. *Wise* is the correct word to call the man who secures additional oil (righteousness), for he does prepare for the inevitable.

Thought 6. Some things cannot be borrowed. Righteousness is one of those things (2 Cor.5:21; Eph.4:24).

DEEPER STUDY # 5
(25:7) **Lamps**: trimming a lamp simply means that the burned top of the wick, the charred top, had to be trimmed or cleaned. Of course, the lamp had to be refilled with oil from the additional supply.

5 (25:10) **Jesus Christ, Return**: the Lord will return and gather the wise. Christ shared two major points.

1. "The bridegroom arrived": three simple but powerful words. So Christ will arrive. The day will come when it will be said, "The bridegroom, Christ Himself, arrived."

> **"When the Son of Man comes in his glory, and all the angels with him, he will sit on his throne in heavenly glory. (Mat 25:31)**
>
> **For the Lord himself will come down from heaven, with a loud command, with the voice of the archangel and with the trumpet call of God, and the dead in Christ will rise first. (1 Th 4:16)**

2. Only they who were *ready* went in with the bridegroom to the marriage. This was their purpose, the reason they were ready. They had looked for His coming; therefore, they were ready. When the summons came, they were able to join in the processional of the Bridegroom and to enter the great marriage feast. The joy of the marriage was theirs (Jn.17:24. See DEEPER STUDY # 2 Great Marriage Feast—Mt.25:1-13.)

> **And he will send his angels with a loud trumpet call, and they will gather his elect from the four winds, from one end of the heavens to the other. (Mat 24:31)**

Thought 1. "The fulness of time" is to come again: the time for the great marriage feast of the Lamb and His church.

Thought 2. The "ready" will enter the marriage feast. Only those who are *ready* will be allowed to enter. It is God who makes us ready (2 Cor.5:5).

6 (25:10-12) **Jesus Christ, Return**: the door is to be shut to the foolish.

1. The door was shut. This was a custom in the East. When all the guests had arrived, the doors were closed. They were closed in order to *secure* the marriage party and to *exclude* intruders. Only the guests belonged; others were to be kept out. When Christ comes, the door to heaven will be closed. Only the *ready*, the genuine guests will be *secured* in the joys of the great marriage feast. The unprepared will find the door shut *in order to exclude them.*

2. The foolish cry for entrance. Very simply, the foolish were *too late*. They were too late to join in the procession and too late to enter the door. Note the Lord's emphasis upon their desperation: they cry out, "Sir, Sir." They now know something they had not paid much attention to before: *preparation was essential.* The door has now been closed, and they are excluded. They are shut out from the Bridegroom's great wedding feast. It is too late for them.

3. The foolish will be rejected. The reason is simple: the Bridegroom does not know them. They were not ready when He arrived nor were they in the processional; therefore, He does not recognize them. He has to say, "I don't know you." He can say nothing else, for...

- they had not *prepared* themselves: they were not ready when He came.
- they had not *participated* in His journey to the marriage feast: He did not recognize them; He did not know them.

Christ taught time and again that the day is coming when the door will be shut (cp. Jn.10:9).

> **"Not everyone who says to me, 'Lord, Lord,' will enter the kingdom of heaven, but only he who does the will of my Father who is in heaven. Many will say to me on that day, 'Lord, Lord, did we not prophesy in your name, and in your name drive out demons and perform many miracles?' Then I will tell them plainly, 'I never knew you. Away from me, you evildoers!' (Mat 7:21-23)**
>
> **Once the owner of the house gets up and closes the door, you will stand outside knocking and pleading, 'Sir, open the door for us.' "But he will answer, 'I don't know you or where you come from.' "Then you will say, 'We ate and drank with you, and you taught in our streets.' "But he will reply, 'I don't know you or where you come from. Away from me, all you evildoers!' (Luke 13:25-27)**

Note the words, "I don't know you." The importance of Christ's *knowing us* is also stressed time and again in Scripture. Of course, the way Christ gets to know us is by our participating in His journey, simply walking with Him day by day.

> **"I never knew you: away from me" (Mat 7:23).**
>
> **"I am the good Shepherd; I know my sheep" (John 10:14).**
>
> **"But now that you know God, or rather are known by God" (Gal 4:9).**
>
> **"I know you by name" (Exo 33:12. God said this of Moses.)**
>
> **"I have redeemed you, I have called you by name: you are mine" (Isa 43:1).**

Thought 1. The idea of the shut door is twofold.

1) To *secure* the wise (believer). The wise person is brought and welcomed into the great marriage feast of the Lord, and he participates in all the joy of the festive occasion. Whatever goes on within the great banqueting hall is his to enjoy. Other Scriptures point out that love, joy, and peace will be perfected and will be the unbroken experience of the believer. He will never again have to go out into an unjoyful, unhappy, corruptible, or painful world.

> **Him who overcomes I will make a pillar in the temple of my God. Never again will he leave it. I will write on him the name of my God and the name of the city of my God, the new Jerusalem, which is coming down out of heaven from my God; and I will also write on him my new name. (Rev 3:12)**

2) To exclude the foolish (who profess only). There has been plenty of time and plenty of signs and warnings to prepare, but the foolish have refused to prepare for the Lord's return (see outline—Ro.1:18-23; 2:11-15).

Thought 2. The foolish believer is a person who fails at two points.

1) Preparation: he does not provide any oil (righteousness) for his lamp *except* what oil is

already there. He sees no need for additional oil or righteousness. Therefore, he does not prepare.

2) Participation: he is unable to join the Bridegroom on His journey to the great marriage feast. He has no additional oil (righteousness), so his lamp (life) is no good to the bridegroom. His lamp (life) is not able to provide light for the bridegroom.

7 (25:13) **Watch—Jesus Christ, Return**: the point is that we must *watch* and expect the Lord's return at any moment.

1. The exhortation is strong: "Therefore keep watch." The believer must prepare and participate in the journey to the great marriage feast. He must walk with the Lord, the bridegroom. (See note, Watch—Mt.24:42.)

2. The reason for watching is strong: "You do not know the day or the hour [when the Son of man is coming]." Unbroken preparation is essential, for He can come at any moment.

"Therefore keep watch, because you do not know the day or the hour. (Mat 25:13)

It will be good for those servants whose master finds them watching when he comes. I tell you the truth, he will dress himself to serve, will have them recline at the table and will come and wait on them. (Luke 12:37)

You are all sons of the light and sons of the day. We do not belong to the night or to the darkness. So then, let us not be like others, who are asleep, but let us be alert and self-controlled. (1 Th 5:5-6)

I am coming soon. Hold on to what you have, so that no one will take your crown. (Rev 3:11)

"Behold, I come like a thief! Blessed is he who stays awake and keeps his clothes with him, so that he may not go naked and be shamefully exposed." (Rev 16:15)

1 The Lord went on a journey

2 The Lord entrusted His property to His servants[DS2]
- a. Called His servants
- b. Gave each servant a different portion
- c. Gave each servant according to his ability

3 The servants treated the Lord's goods differently
- a. Two were responsible: Immediately worked
  - 1) Were faithful & diligent
  - 2) Were successful
- b. One was irresponsible: Did not try

4 The day of settling accounts came
- a. After a long time
- b. The Lord returned

5 The reward for work well done: More work to do
- a. The first servant
  - 1) Acknowledged God's gifts & grace
  - 2) Labored 100% for the Lord
  - 3) Was commended & given a great reward: Rulership & joy
- b. The second servant
  - 1) Acknowledged God's gifts & grace
  - 2) Labored 100% for the Lord
  - 3) Was commended & given a great reward: Rulership & joy

6 The punishment for work not done: Stripping & separation
- a. The servant's reasons for not working
  - 1) He misunderstood God: Thought God was too demanding
  - 2) He feared loss while on earth
- b. God's reasons for condemning the servant
  - 1) He was wicked & lazy
  - 2) He was inconsistent
  - 3) He failed to use his gift
- c. The judgment
  - 1) He was stripped of what he had[DS3]
  - 2) He was thrown into the darkness[DS4]

G. The Parable of the Talents: The Believer's Duty to Work,[DS1] **25:14-30**

14 "Again, it will be like a man going on a journey, who called his servants and entrusted his property to them.
15 To one he gave five talents of money, to another two talents, and to another one talent, each according to his ability. Then he went on his journey.
16 The man who had received the five talents went at once and put his money to work and gained five more.
17 So also, the one with the two talents gained two more.
18 But the man who had received the one talent went off, dug a hole in the ground and hid his master's money.
19 "After a long time the master of those servants returned and settled accounts with them.
20 The man who had received the five talents brought the other five. 'Master,' he said, 'you entrusted me with five talents. See, I have gained five more.'
21 "His master replied, 'Well done, good and faithful servant! You have been faithful with a few things; I will put you in charge of many things. Come and share your master's happiness!'
22 "The man with the two talents also came. 'Master,' he said, 'you entrusted me with two talents; see, I have gained two more.'
23 "His master replied, 'Well done, good and faithful servant! You have been faithful with a few things; I will put you in charge of many things. Come and share your master's happiness!'
24 "Then the man who had received the one talent came. 'Master,' he said, 'I knew that you are a hard man, harvesting where you have not sown and gathering where you have not scattered seed.
25 So I was afraid and went out and hid your talent in the ground. See, here is what belongs to you.'
26 "His master replied, 'You wicked, lazy servant! So you knew that I harvest where I have not sown and gather where I have not scattered seed?
27 Well then, you should have put my money on deposit with the bankers, so that when I returned I would have received it back with interest.
28 "'Take the talent from him and give it to the one who has the ten talents.
29 For everyone who has will be given more, and he will have an abundance. Whoever does not have, even what he has will be taken from him.
30 And throw that worthless servant outside, into the darkness, where there will be weeping and gnashing of teeth.

DIVISION XV

THE MESSIAH'S PROPHECY OF HIS RETURN AND THE END OF THE AGE: THE OLIVET DISCOURSE, 24:1-25:46

G. The Parable of the Talents: The Believer's Duty to Work, 25:14-30

(25:14-30) **Introduction**: Jesus said that the point of this parable was twofold.

First, while Jesus is away, the believer is to do something: work—work faithfully and diligently.

Second, while Jesus is away, the believer is to know something: his work will be greatly rewarded or severely judged.

Again, Christ was dealing with His return. He went "on a journey" (v.14), and "after a long time, the Master" returned (v.19). Christ was teaching a much needed lesson: we must be faithful and diligent, for if we are not, when He returns there will be severe judgment. (See outline and notes—Eph.4:7-16; 1 Cor.12:1-14:40.)

1. The Lord went on a journey (v.14).
2. The Lord entrusted His property to His servants (v.14-15).
3. The servants treated the Lord's property differently (v.16-18).
4. The day of settling accounts came (v.19).
5. The reward for work well done: more work to do (v.20-23).
6. The punishment for work not done: stripping and separation (v.24-30).

DEEPER STUDY # 1

(25:14-30) **Talents—Gifts**: the talent spoken of is a weight not a coin. The value of a talent varied as to whether it was gold, silver, or copper. Christ is probably using money to describe what He is talking about because money is one of the most understood commodities anywhere on earth.

Christ was teaching that His followers are to be faithful and diligent in whatever He gives them, whether a gift, ability, responsibility, or blessing.

1 (25:14) **Jesus Christ, Ascension—Exaltation**: Christ foretold that He was like a man who was travelling to a far country, and what He foretold happened. He travelled away from the earth and ascended into heaven for a specific purpose: to sit at the right hand of God. He is to sit there until His servants complete the work He has given them to do. When He returns, it will be the time for reward and for judgment.

> **In my Father's house are many rooms; if it were not so, I would have told you. I am going there to prepare a place for you. And if I go and prepare a place for you, I will come back and take you to be with me that you also may be where I am. (John 14:2-3)**
>
> **Exalted to the right hand of God, he has received from the Father the promised Holy Spirit and has poured out what you now see and hear. For David did not ascend to heaven, and yet he said, "'The Lord said to my Lord: "Sit at my right hand until I make your enemies a footstool for your feet."' (Acts 2:33-35)**
>
> **God exalted him to his own right hand as Prince and Savior that he might give repentance and forgiveness of sins to Israel. (Acts 5:31)**
>
> **Therefore God exalted him to the highest place and gave him the name that is above every name, that at the name of Jesus every knee should bow, in heaven and on earth and under the earth, and every tongue confess that Jesus Christ is Lord, to the glory of God the Father. (Phil 2:9-11)**

2 (25:14-15) **Gifts**: the Lord has entrusted His *property* (gifts, abilities, responsibilities) to His servants. There is a verse that says it all: "This is why it says: 'When he ascended on high, he led captives in his train and gave gifts to men.'" (Eph.4:8).

In this particular point Christ says three things.

1. The Lord called His *own* servants. The word for *servant* is bond-slave. He called those who were supposedly His own (a precious thought) and who were *supposedly* faithful and responsible to His service. He had bought them. They were to be His own and to serve Him (see note—Ro.1:1). Note why He called them: to put His *property* (gifts) into their hands while He was away. His property had to be looked after and increased and bettered while He was away. The property of the Lord means the world and the souls of men. The servants are given the very same mission and work that Christ had: to minister to the souls of men and to the desperate of the world.

2. The Lord gave each servant a different portion of His property to look after. The point is that each person was given a special talent (gift or responsibility). No one was left out (Eph.4:7). Each servant was therefore expected to work and serve.

3. The Lord gave to each servant according to his ability. Four factors are important here.

a. No two servants have the same ability: environment, opportunity, genes, heritage, training, mind, heart, discipline, initiative. Each is different.

> **To one he gave five talents of money, to another two talents, and to another one talent, each according to his ability. Then he went on his journey. (Mat 25:15)**
>
> **For who makes you different from anyone else? What do you have that you did not receive? And if you did receive it, why do you boast as though you did not? (1 Cor 4:7)**

b. God endows His *property* (gifts) as He wills, knowing each servant perfectly.

> **All these are the work of one and the same Spirit, and he gives them to each one, just as he determines. (1 Cor 12:11)**

c. Each servant receives all the gifts he needs and can use.

> **Just as each of us has one body with many members, and these members do not all have the same function, so in Christ we who are many form one body, and each member belongs to all the others. We have different gifts, according to the grace given us. If a man's gift is prophesying, let him use it in proportion to his faith. If it is serving, let him serve; if it is teaching, let him teach; if it is encouraging, let him encourage; if it is contributing to the needs of others, let him give generously; if it is leadership, let him govern diligently; if it is showing mercy, let him do it cheerfully. (Rom 12:4-8)**
>
> **There are different kinds of gifts, but the same Spirit. There are different kinds of service, but the same Lord. There are different kinds of working, but the same God works all of them in all men. Now to each one the manifestation of the Spirit is given for the common good. (1 Cor 12:4-7)**

d. Each servant has equal opportunity to be faithful in using what God has given him. We are to be judged on our faithfulness, not on the number of gifts or the size of the work we are assigned (cp. v.21 and v.23).

> **For the Son of Man is going to come in his Father's glory with his angels, and then he will reward each person according to what he has done. (Mat 16:27)**
>
> **Since you call on a Father who judges each man's work impartially, live your lives as strangers here in reverent fear. (1 Pet 1:17)**

Thought 1. There are three precious and wonderful facts here.

1) We are "His own." We are God's, His possession (Eph.1:14). Note: God also says, "I am their possession."

> **"'I am to be the only inheritance the priests have. You are to give them no possession in Israel; I will be their possession. (Ezek 44:28)**
>
> **But now, this is what the LORD says—he who created you, O Jacob, he who formed you, O Israel: "Fear not, for I have redeemed you; I have summoned you by name; you are mine. (Isa 43:1)**

2) We are taken care of by Christ. Each one is given "His property," very special gifts, abilities, and responsibilities to look after for God. God gives us exactly what we need to fulfill our lives and to give us purpose, meaning, and significance in life—to conform us to the very image of Christ Himself.

> **But seek first his kingdom and his righteousness, and all these things will be given to you as well. (Mat 6:33)**
>
> **If you then, though you are evil, know how to give good gifts to your children, how much more will your Father in heaven give the Holy Spirit to those who ask him!" (Luke 11:13)**
>
> **The thief comes only to steal and kill and destroy; I have come that they may have life, and have it to the full. (John 10:10)**
>
> **I give them eternal life, and they shall never perish; no one can snatch them out of my hand. (John 10:28)**
>
> **I will give them a heart to know me, that I am the LORD. They will be my people, and I will be their God, for they will return to me with all their heart. (Jer 24:7)**

3) The church is taken care of by Christ. During His absence, He has provided all that is necessary to care for and to advance the church.

> **It was he who gave some to be apostles, some to be prophets, some to be evangelists, and some to be pastors and teachers, to prepare God's people for works of service, so that the body of Christ may be built up until we all reach unity in the faith and in the knowledge of the Son of God and become mature, attaining to the whole measure of the fullness of Christ. (Eph 4:11-13)**

Thought 2. Note: every believer has at least one gift.

DEEPER STUDY # 2
(25:14-15) **Gifts**: the Lord's *properties* are the gifts, talents, and responsibilities He gives to men. The Lord endows His gifts as He pleases (1 Cor.12:11). Each servant receives all the gifts he needs and can use (Ro.12:4-9; 1 Cor.12:4-30). Note the gifts are the Lord's; they are merely entrusted to His servants. Different men have different capacities for different ministries (v.15).

3 (25:16-18) **Gifts—Faithfulness—Unfaithfulness**: the servants treated the Lord's *property* differently.

1. Two servants were responsible, very responsible. They went to work *immediately*. They *lost no time* and began to serve *quickly*.

a. They were faithful and diligent. They used their abilities and energy immediately. They exerted themselves, expended their energy and effort to use what the Lord had given them.

Note: the less gifted servant worked and labored as much as the more gifted servant. He did not have as many gifts, but he exerted the same initiative, energy, and effort (cp. Lk.12:48).

Again, the picture is that of a business transaction, but the point is that the two servants used what the Lord had given them; and they used their gifts faithfully and diligently.

b. They were successful. Each one gained and doubled what the Lord had given him. Each servant's gifts bore fruit *in proportion* to his gifts. The one given more (five talents) bore more (ten talents). The one given less (two talents) bore less (four talents). But both were *equally successful*, *doubling* what the Lord had given them.

> **Never be lacking in zeal, but keep your spiritual fervor, serving the Lord. (Rom 12:11)**
>
> **Now it is required that those who have been given a trust must prove faithful. (1 Cor 4:2)**
>
> **Therefore, my dear brothers, stand firm. Let nothing move you. Always give yourselves fully to the work of the Lord, because you know that your labor in the Lord is not in vain. (1 Cor 15:58)**
>
> **Each one should use whatever gift he has received to serve others, faithfully administering God's grace in its various forms. (1 Pet 4:10)**
>
> **So then, dear friends, since you are looking forward to this, make every effort to be found spotless, blameless and at peace with him. (2 Pet 3:14)**

2. One servant was irresponsible. He simply did not use the Lord's gift. But note: he was somewhat active. He spent time and energy to go out and bury the Lord's gift—he hid it. His days, his time, and his energy were to be the Lord's; but he took his life and days into his own hands. What was he doing? We are not told, but his efforts were not spent in the Lord's cause. He served only himself. He was worldly, lusting after the flesh (sinful nature) and possessions of this world. He was out to serve himself instead of God

> **But everyone who hears these words of mine and does not put them into practice is like a foolish man who built his house on sand. The rain came down, the streams rose, and the winds blew and beat against that house, and it fell with a great crash." (Mat 7:26-27)**
>
> **The seed that fell among thorns stands for those who hear, but as they go on their way they are choked by life's worries, riches and pleasures, and they do not mature. (Luke 8:14)**
>
> **Then he told this parable: "A man had**

a fig tree, planted in his vineyard, and he went to look for fruit on it, but did not find any. (Luke 13:6)

"Be careful, or your hearts will be weighed down with dissipation, drunkenness and the anxieties of life, and that day will close on you unexpectedly like a trap. For it will come upon all those who live on the face of the whole earth. (Luke 21:34-35)

Anyone, then, who knows the good he ought to do and doesn't do it, sins. (James 4:17)

You have lived on earth in luxury and self-indulgence. You have fattened yourselves in the day of slaughter. (James 5:5)

They will be paid back with harm for the harm they have done. Their idea of pleasure is to carouse in broad daylight. They are blots and blemishes, reveling in their pleasures while they feast with you. (2 Pet 2:13)

But you have planted wickedness, you have reaped evil, you have eaten the fruit of deception. Because you have depended on your own strength and on your many warriors, (Hosea 10:13)

Thought 1. Note four lessons.

1) Immediate work—immediate action—immediate use of God's gifts are expected. Each hesitation—each hour—each day where maximum energy and effort are not given is a lost opportunity. Each lost opportunity equals unfaithfulness and slothfulness. What a strong example the two faithful servants were!
2) The efforts of the faithful and diligent will bear interest (fruit). The servant who uses his gifts faithfully and diligently will witness a manifold increase in the *property* of his Lord.
3) A striking point: the person with one talent is as responsible to use his gift as the person with many talents.
4) Too often, a person who is gifted with little feels his service matters little, that it is not really worth the time and effort it takes. This attitude forgets something: the gift is not ours; the gift is the Lord's. It is to be used, and full energy and effort are to be exerted in its use. The use of a single gift is to occupy what days and hours we have on earth. We are to be faithful, even in the single gifts—always faithful and always using what we have for the Lord, even if it is a single gift.

4 (25:19) **Jesus Christ, Return**: the day of settling accounts came, but it was only "after a long time." By the time Christ returns, it will have been a long time in the eyes of men. However, it will have been only a short time to Christ: "I am coming soon" (Rev.3:11; cp. 2 Pt.3:3-4, 8-11).

Note a second fact: Christ says the Lord did return, and He returned to settle accounts with His servants, not with the world. Christ is talking about His servants in this passage—professing believers and church members, some genuine believers and some only professing believers, who are making a false profession (v.30).

"Therefore, the kingdom of heaven is like a king who wanted to settle accounts with his servants. (Mat 18:23)

When the harvest time approached, he sent his servants to the tenants to collect his fruit. (Mat 21:34)

"After a long time the master of those servants returned and settled accounts with them. (Mat 25:19)

"He was made king, however, and returned home. Then he sent for the servants to whom he had given the money, in order to find out what they had gained with it. (Luke 19:15)

So then, each of us will give an account of himself to God. (Rom 14:12)

Just as man is destined to die once, and after that to face judgment, (Heb 9:27)

They think it strange that you do not plunge with them into the same flood of dissipation, and they heap abuse on you. (1 Pet 4:4)

Thought 1. We must always remember this: the Lord is not slow concerning His promise to return. He is *ready* to judge the living and the dead (1 Pt.4:5). He is ready now, but He is *patient, longsuffering*, wanting more and more to come to repentance (2 Pt.3:9).

5 (25:20-23) **Reward**: the reward for work well done will be more work to do. Note that the experience was the same for the first and second servants.

1. They both acknowledged God's gifts and graces: "Master...you entrusted me." All that the servant had was given to him by Christ. There is *appreciation*, *thankfulness*, *privilege*, and a sense of responsibility expressed. The two servants had counted it a privilege to serve their Lord. He had given them purpose and meaning in life and the greatest privilege in all the world: the privilege of serving the Lord Himself. They were appreciative and thankful.

2. Therefore, they were bold in approaching the Lord: "See, I have gained." Their boldness was not in a boastful spirit, but in a spirit that knew it had been faithful in what the Lord had said to do.

In this way, love is made complete among us so that we will have confidence on the day of judgment, because in this world we are like him. (1 John 4:17)

3. The Lord commended the two servants and gave them great rewards: rulership and joy, the joy of the Lord. The Lord commended them for being *good* men (kind, gracious, moral, disciplined) and faithful in the trust (gifts) He had given them. They had worked and worked hard. They had been the kind of men He had wanted them to be and they had done the work He had wanted them to do. They were both *good and faithful* servants. The point is this: the first two servants worked at full capacity, exerting 100 percent energy and effort. Both increased the Lord's property 100 percent. Note the reward: both received responsibility over many things in the Kingdom of Heaven.

The Lord rewarded both servants greatly. He gave them a twofold reward.

First, they were given rulership: the responsibility and rule over many things in the Kingdom of Heaven *after the*

Master returned (see notes and DEEPER STUDY # 1—Mt.19:28; 19:29; Lk.19:15-23).

Second, they were given entrance into the joy of the Lord. The servants were to be ushered into the everlasting kingdom of our Lord and Savior Jesus Christ, where there is nothing but joy. The joy is the joy "of the Lord" Himself—a joy which He Himself possesses within His very being. Joy is the state of the Lord's being because He is perfect; His perfection gives rise to a *fulness of joy*. Believers also experience this joy because of heaven, for heaven is perfect; and where perfection is, there are no tears, pain, or sorrow. There is only joy.

> **"His master replied, 'Well done, good and faithful servant! You have been faithful with a few things; I will put you in charge of many things. Come and share your master's happiness!' (Mat 25:23)**
>
> **"Then the King will say to those on his right, 'Come, you who are blessed by my Father; take your inheritance, the kingdom prepared for you since the creation of the world. (Mat 25:34)**
>
> **But love your enemies, do good to them, and lend to them without expecting to get anything back. Then your reward will be great, and you will be sons of the Most High, because he is kind to the ungrateful and wicked. (Luke 6:35)**
>
> **You are those who have stood by me in my trials. And I confer on you a kingdom, just as my Father conferred one on me, (Luke 22:28-29)**
>
> **For if, by the trespass of the one man, death reigned through that one man, how much more will those who receive God's abundant provision of grace and of the gift of righteousness reign in life through the one man, Jesus Christ. (Rom 5:17)**
>
> **Do you not know that the saints will judge the world? And if you are to judge the world, are you not competent to judge trivial cases? Do you not know that we will judge angels? How much more the things of this life! (1 Cor 6:2-3)**
>
> **If we endure, we will also reign with him. If we disown him, he will also disown us; (2 Tim 2:12)**
>
> **And from Jesus Christ, who is the faithful witness, the firstborn from the dead, and the ruler of the kings of the earth. To him who loves us and has freed us from our sins by his blood, and has made us to be a kingdom and priests to serve his God and Father—to him be glory and power for ever and ever! Amen. (Rev 1:5-6)**
>
> **To him who overcomes and does my will to the end, I will give authority over the nations— (Rev 2:26)**
>
> **To him who overcomes, I will give the right to sit with me on my throne, just as I overcame and sat down with my Father on his throne. (Rev 3:21)**
>
> **There will be no more night. They will not need the light of a lamp or the light of the sun, for the Lord God will give them light. And they will reign for ever and ever. (Rev 22:5)**

Thought 1. Two things are highly commendable among God's servants:
1) To acknowledge that their gifts are of God.
2) To be so faithful and diligent that they can be bold in the day of judgment.

Thought 2. Just how *wise* we are is shown by how much work we do for God and how well we use our gifts.

> **Who is wise and understanding among you? Let him show it by his good life, by deeds done in the humility that comes from wisdom. (James 3:13)**

Our *works* will follow us.

> **Then I heard a voice from heaven say, "Write: Blessed are the dead who die in the Lord from now on." "Yes," says the Spirit, "they will rest from their labor, for their deeds will follow them." (Rev 14:13)**

Thought 3. A precious, precious truth: God will be accepting both our person ("good...servant") and our labor ("faithful servant"). Amen!

6 (25:24-30) **Minister—Servant**: the punishment for work not done will be stripping and separation. Christ covers three points in discussing this worthless servant. Remember: Christ is speaking of a person who professes and is in the church (see note, Kingdom of Heaven—Mt.25:1).

1. Note the servant's reasons for not using the gifts the Lord had entrusted into his care.
   a. He misunderstood God. The worthless servant said that the Lord was too demanding, exacting, stern, and unsympathetic. He was a Lord who demanded too much and was too strict. He did not allow man the right to enjoy this world and its pleasures enough. The servant felt that if he spent his time in the service of the Lord, he would miss out on life. The demands of the Lord upon his time and affairs were just too burdensome. The servant was too involved in the world and its affairs to give that much time and effort to labor for the Lord and to concentrate upon His demands.
   b. He added that he feared—feared using and putting his talent to work for the Lord. Therefore, he hid the Lord's talent and did not use it to increase the Lord's kingdom.

2. Note God's reasons for condemning the servant; note the vast difference between what the Lord said and what the servant had to say.
   a. The worthless servant was wicked and worthless. He was *wicked* because he went about doing exactly what he wished to do, spending his time and energy on his own thing. He transgressed God's command and will. He was *worthless* because he did nothing with God's gift. He buried and hid it.
   b. The worthless servant was inconsistent, or perhaps a better description would be deceptive, double-minded, and self-contradictory. If he really believed the Lord was harsh and stern, he would have labored and worked his fingers to the bone. The servant was either lying or terribly deceived and self-contradictory—all in an attempt to justify his behavior.

c. The worthless servant failed to use his gift. Christ was direct: the servant should have used the gift and served (v.27). He was without excuse.

3. Note the judgment of the worthless servant (v.28-30). Christ pronounced a twofold judgment upon him.

a. The worthless servant was stripped of what he had. All that he had was taken from him. The servant's responsibility—*the glorious privilege of* working for and serving the Lord—was not to be his any more. *He was to have nothing else to do with the Lord. His responsibility* was taken from him and given to the one who proven most faithful.

b. The worthless servant was thrown outside into the darkness. He was cast out of the Lord's presence and banished forever. And there was no joy there, nothing but darkness and weeping and gnashing of teeth (see notes—Mt.8:12 and DEEPER STUDY # 4—25:30 for discussion and verses).

Thought 1. There are two gross errors in the thinking of the world.

1) Many persons think God is hard, stern, demanding, and unsympathetic. They are unwilling to follow such a hard, narrow way. So they bury, hide their God-given gifts and travel along the easy, broad way.
2) Others think that what they have is their own, and they can use it to live as they please. They think that what they do is no one's affair except their own, not even God's.

Thought 2. Few persons feel any responsibility to God for what they have, and even fewer feel the necessity to serve God faithfully and diligently.

Thought 3. Laziness or slothfulness, doing nothing for God, is one of the great sins of professing Christians (Ro.12:11; 2 Th.3:11; Heb.6:12; Pr.18:9; cp. 1 Cor.15:58).

Thought 4. Sins of omission are as serious as sins of commission. Being idle and worthless, being complacent and doing nothing, being lethargic and self-satisfied—all are condemning sins: sins that condemn a person to outer darkness where there will be weeping and gnashing of teeth.

Thought 5. Men deceive themselves. They rationalize their comfort, ease, and slothfulness by minimizing their gift. They think that they will be excused by *downing* or denying their gift.

⇒ Inactive righteousness is as condemning as active wickedness.
⇒ Idle service is as condemning as a busy sin.
⇒ Sleepy concern is as condemning as stimulating flesh.
⇒ Indulging comfort is as condemning as assault and robbery.
⇒ Being *worthless* is as condemning as being evil (cp. Mt.25:42-46).

DEEPER STUDY # 3
(25:28-29) **Judgment**: see note—Lk.8:18 for discussion.

DEEPER STUDY # 4
(25:30) **Outer Darkness**: a darkness outside some realm or space of light. The rewards have to do with the assignment of responsibility. Therefore, it is probably accurate to say that the judgment is a darkness outside the joy (light) of the Lord's presence and outside the joy of responsibility. What a darkness! To be cast outside into the darkness away from the Lord's presence and to be stripped of responsibility—to be responsible for nothing throughout all eternity.

But the subjects of the kingdom will be thrown outside, into the darkness, where there will be weeping and gnashing of teeth." (Mat 8:12)

They will throw them into the fiery furnace, where there will be weeping and gnashing of teeth. (Mat 13:42)

"Then the king told the attendants, 'Tie him hand and foot, and throw him outside, into the darkness, where there will be weeping and gnashing of teeth.' (Mat 22:13)

He will cut him to pieces and assign him a place with the hypocrites, where there will be weeping and gnashing of teeth. (Mat 24:51)

And throw that worthless servant outside, into the darkness, where there will be weeping and gnashing of teeth.' (Mat 25:30)

These men are springs without water and mists driven by a storm. Blackest darkness is reserved for them. (2 Pet 2:17)

And the angels who did not keep their positions of authority but abandoned their own home—these he has kept in darkness, bound with everlasting chains for judgment on the great Day. (Jude 1:6)

"The lamp of the wicked is snuffed out; the flame of his fire stops burning. (Job 18:5)

The wicked man will see and be vexed, he will gnash his teeth and waste away; the longings of the wicked will come to nothing. (Psa 112:10)

If a man curses his father or mother, his lamp will be snuffed out in pitch darkness. (Prov 20:20)

Outline	Scripture
	G. The Parable of the Sheep and Goats: The Final Judgment of Nations, 25:31-46
1 The Son of Man is coming to judge a. Coming in glory b. Coming with angels[DS1] c. Coming to be enthroned d. Coming to gather all nations e. Coming to separate the nations, both sheep & goats 1) Sheep—favored seat 2) Goats—unfavored seat	31 "When the Son of Man comes in his glory, and all the angels with him, he will sit on his throne in heavenly glory. 32 All the nations will be gathered before him, and he will separate the people one from another as a shepherd separates the sheep from the goats. 33 He will put the sheep on his right and the goats on his left.
2 The judgment of sheep will occur a. The Judge: The King b. The invitation: Come c. The reward: The Kingdom d. The basis of judgment: Ministering to Christ	34 "Then the King will say to those on his right, 'Come, you who are blessed by my Father; take your inheritance, the kingdom prepared for you since the creation of the world. 35 For I was hungry and you gave me something to eat, I was thirsty and you gave me something to drink, I was a stranger and you invited me in, 36 I needed clothes and you clothed me, I was sick and you looked after me, I was in prison and you came to visit me.'
e. The ministry defined 1) A humble, instinctive ministry: No thought of reward, only of helping people in need	37 "Then the righteous will answer him, 'Lord, when did we see you hungry and feed you, or thirsty and give you something to drink? 38 When did we see you a stranger and invite you in, or needing clothes and clothe you? 39 When did we see you sick or in prison and go to visit you?'
2) A ministry to the Lord's "brothers"[DS2]	40 "The King will reply, 'I tell you the truth, whatever you did for one of the least of these brothers of mine, you did for me.'
3 The judgment of goats will occur a. The judgment 1) Cut off from God 2) Eternal fire[DS3] b. The basis of judgment 1) A failure to minister 2) A selfish life 3) A spiritual blindness	41 "Then he will say to those on his left, 'Depart from me, you who are cursed, into the eternal fire prepared for the devil and his angels. 42 For I was hungry and you gave me nothing to eat, I was thirsty and you gave me nothing to drink, 43 I was a stranger and you did not invite me in, I needed clothes and you did not clothe me, I was sick and in prison and you did not look after me.' 44 "They also will answer, 'Lord, when did we see you hungry or thirsty or a stranger or needing clothes or sick or in prison, and did not help you?' 45 "He will reply, 'I tell you the truth, whatever you did not do for one of the least of these, you did not do for me.'
4 The judgment is for eternity	46 "Then they will go away to eternal punishment, but the righteous to eternal life."

DIVISION XV

THE MESSIAH'S PROPHECY OF HIS RETURN AND THE END OF THE AGE: THE OLIVET DISCOURSE, 24:1-25:46

G. The Parable of the Sheep and Goats: The Final Judgment of Nations, 25:31-46

(25:31-46) **Introduction—The Final Judgment**: a person must guard against confusing the judgment of a nation's works with the judgment of individuals (sheep and goats). Judging nations is really judging individuals within them. Christ was painting a picture of the final judgment of all men. The final judgment will include *all nations* of men; it will be the judgment of the *whole world.*

It is important to see that Jesus was judging two types of beings, sheep and goats, not the same type of being of whom some behaved in one way and some another. Note the sheep (truly born again believers) serve with Christ's heart of love *because they are sheep.* The ministry they rendered came from within. It was a natural ministry performed by sheep. It arose from a selfless, God-centered nature. Goats do not serve with Christ's heart of love *because they are goats.* The acts of kindness identified the sheep as sheep. The neglect of the goats identified them as goats. The sheep acted like sheep; that is, they served because they were sheep. And the goats acted like goats When Christ sets them at His hand, they are already sheep and goats. Judgment is passed upon the goats because they did not serve Christ, and blessing is bestowed upon the sheep because they served Christ. Scripture says, "Show me your faith without deeds, and I will show you my faith by what I do" (Jas.2:18). The only faith that God knows and accepts is the faith that serves Christ by ministering to people. A man who says he has faith and does not minister to people is *only professing* faith in Christ. The true believer is "God's workmanship created in Christ Jesus to do good works" (Eph.2:10). God knows no faith apart from good works, that is, apart from ministering to the needs of people.

1. The Son of Man is coming to judge (v.31-33).
2. The judgment of sheep will occur (v.34-40).
3. The judgment of goats will occur (v.41-45).
4. The judgment is for eternity (v.46).

1 (25:31-33) **Jesus Christ, Return**: the Son of Man is coming to judge. Christ said five things about His coming in these three verses.

1. When He comes, He is coming in glory. This means at least two things. First, He is coming in His glorified body, that is, His transfigured body (Mt.17:2); in a body full of light and splendor; in a body shining as the sun in all the brilliance of God's glory. Second, He is not coming in the humiliation which He suffered as a man, but He is coming as the Son of Man and as the King of the universe.

2. When He comes, He is coming with His holy angels. An innumberable number of glorious beings will accompany Him, demonstrating the glory and honor of His person as God. The holy angels will be the attendants and ministers of His justice.

3. When He comes, He is coming to be enthroned. When He sits on "his throne in heavenly glory," He sits in judgment. He will become the One before whom every knee shall bow (Ph.2:9-11). He will become the Judge of the whole universe, the Judge who is exalted above all (Rev.20:11f).

4. When He comes, He is coming to gather all nations. All men will be gathered by the angels and brought before Him. The word *nations* stresses that every single country, place, nationality, race, creed, color, language—every living citizen will be gathered before Him in judgment.

5. When He comes, He is coming to separate the nations.

a. Throughout history, there has been a mixture of sheep and goats, of good and evil. The tares and the wheat have grown together. The sinner and the godly have lived together...
   - in the same world
   - in the same nations
   - in the same cities
   - in the same employments
   - in the same churches
   - in the same families

   When Christ comes, however, there is going to be a separation—a separation of the good from the bad, of the sheep from the goats (cp. Mt.13:49; Ezk. 34:17).

b. The sheep will be placed on His right hand and the goats on His left hand. The sheep represent genuine believers. They are...
   - the ones who believe in God's "one and only Son" (Jn.3:16).
   - the ones who are truly "born again" (Jn.3:3, 7).
   - the "good and faithful" servants (Mt.25:21, 23).
   - the "righteous" (Mt.25:37).
   - the ones who are "persistent in doing good" (Ro.2:7).
   - the ones who "seek glory, honor and immortality" (Ro.2:7).
   - the ones who "do good" (Ro.2:10).

   Note that God sets the sheep at His right hand, the position of honor, glory, acceptance, and favor.

   The goats represent *all* unbelievers, those who never professed Christ and those who professed Christ but were not genuine believers. They are...
   - the "worthless servants" (Mt.25:30).
   - the "wicked and lazy servants" (Mt.25:26).
   - the "cursed" (Mt.25:41).
   - the ones who "are self-seeking" (Ro.2:8).
   - the ones who "do not obey the truth" (Ro.2:8).
   - the ones who "follow evil" (Ro.2:9).

Thought 1. Judgment is coming. It is inevitable; it cannot be avoided nor evaded. No person can escape the coming judgment of God. God is going to judge the world by His Son, the Lord Jesus Christ.

Moreover, the Father judges no one, but has entrusted all judgment to the Son, (John 5:22)

He commanded us to preach to the people and to testify that he is the one whom God appointed as judge of the living and the dead. (Acts 10:42)

For he has set a day when he will judge the world with justice by the man he has appointed. He has given proof of this to all men by raising him from the dead." (Acts 17:31)

This will take place on the day when God will judge men's secrets through Jesus Christ, as my gospel declares. (Rom 2:16)

So then, each of us will give an account of himself to God. (Rom 14:12)

In the presence of God and of Christ Jesus, who will judge the living and the dead, and in view of his appearing and his kingdom, I give you this charge: (2 Tim 4:1)

And I saw the dead, great and small, standing before the throne, and books were opened. Another book was opened, which is the book of life. The dead were judged according to what they had done as recorded in the books. (Rev 20:12)

Thought 2. Very simply put, the day is coming when every citizen of every nation and tribe on earth will stand before Christ—stand either in His *favor* or in His *disfavor*.

Thought 3. Note the two claims to deity that Christ makes.

1) He calls Himself "the Son of Man": He is the Ideal Man. As the Ideal Man, He is to judge the sons of men.
2) He says that "the Son of Man will sit upon his throne in heavenly glory." He said this three days before He was killed.

Thought 4. Note a significant fact: Christ is *now* sitting on the throne at the right hand of God. There is a difference between the throne of grace and the throne of judgment pictured in this passage. We can now come to the throne of grace for help (Heb.4:16). But when Christ returns in glory, it will be too late to receive help. His throne will be a *throne of judgment* to which there will be no approach apart from judgment.

DEEPER STUDY # 1

(25:31) **Angels—Jesus Christ, Return**: when Christ returns, He will be accompanied by angels who will serve as His ministers throughout the judgment.

⇒ They will gather the weeds, the children of the evil one (Mt.13:38-40).

> ⇒ They will gather the elect (Mt.24:31).
> ⇒ They will witness the believers' glory (Lk.12:8).
> ⇒ They will call believers together to meet the Lord in the air (Mt.24:31; 1 Th.4:16).
> ⇒ They will witness the torment of the wicked (Rev.14:10).

2 (25:34-40) **Judgment**: the judgment of sheep will occur.

1. The Judge is the King. Christ sits on His *throne in heavenly glory* and reigns as "King of Kings, and Lord of Lords" (Rev.19:16).

2. The invitation is "come, you who are blessed by my Father." The sheep are the blessed, the beloved of God (see note—Eph.1:3). The word *come* is the picture of entering the very presence of God Himself and being privileged to remain there forever.

3. The reward is an inheritance—the inheritance of the Kingdom of God.

a. *An inheritance* is a gift. It is given because the giver cares enough to give it, and it becomes one's own possession as much as it was the former owner's.
b. The inheritance is a *kingdom.* It is a place of responsibility and duty, of ruling and reigning, of honor and joy, of wealth and glory.
c. The inheritance or the kingdom had been *prepared* for the sheep (cp. Jn.14:2-3). It was built to suit them and designed for their habitation. "All this is for your benefit" (2 Cor.4:15).
d. The kingdom had been prepared from *the foundation of the world.* It was in the eternal plan and will of God (Eph.1:4-5, 11-12).

4. The basis of judgment—the reason the sheep are given the kingdom—is because they ministered to Christ. Several important facts need to be noted.

a. The sheep ministered *to Christ*; that is, what they did was done "for Christ's sake." They ministered "as believers" in Him.
b. The sheep ministered because they loved their brothers (see DEEPER STUDY # 2—Mt. 25:40; cp. 1 Jn.4:7-8, 12, 20-21).
c. Christ is not disregarding or minimizing the part of faith in salvation. We will be judged for both our confession of faith and our works (Mt.10:32; Lk.12:8; Ro.10:9-10; 2 Cor.5:10).
d. Note that the works are simple works, some of which anyone can do. They are expressions of care and love that *can* serve as the basis of judgment, as the basis for judging anyone.

5. The ministry is defined by Christ; He shares just what He means by ministering. Note it is the righteous who ask Him what He means.

a. The ministry is a humble, instinctive ministry. It has no thought of reward, only of helping people in need. The true believer serves Christ because Christ has done so much for him. It is "the love of Christ" which compels him (2 Cor.5:14). *Even while he is serving, a humble servant knows something…*
    - He is not even worthy to be serving.
    - He has done, is doing, and will do so little.
    - He deserves nothing.

    He is serving simply because he loves Jesus and the people of the earth. All he knows and wishes to know is Jesus. To serve Jesus and to help all those for whom Jesus died is within him instinctively.
b. The ministry is a ministry to the Lord's brothers (see DEEPER STUDY # 2—Mt.25:40). The thought here is of critical importance. It determines a man's destiny.

    Christ has so *identified* Himself with men in their pain and suffering that He counts men as one with Himself. Christ clearly said that if we minister to men, we are ministering to Him personally. He is identified as one with His people (Mt.8:17; cp. Is.53:4). He accused Saul of actually persecuting Him when Saul was threatening and slaughtering Christians (Acts 9:4).

And if anyone gives even a cup of cold water to one of these little ones because he is my disciple, I tell you the truth, he will certainly not lose his reward." (Mat 10:42)

Not so with you. Instead, whoever wants to become great among you must be your servant, and whoever wants to be first must be slave of all. (Mark 10:43-44)

"Which of these three do you think was a neighbor to the man who fell into the hands of robbers?" The expert in the law replied, "The one who had mercy on him." Jesus told him, "Go and do likewise." (Luke 10:36-37)

Now that I, your Lord and Teacher, have washed your feet, you also should wash one another's feet. (John 13:14)

Again Jesus said, "Simon son of John, do you truly love me?" He answered, "Yes, Lord, you know that I love you." Jesus said, "Take care of my sheep." (John 21:16)

Carry each other's burdens, and in this way you will fulfill the law of Christ. Therefore, as we have opportunity, let us do good to all people, especially to those who belong to the family of believers. (Gal 6:2, 10)

Serve wholeheartedly, as if you were serving the Lord, not men, (Eph 6:7)

Thought 1. Several points are clearly pictured in these verses.
1) The rightful position of Christ before the world: He is the King.
2) The glorious inheritance of the believer.
3) The initial importance of ministry.

Thought 2. Think how many *lonely* of this world become His. How many of the hungry, the thirsty, the strangers, the naked, the sick, the prisoners become His? (Cp. Mt.1:26-27.)

Thought 3. No ministry and no amount of suffering on this earth are so lowly that the ministry and suffering will not be worth the glory that will be revealed in us (Ro.8:18).

Thought 4. There are those who will give huge sums of money and help enormously if they can be recognized. But such is rooted in selfishness; it is pandering to our egos and desires for recognition and esteem.

DEEPER STUDY # 2
(25:40) **Brothers**: without exception, Christ is consistent in His use of the word brothers. His brothers are His disciples (cp. Mt.23:8; 12:46-50; 28:10; Mk.3:31-35; Lk.8:21; Jn.20:17-18). Jesus is saying that the nations (the leaders and citizens of the nations) are to be judged for their actions toward His followers and their message. If they have received His people and their message with open arms and with righteous and brotherly behavior, then they will show that they have definitely received Him.

3 (25:41-45) **Judgment**: the judgment of goats will occur.

1. The judgment will be twofold.
   a. The goats will be cut off and separated from God. Christ will say, "Depart from me"—words that mean a world of misery, a world of darkness, a world of weeping and gnashing of teeth, a world of eternal punishment, a world without God and hope (cp. Mt.25:30, 46). The goats rejected Christ and refused to be identified with Him while on earth. When they stand before Him, they will never have been associated with Him. Therefore, they will not be allowed to associate with Him.

      Note what Christ calls the goats: "You who are cursed." They did not choose to be called "brothers" (v.40), nor did they choose to inherit the kingdom. They will, therefore, be called "cursed;" and they will inherit the curse (Gal.3:10). As Scripture says "It is a dreadful thing to fall into the hands of the living God" (Heb.10:31).
   b. The goats will be placed into "eternal fire" (see DEEPER STUDY # 2—Mt.5:22; DEEPER STUDY # 4—Lk.16:24; note—Rev.9:2. Cp. Rev.20:2.) Note three things. It is a place of anguish, torment, and punishment (cp. Mt.25:30, 46 with notes listed above). It is eternal, having no end. It is prepared for the devil and his angels, not for man.
2. The basis of judgment and the reasons why the goats will be separated from God are revealing.
   a. The goats failed to minister. Very simply, the goats are persons who fail to help the hungry, the thirsty, the stranger, the naked, the sick, and the prisoner. They are persons who do not become *involved* in meeting the needs of people. They are persons who do not dedicate themselves to meeting the desperate needs of a corruptible world (cp. Mt.20:28. Cp. Jn.20:21; Lk.9:23.)
   b. The goats lived a selfish life. The goats are people who live a life of comfort and ease, a life of no concern and care, a life of materialism and things, a life of pleasure and indulgence, a life of money and plenty. They live selfishly while the world around them is suffering with hunger and sickness and death.
   c. The goats were spiritually blind. The goats are people who refuse to see the truth about Christ, that He *identifies Himself* with the suffering masses, with the pain and need of individuals. The goats refuse to open their eyes to see those lying all around, those desperately in need: the hungry, the thirsty, the stranger, the naked, the sick, the prisoner. They refuse to see the *stamp* of God, His glorious love for every man. They refuse to see that they are failing to help Christ when they fail to help the needy.

Jesus answered, "If you want to be perfect, go, sell your possessions and give to the poor, and you will have treasure in heaven. Then come, follow me." (Mat 19:21)

I was a stranger and you did not invite me in, I needed clothes and you did not clothe me, I was sick and in prison and you did not look after me.' (Mat 25:43)

But the worries of this life, the deceitfulness of wealth and the desires for other things come in and choke the word, making it unfruitful. (Mark 4:19)

At his gate was laid a beggar named Lazarus, covered with sores and longing to eat what fell from the rich man's table. Even the dogs came and licked his sores. (Luke 16:20-21)

People who want to get rich fall into temptation and a trap and into many foolish and harmful desires that plunge men into ruin and destruction. (1 Tim 6:9)

Religion that God our Father accepts as pure and faultless is this: to look after orphans and widows in their distress and to keep oneself from being polluted by the world. (James 1:27)

Anyone, then, who knows the good he ought to do and doesn't do it, sins. (James 4:17)

If anyone has material possessions and sees his brother in need but has no pity on him, how can the love of God be in him? (1 John 3:17)

If there is a poor man among your brothers in any of the towns of the land that the LORD your God is giving you, do not be hardhearted or tightfisted toward your poor brother. (Deu 15:7)

You lie on beds inlaid with ivory and lounge on your couches. You dine on choice lambs and fattened calves. (Amos 6:4)

Thought 1. Christ says to the goats, "Depart from me." Where are the goats sent?

⇒ It is not a place of comfort and pleasure. It is a place of weeping and gnashing of teeth.

And throw that worthless servant outside, into the darkness, where there will be weeping and gnashing of teeth.' (Mat 25:30)

⇒ It is not a place of light and justice. It is outer darkness.

"Then the king told the attendants, 'Tie him hand and foot, and throw him outside, into the darkness, where there will be weeping and gnashing of teeth.' (Mat 22:13; cp. Mt.25:30)

⇒ It is not a place of short duration. It is eternal.

"Then he will say to those on his left, 'Depart from me, you who are cursed, into the eternal fire prepared for the devil and his angels. (Mat 25:41)

⇒ It is not a place of good friends and fellowship. It is the company of the devil.

And the devil, who deceived them, was thrown into the lake of burning sulfur, where the beast and the false prophet had been thrown. They will be tormented day and night for ever and ever. Then I saw a great white throne and him who was seated on it. Earth and sky fled from his presence, and there was no place for them. And I saw the dead, great and small, standing before the throne, and books were opened. Another book was opened, which is the book of life. The dead were judged according to what they had done as recorded in the books. The sea gave up the dead that were in it, and death and Hades gave up the dead that were in them, and each person was judged according to what he had done. Then death and Hades were thrown into the lake of fire. The lake of fire is the second death. If anyone's name was not found written in the book of life, he was thrown into the lake of fire. (Rev 20:10-15; cp. Mt.25:41)

Thought 2. Note the *striking* difference between the sheep and the goats.

- ⇒ The sheep heard "come"; the goats heard "depart."
- ⇒ The sheep are called "blessed"; the goats are called "cursed."
- ⇒ The sheep are invited to "inherit"; the goats are "cursed."
- ⇒ The sheep receive a kingdom; the goats receive "eternal fire."
- ⇒ The sheep dwell in a place *prepared* for God's people; the goats dwell in a place prepared for the devil and his angels.
- ⇒ The sheep spend eternity with God and their Christian brothers; the goats spend eternity with the devil and his angels.

Thought 3. Note a critical point. Goats are not condemned for what they did, but for what they did not do. Their sin was the sin of omission, not commission. But note how terrible the sin is, how many destitute people were left suffering all through life because a goat did not help them.

Thought 4. Selfishness, indulgence, extravagance, hoarding—all that leads to and indicates the neglect of others—will visibly condemn a man when he stands before Christ. (For a clear study of this point see outline and notes—Mt.19:16-22; 19:23-26; 19:27-30.)

Thought 5. Note that the worthless servant's sin is the same as the goats: the sin of neglect and omission. Each neglected to do what they should have done. (See outline and notes—Mt.25:14-30.)

DEEPER STUDY # 3

(25:41) **Eternal fire** (to pur to aionion): this literally reads, "fire which is everlasting." It is a fire that lasts forever, burns on and on. Note the fire is not prepared for men, but for the devil and his angels. God never intended men to spend eternity in everlasting fire. Men who choose to follow the devil in his evil ways are choosing to be with the devil wherever he is. (See DEEPER STUDY # 2, Hell—Mt.5:22 for more discussion.)

4 (25:46) **Judgment**: it is critical to note the words of Christ: "They will go away to eternal punishment." The judgment is for eternity. There is no second chance; judgment is unchangeable.

"The righteous [will go] into eternal life." Life eternal is also permanent and unchangeable. Note: it is *life* that is eternal, not some dreamy, unconscious, or semiconscious state of being. The sheep will live, and their life will be eternal, never ending.

Outline	Heading	Scripture	Outline
	CHAPTER 26	2 "As you know, the Passover is two days away—and the Son of Man will be handed over to be crucified."	a. Was tied to the Passover[DS1] b. Was Son of Man dying c. Was caused by betrayal d. To be by crucifixion
	XVI. THE MESSIAH'S ARREST, TRIAL, AND CRUCIFIXION, 26:1-27:66	3 Then the chief priests and the elders of the people assembled in the palace of the high priest, whose name was Caiaphas,	**2 Jesus' death was plotted by the religionists**[DS2] a. Was planned by all the leaders
	A. The Messiah's Death Explained & Plotted, 26:1-5 (Mk.14:1-2; Lk.22:1-2)	4 And they plotted to arrest Jesus in some sly way and kill him.	b. Was to be by deception 1) To arrest on false charges & kill
1 Jesus' death was explained to His disciples	When Jesus had finished saying all these things, he said to his disciples,	5 "But not during the Feast," they said, "or there may be a riot among the people."	2) To arrest quietly, after the pilgrims had left the feast[DS3]

DIVISION XVI

THE MESSIAH'S ARREST, TRIAL AND CRUCIFIXION, 26:1-27:66

A. The Messiah's Death Explained and Plotted, 26:1-5

(26:1-5) **Introduction**: it was apparently Wednesday of Jesus' last week (see notes—Mt.21:1-11; 21:12-16; 21:17-22; 21:23-27). He was to be killed on Friday, just two days away. In these few verses, Matthew gives a glimpse into the drama that was rapidly building. Two scenes are pictured: Jesus was intensely preparing His disciples for His death, and the religionists were behind closed doors demonically plotting His death.

What Jesus explained about His death is explicit: He was to be betrayed and crucified. What the religionists plotted was explicit: they were going to kill Jesus.

1. Jesus' death was explained to His disciples (v.1-2).
   a. His death was tied to the Passover.
   b. His death was the Son of Man dying.
   c. His death was caused by betrayal.
   d. His death was to be by crucifixion.
2. Jesus' death was plotted by the religionists (v.3-5).
   a. His death was planned by all the leaders.
   b. His death was to be by deception
      1) He was to be arrested on false charges and killed.
      2) He was to be arrested quietly after the pilgrims had left the feast.

1 (26:1-2) **Jesus Christ, Death**: Jesus' death was explained to His disciples. In just two days, He was to be crucified. The disciples had to be strengthened for the hour of trial lest their dreams become dashed upon the rocks of despair and they loose faith. Remember, their thoughts were focused on the Messiah's restoring the kingdom of David to Israel. They were thinking that He, the Messiah, was going to deliver Israel from Roman bondage. The Messiah would free the nation and establish it as the greatest nation on earth under the rule of God Himself (see notes—Mt.1:1; DEEPER STUDY # 2—1:18; DEEPER STUDY # 3—3:11; notes—11:1-6; 11:2-3; DEEPER STUDY # 1—11:5; DEEPER STUDY # 2—11:6; DEEPER STUDY # 1—12:16; notes—22:42; Lk.7:21-23). There was the very live possibility that the apostles could lose faith when they saw His being put to death by the hands of mere men. It could appear as though He were being forsaken by God! Christ had to do everything He could to prepare them. There were four basic facts about His death that would help and help tremendously.

1. Christ's death was tied to the Passover (see DEEPER STUDY # 1—Mt.26:2; DEEPER STUDY # 1—Lk.22:7; DEEPER STUDY # 2—22:19-20). He was foretelling the disciples the exact day He was to be killed, and it was to be the very same day the Passover lamb was to be sacrificed. And note, He was tying His death to the sacrifice of the lamb. As John the Baptist had proclaimed earlier, "Look, the Lamb of God, who takes away the sin of the world" (Jn.1:29, 36).

> **Whoever eats my flesh and drinks my blood has eternal life, and I will raise him up at the last day. For my flesh is real food and my blood is real drink. Whoever eats my flesh and drinks my blood remains in me, and I in him. Just as the living Father sent me and I live because of the Father, so the one who feeds on me will live because of me. This is the bread that came down from heaven. Your forefathers ate manna and died, but he who feeds on this bread will live forever." (John 6:54-58)**
>
> **In him we have redemption through his blood, the forgiveness of sins, in accordance with the riches of God's grace (Eph 1:7)**
>
> **But with the precious blood of Christ, a lamb without blemish or defect. (1 Pet 1:19)**
>
> **But if we walk in the light, as he is in the light, we have fellowship with one another, and the blood of Jesus, his Son, purifies us from all sin. (1 John 1:7)**
>
> **My dear children, I write this to you so that you will not sin. But if anybody does sin, we have one who speaks to the Father in our defense—Jesus Christ, the Righteous One. He is the atoning sacrifice for our sins, and not only for ours but also for the sins of the whole world. (1 John 2:1-2)**

2. Christ's death was the Son of Man Himself dying (see DEEPER STUDY # 3—Mt.8:20). "Son of Man" means that He perfectly identified with man in human flesh. But it means more, much more: it means that He is the Ideal Man, the Man who lived a perfect and sinless life. By living without sin, He has become the Ideal and Perfect Man, the Pattern Man for all men. It is the Son of Man who

knows our trials and hurts, pain and suffering. It was the Son of Man who lived a perfect life and who secured a perfect righteousness—the Son of Man who died for us. And because He died, His Ideal righteousness and Ideal death can *stand* for our righteousness and death.

> **"I am the good shepherd. The good shepherd lays down his life for the sheep. (John 10:11)**
> **You see, at just the right time, when we were still powerless, Christ died for the ungodly. (Rom 5:6)**
> **For what I received I passed on to you as of first importance : that Christ died for our sins according to the Scriptures, (1 Cor 15:3)**
> **Who gave himself for our sins to rescue us from the present evil age, according to the will of our God and Father, (Gal 1:4)**
> **And live a life of love, just as Christ loved us and gave himself up for us as a fragrant offering and sacrifice to God. (Eph 5:2)**
> **Who gave himself for us to redeem us from all wickedness and to purify for himself a people that are his very own, eager to do what is good. (Titus 2:14)**
> **So Christ was sacrificed once to take away the sins of many people; and he will appear a second time, not to bear sin, but to bring salvation to those who are waiting for him. (Heb 9:28)**
> **But you know that he appeared so that he might take away our sins. And in him is no sin. (1 John 3:5)**
> **This is how we know what love is: Jesus Christ laid down his life for us. And we ought to lay down our lives for our brothers. (1 John 3:16)**
> **And they sang a new song: "You are worthy to take the scroll and to open its seals, because you were slain, and with your blood you purchased men for God from every tribe and language and people and nation. (Rev 5:9)**

He is our Ideal righteousness and life. When we seek for a Savior, it is He for whom we must seek. It was the Son of Man Himself who was to die, the only Man who could die as the Ideal Man; and because He was the Ideal Man, His death can cover all men. His death is the Ideal death, the Pattern death which covers any man who calls upon Him.

> **But God demonstrates his own love for us in this: While we were still sinners, Christ died for us. (Rom 5:8)**
> **He himself bore our sins in his body on the tree, so that we might die to sins and live for righteousness; by his wounds you have been healed. (1 Pet 2:24)**
> **For Christ died for sins once for all, the righteous for the unrighteous, to bring you to God. He was put to death in the body but made alive by the Spirit, (1 Pet 3:18)**

3. Christ's death was caused by betrayal. One of the disciples was going to betray Him (see notes—Mt.26:20-25; 27:3-5; Mk.14:10-11; Lk.22:4-6; note and DEEPER STUDY # 1—Jn.13:18; note—13:21-26). Note that Christ used the future tense, "will be handed over." The betrayal was certain, immediate, staring Him right in the face.

4. Christ's death was to be by crucifixion. (Death by crucifixion is graphically described in the outline, notes, and DEEPER STUDY # 1—Mt.27:26-44; notes—Mk.15:16-41; Lk.23:26-49; Jn.19:16-37.)

> **He himself bore our sins in his body on the tree, so that we might die to sins and live for righteousness; by his wounds you have been healed. (1 Pet 2:24)**
> **Christ redeemed us from the curse of the law by becoming a curse for us, for it is written: "Cursed is everyone who is hung on a tree." (Gal 3:13)**
> **But God demonstrates his own love for us in this: While we were still sinners, Christ died for us. Since we have now been justified by his blood, how much more shall we be saved from God's wrath through him! For if, when we were God's enemies, we were reconciled to him through the death of his Son, how much more, having been reconciled, shall we be saved through his life! (Rom 5:8-10)**

Thought 1. The Passover clearly shows *the glorious preparation* of God for salvation, for taking away the sins of the world. The Paschal lamb was given by God as a picture of the giving of His Son for the sins of the world.

Thought 2. Jesus died for us. He has taken away the sins of the world.

> **He himself bore our sins in his body on the tree, so that we might die to sins and live for righteousness; by his wounds you have been healed. (1 Pet 2:24)**
> **For Christ died for sins once for all, the righteous for the unrighteous, to bring you to God. He was put to death in the body but made alive by the Spirit, (1 Pet 3:18. See note—Mt.17:22-23; note and DEEPER STUDY # 1—20:18)**

Thought 3. Jesus did all He could to prepare His disciples for the great trial they were to face in witnessing His death. He does all He can to prepare us for whatever lies ahead. Just think of the things He has told us that lie out in the future. How well He has prepared us—lest we be caught off guard (see outlines and notes—Mt.24:1-25:46).

Thought 4. Jesus' death not only saves us, but it encourages us to bear the trials of life.

> **Consider him who endured such opposition from sinful men, so that you will not grow weary and lose heart. (Heb 12:3)**

DEEPER STUDY # 1

(26:2) **Passover—Jesus Christ, Death**: note Jesus' words "you know." The disciples did know both facts. The Passover was only two days away, and Jesus had been telling them for months that He was to be killed. Why, then, was He pointing out facts that the disciples already knew? What Jesus was doing was *revealing* to the disciples that His death was tied to the Passover (see outline and notes—Mt.26:17-19). The Passover throughout history had pictured His death. Christ was fulfilling the Passover with the shedding of His own blood upon the cross.

1. Historically, the Passover refers back to the time when God delivered Israel from Egyptian bondage (Ex.11:1f). God had pronounced judgment, the taking of the firstborn, upon the people of Egypt for their injustices. As God prepared to execute the final judgment, those who believed God were instructed to slay a pure lamb and sprinkle its blood over the door frames of their homes. The blood of the innocent lamb would then serve as a sign that the coming judgment had already been carried out. When seeing the blood, God would *pass over* that house.

2. Symbolically, the passover pictured the coming of Jesus Christ as the Savior. The "lamb without defect" pictured His sinless life (cp. Jn.1:29), and the "blood sprinkled on the door frames" pictured His blood shed for the believer. It was a sign that the life and blood of the innocent lamb had been substituted for the firstborn. The "eating of the lamb" pictured the need for spiritual nourishment gained by feeding on Christ, the Bread of Life. The unleavened bread (bread without yeast) pictured the need for putting evil out of one's life and household (see DEEPER STUDY # 1, Feast of Unleavened Bread—Mt.26:17).

2 (26:3-5) **Religionists, Plot Jesus' Death**: Jesus' death was plotted by the religionists. Matthew painted a dramatic picture. While Christ was on one side of town preparing His disciples for His death, the religionists were on the other side of town plotting His death. And note: they were in the house of the high priest behind closed doors.

1. Christ's death was plotted by all the leaders: the chief priests, the Scribes, and the elders (see DEEPER STUDY # 1—Mt.16:21; DEEPER STUDY # 2—26:3).
   a. Note where they met, how deceptive it was. They met in the home (palace) of the high priest, not in the official court. It was a secret plot, to be kept quiet until the right moment for the arrest and murder.
   b. Note who it was that took the lead in the plot: Caiaphas, the high priest himself, the very person who was supposed to be the spiritual leader of the people.

2. Christ's death was to be wrought by deception and lies.
   a. He was to be arrested on false charges and killed (see outline and notes—Mt.26:60-66).
   b. He was to be arrested quietly, after all the pilgrims had left the feast to return home. The *feast* refers to all eight days of the feast. The danger of an uprising would not have passed until they had all left the city. Of course, the threat of an uprising was removed by the willingness of Judas' to betray Christ. In the crowded masses of about two million bodies within the city, Judas was able to show them where Christ was and to quietly identify Him. He was able to show them how Christ could be quietly taken in the dark of the night (cp. Mt.26:47-50).

"Their throats are open graves; their tongues practice deceit." "The poison of vipers is on their lips." (Rom 3:13)

Do you not know that the wicked will not inherit the kingdom of God? Do not be deceived: Neither the sexually immoral nor idolaters nor adulterers nor male prostitutes nor homosexual offenders (1 Cor 6:9)

Do not be deceived: God cannot be mocked. A man reaps what he sows. (Gal 6:7)

Let no one deceive you with empty words, for because of such things God's wrath comes on those who are disobedient. (Eph 5:6)

Dear children, do not let anyone lead you astray. He who does what is right is righteous, just as he is righteous. He who does what is sinful is of the devil, because the devil has been sinning from the beginning. The reason the Son of God appeared was to destroy the devil's work. (1 John 3:7-8)

Do not merely listen to the word, and so deceive yourselves. Do what it says. (James 1:22)

For in his own eyes he flatters himself too much to detect or hate his sin. (Psa 36:2)

Those who are pure in their own eyes and yet are not cleansed of their filth; (Prov 30:12)

Many a man claims to have unfailing love, but a faithful man who can find? (Prov 20:6)

Friend deceives friend, and no one speaks the truth. They have taught their tongues to lie; they weary themselves with sinning. (Jer 9:5)

The heart is deceitful above all things and beyond cure. Who can understand it? (Jer 17:9)

Thought 1. Note how even the most religious can be gripped by the fear of losing position, power, recognition, esteem, and security (see notes—Mt.12:1-8; note and DEEPER STUDY # 1—12:10; note—15:1-20; DEEPER STUDY # 2—15:6-9; DEEPER STUDY # 3—16:12). How worldly, how attached to the things of the world even the most religious become!

DEEPER STUDY # 2

(26:3) **High Priest—Chief Priests—Caiaphas**: the office of High Priest began with Aaron and his sons (Ex.28:1). The office was hereditary and was for life, but when the Romans conquered Palestine, they made the office political. They chose their own man, a man who would cooperate with the Roman government. Finding such a man was often difficult. For example, between 37 B.C. and 67 A.D. there were at least twenty-eight High Priests. These men were greatly respected and highly honored throughout life, and even when they were removed from power by the Romans, they were still consulted by other Jewish leaders. The ex-High Priest, Annas, was a prime example. He still wielded unusual power (cp. Jn.18:13; Acts 4:6). He and the others who had served as High Priests or else held the top positions of leadership were also called *chief priests*.

The term of office for a High Priest was determined solely by the Romans. The Romans let a High Priest reign so long as he pleased them. The reign of the twenty-eight averaged only about three years, except for Caiaphas. Caiaphas was High Priest for about eighteen years

(18 A.D. to 36 A.D.). Apparently he was a master at intrigue and compromise. This throws great light on his fearing an uproar and wishing to wait until the feast was over to arrest Jesus (Mt.26:5). There was the danger that the people might rally to support Jesus if they saw Him arrested; so many believed Him to be a great prophet that a serious uprising was a real possibility. Caiaphas knew the Romans would hold him responsible and remove him from office. He would lose everything he had. The shrewdness of the man was seen in the strategy he laid. They were to arrest Jesus quietly after the masses had left the feast.

DEEPER STUDY # 3

(26:5) **Passover**: the atmosphere of Jerusalem at the Passover Feast was always explosive. The city was overly packed with pilgrims. Josephus, the notable Jewish historian, says that by law each sacrifice had to represent at least ten persons. He reports over a quarter million sacrificial lambs were slain; therefore, he estimates that two million or more pilgrims were celebrating at this particular feast (Josephus, Wars. 6. 9:3). (See notes—Mt.26:3-5.)

	B. The Messiah Anointed for Death: A Picture of Sacrificial Love & Faith, 26:6-13 (Mk.14:3-9; Jn.12:1-8)	9 "This perfume could have been sold at a high price and the money given to the poor." 10 Aware of this, Jesus said to them, "Why are you bothering this woman? She has done a beautiful thing to me.	**4 The anointing was a grasping of opportunity**
1 In Bethany, in the house of Simon the Leper, a woman anointed Jesus[DS1]	6 While Jesus was in Bethany in the home of a man known as Simon the Leper,	11 The poor you will always have with you, but you will not always have me.	
2 The anointing was an act of love & faith in the Lord Jesus[DS2]	7 A woman came to him with an alabaster jar of very expensive perfume, which she poured on his head as he was reclining at the table.	12 When she poured this perfume on my body, she did it to prepare me for burial.	**5 The anointing pointed toward the burial of Jesus, toward His death**
3 The anointing was a sacrificial gift, a commitment beyond common sense	8 When the disciples saw this, they were indignant. "Why this waste?" they asked.	13 I tell you the truth, wherever this gospel is preached throughout the world, what she has done will also be told, in memory of her."	**6 The anointing was an eternal memorial**

DIVISION XVI

THE MESSIAH'S ARREST, TRIAL AND CRUCIFIXION, 26:1-27:66

B. The Messiah Anointed for Death: A Picture of Sacrificial Love and Faith, 26:6-13

(26:6-13) **Introduction—Jesus Christ, Anointed—Jesus Christ, Death—Love—Worship**: Mark and John also record this anointing of Jesus. John says it actually took place six days before the Passover (Jn.12:1). Matthew, as pointed out before, arranges events by subjects. He is discussing the death of Christ, so He places it here. John also identifies the woman as Mary, the sister of Lazarus and Martha. Matthew says that they were in the house of Simon the leper, and John says Martha served (Jn.12:2). Apparently Simon the leper was the husband of Martha (although others feel that he could be her father or father-in law) (Mt.26:6; cp. Jn.12:2).

What happened was this: the crowds were flowing into the city for the Passover, and the excitement of the Passover was filling the air. There was a sense that something significant was about to happen. Of course, Mary had no idea of the events that were to take place in the last week of Jesus' life, events which were to begin the very next morning with the triumphal entry. But Mary, along with everyone else, sensed that the time for the kingdom to be established was at hand. Mary, who was always sitting at Jesus' feet, sat there again, gazing into His eyes. As she gazed, she sensed two things. She sensed the need to repent of her recent criticism of Jesus (cp. Jn.12:3; see note—Jn.12:3), and she sensed a foreboding of trouble surrounding Him. She saw within His eyes a weight so heavy that she was *drawn* to express the most profound faith and appreciation in Him possible. She took the most precious thing she had, an invaluable bottle of perfume, and anointed Him as the Messiah, the anointed One of her life.

Mary's act was one of the most loving and precious acts, if not *the* most loving and precious, ever shown to Jesus. It was an act of supreme love and adoration. What Jesus had to say about it shows this (v.10-13). Just how loving an act it was can be seen by picturing all that was going on throughout the city at this time and all that was yet to happen: the plotting, the intrigue, the hostility, the attacks, the planned murder, the crowds streaming into the city by the teeming thousands—crowds who created a worldly, carnival atmosphere. Even Simon's own household had an enormous crowd in it with all the disciples present. Just imagine the noise from the conversation alone. Yet there sat Mary at Jesus' feet, once again soaking up all He said, loving and adoring Him. He had done so much for their family. Simon the Leper was apparently her brother-in-law (husband to Martha). He had probably been healed by her Lord. Her brother, Lazarus, had been raised from the dead. They had all been saved by Him. How she loved Him! How she wished to express her love and faith in Him! He seemed so tired, so weary, so foreboding; there was something in His eyes that expressed His concern and preoccupation as she gazed into them. She wanted to help and encourage Him, to show Him that she cared for and loved Him, so she arose and went to get the most precious thing she had to give Him. And she gave it in the most precious way she knew: she anointed her Lord, even as David and all the kings of Israel had been anointed in the past. She anointed Him, not from any official position, but from her heart. It is for this reason that she lives in the memory of all as a memorial. In the behalf of all, she anointed the Lord to be the One who was to experience death for all. In behalf of all, she anointed Him as the Lord and Savior, the true Messiah of all hearts and lives who worship and serve Him as the anointed One of God.

1. In Bethany, in the house of Simon the Leper, a woman anointed Jesus (v.6).
2. The anointing was an act of love and faith in the Lord Jesus (v.7).
3. The anointing was a sacrificial gift, a commitment beyond common sense (v.8-9).
4. The anointing was a grasping of opportunity (v.10-11).
5. The anointing pointed toward the burial of Jesus, His death (v.12).
6. The anointing was an eternal memorial (v.13).

1 (26:6) **Bethany**: see note—Mt.21:17.

DEEPER STUDY # 1

(26:6) **Simon the Leper**: Jesus was in the house of Simon the Leper. Little is known about Simon. He was probably a leper who had been healed by Jesus. Tradition says he was the husband of Martha. Scripture also seems to indicate this. Matthew says Jesus was dining in the house of Simon the Leper, and John says Martha was serving. This would seem to indicate a close relationship. Martha was probably his wife or older daughter. If she were Simon's wife, then her brother and sister, Lazarus and Mary, seemed to be living with her and Simon. Note that Simon's house was large enough to entertain Jesus and His disciples all at once. On such occasions, he would probably have had servants serving under the direction of his wife and not an older daughter. However, if Martha were Simon's oldest daughter, then Simon was the father of Mary and Lazarus as well. It was while Jesus was in Simon the Leper's home that Mary came up to Jesus and anointed Him.

Thought 1. Note a striking point: the man who welcomes the Lord into his home will learn much about the Lord. Just imagine the experience Simon the Leper had by inviting Jesus to dinner! The important thing to know about Simon the Leper is this: he welcomed Jesus into his home.

Thought 2. Note the closeness of the family. Throughout Scripture they are mentioned together, in particular Mary, Martha, and Lazarus. When Christ is a constant guest in a family's home, there is usually a close bond that does not exist otherwise.

Thought 3. Mary's love for Jesus was a most unusual love. Its depth is clearly seen in this most wonderful act (see note—Mt.26:6-13).

2 (26:7) **Faith—Love**: the anointing was an act of love and faith in the Lord Jesus. Very simply put, Mary anointed Jesus to show Him how deeply she loved Him and believed Him to be the true Messiah, "the anointed One of God" (see notes—Mt.26:6-13; cp. Mt.1:18). He was her Savior, Lord, and King. He had done so much for her and her family. She wanted Him to know how much she appreciated, loved, and believed Him.

Something else needs to be noted as well. Mary sensed something within Jesus: a foreboding, a preoccupation of mind, a heaviness of heart, a weight of tremendous pressure. Her heart reached out to Him and wanted to encourage and help Him. Being a young woman in the presence of so many men, she was not allowed to vocally express herself that much. Such a privilege was not allowed women of that day, so she did all that she could: she acted. She arose and went for the most precious gift she could think of—a most costly bottle of perfume. And she gave it to Him in such a way that He would know that at least one person truly loved Him and believed Him to be the Messiah. Her hope was that such faith and love would boost His spirit.

Thought 1. How do we show our love and faith in Christ? Imagine how difficult it was for Mary to do what she did in the presence of so many. She set aside pride and shyness in order to demonstrate her love and faith in Him. How far are we willing to go in order to show our love and faith for Christ?

Thought 2. Note how Mary demonstrated her love and faith.

1) Mary gave the most precious thing she had to the Lord.

But store up for yourselves treasures in heaven, where moth and rust do not destroy, and where thieves do not break in and steal. (Mat 6:20)

Sell your possessions and give to the poor. Provide purses for yourselves that will not wear out, a treasure in heaven that will not be exhausted, where no thief comes near and no moth destroys. (Luke 12:33)

In the same way, any of you who does not give up everything he has cannot be my disciple. (Luke 14:33)

What is more, I consider everything a loss compared to the surpassing greatness of knowing Christ Jesus my Lord, for whose sake I have lost all things. I consider them rubbish, that I may gain Christ (Phil 3:8)

In this way they will lay up treasure for themselves as a firm foundation for the coming age, so that they may take hold of the life that is truly life. (1 Tim 6:19)

2) Mary bore the witness of her love and faith in Christ publicly. Her love and faith in Christ was demonstrated for all to witness.

DEEPER STUDY # 2
(26:7) **Anointing**: see DEEPER STUDY # 1—Acts 10:38.

3 (26:8-9) **Commitment—Sacrifice**: the anointing was a sacrificial gift, a commitment beyond common sense.

1. The anointing was sacrificial. It was worth 300 denarii. A denarius was a small silver coin worth a laborer's daily wage (Mt.20:2); so the perfume was costly, valued at approximately a year's wage (based on a six-day working week).

There is another fact to note about the sacrificial gift. Perfume was a precious item to Eastern women. Mary was taking a most precious possession and giving it to her Lord.

2. The anointing was a commitment beyond common sense. Imagine the scene: a bottle of perfume worth a whole year's wage being broken and poured upon the head of Christ. Common sense would say to the genuine Christian, "Sell it. Use the money for the poor, the hungry, and the homeless." This is just what the disciples did; in fact, they were indignant and vexed about it. They questioned the act; they considered it a waste. After all, if she wished to anoint Christ, she could have used a less expensive perfume. But the disciples failed to see two points.

a. Mary was driven to express her faith in her Lord and her love for Him *personally*. The most meaningful way she could do this was to anoint Him as her Lord with the most expensive perfume she possessed.
b. The most significant person in Mary's life was the Lord. He was the Messiah, the Savior and Lord of her life and family. She wished to show Him that He was deserving of all she was and had.

The point is this: the disciples questioned what Mary did, just as most people would. In the eyes of the world, they would be right. A cheaper perfume could have been used, and not just a few, but a multitude of poor could have been helped with so much money. But what they and the world fail to see is that true love has to be expressed in a personal way. Love is never known unless it is experienced and shared by the believer.

"Why do you look at the speck of sawdust in your brother's eye and pay no attention to the plank in your own eye? (Mat 7:3; cp. v.1-5)

Who are you to judge someone else's servant? To his own master he stands or falls. And he will stand, for the Lord is able to make him stand. (Rom 14:4)

Therefore let us stop passing judgment on one another. Instead, make up your mind not to put any stumbling block or obstacle in your brother's way. (Rom 14:13)

Therefore judge nothing before the appointed time; wait till the Lord comes. He will bring to light what is hidden in darkness and will expose the motives of men's hearts. At that time each will receive his praise from God. (1 Cor 4:5)

You want something but don't get it. You kill and covet, but you cannot have what you want. You quarrel and fight. You do not have, because you do not ask God. (James 4:2)

Thought 1. True love sacrifices self, gives of itself—all that one is and has. Love is not really shown when we give only what we can afford. It is when we sacrifice, dig deep into our lives and money, giving of ourselves all we are and have, that we really show love. The more we sacrifice, the more we demonstrate our love.

Thought 2. There is a strong message in Mary's act—a strong message on giving much and giving sacrificially. But note: the gift and sacrifice were made out of a heart of genuine love and faith in Christ. This is the most important thing to keep in mind about Mary's gift: her heart and life were wholly focused upon Christ.

Thought 3. Sacrifice is sometimes more important than common sense. Sometimes sacrifice should take precedence over common sense. Sometimes common sense must be stretched into sacrifice. Sacrifice is what brings about enlarged horizons, growth, development, advancement, more and more of whatever we are doing. In fact, the more we sacrifice under God's care, the more growth, development, and advancement we see. Name the field, name the area, name the work—the principle holds truth. The more we (or society) sacrifice under God's care, the more advancement we witness. There is a place for common sense, but there is a greater place for sacrifice.

However, there is one area that we often shrink from and ignore and do not allow the principle to take effect: the area of giving money or of tithing. We do not want our easy living and wealth to be touched. Because of evil hearts, men have allowed money and the power to purchase to become the object and judge of life. Too often a man's image, esteem, power, influence, and rights are determined by how much he has.

4 (26:10-11) **Love—Works—Service**: the anointing was a grasping of opportunity. The disciples censored Mary and condemned her act, but Christ defended her. He gave two reasons why Mary's act was justified.

1. Mary's anointing was a *beautiful thing*, a work poured out upon Him *personally*; that is, it was a *personal* gift. Yes, it was an extravagant gift, but it was a gift to Christ Himself. It was not a gift to an idea or program of His. This fact, that it was done to Him personally, makes the difference.

2. Mary's opportunity to show her love for Christ would not always be present. Christ was soon to be gone and ascended to the Father. Bodily, He would not be present for Mary to show her love. The poor would always be present to whom Mary could minister, but not Jesus. He would be gone. If she were ever going to demonstrate her love and faith, she had to do it now. The opportunity had to be grasped now; it would soon be gone.

"My food," said Jesus, "is to do the will of him who sent me and to finish his work. (John 4:34)

As long as it is day, we must do the work of him who sent me. Night is coming, when no one can work. (John 9:4)

Making the most of every opportunity, because the days are evil. (Eph 5:16)

Brothers, I do not consider myself yet to have taken hold of it. But one thing I do: Forgetting what is behind and straining toward what is ahead, I press on toward the goal to win the prize for which God has called me heavenward in Christ Jesus. (Phil 3:13-14)

Be wise in the way you act toward outsiders; make the most of every opportunity. (Col 4:5)

Thought 1. Note four lessons.

1) Opportunities do pass. In fact, they pass ever so rapidly. If we do not act and act immediately, we miss the chance forever. The privilege of witnessing, helping, growing, advancing, improving, and discovering—on and on the opportunities arise. If we fail to act, the opportunities pass on never to return, and we lose the chance to ever reach out and help and improve.
2) The great tragedy of most lives can be summed up in two simple words: missed opportunity.
3) What others think, even their condemnation and censorship, should never keep us from showing our love and faith in the Lord Jesus. Our witness should always be strong for Christ, just as strong as Mary's was: strong in grace and kindness, in courage and unashamedness.
4) Our works and gifts should first of all be given to Christ personally. Our thoughts should be upon Him, concentrating and not wandering as we serve and give. They should be performed and given as though they were being laid at His feet.

5 (26:12) **Jesus Christ, Death**: the anointing pointed toward the burial of Jesus, that is, His death. This is exactly what Christ said: "She did it to prepare me for burial."

Some commentators think that Mary knew what she was doing, that she understood what Christ had been predicting, that He was to die soon. They feel Mary grasped the fact when others did not, but this is unlikely. The atmosphere surrounding the Lord's followers was that the kingdom was about to be set up. However, whether she knew what she was doing or not, Christ took her act and *applied it* to His death. He said that her love and faith and the anointing of His body pointed toward His death. In simple terms, Mary's love and faith, gift and anointing was *a witness of anticipation*. She was witnessing to the Lord's death by looking ahead to it.

Today, the believer's love and faith, gift and anointing *are a witness of fact*. The believer is to witness to the Lord's death by looking back to it. It is a fact: He did die for the sins of the world (cp. 1 Jn.2:1-2).

> **But God demonstrates his own love for us in this: While we were still sinners, Christ died for us. (Rom 5:8)**
>
> **For what I received I passed on to you as of first importance : that Christ died for our sins according to the Scriptures, that he was buried, that he was raised on the third day according to the Scriptures, (1 Cor 15:3-4)**
>
> **He himself bore our sins in his body on the tree, so that we might die to sins and live for righteousness; by his wounds you have been healed. (1 Pet 2:24)**
>
> **For Christ died for sins once for all, the righteous for the unrighteous, to bring you to God. He was put to death in the body but made alive by the Spirit, (1 Pet 3:18)**
>
> **My dear children, I write this to you so that you will not sin. But if anybody does sin, we have one who speaks to the Father in our defense—Jesus Christ, the Righteous One. He is the atoning sacrifice for our sins, and not only for ours but also for the sins of the whole world. (1 John 2:1-2)**

Thought 1. Every act of love and faith for Christ is a witness to Christ's death, and the more we sacrifice in giving money and in working, the stronger our witness is to His death. The depth and strength of our belief in His death can be measured by the depth and strength of our sacrifice. The death of Christ would be seen much clearer if we demonstrated stronger love and faith in Him, or to put it another way, if we sacrificed more for Him.

Thought 2. Mary witnessed and pointed to the Lord's death by honoring and anointing His body publicly. We witness and point to the Lord's death by honoring and anointing (proclaiming) the fact of His death.

6 (26:13) **Devotion**: the anointing was an eternal memorial. Christ honored Mary because she had so greatly honored Him.

Several things about Mary stand as an ideal for all: her deep love and faith in Christ, her sacrificial gift, her courage in proclaiming her strong love and faith by anointing Jesus before a room full of men. Such devotion and love could not be allowed to fade from history. Christ memorialized it. He will memorialize the faith and love of any believer who so sacrifices for Him—throughout all of eternity.

> **I tell you the truth, wherever this gospel is preached throughout the world, what she has done will also be told, in memory of her." (Mat 26:13)**
>
> **I have been reminded of your sincere faith, which first lived in your grandmother Lois and in your mother Eunice and, I am persuaded, now lives in you also. (2 Tim 1:5)**
>
> **Surely he will never be shaken; a righteous man will be remembered forever. (Psa 112:6)**
>
> **The memory of the righteous will be a blessing, but the name of the wicked will rot. (Prov 10:7)**

Thought 1. Mary proclaimed the gospel, the death of Christ from a heart of love and faith. This is what Christ wants: hearts that love and believe Him and will proclaim His death. Thus, He has seen to it that Mary's act lives on eternally.

	C. The Messiah Betrayed by Judas: The Picture of a Ruined Life, 26:14-16 (Mk.14:10-11;Lk.22:3-6)
1 Picture 1: A great call rejected	14 Then one of the Twelve—the one called Judas Iscariot—went to the chief priests
2 Picture 2: The gnawing sin of greed & the love of money	15 And asked, "What are you willing to give me if I hand him over to you?" So they counted out for him thirty silver coins.
3 Picture 3: Deceit and intrigue	16 From then on Judas watched for an opportunity to hand him over.

DIVISION XVI

THE MESSIAH'S ARREST, TRIAL, AND CRUCIFIXION, 26:1-27:66

C. The Messiah Betrayed by Judas: The Picture of a Ruined Life, 26:14-16

(26:14-16) **Introduction**: Judas stands as a great warning to every man including the strongest believer. Judas was one of the original twelve apostles chosen by Christ. He was a man with so much potential that he was chosen to serve with God's very own Son during His earthly journey, but he failed and came ever so short. Just why he failed needs to be closely studied and heeded by all.

1. Picture 1: a great call rejected (v.14).
2. Picture 2: the gnawing sin of greed and the love of money (v.15).
3. Picture 3: deceit and intrigue (v.16).

1 (26:14) **Judas**: the first picture is that of Judas' great call. Judas' great tragedy was his failure as one of the twelve apostles. Just think about the fact. Judas had been personally chosen by Christ. He had some great potential, some unique qualities that attracted the Lord. Therefore, the Lord gave Judas the most honored opportunity in all the world to develop his abilities—the privilege of walking with Him personally.

⇒ Judas knew Christ face to face.
⇒ Judas walked with Christ day after day.
⇒ Judas heard most, if not all, that Christ taught.
⇒ Judas saw most, if not all, that Christ did.
⇒ Judas was trained to be an apostle by Christ Himself.
⇒ Judas served as an apostle, even on witnessing tours, under Christ's personal command (Mk.6:7f).
⇒ Judas was warned of sin's consequences by Christ Himself.

Nevertheless, despite all the opportunities, Judas' life was a terrible tragedy. He was so gifted and had so much opportunity, yet he lost it all. Why? Simply because he turned his back on the Lord Jesus Christ. He went to "the chief priests" of this earth and put his fate into their hands instead of placing his life into the hands of Christ. He had allowed his craving for more and more to blind him to the truth about Christ—that He was truly the Son of God who demanded loyalty, even when man could not understand the events and happenings that surrounded Him (see note—Mt.26:15. This note will explain what is behind this statement.) Judas simply did not believe that Christ was truly God's Son. Therefore, he did not give his heart and life to Christ—not really. He was a follower of Christ; he was even one of the first twelve apostles, but he was not a genuine believer who entrusted his life to Christ.

> **Not so with you. Instead, whoever wants to become great among you must be your servant, and whoever wants to be first must be your slave— just as the Son of Man did not come to be served, but to serve, and to give his life as a ransom for many." (Mat 20:26-28)**
> **For whoever exalts himself will be humbled, and whoever humbles himself will be exalted. (Mat 23:12)**
> **Then he said to them all: "If anyone would come after me, he must deny himself and take up his cross daily and follow me. (Luke 9:23)**
> **How can you believe if you accept praise from one another, yet make no effort to obtain the praise that comes from the only God ? (John 5:44)**

Thought 1. Judas' great potential and terrible tragedy teaches so much.
1) It is not ability, but availability that counts.
2 Gifts do not assure permanent success; Christ alone assures permanent (eternal) success.
3) Walking among godly people does not assure salvation; allowing Christ to enter one's heart and life is the only assurance of salvation.
4) Christ sees the potential of every man's gifts. What is lacking is man's seeing the necessity of Christ in the use of his gifts.

Thought 2. Think of the people who have heard the truth of Christ time after time, yet they still have not trusted Him as the Son of God. They are traitors, having turned their backs upon God; therefore, they are guilty of high treason against God.

2 (26:15) **Judas Iscariot**: the second picture is Judas' gnawing sin of greed and love of money. Various commentators give different reasons why Judas betrayed Christ, but Scripture clearly says that the reason was greed: "What are you willing to give me if I hand him over to you?"

Judas' gnawing greed was a *growing* sin. This is seen by looking at what is said about him in the Scripture.

1. Judas was chosen by Christ to be an apostle (Mt.10:4); therefore, we know he was sincere in the beginning. There was something within Judas—qualities that attracted Christ, qualities that Christ knew could mean a lot to the Kingdom of God.
2. Judas was a man gifted in financial affairs, apparently even more so than Matthew, the wealthy tax collector, and the businessmen among the apostles such as Peter, James, and John (see Master Subject Index under each name for discussions on their business backgrounds). Among all these, Judas was placed in charge of the Lord's funds and the purchasing of whatever was needed (Jn.12:6; 13:29; cp. Lk.8:2-3 for some who supported Jesus' ministry). His appointment from among so many was bound to be due to unusual spiritual qualities as well as to unusual ability in financial management.
3. Judas, at some unknown point, began to embezzle from the Lord's funds. John says unmistakably that Judas was a thief (Jn.12:6). John relates this fact when he says that Judas was greatly disturbed with Mary, the sister of Martha. Mary used some very expensive perfume to anoint Christ instead of selling it to secure money for the Lord's treasury. John says the reason for Judas' disturbance was because Judas was a thief and could have embezzled some of the money (Jn.12:5-6).
4. Judas refused to repent, and he hardened his heart more and more in his sin. Christ knew of Judas' embezzlement and hinted at it, giving Judas opportunity after opportunity to repent.

> **Yet there are some of you who do not believe." For Jesus had known from the beginning which of them did not believe and who would betray him. Then Jesus replied, "Have I not chosen you, the Twelve? Yet one of you is a devil!" (He meant Judas, the son of Simon Iscariot, who, though one of the Twelve, was later to betray him.) (John 6:64, 70-71)**

Judas was bound to feel the pangs of guilt at such times, yet he continued to deceive himself that Christ did not really know and had no real proof. Judas kept right on taking what he felt he could safely embezzle, hardening his heart more and more.

5. Judas apparently followed Christ out of a heart of greed and worldly ambition, and not out of a heart of love and faith in Him as the Son of God. This seems to be indicated by two facts.
   a. He felt that wealth, power, and position would be his when Christ set up his kingdom. The other apostles thought the same, but there was a vast difference. They mistook the Messiah's method of saving the world, not His person; whereas Judas mistook both the Lord's method and person. He did not believe and trust the Lord to be the Son of God. The others did.
   b. He apparently was disillusioned with Christ after the triumphal entry. Christ did not immediately set up His kingdom, and as the days passed, the fact that He was not going to set up His kingdom became more and more apparent. The authorities were mobilizing against Christ to kill Him, and it seemed as though they were going to be successful. Jesus had even been teaching that they were to be successful. He was to be killed by their hands (cp. Mt.26:1-2).

      Judas became convinced that he was mistaken about Christ. Christ was not the real Messiah. He was just another mistaken self-proclaimed messiah. He was doomed, and there was no way out. Judas experienced his dreams of wealth, power, and position with Christ being shattered. Thus what he was trying to do was to get what he could out of the situation. He wanted to be in good standing with what he perceived to be the winning side.
6. Judas filled his heart with the lust for more and more instead of filling it with Christ. He went too long without repenting and letting Christ in his life, and the devil was able to fill his being. The devil blinded and took control of his thoughts (Lk.22:3). Hence Judas was able to justify his betrayal in his own mind. He was, after all, helping the leading religionists of his day as well as himself. Thus he betrayed Jesus of Nazareth, who apparently in Judas' mind was just another mistaken self-proclaimed messiah.

In looking at the bargain to which Judas agreed in betraying Christ, thirty pieces of silver seems to be a small price for betraying someone of the Lord's stature. It amounted to only about four to five months' wages. However, two things need to be kept in mind.

1. Judas probably expected to get much more. But he did not dictate the terms, the chief priests did. They were going to arrest Christ in just a few days anyway, just as soon as the pilgrims left the city (Mt.26:5). All Judas did was move their schedule up a few days.
2. Judas felt Christ was doomed, without any hope of escape. Again, he had become convinced that Christ was not the true Messiah, but just another mistaken self-proclaimed messiah. There is a possibility that Judas betrayed Christ because he was angry for having been deceived as well as for having been disillusioned. He was willing to get what he could, no matter how small the amount.

> **Then he said to them, "Watch out! Be on your guard against all kinds of greed; a man's life does not consist in the abundance of his possessions." (Luke 12:15)**
>
> **For the love of money is a root of all kinds of evil. Some people, eager for money, have wandered from the faith and pierced themselves with many griefs. (1 Tim 6:10)**
>
> **Your gold and silver are corroded. Their corrosion will testify against you and eat your flesh like fire. You have hoarded wealth in the last days. (James 5:3)**
>
> **A greedy man brings trouble to his family, but he who hates bribes will live. (Prov 15:27)**
>
> **They are dogs with mighty appetites; they never have enough. They are shepherds who lack understanding; they all turn to their own way, each seeks his own gain. (Isa 56:11)**

Thought 1. Greed is a growing sin. It has to be fed to grow. Desire for things is normal and natural. It is when we feed the desire time and again, indulging and hoarding more and more, that our desire becomes sin and grows and grows (see notes—Jas.4:1-6. These notes will stir additional thoughts for application in dealing with desires and lust.)

Thought 2. Greed is very dangerous. It is one of the most dangerous sins.
- ⇒ Greed enslaves quickly.
- ⇒ Greed can lead to all other sins.
- ⇒ Greed can make a person sell his country, body, or friends—anything and anyone—all for greed.

Thought 3. Covetousness, the desire for more and more, will eat at us just like a cancer. Judas had what he needed: food, clothing, housing, purpose, meaning, and significance. He did not go without. What was he after? The sin of lust—lusting for more and more—ate away at him, causing him to put his hand into the till.

Thought 4. It is not money that is sinful. It is the love of money (1 Tim.6:10). Money is a *thing*; it is inanimate, lifeless. It has no feelings, no desires, no will to act. Man is the culprit. Man is the one who lusts for more and more; thus man is the one who sins, not a piece of paper or metal.

Thought 5. Many follow Christ not out of a deep conviction and belief but out of the desire to get what they can out of Him. They are religious in order to *fit in* with a so-called Christian society. They want to promote themselves or their business within the community. To profess Christ and to belong to a church is the thing to do. But their profession in Christ does not hamper their human lusts at all. They live just as all other men live, paying little if any attention to true morality and just relationships, pure behavior and honest dealing, clean living and fair treatment.

Thought 6. Judas allowed his strength to become his weakness. This is often true with us.
- ⇒ Gifts of administration can lead to being overbearing.
- ⇒ Gifts of loveliness can lead to being sensual.
- ⇒ Gifts of humility can lead to no service.
- ⇒ Gifts of leadership can lead to being self-seeking.
- ⇒ Gifts of speaking can lead to being super-spiritual.

3 (26:16) **Judas**: the third picture is that of Judas' carrying out a deceitful intrigue against Christ. Note the words "He watched for an opportunity to hand him over." The picture is that of being on the prowl, searching and seeking, looking here and there for the right moment. Judas' heart was set, full of intrigue, plotting evil and planning its strategy. He did not believe Jesus was the Son of God, but he did not stop at unbelief. He willed to do evil against Christ, to hurt Him and to destroy Him, and he sought opportunity to do so. Just how deceitful Judas was can be seen by noticing that immediately after bargaining with the authorities, he sat down to eat with Jesus. He sat at the very table where the Lord's Supper was being instituted.

Thought 1. Judas not only rejected but also sought to destroy Jesus. Many reject Christ, but they do not all seek to harm and destroy Him. Some do, but not all.
- ⇒ Some curse Him, consciously and unconsciously dishonoring His name.
- ⇒ Some talk and teach against His divine nature, that He is the Son of God.
- ⇒ Some talk and teach against the written revelation of Christ Himself and the truth, that is, the Word.
- ⇒ Some talk and teach against His active presence in the life of the genuine believer.

> **"Watch out for false prophets. They come to you in sheep's clothing, but inwardly they are ferocious wolves. (Mat 7:15)**
>
> **The Spirit clearly says that in later times some will abandon the faith and follow deceiving spirits and things taught by demons. Such teachings come through hypocritical liars, whose consciences have been seared as with a hot iron. (1 Tim 4:1-2)**
>
> **But mark this: There will be terrible times in the last days. People will be lovers of themselves, lovers of money, boastful, proud, abusive, disobedient to their parents, ungrateful, unholy, without love, unforgiving, slanderous, without self-control, brutal, not lovers of the good, treacherous, rash, conceited, lovers of pleasure rather than lovers of God— having a form of godliness but denying its power. Have nothing to do with them. (2 Tim 3:1-5)**

Thought 2. Note something: even after Judas' bargain to betray Christ, Christ gave him opportunity to repent.

D. The Messiah's Last Supper: The Lord's Supper Instituted, 26:17-30
(Mk.14:12-26;Lk.22: 7-23; cp. Jn.13:1-30)

1 The Lord's supper was based upon the Passover
- a. Christ tied the Lord's supper to the Feast of Unleavened Bread[DS1]
- b. Christ tied the Lord's supper to His death: His "appointed time was near"
- c. Christ tied the Lord's supper to religious obedience: "I am going to celebrate the passover"

2 The Lord's supper was used as an appeal to a sinner
- a. He revealed the treachery
  - 1) The sinner was a disciple
  - 2) The revelation caused a stir
  - 3) The sinner committed a monstrous deception
- b. He warned the sinner of terrible judgment
- c. He identified the sinner

3 The Lords' supper was given as a permanent ordinance
- a. Christ took the bread, gave thanks, broke it & gave it: His body[DS2]
- b. Christ took the cup, gave thanks and gave it: His blood[DS3]
- c. Christ instituted a new covenant: Forgiveness[DS4]
- d. Christ promised to celebrate the supper with His followers in the future
- e. Christ and His disciples sang a hymn & departed

17 On the first day of the Feast of Unleavened Bread, the disciples came to Jesus and asked, "Where do you want us to make preparations for you to eat the Passover?"
18 He replied, "Go into the city to a certain man and tell him, 'The Teacher says: My appointed time is near. I am going to celebrate the Passover with my disciples at your house.'"
19 So the disciples did as Jesus had directed them and prepared the Passover.
20 When evening came, Jesus was reclining at the table with the Twelve.
21 And while they were eating, he said, "I tell you the truth, one of you will betray me."
22 They were very sad and began to say to him one after the other, "Surely not I, Lord?"
23 Jesus replied, "The one who has dipped his hand into the bowl with me will betray me.
24 The Son of Man will go just as it is written about him. But woe to that man who betrays the Son of Man! It would be better for him if he had not been born."
25 Then Judas, the one who would betray him, said, "Surely not I, Rabbi?" Jesus answered, "Yes, it is you."
26 While they were eating, Jesus took bread, gave thanks and broke it, and gave it to his disciples, saying, "Take and eat; this is my body."
27 Then he took the cup, gave thanks and offered it to them, saying, "Drink from it, all of you.
28 This is my blood of the covenant, which is poured out for many for the forgiveness of sins.
29 I tell you, I will not drink of this fruit of the vine from now on until that day when I drink it anew with you in my Father's kingdom."
30 When they had sung a hymn, they went out to the Mount of Olives.

DIVISION XVI

THE MESSIAH'S ARREST, TRIAL, AND CRUCIFIXION, 26:1-27:66

D. The Messiah's Last Supper: The Lord's Supper Instituted, 26:17-30

(26:17-30) **Introduction—The Lord's Supper—The Passover**: this is the passage where Christ instituted the Lord's Supper, one of the ordinances which He charged His followers to practice on a regular basis (Mt.26:2). He instituted the Supper in verses 26-30. Note that the preparations made in verses 17-25 are the preparations for the Passover. The disciples knew nothing about the Lord's intentions to institute a new ordinance in His name. They thought Christ was preparing to celebrate the Jewish Passover. This is significant, for it shows that Christ tied both His death and the Lord's Supper to the Passover. By so doing, Christ was saying two things.

1. Jewish tradition held that the Messiah was going to redeem Israel during the Passover. In fact, they believed He would redeem them on the very day that God delivered Israel out of Egyptian bondage. By tying His supper to the Passover, Christ was proclaiming Himself to be the Messiah whom Israel anticipated.

2. The sacrificial lamb used in the Passover was a picture of Christ, the Lamb of God, sacrificing Himself for man. By instituting the Lord's Supper on this day, Christ was not only tying His death to the Passover, He was proclaiming two new things:
   a. He was proclaiming Himself to be the Lamb of God who was to be slain for the sins of men.
   b. He was proclaiming the Lord's Supper to be the new celebration which was to be observed by His followers. The Lord's Supper was to replace the Passover, a man's celebration of God's deliverance from bondage.

1. The Lord's Supper was based upon the Passover (v.17-19).
2. The Lord's Supper was used as an appeal to a sinner (v.20-25).
3. The Lord's Supper was given as a permanent ordinance (v.26-30).

1 (26:17-19) **Lord's Supper—Passover**: the Lord's Supper is based upon and tied to the Passover. 1.The Lord's Supper is tied to the Feast of Unleavened Bread, to the first day of the Feast, the day of preparation and the sacrifice of the lamb (see DEEPER STUDY # 1—Mt.26:17).

a. It was on the first day of the Feast that the disciples came to Christ. Again, they knew nothing about Christ's plans to institute a new celebration. They just assumed He was going to celebrate the Passover as always. But by instituting the Lord's Supper on this day, Christ definitely tied the Supper to the Passover (see DEEPER STUDY # 1—Mt.26:17).

b. It was the disciples who came to Christ. Christ did not have to approach them. They knew that it was His practice to observe the celebration.

c. Christ faced *great difficulty* in observing the celebration. He had no home, no place of His own for the observance. But there was a much greater obstacle confronting Him at this particular celebration: enemies within the city were seeking to kill Him. Note His faithfulness in observing the celebration despite this fact.

2. The Lord's Supper is tied to *Christ's death*. Christ said "My appointed time is near." "My appointed time" or "My appointed hour" is a term which Christ constantly used to refer to His death (see note, pt.2—Jn.2:3-5). He tied His death to the Passover with the words, "My appointed time [death] is near; I will keep the Passover." And, of course, His death is what the Lord's Supper celebrates (v.26-28).

3. The Lord's supper is tied to *religious obedience*. Christ said, "I am going to celebrate the Passover." Jewish tradition held that the Messiah was going to redeem Israel during the Passover. In fact, the Jews believed the Messiah would redeem them on the very day God delivered Israel out of bondage to Egypt. By obeying this religious celebration, the Passover, Christ was doing three significant things.

a. He was proclaiming Himself to be the Messiah whom Israel had always anticipated.

b. He was, again, definitely tying the Lord's Supper to the Passover.

c. He was stressing the importance of *religious obedience*, that is, being obedient in celebrating the Lord's Supper.

Thought 1. Christ kept the Passover. *Religious obedience* is important to God; therefore, we are to be obedient and faithful to religious observances. Note how Christ was faithful in His observance, even in the face of death. What a rebuke to us—we who allow the comfort of our homes, the enjoyment of our recreation, the pleasing of our flesh to keep us away from the Lord's Supper and other religious observances!

Whoever has my commands and obeys them, he is the one who loves me. He who loves me will be loved by my Father, and I too will love him and show myself to him." (John 14:21)

Jesus replied, "If anyone loves me, he will obey my teaching. My Father will love him, and we will come to him and make our home with him. (John 14:23)

If you obey my commands, you will remain in my love, just as I have obeyed my Father's commands and remain in his love. (John 15:10)

You are my friends if you do what I command. (John 15:14)

For whenever you eat this bread and drink this cup, you proclaim the Lord's death until he comes. (1 Cor 11:26)

Although he was a son, he learned obedience from what he suffered (Heb 5:8)

Thought 2. The Lord's "appointed time was near." He had to grasp the opportunity while it was at hand. So must we. But the day is coming when it will be too late to celebrate the Lord's Supper. We must celebrate it while we can.

DEEPER STUDY # 1

(26:17) **Feast of Unleavened Bread**: this feast is another name for the Passover Feast (see Lev.23:5-8; Lk.22:1). However, on the first day of the Passover week, the Feast of Unleavened Bread had special significance. It was the day that all preparations were made to celebrate the Passover. (See DEEPER STUDY # 1—Mt.26:2; cp. Ex.12:1-51, esp. 11-28 for the background of the Passover.) Preparations included securing the lamb and taking it to the temple to be sacrificed. Preparations also included securing the food and drink items necessary for the Passover and arranging the room for the Feast. But there were two preparations for which the Feast of Unleavened Bread received its name.

1. There was the baking of unleavened bread. On the very night of the Passover, God had told Israel to make final preparations for being delivered from Egyptian bondage. But the Israelites did not have time to bake leavened bread. They had to bake bread without leaven because of the time it takes for leavened bread to rise. The Feast of Unleavened Bread was simply one of the Passover ceremonies by which Israel remembered God's glorious deliverance of their forefathers from Egyptian bondage. (See DEEPER STUDY # 1—Mt.26:2.)

2. There was a ceremony by which all leaven within the house had to be removed. It must be remembered that leaven was a symbol of evil to the Jews. Therefore, in removing all leaven, they were picturing the need for putting evil out of their lives and households. There was an actual search made throughout the rooms of the house looking for any crumb of leaven that might have fallen upon the floor or between some furniture. Whatever leaven was found, no matter how small a crumb, it was removed from the house. By removing all leaven from their households, the Jews were saying they wanted to be included among the faithful of their forefathers, the faithful who had cleansed their lives and households for the journey of deliverance from bondage.

2 (26:20-25) **Judas—Lord's Supper**: the Lord's Supper was used as an appeal to a sinner. Christ used the occasion of the Supper to appeal to Judas. He gave Judas a last chance to repent of his sin. Christ took three steps with Judas.

1. Christ revealed the sin and the treachery of Judas. It was a shock, for the Lord said the betrayer was a disciple: "One of you will betray me" (v.21). It was treachery and deception. Judas had tried to hide his sin, and he had done a good job. No one knew about his plot, not even the disciples, his closest associates. But Jesus knew.

The apostles were, of course, stirred: "they were very sad" (v.22). They became so heavily burdened over the news that they began to question their own loyalty. "Surely not I, Lord?" each began to ask.

The sinner committed a monstrous deception (v.23). It was the one who "dipped his hand into the bowl." Imagine the deception: the sinner sat with Christ, partook of the Lord's Last Supper, plotted and was guilty of the most terrible sin.

Even my close friend, whom I trusted, he who shared my bread, has lifted up his heel against me. (Psa 41:9)

2. Christ warned the sinner of terrible judgment (v.24). Jesus knew the destiny of the sinner, the terrible fate that awaited him. It would have been better had the sinner never been born.

3. Christ identified the sinner (v.25). He answered Judas, letting him know that his sin was not hid. Christ knew. Note what Judas called Christ: "Rabbi," teacher. The other disciples had called Him, "Lord" (v.22).

> **I tell you, no! But unless you repent, you too will all perish. I tell you, no! But unless you repent, you too will all perish." (Luke 13:3, 5)**
>
> **Repent, then, and turn to God, so that your sins may be wiped out, that times of refreshing may come from the Lord, (Acts 3:19)**
>
> **Repent of this wickedness and pray to the Lord. Perhaps he will forgive you for having such a thought in your heart. (Acts 8:22)**

Thought 1. The Lord's Supper is an occasion that speaks to sinners. It can be used to point out sin for which Christ died and to warn about the consequences of sin if a person does not repent.

Thought 2. Judas sat at Jesus' Last Supper, and he deceptively partook of it with sin in his life. Too many believers do the same. Their close associates and fellow believers may be deceived, but not God. He knows all about the sin.

Thought 3. Judas deceived the apostles. People can deceive others, even family and friends, and never be discovered, but God knows the heart and the sin.

Thought 4. The disciples examined themselves. They looked at themselves to see if they were the sinner. Believers are exhorted to examine themselves before partaking of the Supper (1 Cor.11:27-28). Examining oneself is necessary. No believer is sinless nor beyond sin. The exhortation is clear: "Do not be arrogant, but be afraid" (Ro.11:20).

Thought 5. Christ revealed that He was to be betrayed in order to strengthen the faith of the disciples (Jn.13:19). He revealed His omniscience, that He was truly God (cp. Jn.14:29).

Thought 6. Note how Judas tried to continue His deception. Even after the Lord had revealed that a sinner sat among them, Judas turned to the Lord and asked, "Surely not I, Rabbi?" How like so many! They continue to deceive and deceive, ever seeking to satisfy the lust of their sin.

Thought 7. Judas illustrated a significant point: the reason for continuous sin. The reason was unbelief in Jesus. Jesus was not *Lord* to Judas. To Judas Jesus was only a man, a misguided and self-proclaimed messiah (see outline and notes—Mt.26:14-16).

3 (26:26-30) **Lord's Supper**: the Lord's Supper was given as a permanent ordinance.

1. It was while "they were eating" the Passover meal that Christ instituted the Lord's Supper. He was replacing the Passover with the Lord's Supper. The Lord's Supper is the new ordinance of God to celebrate His deliverance of man from bondage and slavery (see DEEPER STUDY # 1—Mt.26:2).

2. In God's eternal plan, the sacrificial lamb used in the Passover had always been a picture of Christ, the real Lamb of God who was to be sacrificed for man. By instituting the Lord's Supper during the Passover meal, Christ was not only tying His Supper to the Passover, He was proclaiming Himself to be the Lamb of God who was to be slain for the sins of men (v.27-28; cp. 1 Cor.5:7; Rev.13:8).

3. Christ instituted the Lord's Supper before He died, not after His resurrection. This is very significant. It means that His death was voluntary. He had not yet died; He did not have to die. He could have slipped out of town and escaped, but He chose to willingly lay down His life for the sins of men. Therefore, the Lord's Supper is the great celebration of *the voluntary* sacrifice of God's Son for man. The broken bread and poured wine picture the *willingness* of God's Son to lay down His life for man's sins.

Christ instituted the Lord's Supper by doing five things.

1. Christ took the bread, His body, and He gave thanks, broke it, and gave it to the disciples (v.26).

a. By taking the bread into His hands, Christ was indicating that His death was a voluntary act. His destiny was in His hands.

> **Just as the Father knows me and I know the Father—and I lay down my life for the sheep. (John 10:15)**
>
> **The reason my Father loves me is that I lay down my life—only to take it up again. No one takes it from me, but I lay it down of my own accord. I have authority to lay it down and authority to take it up again. This command I received from my Father." (John 10:17-18)**

b. By giving thanks, Christ was offering praise for deliverance and for a life full of provision, a provision that came from God Himself.

c. By breaking the bread, Christ was saying that His body was to be broken and sacrificed as a victim for man's deliverance (Is.53:5). This act was so significant that the early church sometimes called the Lord's Supper simply "the breaking of bread" (Acts 2:42, 46; 1 Cor.10:16). Under the Old Testament the broken bread pictured the sufferings of the Israelites. Now, under the New Testament, the bread is to picture the broken body of Christ (1 Cor.11:24).

> **But he was pierced for our transgressions, he was crushed for our iniquities; the punishment that brought us peace was upon him, and by his wounds we are healed. (Isa 53:5)**

d. By giving the bread and saying, "Take and eat: this is my body," Christ was saying that He is to be received into a man's life. And that moment of redemption is to be remembered in this ordinance (see note—Mt.26:26).

> **But here is the bread that comes down from heaven, which a man may eat and not die. I am the living bread that came down from heaven. If anyone eats of this bread,**

he will live forever. This bread is my flesh, which I will give for the life of the world." (John 6:50-51)

2. Christ took the cup, gave thanks, and gave it to the disciples (v.27).

a. By taking the cup into His own hands, Christ was again teaching that His death was voluntary (cp. Jn.10:11, 17-18).
b. By giving thanks, Christ was again expressing praise and appreciation for deliverance promised through sacrifice.
c. By giving the cup and saying, "Drink from it, all of you," Christ was again saying that He must become a part of man's very being if man wished deliverance. Note: the word "offered" (edoken) is in the Greek aorist tense which means that Christ gave the cup *once for all*. He died once and only once, and man partakes of His death once and only once.

For we know that our old self was crucified with him so that the body of sin might be done away with, that we should no longer be slaves to sin— (Rom 6:6)

The death he died, he died to sin once for all; but the life he lives, he lives to God. (Rom 6:10)

3. Christ instituted a new covenant: forgiveness (v.28). Note the Lord's exact words.

a. "This is my blood." His blood was to become the sign and symbol of the new covenant. His blood was to take the place of the sacrificial lamb of the Passover.
b. "The covenant." His blood, the sacrifice of His life, established a New Testament, a new covenant between God and man (cp. Heb.9:11-15). Faith in His blood and sacrifice is the way man is to approach God. Before, under the Old Testament or Old Covenant, a man who wanted a right relationship with God approached God through the sacrifice of an animal's blood. The Old Testament believer believed that God accepted him because of the sacrifice of the animal. Now, under the New Testament, the believer believes that God accepts him because of the sacrifice of Christ. This is what Christ said: "This is my blood of the New Covenant, which is poured out for many for the forgiveness of sins" (see DEEPER STUDY # 4—Mt.26:28; cp. Eph.1:7; 1 Jn.2:1-2; Heb.9:22). A man's sins are forgiven and he becomes acceptable to God by believing that Christ's blood was shed for him (1 Jn.1:7. See DEEPER STUDY # 2, Justification—Ro.4:22; 5:1.)

In him we have redemption through his blood, the forgiveness of sins, in accordance with the riches of God's grace (Eph 1:7)

But if we walk in the light, as he is in the light, we have fellowship with one another, and the blood of Jesus, his Son, purifies us from all sin. (1 John 1:7)

My dear children, I write this to you so that you will not sin. But if anybody does sin, we have one who speaks to the Father in our defense—Jesus Christ, the Righteous One. He is the atoning sacrifice for our sins, and not only for ours but also for the sins of the whole world. (1 John 2:1-2)

Whoever eats my flesh and drinks my blood has eternal life, and I will raise him up at the last day. For my flesh is real food and my blood is real drink. Whoever eats my flesh and drinks my blood remains in me, and I in him. Just as the living Father sent me and I live because of the Father, so the one who feeds on me will live because of me. This is the bread that came down from heaven. Your forefathers ate manna and died, but he who feeds on this bread will live forever." (John 6:54-58)

c. Now note the words, "Drink from it, all of you." A man must receive what Christ has done for him. He must drink, partake, absorb, assimilate Christ's blood into his life. That is, a man must believe and trust the death of Christ to forgive his sins. He must allow Christ's death to become the very nourishment, the innermost part and energy and flow of his life (see DEEPER STUDY # 3—Mt.26:27-28).

4. Christ promised to celebrate the Supper with His followers in the future (v.29). This is the glorious promise to all genuine believers: they shall sit down with Christ at the great marriage Feast of the Lamb (see outline and notes—Mt.22:1-14). It is the promise of perfection and of being a part of the new heavens and earth, of sitting with Christ in the Kingdom of God which is to be established in the future (see DEEPER STUDY # 3—Mt.19:23-24). Note that Christ again predicted His death.

The Spirit himself testifies with our spirit that we are God's children. Now if we are children, then we are heirs—heirs of God and co-heirs with Christ, if indeed we share in his sufferings in order that we may also share in his glory. (Rom 8:16-17)

When Christ, who is your life, appears, then you also will appear with him in glory. (Col 3:4)

For our light and momentary troubles are achieving for us an eternal glory that far outweighs them all. (2 Cor 4:17)

To the elders among you, I appeal as a fellow elder, a witness of Christ's sufferings and one who also will share in the glory to be revealed: (1 Pet 5:1)

And you will receive a rich welcome into the eternal kingdom of our Lord and Savior Jesus Christ. (2 Pet 1:11)

5. Christ and His disciples sang a hymn and departed. Christ closed the Lord's Supper with a hymn. In the midst of great sorrow and perplexity, of a heavy and burdening atmosphere, Christ led His people in a hymn. It was probably the Hallel (Ps.115-118).

I have told you this so that my joy may be in you and that your joy may be complete. (John 15:11)

Sorrowful, yet always rejoicing; poor, yet making many rich; having nothing, and yet possessing everything. (2 Cor 6:10)

Rejoice in the Lord always. I will say it again: Rejoice! (Phil 4:4)

Let the word of Christ dwell in you richly as you teach and admonish one an-

other with all wisdom, and as you sing psalms, hymns and spiritual songs with gratitude in your hearts to God. (Col 3:16)

Thought 1. How do we become sons or children of God and receive eternal life? Christ said (1) by receiving Him (Jn.1:12), and (2) by feeding upon Him (Jn.6:53-54, 57-58).

Thought 2. Under the Old Testament (covenant), the blood of Christ was symbolized in the blood of animals. Under the New Testament (covenant), the blood of Christ is symbolized in the wine of the Lord's Supper.

Thought 3. Note the glorious confidence and surety of Christ. In the face of being murdered, He promised that He would sit down with his followers in the coming kingdom. The death of Christ was not the end; it was the beginning of eternal life for the person who really believed in the death of Christ.

DEEPER STUDY # 2

(26:26) **Lord's Supper**: the words "Take and eat: this is my body" are not cannibalism (see outline and notes—Jn.6:52-58). The words simply mean that a man is to receive Christ into his life. A man's deliverance from the bondage of sin and death is by *taking or eating* of Christ's body. That is, the man must receive, partake, consume, absorb, and assimilate Christ into His life. He must allow Christ to become the very nourishment, the innermost part and energy, the very consumption of his being.

DEEPER STUDY # 3

(26:27-28) **Lord's Supper**: the words "Drink from it, all of you" (the blood of Christ) mean to receive the death of Christ in place of one's own death. A man's deliverance from sin and death comes by receiving Christ's death as his own. The man must identify with Christ's death. He must drink, partake, absorb, and assimilate the Lord's death. The death of Christ must become the very nourishment, the innermost part and energy, the very flow of his life. (Cp. 1 Cor.2:2.)

DEEPER STUDY # 4

(26:28) **Forgiveness** (aphesin): to send off, to send away. The wrong is cut out, sent off, and sent away from the wrongdoer. The sin is separated from the sinner.

There are four main ideas in the Biblical concept of forgiveness.

1. There is the idea of why forgiveness is needed. Forgiveness is needed because of wrongdoing and guilt and the penalty arising from both (cp. Ro.3:23; 6:23; 8:1).

2. There is the idea of a *once-for-all* forgiveness, a total forgiveness. A man is *once-for-all* forgiven when he receives Jesus Christ as his Savior. Belief in Jesus Christ is the only condition for being forgiven *once-for-all* (Eph.1:7; Ro.4:5-8).

3. There is the idea of forgiveness that maintains fellowship. Fellowship exists between God as Father and the believer as His child. When the child does wrong, the fellowship is disturbed and broken. The condition for restoring the fellowship is confessing and forsaking the sin (Ps.66:18; Pr.28:13; 1 Jn.1:7).

4. There is the idea of a *releasing from guilt*. This is one of the differences between man's forgiving a man and God's forgiving a man. A man may forgive a person for wronging him, but he can never remove the guilt that his friend feels. And often he cannot remove the resentment he feels within his own heart. Only God can remove the guilt and assure the removal of resentment, and God does both. God forgives and erases the guilt and resentment (Ps.51:2, 7-12; 103:12; 1 Jn.1:9).

	E. The Messiah Foretells the Disciples' Failure: Stumbling & Falling Away in Life, 26:31-35 (Mk.14:27-31; Lk.22:31-34; Jn.13:36-38)	will go ahead of you into Galilee."	resurrection[DS2]
		33 Peter replied, "Even if all fall away on account of you, I never will."	**2 There is the claim of over-confidence** a. Caused by comparing oneself with others
1 There is the prediction: All shall fall away a. Fall away[DS1] because of Christ b. Fall away because Christ is rejected c. The remedy: The Lord's	31 Then Jesus told them, "This very night you will all fall away on account of me, for it is written: "'I will strike the shepherd, and the sheep of the flock will be scattered.'" 32 But after I have risen, I	34 "I tell you the truth," Jesus answered, "this very night, before the rooster crows, you will disown me three times." 35 But Peter declared, "Even if I have to die with you, I will never disown you." And all the other disciples said the same.	b. Caused by being blind to the cross c. Caused by not knowing oneself, one's flesh (sinful nature) d. Caused by contradicting Christ

DIVISION XVI

THE MESSIAH'S ARREST, TRIAL, AND CRUCIFIXION, 26:1-27:66

E. The Messiah Foretells the Disciples' Failure: Stumbling and Falling Away in Life, 26:31-35

(26:31-35) **Introduction**: one of the great convictions of believers is that they must warn the world of sin and its consequences. Yet in the midst of this warning and its fervor, something is often missed: believers, too, must be warned of sin and its consequences. Believers are not above sin; they are not removed from the sinful nature. However, there is something that makes them different: they have been given a spiritual nature. They now live *in the spirit* as well as *in the flesh*. The flesh is still with every believer. Therefore, every believer must be warned: here and there he will stumble and fall. But Christ is ever waiting to receive and forgive him if he will do but one thing: genuinely confess and repent. Such is the warning that Christ gives to His disciples in this most meaningful passage.

1. There is the prediction: all shall fall away (v.31-32).
2. There is the claim of over-confidence (v.33-35).

(26:31-35) **Another Outline**: The Warning about Falling Away (Mt.26:31-35).

1. Some fall because they are offended "in" Christ, v.31.
2. Some fall because Christ is rejected by the crowd (v.31).
3. Some fall because they fail to see and believe the resurrection of Christ, (v.32).
4. Some fall because of over-confidence (v.33).
5. Some fall because they are blind to the cross (v.34).
6. Some fall because they do not know self, that is, the flesh (sinful nature) (v.35).

1 (26:31-32) **Backsliding**: there is the prediction—*all* shall fall away. "You will all" is emphasized; not a single one will stand fast. Every disciple will fall away.

Christ shared two reasons why the disciples would fall away, two reasons that are common to every man.

1. "You will fall away on account of me" (en emoi, *of me*). Men question who Christ is, wondering about Him and sometimes being turned off by Him. The words fall away means to stumble, to fall (see DEEPER STUDY # 1—Mt.26:31). When facing Christ, men stumble over three things. (For a thorough discussion see DEEPER STUDY # 9,10—Mt.21:44; cp. note—Lk.20:17-18.)

   a. Men stumble over the identity of Christ (Jn.6:54-58, 60, 66).
   b. Men stumble over the cross of Christ (1 Cor.1:21-23, esp.23).
   c. Men stumble over the cross God calls them to bear (see note and DEEPER STUDY # 1—Lk.9:23).

Very simply, when men look at Jesus Christ and His cross, many react. They...

- doubt
- deny
- ignore
- reject
- close their hearts
- spiritualize
- consider Him and His cross to be irrational in the modern, scientific world

When Christ was arrested, the apostles questioned and wondered if Christ were really the Messiah. He did not resist arrest, and He did not use His mighty power. He was not leading the people in an uprising against the Romans, nor was He freeing Israel and setting up the nation as the center of God's kingdom. The apostles were disillusioned and perplexed; they simply could not understand. Their hopes were hanging upon a cross of despair. In this passage, Christ was foretelling them of their falling away. He knew that after His resurrection, they would remember His words and be able to return more easily and understand more fully. Remembering that He had foretold them would help them to return and to become stronger (cp. Jn.14:29; 13:19).

2. The disciples would fall away because Christ was rejected. Visibly, He was rejected by the crowd. But behind the scenes, in the invisible world, it was God who smote the Shepherd; that is, God put Christ to death (cp. Zech.13:7). It was in "God's set purpose and foreknowledge" that Christ was to die (Acts 2:23). Christ had to give His life for man if man were to be saved.

> **David said about him: "'I saw the Lord always before me. Because he is at my right hand, I will not be shaken. (Acts 2:25)**
>
> **But God demonstrates his own love for us in this: While we were still sinners, Christ died for us. (Rom 5:8)**
>
> **He himself bore our sins in his body on the tree, so that we might die to sins and**

> **live for righteousness; by his wounds you have been healed. (1 Pet 2:24)**
> **For Christ died for sins once for all, the righteous for the unrighteous, to bring you to God. He was put to death in the body but made alive by the Spirit, (1 Pet 3:18)**

When the crowd rejected Christ, the disciples felt threatened. They feared the crowd and lacked the courage to take a stand with Him. They turned away, fled, and deserted. Peter even denied Him vocally (Mt.26:69-75).

There is a remedy for *falling away*: the resurrection. Note the Lord's words, "I will go ahead of you." Christ was telling the apostles two things:

1. They were to come to Him after His resurrection (see DEEPER STUDY # 2—Mt.26:32). Despite their fall, He would still accept them. In fact, He would be waiting for them.
2. They would be *forgiven* for having denied Him.

> **Repent of this wickedness and pray to the Lord. Perhaps he will forgive you for having such a thought in your heart. (Acts 8:22)**
> **If we confess our sins, he is faithful and just and will forgive us our sins and purify us from all unrighteousness. (1 John 1:9)**
> **He who conceals his sins does not prosper, but whoever confesses and renounces them finds mercy. (Prov 28:13)**

Thought 1. How quickly a *fall* can come. Picture the disciples' sitting in the Upper Room with Christ as He shared with them. It was this very night that they would fall—not the next week, not the next month, but this night—the very night that He and they were sharing so much, so intimately (v.34). (Cp. Jn.14-16 to see just how much Jesus shared and how precious and intimate the occasion was.)

Thought 2. Christ knew His disciples would stumble and fall. He knew they would be extremely discouraged. Knowing this, note what He did.
1) He did not upbraid, scold, reproach, or condemn them.
2) He planned to meet them, forgiving and receiving them—all in the power of His love and resurrection.

Thought 3. Christ knows nothing but love for the believer who stumbles and falls, even if the believer commits the most terrible sin, that of denying Christ with his lips. However, one thing is essential for forgiveness: repentance.

DEEPER STUDY # 1
(26:31) **Fall Away** (skandalizo): to stumble, to cause to stumble, to fall.

DEEPER STUDY # 2
(26:32) **Resurrection—Galilee**: Galilee was not to be the first place where Christ was to appear after His resurrection. He made a number of appearances over several days to different groups of the disciples. Galilee was to be the official meeting place, a meeting place where all the disciples were to be present and receive the renewing of their commission (Mt.28:16-20).

2 (26:33-35) **Self-Confidence—Flesh—Sinful Nature, Weakness of**: there was the claim of over-confidence by Peter. Peter's over-confidence was caused by four things.

1. His over-confidence was caused by comparing himself with others. Peter could not believe what he was hearing. Christ said, "All will fall away," including him. Others may, Peter thought, but not him. There was not a chance, and he wanted Christ to know it. Note that Peter compared himself with others, in fact, with "all others": "Even if all fall away...I never will." Peter saw the weaknesses and the flaws of others. Perhaps they could fail, but not him; he could never fall away from Christ. Others may be weak, but not him. Peter committed the terrible sin of humanity: pride (1 Cor.10:12). Peter thought himself stronger than others, above and beyond them spiritually.
2. Peter's over-confidence was caused by being blind to the cross (v.34). Peter just did not see the cross. It was Christ's hanging upon the cross that was going to cause Peter to deny Christ. Christ had told him all about the cross, but he had refused to believe it (see notes—Mt.17:22; 18:1-2). The fact that human flesh or nature was so sinful, so depraved that God would have to crucify it was just too much to grasp (see outline, notes, and DEEPER STUDY # 1—Lk.9:23; Ro.6:1-10; 6:10-13; Gal.2:19-21; 5:24; 6:14-17. Cp. Ro.6:2; Col.3:3.)
3. Peter's over-confidence was caused by not knowing himself, his own personal weaknesses, the weaknesses of his sinful nature. Peter's self-image was strong. He saw himself above *serious* sin and failure. He asserted with all the confidence in the world that he would die for Christ before denying Him.

   Note several things.
   a. Peter was a strong believer, one of the strongest.
   b. Peter really failed to understand himself and his flesh (sinful nature). The one sin that a believer should not commit is to deny Christ. To die for Christ rather than to deny Him is the one thing a genuine believer would be expected to do.
   c. Peter believed and believed strongly that he, his flesh (sinful nature), was above serious sin (cp. Ro.3:9f; 7:8, 14-18; Gal.5:19f).
   d. Peter failed not once, but three times, and all three times were in the same night when Christ was right off to his side being tried for His life (Lk.22:61).
4. Peter's over-confidence was caused by contradicting Christ instead of listening to Him. Christ was warning the disciples about the deceitfulness and weakness of the human heart. Peter and the rest just refused to accept the fact. They denied personal weaknesses.

Thought 1. The fact that others fail is not reason for confidence in oneself but a reason for guarding oneself even more.

Thought 2. All men come short, stumble, and fall. Falling and stumbling are the way of sinful nature. One falls in a particular area; another falls in another area. The difference between men is that one confesses and repents in his heart and the other does not. In fact, many do not even acknowledge the need to repent.

Thought 3. Over-confidence is a dangerous sin.

Pride goes before destruction, a haughty spirit before a fall. (Prov 16:18)

Let another praise you, and not your own mouth; someone else, and not your own lips. (Prov 27:2)

He who trusts in himself is a fool, but he who walks in wisdom is kept safe. (Prov 28:26)

Woe to those who are wise in their own eyes and clever in their own sight. (Isa 5:21)

"Now then, listen, you wanton creature, lounging in your security and saying to yourself, 'I am, and there is none besides me. I will never be a widow or suffer the loss of children.' Both of these will overtake you in a moment, on a single day: loss of children and widowhood. They will come upon you in full measure, in spite of your many sorceries and all your potent spells. (Isa 47:8-9)

To some who were confident of their own righteousness and looked down on everybody else, Jesus told this parable: (Luke 18:9)

The man who thinks he knows something does not yet know as he ought to know. (1 Cor 8:2)

So, if you think you are standing firm, be careful that you don't fall! (1 Cor 10:12)

If anyone thinks he is something when he is nothing, he deceives himself. (Gal 6:3)

Thought 4. We are not to compare ourselves with others. We are to "bear ye one another's burdens" (Gal.6:2).

Live in harmony with one another. Do not be proud, but be willing to associate with people of low position. Do not be conceited. (Rom 12:16)

Brothers, if someone is caught in a sin, you who are spiritual should restore him gently. But watch yourself, or you also may be tempted. Carry each other's burdens, and in this way you will fulfill the law of Christ. If anyone thinks he is something when he is nothing, he deceives himself. (Gal 6:1-3)

Thought 5. Peter really felt he was above serious sin. How like human nature! How common to us all, how self-righteous!

Thought 6. No believer is above serious sin, and all sin is serious. In particular, the very thought that one is above serious sin *is* serious sin.

F. The Messiah's Agony in Gethsemane: Confronting Death & The Terrifying Trials of Life, 26:36-46
(Mk.14:32-42; Lk.22:39-46; Jn.18:1; cp. Heb.5:7-8; 12:3-4)

1 Christ entered the garden of Gethsemane[DS1]
a. With all the disciples
b. For the purpose of praying
c. With just three disciples

2 He suffered—agonizing grief & pain[DS2,3]
a. Felt pain to the point of death
b. Requested companionship
c. Warned: Watch & pray for yourselves as well

3 He turned to God—crying
a. Prostrated Himself
b. Prayed: "My Father"
c. Asked God to remove the cup[DS4]

4 He stood alone—neglected by His closest friends
a. He found them asleep
b. He warned of temptation
c. He warned of the body & its weakness, v.43,45

5 He continued to pray—agonizing for release
a. He asked His Father to remove the cup a second time
b. He found the disciples asleep a second time
c. He prayed a third time—the same words

6 He received release—great peace & courage
a. The words of great release
b. The words of great courage

36 Then Jesus went with his
disciples to a place called
Gethsemane, and he said to
them, "Sit here while I go
over there and pray."
37 He took Peter and the two
sons of Zebedee along with
him, and he began to be sorrowful and troubled.
38 Then he said to them,
"My soul is overwhelmed
with sorrow to the point of
death. Stay here and keep
watch with me."
39 Going a little farther, he
fell with his face to the
ground and prayed, "My Father, if it is possible, may this
cup be taken from me. Yet
not as I will, but as you will."
40 Then he returned to his
disciples and found them
sleeping. "Could you men not
keep watch with me for one
hour?" he asked Peter.
41 "Watch and pray so that
you will not fall into temptation. The spirit is willing, but
the body is weak."
42 He went away a second
time and prayed, "My Father,
if it is not possible for this
cup to be taken away unless I
drink it, may your will be
done."
43 When he came back, he
again found them sleeping,
because their eyes were
heavy.
44 So he left them and went
away once more and prayed
the third time, saying the
same thing.
45 Then he returned to the
disciples and said to them,
"Are you still sleeping and
resting? Look, the hour is
near, and the Son of Man is
betrayed into the hands of
sinners.
46 Rise, let us go! Here
comes my betrayer!"

DIVISION XVI

THE MESSIAH'S ARREST, TRIAL, AND CRUCIFIXION, 26:1-27:66

F. The Messiah's Agony in Gethsemane: Confronting Death and the Terrifying Trials of Life, 26:36-46

(26:36-46) **Introduction—Death—Jesus Christ, Sacrifice and Death**: death for Jesus Christ was different than death for all other men. In death, Jesus took all the sins of the world upon Himself and stood before God the Judge and…

- accepted the verdict of *guilty* for every man.
- accepted the penalty and punishment of death for every man.

It is in the word *death* that the difference lies. *Death* is not what some persons conceive it to be: some dreamy state of being; or some euphoric existence in another world; or the end (disfunctioning) of the body with only the spirit of one's work or life left behind in the memory of others; or simply annihilation. Death means separation from God (see DEEPER STUDY # 1—Heb.9:27), and it is this that makes Christ's death different from the deaths of other men. He did not experience death for *one man's sins*; He experienced death for *every man's sins*. In confronting death, He experienced unbelievable agony and pain because He was to be separated from His Father; and the one thing Christ did not want to face was having to be cut off from His Father. If there were any other way to save man, He wanted it (His human nature).

This is the terrifying struggle Christ was suffering in the Garden of Gethsemane—a struggle so terrible that it would have killed Him if God had not sent an angel to strengthen Him (Lk.22:43). In His great struggle and persevering prayer, Christ shows us how to confront death and the terrifying trials of life.

1. Christ entered the Garden of Gethsemane (v.36-37).
2. He suffered—agonizing grief and pain (v.37-38).
3. He turned to God—crying (v.39).
4. He stood alone—neglected by His closest friends (v.40-41).
5. He continued to pray—agonizing for release (v.42-44).
6. He received release—great peace and courage (v.45-46).

1 (26:36-37) **Jesus Christ, Prayer Life—Prayer**: Christ entered the Garden of Gethsemane.

1. He entered with all the disciples except Judas who had already begun his terrible betrayal. The disciples were all still with Him. Knowing the dark hour and terrible tragedy He was about to endure, He was doing all He could to keep them close to Himself. He wanted them to remember His great dependence upon God. By having the experience of Gethsemane fresh in their minds, they would be better able to face their disillusionment, blindness, unbelief, and desertion. They would be better able to overcome their weaknesses when He arose and confronted them. Thus He was holding them together as closely as possible as long as He could.

2. Christ entered the garden to pray. His words suggested that they, too, should begin seeking God in prayer: "Sit here while I go over there and pray." Luke actually says that He told them all to pray: "Pray that you will not fall into temptation" (Lk.22:39-40).

3. Christ withdrew some distance farther into the garden, taking Peter, James, and John with Him. Why these three? The reason seemed clear. Christ had a double need: a need to be alone with God and a need for close companionship and prayer from those closest to Him. This becomes clearer in the discussion of v.38.

> **Look to the LORD and his strength; seek his face always. (1 Chr 16:11)**
>
> **"Ask and it will be given to you; seek and you will find; knock and the door will be opened to you. (Mat 7:7)**
>
> **Then Jesus told his disciples a parable to show them that they should always pray and not give up. (Luke 18:1)**
>
> **Is any one of you in trouble? He should pray. Is anyone happy? Let him sing songs of praise. (James 5:13)**

Thought 1. A man needs a garden, a private spot where he can get all alone with God in times of great trial.

Thought 2. Two things are essential when we face a desperate hour of need.
1) Withdrawing, getting all alone in some private spot.
2) Praying and sharing our need with God.

Thought 3. Note something of paramount importance: How does our desperate hour affect our loved ones? Christ was thinking as much of His disciples as He was of His own need. He was holding them together and encouraging them to pray for themselves as well as for Him.

DEEPER STUDY # 1
(26:36) **Gethsemane**: the word "Gethsemane" means *oil press* or *olive press*. Gethsemane was a garden sitting on the Mount of Olives. It was probably a garden of olive trees, beautifully situated on the slopes of the mountain overlooking all the surrounding area including the city of Jerusalem. Private and public gardens on the surrounding mountains were common because of the beauty of the mountains and because of the lack of space within the city. It was to such a garden that Christ withdrew in His desperate hour of need.

2 (26:37-38) **Jesus Christ, Death**: in confronting death, Christ suffered agonizing grief and pain (see DEEPER STUDY # 3—Mt.26:37). Note three things.

1. Christ felt so much sorrow and heaviness, so much inner pain, that it almost killed Him. Note His words: "My soul is overwhelmed with sorrow to the point of death." The pain and agony were so intense that He sweated great drops of blood.

God the Father had to send an angel to strengthen Him (Lk.22:43-44. Cp. the reference to this experience in Heb.12:3-4, esp. 4.) Apparently, all that Christ had been through and was about to go through was opened up to His mind. His whole being was now focusing upon the suffering He had to experience as the sin-bearer for the world. The mental vision literally compressed His physical body, almost to the point of crushing Him. (See DEEPER STUDY # 2—Mt.26:37-38.)

2. Christ was suffering so much agonizing grief and pain that He requested the presence of close friends. He needed them to *pray* for Him and be a *comfort* to Him. This is seen in His words, "Keep watch with me." Christ needed to be alone with God, but He also needed friends close by who were also praying for Him. Just knowing that they were close by praying and feeling for Him would be a strong encouragement.

3. Christ warned: watch and pray for yourselves as well. The greatest trial the disciples were to ever know was at hand, and they did not know it. In just a few hours, they were going to fall away. They desperately needed to pray that they "will not fall into temptation" (v.41); that the depth of sin would not discourage them to the point that they would feel too unworthy to repent.

Thought 1. The greatest lesson to be learned from Gethsemane is probably this: we are to strive against sin at any cost. The Scripture clearly proclaims this lesson:

> **Consider him who endured such opposition from sinful men, so that you will not grow weary and lose heart. In your struggle against sin, you have not yet resisted to the point of shedding your blood. (Heb 12:3-4)**

Christ strove against sin, against the temptation to save the world by some other way than the cross (being separated from God the Father). He strove and strove against the temptation, experiencing so much pressure that His sweat was like "drops of blood" (Lk.22:44). Just imagine striving against sin to such a point! (See note—Mt.27:26-44.)

Thought 2. Something needs to be meditated upon time and again: the great agony that Christ bore for us. Nothing pictures His great agony any more than the Garden of Gethsemane.

Thought 3. Think of the Lord's enormous love for us. He foresaw all that He was to bear for us. All was opened up to His mind, yet He willingly surrendered Himself to bear it all (to get a quick picture of all that He was to bear, glance quickly at note, pt. 1—Mt.26:37-38).

Thought 4. The presence, prayer, and comfort of close friends can be a tremendous source of help when we face desperate needs.

DEEPER STUDY # 2
(26:37-38) **Jesus Christ, Suffering—Death**: words could never express what Christ experienced. Words are just inadequate, totally inadequate. Using all the descriptive words in the world would be as inadequate in describing the sufferings of Christ as using a syringe to drain an ocean.

1. There was the *mental and emotional agony*: the weight, pressure, anguish, sorrow, and excessive strain such as no man has ever experienced. He was the Son of God, Maker of heaven and earth, yet images and thoughts were pressing ever so heavily in upon His spirit, the images and thoughts of...

- the *unbelief* of all men everywhere.
- the *rejection* of His own people, the Jews.
- the *malice* of the world's leaders, both Jew and Gentile, religious and civil.
- the *betrayal* of one of His own, Judas.
- the *desertion* of all His men.

- the *denial* by the leader of His own men, Peter.
- the *injustice and condemnation* of His trial.
- the *ridicule and pain* of being scourged, spit upon, slugged, cursed, mocked, crowned with thorns, and nailed to the cross and killed.

2. There was the *physical experience of death while being the Son of God.* What is it like for the Son of God to die just as all men die? If just the physical aspect of Christ's death is considered, His death is still different from all other men.

a. Christ as the Son of God possessed the very seed, quality, ingredient, and energy of life within His being (see DEEPER STUDY # 1—Jn.17:2-3).

b. Christ as the Son of God possessed no seed, quality, or ingredient of death (Jn.14:6; 1 Tim.6:16; 1 Jn.1:1-2; cp. Jn.1:4); but man does. Man possesses the seed of corruption and death. Man's sinful nature knows nothing and expects nothing but death, but the sinless nature of Christ knows nothing of sin and death. His sinless nature and the agony and pain of death were bound to be as different from man's death as white is different from black.

There is another point to note as well. Man suffers humiliation in death. No matter how much man struggles to live, he wastes and wastes away until he is carried into the grave to become dust of the ground. But not Christ; He was sinless and perfect even in His human nature. His sinless nature knew nothing of death. Imagine the humiliation: the Son of God—the Perfect Man, the Perfect God—having to die upon this earth! No wonder He "began to be sorrowful and troubled!" No wonder He could say, "My soul is overwhelmed with sorrow to the point of death." In some mysterious way, God made Christ to become sin for us (2 Cor.5:21).

3. There was *the spiritual experience of death while being the Son of Man* (see note—Mt.5:17-18; DEEPER STUDY # 3—8:20; note—Ro.8:2-4). There is so much here, yet so little can ever be known.

a. First, what is it like to be without sin? Christ, made in the image of man and being fully man, was sinless. He lived as all men live facing all the trials and temptations that men face, yet He never sinned. He was without sin. He became the Perfect and Ideal Man—all that God wants man to be. He became the Pattern for all men.

For we do not have a high priest who is unable to sympathize with our weaknesses, but we have one who has been tempted in every way, just as we are—yet was without sin. (Heb 4:15; cp. 2 cor.5:21; 1 Pt.2:22; 1 Jn.3:5)

Although he was a son, he learned obedience from what he suffered and, once made perfect, he became the source of eternal salvation for all who obey him (Heb 5:8-9)

b. Second, what is it like to bear all the sins of the world? What is it like to be perfect and sinless and then, all of a sudden, to have all the sins of the world laid upon Oneself? In some mysterious way, God took all the sins of the world and laid the whole *body of sin* upon Christ. In some mysterious way, God made Christ to become sin for us (2 Cor.5:21). Christ, as the Ideal Man, became the Ideal Sin-Bearer. He bore all the sins and all that sin causes—all the...

- darkness
- pollution
- filthiness
- dirt
- weight
- pressure
- anxiety
- turmoil
- worry
- guilt
- savagery
- conflict
- strife
- war
- torture
- enmity
- poison
- corruption
- consumption
- disturbance

We all, like sheep, have gone astray, each of us has turned to his own way; and the LORD has laid on him the iniquity of us all. (Isa 53:6)

You see, at just the right time, when we were still powerless, Christ died for the ungodly. (Rom 5:6)

For what I received I passed on to you as of first importance : that Christ died for our sins according to the Scriptures, (1 Cor 15:3)

God made him who had no sin to be sin for us, so that in him we might become the righteousness of God. (2 Cor 5:21)

So Christ was sacrificed once to take away the sins of many people; and he will appear a second time, not to bear sin, but to bring salvation to those who are waiting for him. (Heb 9:28)

He himself bore our sins in his body on the tree, so that we might die to sins and live for righteousness; by his wounds you have been healed. (1 Pet 2:24)

c. Third, what is it like to bear all the judgment and condemnation of sin for all men? Christ suffered for the sins of the whole world, suffered *separation* from God. The terrifying mystery of this hellish experience is seen in His cry upon the cross, "My God, My God, why have you forsaken me?" (see note and DEEPER STUDY # 1—Mt.27:26-44; note—27:46-49; note and DEEPER STUDY # 1—1 Pt.2:21-25).

But he was pierced for our transgressions, he was crushed for our iniquities; the punishment that brought us peace was upon him, and by his wounds we are healed. (Isa 53:5)

Christ redeemed us from the curse of the law by becoming a curse for us, for it is written: "Cursed is everyone who is hung on a tree." (Gal 3:13)

But we see Jesus, who was made a little lower than the angels, now crowned with glory and honor because he suffered death, so that by the grace of God he might taste death for everyone. (Heb 2:9)

For Christ died for sins once for all, the righteous for the unrighteous, to bring you to God. He was put to death in the body but made alive by the Spirit, (1 Pet 3:18)

DEEPER STUDY # 3

(26:37) **Sorrowful (lupeisthai)—Troubled (ademonein)**: *sorrowful* means to be distressed, grieved, pained. It means to be *consumed* with intense sorrow of heart. *Troubled* means to be troubled, dismayed, disturbed. It means to be *gripped* with intense heaviness of soul. *Troubled* pictures the trouble and dismay that is caused by an *unexpected calamity*. It is consternation, a heaviness that drives a man to be alone, for he is unfit for company. He desperately needs quiet, and he needs a few companions to understand and help him bear the trouble.

3 (26:39) **Jesus Christ, Death**: in confronting death Christ turned to God, crying with strong cries and tears (cp. Heb.5:7). Four things are seen in this verse.

1. Christ got all alone and prostrated Himself before God. Luke says He withdrew "about a stone's throw" from the three apostles (Lk.22:41). Note two significant points: (a) He needed to be alone with God—He was desperate. (b) He fell on His face—the pressure and weight were unbearable.

2. Christ prayed, "My Father [pater mou]." Note that Christ called God "My Father." This is what a small child calls his father day by day. It is the address of a child's love, of dependency and trust. The child knows that His father will hear and turn to him when he calls *Father*. But note also the words, "My Father." Christ was broken, weighed down, fallen, prostrated on the ground. In desperation He cried out "My Father." Just like a child, He cried out to His Father in childlike brokenness and dependency; He knew that His Father would hear and turn to help Him.

3. Christ asked God to remove the cup from Him. (See DEEPER STUDY # 4, Cup—Mt.26:39. Also see DEEPER STUDY # 1—Mt.27:26-44; cp. Mt.20:19.) The human nature and will of Christ are clearly seen here. He was as much man as any man is. Thus He begged God to choose another way other than the cup (cross), if possible. The experience of being separated from God upon the cross was too much to bear.

4. The Divine nature and will of Christ were also clearly seen. Note the Lord's words: "May this cup be taken away." The first act and impulse, the first struggle and movement of His will had come from His flesh: to escape the cup of separation from God. But the second act and impulse, the second struggle and movement of His will came from His Divine nature: to do not as He willed, but as God willed.

Christ's surrender to do God's perfect will was critical.

⇒ It was through His surrender that He was made perfect and stood before God as the Ideal and Perfect Man.

⇒ It was through His surrender to be the Ideal and Perfect Man that His righteousness is still able to stand for every man.

⇒ It was through His surrender to be the Ideal and Perfect Man that He was able to bear the cup of God's wrath against sin *for every man*.

⇒ It was through His surrender to be the Ideal and Perfect Man that His sacrifice and sufferings are still able to stand for every man.

But we see Jesus, who was made a little lower than the angels, now crowned with glory and honor because he suffered death, so that by the grace of God he might taste death for everyone. In bringing many sons to glory, it was fitting that God, for whom and through whom everything exists, should make the author of their salvation perfect through suffering. (Heb 2:9-10)

Although he was a son, he learned obedience from what he suffered and, once made perfect, he became the source of eternal salvation for all who obey him (Heb 5:8-9)

God made him who had no sin to be sin for us, so that in him we might become the righteousness of God. (2 Cor 5:21)

Thought 1. There are three vivid pictures in this point that should speak to our hearts.

1) The picture of Christ's child-like dependency and trust in His Father.
2) The picture of Christ's bearing the awful cup of God's wrath *for us*.
3) The picture of our enormous obligation to Christ: the obligation to be appreciative and to express our appreciation in love, adoration, worship, and service.

Thought 2. Note both the human will and the Divine will of Christ. The first impulse of the human will is to get and possess what one desires, but the second impulse of the Divine will is to do as God wills. Genuine believers are "participates in the divine nature" (2 Pt.1:4). Therefore, they too possess both wills. Note that this is a good way to describe temptation. The first impulse to do as one wishes comes from the human will, but the second impulse to do as God wills comes from the divine will. What we must do is learn to surrender to the divine will, to the godly impulse, just as Christ did.

But we see Jesus, who was made a little lower than the angels, now crowned with glory and honor because he suffered death, so that by the grace of God he might taste death for everyone. In bringing many sons to glory, it was fitting that God, for whom and through whom everything exists, should make the author of their salvation perfect through suffering. (Heb 2:9-10)

Although he was a son, he learned obedience from what he suffered and, once made perfect, he became the source of eternal salvation for all who obey him (Heb 5:8-9)

God made him who had no sin to be sin for us, so that in him we might become the righteousness of God. (2 Cor 5:21)

DEEPER STUDY # 4

(26:39) **Cup**: Jesus Christ was not fearing nor shrinking from death itself. This is clearly seen in Jn.10:17-18. Death for a cause is not such a great price to pay. Many men have so died—fearlessly and willingly, some perhaps more cruelly than Christ Himself. Shrinking from betrayal, beatings, humiliation and death, increased by foreknowledge is not what was happening to Christ. As stated, some men have faced such persecution courageously, even inviting martyrdom for a cause. The Lord knew He was to die from the very beginning, and He had been preparing His disciples for His death (cp. Mt.26:1-2). It was not just human or physical suffering that Christ was shrinking from. Such an explanation is totally inadequate in explaining

Gethsemane. The great cup or trial that Jesus was facing was separation from God (see DEEPER STUDY # 2—Mt.26:37-38). He was to be the sacrificial "Lamb of God" who takes away the sins of the world (Jn.1:29). He was to bear the judgment and wrath of God for the sins of the world (see note—Mt.27:46-49; cp. Is. 53:10). Jesus Himself had already spoken of the *cup* when referring to His sacrificial death (see DEEPER STUDY # 2—Mt.20:22-23; note—Mk.14:35-36; DEEPER STUDY # 2—Jn.18:11).

Scripture speaks of the cup in several ways.

1. The cup is called "the cup of the Lord's wrath."

> **Awake, awake! Rise up, O Jerusalem, you who have drunk from the hand of the LORD the cup of his wrath, you who have drained to its dregs the goblet that makes men stagger. (Isa 51:17)**

2. The cup is associated with suffering and God's wrath.

> **On the wicked he will rain fiery coals and burning sulfur; a scorching wind will be their lot. (Psa 11:6)**
>
> **"Father, if you are willing, take this cup from me; yet not my will, but yours be done." (Luke 22:42)**

3. The cup is also associated with salvation. Because Jesus drank the cup of suffering and wrath for us, we can "lift up the cup of salvation and call on the name of the Lord" (Ps.116:13). He bears the judgment of God for the sins of the world.

> **Yet it was the Lord's will to crush him and cause him to suffer, and though the LORD makes his life a guilt offering, he will see his offspring and prolong his days, and the will of the LORD will prosper in his hand. (Isa 53:10)**

4 (26:40-41) **Jesus Christ, Death**: in confronting death Christ stood alone, neglected by His closest friends.

1. He arose from prayer and went to the three who were supposed to be praying with Him. They were asleep. The companionship, the spirit of prayer and comfort He had sought, was not there. All were asleep. He had been left alone to wrestle with God by Himself.

2. Christ warned of temptation. The disciples had failed to pray for Him, but they must not fail to pray for themselves. Christ said, "Watch and pray." Both were important. *Watchfulness* sees and *praying* prepares. They were to watch in order to see temptation coming, and they were to pray in order to be prepared when temptation struck.

3. Christ warned of the body (flesh) and its weakness. They were sleeping because of the emotional strain and distress of the evening. As Luke says, they slept because of *sorrow*, that is, sadness (Lk.22:45). The evening had been shocking and taxing. They were weary, fatigued, and preoccupied. Concentration in prayer was difficult. They probably fought to stay awake and to pray for their Lord. But the importance of prayer and spiritual dependency upon God in facing trials had not yet been learned. They were making two mistakes common among believers.

a. The disciples were depending upon their own wisdom and strength instead of God's Spirit to fight whatever battles lay ahead.

b. The disciples were taking God's deliverance for granted instead of assuring His deliverance through the testimony of prayer. They believed Christ to be the Messiah; therefore, they believed God was going to deliver them against the Romans no matter what. As carnal, fleshly men are apt to do, the disciples no doubt thought prayer mattered little. They were just presuming upon God, taking His deliverance for granted. What Christ said was, "Watch and pray; for only as you watch and pray can you keep from falling when the trial comes." Watchfulness and prayer bear *testimony* to God.

This point needs to be noted: watchfulness and prayer bear *testimony* to God. When men watch and pray, they demonstrate that dependency and trust in God are well founded. When God answers the prayers of men, He demonstrates that He loves and cares and delivers those who truly look up to Him. Without watching and praying, God allows men to fall in order to teach that dependency and trust in Him are absolutely essential.

4. They were failing to stay awake to pray, to watch and to be watchful in prayer. Their spirits were not alive and alert enough to overcome the flesh. The drowsiness and slumber of the body were stronger than the spirit (see note 5, pt.2—Mt.26:42-44; cp. Eph.6:18).

> **It will be good for those servants whose master finds them watching when he comes. I tell you the truth, he will dress himself to serve, will have them recline at the table and will come and wait on them. (Luke 12:37)**
>
> **You are all sons of the light and sons of the day. We do not belong to the night or to the darkness. So then, let us not be like others, who are asleep, but let us be alert and self-controlled. (1 Th 5:5-6)**
>
> **Be self-controlled and alert. Your enemy the devil prowls around like a roaring lion looking for someone to devour. (1 Pet 5:8)**
>
> **I know, O LORD, that a man's life is not his own; it is not for man to direct his steps. (Jer 10:23)**

Thought 1. No believer is ever alone. Even if his closest friends neglect the spirit of prayer and comfort, God is with him.

Thought 2. Many trials arise immediately and unexpectedly. They jump right up in front of us. Only persistent, sleepless prayer will prepare us for such crises (cp. Eph.6:18).

Thought 3. The flesh (sinful nature) struggles against the Spirit (Gal.5:17).

5 (26:42-44) **Jesus Christ, Death**: in confronting death, Christ continued to pray—agonizing for release.

1. He asked His Father to remove the cup a second time. Matthew is the only writer to give the words of Christ in this second prayer. Mark simply says that He "prayed the same thing" (Mk.14:39). There are two views about what Jesus was saying.

a. Some commentators say that He was accepting the cup and consenting to the fact that He must drink it: "If it is not possible for this cup to be taken away unless I drink it, may your will be done."

When reading the verse this way, the battle does seem to be already won. Christ seems to have already accepted the fact that there just was no other way than to bear the cup. His human nature already seems to be subjected to the Divine nature.

b. Other commentators understand the verse to say what Mark seems to be saying: "Once more He went away; and prayed the same thing" (Mk.14:39). Christ was continuing to pray and to agonize for release from the cup. He, of course, was willing to bear it, but His soul was crying out with "strong tears" for another way. Two facts always need to be remembered.

First, Christ was not shrinking from death; He was shrinking from drinking the cup of separation from God.

Second, the pressure of bearing all the suffering of the world as the Son of Man was unbearable. He felt as though He would die, and Scripture seems to indicate this by mentioning that an angel had to be sent to strengthen Him against the pressure.

2. Christ found the disciples asleep again. Note "their eyes were heavy." This indicates they fought against drowsiness but lost the fight. They could not shake off their...

- physical drowsiness.
- spiritual blindness (not accepting Christ's former prophecies of death).
- carnal security (taking God for granted).

3. Christ prayed a third time, praying the same words (v.44). The pressure was unbearable. He must have release. Note: this was the third time Christ prayed, and note the statement "the same thing" (ton auton logon). This seems to be saying that He was struggling in the *same agonizing spirit*, struggling *to be released* from the life-threatening pressure. *Three times* He came before God pouring out His soul, with "strong tears," begging for *release*. In so doing, He has demonstrated forever the necessity of persevering in prayer in order to secure release from agonizing pressure. God answers persevering prayer.

"Ask and it will be given to you; seek and you will find; knock and the door will be opened to you. (Mat 7:7)

Devote yourselves to prayer, being watchful and thankful. (Col 4:2)

Submit yourselves, then, to God. Resist the devil, and he will flee from you. Come near to God and he will come near to you. Wash your hands, you sinners, and purify your hearts, you double-minded. (James 4:7-8)

Thought 1. Persevering prayer is the great lesson of Gethsemane, and our Lord Himself gives us the greatest example of persevering prayer. When facing the pressuring and terrifying trials of life, Christ teaches us by example to seek release by coming before God in prayer. And He teaches us to stay before God—asking and asking, praying and praying—continuing and persevering in prayer until God answers. (See outlines and notes—Mt.7:7-11. Cp. Eph.6:18; Lk.18:1-8.)

Thought 2. There are three enemies that constantly fight against persevering prayer, that must be struggled and struggled against (see note, pt.2—Mt.26:42-44).

1) Physical drowsiness.
2) Spiritual blindness: not believing the Lord's words, wanting to understand and interpret Him as we wish instead of letting Him speak for Himself.
3) Carnal security: presuming upon and taking God for granted.

6 (26:45-46) **Jesus Christ, Death**: in confronting death, Christ received great release, great peace and courage.

1. There were His words, the evidence of great release: "Are you still sleeping and resting?" Christ's agony, His desperate need for friends to "watch" with Him was now gone. God had given Him great relief of soul. The very tone of His words to His disciples revealed a calmness of spirit, a peace of mind, a relief of the physical and emotional strain that was about to kill Him. God had met His need in a most wonderful way.

When I called, you answered me; you made me bold and stouthearted. (Psa 138:3)

An angel from heaven appeared to him and strengthened him. (Luke 22:43)

During the days of Jesus' life on earth, he offered up prayers and petitions with loud cries and tears to the one who could save him from death, and he was heard because of his reverent submission. (Heb 5:7; cp. 5:7-9)

2. There were His words, the evidence of great courage: "Look, the hour is near, and the Son of Man is betrayed into the hands of sinners."

Note two things:

a. There was no shrinking now, no agony, no desperation. Christ was relieved and strengthened, ready to face the sufferings necessary to secure the salvation of man.

b. Christ said He was being "betrayed into the hands of sinners." All those taking part in His death were *sinners*. His death was the most heinous crime of history. He, the Son of Man, the Ideal and Perfect Man, was killed by men. But there is more here: He died for the sins of the world. It was every man's sin that caused Him to be crucified. Every sin is an act of rebellion, of simply saying "No!" to God (Ro.3:23). Therefore, every man is guilty of putting Christ to death. There is a sense in which every sin and every act of rebellion crucifies "the Son of God all over again and subjecting him to public disgrace" (Heb.6:6).

Thought 1. Note a critical point: God did not give Christ what He asked; that is, God did not remove the cup. Christ had to drink the cup, but God did answer His prayer. God relieved the agony and strengthened Him to bear the cup. God kept Him from failing. The lesson is clear: God sometimes answers our prayers with "No." But He strengthens us and gives us something much better.

I desire to do your will, O my God; your law is within my heart." (Psa 40:8)

By myself I can do nothing; I judge only as I hear, and my judgment is just, for I seek not to please myself but him who

sent me. (John 5:30)

Who gave himself for our sins to rescue us from the present evil age, according to the will of our God and Father, (Gal 1:4)

And live a life of love, just as Christ loved us and gave himself up for us as a fragrant offering and sacrifice to God. (Eph 5:2)

Then I said, 'Here I am—it is written about me in the scroll— I have come to do your will, O God.'" First he said, "Sacrifices and offerings, burnt offerings and sin offerings you did not desire, nor were you pleased with them" (although the law required them to be made). Then he said, "Here I am, I have come to do your will." He sets aside the first to establish the second. And by that will, we have been made holy through the sacrifice of the body of Jesus Christ once for all. But when this priest had offered for all time one sacrifice for sins, he sat down at the right hand of God. (Heb 10:7-10, 12)

Outline	Section / Scripture	Scripture (cont.)	Outline (cont.)
	G. The Messiah Betrayed, Arrested & Deserted: Four Pictures of Commitment, 26:47-56 (Mk.14:43-52; Lk.22:47-53; Jn.18:3-11)	sword, drew it out and struck the servant of the high priest, cutting off his ear.	**militancy** a. He misunderstood Jesus' kingdom & "warred in the flesh"
		52 "Put your sword back in its place," Jesus said to him, "for all who draw the sword will die by the sword.	b. Jesus rebuked carnal commitment: Rebuked "warring in the flesh"
1 Judas betrayed Jesus a. Was one of the apostles b. Headed a large crowd c. Had them armed d. Was sent by the religionists	47 While he was still speaking, Judas, one of the Twelve, arrived. With him was a large crowd armed with swords and clubs, sent from the chief priests and the elders of the people.	53 Do you think I cannot call on my Father, and he will at once put at my disposal more than twelve legions of angels?	**4 Picture 3: A purposeful commitment—Jesus' willingness to die for man** a. He could save Himself
		54 But how then would the Scriptures be fulfilled that say it must happen in this way?"	b. He purposed to fulfill Scripture & die (cp.v.56)
2 Picture 1: A deceptive commitment—Judas' betrayal a. The deceiver laid his plans	48 Now the betrayer had arranged a signal with them: "The one I kiss is the man; arrest him."	55 At that time Jesus said to the crowd, "Am I leading a rebellion, that you have come out with swords and clubs to capture me? Every day I sat in the temple courts teaching, and you did not arrest me.	**5 Picture 4: Two tragic commitments** a. A commitment that opposes Jesus: The world's treatment
b. The deceiver carried out his plan	49 Going at once to Jesus, Judas said, "Greetings, Rabbi!" and kissed him.		
c. The deceiver was given a clear-cut charge: Told to do what he came for ?	50 Jesus replied, "Friend, do what you came for." Then the men stepped forward, seized Jesus and arrested him.	56 But this has all taken place that the writings of the prophets might be fulfilled." Then all the disciples deserted him and fled.	b. A commitment that forsakes Jesus: The disciples' fleeing
3 Picture 2: A carnal commitment—Peter's carnal	51 With that, one of Jesus' companions reached for his		

DIVISION XVI

THE MESSIAH'S ARREST, TRIAL, AND CRUCIFIXION, 26:1-27:66

G. The Messiah Betrayed, Arrested, and Deserted: Four Pictures of Commitment, 26:47-56

(26:47-56) **Introduction**: humanly speaking, this is a tragic scene. Jesus was betrayed, arrested, and deserted within a few minutes. Just imagine facing all three events within so short a time: being betrayed by one of His own disciples; being falsely arrested by a mob determined to kill Him; and being deserted by all His closest friends, the apostles themselves. Jesus stood alone. He did not *have* to; not a single hand or abusive word or indignity *had* to be borne. But He chose to stand there. He willingly suffered all the abuse and indignity that He might save the world.

Much can be learned from what happens in this event. There are four separate events or pictures seen.

1. Judas betrayed Jesus (v.47).
2. Picture 1: a deceptive commitment—Judas' betrayal (v.48-50).
3. Picture 2: a carnal commitment—Peter's carnal militancy (v.51-52).
4. Picture 3: a purposeful commitment—Jesus' willingness to die for man (v.53-54).
5. Picture 4: two tragic commitments (v.55-56).
   a. A commitment that opposes Jesus: the world's treatment.
   b. A commitment that forsakes Jesus: the disciples' fleeing.

1 (26:47) **Judas—Jesus Christ, Betrayed**: Judas betrayed Jesus. Judas is seen leading a large crowd to arrest Jesus. Note the four facts stated.

1. Judas was one of the twelve apostles, a disciple, a professing follower of the Lord. Just a few hours before, that very evening, he had been sitting at the table of the Lord eating bread with Him. Now, ever so quickly, he had turned away and had actually taken the lead in betraying the Lord (cp. Acts 1:16).

> **Thought 1.** There are too many within the church just like Judas. They profess Christ, yet ever so quickly they turn away. Some even give leadership to others in opposing Christ (or righteousness).

2. Judas led a large crowd to arrest Jesus (see note—Lk.22:47-48).

3. Judas made sure they were armed. He feared Jesus ("arrest Him," he had said, v.48). Judas had witnessed Jesus' power and His escaping from crowds before (cp. Lk.4:30; Jn.8:59).

4. Judas was officially sent by the religionists: the chief priests and leaders (Mt.26:3-5, 14-16). The very people who should have received Him rejected Him. His severest enemies were those who professed to believe in God and who gave religious leadership to the people.

> **Thought 1.** If Jesus returned to earth today, how many religionists would reject and oppose Him? In fact, how many religionists are already rejecting Him? How many reject Him as He is revealed by those who follow Him? How many go about formulating an image of Christ as they wish, after their own lusts?

2 (26:48-50) **Commitment—Deception—Judas**: the first picture of commitment is a deceptive commitment—that of Judas' betrayal.

1. The deceiver Judas laid his plans. It would be dark. How would the temple guard be able to recognize Jesus in the dark and keep Him from slipping away? Judas thought and thought and came up with a plan. He would identify Jesus for them by walking up and greeting Jesus with a kiss. A kiss was a sign of friendship and commitment among people in the East, in particular among friends. Judas felt he could deceive the disciples; they would never suspect his sin.

Thought 1. The point here is the planning and plotting of evil while professing Christ. How many profess Christ and yet lay plans to steal, lie, cheat, sin? How many profess loyalty to Christ and yet plan to give their allegiance to someone else? How many of us profess Christ and yet, just like Judas, plan to serve our own self-interest?

Thought 2. When we plan and plot to sin, we play the deceiver.

2. The deceiver Judas carried out his plan. What he planned he did: "Going at once to Jesus, Judas said, 'Greetings Rabbi!,' and kissed Him." The word for "kissed Him" (katephilesen) is strong. It means to kiss strongly, forcefully, passionately, fervently, repeatedly. Either Judas had planned to really put on a show to hide his sin or else his nervousness caused him to act passionately. The sin was bad enough, but the deception was worse.

Thought 1. What we plan, we often do, both good and evil.

Thought 2. Professing Christ and living in sin makes two things out of us: a betrayer and a deceiver. We betray Christ and deceive others.

3. The deceiver Judas was given a clear-cut charge:: "Friend, do what you came for." Note that Jesus did not rebuke or reproach Judas. By addressing Judas so directly, He forced Judas to search his deceptive heart. Christ still wanted to reach Judas, if possible. By His clear-cut charge, He was in essence saying, "You have greeted me as a loyal companion. Have you come committed and loyal to Me?" The clear-cut charge was bound to pierce and arouse a searching conviction within the deceptive heart. The deception and sin were completed. Christ was arrested (v.50).

Friend deceives friend, and no one speaks the truth. They have taught their tongues to lie; they weary themselves with sinning. (Jer 9:5)

The heart is deceitful above all things and beyond cure. Who can understand it? (Jer 17:9)

Then we will no longer be infants, tossed back and forth by the waves, and blown here and there by every wind of teaching and by the cunning and craftiness of men in their deceitful scheming. (Eph 4:14)

While evil men and impostors will go from bad to worse, deceiving and being deceived. (2 Tim 3:13)

For there are many rebellious people, mere talkers and deceivers, especially those of the circumcision group. (Titus 1:10)

See to it, brothers, that none of you has a sinful, unbelieving heart that turns away from the living God. (Heb 3:12)

They will be paid back with harm for the harm they have done. Their idea of pleasure is to carouse in broad daylight. They are blots and blemishes, reveling in their pleasures while they feast with you. With eyes full of adultery, they never stop sinning; they seduce the unstable; they are experts in greed—an accursed brood! (2 Pet 2:13-14)

Many deceivers, who do not acknowledge Jesus Christ as coming in the flesh, have gone out into the world. Any such person is the deceiver and the antichrist. (2 John 1:7)

Thought 1. Note that God's glorious patience or long-suffering toward us was demonstrated by Christ (cp. 2 Pt.3:9).
1) Christ submitted to the hypocritical profession of Judas and the mistreatment of the barbarious crowd.
2) Christ tried to reach Judas again, just as He had tried and tried before.

Thought 2. Christ tells everyone of us: "Friend, do what you came for. Why have you come to me? To the church?"
1) Because you are really committed and loyal?
2) Because you want gain: social standing, business, livelihood, security, influence, position, religious recognition?
3) Because you want acceptability within the community?
4) Because you want to satisfy conscience: to have just enough religion to keep you from feeling guilty?
5) Because you want to please family or friends?
6) Because you were taught to come?
7) Because all your friends come?

Thought 3. The statement of Christ should pierce every one of our hearts and arouse a searching conviction.

3 (26:51-52) **Carnal—Peter**: the second picture of commitment is a carnal commitment—that of Peter's carnal militancy.

1. Peter misunderstood Jesus' kingdom and he "warred in the flesh (sinful nature)." The disciple was Peter and the servant whose ear was cut off was Malchus (Jn.18:10). Jesus restored the ear; He miraculously healed it (Lk.22:51).

Peter thought the Messiah's hour had come. Christ was now ready to free Israel and establish the throne of David as the dominant nation in the world (see notes—Mt.1:1; DEEPER STUDY # 2—1:18; DEEPER STUDY # 3—3:11; notes—11:1-6; 11:2-3; DEEPER STUDY # 1—11:5; DEEPER STUDY # 2—11:6; DEEPER STUDY # 1—12:16; notes— 22:42; Lk.7:21-23). Peter drew his sword (note that he had one) and struck, slashing off the ear of Malchus.

2. Christ rebuked Peter and his carnal commitment, his warring in the flesh (sinful nature).
a. He told Peter to put his sword back into its sheath where it belonged.
b. He healed Malchus' ear (Lk.22:51).

c. He told Peter that "for all who draw the sword will die by the sword."

The picture painted by Peter's behavior is carnal commitment, acting and struggling in the flesh (sinful nature). Peter took his stand for Christ *in the flesh*; therefore, he failed. Eventually, he deserted Christ. Acting in the flesh will always result in failing and deserting Christ. Peter's carnal commitment is seen in four mistakes. Each mistake is too often seen in the lives of believers.

1. Peter misunderstood the Lord's Word. First, Peter thought Christ was to establish an earthly kingdom. He thought in terms of the earthly, the physical, the material. Therefore, he failed to grasp the spiritual and eternal kingdom (the spiritual world, the spiritual dimension of being) proclaimed by Christ. Second, Peter never accepted the Lord's word. Christ had predicted His death and forewarned the apostles, giving them extensive training for months (see notes—Mt.16:13-20; 16:21-28; 17:1-13; 17:22; 17:24-27). Yet Peter refused to give up his preconceived ideas and accept what Christ was saying. Therefore, he did not see the eternal world of the Spirit nor the eternal salvation which Christ was securing.

2. Peter did not wait for instructions from Christ. He acted on his own; he took matters into his own hands. The disciples had asked, "Lord, should we strike with our swords?" (Lk.22:49). But Jesus had not yet answered. However, this did not stop Peter. He acted on his own. How like so many of us! Too often, we act without waiting on the Lord.

3. Peter did not ask Christ what to do, not again and again. He did not persist until Christ answered.

> **"Watch and pray so that you will not fall into temptation. The spirit is willing, but the body is weak." (Mat 26:41)**
>
> **Be always on the watch, and pray that you may be able to escape all that is about to happen, and that you may be able to stand before the Son of Man." (Luke 21:36)**
>
> **Look to the LORD and his strength; seek his face always. (1 Chr 16:11)**

4. Peter did not think clearly nor use discretion nor act wisely. His action could have led to the failure of God's will. It could have led to the death of many. That is what Christ said: "Violence leads to violence. If you draw the sword, the soldiers will cut you down." Among God's people, the place of the sword is in the sheath, not drawn and slashing at people. God's people are to proclaim love and peace, not war and violence, not carnal and fleshly behavior.

> **So he said to me, "This is the word of the LORD to Zerubbabel: 'Not by might nor by power, but by my Spirit,' says the LORD Almighty. (Zec 4:6)**
>
> **Those whom I love I rebuke and discipline. So be earnest, and repent. (Rev 3:19)**
>
> **But in your hearts set apart Christ as Lord. Always be prepared to give an answer to everyone who asks you to give the reason for the hope that you have. But do this with gentleness and respect, (1 Pet 3:15)**

> **Thought 1.** The weapons of the believers warfare are spiritual, not physical or carnal (cp. 2 Cor.10:3-5; cp. Ro.8:5-8; Gal.5:17).

4 (26:53-54) **Jesus Christ, Love—Obedience**: the third picture of commitment is a purposeful commitment—that of Jesus' willingness to die for man.

1. Jesus could have saved Himself. He could have prayed to His Father and seventy-two thousand angels would have rallied to His defense and blasted His enemies away. He does not need the weak efforts of men to defend Him. He is God's Son, God's only Son, and God will defend His Son as He wills.

2. However, Jesus was determined to fulfill Scripture: He had to die, and He was willing to die for man. His life was not being taken from Him by men. He was laying it down willingly as God had purposed.

> **But he was pierced for our transgressions, he was crushed for our iniquities; the punishment that brought us peace was upon him, and by his wounds we are healed. We all, like sheep, have gone astray, each of us has turned to his own way; and the LORD has laid on him the iniquity of us all. He was oppressed and afflicted, yet he did not open his mouth; he was led like a lamb to the slaughter, and as a sheep before her shearers is silent, so he did not open his mouth. (Isa 53:5-7)**
>
> **The reason my Father loves me is that I lay down my life—only to take it up again. No one takes it from me, but I lay it down of my own accord. I have authority to lay it down and authority to take it up again. This command I received from my Father." (John 10:17-18)**
>
> **This man was handed over to you by God's set purpose and foreknowledge; and you, with the help of wicked men, put him to death by nailing him to the cross. (Acts 2:23)**

> **Thought 1.** Christ is the perfect example of purposeful commitment. The commitment God wants from us is a purposeful commitment: a commitment to die daily for Christ and His cause (see note and DEEPER STUDY # 1—Lk.9:23).

> **Thought 2.** Purpose, meaning, and significance are what every man desires and needs. Such is found in Christ alone. He and His cause alone fill the heart of man with purpose, meaning, and significance.

5 (26:55-56) **Commitment**: the fourth picture of commitment is that of two tragic commitments.

1. A commitment to oppose Jesus: the world's treatment of Jesus.
   a. Note how the world treated Jesus: they treated Him as (1) a thief, as though He were going to steal from them; (2) as a dangerous man who must be opposed with weapons; and (3) as a man who must be opposed in the dark and in secret.
   b. Note how the world opposed Jesus and cut His heart. The words of Jesus are spoken with feeling, hurt, and intense sorrow.

At that time Jesus said to the crowd, "Am I leading a rebellion, that you have come out with swords and clubs to capture me? Every day I sat in the temple courts teaching, and you did not arrest me. (Mat 26:55)

Jesus allowed such indignities and shameful behavior, but it hurt and broke His heart. He was, after all, the Son of God.

He was in the world, and though the world was made through him, the world did not recognize him. He came to that which was his own, but his own did not receive him. (John 1:10-11)

Father, glorify your name!" Then a voice came from heaven, "I have glorified it, and will glorify it again." (John 12:28)

The people of Jerusalem and their rulers did not recognize Jesus, yet in condemning him they fulfilled the words of the prophets that are read every Sabbath. (Acts 13:27)

2. A commitment that forsakes Jesus: the disciples' fleeing. They fled for at least two reasons.
   a. They feared for their own lives. Jesus was not using His power to free Himself. They could not understand. They fled to save themselves.
   b. They were disillusioned; they could not understand Jesus' behavior and why He would not blast His enemies away to free Himself. A point needs to be noted about their disillusionment: it was their own fault.

   First, they were close-minded; therefore, they were weak in faith. They had closed their minds to His full mission and purpose. They had *refused* to literally accept His word about dying and rising again. They had failed to grasp the spiritual and eternal nature of His kingdom. They symbolized what He was saying. Now that it was happening, they were not prepared for it. Their faith was too weak.

   Second, they were worldly and materialistic-minded. They had hung on to their earthly concept of the Messiah: the Messiah who was coming to bring utopia to this material and physical world. They were, therefore, not prepared to deal with their earthly Messiah's being bound and taken prisoner by men of this earth. Their faith lacked the strength to bear such a trial.

Therefore, dear friends, since you already know this, be on your guard so that you may not be carried away by the error of lawless men and fall from your secure position. But grow in the grace and knowledge of our Lord and Savior Jesus Christ. To him be glory both now and forever! Amen. (2 Pet 3:17-18)

Jesus replied, "No one who puts his hand to the plow and looks back is fit for service in the kingdom of God." (Luke 9:62)

He is a double-minded man, unstable in all he does. (James 1:8)

Blessed is the man who perseveres under trial, because when he has stood the test, he will receive the crown of life that God has promised to those who love him. (James 1:12)

Come near to God and he will come near to you. Wash your hands, you sinners, and purify your hearts, you double-minded. (James 4:8)

Thought 1. The world opposes Christ.
1) Many treat Him as a thief. They believe He withholds pleasure and prevents (cheats) people from really living. They believe that His commandments cause people to miss out on life.
2) Others oppose Him as though He is dangerous. They actually curse and try to stamp out His name and church. They oppose Him and His church with every weapon they can find.
3) Still others oppose Him by plotting and sinning in the dark and in secret.

Thought 2. All opposition and shameful behavior—all sin cuts the heart of Jesus. It was because of sin that He died (2 Pt.2:24).

Thought 3. Too many disciples forsake Jesus for the same reason: disillusionment. And too often our disillusionment is caused by the same two reasons: either being close-minded or being worldly and materialistic-minded.

	H. The Messiah's Trial before Caiaphas & the Sanhedrin: Lessons under Trial, 26:57-68 (Mk.14:53-65; Lk.22:54, 63-71; cp. Jn.18:12-14, 19-24)	62 Then the high priest stood up and said to Jesus, "Are you not going to answer? What is this testimony that these men are bringing against you?"	**5 There was the calm assurance of Jesus**
		63 But Jesus remained silent. The high priest said to him, "I charge you under oath by the	**6 There was the claim of Jesus: He is the Messiah, the Son of God**
1 Jesus was led to trial	57 Those who had arrested Jesus took him to Caiaphas, the high priest, where the teachers of the law and the elders had assembled.	living God: Tell us if you are the Christ, the Son of God."	a. He was questioned: Put under oath to answer
2 There was the confused faith & loyalty of Peter a. He could not understand b. But he loved: He came back to see the end	58 But Peter followed him at a distance, right up to the courtyard of the high priest. He entered and sat down with the guards to see the outcome.	64 "Yes, it is as you say," Jesus replied. "But I say to all of you: In the future you will see the Son of Man sitting at the right hand of the Mighty One and coming on the clouds of heaven."	b. He claimed to be the Messiah[DS2] c. He gave two proofs 1) His resurrection & exaltation[DS3] 2) His second coming
3 There was the stacked court: Predetermined rejection & opposition[DS1]	59 The chief priests and the whole Sanhedrin were looking for false evidence against Jesus so that they could put him to death.	65 Then the high priest tore his clothes and said, "He has spoken blasphemy! Why do we need any more witnesses? Look, now you have heard the blasphemy.	**7 There was the tragic verdict** a. The crime: Blasphemy b. The evidence: His claim
4 There was the false charge: A revolutionary a. Many false witnesses: The charges were unconvincing b. Two false witnesses: The charge was convincing—a revolutionary	60 But they did not find any, though many false witnesses came forward. Finally two came forward 61 and declared, "This fellow said, 'I am able to destroy the temple of God and rebuild it in three days.'"	66 What do you think?" "He is worthy of death," they answered. 67 Then they spit in his face and struck him with their fists. Others slapped him 68 And said, "Prophesy to us, Christ. Who hit you?"	c. The sentence: Death **8 There was the physical abuse inflicted** a. Bitter hatred & behavior b. Ridicule of His claim to be the Messiah

DIVISION XVI

THE MESSIAH'S ARREST, TRIAL, AND CRUCIFIXION, 26:1-27:66

H. The Messiah's Trial before Caiaphas and The Sanhedrin: Lessons under Trial, 26:57-68

(26:57-68) **Introduction**: Christ had been rejected and opposed throughout all His ministry. Now He was being officially condemned to die by the high court of the Jews, the Sandedrin. Christ was standing before the court, and all the negative feelings of humanity against God were beginning to seep through: confusion, disloyalty, unbelief, rejection, disregard, opposition, bitterness, enmity, hatred.

A glance at the major points of the passage gives some insight into what really lies within the heart of man toward God. Because Christ stood so magnificently before the court, the believer can look and learn lesson after lesson that helps him to stand before the great trials of his own life.

1. Jesus was led to trial (v.57).
2. There was the confused faith and loyalty of Peter (v.58).
3. There was the stacked court: predetermined rejection and opposition (v.59).
4. There was the false charge: a revolutionary (v.60-61).
5. There was the calm assurance of Jesus (v.62).
6. There was the claim of Jesus: He is the Messiah, the Son of God (v.63-64).
7. There was the tragic verdict (v.65-66).
8. There was the physical abuse inflicted (v.67-68).

1 (26:57) **Jesus Christ, Trials**: Jesus was led to trial. He had been arrested and now He was being put on trial for His life. In the span of just a few hours, He was to be tried at least six times (see DEEPER STUDY # 1—Lk.22:66-71). The first trial was an informal trial before Annas, the retired High Priest who was highly respected by the Jewish leaders (Jn.18:13, 19-24). The trial before Caiaphas, in the present passage, was the second trial. The court (Sanhedrin) was already assembled. These were the very men who had Jesus arrested (Mt.26:3-5). They were the High Priest, the Scribes and the elders, that is, the Sanhedrin, the council who ruled the Jewish people for the Romans (v.59). In a hastily called meeting, the council was sitting there waiting for the guards to bring Jesus to them. Several facts reveal the evil of their hearts (see note and DEEPER STUDY # 1—Mt.12:10; note—15:1-20; DEEPER STUDY # 2—15:6-9; note—16:1-12; DEEPER STUDY # 3—16:12).

1. They had hastily assembled the court *at night*. It was illegal to try cases at night. All criminals had to be tried in the day.

2. They were meeting in Caiaphas' palace (home), not in the official court. This, too, was illegal. All cases had to be tried in court.

3. Jesus was being tried during the Passover week. No cases could be tried during the Passover week.

4. They had not met to try Jesus but to secretly devise charges that would condemn Him to death.

Thought 1. A heart that wants to do evil will twist the rules. These religionists had to twist the law if they were going to condemn Christ.

Thought 2. A person often finds it easier to oppose Christ within a group than when alone. Not all among these religionists felt malice toward Christ, but most went along with those who did. They did not stand against the malicious and unjust treatment of our Lord. (It is doubtful if Nicodemus and Joseph of Arimathaea had been summoned to the hastily called illegal meeting. Their favorable feelings toward Christ were probably well known to the council. However, this is disputable, cp. Mt.27:57; Jn.3:1f.)

Thought 3. The house of Caiaphas, the religious leader, should have been an ideal home, a home that stood forth as a strong testimony for God. Yet, here it is seen as a center for evil.

Thought 4. Two things need to be observed and searched out in our lives.
1) How far institutional religion twisted the minds of these men. Has it twisted our minds?
2) How much these men were concerned for personal security, position, and influence (power). How far away these men were from God, and they were religionists (see note and DEEPER STUDY # 1—Mt.12:10; note—15:1-20; DEEPER STUDY # 2—15:6-9). How far have we allowed security, position, and influence to lead us away from God?

2 (26:58) **Peter**: there was the confused faith and loyalty of Peter. Peter was confused. He just could not understand why Jesus was not blasting His enemies and setting up His earthly kingdom (see note—Mt.26:51-52). When it was clear that Jesus was not going to act, Peter fled for his life, but he had not gone far. His love for Christ had stopped him, and now his love was turning him around to follow Christ along the trail to Caiaphas' palace. He wanted to see the end, just what would happen to His Lord.

For this reason I remind you to fan into flame the gift of God, which is in you through the laying on of my hands. For God did not give us a spirit of timidity, but a spirit of power, of love and of self-discipline. (2 Tim 1:6-7)

There is no fear in love. But perfect love drives out fear, because fear has to do with punishment. The one who fears is not made perfect in love. (1 John 4:18)

Thought 1. Peter was caught between two forces: loyalty to Christ and fear for self. We are often caught between the same two forces. If we stand for Christ, we often find that we suffer ridicule or abuse or being passed over for some position, or a host of other possible acts of persecution.

Thought 2. Peter's failure was due to misunderstanding the truth about Christ (see note—Mt.26:51-52). Failure to understand Christ will lead to failure now and doom us to eternal failure.

3 (26:59) **Religionists**: there was the stacked court against Christ—predetermined rejection and opposition. The court was not convening to see if Jesus were guilty. The court was meeting to seek false witnesses against Christ (cp. Ps.35:11). They wanted to sentence Him to death. They had already determined in their hearts to reject and oppose Him. He was a threat to both their nation and their personal security and position. They feared the loss of both, so they were set on killing Him. (For a discussion of the reasons for their opposition, see note—Mt.12:1-8; note and DEEPER STUDY # 1—12:10; note—15:1-20; DEEPER STUDY # 2—15:6-9; DEEPER STUDY # 3—16:12.)

Thought 1. The religionists rejected and opposed Christ for two primary reasons, the same two reasons that men reject and oppose Him today.
1) They were unwilling to deny self, to surrender all they were and had to Christ. They feared loss, the loss of some security, money, position, pleasure. They loved the world and self more than they loved God.

"Therefore come out from them and be separate, says the Lord. Touch no unclean thing, and I will receive you." "I will be a Father to you, and you will be my sons and daughters, says the Lord Almighty." (2 Cor 6:17-18)

2) They were unwilling to deny their institutional religion, their rituals and ceremonies and their religious practices that were *man-made*, *man-conceived,* and *man-honoring*.

Anyone, then, who knows the good he ought to do and doesn't do it, sins. (James 4:17)

Dear friend, do not imitate what is evil but what is good. Anyone who does what is good is from God. Anyone who does what is evil has not seen God. (3 John 1:11)

DEEPER STUDY # 1
(26:59) **Sanhedrin**: the ruling body of the nation of Israel, both the governing council and supreme court of the Jews. It had seventy-one members and was presided over by the High Priest. Its membership was made up of the Pharisees, Sadducees, Scribes or lawyers, and the elders who were leaders from among the people. A quorum was twenty-three. The legal power of the Sanhedrin to pass the death sentence was restricted about twenty some years before the trial of Jesus. However, they did retain the right of excommunication (cp. Jn.9:22). To secure Jesus' death, they were forced by law to appeal to the Romans for the death sentence.

4 (26:60-61) **Jesus Christ, Charges Against**: there was the false charge—a revolutionary. Note the words "But they did not find any" are repeated twice. The religionists sought false witnesses but found none whose charges were strong enough. The law required two witnesses who had no contact with each other and who agreed on the same evidence. The court was to examine each separately. Apparently, the religionists ran into several problems…
- The evidence of the false charges was just too weak to convince the Roman authorities of Jesus' guilt.

- A strong case could not be formulated from the charges made.
- Two witnesses who agreed on a single charge could not be found.

Finally, two witnesses did come forth with a charge that seemed to be strong enough. Note the word "finally." The case almost broke down and failed. Imagine! Even in seeking false witnesses, the case against our Lord could not be established.

Note the following facts.

1. The two witnesses with adequate testimony were false witnesses.

2. The two were crude and base. This is shown by their contemptuous attitude and public animosity: "this fellow" (autos)—a disrespectful, contemptuous address.

3. The two distorted Jesus' words. Jesus had said, "Destroy this temple, and I will raise it again in three days" (Jn.2:19). Jesus had actually said the Jews were to be the destroyers. But the false witnesses said, "This fellow said, I am able to destroy the temple of God." They distorted His words, making Him the destroyer.

The false witnesses also misunderstood Jesus' words. Jesus was referring to His body, to the temple of His body and to the resurrection of His body. The Jews apparently thought He meant He would destroy and rebuild the Jerusalem temple in three days. It was this charge, the charge of being a revolutionary, that the religionists believed they could use to convince the Romans to execute Jesus.

> **"But his subjects hated him and sent a delegation after him to say, 'We don't want this man to be our king.' (Luke 19:14)**
>
> **The world cannot hate you, but it hates me because I testify that what it does is evil. (John 7:7)**
>
> **"If the world hates you, keep in mind that it hated me first. But this is to fulfill what is written in their Law: 'They hated me without reason.' (John 15:18, 25)**

Thought 1. When men are bent on doing something, they often go ahead and do it—regardless of the method.
1) When a man is bent on rejecting Christ, he rationalizes and justifies himself and rejects Christ.
2) When a man is bent on doing something wrong, he rationalizes and justifies himself and does it.

Thought 2. One of the greatest mistakes we make is to distort the Word of Christ. The two false witnesses distorted and twisted His Word. When we distort and twist what He said, we condemn ourselves to destruction.

> **Bear in mind that our Lord's patience means salvation, just as our dear brother Paul also wrote you with the wisdom that God gave him. He writes the same way in all his letters, speaking in them of these matters. His letters contain some things that are hard to understand, which ignorant and unstable people distort, as they do the other Scriptures, to their own destruction. (2 Pet 3:15-16)**

5 (26:62) **Jesus Christ, Trials**: there was the calm assurance of Jesus. Note these facts.

1. The two witnesses who charged Jesus with being a revolutionary could not agree (Mk.14:59).

2. Jesus "remained silent." He was silent; He said nothing in defending Himself against the false charges.

3. The High Priest and court become disturbed and perhaps confused by Jesus' silence. They needed Him to begin speaking, hoping He would add evidence to the charge, thereby incriminating Himself. The High priest turned and attempted to pressure and browbeat Jesus: "Are you not going to answer?"

"But Jesus remained silent" (v.63). He was calm, assured, peaceful, and confident in the midst of turmoil. Why did He say nothing?

1. He stood in the will of God. He had been and was obedient to God. In the "God's set purpose and foreknowledge," it was God's will for Him to die (Acts 2:23; cp. Is. 53:7; Ps.38:13-14). Therefore, He would surrender to the false charge and murderous intention of the council.

2. He said nothing because He would not become entangled in a useless argument. To answer would be useless, for He would be defending Himself against a false charge and against a group of men who were set on opposing and destroying Him.

3. He would answer only when an opportunity arose to proclaim the truth of the gospel: that He is the Messiah and that God does love the world (Mt.26:63-64; cp. Jn.3:16).

> **For, "Whoever would love life and see good days must keep his tongue from evil and his lips from deceitful speech. (1 Pet 3:10)**
>
> **He who guards his lips guards his life, but he who speaks rashly will come to ruin. (Prov 13:3)**
>
> **He who guards his mouth and his tongue keeps himself from calamity. (Prov 21:23)**

Thought 1. Christ taught that there are times when silence is the best policy.
1) When words would entangle us in *useless argument*.
2) When men are *set on opposing and destroying* us.
3) When men *persecute* us (see note—Mt.10:23).
4) When men *reject* our message (Mt.10:12-14).

Thought 2. God will give us an inner peace and calm assurance in great trial (cp. Jn.14:27; 16:33).

> **No temptation has seized you except what is common to man. And God is faithful; he will not let you be tempted beyond what you can bear. But when you are tempted, he will also provide a way out so that you can stand up under it. (1 Cor 10:13)**
>
> **Who through faith are shielded by God's power until the coming of the salvation that is ready to be revealed in the last time. In this you greatly rejoice, though now for a little while you may have had to suffer grief in all kinds of trials. These have come so that your faith—of greater worth than gold, which perishes even though refined by fire—may be proved genuine and may result in praise, glory and honor when Jesus Christ is revealed. (1 Pet 1:5-7)**
>
> **Dear friends, do not be surprised at the painful trial you are suffering, as though**

something strange were happening to you. But rejoice that you participate in the sufferings of Christ, so that you may be overjoyed when his glory is revealed. (1 Pet 4:12-13)

Thought 3. Jesus Christ willingly submitted to such false charges so that no man could "bring any charge against those whom God has chosen" (Ro.8:33). Jesus Christ was falsely accused that we might not be condemned (Ro.8:34).

6 (26:63-64) **Jesus Christ, Deity**: there was the claim of Jesus: He is the Messiah, the Son of God. Four things happened here.

1. The High Priest questioned Jesus and put Him under oath to answer. The words "I charge you under oath by the living God" was an official oath which demanded an answer. The High Priest used his office as God's representative to demand an answer: "By the living God, answer. Are you claiming to be the Messiah, the Son of God?" he asked Jesus.

2. Jesus claimed to be the Messiah, the Son of God (see note—Mt.1:18). Jesus answered, "Yes, it is as you say." It was a strong assertion. All that Caiaphas had said was true. Mark added the striking words of deity, "I am" (ego eimi) (Mk.14:62; see DEEPER STUDY # 1—Jn.6:20; note—18:6).

Note that Christ also called Himself "the Son of Man" (see DEEPER STUDY # 3—Mt.26:64).

Thought 1. Jesus claimed beyond question to be the promised Messiah, the Son of God. He was claiming to be God of gods, Lord of lords, One with the Father in every respect (see DEEPER STUDY # 1—Jn.6:20; note—18:4-6. See outline and notes—Ph.2:5-11.)

Thought 2. What if Jesus had said, "No. I am not the Messiah. I am not the Son of God." Where would we be today? Honestly and objectively, where would the world be today? Just imagine a world without the cross of Christ!

3. Jesus gave two proofs for His claim. His resurrection and exaltation and His second coming prove both His person and authority.

Thought 1. The believer hopes in the resurrection and exaltation and in the second coming of Christ, but the emphasis of Christ to these unbelievers is judgment.

⇒ His resurrection declares Him to be the Son of God (Ro.1:4).

And who through the Spirit of holiness was declared with power to be the Son of God by his resurrection from the dead: Jesus Christ our Lord. (Rom 1:4)

⇒ His exaltation declares His position and authority to rule and reign over all men (Ph.2:9-11).

Therefore God exalted him to the highest place and gave him the name that is above every name, that at the name of Jesus every knee should bow, in heaven and on earth and under the earth, and every tongue confess that Jesus Christ is Lord, to the glory of God the Father. (Phil 2:9-11)

⇒ His return will declare His execution of justice and judgment (Mt.24:30; Jn.5:28).

"At that time the sign of the Son of Man will appear in the sky, and all the nations of the earth will mourn. They will see the Son of Man coming on the clouds of the sky, with power and great glory. (Mat 24:30)

"Do not be amazed at this, for a time is coming when all who are in their graves will hear his voice (John 5:28)

DEEPER STUDY # 2
(26:64) **Christ**: see DEEPER STUDY # 2—Mt.1:18.

DEEPER STUDY # 3
(26:64) **Son of Man**: see DEEPER STUDY # 3—Mt.8:20.

7 (26:65-66) **Jesus Christ, Condemned**: there was the tragic verdict. Note that Caiaphas tore his clothes. Mark even says he tore his under garments (tunic). This was a custom among Jews when they heard or saw God's name dishonored or disgraced (2 Ki.18:37; 19:1 cp. Is.36:22; 27:1; Acts 14:14). Caiaphas had gotten what he wanted. Christ had committed blasphemy which was punishable by death among the Jews (Lev.24:16; cp. Acts 7:58). No other witnesses were needed. *A vote by acclamation* was quickly called for: "What do you think? They answered and said, He is worthy of death."

8 (26:67-68) **Jesus Christ, Death**: there was the physical abuse inflicted. The bitter enmity and hatred of the Jews broke through. The rights and expectation of justice was completely forgotten. The abuse took two forms.

1. Bitter hatred and behavior. Spitting in the face was a sign of monstrous disrespect. Beating with the fists and palms (erra pisan, rods) was an outburst of the inner bitterness within the hearts of the religionists against Christ.

I offered my back to those who beat me, my cheeks to those who pulled out my beard; I did not hide my face from mocking and spitting. (Isa 50:6; cp. Isa 52:14)

Marshal your troops, O city of troops, for a siege is laid against us. They will strike Israel's ruler on the cheek with a rod. (Micah 5:1)

2. Ridicule of His claim, mocking His supernatural power and sarcastically calling Him "Christ."

Thought 1. Rejecting and opposing can cause bitterness. Too many harbor an inner bitterness against God and Christ. Too many have allowed their rejection and opposition and the events which happened to them to grow into bitterness. Thus when opportunity arises, they vent their feelings and hostility. Too many believers, in rejecting or opposing Christ, allow bitterness to seep into their hearts. Too many vent their feelings and bitterness when they have a chance to attack some movement of God or some true believer who faithfully follows Christ day by day.

	I. The Messiah Denied by	72 He denied it again, with	b. Denial by oath: Called
	Peter: A Look at Deny-	an oath: "I don't know the	Jesus "the man"—
	ing Christ, 26:69-75	man!"	downgraded Him
	(Mk.14:66-72; Lk.22:54-62;	73 After a little while, those	**4 The denial by cursing &**
	Jn.18:15-18, 25-27)	standing there went up to	**swearing**
		Peter and said, "Surely you	a. Charge: Peter was a
1 The cause of denial:	69 Now Peter was sitting out	are one of them, for your ac-	disciple
Sitting with the crowd[DS1]	in the courtyard, and a ser-	cent gives you away."	1) A crowd came
2 The denial by pretension	vant girl came to him. "You	74 Then he began to call	2) Speech betrayed
a. Charge: Peter had been	also were with Jesus of Gali-	down curses on himself and	b. Denial by cursing &
with Jesus	lee," she said.	he swore to them, "I don't	swearing
b. Denial: Peter pretended	70 But he denied it before	know the man!" Immediately	
he did not know Jesus	them all. "I don't know what	a rooster crowed.	
	you're talking about," he said.	75 Then Peter remembered	**5 The answer to denial:**
3 The denial by oath	71 Then he went out to the	the word Jesus had spoken:	**Repentance**[DS2]
a. Charge: Peter had	gateway, where another girl	"Before the rooster crows,	a. Remembering the
been with Jesus	saw him and said to the peo-	you will disown me three	Lord's Word
1) Made by a girl	ple there, "This fellow was	times." And he went outside	b. Getting alone
2) Made before a crowd	with Jesus of Nazareth."	and wept bitterly.	c. Godly sorrow: Repent

DIVISION XVI

THE MESSIAH'S ARREST, TRIAL, AND CRUCIFIXION, 26:1-27:66

I. The Messiah Denied by Peter: A Look at Denying Christ, 26:69-75

(26:69-75) **Introduction—Apostasy—Jesus Christ, Denied**: denying Christ is serious, very serious. It is a tragic and terrible sin, yet Christ forgives even a man who denies Him. He forgave Peter; and in forgiving Peter, He has demonstrated forever God's unbelievable love for man, no matter how terrible man's sin. Just think for a momemt. Christ forgave a man who professed an undying loyalty to Him yet who ended up denying Him three times when the man felt pressured and threatened by a crowd. No greater picture of God's great love and marvelous grace can be found.

Note another point as well: Peter wanted the world to know about the Lord's great love. The story of His denying Christ originates with him. No other disciple was there to witness it. He shared the terrible experience and God's wondrous grace in forgiving him. Mark was Peter's disciple, and Mark is the gospel writer who shares the most detail about Peter's denials.

Peter's tragic experience in denying Christ says much to believers of all generations.

1. The cause of denial: sitting with the crowd (v.69).
2. The denial by pretension (v.69-70).
3. The denial by oath (v.71-72).
4. The denial by cursing and swearing (v.73-74).
5. The answer to denial: repentance (v.75).

1 (26:69) **Apostasy—Denial**: the cause of Peter's denial was that he "was sitting out in the courtyard." He sat down with the crowd, the crowd which represented the world of rejecters. Very frankly, Peter was failing Christ and failing Him miserably. Sitting down among the crowd was the last place he should have been. Of course, He should have never forsaken Christ. But having fled, he should have been off alone with God in prayer, seeking answers and understanding from God (see notes—Mt.26:51-52; 26:55-56). Or he should have been with the other apostles, leading them to seek the face of God for understanding and direction.

There are at least three causes for denial—three things that can lead a person to deny Christ. All three are seen in Peter's experience (also see notes—Jn.18:12-27).

1. Deserting Christ: turning away from Him and fleeing from Him (cp. Mt.26:56).

2. "Following Christ at a distance": not walking close to Him, not standing and being identified with Him (cp. Mt.26:58).

> **For God did not give us a spirit of timidity, but a spirit of power, of love and of self-discipline. So do not be ashamed to testify about our Lord, or ashamed of me his prisoner. But join with me in suffering for the gospel, by the power of God, (2 Tim 1:7-8)**

3. "Sitting out" or sitting with the crowd: not being where one should be, with the disciples of the Lord.

> **"Therefore come out from them and be separate, says the Lord. Touch no unclean thing, and I will receive you." "I will be a Father to you, and you will be my sons and daughters, says the Lord Almighty." (2 Cor 6:17-18)**
>
> **In the name of the Lord Jesus Christ, we command you, brothers, to keep away from every brother who is idle and does not live according to the teaching you received from us. (2 Th 3:6)**

DEEPER STUDY # 1

(26:69) **Courtyard**: Peter was in the courtyard. The first denial took place in the courtyard, the second on the porch of the palace.

2 (26:69-70) **Apostasy—Denial**: there was the denial by pretension. This is always a denial that pretends to have nothing to do with Christ.

The guard at the gate (a woman) knew John and allowed him to enter (Jn.18:15). Apparently John requested her to let Peter enter. Note the words, "You also were with Jesus of Nazareth." She seemed to be making a simple statement to Peter, perhaps for identification purposes. There seemed to be no threat or danger to Peter, yet Peter pretended to know nothing about Jesus. Again, note his exact words: "I don't know what you are talking about"; that is, he pretended to know nothing about what she was saying or to know nothing about this Jesus of Nazareth. In either case, Peter denied and pretended to have nothing to do with Jesus.

> **If anyone is ashamed of me and my words in this adulterous and sinful generation, the Son of Man will be ashamed of him when he comes in his Father's glory with the holy angels." (Mark 8:38)**
> **Fear of man will prove to be a snare, but whoever trusts in the LORD is kept safe. (Prov 29:25)**
> **But in your hearts set apart Christ as Lord. Always be prepared to give an answer to everyone who asks you to give the reason for the hope that you have. But do this with gentleness and respect, (1 Pet 3:15)**

Thought 1. Pretending is one of the constant sins of men.

⇒ We are asked if we think something. We do, yet we deny it.
⇒ We are asked if we feel something. We do, yet we deny it.
⇒ We are asked if we fear something. We do, yet we deny it.
⇒ We are asked if we did something. We did, yet we deny it.

Thought 2. Too many believers deny Christ by pretension. Very simply, they pretend not to know Christ when out in the world...

- at their employment
- at their school
- at their social functions
- among their neighbors
- among their friends
- among strangers

Thought 3. Pretension is two things.

1) Pretention is hypocrisy. It is pretending to be something we are not.
2) Pretension is denial of Christ. It is shying away from or lying about one's confession of Christ.

3 (26:71-72) **Apostasy—Denial**: there was the denial by oath. This is a denial that is strong and emphatic, "I swear by God, I do not know the man. I know nothing about Him."

1. This charge was made by a girl, and it was made before a crowd of people. By being made before a crowd, Peter felt more threatened. The charge is the same, "This fellow was with Jesus." Note the charge was true.

⇒ Peter had been with Jesus. He was an apostle; in fact, he was supposedly the leader of the apostles.
⇒ Peter was the disciple who had professed that Jesus was the Christ, the Son of God (Mt.16:16).
⇒ Peter was the disciple who had sworn loyalty to Christ even if it meant death (Mt.26:33-35).

2. The denial which uses an oath downgrades Christ. Note that Peter called Christ, "the man!" He, of course, was the Man; but Peter did not mean the Man in this sense. Peter ignored who Jesus really was, pushing his responsibility to profess Christ out of his mind. Embarrassment, ridicule, abuse, persecution, and the threat of arrest and death intimidated him; so he denied any knowledge of Christ with an emphatic oath: "I swear to God, I do not know the man."

> **But whoever disowns me before men, I will disown him before my Father in heaven. (Mat 10:33)**
> **So do not be ashamed to testify about our Lord, or ashamed of me his prisoner. But join with me in suffering for the gospel, by the power of God, (2 Tim 1:8)**
> **Be strong and courageous. Do not be afraid or terrified because of them, for the LORD your God goes with you; he will never leave you nor forsake you." (Deu 31:6)**

Thought 1. Note something important. In the first denial, Peter was charged by only one person. His denial was a simple denial by pretension, of simply ending the issue: "I don't know what you are talking about." But in this second denial, Peter was charged before a crowd. He felt more threatened; therefore, his denial was stronger and more emphatic: he used an oath. The lesson for us is clear. The more we are among the crowds of the world, the more we are threatened with ridicule, embarrassment, abuse, and persecution for our profession in Christ. And the more we are threatened, the more likely we are to deny Christ (cp. Ro.12:1-2; 2 Cor.6:17-18; 1 Jn. 2:15-16).

Thought 2. There is a strong warning for us in Peter's denials.

⇒ Peter was a strong disciple.
⇒ Peter knew and had trusted Christ as the Messiah, the Son of God.
⇒ Peter had a strong profession of loyalty to Christ.
⇒ Peter had just partaken of the Lord's Supper; in fact, he had just been privileged to partake of the very first Supper.
⇒ Peter had left all to follow Christ.
⇒ Peter had been taught about God, taught by Christ Himself.
⇒ Peter had even been forewarned that the body or flesh was weak and that he would fail.

Thought 3. Every denial (in fact, every neglect) of Christ downgrades the Lord. Denial (and neglect) ignores just who Christ is, the Son of God who possesses all power and majesty and dominion. Denial shows that we fear men more than we fear and reverence God. Neglect of Christ shows how little we fear and reverence Him. The Biblical exhortation always needs to be kept in mind: "The Lord will judge His people. It is a dreadful thing to fall into the hands of the living God" (Heb.10:30-31).

Thought 4. Peter had forgotten Christ's exhortation: "Do not swear at all...." (Mt.5:34-37).

Thought 5. Too many believers fear, and because they fear, they lose their testimony for Christ and the opportunity to witness and win others to Christ. Too many fear...

- embarrassment
- ridicule
- abuse
- loss of position
- worldly friends
- worldly neighbors
- business management
- loss of promotion

4 (26:73-74) **Apostasy—Denial**: there was the strongest and most terrible denial of all, the denial by cursing snd swearing.

1. The charge was made by a crowd this time, a crowd who actually came up to Peter to charge him. Luke says it happened about one hour after the second charge (Lk.22:59). And John says that one of the persons in the crowd was a kinsman of Malchus, whose ear Peter had cut off in the garden of Gethsemane (Jn.18:26). Note that the third charge differed from the other two: Peter was no longer charged with having been with Jesus; he was now charged with being "one of them," one of the disciples. Note also that it was his speech, his accent that gave him away. Peter was from the north, from Galilee, and his northern accent differed significantly from the speech of Judaea and Jerusalem.

2. The denial by cursing and swearing is a terrible sin. A man who is put under pressure to prove himself often resorts to cursing and swearing. Note three things.

a. Peter *began* to curse. His cursing was a continuous thing.

b. Peter's failure was a deteriorating failure. His first denial was simply pretending not to know Christ, simply evading the issue. His second denial was stronger, using a socially acceptable oath (although it was wrong and a sin). His third denial declines into depraved cursing, totally unacceptable to righteous hearts and pure minds and clean lips.

c. As soon as Peter had cursed and swore for a while, "Immediately a rooster crowed."

Thought 1. A crowd of unbelievers can put pressure upon any of us. Peter was where he did not belong. He was hanging around in the midst of a worldly crowd. He belonged in one of three places: by the side of Christ, or alone with God seeking answers and understanding, or with the other apostles, rallying them in prayer for understanding and direction.

> **Have nothing to do with the fruitless deeds of darkness, but rather expose them. (Eph 5:11)**
>
> **They claim to know God, but by their actions they deny him. They are detestable, disobedient and unfit for doing anything good. (Titus 1:16)**
>
> **Therefore, dear friends, since you already know this, be on your guard so that you may not be carried away by the error of lawless men and fall from your secure position. (2 Pet 3:17)**
>
> **Do not set foot on the path of the wicked or walk in the way of evil men. (Prov 4:14)**

Thought 2. Our speech should give us away. Our speech should be kind, gentle, yet strong—strong for the Lord. A person should be able to tell we are believers by our speech. Note that Peter used his speech, his cursing to try to deceive the crowd into thinking that he was anything but a disciple. The Lord's disciples are not to curse and swear. Cursing and swearing are terrible sins in the eyes of the Lord (see outline and notes—Mt.5:33-37).

Thought 3. Sin causes man to deteriorate: it causes him to deteriorate more and more, to wax worse and worse. Note what happened to Peter.

1) Peter's first denial: he pretended ignorance, simply sinned.
2) Peter's second denial: he committed apostasy, infidelity.
3) Peter's third denial: he committed perjury, blasphemy.

5 (26:75) **Denial**: there was the answer to denial—repentance. Three steps were involved in Peter's repentance.

1. Remembering the Lord's words: apparently while the rooster was crowing, the Lord, standing in the chamber of the palace, turned around and caught Peter's eye (Lk.22:61). And Peter, eye to eye with the Lord, remembered the words the Lord had spoken to him:

> **"Simon, Simon, Satan has asked to sift you as wheat. But I have prayed for you, Simon, that your faith may not fail. And when you have turned back, strengthen your brothers." (Luke 22:31-32)**

In the midst of all His own pain and suffering, the Lord took time to look at Peter. His look told Peter that His Lord had not forgotten him. The Lord still loved and cared for Him and wanted his loyalty and service. Christ had prayed for Peter, and the power of that prayer was now moving in Peter's heart and life. Peter now remembered His Lord's word and that word began to take effect.

2. Getting alone: Peter left the courtyard as fast as he safely could. He rushed out through the gate into the night to get alone with God. He was broken and full of anguish and pain for having failed his Lord: he "wept bitterly."

3. Repenting and experiencing godly sorrow. Peter repented and expressed godly sorrow (see DEEPER STUDY # 1—2 Cor.7:10).

> **If we confess our sins, he is faithful and just and will forgive us our sins and purify us from all unrighteousness. (1 John 1:9)**
>
> **Repent of this wickedness and pray to the Lord. Perhaps he will forgive you for having such a thought in your heart. (Acts 8:22)**
>
> **Now make confession to the LORD, the God of your fathers, and do his will. Separate yourselves from the peoples around you and from your foreign wives." (Ezra 10:11)**
>
> **He who conceals his sins does not prosper, but whoever confesses and renounces them finds mercy. (Prov 28:13)**
>
> **Only acknowledge your guilt— you have rebelled against the LORD your God, you have scattered your favors to foreign gods under every spreading tree, and have not obeyed me,'" declares the LORD. (Jer 3:13)**

Thought 1. The same steps Peter took are the steps we need to take in repenting of sin.

DEEPER STUDY # 2

(27:75) **Repentance**: see note and DEEPER STUDY # 1—Acts 17:29-30.

CHAPTER 27

J. The Messiah's Traitor, Judas, & His End: A Picture of Wrong Repentance & Human Religion, 27:1-10
(cp. Acts 1:16-19)

1 Jesus was condemned by the Sanhedrin
- a. They met to finalize the charge to convince the Romans
- b. They bound Jesus
- c. They led Jesus away—to Pilate

2 Judas' wrong repentance
- a. He saw his sin: Jesus was condemned
- b. He felt remorse, but to the priests not to God
- c. He made restitution, but too late
- d. He confessed, but to the priests not to God
- e. He was not helped; he was left to himself
- f. He cast the money at the priests
- g. He fell into utter despair & hanged himself

3 The religionists' human religion
- a. They were inconsistent: In behavior & religious rules
- b. They were deceptive: They tried to hide their evil by public service—bought a cemetary
  - 1) Became known as the "Field of Blood"
  - 2) Fulfilled Scripture[DS1]

Early in the morning, all
the chief priests and the elders of the people came to
the decision to put Jesus to
death.
2 They bound him, led him
away and handed him over to
Pilate, the governor.
3 When Judas, who had be-
trayed him, saw that Jesus
was condemned, he was
seized with remorse and returned the thirty silver coins
to the chief priests and the elders.
4 "I have sinned," he said,
"for I have betrayed innocent
blood." "What is that to us?"
they replied. "That's your responsibility."
5 So Judas threw the money
into the temple and left. Then
he went away and hanged
himself.
6 The chief priests picked up
the coins and said, "It is
against the law to put this
into the treasury, since it is
blood money."
7 So they decided to use the
money to buy the potter's
field as a burial place for
foreigners.
8 That is why it has been
called the Field of Blood to
this day.
9 Then what was spoken by
Jeremiah the prophet was fulfilled: "They took the thirty
silver coins, the price set
on him by the people of Israel,
10 And they used them to
buy the potter's field, as the
Lord commanded me."

DIVISION XVI

THE MESSIAH'S ARREST, TRIAL, AND CRUCIFIXION, 26:1-27:66

J. The Messiah's Traitor, Judas, and His End: A Picture of Wrong Repentance and Human Religion, 27:1-10

(27:1-10) **Introduction—Judas**: there were two misguided culprits involved in the death of Christ—Judas Iscariot and the Sanhedrin, the ruling body of the Jews. Judas was the culprit who betrayed Christ; the body of the Sanhedrin was the culprit who condemned Christ in a stacked and unjust trial.

There is recorded in this passage something often overlooked: Judas did repent (v.3). He turned away from his terrible sin and tried to make restitution. However, his repentance was a wrong repentance. What he did fell far short of what he needed to do. Nevertheless, he did try to right his wrong. It is this picture, the picture of wrong repentance, that is discussed in the first part of this passage.

The second part of the passage pictures the humanistic religion of the priests. It discusses how they treated Judas' repentance and blood money, that is, the money they themselves had paid him for betraying Christ. The incident shows just how much man uses and twists religion to suit his own desires and lusts.

1. Jesus was condemned by the Sanhedrin (v.1-2).
2. Judas' wrong repentance (v.3-5).
   a. He saw his sin: Jesus was condemned.
   b. He repented, but to the priests not to God.
   c. He made restitution, but too late.
   d. He confessed, but to the priests not to God.
   e. He was not helped; he was left to himself.
   f. He cast the money at the priests.
   g. He fell into utter despair and hanged himself.
3. The religionists' human religion (v.6-10).
   a. They were inconsistent: in behavior and religious rules.
   b. They were deceptive: they tried to hide their evil by public service—bought a cemetary.

1 (27:1-2) **Jesus Christ, Trial—Sanhedrin**: Jesus was condemned by the Sanhedrin (see notes—Mt.26:57-68). They had met the evening before in a hastily called meeting to put Christ on trial for His life. They had secured the false witnesses and charges they sought. Now, in these verses, they are seen meeting to formulate the charges in such a way that the Romans would be forced to condemn Christ as a revolutionary. As soon as the charge was worded, they bound and led Christ away in an atmosphere of triumph.

The fact to note is that Judas apparently witnessed these unjust proceedings against Christ. He "saw that Jesus was condemned" (v.3), and it was his witnessing the unjust condemnation of Christ that led to the two events of the present passage.

2 (27:3-5) **Judas—Repentance**: Judas' wrong repentance. Judas did repent, but his repentance was a worldly repentance, not a godly repentance. Seven things are said about Judas.

1. Judas saw his sin; he saw Jesus condemned. Note the words, "When he saw that Jesus was condemned." It was seeing Jesus so unjustly condemned that caused Judas to do what he now did. He knew Christ, how good Christ was. He did not believe Jesus to be the Messiah, but he knew that Jesus was a tremendously good man, and he knew that it was because of his sin that Jesus was being condemned to death in a most unjust and savage way (see notes—

Mt.26:57-68). This fact—plus the fact that Jesus was definitely God's Son and that God was causing a sharp pang of guilt in the chest of Judas—drove Judas to seek relief. He felt boiling up within him an intense remorse and grief, the sense of being all alone, even without God, and a sense of not knowing what to do. It was too much, more than he could bear. He felt he would explode if he did not get relief of soul and some deliverance.

Note: Judas knew the religionists were seeking to kill Jesus. Apparently many knew of the plot (Jn.5:18; 7:1, 19-20). This was the very reason Judas went to the authorities and betrayed Christ into their hands. Some say there is a possibility that he thought sufficient charges could never be formulated against Christ. However, this is not likely, and Scripture gives no hint of this possibility. Jesus was a revolutionary. The religionists feared for their religion (Judaism), position, and security (see notes—Mt.12:1-8; note and DEEPER STUDY # 1—12:10; note—15:1-20; DEEPER STUDY # 2—15:6-9). Judas knew Christ was making changes, and when the authorities began to make their move, Judas set out to get what he could out of a bad situation. He wanted to assure his own safety and security (see outline and notes—Mt.26:14-16). The guilt and remorse boiling up within him seems to be the explanation for his deep conviction of sin and repentance.

When the people heard this, they were cut to the heart and said to Peter and the other apostles, "Brothers, what shall we do?" (Acts 2:37)

As Paul discoursed on righteousness, self-control and the judgment to come, Felix was afraid and said, "That's enough for now! You may leave. When I find it convenient, I will send for you." (Acts 24:25)

My guilt has overwhelmed me like a burden too heavy to bear. (Psa 38:4)

For I know my transgressions, and my sin is always before me. (Psa 51:3)

Thought 1. Believers see Christ condemned practically every day, that is, cursed, ridiculed, and abused by various people standing around talking. Such condemnation should convict us. Our silence should stir turmoil within our hearts. We need to speak up and take a position by the side of our Lord. Too many betray our Lord in such moments. Jesus is God's Son, and He deserves the utmost respect from every man.

2. Judas repented. However, he repented to the priests, not to God. Note the words "Judas...was seized with remorse...[and] returned to the chief priests and the elders." There is no mention of God at all. This was his mistake. Repentance means to change and to turn away from sin to God (see note and DEEPER STUDY # 1—Acts 17:29-30). Judas needed to change, to turn from his terrible sin. But he needed to turn to God, not to other men.

Repent of this wickedness and pray to the Lord. Perhaps he will forgive you for having such a thought in your heart. (Acts 8:22)

Let the wicked forsake his way and the evil man his thoughts. Let him turn to the LORD, and he will have mercy on him, and to our God, for he will freely pardon. (Isa 55:7)

"But if a wicked man turns away from all the sins he has committed and keeps all my decrees and does what is just and right, he will surely live; he will not die. (Ezek 18:21)

'Even now,' declares the LORD, 'return to me with all your heart, with fasting and weeping and mourning.' (Joel 2:12)

Thought 1. Sin should lead to repentance. When we sense *guilt* for real sin, we should repent and turn from the sin. *But to whom we turn* is the critical factor: we are to turn to God. Turning away from sin is not enough. Changing and turning our backs and walking away from sin is not enough. We must turn our faces toward God and walk with Him.

3. Judas made restitution. Judas did what God wants every man to do: make restitution for his sin. But he was too late. He should have made restitution while events could be changed. He should have shown a repentance to God and returned the money *before Christ was condemned.* It was too late now. Christ was already condemned, and his life was doomed.

Note that this was the second mistake Judas made. He repented to the priests, not to God; and here he made restitution, but too late.

Thought 1. We should make restitution for our sins, but we must act soon enough to make amends and to change events. We must act soon enough to save the situation. The first step, of course, is to repent before God; and then we can make restitution. But note, there is a right way and a wrong way to do both. Judas repented, but he repented in a wrong way. He turned in remorse to men instead of turning to God. He made restitution, but he made restitution too late. We must *turn to God and make restitution,* being sure to correct the situation soon enough.

Thought 2. Money and other things which are secured through evil ways will eat away at a person's mind and heart.

Your gold and silver are corroded. Their corrosion will testify against you and eat your flesh like fire. You have hoarded wealth in the last days. (James 5:3)

4. Judas confessed, but he confessed to the priests not to God. Note Judas' words, "I have sinned." But he was speaking to the chief priests and elders, not to God. Note something important: Judas accepted personal responsibility for his sin; he blamed no one else. He said, "I have sinned." His problem was that he went to men instead of going to God. He should have confessed his sin to God; instead, he carried his burden to men. He should have gone to God for relief and confession, for only God could have saved and relieved him.

Note: Judas was gripped with a worldly sorrow, not a godly sorrow (see DEEPER STUDY # 1—2 Cor.7:10).

If we confess our sins, he is faithful and just and will forgive us our sins and purify us from all unrighteousness. (1 John 1:9)

Now make confession to the LORD, the God of your fathers, and do his will. Separate yourselves from the peoples around you and from your foreign wives." (Ezra 10:11)

Only acknowledge your guilt—you have rebelled against the LORD your God, you

have scattered your favors to foreign gods under every spreading tree, and have not obeyed me,'" declares the LORD. (Jer 3:13)

Thought 1. Confession is essential if we wish forgiveness, but confession is to be made to God not to men.

Thought 2. We sin and are personally responsible for our own sin. No one else is responsible for our sin. Blame cannot be laid at anyone else's feet.

Thought 3. There is a wrong confession, a worldly sorrow, as well as a right confession, a godly sorrow (see DEEPER STUDY # 1—2 Cor.7:10).

5. Judas was not helped, and he was left to himself. Judas felt guilt, for he had betrayed Christ. The religionists did not feel guilt for they saw Christ as a threat to their religion and nation (Mt.12:1-8; 12:10; 15:1-20; 15:6-9). Therefore, in their minds, they were serving their religion (God) and their nation (God's chosen people). If Judas were bothered with a guilty conscience, he was a fool. They had no time, especially right now in the *busyness* of the moment. They did not have time to be concerned with a guilt stricken fool who could not see *the good* he had done in helping his nation and religion. Note the words of the religionists to Judas, and keep in mind that Judas was a man who was desperately crying out for help: "What is that to us? That's your responsibility."

Four terrible things are seen in the action and words of the religionists.

a. Hardness of heart: a hardness that keeps a man from helping those in need, even those who are desperate for help.
b. Misunderstanding the ministry: not understanding the true ministry and call of God which is to help people at any cost. (The religionists were the priests of God; yet instead of helping, they just left Judas to himself.)
c. Extreme blindness: a blindness of mind caused by rationalizing and twisting the truth. They were able to justify their behavior in their minds, so they were able to turn from Judas and to continue on in their sin of putting Christ to death.
d. Obstinate unbelief: unbelief that persists, that just marches on in its own will and way, rejecting and rejecting the truth (see DEEPER STUDY # 4—Mt.12:24; note—12:31-32).

But because of your stubbornness and your unrepentant heart, you are storing up wrath against yourself for the day of God's wrath, when his righteous judgment will be revealed. (Rom 2:5)

But encourage one another daily, as long as it is called Today, so that none of you may be hardened by sin's deceitfulness. (Heb 3:13)

Blessed is the man who always fears the LORD, but he who hardens his heart falls into trouble. (Prov 28:14)

A man who remains stiff-necked after many rebukes will suddenly be destroyed—without remedy. (Prov 29:1)

Thought 1. The mind can easily twist the truth and rationalize. It can easily take misbehavior and justify it. If we lust to do something, the mind can usually find a way to do it, a way that allows us to justify ourselves. But, just as the priests were guilty of terrible sin, so are we. No matter how much we rationalize and justify our behavior, the truth condemns us. The truth of righteousness cannot be changed.

Thought 2. *Busyness* to some degree kept the religionists from helping Judas. The claim is too often made that we are too busy to help. The first priority of ministry is to help those in need.

Thought 3. Note the four terrible things seen in the action of the religionists. They are applicable to many.

Thought 4. What would have happened if Judas had run up to Christ, begging forgiveness? If he had run to the disciples for help?

6. Judas threw the money at the feet of the priests. This was an act of frustration and anger, of hopelessness and helplessness. What could he do? The religionists were not going to change their verdict against Christ. Neither were they going to help him in his desperate need. In his mind, there was no one to help. He was stricken with guilt, standing all alone with no hand to help. Hopelessness and helplessness set in. In anger against the priests, he threw the blood money into the court at the feet of the priests and raced out of the temple into the streets of the city. He passed through the city gate into the country, seeking to escape his gnawing conscience, the glare of human eyes, and the haunting face of Him whom he had betrayed.

My God. My soul is downcast within me; therefore I will remember you from the land of the Jordan, the heights of Hermon—from Mount Mizar. (Psa 42:6)

But as for me, my feet had almost slipped; I had nearly lost my foothold. (Psa 73:2)

Do not run until your feet are bare and your throat is dry. But you said, 'It's no use! I love foreign gods, and I must go after them.' (Jer 2:25)

Thought 1. There is a fact that always needs to be remembered. When facing spiritual need, God is the One to whom we should turn, not man. The help of man in providing spiritual deliverance is empty. The end result of man's deliverance is always frustration, helplessness, and hopelessness. Man cannot erase guilt and liberate the anguished soul of man.

7. Judas fell into utter despair and hung himself. He was gripped by guilt, grief, despair, and helplessness. He was haunted and saw no hope. Left alone with his thoughts, he felt his sin was too terrible to be forgiven. He felt God could never forgive him for so great a sin. So he took his belt, and as Peter seems to indicate, tied it to an overhanging rock on a mountain precipice and hanged himself. The belt broke and Judas fell headlong, bursting his body open (Acts 1:18).

Note a significant fact: Judas' sin was not unpardonable. He could have been forgiven. Throughout history many murderers have been forgiven, but Judas make a common mistake, a mistake that is more clearly seen by being stated in several ways.

⇒ He felt his sin was too great to be forgiven.

⇒ He thought the mercy of God was limited, too small to forgive his sin.
⇒ He thought his sin was greater than the mercy of God.
⇒ He allowed his sin to overshadow and blot out the mercy of God.

"I loathe my very life; therefore I will give free rein to my complaint and speak out in the bitterness of my soul. (Job 10:1)
I sink in the miry depths, where there is no foothold. I have come into the deep waters; the floods engulf me. (Psa 69:2)
When I tried to understand all this, it was oppressive to me (Psa 73:16)
But Zion said, "The LORD has forsaken me, the Lord has forgotten me." (Isa 49:14)
Remember that at that time you were separate from Christ, excluded from citizenship in Israel and foreigners to the covenants of the promise, without hope and without God in the world. (Eph 2:12)

Thought 1. We should never abandon ourselves to despair nor become suffocated with grief. We should never be haunted with helplessness and hopelessness. Christ Jesus delivers and helps meet our need perfectly.

Thought 2. God's mercy is so great and so sufficient it will cover any sin. We just need to come to Him, confess and repent, then He will forgive and deliver us unto eternal life.

Thought 3. Note the difference between Judas and Peter. Both sinned against the Lord and regretted their sinful acts, but only Peter repented. He repented and was received by the Lord and recommissioned for service (Jn.21:15-17). But Judas gave up in utter despair and destroyed himself. Regret can lead to repentance or to remorse and destruction.

3 (27:6-10) **Religionists**: the religionists' human religion. These verses show just how the chief priests took their religion and twisted it to suit their own desires. The corruption of their lives and religion is clearly seen.

1. Their corruption is seen in their inconsistency. They were inconsistent in both their behavior and their religious rules. They held the position of serving God, yet they sought false witnesses against an innocent man and condemned Him to death (Mt.26:57-68). They claimed to be the servants of God, yet they turned away from ministering to a man (Judas) in desperate need. Neither their behavior nor their religion matched their profession.

They were also inconsistent in their religious rules. They took the money out of the temple treasury to pay a bribe, but they would not put the same money back into the treasury. They were careful to keep the religious rules that suited them, but they were loose in true justice and mercy.

The law said that money gained or used in an evil way was not acceptable for God's service (Dt.23:18). It was this rule that they haggled over, this rule that shows how inconsistent they had become in behavior and religion. They had taken the religion given by God and twisted it to suit their own wills and desires. They had developed a man-made religion that allowed them to do as they wished.

2. Their corruption is also seen in their deception. They tried to hide their evil by public service. They took the blood-money of Judas and purchased land for a public cemetary. The purpose of the religionists seems clear. They had hoped that such a service to the public would help in quieting any grumbling over the death of Christ. But note: their scheme failed. The public, discovering through talk and rumor that the field had been purchased with the blood-money of Jesus' betrayer, began to call the cemetary "the Field of Blood."

In the same way, on the outside you appear to people as righteous but on the inside you are full of hypocrisy and wickedness. (Mat 23:28)
God saw how corrupt the earth had become, for all the people on earth had corrupted their ways. (Gen 6:12)
And these also stagger from wine and reel from beer: Priests and prophets stagger from beer and are befuddled with wine; they reel from beer, they stagger when seeing visions, they stumble when rendering decisions. All the tables are covered with vomit and there is not a spot without filth. (Isa 28:7-8)
And have grown fat and sleek. Their evil deeds have no limit; they do not plead the case of the fatherless to win it, they do not defend the rights of the poor. (Jer 5:28)

DEEPER STUDY # 1

(27:9-10) **Old Testament Quotation**: this quotation is from Zech.11:12-13, not from Jeremiah. There are several explanations for Jeremiah's being credited with the statement. Two of the more reasonable explanations are as follows.

1. Some later writer added the word "Jeremiah" to the Scripture while making a copy. The word is omitted in the Syriac, Persic, and other Latin copies.

2. Many Hebrew manuscripts list Jeremiah as the first prophetic book. Matthew, unable to remember exactly where the prophecy was found, uses the first prophetic book, Jeremiah, to stand for the roll of the prophets. Jeremiah, by being the first prophet, represented the prophets.

K. The Messiah's Tragic Trial before Pilate: The Tragedy of an Indecisive Man,[DS1] **27:11-25**
(Mk.15:1-15; Lk.23:1-25; Jn.18:28-40)

1 He rejected the Lord's strong confession
- a. Jesus' strong & straightforward claim: He is King
- b. Jesus' strong & controlled behavior: Under severe accusation, He was silent & purposed
- c. Jesus' strong & enduring purpose: Under repeated questioning, He endured
- d. Jesus' impact: Pilate was impressed but still indecisive

2 He compromised clear evidence
- a. A custom of Rome to humor the Jews
- b. A notorious criminal: Barabbas
- c. Pilate's planned compromise: Offering Barabbas for Jesus
- d. Pilate's reason: He knew Jesus was innocent

3 He failed to listen to a strong warning

4 He ignored the influence of evil men upon people

5 He gave in to worldly pressure

6 He tried to escape responsibility for evil

7 The conclusion: The responsibility for Jesus' blood is cried out for by the Jews

11 Meanwhile Jesus stood before the governor, and the governor asked him, "Are you the king of the Jews?" "Yes, it is as you say," Jesus replied.
12 When he was accused by the chief priests and the elders, he gave no answer.
13 Then Pilate asked him, "Don't you hear the testimony they are bringing against you?"
14 But Jesus made no reply, not even to a single charge—to the great amazement of the governor.
15 Now it was the governor's custom at the Feast to release a prisoner chosen by the crowd.
16 At that time they had a notorious prisoner, called Barabbas.
17 So when the crowd had gathered, Pilate asked them, "Which one do you want me to release to you: Barabbas, or Jesus who is called Christ?
18 For he knew it was out of envy that they had handed Jesus over to him.
19 While Pilate was sitting on the judge's seat, his wife sent him this message: "Don't have anything to do with that innocent man, for I have suffered a great deal today in a dream because of him."
20 But the chief priests and the elders persuaded the crowd to ask for Barabbas and to have Jesus executed.
21 "Which of the two do you want me to release to you?" asked the governor "Barabbas," they answered.
22 "What shall I do, then, with Jesus who is called Christ?" Pilate asked. They all answered, "Crucify him!"
23 "Why? What crime has he committed?" asked Pilate. But they shouted all the louder, "Crucify him!"
24 When Pilate saw that he was getting nowhere, but that instead an uproar was starting, he took water and washed his hands in front of the crowd. "I am innocent of this man's blood," he said. "It is your responsibility!"
25 All the people answered, "Let his blood be on us and on our children!"

DIVISION XVI

THE MESSIAH'S ARREST, TRIAL, AND CRUCIFIXION, 26:1-27:66

K. The Messiah's Tragic Trial before Pilate: The Tragedy of an Indecisive Man, 27:11-25

(27:11-25) **Introduction**: Pilate's treatment of Jesus is better understood by referring to note three, which discusses Pilate himself (see DEEPER STUDY # 1—Mt.27:11-25). Despite his enormous and proven ability as a leader, he was indecisive as he stood before Christ. He knew Christ was innocent, for he saw no evil in Him (cp. Lk.23:22). Yet he had to tread carefully with the Jewish authorities lest he fall into their disfavor. If they reported him to Rome, he could lose his position and wealth.

In the behavior of Pilate is seen the picture and tragedy of an indecisive man. (Also see outline, notes, and DEEPER STUDY # 1—Mk.15:1-15; outline and notes Lk.23:1-25; Jn.18:28-19:15.)

1. He rejected the Lord's strong confession (v.11-14).
2. He compromised clear evidence (v.15-18).
3. He failed to listen to a strong warning (v.19).
4. He ignored the influence of evil men upon people (v.20).
5. He gave in to worldly pressure (v.21-23).
6. He tried to escape responsibility for evil (v.24).
7. Conclusion: the responsibility for Jesus' blood is cried out for by the Jews (v.25).

(27:11-25) **Another Outline**.

1. Pilate was amazed, was impressed with Jesus (v.11-14).
2. Pilate sought an escape for Jesus (v.15-18).
3. Pilate received a warning from his disturbed wife (v.19-21).
4. Pilate sought the counsel of a frenzied mob (v.20-23).
5. Pilate sought to unshoulder the responsibility (v.24-25).

DEEPER STUDY # 1

(27:11-25) **Pilate**: the procurator of Judaea. He was directly responsible to the Emperor for the administrative and financial management of the country. A man had to work himself up through the political and military ranks to become a procurator. Pilate was, therefore, an able man, experienced in the affairs of politics and government as well as the military. He had held office for ten years, which shows that he was deeply trusted by the Roman government. However, the Jews despised Pilate, and Pilate despised the Jews; in particular, he despised their intense practice of religion. When Pilate became procurator of Judaea, he did two things that aroused the people's bitter hatred against him forever. First, on his state visits to Jerusalem, he rode into the city with the Roman standard, an eagle sitting atop a pole. All previous governors had removed the standard because of the Jews' opposition to idols. Second, Pilate launched the construction of a new water supply for Jerusalem. To finance the project, he took the money out of the temple treasury. The Jews never forgot nor forgave this act. They bitterly opposed Pilate all through his reign, and he treated them with equal contempt (see note—Mk.15:9). On several occasions, Jewish leaders threatened to exercise their right to report Pilate to the emperor. This, of course, disturbed Pilate greatly, causing him to become even more bitter and contemptuous toward the Jews.

1 (27:11-14) **Jesus Christ, Trials**: Pilate (the indecisive man) rejected the Lord's clear confession. Paul refers to the Lord's strong confession before Pilate: "Christ Jesus, who while testifying before Pontius Pilate made the good confession" (1 Tim.6:13). Note the strength of that confession.

1. Jesus' strong, straightforward claim: He is King. This is one of the charges brought against Christ, that He claimed to be a King (Lk.23:2). Pilate, somewhat surprised, reacted scornfully, asking Christ: "Are you the King of the Jews?" Christ strongly claimed He was King: "Yes, it is as you say" (cp. Mt.26:25, 64. See esp. Jn.18:36-37.)

2. Jesus' strong, controlled behavior: under severe accusation, Jesus was silent and purposed (cp. Is.53:7). The religionists, fitfully aroused, accused and accused Jesus, yet He remained silent. Note His control and nobility. (a) He knew there was no need to argue with a close-minded person. He would not dignifiy their behavior by being drawn into argument with them. (b) He was purposed to do God's will by dying for the sins of the world. His hour to die had come. There was no need to argue, no need to try to escape death by argument. The depth of man's depravity was to be demonstrated for now. He would be noble: silent, purposed in His behavior.

3. Jesus' strong, enduring purpose: under repeated questioning He endured. Apparently Pilate wished to release Jesus (cp. v.18). He knew Jesus was innocent and to release Him would be a way to get at these contemptible religionists. Thus Pilate tried to get Jesus to answer the charges. He did not understand why Jesus would not answer, what Jesus was doing. All Jesus did was stand there, silent, portraying an image of strength, of some enduring purpose. But Pilate was unable to grasp its meaning.

4. Jesus' impact: Pilate was impressed, but still indecisive. He was amazed at Jesus' claim to be King and at His silence. Yet he still lacked the courage to make the right decision. He still waivered under the pressure of the accusers and failed to release Jesus.

> **"No one can serve two masters. Either he will hate the one and love the other, or he will be devoted to the one and despise the other. You cannot serve both God and Money. (Mat 6:24)**
>
> **You cannot drink the cup of the Lord and the cup of demons too; you cannot have a part in both the Lord's table and the table of demons. (1 Cor 10:21)**
>
> **He is a double-minded man, unstable in all he does. (James 1:8)**
>
> **Elijah went before the people and said, "How long will you waver between two opinions? If the LORD is God, follow him; but if Baal is God, follow him." But the people said nothing. (1 Ki 18:21)**

Thought 1. Christ has given man a strong confession.
1) A strong claim: He is King (Jn.18:36-37).
2) A strong, controlled behavior: perfection (Heb. 5:8-9; cp. 2 Cor.5:21).
3) A strong, enduring purpose: to die for the sins of the world (1 Pt.2:24; 3:18).

Thought 2. An indecisive man is just like Pilate: he rejects the clear confession of our Lord.

Thought 3. Christ teaches a lesson here about arguing. It is futile to argue with a close-minded or fitfully aroused person. To argue only dignifies their behavior.

Thought 4. Christ endured in His great purpose, even unto death. We must be just as enduring.

2 (27:15-18) **Indecision—Compromise—Pilate—Jesus Christ, Trials**: Pilate (the indecisive man) compromised clear evidence. Pilate saw the evidence. Jesus was innocent; the religionists were envious of Christ and His threat to their security (v.18). He wanted to declare Christ innocent, but he felt he had to satisfy the cries of these religious worldlings as well. Thus, he conceived a compromise. It was a long-time custom for Rome to release a prisoner to the Jews at the Passover Feast. By such, Rome sought to humor and secure more cooperation from the Jews. Within the prison was a notorious criminal, Barabbas. Pilate had him brought before the people along with Christ and shouted out that the people could choose which one was to be released. At this point Pilate walked back into the Judgment Hall giving the crowd time to decide (v.19).

Note two things.

1. Pilate was seeking a compromise. He was trying to declare Christ innocent and to please the worldlings who were accusing Christ. Despite the clear evidence that Christ was innocent, he still lacked the courage and decisiveness to take a stand for Christ.

2. Pilate fully expected the people to choose to release Christ. He thought his compromise had worked, for who would not choose a great teacher over a notorious criminal?

> **"He who is not with me is against me, and he who does not gather with me, scatters. (Luke 11:23)**
>
> **That all may honor the Son just as they honor the Father. He who does not honor the Son does not honor the Father, who sent him. "I tell you the truth, whoever hears my word and believes him who sent me has eternal life and will not be condemned; he has crossed over from death to life. (John 5:23-24)**
>
> **And this is the testimony: God has given us eternal life, and this life is in his Son. He who has the Son has life; he who does not have the Son of God does not have life. (1 John 5:11-12)**
>
> **Submit yourselves, then, to God. Resist the devil, and he will flee from you. Come near to God and he will come near to you.**

Wash your hands, you sinners, and purify your hearts, you double-minded. Grieve, mourn and wail. Change your laughter to mourning and your joy to gloom. Humble yourselves before the Lord, and he will lift you up. (James 4:7-10)

Thought 1. Two facts about the nature of man need to be noted.
1) Compromising with a man set on doing evil will not work. He will go on with his evil no matter the compromise. It is the way of nature.
2) Compromising when the evidence is clear will not work. It weakens character and principle and position.

Thought 2. We need to declare Christ innocent, declare loudly and clearly that He is the Son of God. This is not a day for indecision and compromise of the truth. Christ is King, perfectly innocent of sin and evil. We need to be decisive, to take a stand for Christ.

3 (27:19) **Warning—Pilate**: Pilate (the indecisive man) failed to listen to strong warning. While Pilate was sitting on his judgment seat waiting on the people's decision, his wife came to him. She had had a dream about Christ. Note three things.

1. She declared Jesus to be just, righteous. She was declaring that Christ was not only an innocent man, but a righteous and good man.
2. She warned there was something very unusual about Jesus, something that could cause suffering and sorrow. She warned Pilate that he must declare Jesus to be innocent or hereafter be sorry.
3. Pilate listened to the warning but still chose to seek a compromise, still lacked the courage to declare Christ innocent.

Thought 1. The indecisive man is warned: suffering and sorrow lie ahead. Judgment is coming upon any man who does not take his stand for Christ (Mt.10:32; Lk.12:8).

Thought 2. God uses many ways in His attempt to reach men. He used the dream of a wife to warn Pilate. He also warns us: we must be courageous, not indecisive. Today is the day of salvation.

For he says, "In the time of my favor I heard you, and in the day of salvation I helped you." I tell you, now is the time of God's favor, now is the day of salvation. (2 Cor 6:2)

But encourage one another daily, as long as it is called Today, so that none of you may be hardened by sin's deceitfulness. (Heb 3:13)

Now listen, you who say, "Today or tomorrow we will go to this or that city, spend a year there, carry on business and make money." (James 4:13)

4 (27:20) **Evil, Ignoring—Pilate**: Pilate (the indecisive man) ignored the influence of evil men upon people. The picture is tragic. Religious leaders were either moving or sending their emissaries among the people to influence them to do this evil deed—the deed of murdering Christ. All the while Pilate sat indecisively upon his throne, ignoring the reality of the situation.

As it is written: "God's name is blasphemed among the Gentiles because of you." (Rom 2:24)

While evil men and impostors will go from bad to worse, deceiving and being deceived. (2 Tim 3:13)

Who is the liar? It is the man who denies that Jesus is the Christ. Such a man is the antichrist—he denies the Father and the Son. No one who denies the Son has the Father; whoever acknowledges the Son has the Father also. I am writing these things to you about those who are trying to lead you astray. (1 John 2:22-23, 26)

Thought 1. Evil men will try to influence others in order to get their way. To ignore the fact is to hide one's head as an ostrich in the sand.

Thought 2. Indecision and compromise are not the way to stop the influence of evil men. Evil men will continue to influence people as long as we are indecisive and compromising.

Thought 3. The perfect innocency and righteousness of Christ must be proclaimed. Proclaiming His righteousness is the only way to stop the influence of evil men in the world. We cannot ignore the fact.

5 (27:21-23) **Pilate**: Pilate (the indecisive man) gave in to worldly pressure. The scene is again tragic. Pilate walked back out to the people for their decision. They shocked him, crying for the release of Barabbas and the crucifixion of Jesus.

Pilate had cornered himself, creating the most terrible dilemma imaginable. Stunned, somewhat in a state of shock, he cried back to the people, "Why? What crime has he committed?" But it was too late. The people, aroused by the worldly religionists, fitfully and repeatedly shouted back, "Crucify Him!" Note several things.

1. The people preferred an evil man to the Holy Man, preferred a man who *took* life to the Prince who *gave* life (cp. Acts 3:14-15).
2. Pilate was weak, indecisive, non-courageous throughout the whole episode. He would not act decisively; he would not courageously declare Christ to be what he knew: innocent.
3. The people asked for Jesus to be executed in the most horrible and painful way—by crucifixion. This was just as Christ had foretold (Mt.20:19).

Do not love the world or anything in the world. If anyone loves the world, the love of the Father is not in him. For everything in the world—the cravings of sinful man, the lust of his eyes and the boasting of what he has and does—comes not from the Father but from the world. (1 John 2:15-16)

Do not conform any longer to the pattern of this world, but be transformed by the renewing of your mind. Then you will be able to test and approve what God's will is—his good, pleasing and perfect will. (Rom 12:2)

By faith Moses, when he had grown up, refused to be known as the son of Pharaoh's daughter. He chose to be mistreated along with the people of God rather than to enjoy the pleasures of sin for a short time. (Heb 11:24-25)

Thought 1. The pressure of the world to do evil is great. Indecision and compromise are not the way to face the world: decisive dedication and separation are (Ro.12:1-2; 2 Cor.6:17-18; 1 Jn.2:15-16).

Thought 2. Most do prefer the company of evil, sinful men to that of the Prince of life. Note: even worldly religionists choose the worldly over the Prince of life.

Thought 3. Note a critical point. It is when we are indecisive or willing to compromise that the pressure of the world to do evil gets to us. Hesitating and being indecisive will cause us to give in to pressure and sin. We usually choose to go along with sin when we are indecisive.

6 (27:24) **Man, Weakness—Pilate**: Pilate (the indecisive man) tried to escape responsibility for evil. The picture is dramatic. Pilate was overruled by the people's choice. His own opinion availed nothing, had no influence whatsoever over Jesus' death. Thus he took a bowl of water and lifted it high; he washed his hands and dried them off. By such an act, Pilate was symbolizing two things.

1. He was declaring the innocence of Jesus.
2. He was washing his hands of the whole affair, declaring the people to be the guilty party in the death of Jesus.

But Pilate was not free of guilt. He was the governor, and he knew Christ was innocent of the charge. The responsibility to declare Jesus innocent was his, even if he had to override the accusers. Pilate had the authority and responsibility to do right, to see that justice was done.

This day I call heaven and earth as witnesses against you that I have set before you life and death, blessings and curses. Now choose life, so that you and your children may live (Deu 30:19)

Elijah went before the people and said, "How long will you waver between two opinions? If the LORD is God, follow him; but if Baal is God, follow him." But the people said nothing. (1 Ki 18:21)

Thought 1. We cannot wash our hands from guilt. If we act irresponsibly, we stand guilty. We stand guilty...

- for rejecting the Lord's strong confession.
- for compromising.
- for failing to listen to strong warning.
- for ignoring the influence of evil men.
- for giving in to worldly pressure.
- for trying to escape the responsibility for evil.

Thought 2. Everyone is responsible for his actions. Decisive action is what God calls for, decisive action that declares Christ to be innocent and righteous (2 Cor.5:21).

7 (27:25) **Jews—Israel**: the crowd cried out for the responsibility of Jesus' blood to be laid to their charge. This is a tragic and unbelievable scene. The mob cried out for God to hold them responsible for the death of Christ. The people did not know what they were saying, yet they were still killing Christ and still acting in an unjust, sinful, savage spirit. Because of their evil spirit against God's Son, all the evidence of history points toward their request's being granted.

⇒ Their nation and its capital, Jerusalem, were destroyed and taken from them.
⇒ Their people have been exiled and scattered for centuries.
⇒ Their very name is often the object of prejudice and hatred.
⇒ Annihilation of their race has been attempted time and again.

Amazingly, the Jewish people remain a nationality, yet the evoked vengeance has fallen upon them for centuries. Despite their terrible sin, the Jews hold a very special place in God's heart and plan. He will continue to hold them together as a race until the full number of the Gentiles has come in (cp. Ro.11:25f).

"Therefore I tell you that the kingdom of God will be taken away from you and given to a people who will produce its fruit. (Mat 21:43)

I tell you, not one of those men who were invited will get a taste of my banquet.'" (Luke 14:24)

He will come and kill those tenants and give the vineyard to others." When the people heard this, they said, "May this never be!" (Luke 20:16)

If some of the branches have been broken off, and you, though a wild olive shoot, have been grafted in among the others and now share in the nourishing sap from the olive root, (Rom 11:17)

My God will reject them because they have not obeyed him; they will be wanderers among the nations. (Hosea 9:17)

	L. The Messiah's Suffering & Crucifixion: A Picture of the World's Treatment of God's Son, *DS1* **27:26-44** (Mk.15:16-32; Lk.23:43; Jn.19:16-24)	34 There they offered Jesus wine to drink, mixed with gall; but after tasting it, he refused to drink it.	
		35 When they had crucified him, they divided up his clothes by casting lots.	m. They crucified Him n. They gambled His clothes away
		36 And sitting down, they kept watch over him there.	o. They sat down & stared at Him
1 The rulers passed judgment upon Christ	26 Then he released Barabbas to them. But he had Jesus flogged, and handed him over to be crucified.	37 Above his head they placed the written charge against him: THIS IS JESUS, THE KING OF THE JEWS.	p. They ridiculed His claim again
2 The soldiers mocked & tortured Christ a. They flogged Him b. They humiliated Him before a hundred or more soldiers	27 Then the governor's soldiers took Jesus into the Praetorium and gathered the whole company of soldiers around him.	38 Two robbers were crucified with him, one on his right and one on his left.	q. They crucified Him between two thieves
c. They stripped Him & put a scarlet robe on Him	28 They stripped him and put a scarlet robe on him,	39 Those who passed by hurled insults at him, shaking their heads	**3 The average persons, the passers-by, mocked & abused Christ**
d. They put a crown of thorns on His head & a staff in His hand	29 and then twisted together a crown of thorns and set it on his head. They put a staff in his right hand and knelt in front of him and mocked him.	40 And saying, "You who are going to destroy the temple and build it in three days, save yourself! Come down from the cross, if you are the Son of God!"	a. Mocked His power to destroy & rebuild the temple b. Mocked His claim to be God's Son
e. They bowed & ridiculed His claim to be King	"Hail, king of the Jews!" they said.	41 In the same way the chief priests, the teachers of the law and the elders mocked him.	**4 The religionists & government leaders mocked & taunted Christ**
f.. They spat upon Him g. They beat Him on the head with the staff	30 They spit on him, and took the staff and struck him on the head again and again.		a. Mocked His claim to be the Savior, to save others
h. They ridiculed Him & aggravated the wounds i. They forced Him to carry the cross until He was exhausted	31 After they had mocked him, they took off the robe and put his own clothes on him. Then they led him away to crucify him.	42 "He saved others," they said, "but he can't save himself! He's the King of Israel! Let him come down now from the cross, and we will believe in him.	b. Mocked His claim to be the King of Israel c. Mocked His claim to trust God perfectly
j. They enlisted a Gentile to help carry His cross	32 As they were going out, they met a man from Cyrene, named Simon, and they forced him to carry the cross.	43 He trusts in God. Let God rescue him now if he wants him, for he said, 'I am the Son of God.'"	d. Mocked His claim to be the Son of God
k. They escorted Him to a terrible place for execution l. They gave Him wine mixed with gall	33 They came to a place called Golgotha (which means The Place of the Skull).	44 In the same way the robbers who were crucified with him also heaped insults on him.	**5 The criminals mocked Christ**

DIVISION XVI

THE MESSIAH'S ARREST, TRIAL, AND CRUCIFIXION, 26:1-27:66

L. The Messiah's Suffering and Crucifixion: A Picture of the World's Treatment of God's Son, 27:26-44

(27:26-44) **Introduction—Jesus Christ, Death**: this Scripture covers the sufferings and crucifixion of our Lord. Matthew, in his organized way, presented a picture of the world's treatment of God's Son. He saw various classes of people, symbolizing the world, stand before Christ. Their treatment of Him was unbelievable and horrible. The people of *God's world* were not only rejecting God's Son, they were torturing and destroying Him.

1. There were the rulers: they passed judgment upon Christ—the judgment that He was a threat and must be destroyed (v.26).
2. There were the soldiers: they mocked and tortured Christ (v.26-38).
3. There were the average persons, the passers-by: they mocked and abused Christ (v.39-40).
4. There were the religionists and government leaders: they mocked and taunted Christ (v.41-43).
5. There were the criminals: they mocked Christ (v.44).

(27:26-44) **Another Outline**: The Crucifixion.

1. The flogging of Jesus (v.26).
2. The soldiers' horseplay and torture (v.27-31).
3. The journey to Golgotha—Simon of Cyrene (v.32-33).
4. The drugging (v.34).
5. The crucifixion (v.35).
6. The gambling for His clothes (v.35).
7. The title of accusation on the cross (v.36-37).
8. The two thieves (v.38).
9. The passers-by who taunted and mocked (v.39-43).
10. The thieves who taunted and mocked (v.44).

DEEPER STUDY # 1

(27:26-44) **Jesus Christ, Death**: the Lord's sufferings and torture were marked by Divine pain and human cruelty.

1. The divine pain of the Lord Jesus came from being fully conscious of the judgment He was to bear for man—separation from God (see note—Mt.27:46-49). The pressure of this hellish experience is seen in Gethsemane. Under great emotional stress, the tiny capillaries right under His skin which lined the sweat glands apparently gave way and burst. Jesus sweated great drops of blood. Such an experience causes marked weakness and sometimes a state of shock. The terrifying mystery of this hellish experience is seen in His cry upon the cross, "My God, my God, why have you forsaken me?" This was the point at which the great separation from God began (see notes—Mt.27:46-49; Eph.4:8-10; DEEPER STUDY # 1—1 Pt.3:19-20).

2. The physical torture He bore at the hands of men was abhorrent. Before the High Priest, an officer struck Jesus across the face (Jn.18:22). The palace guards blindfolded, mocked, spat upon, and slapped Him in the face; and they kept Him up all night (Lk.22:63-66).

Before Pilate, the Roman trial: His hands were tied to a post above His head and He was flogged (Jn.19:1). The prisoner was lashed until He was judged near death by the presiding centurion (Jewish trials allowed only forty lashes).

Still before Pilate: the guards called the whole band of soldiers together and began to mock His claim to be King of the Jews (Mk.15:16). They threw a robe around Him and continued to strike Him across the face. They took the scepter from His hand and used it to whip Him and to drive the thorns even deeper. Finally, they ceased this sadistic treatment and ripped the robe from His back. This tore open the dried blood caked to its lining. Excruciating pain followed (cp. Mt.27:28-31; Mk.15:16-20; Jn.10:1-5).

Bearing the cross itself: it was heavy, very heavy. He had to carry it up and down the streets of the city, taking a meandering route. The Romans did this as a living lesson to all that crime does not pay. Christ just broke down under the load; and Simon, the Cyrene, was forced to carry the cross for Him (Mt.27:32; Mk.15:21; Lk.23:26).

1 (27:26) **Sanhedrin—Pilate**: the rulers passed judgment. Christ was a threat; He must be destroyed. The Sanhedrin, both its religious and civil (elders) leaders, and Pilate passed judgment upon Christ. In their minds, Christ was a threat to them. Even Pilate gave in, despite his doubts, to the execution of Christ in order to preserve the peace of his rule and the security of his position (see outline, notes, and DEEPER STUDY # 1—Mt.27:11-25).

> **Thought 1.** Position, power, wealth, security, envy, and much more—all cause the powerful of this earth to seek to destroy Christ and His influence.

2 (27:26-38) **Jesus Christ, Suffering**: the soldiers mocked and tortured Christ. Their treatment included at least seventeen abuses.

1. They *flogged* Christ (v.26). He was stripped and beaten with a whip. This was a savage, excruciating punishment. The whip (phagellow) was made of leather straps with two small balls attached to the end of each strap. The balls were made of rough lead or sharp bones or spikes, so that they would cut deeply into the flesh. His hands were tied to a post above His head and He was flogged (Jn.19:1). It was the custom for the prisoner to be lashed until He was judged near death by the presiding centurion (Jewish trials allowed only forty lashes.) The criminal's back was, of course, nothing more than an unrecognizable mass of torn flesh.

> **Thought 1.** Two important facts.
>
> 1) Christ was being *punished* and *chastised for our sins*:
>
> **But he was pierced for our transgressions, he was crushed for our iniquities; the punishment that brought us peace was upon him, and by his wounds we are healed. (Isa 53:5)**
>
> 2) Christ suffered the punishment for our sins *willingly*:
>
> **I offered my back to those who beat me, my cheeks to those who pulled out my beard; I did not hide my face from mocking and spitting. (Isa 50:6)**

2. They humiliated Christ before a hundred or more soldiers (v.27). Note the words, "the whole company" (speiran). A *company* of soldiers usually meant a *cohort* which was made up of six hundred soldiers. However, "company" (speiran) sometimes meant maniple. Every cohort consisted of three maniples, about two hundred soldiers. Which is meant here is not known. Most believe the number of soldiers was large, certainly close to the two hundred serving in a maniple.

> **Thought 1.** Christ was humiliated and made a spectacle in order to save us. We are to become spectacles for Christ in order to reach some for Him.
>
> **For it seems to me that God has put us apostles on display at the end of the procession, like men condemned to die in the arena. We have been made a spectacle to the whole universe, to angels as well as to men. (1 Cor 4:9)**
>
> **Remember those earlier days after you had received the light, when you stood your ground in a great contest in the face of suffering. Sometimes you were publicly exposed to insult and persecution; at other times you stood side by side with those who were so treated. (Heb 10:32-33)**

3. They stripped Christ and put a scarlet robe on Him (v.28). Christ was stripped *naked and shamed* and made to appear *ridiculous* by being clad with a royal robe.

> **Thought 1.** Sin made man naked and shamed him (Gen.3:7). We are naked before Him who is to judge the world. Christ was stripped naked and shamed that He might secure clothing that is white and pure for us (that is, righteousness).
>
> **I counsel you to buy from me gold refined in the fire, so you can become rich; and white clothes to wear, so you can cover your shameful nakedness; and salve to put on your eyes, so you can see. (Rev 3:18; cp. Eph4:23-24)**

Thought 2. Christ *wore* (*bore*) the scarlet robe for us. The scarlet robe symbolized that He was to bear our sins.

1) Because He wore the scarlet robe of our sins, our sins can be as white as snow.

"Come now, let us reason together," says the LORD. "Though your sins are like scarlet, they shall be as white as snow; though they are red as crimson, they shall be like wool. (Isa 1:18)

2) Because He wore the scarlet robe of our sins, we can wash our robes in the blood of the lamb.

I answered, "Sir, you know." And he said, "These are they who have come out of the great tribulation; they have washed their robes and made them white in the blood of the Lamb. (Rev 7:14)

4. They put a crown of thorns on the head of Christ and a staff in His hands (v.29). A mock crown was made out of some limbs from a thorn bush and jammed upon His head. The thorns pierced through the skin of His brow and under His hair. Blood streamed down his head and face. A mock sceptre was made out of the weak, limber reed and thrust into His hand.

Thought 1. Thorns are a symbol of God's *curse* upon the earth, a result of sin (Gen.3:18). Christ was bearing the sin that brought about the curse. He became a curse for us.

Christ redeemed us from the curse of the law by becoming a curse for us, for it is written: "Cursed is everyone who is hung on a tree." (Gal 3:13)

Thought 2. Christ held the limber, weak staff, the staff that is so easily shaken with the wind (Mt.11:7), that wavers and withers and wastes away. He held the staff that symbolizes the weak kingdoms of the world, kingdoms that are so easily shaken and withered and wasted away. He held it as part of His sufferings so that He might secure an eternal sceptre, an eternal throne and kingdom.

But about the Son he says, "Your throne, O God, will last for ever and ever, and righteousness will be the scepter of your kingdom. (Heb 1:8)

5. They bowed and ridiculed the claim of Christ to be king (v.29). They ridiculed His claim to be king by *jokingly* bowing the knee before Him and mockingly shouting, "Hail, King of the Jews." They scorned Him as a sham king.

Thought 1. The day is coming when bowing the knee and confessing Christ to be Lord will be no joke. There will be no mocking and no scorning in that day.

Therefore God exalted him to the highest place and gave him the name that is above every name, that at the name of Jesus every knee should bow, in heaven and on earth and under the earth, and every tongue confess that Jesus Christ is Lord, to the glory of God the Father. (Phil 2:9-11)

6. They spat on Christ (v.30). (Cp. Is.50:6.) It was the custom for subjects to kiss their rulers as a sign of homage and allegiance. The soldiers gave the Lord a mock allegiance by spitefully spitting in His face.

Thought 1. Christ bore the spite, spitting, and mocking homage in order to deliver men from perishing. But the day has now come when the Lord is not to be spit upon, but kissed. He is to be given a genuine, not a mocking, allegiance.

Kiss the Son, lest he be angry and you be destroyed in your way, for his wrath can flare up in a moment. Blessed are all who take refuge in him. (Psa 2:12)

7. They beat Christ on the head with the staff (v.30). The Greek word for "struck Him" (etupton, imperfect tense) means they *kept on beating Him.* They took the staff, the mock scepter, and used it as a weapon, beating Him on the head continuously. They probably passed the staff from one soldier to another, giving many an opportunity to vent their folly and spite. He was bruised and bleeding, a horrible sight.

Thought 1. Two important facts.

1) **But he was pierced for our transgressions, he was crushed for our iniquities; the punishment that brought us peace was upon him, and by his wounds we are healed. (Isa 53:5)**
2) **Yet it was the Lord's will to crush him and cause him to suffer, and though the LORD makes his life a guilt offering, he will see his offspring and prolong his days, and the will of the LORD will prosper in his hand. (Isa 53:10)**

8. They stripped Christ of the kingly robe and put His own robe back on Him, aggravating the wounds. They were now ready to get to the matter at hand, His crucifixion. As they stripped the kingly robe off, two things happened.

a. The dried blood clinging to the robe ripped away from the wounds. As Christ suffered excruciating pain, His blood began to flow from the wounds again.
b. In removing the kingly robe, the soldiers were stripping Him of the authority they had given Him. It was just a mock authority and homage, but it had symbolized the attitude of the world toward paying homage to God's Son.

Thought 1. No man determines the authority of God's Son. He possesses authority because He is God's Son, not because man gives Him authority. God has given Him all authority and rule because He has borne the sufferings and death of the cross for man.

Then Jesus came to them and said, "All authority in heaven and on earth has been given to me. (Mat 28:18)

Moreover, the Father judges no one, but has entrusted all judgment to the Son, that all may honor the Son just as they honor the Father. He who does not honor the Son does not honor the Father, who sent him. (John 5:22-23)

Thought 2. "The blood of Jesus Christ, His (God's) Son, purifies us from all sin" (1 Jn.1:7).

9. They forced Christ to carry the cross until He was exhausted (v.32). The condemned criminal's carrying his own cross was the common practice. A centurion riding upon his stallion led the way. A herald followed, shouting out the criminal charges against the condemned. Immediately behind the herald was the condemned man bearing his cross and a small detachment of soldiers. The criminal had to carry his cross up and down through the streets of the city, taking a meandering route. The Romans did this as a living lesson to the citizens of a city that crime did not pay.

Thought 1. Note two important facts.
1) Man forced Christ to carry the cross to Golgotha. There is a spiritual symbol here. Spiritually, it is man's sin that forced Christ to bear the cross for man.

He himself bore our sins in his body on the tree, so that we might die to sins and live for righteousness; by his wounds you have been healed. (1 Pet 2:24)

2) God forced Christ to bear the cross for man.

This man was handed over to you by God's set purpose and foreknowledge; and you, with the help of wicked men, put him to death by nailing him to the cross. (Acts 2:23)

10. They enlisted a Gentile to help with the cross of Christ (v.32). Christ broke under the weight of the cross. This is not surprising, for He had just suffered so much...
- suffered the agony of the Garden.
- suffered the tension and excitement of the trials.
- suffered the ridicule and torture of the soldiers.

He had lost too much blood from the savage torture, and He had gone without food and sleep for hours. The soldiers had the legal authority to tap a bystander upon the shoulder and enlist the citizen to help with whatever load needed carrying. In this case, of course, they needed someone to carry the cross for Christ. They tapped Simon of Cyrene, and he bore the cross for Christ. It is an event used by God to change the life of Simon forever (see note—Mk.15:21).

Thought 1. Christ bore the cross for us that He might enlist us in the service of God. Even as He bore the cross, we are now to bear the cross for Him. Simon literally bore the cross, symbolizing that we are to bear the cross for Christ spiritually (see note—Lk.9:23).

Then he said to them all: "If anyone would come after me, he must deny himself and take up his cross daily and follow me. (Luke 9:23)

11. They escorted Christ to a terrible place for execution (v.33). The place was called Golgotha, the place of a skull. Why it was given this name is not known. But note that it was known as a place of death, of dead men's bones. It was a rugged place which stirred thoughts of death, of corruptible and decaying flesh. It was a terrible place to die.

Thought 1. Even the very place where Christ was crucified symbolized death itself. Every act seemed to point to His dying for the deliverance of man. Here upon Golgotha was the picture or thought of death, and here upon Golgotha He was to die to deliver all men from the bondage of death.

Since the children have flesh and blood, he too shared in their humanity so that by his death he might destroy him who holds the power of death—that is, the devil— and free those who all their lives were held in slavery by their fear of death. (Heb 2:14-15)

Thought 2. Christ was judged unworthy to live among the people of the world, so He was led out of the city and sent out of the world through execution. He was cast out of the vineyard (Mt.21:39). In the Old Testament, the sacrifice of animals took place outside the camp, and the blood was brought into the congregation. The Lamb of God was led outside the gate as a sheep is led to the slaughter.

The high priest carries the blood of animals into the Most Holy Place as a sin offering, but the bodies are burned outside the camp. And so Jesus also suffered outside the city gate to make the people holy through his own blood. (Heb 13:11-12)

Thought 3. He bore the disgrace of sin for us. We should, therefore, bear the disgrace of righteousness for Him.

Let us, then, go to him outside the camp, bearing the disgrace he bore. (Heb 13:13)

12. They gave Christ wine mixed with gall (v.34). It was the custom to give the criminal spiked wine right before he was raised on the cross. The spiked wine was a strong stupefying liquor used as a narcotic drink. Scripture foretold this event (Ps.69:21).

Thought 1. Christ came to do the will of God, to die as a sacrifice for man. He refused to do God's will unthoughtfully, with deadened senses and a semiconscious mind. He had work to do in sacrificing His life for man: He was to taste death for all men, and He would taste it in full consciousness and by being as mentally alert as possible.

But we see Jesus, who was made a little lower than the angels, now crowned with glory and honor because he suffered death, so that by the grace of God he might taste death for everyone. (Heb 2:9)

With burnt offerings and sin offerings you were not pleased. Then I said, 'Here I am—it is written about me in the scroll— I have come to do your will, O God.'" And by that will, we have been made holy through the sacrifice of the body of Jesus Christ once for all. (Heb 10:6-7, 10)

13. They crucified Christ (v.35). The crucifixion itself was the most horrible of deaths. The ancient writer, Tacitus, called it "a despicable death." Cicero called it "the most cruel and horrifying death." He simply said it was "incapable of description." There was the pain of the driven spikes forced through the flesh of Jesus' hands and feet or ankles. There was the weight of His body jolting and pulling against the spikes as the cross was lifted and rocked into place. There was the scorching sun and the unquenchable thirst gnawing away at His dry mouth and throat. There was the blood oozing from His flogged back, His thorn crowned brow, His feet, and His stick-beaten head. In addition, just imagine the aggravation of flies, gnats, and other insects. There was also the piercing of the spear thrust into His side. On and on the sufferings could be described. There has never been a more cruel form of execution than crucifixion upon a cross.

Thought 1. In the simplest of terms, Christ was crucified for our sins in order to bring us to God.

He himself bore our sins in his body on the tree, so that we might die to sins and live for righteousness; by his wounds you have been healed. (1 Pet 2:24)

For Christ died for sins once for all, the righteous for the unrighteous, to bring you to God. He was put to death in the body but made alive by the Spirit, (1 Pet 3:18)

14. They gambled for the clothes of Christ (v.35). Apparently, it was a custom for the executing soldiers to claim whatever they wished of the clothes of the crucified criminal. The soldiers stripped Christ and divided His clothes among themselves. His coat was valuable. It was seamless, one piece of cloth, woven from top to bottom just as the high Priest's coat or cloak was. The soldiers, therefore, decided to gamble by casting lots for it (Jn.19:23-24). This event was foretold in Ps.22:18.

Thought 1. Note two things.

1) Christ was stripped by the soldiers. But He stripped Himself of His glory in order to become man and die for us.

Since the children have flesh and blood, he too shared in their humanity so that by his death he might destroy him who holds the power of death—that is, the devil— and free those who all their lives were held in slavery by their fear of death. (Heb 2:14-15)

2) The coat was a symbol of Christ, *the Mediator*, the Pontifex, which means in Latin, *the bridge-builder* between God and man.

For there is one God and one mediator between God and men, the man Christ Jesus, who gave himself as a ransom for all men—the testimony given in its proper time. (1 Tim 2:5-6)

15. They sat down and stared at Christ (v.36). Death by crucifixion was usually slow, very slow. It sometimes took days for the sufferer to die from his agony. Hence, soldiers had to be posted to guard the sufferer to keep any friends from trying to save him from death. In dealing with Christ, the soldiers' horseplay and work in crucifying Him was now done. They had only to wait. They sat down and watched His hanging there. We can imagine what they saw by picturing what He looked like after all the torture and by reviewing the seven sayings of the cross. Jesus hung there naked, being stared at, the whole scene was a shameful sight. The embarrassment of the shame must have cut the heart of Christ to the core. The stare of the soldiers was prophesied (Ps.22:17).

Thought 1. Sin is the nakedness, the shame, of man. Sin strips man and makes him naked before God. The cross is the shame of Christ, yet He bore the shame of the cross for us.

I counsel you to buy from me gold refined in the fire, so you can become rich; and white clothes to wear, so you can cover your shameful nakedness; and salve to put on your eyes, so you can see. (Rev 3:18)

Let us fix our eyes on Jesus, the author and perfecter of our faith, who for the joy set before him endured the cross, scorning its shame, and sat down at the right hand of the throne of God. (Heb 12:2)

Thought 2. God, in His providence, saw that guards were posted around the cross. Why? So that there could never be any legitimate question about His Son's really dying.

Thought 3. What the honest and thinking soldier saw was a noble, righteous man being unjustly put to death.

And when the centurion, who stood there in front of Jesus, heard his cry and saw how he died, he said, "Surely this man was the Son of God!" (Mark 15:39)

16. They shamed Christ and disgraced His claim again (v.37). It was the custom for the charges against a crucified criminal to be written out on a board and nailed to the cross above his head. This served both as information and as a warning to the public. It, of course, added shame and reproach to the crucified sufferer. In Christ's case, the charges were written in three different languages (Jn.19:20). Note the exact words, "This is Jesus the King of the Jews." This inscription disturbed the religious leaders. They went to Pilate and said, "Do not write, 'the King of the Jews,' but that this man claimed to be King of the Jews." Pilate simply answered, "What I have written, I have written" (Jn.19:21-22).

Thought 1. God overruled the shame and disgrace of our Lord. God saw to it that the very charges against Him proclaimed His deity and honor. He was proclaimed King in three languages, languages which symbolized the world: the Aramaic (Jews), the Latin (the Gentiles), and the Greek (the intellectual Jew and Gentile).

And being found in appearance as a man, he humbled himself and became obedient to death— even death on a cross! Therefore God exalted him to the highest

place and gave him the name that is above every name, that at the name of Jesus every knee should bow, in heaven and on earth and under the earth, and every tongue confess that Jesus Christ is Lord, to the glory of God the Father. (Phil 2:8-11)

To keep this command without spot or blame until the appearing of our Lord Jesus Christ, which God will bring about in his own time—God, the blessed and only Ruler, the King of kings and Lord of lords, who alone is immortal and who lives in unapproachable light, whom no one has seen or can see. To him be honor and might forever. Amen. (1 Tim 6:14-16)

17. They added shame and disgrace by crucifying Christ between two thieves (v.38). Perhaps this was a day set aside for execution. Or perhaps the Jewish leaders pressed Pilate to execute Jesus with other criminals. Such would add weight to their position that He was no more than a mere man, an imposter who deserved to die just as other criminals. Whatever the reason, the fact that the Son of God was executed right along with other criminals added to the shame and disgrace He bore. Again, this event had been prophesied (Is.53:12).

Thought 1. Christ was counted as a sinner that He might bear the sin of many.

Therefore I will give him a portion among the great, and he will divide the spoils with the strong, because he poured out his life unto death, and was numbered with the transgressors. For he bore the sin of many, and made intercession for the transgressors. (Isa 53:12)

Here is a trustworthy saying that deserves full acceptance: Christ Jesus came into the world to save sinners—of whom I am the worst. (1 Tim 1:15)

3 (27:39-40) **Jesus Christ, Mocked**: the average persons and the passers-by mocked and abused Christ. There were a large number of passers-by (Jn.19:20). Golgotha was close to the city, sitting on a hill that was probably close to a main road and a large gate leading into the city.

First, only Christ was mocked and abused; the two criminals were not. No abuse was heaped upon them. The murderers of the Lord were not satisfied with His death; they were filled with enmity and a bitterness that sought revenge and humiliation. Therefore, they sowed the seeds of enmity and mockery among those who passed by, and they too were caught up in the excitement of the sin and shame of the evil crowd.

Second, the passers-by saw Christ's hanging there, believing He had claimed to be a King. Being spurred on by His accusers, they hurled insults at Him. The word for hurl insult (blasphemoun) is strong, meaning to blaspheme, profane, rail at. They also shook their heads at Him. This was a gesture of that day which showed insult, contempt, and mockery.

The passers-by mocked Christ for two things: His claim to have the power to destroy and rebuild the temple (see note—Mt.26:60-61), and His claim to be the Son of God (Mt.26:64). Note that the crowd used the very same words that the devil had tempted Jesus with at the begining of His ministry: "If you are the Son of God" (Mt.4:6).

Thought 1. Too many curse and profane Christ when they hear about the claim that He makes upon their lives as the Messiah, the Son of God. The reaction of most men was predicted generations ago.

All who see me mock me; they hurl insults, shaking their heads: (Psa 22:7)

I am an object of scorn to my accusers; when they see me, they shake their heads. (Psa 109:25)

Thought 2. Christ possessed the deity and all the dignity, power, and riches of God. Yet for our sake, He became weak and poor for us. He surrendered to the mockery and abuse of men in order to die.

For to be sure, he was crucified in weakness, yet he lives by God's power. Likewise, we are weak in him, yet by God's power we will live with him to serve you. (2 Cor 13:4)

For you know the grace of our Lord Jesus Christ, that though he was rich, yet for your sakes he became poor, so that you through his poverty might become rich. (2 Cor 8:9)

Thought 3. The average person, the passer-by, often mocks and abuses Christ. How?

⇒ By ridiculing Christ's claim to be the Son of God.
⇒ By cursing and profaning the name of Christ.
⇒ By challenging Christ to prove His power by meeting his needs when he has not lived for Christ.
⇒ By acting worse toward Christ and His followers than toward the rest of society, even criminals.

4 (27:41-43) **Jesus Christ, Mocked**: the religionists and government leaders (elders) mocked and taunted Christ. Men of religion and government should be above this kind of behavior. However, being part of a sinful unbelieving crowd, men filled with enmity and bitterness are led to do shameful things. These leaders ridiculed the four major claims of Christ:

⇒ that He was the Savior
⇒ that He was the King
⇒ that He was the Son of Man who trusted God perfectly
⇒ that He was the Son of God

Their purpose was to vent their enmity and humiliate Christ, hoping to reinforce in the minds of the crowd that He was an imposter and deceiver. The religionists completely misunderstood God's Messiah, even the Lord Jesus Christ.

Here is a trustworthy saying that deserves full acceptance: Christ Jesus came into the world to save sinners—of whom I am the worst. (1 Tim 1:15)

For there is one God and one mediator between God and men, the man Christ Jesus, who gave himself as a ransom for all men—the testimony given in its proper time. (1 Tim 2:5-6)

Thought 1. Christ was all that He claimed to be.
1) The Savior.

For the Son of Man came to seek and to save what was lost." (Luke 19:10. See note—Mt 8:20)

2) The King.

Meanwhile Jesus stood before the governor, and the governor asked him, "Are you the king of the Jews?" "Yes, it is as you say," Jesus replied. (Mat 27:11)

"You are a king, then!" said Pilate. Jesus answered, "You are right in saying I am a king. In fact, for this reason I was born, and for this I came into the world, to testify to the truth. Everyone on the side of truth listens to me." (John 18:37)

3) The Son of Man who trusted God perfectly.

"My food," said Jesus, "is to do the will of him who sent me and to finish his work. (John 4:34)

By myself I can do nothing; I judge only as I hear, and my judgment is just, for I seek not to please myself but him who sent me. (John 5:30)

So if the Son sets you free, you will be free indeed. (John 8:36)

4) The Son of God.

"For God so loved the world that he gave his one and only Son, that whoever believes in him shall not perish but have eternal life. For God did not send his Son into the world to condemn the world, but to save the world through him. Whoever believes in him is not condemned, but whoever does not believe stands condemned already because he has not believed in the name of God's one and only Son. (John 3:16-18)

What about the one whom the Father set apart as his very own and sent into the world? Why then do you accuse me of blasphemy because I said, 'I am God's Son'? (John 10:36)

Thought 2. Leaders, civil and religious, are still men. It is not the position or profession that makes a man, but the heart. A heart of unbelief and enmity, a heart willing to become a participant with the sinful crowd will stoop to do shameful things, no matter the position or profession.

Thought 3. If Christ had used His power to save Himself, what would have happened to our salvation?

5 (27:44) **Jesus Christ, Mocked**: the criminals mocked Christ. The picture of the thieves joining in the mockery of Christ shows...

- the intensity of the ridicule and abuse.
- the bitterness and enmity against Christ within hearts.
- the depraved heart of a man who lets loose in a crowd, even when he is facing, or is going to face, punishment.
- the depth of shame to which men will stoop.

When they hurled their insults at him, he did not retaliate; when he suffered, he made no threats. Instead, he entrusted himself to him who judges justly. He himself bore our sins in his body on the tree, so that we might die to sins and live for righteousness; by his wounds you have been healed. (1 Pet 2:23-24)

Outline	Scripture
	M. The Messiah's Great Triumph: The Miraculous Events Surrounding the Cross, 27:45-56 (Mk.15:33-41; Lk.23:44-49; Jn.19:30-37)
1 The terrifying darkness a. For three hours b. Over all the land	45 From the sixth hour until the ninth hour darkness came over all the land.
2 The mysterious loud cry a. The great separation—God forsook Him	46 About the ninth hour Jesus cried out in a loud voice, "Eloi, Eloi, lama sabachthani?"—which means, "My God, my God, why have you forsaken me?"
b. The cry misunderstood	47 When some of those standing there heard this, they said, "He's calling Elijah."
1) One showed compassion	48 Immediately one of them ran and got a sponge. He filled it with wine vinegar, put it on a stick, and offered it to Jesus to drink.
2) Others superstitiously mocked	49 The rest said, "Now leave him alone. Let's see if Elijah comes to save him."
3 The great shout of triumph & the yielding up of Jesus' spirit	50 And when Jesus had cried out again in a loud voice, he gave up his spirit.
4 The great curtain or veil of the temple torn: From top to bottom	51 At that moment the curtain of the temple was torn in two from top to bottom.
5 The terrifying earthquake	The earth shook and the rocks split.
6 The resurrection of many holy people	52 The tombs broke open and the bodies of many holy people who had died were raised to life. 53 They came out of the tombs, and after Jesus' resurrection they went into the holy city and appeared to many people.
7 The confession of the centurion & others	54 When the centurion and those with him who were guarding Jesus saw the earthquake and all that had happened, they were terrified, and exclaimed, "Surely he was the Son of God!"
8 The courage & love of the women a. Many women	55 Many women were there, watching from a distance. They had followed Jesus from Galilee to care for his needs.
b. Some identified	56 Among them were Mary Magdalene, Mary the mother of James and Joses, and the mother of Zebedee's sons.

DIVISION XVI

THE MESSIAH'S ARREST, TRIAL, AND CRUCIFIXION, 26:1-27:66

M. The Messiah's Great Triumph: The Miraculous Events Surrounding the Cross, 27:45-56

(27:45-56) **Introduction**: while Christ hung on the cross, some miraculous events happened—events which demonstrated perfectly that the cross was a triumph, not a tragedy. The cross was the Messiah's great triumph. Eight events show this clearly.

1. The terrifying darkness (v.45).
2. The mysterious, loud cry (v.46-49).
3. The great shout of triumph and the yielding up of Jesus' spirit (v.50).
4. The great curtain or veil of the temple torn: from top to bottom (v.51).
5. The terrifying earthquake (v.51).
6. The resurrection of many holy people (v.52-53).
7. The confession of the centurion and others (v.54).
8. The courage and love of the women (v.55-56).

1 (27:45) **Jesus Christ, Death—Earth, Darkness**: the terrifying darkness. A supernatural darkness hung over the land from the sixth to the ninth hour, or according to our time from noon to 3 p.m.

Think for a moment. Just imagine...

Who it was hanging on the cross...

- God's only Son, the Sovereign Lord of all beings, both visible and invisible (cp. Col.1:16).
- The great architect and creator of the whole universe, of all nature.

What He was doing there on the cross...

- Bearing the sins of all men.
- Bearing the judgment and wrath of God against sin *for all men.*
- Dying the death of man for all men.
- Doing all that was necessary to free men from sin, death, and judgment so that they might live forever.

What the depth of God's plan is...

> **Oh, the depth of the riches of the wisdom and knowledge of God! How unsearchable his judgments, and his paths beyond tracing out! "Who has known the mind of the Lord? Or who has been his counselor?" "Who has ever given to God, that God should repay him?" For from him and through him and to him are all things. To him be the glory forever! Amen. (Rom 11:33-36)**

When one really meditates upon the facts, is there any wonder that all things, including nature itself, were drastically affected by the death of God's Son? The darkness demonstrated and symbolized several things.

1. The darkness demonstrated that Christ was definitely God's Son. Before Him, all mouths are to be stopped in fear and reverence. There is no doubt that fear and wonder stopped the mocking mouths of the crowd standing around the cross. There is no mention of jeering taking place during these hours. The crowd was stricken with a sense of terror, wondering just what was happening (v.54).

He took Peter, James and John along with him, and he began to be deeply distressed and troubled. (Mark 14:33)

"For God so loved the world that he gave his one and only Son, that whoever believes in him shall not perish but have eternal life. For God did not send his Son into the world to condemn the world, but to save the world through him. Whoever believes in him is not condemned, but whoever does not believe stands condemned already because he has not believed in the name of God's one and only Son. (John 3:16-18)

And being found in appearance as a man, he humbled himself and became obedient to death—even death on a cross! Therefore God exalted him to the highest place and gave him the name that is above every name, that at the name of Jesus every knee should bow, in heaven and on earth and under the earth, and every tongue confess that Jesus Christ is Lord, to the glory of God the Father. (Phil 2:8-11)

2. The darkness symbolized the darkest day of human history. This was the day when the Son of God Himself was being put to death for the sins of men.

He himself bore our sins in his body on the tree, so that we might die to sins and live for righteousness; by his wounds you have been healed. (1 Pet 2:24)

For Christ died for sins once for all, the righteous for the unrighteous, to bring you to God. He was put to death in the body but made alive by the Spirit, (1 Pet 3:18)

3. The darkness symbolized the darkness of sin:
   ⇒ sin which demands darkness to carry on its acts.

This is the verdict: Light has come into the world, but men loved darkness instead of light because their deeds were evil. Everyone who does evil hates the light, and will not come into the light for fear that his deeds will be exposed. But whoever lives by the truth comes into the light, so that it may be seen plainly that what he has done has been done through God." (John 3:19-21)

⇒ sin which leads to the most terrible darkness of all—death.

For the wages of sin is death, but the gift of God is eternal life in Christ Jesus our Lord. (Rom 6:23)

4. The darkness symbolized the darkness of the human soul and its works. The darkness of the human soul was now being borne by the Son of God—all for man.

So Christ was sacrificed once to take away the sins of many people; and he will appear a second time, not to bear sin, but to bring salvation to those who are waiting for him. (Heb 9:28)

As for you, you were dead in your transgressions and sins, in which you used to live when you followed the ways of this world and of the ruler of the kingdom of the air, the spirit who is now at work in those who are disobedient. All of us also lived among them at one time, gratifying the cravings of our sinful nature and following its desires and thoughts. Like the rest, we were by nature objects of wrath. But because of his great love for us, God, who is rich in mercy, made us alive with Christ even when we were dead in transgressions—it is by grace you have been saved. But now in Christ Jesus you who once were far away have been brought near through the blood of Christ. (Eph 2:1-5, 13)

But I am a worm and not a man, scorned by men and despised by the people. (Psa 22:6)

5. The darkness symbolized the withdrawal of the light of God's presence from the sinner. Christ hung upon the cross as the sinner—all for us—the sinner who was becoming sin for us.

About the ninth hour Jesus cried out in a loud voice, "Eloi, Eloi, lama sabachthani?"—which means, "My God, my God, why have you forsaken me?" (Mat 27:46)

God made him who had no sin to be sin for us, so that in him we might become the righteousness of God. (2 Cor 5:21)

6. The darkness symbolized the anger of God at sin. Sin and the sinner deserve nothing but the judgment of darkness. Sin deserves no light from God's presence, none whatsoever.

Christ redeemed us from the curse of the law by becoming a curse for us, for it is written: "Cursed is everyone who is hung on a tree." (Gal 3:13)

My dear children, I write this to you so that you will not sin. But if anybody does sin, we have one who speaks to the Father in our defense—Jesus Christ, the Righteous One. He is the atoning sacrifice for our sins, and not only for ours but also for the sins of the whole world. (1 John 2:1-2)

Surely he took up our infirmities and carried our sorrows, yet we considered him stricken by God, smitten by him, and afflicted. But he was pierced for our transgressions, he was crushed for our iniquities; the punishment that brought us peace was upon him, and by his wounds we are healed. We all, like sheep, have gone astray, each of us has turned to his own way; and the LORD has laid on him the iniquity of us all. (Isa 53:4-6)

2 (27:46-49) **Jesus Christ, Separated from God**: the mysterious, loud cry: "My God, my God, why have you forsaken me." This was the great separation, the moment when God forsook Christ, His only Son. What is the meaning of this shocking statement? The very idea that God could and would "forsake" His only Son staggers the human mind. Yet Christ shouted out: "My God, my God, why have you forsaken me?" The meaning cannot be ventured into lightly. The meaning requires reverence and much prayerful thought. But even then, even after an eternity of prayerful thought. But even then, even after an eternity of prayerful thought, the depth of the meaning remains fathomless and unreachable to man. (See note—Mt.20:19.)

Scripture indicates at least the following meanings.

1. "Why have you forsaken me?" Jesus sensed that God had withdrawn His presence from Him. He sensed that God was no longer with Him.

2. "Why have you forsaken me?" Jesus sensed that God had withdrawn His deliverance. Always in the past when Jesus was troubled, God had met His need. For example, God had sent a voice from heaven to assure Him (Jn.12:27-28); and when He was facing the cup in the garden of Gethsemane, God had even sent an angel to strengthen Him. But now, hanging upon the cross, God had forsaken Him. There was no deliverance from God. He was left all alone.

3. "Why have you forsaken me?" Jesus sensed that He was bearing the *curse* of God, the curse of separation from God, the curse of the judgment and condemnation of God against sin (cp. Ga.3:13. See DEEPER STUDY # 1—Heb.9:27.)

4. "Why have you forsaken me?" Jesus sensed that God's life and holiness had left Him, that He had been delivered into the hands of the enemies of life and holiness, that is, into the hands of sin and death. He was being made sin and having to die. And both sin and death were foreign to God, alien to God's nature which is life and holiness. Both sin and death stood as enemies of God and enemies to all that belonged to God.

⇒ In becoming sin and in dying, Christ experienced all that was contrary to the nature of God—all that was involved in God's separating Himself from sin and death. (See DEEPER STUDY # 1—Jn.10:10; DEEPER STUDY # 1—17:2-3. Cp. 2 Cor.5:21; Heb.2:14-15. Cp. Col.2:15 with Eph.6:12 and note—Eph.4:8-10; DEEPER STUDY # 1—1 Pt.3:19-20.)

Jesus' cry was prophesied in Ps.22:1. The reason God had to forsake Jesus is given in Ps.22:3: "You are…the Holy One." Jesus had "become sin" for many (2 Cor.5:21).

⇒ Christ bore sin for man; therefore, He had to bear the penalty due man—the penalty of separation from a perfectly holy God (see note and DEEPER STUDY # 2—Mt.26:37-38; DEEPER STUDY # 4—26:39). In all the mystery of His death, Scripture proclaims: "He himself [Jesus] bore our sins in His body on the tree…." (1 Pt.2:24).

Note that some of the crowd misunderstood the words of Jesus' cry. One had compassion and sought to help Him by giving Him a drink. But others stopped the man and superstitiously mocked by demanding that He be left alone to see if Elijah would come to save Him.

> **God made him who had no sin to be sin for us, so that in him we might become the righteousness of God. (2 Cor 5:21)**
>
> **Christ redeemed us from the curse of the law by becoming a curse for us, for it is written: "Cursed is everyone who is hung on a tree." (Gal 3:13)**
>
> **But we see Jesus, who was made a little lower than the angels, now crowned with glory and honor because he suffered death, so that by the grace of God he might taste death for everyone. (Heb 2:9)**
>
> **So Christ was sacrificed once to take away the sins of many people; and he will appear a second time, not to bear sin, but to bring salvation to those who are waiting for him. (Heb 9:28)**
>
> **For zeal for your house consumes me, and the insults of those who insult you fall on me. (Psa 69:9)**
>
> **But he was pierced for our transgressions, he was crushed for our iniquities; the punishment that brought us peace was upon him, and by his wounds we are healed. (Isa 53:5)**
>
> **Therefore I will give him a portion among the great, and he will divide the spoils with the strong, because he poured out his life unto death, and was numbered with the transgressors. For he bore the sin of many, and made intercession for the transgressors. (Isa 53:12)**

3 (27:50) **"It is finished"**: the great shout of triumph and the yielding up of Jesus' spirit. There are three important points here.

1. Jesus cried, "It is finished" (Jn.19:30). The Greek word *tetelestai* is the shout of victorious purpose. Christ had completed His work, mission, and task. He was not crying the cry of a defeated martyr; He was crying the cry of a victorious conqueror.

2. "He gave up his spirit" (apheken to pneuma) means that He willingly yielded and gave up His spirit. It must always be remembered that Jesus *willingly* died. He willingly came to this moment of yielding and giving up His spirit unto death. Both Paul and Peter cover the Lord's work during the three days immediately following His death until the resurrection.

a. On the cross:

> **And having disarmed the powers and authorities, he made a public spectacle of them, triumphing over them by the cross. (Col 2:15. Cp. Eph.6.12)**

b. On the cross and after death:

> **For Christ died for sins once for all, the righteous for the unrighteous, to bring you to God. He was put to death in the body but made alive by the Spirit, through whom also he went and preached to the spirits in prison who disobeyed long ago when God waited patiently in the days of Noah while the ark was being built. In it only a few people, eight in all, were saved through water, (1 Pet 3:18-20. See note—1 Pet 3:19-20)**

c. After death:

> **This is why it says: "When he ascended on high, he led captives in his train and gave gifts to men." (What does "he ascended" mean except that he also descended to the lower, earthly regions ? He who descended is the very one who ascended higher than all the heavens, in order to fill the whole universe.) (Eph 4:8-10. See note—Eph 4:8-10)**

3. Christ died at the ninth hour, that is, 3:00 p.m. (v.45, 50). This was the very hour when the priests began to make the evening offering of the Passover Lamb. While the priests were going about sacrificing the symbolic lamb for the people, the true Lamb of God was being sacrificed for the people's sins outside the city walls (1 Cor.5:7; Heb.13:12).

4 (27:51) **Curtain—Veil Torn**: the great curtain or veil of the temple was torn from top to bottom. In the minds of the Jews, the curtain or veil was one of the most important things in the temple. Why? Because it surrounded the ark of the covenant which symbolized the very presence of God Himself. It was huge and beautiful, made of the very finest materials. It was sixty or more feet high. To get some idea of the magnificence of the curtain or veil, imagine one of the other temple veils described by Josephus:

> "...before these doors there was a veil of equal largeness with the doors. It was embroidered with blue and fine linen, and scarlet, and purple, and of a contexture that was truly wonderful. This mixture of colors [had] its mystical interpretation, but [it] was a kind of image of the universe; for by the scarlet, there seemed to be signified fire, by the fine flax the earth, by the blue the air and by the purple the sea....This curtain had also embroidered upon it all that was mystical in the heavens" (Josephus, Wars. 5. 5:4).

The significant point to note is that the curtain or veil was torn from top to bottom. This symbolizes that it was torn by an act of God himself. It symbolizes direct access to God (Heb.6:19; 9:3-12, 24; 10:19-23). It was the curtain or veil that separated the Most Holy Place from the Holy Place. Up until this time, only the High Priest could enter the Most Holy Place; and He could enter only one day a year, the Day of Atonement (Ex.26:33). Now through the body of Christ, any man can enter the presence of God. He can enter God's presence and pray any time, any place.

> **For he himself is our peace, who has made the two one and has destroyed the barrier, the dividing wall of hostility, by abolishing in his flesh the law with its commandments and regulations. His purpose was to create in himself one new man out of the two, thus making peace, (Eph 2:14-15)**
>
> **We have this hope as an anchor for the soul, firm and secure. It enters the inner sanctuary behind the curtain, where Jesus, who went before us, has entered on our behalf. He has become a high priest forever, in the order of Melchizedek. (Heb 6:19-20)**
>
> **For Christ did not enter a man-made sanctuary that was only a copy of the true one; he entered heaven itself, now to appear for us in God's presence. (Heb 9:24)**
>
> **And by that will, we have been made holy through the sacrifice of the body of Jesus Christ once for all. (Heb 10:10)**
>
> **Therefore, brothers, since we have confidence to enter the Most Holy Place by the blood of Jesus, by a new and living way opened for us through the curtain, that is, his body, and since we have a great priest over the house of God, let us draw near to God with a sincere heart in full assurance of faith, having our hearts sprinkled to cleanse us from a guilty conscience and having our bodies washed with pure water. Let us hold unswervingly to the hope we profess, for he who promised is faithful. (Heb 10:19-23)**

5 (27:51) **Earthquake**: the terrifying earthquake. The symbolism could be threefold.

1. The earth could have quaked under the weight of the sin placed upon its Architect and Creator.

> **He himself bore our sins in his body on the tree, so that we might die to sins and live for righteousness; by his wounds you have been healed. (1 Pet 2:24)**
>
> **But he was pierced for our transgressions, he was crushed for our iniquities; the punishment that brought us peace was upon him, and by his wounds we are healed. (Isa 53:5)**

2. The earth could have quaked and torn at its rocks to symbolize the fatal blow to Satan's domain.

> **Now is the time for judgment on this world; now the prince of this world will be driven out. But I, when I am lifted up from the earth, will draw all men to myself." (John 12:31-32)**
>
> **And having disarmed the powers and authorities, he made a public spectacle of them, triumphing over them by the cross. (Col 2:15)**
>
> **Since the children have flesh and blood, he too shared in their humanity so that by his death he might destroy him who holds the power of death—that is, the devil— and free those who all their lives were held in slavery by their fear of death. (Heb 2:14-15)**

3. The earth could have quaked to symbolize that it, too, is stirred to await the glorious day of redemption.

> **That the creation itself will be liberated from its bondage to decay and brought into the glorious freedom of the children of God. (Rom 8:21)**
>
> **But the day of the Lord will come like a thief. The heavens will disappear with a roar; the elements will be destroyed by fire, and the earth and everything in it will be laid bare. Since everything will be destroyed in this way, what kind of people ought you to be? You ought to live holy and godly lives as you look forward to the day of God and speed its coming. That day will bring about the destruction of the heavens by fire, and the elements will melt in the heat. But in keeping with his promise we are looking forward to a new heaven and a new earth, the home of righteousness. (2 Pet 3:10-13)**

6 (27:52-53) **Believers, Resurrected**: the resurrection of many saints. Just who these saints were is not known, not for certain. But several facts mentioned in Scripture need to be noted.

1. The graves were opened during the terrifying earthquake (v.51), but the bodies did not arise until after Jesus' resurrection (v. 53). Christ had to be the first to arise from the dead—the first who was never to die again (1 Cor.15:20; Col.1:18; Rev.1:5).

2. Between these two events, the cross and the resurrection, was evidently the time that Jesus bore the full punishment of death and hell for man's sins. He tasted death for every man—both physical and spiritual death (Heb.2:9, 14).

3. Peter adds, "He went and preached to the spirits in prison" (1 Pt.3:19). This probably means that He confronted the lost in hell and proclaimed that the way of the righteous is now vindicated. John quotes Christ in Rev.1:18, "[I] was dead; and behold, I am alive for ever and ever! And I hold the keys of death and Hades."

Many believe that before the resurrection of Christ all dead people went to a place known in Scripture as Hades (see DEEPER STUDY # 2—Lk.16:23). Hades was divided into two areas, paradise and hell. The spirits of believers went to paradise; the spirits of unbelievers went to hell. Some commentators believe that when Christ arose He took the saints of paradise with Him to live in the presence of God forever. Now, since Christ's resurrection, all believers go immediately into the presence of God.

4. Paul adds "When He ascended on high, He led captives in his train...He also descended to the lower earthly regions...." (Eph.4:8-10; cp. the graves' opening in Mt.27:51 and the bodies' being raised in Mt.27:52). The idea is that Christ led captivity—sin, death and hell—captive. He conquered all the enemies of man, setting man free to arise and live forever in the presence of God.

The resurrection of these saints symbolized at least two things.

1. It symbolized the conquest of death by Christ. The sting is now taken from death; the power of death is now broken.

For he must reign until he has put all his enemies under his feet. The last enemy to be destroyed is death. (1 Cor 15:25-26)

Listen, I tell you a mystery: We will not all sleep, but we will all be changed—in a flash, in the twinkling of an eye, at the last trumpet. For the trumpet will sound, the dead will be raised imperishable, and we will be changed. For the perishable must clothe itself with the imperishable, and the mortal with immortality. When the perishable has been clothed with the imperishable, and the mortal with immortality, then the saying that is written will come true: "Death has been swallowed up in victory." "Where, O death, is your victory? Where, O death, is your sting?" The sting of death is sin, and the power of sin is the law. But thanks be to God! He gives us the victory through our Lord Jesus Christ. (1 Cor 15:51-57)

Since the children have flesh and blood, he too shared in their humanity so that by his death he might destroy him who holds the power of death—that is, the devil— (Heb 2:14)

2. It symbolized the resurrection of believers. Believers shall arise and be recognized and know one another (Mt.27:53).

"Do not be amazed at this, for a time is coming when all who are in their graves will hear his voice and come out—those who have done good will rise to live, and those who have done evil will rise to be condemned. (John 5:28-29)

For my Father's will is that everyone who looks to the Son and believes in him shall have eternal life, and I will raise him up at the last day." (John 6:40)

Because we know that the one who raised the Lord Jesus from the dead will also raise us with Jesus and present us with you in his presence. (2 Cor 4:14)

For the Lord himself will come down from heaven, with a loud command, with the voice of the archangel and with the trumpet call of God, and the dead in Christ will rise first. After that, we who are still alive and are left will be caught up together with them in the clouds to meet the Lord in the air. And so we will be with the Lord forever. (1 Th 4:16-17)

7 (27:54) **Centurion**: the confession of the centurion and others. A magnificent thing happened to some of those standing at the foot of the cross. When the earth quaked upon the heels of the darkness, the centurion and his soldiers feared and exclaimed: "Surely he was the Son of God." The confession was probably genuine, much more than just feeling that Christ was innocent and a special person to His God. Of course, the soldiers could not fully understand what *Son of God* meant; but they knew Christ claimed to be the Son of God. And in witnessing Christ's words and purposeful behavior on the cross, they more than likely believed His claim to be true.

That if you confess with your mouth, "Jesus is Lord," and believe in your heart that God raised him from the dead, you will be saved. For it is with your heart that you believe and are justified, and it is with your mouth that you confess and are saved. (Rom 10:9-10)

Thought 1. The magnetic power of the cross begins its work with the centurion and his soldiers.

But I, when I am lifted up from the earth, will draw all men to myself." (John 12:32)

Thought 2. Truly believing the claim of Christ to be the Son of God is what it takes to be saved.

8 (27:55-56) **Women**: the courage and love of the women. Note the following phrases.

⇒ "Many women": many were there. When the men fled, many women demonstrated courage.

⇒ "Watching from a distance": some did stand far off, but some stood at the very foot of the cross (Jn.19:25). Their love ran deep and their devotion and courage clear. They triumphed over fear. They did not fear the enemies of Christ: they triumphed simply because they loved (1 Jn.4:18).

For whoever wants to save his life will lose it, but whoever loses his life for me and for the gospel will save it. (Mark 8:35)

There is no fear in love. But perfect love drives out fear, because fear has to do with punishment. The one who fears is not made perfect in love. (1 John 4:18)

N. The Messiah's Burial: Reactions to His Death, 27:57-66
(Mk.15:42-47; Lk.23: 50-56; Jn.19:38:42)

1 A secret disciple: Was stirred to step forward for Christ
a. He was a disciple, but secret
b. He was stirred to step forward for Christ: He requested Jesus' body
c. He embalmed the body
d. He buried the body
1) In his own tomb
2) Closed the entrance with a great stone

2 Two believing women: Showed loyalty & affection

57 As evening approached,
there came a rich man from
Arimathea, named Joseph,
who had himself become a
disciple of Jesus.
58 Going to Pilate, he asked
for Jesus' body, and Pilate
ordered that it be given to
him.
59 Joseph took the body,
wrapped it in a clean linen
cloth,
60 And placed it in his own
new tomb that he had cut out
of the rock. He rolled a big
stone in front of the entrance
to the tomb and went away.
61 Mary Magdalene and the
other Mary were sitting there
opposite the tomb.
62 The next day, the one after Preparation Day, the chief
priests and the Pharisees went
to Pilate.
63 "Sir," they said, "we remember that while he was
still alive that deceiver said,
'After three days I will rise
again.'
64 So give the order for the
tomb to be made secure until
the third day. Otherwise, his
disciples may come and steal
the body and tell the people
that he has been raised from
the dead. This last deception
will be worse than the first."
65 "Take a guard," Pilate answered. "Go, make the tomb
as secure as you know how."
66 So they went and made
the tomb secure by putting a
seal on the stone and posting
the guard.

3 Unbelievers & worldly religionists: Faced a serious problem
a. Their twofold problem
1) The Lord's claim: He would arise
2) The message of a risen Messiah
b. Their request: Secure the tomb
c. Their error: Believing Jesus' claims were false
d. Their extensive security of the tomb[DS1]
1) The sealing of the tomb
2) A military guard

DIVISION XVI

THE MESSIAH'S ARREST, TRIAL, AND CRUCIFIXION, 26:1-27:66

N. The Messiah's Burial: Reactions to His Death, 27:57-66

(27:57-66) **Introduction**: Jesus was now dead. In this passage, there are three reactions to His death, reactions that reveal how we should and should not react to His death.

1. A secret disciple: was stirred to step forward for Christ (v.57-60).
2. Two believing women: showed loyalty and affection (v.61).
3. Unbelievers and worldly religionists: faced a serious problem (v.62-66).

1 (27:57-60) **Joseph of Arimathaea**: there was the reaction of a secret disciple. He was stirred to step forward for Christ. Several things are said about Joseph of Arimathaea that show the kind of man he was.

⇒ He was a prominent member of the Council, that is, a member of the Sanhedrin (Mk.15:43).
⇒ He was a good and upright man (Lk.23:50).
⇒ He waited for the Kingdom of God (Mk.15:43).
⇒ He was rich (Mt.27:57).
⇒ He did not vote for Jesus' death when the Sanhedrin voted (Lk.23:51).
⇒ He was a disciple, but a secret disciple, fearing his fellow Jews (Jn.19:38).

It is this last fact that reveals a marked change in Joseph. Up until the death of Jesus, He had been a secret disciple. He had probably had several meetings with Christ when the Lord visited Jerusalem. But after the Lord's death, he was no longer secret. He became bold.

Four acts show a remarkable boldness, a boldness that reveals the strength of Joseph's discipleship.

1. Joseph actually marched in "boldly to Pilate" and requested the body of Jesus (Mk.15:43). This was a tremendous act of courage. The Romans either dumped the bodies of crucified criminals in the trash heaps or left the bodies hanging upon the cross for the vultures and animals to consume. The latter served as an example of criminal punishment to the public. Joseph also braved the threat of Pilate's reaction, for Pilate was fed up with the *Jesus matter*. Jesus had proven to be very bothersome to Pilate. Pilate could have reacted severely against Joseph.

2. Joseph risked the disfavor and discipline of the Sanhedrin. They were the ruling body who had instigated and condemned Christ, and Joseph was a member of the council. Unquestionably, he would face some harsh reaction from some of his fellow Sanhedrin members and from certain of his closest friends.

3. Joseph demonstrated a care, even an affection, for Jesus by giving his own tomb for the burial of Jesus. This act alone would leave no question about his stand with Christ.

4. Joseph also eliminated himself from taking part in the great Passover Feast. This was just never done, even for the most serious reasons. Joseph, by handling Jesus' body, was considered defiled for seven days for having come in contact with a corpse. Once defiled, Jewish law forbade a person from taking part in Jewish ceremonies.

The thing that turned Joseph from being a secret disciple to a bold disciple seems to be the phenomenal events surrounding the cross (the behavior and words of Christ, the darkness, the earthquake, and the torn veil). When Joseph witnessed all this, his mind connected the claims of Christ with the Old Testament prophecies of the Messiah. Joseph saw the prophecies fulfilled in Jesus. He stepped forward and braved all risks: he took his stand with Christ. A remarkable courage! A courage stirred by the death of Christ.

Note that Joseph embalmed the body and laid it in *his own tomb*, and he closed the tomb's entrance with a huge stone (see DEEPER STUDY # 1—Mt.27:65-66). (Cp. Is.53:9.)

Thought 1. Every secret believer needs to study the cross of Christ. Really seeing the cross will turn any secret believer into a bold witness for Christ.

> **"For God so loved the world that he gave his one and only Son, that whoever believes in him shall not perish but have eternal life. (John 3:16)**
> **But God demonstrates his own love for us in this: While we were still sinners, Christ died for us. (Rom 5:8)**
> **He himself bore our sins in his body on the tree, so that we might die to sins and live for righteousness; by his wounds you have been healed. (1 Pet 2:24)**
> **For Christ died for sins once for all, the righteous for the unrighteous, to bring you to God. He was put to death in the body but made alive by the Spirit, (1 Pet 3:18)**

Thought 2. Position, power, wealth, and fame—none of these make us bold for Christ. Only true affection for Christ will make us bold, and only as we see the cross of Christ will affection for Christ be aroused.

Thought 3. Christ identified with men perfectly.
⇒ He lived as a man, but perfectly.
⇒ He died as a man, but perfectly (as the Ideal Man).
⇒ He was buried as a man, but perfectly.

> **He was assigned a grave with the wicked, and with the rich in his death, though he had done no violence, nor was any deceit in his mouth. (Isa 53:9)**
> **For this reason he had to be made like his brothers in every way, in order that he might become a merciful and faithful high priest in service to God, and that he might make atonement for the sins of the people. (Heb 2:17)**

Thought 4. God's own Son had nothing when He was on earth. This means two things.
⇒ Christ is the Savior of the poorest. He was born in a stable. He had no place of His own to lay His head (Mt.8:20; Lk.9:58). His tomb was a borrowed tomb.
⇒ Yet the rich can serve Him just as Joseph of Arimathaea did.

2 (27:61) **Women Believers**: there was the reaction of two believing women. They showed affection and loyalty. There are three facts to note about these women.

1. The women were loyal to Christ despite all danger. The men forsook Christ, but not the women (Mt.26:56, 69-75; cp. 27:55-56, 61).

2. The women had a deep affection for Christ. They took what they had, money to buy spices and ointments, and used it for Christ. This they did because they loved Him (Mt.27:61; cp. Mk.16:1; Lk.23:56).

3. The women had not yet understood the resurrection of Christ. They were preparing His body to lie, and eventually to decay, in the tomb. The true meaning of living forever, the human body's being remade, recreated, and becoming incorruptible, had not yet been grasped by them (Jn.5:24-29; cp. 1 Cor.15:42f. Cp. 1 Cor.15:1-58.)

Thought 1. The two women were great examples for all men. All men believers...
- should be loyal to Christ no matter how furious the danger.
- should love Christ to such an extent that they give all they are and have to Christ.
- should seek to understand and grasp the full meaning of the resurrection of Christ.

> **I am not ashamed of the gospel, because it is the power of God for the salvation of everyone who believes: first for the Jew, then for the Gentile. (Rom 1:16)**
> **So do not be ashamed to testify about our Lord, or ashamed of me his prisoner. But join with me in suffering for the gospel, by the power of God, (2 Tim 1:8)**

3 (27:62-66) **Jesus Christ, Response to**: there was the reaction of unbelievers and worldly religionists. They faced a serious problem. They were so uneasy and fearful that they went to Pilate in an attempt to prevent the disciples from stealing the body.

1. The unbelievers had a twofold problem.
   a. The unbeliever had the problem of the Lord's claim. He had said He would arise from the dead. These worldly religionists did not believe He would, but they knew He had predicted some kind of resurrection (Mt.12:40; Jn.2:19; 10:17-18). Some of them had heard Him personally talk about rising from the dead. The disciples had shared with their families and closest associates the words of Christ about His death and resurrection; and, as with all matters shared with another, the families and closest associates shared with their closest friends and the prediction had spread. Moreover, during the last months Christ had intensified His prediction in order to drill the truth into the disciples and prepare them for what lay ahead (see notes—Mt.15:21-22; 15:29; 16:21-28; 17:22).

   It should be remembered that the disciples did not take Jesus' words literally. They spiritualized the prediction of His death, resurrection, and return. They probably thought Jesus was referring to some events dealing with the upcoming struggle to free Israel from Roman domination and establishing the Messiah's kingdom in glory.

> **What about the one whom the Father set apart as his very own and sent into the world? Why then do you accuse me of blasphemy because I said, 'I am God's Son'? (John 10:36)**
> **"Yes, Lord," she told him, "I believe that you are the Christ, the Son of God, who was to come into the world." (John 11:27)**
> **If anyone acknowledges that Jesus is the Son of God, God lives in him and he in God. (1 John 4:15)**

Thought 1. Unbelievers of all generations have to deal with the problem of the Lord's claim to be the Messiah, the Son of God.

Thought 2. Many spiritualize Jesus' words even today.

b. The unbeliever had the problem of the message about the risen Messiah. What they feared was that the disciples would come during the night to steal the body and begin to preach that Jesus had arisen from the dead. Note: there was no chance of this.
   ⇒ The disciples were *emotionally destitute*, utterly hopeless and depressed. In addition, they were *terrorized*, thinking they were being hunted down like a pack of wolves.
   ⇒ The disciples, if they lied about the resurrection, would have been deceiving themselves; and above all men, they would have lost the most. They had left everything for Christ: their families, homes, and businesses. They had left all because of their faith in Christ and their hope in the next world. If there were no other world, they would be the most miserable men of all. And remember: at that particular time, they were the most miserable.
   ⇒ The disciples, if they lied about the resurrection, would have been deceiving others. They would have been lying and deceiving people with the very opposite of everything Christ had taught them. There was no chance the disciples could ever pull off so mammouth a deception on the world.

Thought 1. The unbeliever has to deal with the message of the risen Lord. He actually arose.

> **But also for us, to whom God will credit righteousness—for us who believe in him who raised Jesus our Lord from the dead. (Rom 4:24)**
>
> **That if you confess with your mouth, "Jesus is Lord," and believe in your heart that God raised him from the dead, you will be saved. (Rom 10:9)**
>
> **For what I received I passed on to you as of first importance : that Christ died for our sins according to the Scriptures, that he was buried, that he was raised on the third day according to the Scriptures, (1 Cor 15:3-4)**
>
> **Praise be to the God and Father of our Lord Jesus Christ! In his great mercy he has given us new birth into a living hope through the resurrection of Jesus Christ from the dead, (1 Pet 1:3)**

2. The unbelievers requested Pilate to secure the tomb, making it as secure as was humanly possible (see DEEPER STUDY # 1—Mt.27:65-66).

3. The unbelievers made one drastic mistake: they believed that Jesus' claims were false (v.64). Note the wording of what they said. They feared the last deception (Jesus' claim to be the Messiah, the Son of God), and they feared the possibility of a new deception, the message of a risen messiah. Note: they felt the message of a risen Lord might be more powerful than the claims to deity—and it is.

4. The unbelievers planned extensive security of the tomb. Pilate gave permission to post a guard and to seal the tomb. Both measures were taken (see DEEPER STUDY # 1—Mt.27:65-66).

DEEPER STUDY # 1

(27:65-66) **Jesus' Tomb**: cave tombs were closed by rolling a huge cartwheel-like stone in front of the entrance. They were almost impossible to remove. A deep slanting groove was hewn out of the rock at the base of the entrance for the circular stone to rest in. The stone usually weighed several tons. Such precautions were essential because there were so many tombs ransacked in those days of poverty.

The tomb was further secured by being sealed. When it was necessary to seal a tomb, the huge stone was cemented to the entrance walls or else some type of rope or binding was wrapped around the entrance stone and fastened to both sides of the tomb. Then the binding was cemented with a hardening clay or wax-like substance. In the case of some burials, usually political figures, the seal of the Emperor was also attached to the walls of the entrance. This was to strike fear of Roman retaliation against any intruder.

In the case of Jesus' tomb, further precautions were taken by placing a patrol to guard against any foul play. This guard consisted of a large number of men (Mt.28:4, 11f).

1 The time of the resurrection
2 The first witnesses of the resurrection
a. Mary Magdalene
b. The other Mary
3 The miraculous events of the resurrection
a. The great earthquake
b. The great stone rolled back
c. The radiant figure
1) Appearance: Dazzling
2) Clothing: As snow
d. The guards terrified
1) Shook
2) Acted as dead men
4 The appeals of the resurrection
a. Do not fear
1) Your seeking Messiah is known
2) He was crucified
3) He is risen[DS1]
b. Come, see: Believe & live
c. Go quickly & tell:

CHAPTER 28

XVII. THE MESSIAH'S TRIUMPHANT RESURRECTION, 28:1-20

A. The Messiah's Resurrection: Surrounding Events, 28:1-15
(Mk.16:1-13; Lk.24:1-49; Jn.20:1-23)

After the Sabbath, at dawn
on the first day of the week,
Mary Magdalene and the
other Mary went to look at
the tomb.
2 There was a violent earthquake, for an angel of the
Lord came down from heaven
and, going to the tomb, rolled
back the stone and sat on it.
3 His appearance was like
lightning, and his clothes
were white as snow.
4 The guards were so afraid
of him that they shook and
became like dead men.
5 The angel said to the
women, "Do not be afraid,
for I know that you are looking for Jesus, who was crucified.
6 He is not here; he has risen,
just as he said. Come and see
the place where he lay.
7 Then go quickly and tell his
disciples: 'He has risen from
the dead and is going ahead
of you into Galilee. There
you will see him.' Now I
have told you."
8 So the women hurried
away from the tomb, afraid
yet filled with joy, and ran to
tell his disciples.
9 Suddenly Jesus met them.
"Greetings," he said. They
came to him, clasped his feet
and worshiped him.
10 Then Jesus said to them,
"Do not be afraid. Go and tell
my brothers to go to Galilee;
there they will see me."
11 While the women were on
their way, some of the guards
went into the city and reported to the chief priests
everything that had hap-
pened.
12 When the chief priests
had met with the elders and
devised a plan, they gave the
soldiers a large sum of
money,
13 Telling them, "You are to
say, 'His disciples came during the night and stole him
away while we were asleep.'
14 If this report gets to the
governor, we will satisfy him
and keep you out of trouble."
15 So the soldiers took the
money and did as they were
instructed. And this story has
been widely circulated among
the Jews to this very day.

The glorious news
1) He meets you
2) You will see Him
3) The women obeyed: With fear & great joy
d. Greetings:[DS2] The glorious encounter with Jesus Himself
5 The attempt to discredit the resurrection[DS3]
a. The guards reported the resurrection
b. The authorities were baffled: Devised a plan
c. The authorities bribed & assured the soldiers of protection from Pilate
d. The lie was found out: The truth marched on

DIVISION XVII

THE MESSIAH'S TRIUMPHANT RESURRECTION, 28:1-20

A. The Messiah's Resurrection: Surrounding Events, 28:1-15

(28:1-15) **Introduction**: Matthew reports five significant events surrounding the resurrection—events that stir interest and challenge action.
1. The time of the resurrection (v.1).
2. The first witnesses of the resurrection (v.1).
3. The miraculous events of the resurrection (v.2-4).
4. The appeals of the resurrection (v.5-10).
5. The attempt to discredit the resurrection (v.11-15).

1 (28:1) **Jesus Christ, Resurrection**: the time of the resurrection. Jesus arose after the Sabbath was over, that is, on Sunday, the first day of the week. There are four facts to note about this.

1. Matthew said, "After the Sabbath" which means late on the Sabbath. Matthew was not speaking of strict Jewish time. This would mean the Sabbath had ended at 6 p.m. the preceding evening of Saturday (see DEEPER STUDY # 1—Mk.6:48). He was using the common day-to-day idea of time. He was simply adding the night time to the preceding day (cp. Mk.16:1).

2. Jesus arose before dawn, before the sun arose on Sunday morning. This was significant to the early Christian believers, so significant that they broke away from the practice of worshipping on the Sabbath or Saturday. They began to worship on Sunday, the day of the resurrection of their Lord.

> **On the first day of the week we came together to break bread. Paul spoke to the people and, because he intended to leave the next day, kept on talking until midnight. (Acts 20:7)**
> **On the first day of every week, each one of you should set aside a sum of money in keeping with his income, saving it up, so that when I come no collections will have to be made. (1 Cor 16:2)**

3. Jesus arose on the first day of the week, on Sunday morning. This means that He arose on the third day just as He had said (Mt.12:40; 16:21; 17:23; 20:19; Mk.9:31;

10:34; Lk.9:22; 18:33; 24:7, 46). His arising from the dead is a triumph, a conquest over death. Death reigns no more. Its rule has been broken. (See note—Ro.8:2-4.)

> **Indeed, in our hearts we felt the sentence of death. But this happened that we might not rely on ourselves but on God, who raises the dead. He has delivered us from such a deadly peril, and he will deliver us. On him we have set our hope that he will continue to deliver us, (2 Cor 1:9-10)**
>
> **But it has now been revealed through the appearing of our Savior, Christ Jesus, who has destroyed death and has brought life and immortality to light through the gospel. (2 Tim 1:10)**
>
> **But we see Jesus, who was made a little lower than the angels, now crowned with glory and honor because he suffered death, so that by the grace of God he might taste death for everyone. Since the children have flesh and blood, he too shared in their humanity so that by his death he might destroy him who holds the power of death— that is, the devil— and free those who all their lives were held in slavery by their fear of death. (Heb 2:9, 14-15)**

4. Again, Jesus arose on the first day of the week, Sunday morning. He was in the grave on the Sabbath, unable to observe the laws governing the great season of the Passover and the Sabbath. He was dead; therefore, the law and its observances had no authority over Him. This is symbolic of the identification believers gain in Christ. When a man believes in Jesus Christ, God identifies the man with Christ, in particular with the death of Christ. God counts the man as having died with Christ. Therefore, in Christ's death believers become dead to the law (see note—Ro.7:4; DEEPER STUDY # 2—8:3; note—Mt.5:17-18 for more discussion).

> **For we know that our old self was crucified with him so that the body of sin might be done away with, that we should no longer be slaves to sin— (Rom 6:6)**
>
> **I have been crucified with Christ and I no longer live, but Christ lives in me. The life I live in the body, I live by faith in the Son of God, who loved me and gave himself for me. (Gal 2:20)**
>
> **Since you died with Christ to the basic principles of this world, why, as though you still belonged to it, do you submit to its rules: (Col 2:20)**

2 (28:1) **Jesus Christ, Resurrection**: the first witnesses of the resurrection. Note several things.

1. The first witnesses were women, not men, not even his own disciples. The women took the lead in love and care for the Lord Jesus.

2. Two reasons are given for the women's coming to the tomb of Jesus.

a. Matthew says the women "came...to look at the tomb." The Greek word "to look at" (theoresai) means to contemplate, to gaze, to observe in order to grasp. They came to be close to their Lord, the One who meant so much to them, to mourn over Him, to think through all that had happened. This is an important point, for it perhaps explains why the women were more prepared to believe the miracle of the resurrection.

> **When Jesus rose early on the first day of the week, he appeared first to Mary Magdalene, out of whom he had driven seven demons. She went and told those who had been with him and who were mourning and weeping. When they heard that Jesus was alive and that she had seen him, they did not believe it. (Mark 16:9-11)**
>
> **It was Mary Magdalene, Joanna, Mary the mother of James, and the others with them who told this to the apostles. But they did not believe the women, because their words seemed to them like nonsense. (Luke 24:10-11)**

Thought 1. Thinking and meditating upon the Lord will help us to understand the Lord and prepare us to receive the great truth of His resurrection.

> **"Come now, let us reason together," says the LORD. "Though your sins are like scarlet, they shall be as white as snow; though they are red as crimson, they shall be like wool. (Isa 1:18)**

b. Mark says the women came to "anoint Jesus' body" (Mk.16:1). They cared, so they wanted to take care of His body as loved ones do.

Thought 1. The women are an example to us in taking care of the bodies of our loved ones.

3. Mary Magdalene stands out as the most prominent of the women who witnessed the resurrection of the Lord. Her love and devotion must have been deep, very deep. Mary had a very special quality about her, possessing a deeper love and devotion than most (cp. Mk.16:1, 9; Lk.24:10; Jn.20:11-18).

4. The other Mary was the mother of James and Joses. She just could not tear herself away from the body of Jesus which indicates a very special love and devotion for Him (Mt.27:56, 61; 28:1; Mk.15:40; Lk.24:10). She was probably the mother of Cleopas as well (cp. Jn.19:25).

3 (28:2-4) **Jesus Christ, Resurrection**: the miraculous events of the resurrection.

1. There was a "violent earthquake." Nothing more is said, only that it was *violent*. The earthquake symbolized that a *historical convulsion* was taking place, an event that never before had happened: a man was rising from the dead, the man Christ Jesus, the Son of God Himself. Tragically, He had been put to death by the hands of men, but gloriously He was being raised from the dead by the power of God (Ro.1:4; Eph.1:19-20). The historical event was a picture of the unbelievable convulsion that God was planning for the end time: the resurrection of all the dead. The resurrection of God's dear Son paved the way and prefigured the resurrection of all men. History was witnessing the most convulsive event of all time; the quaking of the earth was bound to happen.

2. There was the great stone rolled back (see DEEPER STUDY # 1—Mt.27:65-66). The stone was not rolled back for the benefit of Christ, but for the witnesses to the resurrection. When Christ arose, He was in His resurrection body, the

body of the spiritual dimension of being which has no physical bounds. But the witnesses needed to enter the tomb to see the truth (see outline and notes—Jn.20:1-10).

3. There was the radiant figure, the angel of the Lord. Note two facts about the angel.

a. He rolled back the stone for the sake of the witnesses. He was a ministering spirit of God's, serving by helping God's people (see DEEPER STUDY # 1—Heb.1:4-14).

b. His appearance was dazzling:

⇒ just like lightning—visible, quick, startling, striking, frightening, brilliant.

⇒ just like snow—white, pure, glistening.

4. There were the guards and their terror. Matthew seems to indicate that the guards witnessed the flashing appearance of the angel and the rolling back of the stone. The suddenness of the event, the brilliant appearance and the enormous strength of the angel were like a volcanic eruption to them. They quaked, shook, and fell as dead men to the ground. They were either striken unconscious or were so terrified they pretended to be unconscious.

Thought 1. The power of God is awesome and terrifying. The guards had been told they were to guard a dead body against thieving men. They were totally unprepared and unable to stand against the power of God and His messenger (angel). There is a strong lesson here for every unbeliever.

For nothing is impossible with God." (Luke 1:37)

Then Jesus came to them and said, "All authority in heaven and on earth has been given to me. (Mat 28:18)

No one takes it from me, but I lay it down of my own accord. I have authority to lay it down and authority to take it up again. This command I received from my Father." (John 10:18)

And who through the Spirit of holiness was declared with power to be the Son of God by his resurrection from the dead: Jesus Christ our Lord. (Rom 1:4)

Which he exerted in Christ when he raised him from the dead and seated him at his right hand in the heavenly realms, (Eph 1:20)

By his power he churned up the sea; by his wisdom he cut Rahab to pieces. (Job 26:12)

Who formed the mountains by your power, having armed yourself with strength, (Psa 65:6)

Our God is in heaven; he does whatever pleases him. (Psa 115:3)

Yes, and from ancient days I am he. No one can deliver out of my hand. When I act, who can reverse it?" (Isa 43:13)

4 (28:5-10) **Jesus Christ, Resurrection**: the appeals of the resurrection. When the women arrived at the tomb, they saw the dazzling angel sitting on the stone. Mark says they saw "a young man dressed in a white robe sitting on the right side" (Mk.16:5). Luke says "two men in clothes that gleamed like lightning stood beside them" (Lk.24:4). Apparently, many angels were all about the tomb and the surrounding area attending Christ, joying and rejoicing over what God had done. At the right time, one angel appeared to the women, then two. Note that they appeared as men, that is, as messengers of God.

The appeals of the resurrection are a message within themselves.

1. Do not fear. There are three reasons why the person who seeks after Christ should not fear.

a. God knows the person who is seeking after the Messiah. He knows the movement of every heart. The person who seeks diligently shall find (Mt.7:7).

"Ask and it will be given to you; seek and you will find; knock and the door will be opened to you. For everyone who asks receives; he who seeks finds; and to him who knocks, the door will be opened. (Mat 7:7-8)

But if from there you seek the LORD your God, you will find him if you look for him with all your heart and with all your soul. (Deu 4:29)

For I know the plans I have for you," declares the LORD, "plans to prosper you and not to harm you, plans to give you hope and a future. Then you will call upon me and come and pray to me, and I will listen to you. You will seek me and find me when you seek me with all your heart. (Jer 29:11-13)

b. Christ has been crucified to save every man.

But Jesus said to them, "I have shown you many great miracles from the Father. For which of these do you stone me?" "We are not stoning you for any of these," replied the Jews, "but for blasphemy, because you, a mere man, claim to be God." (John 10:32-33)

You see, at just the right time, when we were still powerless, Christ died for the ungodly. (Rom 5:6)

And he died for all, that those who live should no longer live for themselves but for him who died for them and was raised again. (2 Cor 5:15)

He himself bore our sins in his body on the tree, so that we might die to sins and live for righteousness; by his wounds you have been healed. (1 Pet 2:24)

And they sang a new song: "You are worthy to take the scroll and to open its seals, because you were slain, and with your blood you purchased men for God from every tribe and language and people and nation. (Rev 5:9)

c. Christ has now risen from the dead and conquered death.

But also for us, to whom God will credit righteousness—for us who believe in him who raised Jesus our Lord from the dead. He was delivered over to death for our sins and was raised to life for our justification. (Rom 4:24-25)

And his incomparably great power for

us who believe. That power is like the working of his mighty strength, which he exerted in Christ when he raised him from the dead and seated him at his right hand in the heavenly realms, (Eph 1:19-20)

2. Come see: believe. Note that the angel reminded the women of the Lord's words: "He has risen, just as He said" (cp. Mt.16:21; 17:23; 20:19; 26:32). Note also that the women were told to "come and see the place." They were eyewitnesses of His resurrection.

Thought 1. Believers can become witnesses of the Lord's death and resurrection—clear witnesses. They can see as though they were eye-witnesses—all by God's Spirit.

You foolish Galatians! Who has bewitched you? Before your very eyes Jesus Christ was clearly portrayed as crucified. (Gal 3:1)

But the Counselor, the Holy Spirit, whom the Father will send in my name, will teach you all things and will remind you of everything I have said to you. (John 14:26)

The Spirit himself testifies with our spirit that we are God's children. (Rom 8:16)

3. Go quickly and tell the glorious news. Sharing the glorious news is essential. It is the greatest news of all history: Christ is risen. He shall meet you and you shall see Him.

Note several things.

a. The women obeyed. They became the very first witnesses for the risen Lord.
b. The discouraged believers (disciples) were the first ones the women were to tell. The discouraged were to be encouraged and stirred to join the great force of witnesses.
c. The witnessing was to be done quickly.

4. Greetings: the glorious encounter with Jesus Himself. Note what happened when Christ was personally encountered.

a. He said, "Greetings"; that is, rejoice.

They will put you out of the synagogue; in fact, a time is coming when anyone who kills you will think he is offering a service to God. (John 16:2)

Rejoice in the Lord always. I will say it again: Rejoice! (Phil 4:4)

b. There was the worship of Him: wonder, amazement, adoration, and awe.
c. He said: "Do not be afraid."

For God did not give us a spirit of timidity, but a spirit of power, of love and of self-discipline. (2 Tim 1:7)

d. Go and tell my brothers: the commission was repeated because of the extreme importance of bearing the glorious news.

Therefore go and make disciples of all nations, baptizing them in the name of the Father and of the Son and of the Holy Spirit, and teaching them to obey everything I have commanded you. And surely I am with you always, to the very end of the age." (Mat 28:19-20)

He said to them, "Go into all the world and preach the good news to all creation. (Mark 16:15)

And the things you have heard me say in the presence of many witnesses entrust to reliable men who will also be qualified to teach others. (2 Tim 2:2)

To them God has chosen to make known among the Gentiles the glorious riches of this mystery, which is Christ in you, the hope of glory. We proclaim him, admonishing and teaching everyone with all wisdom, so that we may present everyone perfect in Christ. To this end I labor, struggling with all his energy, which so powerfully works in me. (Col 1:27-29)

DEEPER STUDY # 1

(28:6-7) **Resurrection Predicted**: Christ predicted His resurrection time and again.

From that time on Jesus began to explain to his disciples that he must go to Jerusalem and suffer many things at the hands of the elders, chief priests and teachers of the law, and that he must be killed and on the third day be raised to life. (Mat 16:21)

They will kill him, and on the third day he will be raised to life." And the disciples were filled with grief. (Mat 17:23)

And will turn him over to the Gentiles to be mocked and flogged and crucified. On the third day he will be raised to life!" (Mat 20:19)

But after I have risen, I will go ahead of you into Galilee." (Mat 26:32)

As they were coming down the mountain, Jesus gave them orders not to tell anyone what they had seen until the Son of Man had risen from the dead. (Mark 9:9)

But after I have risen, I will go ahead of you into Galilee." (Mark 14:28)

Jesus answered them, "Destroy this temple, and I will raise it again in three days." (John 2:19)

But I have had God's help to this very day, and so I stand here and testify to small and great alike. I am saying nothing beyond what the prophets and Moses said would happen— that the Christ would suffer and, as the first to rise from the dead, would proclaim light to his own people and to the Gentiles." (Acts 26:22-23)

DEEPER STUDY # 2

(28:9) **Greetings** (chairete): rejoice.

5 (28:11-15) **Jesus Christ, Resurrection**: the attempt to discredit the resurrection. The outline above is adequate to see the event being described.

1. The guards reported the resurrection.
2. The authorities were baffled, and they devised a plan to decide what to do.
3. The authorities bribed and assured the soldiers of protection from Pilate.
4. The lie was found out; the truth marched on.

Thought 1. If the guards were asleep, how would they know what happened? Deception and lying are always contradicted by the truth.

Thought 2. Truth will always prevail (v.15). It may take some time, but its triumph is assured.

Then you will know the truth, and the truth will set you free." (John 8:32)

Stand firm then, with the belt of truth buckled around your waist, with the breastplate of righteousness in place, (Eph 6:14)

Truthful lips endure forever, but a lying tongue lasts only a moment. (Prov 12:19)

DEEPER STUDY # 3
(28:11-15) **Jesus—Plots Against**: note the plots against Jesus. The authorities had used treachery to arrest Him; an illegal court to try Him (Mt.26:59); false charges to accuse Him before Pilate (Mt.27:1, 2, 11f); and now they were using bribery to discredit His resurrection.

Outline	Subject Heading	Scripture	Outline
	B. The Messiah's Final Commission to His Disciples, 28:16-20 (Mk.16:15-18; Lk.24: 46-49; Jn.20:21; cp. Jn.17:18; Acts 1:8)	18 Then Jesus came to them and said, "All authority in heaven and on earth has been given to me.	**2 He assured His followers of His power** a. Is a given power b. Is in heaven & earth
1 The disciples met Jesus in Galilee a. They met on a pre-appointed mountain b. They worshipped Him c. Some doubted	16 Then the eleven disciples went to Galilee, to the mountain where Jesus had told them to go. 17 When they saw him, they worshiped him; but some doubted.	19 Therefore go and make disciples of all nations, baptizing them in the name of the Father and of the Son and of the Holy Spirit, 20 And teaching them to obey everything I have commanded you. And surely I am with you always, to the very end of the age."	**3 He commissioned His followers** a. To make disciples of all nations b. To baptize c. To teach all that He had commanded **4 He promised to be with His followers**

DIVISION XVII

THE MESSIAH'S TRIUMPHANT RESURRECTION, 28:1-20

B. The Messiah's Final Commission to His Disciples, 28:16-20

(28:16-20) **Introduction**: Matthew began his gospel by proclaiming that the baby Jesus was the Son of David, the promised King of Israel (Mt.1:1-2). He now closes his gospel by proclaiming that the Lord Jesus possesses all power and authority in heaven and earth. The Lord Jesus had risen from the dead, and in the power of His resurrection His followers are to go forth proclaiming His glorious kingdom.

In this great passage, Matthew covers the great commission of the resurrected Lord, the King to whom all power and authority belong.

1. The disciples met Jesus in Galilee (v.16-17).
2. He assured His followers of His power (v.18).
3. He commissioned His followers (v.19-20).
4. He promised to be with His followers—always (v.20).

1 (28:16-17) **Disciples**: the disciples met Jesus in Galilee. Note several background facts.

1. Matthew says the eleven disciples met Christ. The eleven were the prominent ones, but apparently there were over five hundred believers present, all seeing Him at once (1 Cor.15:6). The reference to "they" and "some doubted" (v.17) seems to indicate that this was the great appearance to the mass of believers mentioned by Paul. Christ had already appeared to the eleven on several occasions. They already knew the reality of His resurrection. It is unlikely that they were the ones who were questioning at this time (Mk.16:12-14; Lk.24:13-48; Jn.20:19-25; 20:26-31; 21:1-25).

2. The disciples met the Lord in Galilee on a pre-appointed mountain (cp. Mt.26:32; 28:7, 10). The Lord had apparently instructed the apostles to pass the word along and to gather all His disciples to meet Him in a mass meeting in Galilee. A particular mountain was designated as the meeting place. Note that Galilee was where the Lord had conducted most of His ministry and where most of His disciples lived. It was also some distance from Jerusalem, a place somewhat safe from the immediate enemies of Christ.

> **Thought 1.** There are appointed places where we are to meet the Lord: in prayer, devotions, worship, and Bible study. When we meet the Lord as He says, He meets us. We must meet the Lord as He instructs if we are to know the reality of His resurrection.

3. This is significant. They worshipped Him, but some doubted. They just were not sure. Note what Jesus did: He "came to them and said" (v.18). Apparently, His *coming and speaking to them* erased their doubt and questioning.

> **Thought 1.** When we meet Christ as He instructs, He meets us. When He meets us, all fear and doubt vanish. The person who truly seeks after Christ, who truly seeks to meet Him, will have his doubts erased. Christ will *come and speak to him.*

2 (28:18) **Power**: Jesus assured His followers of His power.

1. Jesus' power or authority is a given power. It is given by God, and it is given for one reason: to exalt Christ above and over all.

> **And being found in appearance as a man, he humbled himself and became obedient to death—even death on a cross!**
> **Therefore God exalted him to the highest place and gave him the name that is above every name, (Phil 2:8-9)**

2. Jesus' power is above and over all that is in heaven and in earth. His authority is over all the universe. His authority includes at least three areas.

a. The Lord's authority includes the power to rule and reign...
   - to receive the worship and subjection of all men who willingly surrender to His dominion.

> **Therefore, I urge you, brothers, in view of God's mercy, to offer your bodies as living sacrifices, holy and pleasing to God—this is your spiritual act of worship. Do not conform any longer to the pattern of this world, but be transformed by the renewing of your mind. Then you will be able to test and approve what God's will is—his good, pleasing and perfect will. (Rom 12:1-2)**
> **You were bought at a price. Therefore honor God with your body. (1 Cor 6:20)**
> **That if you confess with your mouth, "Jesus is Lord," and believe in your heart**

that God raised him from the dead, you will be saved. For it is with your heart that you believe and are justified, and it is with your mouth that you confess and are saved. (Rom 10:9-10)

In a loud voice they sang: "Worthy is the Lamb, who was slain, to receive power and wealth and wisdom and strength and honor and glory and praise!" (Rev 5:12)

- to bow the knee of all men and to receive their acknowledgement of His Lordship.

Therefore God exalted him to the highest place and gave him the name that is above every name, that at the name of Jesus every knee should bow, in heaven and on earth and under the earth, and every tongue confess that Jesus Christ is Lord, to the glory of God the Father. (Phil 2:9-11)

b. The Lord's authority includes the power to govern and direct…

- the affairs of men without violating man's freedom.

After the Lord Jesus had spoken to them, he was taken up into heaven and he sat at the right hand of God. (Mark 16:19)

But from now on, the Son of Man will be seated at the right hand of the mighty God." (Luke 22:69)

Everyone must submit himself to the governing authorities, for there is no authority except that which God has established. The authorities that exist have been established by God. (Rom 13:1)

Who has gone into heaven and is at God's right hand—with angels, authorities and powers in submission to him. (1 Pet 3:22)

- the affairs of nature and the world without violating the laws of nature.

The men were amazed and asked, "What kind of man is this? Even the winds and the waves obey him!" (Mat 8:27)

And God placed all things under his feet and appointed him to be head over everything for the church, (Eph 1:22)

c. The Lord's authority includes the power to forgive sins, to judge, receive and reject men, and to save and deliver men through life and death. (See outline and notes—Ro.8:28-39.)

But so that you may know that the Son of Man has authority on earth to forgive sins." Then he said to the paralytic, "Get up, take your mat and go home." (Mat 9:6)

When Jesus saw their faith, he said, "Friend, your sins are forgiven." The Pharisees and the teachers of the law began thinking to themselves, "Who is this fellow who speaks blasphemy? Who can forgive sins but God alone?" (Luke 5:20-21)

Moreover, the Father judges no one, but has entrusted all judgment to the Son, (John 5:22)

And he has given him authority to judge because he is the Son of Man. (John 5:27)

3. Jesus' power assures the believer of deliverance. Note *when* Jesus came to them and spoke about His power: immediately upon the heels of some doubting and immediately before charging His disciples to go into a hostile world. He proclaimed His power in order to erase doubt and to strengthen His disciples in going forth. His power was the disciples' assurance of victory.

Now, in dealing with the supreme power and authority of Jesus Christ, there are two points that must always be remembered.

1. The Lord's supreme reign is not yet fully seen. God has not yet revealed His Son's supremacy in an absolute sense. However, there is *a striking reason* for God's delaying the visible enthronement of His Son. God wants His Son to still be seen as the Savior of the world. He wants more and more persons to be saved before He ends the world and begins the sovereign reign of His Son upon earth.

First of all, you must understand that in the last days scoffers will come, scoffing and following their own evil desires. They will say, "Where is this 'coming' he promised? Ever since our fathers died, everything goes on as it has since the beginning of creation." But do not forget this one thing, dear friends: With the Lord a day is like a thousand years, and a thousand years are like a day. The Lord is not slow in keeping his promise, as some understand slowness. He is patient with you, not wanting anyone to perish, but everyone to come to repentance. (2 Pet 3:3-4, 8-9)

2. The Lord's supreme reign over all the universe is assured.

But the day of the Lord will come like a thief. The heavens will disappear with a roar; the elements will be destroyed by fire, and the earth and everything in it will be laid bare. Since everything will be destroyed in this way, what kind of people ought you to be? You ought to live holy and godly lives as you look forward to the day of God and speed its coming. That day will bring about the destruction of the heavens by fire, and the elements will melt in the heat. But in keeping with his promise we are looking forward to a new heaven and a new earth, the home of righteousness. (2 Pet 3:10-13)

And put everything under his feet." In putting everything under him, God left nothing that is not subject to him. Yet at present we do not see everything subject to him. But we see Jesus, who was made a little lower than the angels, now crowned with glory and honor because he suffered death, so that by the grace of God he might taste death for everyone. In bringing many sons to glory, it was fitting that God, for whom and through whom everything exists, should make the author of their salvation perfect through suffering. (Heb 2:8-10)

Then the end will come, when he hands over the kingdom to God the Father after he has destroyed all dominion, authority and power. For he must reign until he has put all his enemies under his feet. The last enemy to be destroyed is death. For he "has put everything under his feet." Now when it says that "everything" has been put under him, it is clear that this does not include God himself, who put everything under Christ. When he has done this, then the Son himself will be made subject to him who put everything under him, so that God may be all in all. (1 Cor 15:24-28)

3 (28:19-20) **Commission, Great—Disciples, Making**: Jesus commissioned His followers. He commissioned not only the eleven apostles, but all who were present, more than five hundred disciples. However, note something of crucial importance: it was impossible for that generation to reach the whole world in its lifetime. Therefore, the commission given to the first generation of believers extends beyond to all generations of believers. The very same charge given to them is given to us. Our Lord charges us with the very same words, "Therefore go and make disciples of all nations...."

The Lord's commission was threefold.

1. He commissions us to "go...and make disciples of all nations." This is one of the crucial verses in the Bible. No verse is more important for genuine believers.

Teaching and baptizing are not enough to reach the world for Christ. Both are important, and Christ commissions both; but He says something else must precede both: discipleship. "Therefore go and 'matheteuo' all nations" (Mt.28:19). "Matheteuo" means to make disciples. Thus the verse accurately reads, "Therefore go and 'make disciples' of all nations...." Most messages that are preached on this passage stress the objective of our Lord, the reaching of all nations, as though this is what our Lord had in mind. There is no question, the great commission is what Christ had in mind. He has instructed us to go to all nations and evangelize them. But there is the strong conviction that He had more than that objective in mind, more than just an overriding purpose—much more.

Our Lord was not only telling us "to go and evangelize," He was telling us *how* to go and *how* to evangelize. He was not only giving His ultimate *objective* and overriding purpose, He was giving *the method* to use in evangelizing the world.

Think about the word "*matheteuo*" (make disciples). What does our Lord mean by "make disciples"? Does it not mean that we are to do what He did: make disciples and do things with them as He did. Is He not telling us to do exactly as He did?

What *did* He do? Christ "came to seek and save what was lost" (Lk.19:10). He sought the lost, those who were willing to commit their lives to Him. And when He found such a person, He saved that person. When Christ found a person who was willing to commit his life, Christ attached Himself to that person. Christ began to mold and make that person into His image. The word *attach* is the key word. It is probably the word that best describes discipleship. Christ made disciples of men by attaching Himself to them; and through that personal attachment, they were able to observe His life and conversation; and in seeing and hearing, they began to absorb and assimilate His very character and behavior. They began to follow Him and to serve Him more closely. In simple terms, this is what our Lord did. This is the way He made disciples. This was His mission and His method, His obsession: to attach Himself to willing believers.

There is another way to describe what Christ did. Christ envisioned something beyond Himself and beyond His day and time. He envisioned an *extension* of Himself, an *extension* of His very being, and an *extension* of His mission and method. The way He chose to extend Himself was discipleship, attaching Himself to committed persons; and through attachment, the persons absorbed and assimilated the Lord's very character and mission. They in turn attached themselves to others and discipled them. They, too, expected their disciples to make disciples of others who were willing to commit their lives to Christ. Thus was the glorious message of Christ to march down through the centuries (2 Tim.2:2).

There is no question what our Lord's commission is: we are to go; but more than that, we are to make disciples, to attach ourselves to those persons who will follow our Lord until they in turn can make disciples (2 Tim.2:2).

As you go, preach this message: 'The kingdom of heaven is near.' (Mat 10:7)

Therefore go and make disciples of all nations, baptizing them in the name of the Father and of the Son and of the Holy Spirit, and teaching them to obey everything I have commanded you. And surely I am with you always, to the very end of the age." (Mat 28:19-20)

He said to them, "Go into all the world and preach the good news to all creation. (Mark 16:15)

But these are written that you may believe that Jesus is the Christ, the Son of God, and that by believing you may have life in his name. (John 20:31)

But you will receive power when the Holy Spirit comes on you; and you will be my witnesses in Jerusalem, and in all Judea and Samaria, and to the ends of the earth." (Acts 1:8)

"Go, stand in the temple courts," he said, "and tell the people the full message of this new life." (Acts 5:20)

Preach the Word; be prepared in season and out of season; correct, rebuke and encourage—with great patience and careful instruction. (2 Tim 4:2)

But in your hearts set apart Christ as Lord. Always be prepared to give an answer to everyone who asks you to give the reason for the hope that you have. But do this with gentleness and respect, (1 Pet 3:15)

2. He commissioned us to baptize all nations (see DEEPER STUDY # 1—Mk.16:16; note—Lk.3:21; DEEPER STUDY # 1—Acts 2:38). Two things need to be noted here.

a. Baptism is of crucial importance. Christ says that it is as essential as teaching, despite the fact that it is a one-time act. It is as much a part of the commission of Christ as discipling and teaching. Christ is definitely teaching that baptism is to be the immediate sign and the identifying sign that a person is now stepping out of the heathen (unbelieving) ranks and taking his stand with Christ.

b. Baptism "in the name of the Father, and of the Son, and of the Holy Spirit" means more than just saying a formula as one is baptized, much more. It means...

- a statement of faith: of belief in God as the true Father of Jesus Christ; of belief in Christ as the true Son of God, the Savior of the world; of belief in the Holy Spirit as the Comforter of the believer.
- a commitment to follow God: to follow Him as revealed in the Father, the Son, and the Holy Spirit (cp. Christ's constant references to God as His Father, to Himself as the Son, and to the Holy Spirit throughout the Gospel of John. Also cp. Mt.11:27; 24:36. Also see outlines and notes, Holy Spirit—Jn.14:15-26; 16:7-15; Ro.8:1-17.)

Whoever believes and is baptized will be saved, but whoever does not believe will be condemned. (Mark 16:16)

Peter replied, "Repent and be baptized, every one of you, in the name of Jesus Christ for the forgiveness of your sins. And you will receive the gift of the Holy Spirit. (Acts 2:38)

So he ordered that they be baptized in the name of Jesus Christ. Then they asked Peter to stay with them for a few days. (Acts 10:48)

And now what are you waiting for? Get up, be baptized and wash your sins away, calling on his name.' (Acts 22:16)

3. He commissioned us to teach all that Christ had commanded. Teaching is just as essential as making disciples and baptizing. One is not to be emphasized over the other. All are part of the commission of our Lord. Note what is to be taught: "everything I have commanded you."

Therefore go and make disciples of all nations, baptizing them in the name of the Father and of the Son and of the Holy Spirit, and teaching them to obey everything I have commanded you. And surely I am with you always, to the very end of the age." (Mat 28:19-20)

It is written in the Prophets: 'They will all be taught by God.' Everyone who listens to the Father and learns from him comes to me. (John 6:45)

Let the word of Christ dwell in you richly as you teach and admonish one another with all wisdom, and as you sing psalms, hymns and spiritual songs with gratitude in your hearts to God. (Col 3:16)

If you point these things out to the brothers, you will be a good minister of Christ Jesus, brought up in the truths of the faith and of the good teaching that you have followed. (1 Tim 4:6)

Command and teach these things. (1 Tim 4:11)

And the Lord's servant must not quarrel; instead, he must be kind to everyone, able to teach, not resentful. (2 Tim 2:24)

These commandments that I give you today are to be upon your hearts. Impress them on your children. Talk about them when you sit at home and when you walk along the road, when you lie down and when you get up. (Deu 6:6-7)

They are to teach my people the difference between the holy and the common and show them how to distinguish between the unclean and the clean. (Ezek 44:23)

Thought 1. What Christ taught and commanded must be studied and studied, to the point of learning and knowing and practicing. The commandments of Christ will be the first things taught. They should be the rule of society.

Thought 2. Society deteriorates and crumbles when it neglects the teaching and commandments of Christ.

4 (28:20) **Jesus Christ, Presence**: Jesus promised to be with His followers—always.

1. Note the word "Surely," or behold. Christ used this striking word to get the attention of His followers, to startle them to wake up and listen. He was about to encourage them in the great task He had charged to their care.

2. Note the great promise: "I am with you." He gave emphatic assurance: not "I will be with you," but "I am with you." Christ is with the believer as the believer goes forth to make disciples of all nations. Christ is with us...

- every step
- every decision
- every trial
- every joy
- every day
- every hour
- every sorrow
- when without
- when poor
- when having nothing
- when having plenty
- when abused
- when sick
- when facing death

3. Note the boundless promise: "always, to the very end of the age." There is not a moment when Christ is not with the believer to help him in his witness, even if his witness means abuse, persecution, and martyrdom.

For where two or three come together in my name, there am I with them." (Mat 18:20)

And teaching them to obey everything I have commanded you. And surely I am with you always, to the very end of the age." (Mat 28:20)

Keep your lives free from the love of money and be content with what you have, because God has said, "Never will I leave you; never will I forsake you." So we say with confidence, "The Lord is my helper; I will not be afraid. What can man do to me?" (Heb 13:5-6)

I am with you and will watch over you wherever you go, and I will bring you back to this land. I will not leave you until I have done what I have promised you." (Gen 28:15)

So do not fear, for I am with you; do not be dismayed, for I am your God. I will strengthen you and help you; I will uphold you with my righteous right hand. (Isa 41:10)

**When you pass through the waters,
I will be with you; and when you pass
through the rivers, they will not sweep
over you. When you walk through the
fire, you will not be burned; the flames
will not set you ablaze. (Isa 43:2)**

THE
OUTLINE & SUBJECT INDEX

REMEMBER: When you look up a subject and turn to the Scripture reference, you have not only the Scripture, you have *an outline and a discussion* (commentary) of the Scripture and subject.

This is one of the *GREAT VALUES* of **The Preacher's Outline & Sermon Bible®**. Once you have all the volumes, you will have not only what all other Bible indexes give you, that is, a list of all the subjects and their Scripture references, *BUT* you will also have...

- An outline of *every* Scripture and subject in the Bible.
- A discussion (commentary) on every Scripture and subject.
- Every subject supported by other Scriptures or cross references.

DISCOVER THE GREAT VALUE for yourself. Quickly glance below to the very first subject of the Index of Matthew. It is:

ABILITIES (See **TALENTS—GIFTS**)
Duty. To surrender to Christ. Mt.14:18-21

Turn to the reference. Glance at the Scripture and outline of the Scripture, then read the commentary. You will immediately see the *GREAT VALUE* of the *INDEX* of **The Preacher's Outline & Sermon Bible®**.

OUTLINE AND SUBJECT INDEX

INDEX

INDEX

INDEX

INDEX

PURPOSE STATEMENT

LEADERSHIP MINISTRIES WORLDWIDE

exists to equip ministers, teachers, and laymen in their understanding, preaching, and teaching of God's Word by publishing and distributing worldwide *The Preacher's Outline & Sermon Bible*® and related *Outline* Bible materials, to reach & disciple men, women, boys, and girls for Jesus Christ.

•MISSION STATEMENT•

1. To make the Bible so understandable - its truth so clear and plain - that men and women everywhere, whether teacher or student, preacher or hearer, can grasp its Message and receive Jesus Christ as Savior; and...
2. To place the Bible in the hands of all who will preach and teach God's Holy Word, verse by verse, precept by precept, regardless of the individual's ability to purchase it.

The ***Outline*** Bible materials have been given to LMW for printing and especially distribution worldwide at/below cost, by those who remain anonymous. One fact, however, is as true today as it was in the time of Christ:

• The Gospel is free, but the cost of taking it is not •

LMW depends on the generous gifts of Believers with a heart for Him and a love and burden for the lost. They help pay for the printing, translating, and placing ***Outline*** Bible materials in the hands and hearts of those worldwide who will present God's message with clarity, authority and understanding beyond their own.

LMW was incorporated in the state of Tennessee in July 1992 and received IRS 501(c) 3 non-profit status in March 1994. LMW is an international, nondenominational mission organization. All proceeds from USA sales, along with donations from donor partners, go 100% into underwriting our translation and distribution projects of ***Outline*** Bible materials to preachers, church & lay leaders, and Bible students around the world.

9/98

Box 21310 - Chattanooga, TN 37424 • (423) 855-2181 • FAX (423) 855-8616
• E-Mail - outlinebible@compuserve.com — www.outlinebible.org •

Equipping God's Servants Worldwide

1. **PAYMENT PLANS.** Convenient and affordable ways to get/use your FullSet with easy payments.

2. **NEW TESTAMENT.** In 14 volumes. Deluxe version 3-ring binders. Also: SoftBound Set, 3 volume set, and NIV edition. All on 1 CD-ROM disc.

3. **OLD TESTAMENT.** In process; 1 volume releases about every 6-8 months, in sequence.

4. **THE MINISTERS HANDBOOK.** Acclaimed as a "must-have" for every minister or Christian worker. Outlines more than 400 verses into topics like Power, Victory, Encouragement, Security, Restoration, etc. Discount for quantities.

5. **THE TEACHER'S OUTLINE & STUDY BIBLE™.** Verse-by-verse study & teaching; 45 minute lesson or session. Ideal for study, small groups, classes, even home schooling. Each book also offers a STUDENT JOURNAL for study members.

6. **OUTLINE BIBLE CD-ROM.** Includes all current volumes and books; Preacher, Teacher, and Minister Handbook. 1 disc. WORDsearch STEP format. Also 50+ Bible study tools unlockable on same disc.
   FREE Downloads - www.outlinebible.org

7. THE **OUTLINE**. Quarterly newsletter to all users and owners of *POSB*. Complimentary.

8. **LMW AGENT PLAN.** An exciting way any user sells *OUTLINE* materials & earns a second income.

9. **DISTRIBUTION.** Our ultimate mission is to provide *POSB* volumes & materials to preachers, pastors, national church leaders around the world. This is especially for those unable to purchase at U.S. price. USA sales gain goes 100% to provide volumes at affordable prices within the local economy.

10. **TRANSLATIONS.** Korean, Russian, & Spanish are shipping first volumes — Others in-process: Hindi, Tamil, Telugu, Chinese, French, German, Finnish.

11. **FUNDING PARTNERS.** To cover the cost of all the translations, plus print, publish, and distribute around the world is a multi million dollar project.

    Church-to-Church Partners send *Outline* Bible books to their missionaries, overseas church leaders, Bible Institues and seminaries...at special prices.

12. **REFERRALS.** Literally thousands (perhaps even you!) first heard of *POSB* from a friend. Now Referral Credit pays $16.00 for each new person who orders from a customer's Referral.

13. **CURRICULUM & COPYRIGHT.** Permission may be given to copy specific portions of *POSB* for special group situations. Write/FAX for details.

9/98

For Information about any of the above, kindly FAX, E-Mail, Call, or Write

Please PRAY 1 Minute/Day for LMW!

PO Box 21310, Chattanooga, TN 37424 • (423) 855-2181 • FAX (423) 855-8616
• E-Mail - outlinebible@compuserve.com — www.outlinebible.org •

Sharing

With the World!